Fundamentals of Estate Planning

THE
AMERICAN
COLLEGE
OF FINANCIAL SERVICES®

Huebner School Series

Fundamentals of Estate Planning

16th Edition

Randy Gardner, JD, LLM, MBA, CPA, CFP®, RLP®

HS330-16

This publication is designed to provide accurate and authoritative information about the subject covered. While every precaution has been taken in the preparation of this material, the authors, and The American College assume no liability for damages resulting from the use of the information contained in this publication. The American College is not engaged in rendering legal, accounting, or other professional advice. If legal or other expert advice is required, the services of an appropriate professional should be sought.

© 2019 The American College Press
630 Allendale Road, Suite 400
King of Prussia, PA 19406
(888) AMERCOL (263-7265)
theamericancollege.edu
All rights reserved
Library of Congress Control Number 2019939478
ISBN-10: 1-58293-322-7
ISBN-13: 978-1-58293-322-1
Printed in the United States of America

THE AMERICAN COLLEGE OF FINANCIAL SERVICES

The American College of Financial Services® is an independent, nonprofit, accredited institution founded in 1927 that offers professional certification and graduate-degree distance education to men and women seeking career growth in financial services.

The Solomon S. Huebner School® of The American College administers the Chartered Life Underwriter® (CLU®); the Chartered Financial Consultant® (ChFC®); the Chartered Special Needs Consultant® (ChSNC®); the Chartered Leadership Fellow® (CLF®); the Retirement Income Certified Professional® (RICP®); the Financial Services Certified Professional® (FSCP®); Wealth Management Certified Professional® (WMCP®); the Global Leadership & Management Professional™ (GLMP™); and the Global Financial Services Professional™ (GFSP™) professional designation programs. In addition, The College offers an educational preparation program for the CFP® certification.[1]

The Richard D. Irwin Graduate School® of The American College offers a Master of Science in Financial Services (MSFS) degree; and a Master of Science in Management (MSM) degree, a one-year program with an emphasis in leadership. Additionally, it offers the Chartered Advisor in Philanthropy® (CAP®) and several graduate-level certificates that concentrate on specific subject areas.

The American College of Financial Services is accredited by **The Middle States Commission on Higher Education**, 3624 Market Street, Philadelphia, PA 19104 at telephone number 267.284.5000.

The Middle States Commission on Higher Education is a regional accrediting agency recognized by the U.S. Department of Education and the Commission on Recognition of Postsecondary Accreditation. Middle States accreditation is an expression of confidence in an institution's mission and goals, performance, and resources. It attests that in the judgment of the Commission on Higher Education, based on the results of an internal institutional self-study and an evaluation by a team of outside peer observers assigned by the Commission, an institution is guided by well-defined and appropriate goals; that it has established conditions and procedures under which its goals can be realized; that it is accomplishing them substantially; that it is so organized, staffed, and supported that it can be expected to continue to do so; and that it meets the standards of the Middle States Association. The American College of Financial Services has been accredited since 1978.

---

1   Certified Financial Planner Board of Standards, Inc., owns the certification marks CFP®, CERTIFIED FINANCIAL PLANNER™, and CFP (with flame logo)®, which it awards to individuals who successfully complete initial and ongoing certification requirements.

The College does not discriminate on the basis of race, religion, sex, handicap, or national and ethnic origin in its admissions policies, educational programs and activities, or employment policies.

The College is located at 630 Allendale Road, Suite 400, King of Prussia, PA 19406. The toll-free number of the Office of Professional Education is (888) 263-7265; the fax number is (610) 526-1300 and the home page address is theamericancollege.edu.

Table of Contents

The Basis Rules for Property Transferred during Lifetime or at Death

Income Taxation of Estates and Trusts

About the Authors

Randy Gardner, JD, LLM, MBA, CPA, CFP®, RLP®

Randy Gardner is Adjunct Professor of Financial Planning at The American College of Financial Services. He is the founder of Goals Gap Planning LLC, and a former award-winning professor and CFP® Program Director at the University of Missouri. A regular columnist for the Journal of Financial Planning, Gardner is co-author of the books, 101 Tax Saving Ideas and The Closing Wealth Transfer Window.

Randy earned an undergraduate degree in Philosophy from Harvard and a JD and MBA from the University of Kansas. Gardner regularly shares his tax and financial planning ideas on the webinar series of the Garrett Planning Network, Financial Planning Association, and California Society of CPAs.

Contributing Authors

Jamie Hopkins, Esq., LLM, MBA, CFP®, RICP®

Jamie Hopkins, Esq., LLM, MBA, CFP®, RICP®, is the Director of Retirement Research at Carson Wealth and a finance professor of practice at Creighton University's Heider College of Business. In addition, he is a former professor of Taxation at The American College, where he helped co-create the Retirement Income Certified Professional® (RICP®) education program. Jamie strives to increase the retirement income security of Americans by delivering practical and trusted retirement research and education.

Jamie P. Hopkins was an associate professor of taxation at The American College in the Retirement Income program, and he was the co-director of the New York Life Center for Retirement Income. He also held the Larry R. Pike Chair in Insurance and Investments at The American College. While a professor at The College, he taught courses in retirement, estate planning and life insurance. Through his role at The American College, he educated thousands of financial service professionals and moved the needle for retirement income planning. His major course responsibilities were with the RICP® program, HS 326 Planning for Retirement Needs, and HS 330 Fundamentals of Estate Planning.

Matt Goren

Matt is the host of Nothing Funny About Money, a lighthearted personal finance show on WUGA and other NPR stations around the United States. He has earned the Certified Financial Planner(R) marks as well as a PhD in psychology from UC Berkeley. And, many years ago, he was a comedy writer, a performer, a statistician, and a diversity trainer, and a professor of cultural psychology, and he's taught personal finance to over 3,500 students at UGA and UC Berkeley. Now he pays his bills as a financial education consultant: helping universities, non-profits, and businesses make better, more affordable financial products and services for low- and moderate-income families. He is also currently an adjunct professor at The American Colllege.

Sophia Duffy, JD, CPA

Sophia Duffy is Academic Dean and Assistant Professor of Business Planning at The American College of Financial Services. In her role as Academic Dean, Professor Duffy oversees all Academic projects and course revisions, determines curriculum and academic policy matters, maintains a network of highly qualified faculty and adjunct instructors, and monitors the quality of teaching and faculty course development. She also works with the live delivery team to identify staffing needs for courses, and she oversees the department budgets.

Professor Duffy teaches in both the Huebner School and the Irwin Graduate School. She began her academic career at The College in 2012, and continues as instructor of GS 803 Financial Statement and Business Valuation Analysis and GS 950 Business Law, Compliance, Benefits, and Social Responsibility.

Audrey Snell

Audrey holds an MBA in Finance and CFP® and ChFC® designations. She has been a portfolio manager on Wall Street for a large mutual fund family for more than 20 years. She has also been a partner at a national brokerage firm for several years. Audrey specializes in equity analysis of growth stocks.

Audrey has also worked as a financial planner for two major financial firms, where she received her CFP® designation.

Audrey teaches, tutors and guides students in their pursuit of various designations at The American College, focusing on the courses of the CFP®, ChFC® and CLU® designations. In addition, she holds an undergraduate degree in Journalism and has served as an editor and content provider for several textbooks at The American College.

Chapter 1:

Estate Planning—An Overview

Learning Objectives

An understanding of the material in this chapter should enable the student to

LO 1.1   **Explain what is meant by estate planning and the purpose that it serves.**

LO 1. 2   **Briefly summarize the historical development of estate planning.**

LO 1. 3   **Describe the steps in the estate planning process.**

LO 1. 4   **Describe the impediments to a well-developed estate plan.**

LO 1. 5   **Explain the interaction of the estate planning team and the specific functions of different team members.**

The estate planner must combine the talents of an artist with those of an artisan. To develop the necessary rapport with a client, the planner and advisor must deal lightly but deftly with the sometimes fragile threads woven into the tapestry of the client's life. As an artisan, it is necessary for the estate planner to have a solid understanding of the tools of the field, including knowledge of property and tax law as well as financial planning. The art lies in the ability to put clients in touch with their true feelings, dreams, and aspirations as well as to assist them in the crystallization of their estate plans. Estate planning is inherently complex because of the technicalities of the applicable law and the foresight required to develop a program that best suits the client's immediate as well as anticipated needs and desires.

LO 1.1   **Explain what is meant by estate planning and the purpose that it serves.**

Purpose

Before beginning the study of estate planning fundamentals, it is important to understand that estate and gift taxation is part of a transfer tax system that is separate from the income tax system (although there are transfer-tax aspects that interact with income-tax aspects). The generation-skipping transfer tax (GSTT) and qualified domestic trust (QDOT) taxation are additional forms of transfer taxation that impact estate planning.

Tax Systems

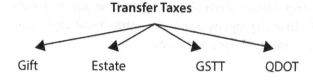

Tax Systems

Transfer Taxes

Gift   Estate   GSTT   QDOT

Income Tax

estate planning

There is a common misconception that an estate is only the property that one leaves at death. In reality, it is much more than that. In its broadest sense, the term **estate planning** encompasses the accumulation, conservation, management, and distribution of an estate. The overall purpose of the estate planning process is to develop a plan that will enhance and maintain the financial security of clients and their families upon the client's incapacitation or death. Estate planning has come to include lifetime financial planning that may lead to increases in a client's estate as well as the conservation of existing assets. Estate planning should provide financial security during retirement years and facilitate the intended and orderly disposition of property at death.

Estate Planning
- accumulation
- conservation
- management
- distribution

LO 1. 2   Briefly summarize the historical development of estate planning.

History

Estate Planning Considerations

When developing an estate plan, a variety of issues must be taken under consideration. The most important aspect of estate planning is to follow the individual's wishes and desires. This might be in the form of transferring property, changing ownership rights, continued control of the property, meeting support obligations, generating liquidity, managing tricky family dynamics, or minimizing taxes. Whatever the client's goals and desires might be, the plan needs to be tailored to the specific client's unique wishes and personal situation. While a certain trust might work perfectly well for one client, it could be a complete disaster for another. Additionally, estate planning is impacted by both state and federal law. Federal law generally controls issues regarding taxation of transfers–either lifetime gifts or transfers upon death. State laws often set forth one's property ownership rights, the ability to transfer property, and provide the legal requirements for wills and trusts.

life estate

estate in fee simple absolute

Before exploring the art of estate planning, it is important to understand the historical meaning of the term estate as well as its meaning today. Under old English common law (discussed in more detail below), the term "estate" referred primarily to an interest in land and the buildings or other permanent improvements on the land. Estate described the proprietary rights of the estate owner projected over time. Different types of estate ownership were classified on the basis of (1) the rights an owner could exercise over the property and (2) the duration of the owner's interest. A **life estate**, for example, is a property interest for the life of the estate owner with certain limitations on the life tenant's use of the property. It is, therefore, a lesser interest than an **estate in fee simple absolute**, which is an interest that belongs absolutely to the estate owner, the heirs, and assigns forever without condition or limitation. Over the course of time, an estate has come to mean more than an interest in land. It encompasses all the property or property rights that a person owns, even those from which a lifetime benefit will never be received, such as life insurance proceeds or survivor annuities. Modern estate planning focuses on all property-ownership rights (real, personal, tangible, and intangible), attempts to make appropriate arrangements for them during the estate owner's life, and provides for their orderly transfer at death.

The need for an orderly disposition of property at the death of the owner of that property has existed since humans began to accumulate and value possessions. Various cultures have resolved this need in different ways. In some cultures, all possessions belonged to families or tribes, so the death of an individual did not affect their ownership. Other cultures that did recognize individual property provided for a system of inheritance to persons related to the deceased through the mother, father, or both. It was a system very similar to today's laws of intestate succession, which provide a rigid scheme for inheritance of a deceased person's property by the heirs. The degree of relationship required to inherit as well as the method of tracing that relationship may have varied considerably from the criteria utilized for intestate succession today. Even in the early days of civilization, a rigid system of inheritance did not meet the needs of every family and it does not do so today. One child may have been favored by the estate owner over others, or may have required special assistance because of physical or mental frailties or prowess. In short, no one knows as much about the interrelationships and needs of a family as do the members of that family. Various cultures have recognized that fact for thousands of years by allowing adult family members to provide for postmortem property transfers designed to meet individual or family needs.

As early as the Fourth Egyptian Dynasty (2575-2465 BC), there appeared a testamentary disposition by an official to endow his tomb. In 2548 BC, an instrument was written on papyrus and witnessed by two scribes in which an Egyptian provided for certain property to be settled on his wife and appointed a guardian for his minor children. The Code of Hammurabi (1750 BC) does not mention wills directly but suggests that the culture had a scheme of intestate succession that the individual could alter, if the individual so desired.

The provision referred to is the right of an estate owner to favor the eldest son by *sealed deed*. If the sealed deed was executed, the eldest son would have had an absolute right to receive the property described within, sharing equally in the remaining property with his brothers. In the absence of a sealed deed, all male children presumably inherited equally. Total disinheritance of a son was allowed only by judicial proceeding during the lifetime of the father.

forced heirship

Both the Greek and Roman civilizations allowed a testamentary disposition of property pursuant to the wishes of the deceased party. In fact, prior to 40 BC, Roman citizens could totally disinherit children or other relatives. Because part of the state's interest in the orderly disposition of property at death has always been the support of the deceased's dependents to prevent them from becoming burdens of the state, the Romans developed a system of forced heirship for a portion of the deceased's property. This system continues to this day in civil-law jurisdictions (those jurisdictions tracing their judicial system to the ancient Romans and the Napoleonic Code rather than to English common law). Louisiana is the only true civil-law state in the United States and has a forced heirship provision that affects not only Louisiana residents but also Louisiana property owned by nonresidents. Other states, however, may also have some form of forced heirship provisions. **Forced heirship** is an estate-planning mechanism found in most civil law societies, which splits the estate into a forced estate portion and a discretionary estate portion. The forced estate portion must be passed along to a legally-mandated family member. The mandated family members are often referred to as forced heirs. While Louisiana, is the only U.S. state that follows a system of forced heirship, many other states protect the surviving spouse in a similar manner under Elective Share statutes.

Although our modern statutes retain some traces of ancient Roman law, the most prevalent influence is the English common law that developed after the invasion of William the Conqueror in 1066 AD. In that feudal society, the only property of consequence that a person could potentially pass at death was interest in land. All land in feudal England belonged ultimately to the king. Vast interests in land were granted by the king to the great nobles in return for various payments and services. The nobles, in turn, granted interests in smaller portions of land to lesser members of the nobility in exchange for services. It is readily apparent that an inherent conflict of interest existed between the tenant in possession of the land, the presumptive heirs, and the immediate overlord. In bargaining for the land grant, the tenant wished to give up as few payments or services as possible and the overlord wished to receive maximum benefits. The overlord wanted the land returned to him at the death of a tenant so that he could make a new and possibly more advantageous bargain with another tenant. On the other hand, the tenant in possession wished to be able to dispose of the land to his or her own heirs who, in turn, desired the certainty of knowing they would not be dispossessed. Conflicts were eventually resolved primarily in favor of the tenant in possession of the land by allowing the lifetime transfer by the tenant, thereby defeating both the claims of the presumptive heirs and the overlord (Statute of Quia Emptores, 1290 AD). A testamentary right of disposition over property, however, did not exist until the Statute of Wills in 1540, which gave all those except married women, infants, idiots, and the insane the right to dispose of most of their property by written instrument.

The English common law (both the statutes and the case law that construed them) became the foundation for American law in most legal areas, including the area of estates. Likewise, the English *use* (by which legal title to property was conveyed to a person in whom the owner had confidence with the instruction that the property be used for the benefit of the original owner's family or other designated persons) became the basis for the modern law of trusts.

The federal government began taxing estates as long ago as 1797. From 1797 to 1898, the tax went through repeal and reenactment, and it was held, albeit indirectly, unconstitutional in *Pollock v. Farmers' Loan & Trust Co.*, 157 U.S. 429, 3 AFTR 2557 (1895). In 1898, the federal estate tax was imposed once again under the War Revenue Act.

Two other historical occurrences are also important in estate planning. The first occurred in the late 19th century when various state legislatures in this country began to enact state inheritance tax laws based on the value of property distributed to a decedent's beneficiaries. The second occurrence was the federal government's taxation of gratuitous transfers of property (property passing at death [1915] and lifetime gifts [1932]).

As the legal complexities surrounding transfers of property at death became complicated further by federal and state estate, gift, or inheritance taxes, more people became concerned about protecting their property from erosion by taxes. Consequently, the process of estate planning evolved. In essence, estate planning today is the art of accumulating, conserving, and possibly transferring portions of one's property during lifetime and disposing of property at death in a manner that minimizes taxes, probate costs, and other related expenses and is consistent with one's lifetime goals.

Historical Notes
- Code of Hammurabi
- Statute of Wills
- state inheritance taxation
- federal transfer taxation
    - at death (1915)
    - lifetime gifts (1932)

LO 1. 3   Describe the steps in the estate planning process.

ESTATE PLANNING PROCESS

The estate planning process has a number of identifiable stages. First, data must be obtained. Then the existing estate plan must be evaluated for potential impairments. After that, a plan is designed that is approved by the client. After the client reviews the plan, it must be implemented. This stage includes the execution of any necessary legal documents and transfers for arrangements of property. Finally, it is important for the client to be made aware that there should be a periodic review of the plan, particularly at times of change in life or tax laws.

The Estate Planning Process
- *Step 1 :* data-gathering interview (personal information)
- *Step 2 :* evaluation of an existing plan
    - use of a financial fact finder (financial data)
    - client interview
- *Step 3 :* development of estate plan
    - preparation
- *Step 4 :* client review and approval of plan
- *Step 5 :* implementation of plan
    - execution of documents
    - transfer of property
- *Step 6 :* periodic review of plan

Data-gathering Interview

The initial stage in creating an estate plan is to gather all relevant facts from the estate owner and to compile them in a systematic manner. These facts should include full disclosure regarding all property ownership (both assets and liabilities), including expected gifts or inheritances. Any known problems connected with a particular property, such as the problems surrounding a closely held business interest, should be noted. Detailed information must also be obtained regarding the family structure, the names of all persons in the family who have some connection with the estate owner, and the relationships and attitudes of family members toward each other. For example, it is important to elicit the attitude of the estate owner toward a spouse and younger generations. Information must be obtained regarding philosophy about assets as well as feelings about work, money, risk, philanthropy, and financial security.

Some questions and areas of exploration that will help the estate planner discover the client's personal attitudes are the following: Does the estate owner have strong feelings about charitable giving or particular charitable organizations? Many individuals who have accumulated a substantial estate do have special feelings for some of the institutions that have aided them in achieving their goals and arriving at positions of financial, professional, or business success. What are the estate owner's obligations to a former spouse or to children of a first marriage? In estate planning today, one cannot ignore the subject of divorce. When an estate owner comes to see you with his or her spouse, it is possible that this may not be the first spouse. Also, there might be an elderly parent or a handicapped person in the family for whom the estate owner has some concern. Does the estate owner have a legal or moral obligation to support such a person? The estate owner should also be questioned regarding gifts that have been made during his or her lifetime as well as gifts that the estate owner anticipates making to various persons in the future.

Evaluation of an Existing Plan

Information should be obtained regarding the provisions of the estate owner's current estate plan, if any. Does the client presently have a valid will? Has the client created trusts that may or may not serve his or her needs? These documents and other legal documents should be brought to the interview to assist the estate planner in both evaluating the client's current plan and in making recommendations for improvement.

Use of a Financial-Fact Finder

To develop or revise an estate plan for a client, the planner needs to have a record containing all the relevant facts and information about the client. The financial fact finder provides a simple, thorough, and accurate way to record the client's information for present and future reference. Fact finders are forms designed to gather data systematically for financial and estate planning. Planners may also create their own fact finders and design them to suit their particular professional needs. Using the information provided in the fact finder, estate planners are able to make decisions by exercising their professional judgment based on their relationships with clients and their assessment of the clients' problems.

It is crucial in gathering facts and information to obtain both objective and subjective information. No questionnaire or fact finder has any value if the personal objectives of the estate owner are not extracted during the interview. Estate planning involves property, but more than that, it is planning for human beings. As such, it should be highly personalized. Good estate planners make sure that they have elicited from clients all their goals and intentions regarding their property, as well as their feelings about all family and nonfamily members whom they may want to protect or benefit in some way.

There are pros and cons regarding the submission of a fact finder to a client before an interview. While mailing the questionnaire in advance saves time during the initial interview, the amount of information requested may intimidate or overwhelm a client. In addition, there are many things the estate planner cannot determine from numbers and names on a piece of paper. It is only in a direct, personal interchange that a climate of trust can be established that will enable the estate owner to be comfortable in fully revealing personal information, beliefs, concerns, and attitudes to the estate planner. A good estate planner is usually able to establish rapport with, and gain the confidence of, a client fairly quickly.

Client Interview

In eliciting or reviewing facts in the initial data-gathering interview, problems that would impede the estate plan should be noted, defined, and explored with the client. As part of the data-gathering process, the estate planner also has a duty to explain to the client various potential options that are available under the current law. The client's responses to these various options provide significant guidance to the estate planner in determining the type of plan that is most suitable for meeting the client's needs and objectives. This involves explaining the law to the client and making certain it is understood. The plan is the client's plan, as is the ultimate decision regarding the arrangement of assets and transfers to beneficiaries. Many clients are intimidated by the professional person, are unfamiliar with the professional's language or terminology, and do not quite know how to ask questions that would help them understand

and feel comfortable with the estate plan. It is very important to make certain clients know what they are doing and why. This outcome can be accomplished by giving the client an analysis of problem areas the planner has identified as well as areas where there may be a choice among alternative solutions. The analysis is helpful to the client only if it is explained in understandable terms.

Development and Implementation of an Estate Plan

The next stage is the actual development of an estate plan. This includes the preparation and presentation of the plan to the client for review and final approval.

The fifth stage is the implementation of the plan. This entails executing the necessary legal documents, making arrangements for any current transfer of ownership, as well as providing for liquidity needs. In choosing between alternative planning options, the estate planner utilizes to the greatest extent possible those vehicles consistent with the client's wishes that provide the most benefits in the areas of estate, gift, and income tax.

Periodic Review

After the appropriate documents are reviewed and executed, the estate owner should be advised that a periodic review of the documents is essential as a final, and ongoing, stage of estate planning. Changes in the tax laws occur at an unprecedented rate, as can changes in financial and interpersonal situations. Through the process of periodic review, the estate owner ensures that such changes are reflected in his or her original estate plan.

When an estate plan is fully implemented and a review procedure is adopted, estate owners have the satisfaction of knowing they have taken an active role in the direction of their lives' plans, and they should have greater peace of mind in the knowledge that they have provided for the financial security of themselves and their families.

It is imperative that planners stress to their clients the critical importance of *accurate and comprehensive information*. Such information forms the foundation on which an effective estate plan is built.

Advantages of a Well-planned Estate
- property distribution according to the decedent's wishes
- tax-saving options
- appropriate ownership of assets
- disability and last illness preparedness
- liquidity needs assessment
- personal peace of mind

LO 1. 4   Describe the impediments to a well-developed estate plan.

IMPEDIMENTS TO A WELL-PLANNED ESTATE

Failure to Plan

Most people do not realize that even if they do not create an estate plan and execute the appropriate documents to implement their plans, a plan has been created and imposed on them by the state in which they reside. Everyone, no matter how poor, has an estate plan. Each state has drafted its own statutory scheme for the disposition of its citizens' property at death in the event that the resident dies either without a valid will or with an incomplete disposition of property.

intestate-succession statutes

escheat

intestate

Each state legislature has drafted a statutory plan that clearly lays out the way in which the property one owns at death will be distributed if the decedent dies without a valid will. These statutes are called **intestate succession statutes** or statutes of descent and distribution. In each of these statutes, the state has set out a standardized line of succession that controls who will succeed to ownership of the deceased person's property. These intestate succession statutes are based on spousal relationships and degrees of consanguinity (blood relationship) to the decedent rather than on the distribution of property according to the intentions and desires of the deceased individual. Note that adopted children are generally treated as bio-logical children of a decedent for intestate succession purposes. Without a will or trust, the decedent may not leave property to charity. Neither may a friend who is not related inherit any property from the deceased. If no relatives exist, the property reverts to the state. The property is said to **escheat** to the state. A decedent who dies **intestate** (without a will) appears to have had little concern for property, family, friends, or any other potential beneficiary, such as a charity.

The same limitations apply to today's statutes of intestate succession that applied to the intestate distribution vehicles of earlier cultures. They are highly standardized and rigid. As a result, they take no account of any special circumstances within families or any special relation-ships with nonrelated parties. Furthermore, lack of planning can destroy family relationships unintentionally, thereby causing bitterness and hardship for innocent family members. Because of those facts, distribution by intestate succession is only used when decedents have failed to advise the state in a legally acceptable manner through a will or similar document what they intend to do with their accumulated property at death.

will

The most basic legal instrument of all estate plans is a **will**. A will is a legal instrument whereby a person makes disposition of his or her property to take effect after death. Once a valid will has been executed, the statutes of intestate succession are largely displaced by the provisions of the will. Executing a will occurs when the testator, the person creating the will, signs it and satisfies any other state requirements to make the will valid, such as having witnesses also sign the will. While the intestate-succession statutes may be largely displaced by a will or other personal disposition by the decedent, they may not be totally displaced. The state is concerned with the support of a spouse and minor children since these individuals may become a financial burden to the state. Therefore, all states either have common-law rules or have enacted statutory provisions that protect a portion of the decedent's property for a surviving spouse under laws that are labeled variously as dower, curtesy, homestead rights, or other statutory provisions, such as a spouse's right of election. These provisions may be operative only if the spouse and children have not been provided for by the will, or they may be absolute rights regardless of the will's provisions, such as forced heirship. The specific provisions of such laws vary from state to state, but they are a form of intestate succession. Individuals should understand what form these provisions take in their states and whether or not they can be displaced by the provisions in a will. The surviving spouse's rights can often be enforced only by an election to take against the provisions in a valid will and often these provisions are not what the decedent would have wanted.

Outdated Plan

While a valid will is a good beginning point for an estate plan, the will must be reviewed periodically to assure that a property owner's most recent intentions are honored at death. The birth of new children or grandchildren, the unexpected illness or disability of family members, and changes in the estate owner's objectives are common reasons for revising an estate plan, will, or trust. Major tax law changes may affect the goals of an existing plan or the tax clauses contained in a will or trust. An owner may perceive beneficiaries and their needs differently over time. Guardianship for minor children or arrangements for special-needs beneficiaries may need to be altered.

Will provisions may be altered by an amendment (called a *codicil*) or completely rewritten by the property owner at any time. The modern technology of word processors and computers makes rewriting an entire will even for minor changes a relatively simple task. If family circumstances or laws have changed dramatically since the will was written, the will's provisions may be seriously out of touch with the property owner's current wishes. Nonetheless, the existing will is the one that will be followed until (or unless) it is replaced with a later valid will. This situation can produce some disturbing results.

EXAMPLE

Jane and her cousin, Martin, were close friends 10 years ago. Jane named Martin as a substantial beneficiary under her will. Later, Martin fell into Jane's disfavor, and for years they seldom spoke. Despite the change in Jane and Martin's relationship, the property set out in Jane's will 10 years ago will pass to Martin at Jane's death unless Jane reviews and revises her will to reflect the change in her feelings toward Martin.

Wills and trusts should be reviewed periodically to make certain that the owner's objectives are met.

Overlooked Provisions

The following provisions are sometimes overlooked or forgotten in an estate plan, will, or trust: guardianship, simultaneous death, residuary estate, tax apportionment, and contingent beneficiaries.

The issue of guardians should be addressed by an estate owner with minor children or special-needs family members. Frequently, a guardian is named for the minor's personal care while another or others supervise and invest the minor's property. Usually guardians are named in the wills of parents and individuals having the responsibility of other family members. Clearly, arrangements should be discussed with potential guardians prior to naming them in the will.

The possibility of simultaneous deaths should also be considered in an estate plan. An owner should devise backup asset arrangements in case spouses and/or beneficiaries die in a common disaster.

A residuary clause is an important will provision. Even though the estate owner believes all property is provided for and is arranged to pass according to his or her wishes, a residuary clause provides for the transfer of unexpected, unknown, or forgotten assets as well as assets acquired in the future.

Tax-apportionment issues are sometimes neglected in an estate plan. Planners should make certain that clients carefully consider tax payment options and the sources from which tax payments are to be made. In other words, a determination should be made concerning which assets and beneficiaries bear the burden of death taxes.

equitable apportionment

For example, if an individual directs under the will that all estate taxes are to be paid from the residuary estate, he or she should recognize that the residuary beneficiaries may not receive what the testator originally intended. Generally speaking, most state statutes direct the payment of taxes to be equitably apportioned. **Equitable apportionment** means that each bequest bears the tax it generates. For instance, if a beneficiary receives 15 percent of the taxable estate, the beneficiary is responsible for 15 percent of the death taxes. State law, however, yields to a specific direction in a will or trust document regarding the apportionment of taxes. A carefully drafted tax-apportionment clause is tailored to meet the estate owner's intentions.

An estate owner should have provisions in place for contingent beneficiaries in case the primary beneficiaries are no longer living at the time of the owner's death or incapacity or in case the primary beneficiaries disclaim assets passing to them.

Improper Tax Planning

The potential estate and gift tax relief that changes in the federal estate and gift tax laws appear to provide may make many individuals think they no longer need a carefully planned estate. However, the truth is that only by utilizing the new tax laws to maximum advantage through professional advice can property owners carry out their postmortem intentions and prevent the unnecessary erosion of their estates due to taxes. For example, the unlimited marital deduction that allows an individual to pass an entire estate free of federal gift and estate taxes to a spouse appears to offer relief from taxation. In reality, use of the unlimited marital deduction (covered in later chapters) may be enormously expensive at the death of the second spouse, since property will pass unprotected by the marital deduction (assuming the surviving spouse does not remarry). Thus, the combined taxes on two estates may be greater than if the unlimited marital deduction had not been used in the estate of the first spouse to die. In short, the need for estate planning has never depended, and does not now depend, solely on whether there is a federal estate tax payable in one particular estate.

While there are important tax planning options that can be utilized in estate planning, tax relief should not be the primary objective of estate planning. The best estate plan is one that accurately reflects the client's wishes, needs, and objectives in a manner that reduces the potential tax liability to the lowest level consistent with the client's aims. This approach means that various tax options must be balanced against rigidity, loss of control over assets, tax liability, and so on. The alternatives must also be explained to clients so they can understand both the limitations and the benefits of these options and choose the ones that reflect their desires and intentions. An estate plan that reduces the estate tax liability to zero is a poor plan if the cost is the perversion of the client's wishes.

Improper Ownership of Assets

Many times the estate tax liability and even the ultimate ownership of an asset is predetermined by the form of ownership in which it is held prior to the owner's death. An example of an asset that is frequently improperly owned or positioned is life insurance. If the insured retains any incident of ownership in life insurance, the proceeds are subject to estate taxation. This unnecessary estate tax drain can be eliminated and more net dollars can be made available to the estate or its beneficiaries by removing all incidents of ownership from the insured and giving them to a spouse or trust. However, the unlimited marital deduction may now make it more desirable for the decedent to retain ownership of life insurance. Proper ownership of assets, including life insurance, must be analyzed on a case-by-case basis.

Another form of property ownership that can be problematic in estate planning is joint ownership with right of survivorship. This tilting includes ownership as joint tenants with right of survivorship (ownership by the deceased and any other person including the surviving spouse) or as tenants by the entireties (a form of joint ownership restricted to married couples). The postmortem succession of property that is owned in either of these forms is not controlled by the provisions in a valid will. Ownership is transferred automatically by operation of law to the surviving joint tenant or tenant by the entireties. If all or most property is owned in this form, the result can be the cause of an improperly balanced estate in which the surviving spouse may inherit too much of the property relative to the children, possibly resulting in an excessive estate tax liability at the second death.

Digital Assets

The law is usually years behind technology. The development of a digital world has created numerous challenges for traditional legal planning devices. Perhaps no legal area has been more impacted than estate planning by the development of a digital world. In the past, bank vaults, safe-deposit boxes, and safes were used to hold assets for an estate. These assets were then passed along through a will or trust to the decedent's heirs. However, many of the assets previously held in safety deposit boxes and safes are being held in digital formats online.

Digital assets are becoming a huge part of our everyday life and make up a large portion of our assets. Just think for a minute about all of the different online accounts you use on a daily basis. It is likely you will use more than twenty different online accounts in a day. In fact, you might have hundreds of these accounts in your name. Most, and perhaps all, of these accounts contain some form of property that you own. Property that is held only online is referred to as a **digital asset**. The term digital assets does not include digital storage devices like computers, phones, and flash drives. Instead, the term describes the valuable property you have stored on those devices.

Digital assets present a variety of issues for estate planners. First, there are real issues about ownership and access. While you might believe you own your digital assets outright in fee simple absolute, it is likely you have some form of split ownership rights. Your ownership rights in digital assets are usually set forth in the service agreement you clicked through when you set up your online account. These service agreements are widely different from company-to-company, but traditionally they all restrict your form of ownership in some way. Some agreements state you have a lifetime lease, some give you outright ownership, and many make the asset nontransferable while alive or upon death. This discrepancy means you might think you own an online account you use for your small business, but upon your death no one else can own or use that account. This risk can cause tremendous estate planning issues.

Currently, there are no federal laws on point that control the ownership rights or distribution of digital assets. However, there are a few states considering adopting a uniform law that allows fiduciaries to have access to digital assets upon the owner's death or incompetency. At the end of 2018, almost every state has enacted some version of the Revised Uniform Fiduciary Access to Digital Assets and Digital Accounts Act.

Digital assets can also be hard to find because the decedent passed away without leaving a comprehensive list. Traditional estate planning devices like wills and trusts offer little protection because they cannot keep track of the vast amount of digital assets and cannot change the service agreements which control ownership and transferability of the digital assets. Instead, individuals will need to keep track of their usernames and passwords in a secure location so their heirs can get access to the digital assets upon their death.

Failure to Plan for Disability, Last Illness, Job Change or Loss

The cost of a protracted period of disability or a prolonged last illness may so erode an otherwise adequate estate that the estate owner leaves nothing to the beneficiaries at death, except a crushing amount of debt. The ownership of adequate medical expense and disability income insurance protection is an important consideration in planning any estate. Disability income protection, in particular, is often ignored or misunderstood by clients despite the fact that statistically there is a greater likelihood of a significant period of disability before retirement age than there is of an early death.

Planners also need to advise clients to plan for the possibility of changes in employment, including job loss and severance packages. At the very least, a significant variation in employment requires a review of the client's existing estate plan.

Failure to Consider Inflation

tax bracket creep

Another impediment to effective estate planning that should not be underestimated is the rate of inflation experienced over the past few years. At the very least, continuing inflation necessitates periodic reviews of existing estate plans to keep abreast of projected estate tax liabilities, as these can be affected by inflation through **tax bracket creep**. Tax bracket creep refers to the adverse effect of inflation pushing individual income and wealth levels into higher tax brackets. The result is higher taxes with no increase in purchasing power. The federal government adjusts individual and estate and trust income tax rate brackets as well as the transfer tax exclusions for inflation, but most states do not adjust their tax brackets, and the rate of increase of the individual's income and wealth may exceed the rate of the government's bracket adjustments.

It is also necessary to review asset valuations, projected income from assets held, and amounts of life insurance in terms of constant dollars to assure that the estate owner's family would continue to be adequately protected. An inflated economic climate will have a direct impact on all estates as the value of the dollar is eroded. Failure to take inflation into consideration when projecting the adequacy of an estate 10, 20, or 30 years into the future will probably make it impossible to carry out the estate owner's desires.

Lack of Liquidity

Lack of liquidity may be a major problem in an otherwise well-planned estate. Four factors are particularly important in assessing liquidity needs in estate planning: (1) the amount and terms of debt of the estate owner, (2) the projected estate tax liability, (3) the type of assets that make up the estate , and (4) the marital status of the testator. The marital status of the decedent is important for liquidity purposes because if a surviving spouse is left the majority of the assets there will likely be lower fees and taxes owed by the estate. However, there could also be a need for liquid assets in the form of retirement or income needs. As such, any liquidity discussion needs to include the marital status of the testator.

At the time of an estate owner's death, the amount and terms of debt for which a decedent is personally responsible may dramatically reduce either the actual assets or the net income stream available to the beneficiaries. The same is true of the estate tax liability.

The types of assets owned at the time of death also affect the cash available to the beneficiaries for their income needs. For example, when a closely held business is the primary estate asset and is the source of income to the decedent and family through the decedent's salary and bonuses, there is frequently a family cash shortage when salary and bonuses cease. This event results in financial stress to a family that is already trying to deal with the death of a family member. It is most important that the possibility of such a situation be considered prior to its occurrence, and both the estate owner and the family make appropriate decisions to avoid these problems. If adequate planning has been done, salary continuation plans are a possible way to soften the financial shock of a breadwinner's death, and additional liquidity may also be available from retirement plans and life insurance proceeds.

If the business is to be sold, it is imperative that the arrangements for the sale be reduced during the lifetime of the shareholder to legally enforceable agreements that are equitable to all parties, including both the persons who will continue the business and the decedent-share-holder's family.

If no such advance planning is done, the estate may be forced to sell assets hurriedly to pay its bills or taxes, and assets may have to be sold under disadvantageous market conditions at greatly reduced prices.

Psychological Impediments

Dealing With One's Own Mortality

Many people avoid making an estate plan because it encompasses planning for the transfer of assets after their death. It is almost as if, by failing to participate in estate planning, these individuals avoid confronting the fact that death will happen to them. They perpetuate their denial of death.

Implementation of an estate plan includes provision for the disposition of assets after death and requires an individual to acknowledge the reality of his or her mortality. Very few people can deal comfortably with this. There are many sophisticated and successful professionals who are very comfortable in the high-pressure atmosphere of finance and international business but who are so distressed when attempting to deal with the inevitability of death that they never implement a cohesive estate plan. In this case, it is the family of the estate owner who ultimately suffers when their standard of living is impaired at the decedent's death or when they try to impose some semblance of order on an estate that is in disarray.

Estate planners must make every reasonable effort to work with clients who are avoiding a confrontation with the inevitability of death. They should avoid getting involved in an intense psychological encounter for which they are not trained; therefore, they must be sensitive in handling the difficulties presented by clients in this situation. It may be possible to assist a client past this obstacle by suggesting that estate planning is purely precautionary, and prudence requires that he or she be prepared for any eventuality. It is also important to educate the client regarding the consequences of failing to do estate planning, including the very real possibility that an unplanned estate may cause the dissolution of the achievements of a lifetime of effort devoted to accumulating and preserving wealth.

Procrastination

While procrastination may be another indication that clients are delaying a confrontation with their own mortality, a more common reason for this delay is the feeling that planning for the distribution of an estate is a task so large that it is impossible to achieve. The client can become overwhelmed and simply do nothing. In this circumstance, it is often sufficient for the estate planner to accept a significant part of the responsibility for completing the estate plan and divide the tasks that must be done by the client into manageable chores.

Obstacles to Effective Estate Planning

- failure to plan for death
  - not executing or updating a will
  - not taking the time to think about who gets what and when
  - believing the state succession statutes will cause property to pass the way the estate owner would want it to
- outdated plan
  - birth and death of family members
  - failure to update decision makers and beneficiaries
  - tax law changes
- overlooked provisions
  - guardianship
  - simultaneous death
  - tax apportionment
- improper tax planning
- improper ownership of assets
- failure to plan for disability, illness, or changes in or loss of employment
- failure to consider inflation
- lack of liquidity
- psychological factors
  - dealing with mortality
  - procrastination

LO 1. 5   Explain the interaction of the estate planning team and the specific

functions of different team members.

ESTATE PLANNING TEAM

The estate planning team has traditionally consisted of an attorney, an insurance specialist, a bank trust officer, an accountant, and an investment counselor (see the figure below). A newer member of the team is the financial planner. It is frequently the financial planner or the insurance specialist who makes the first contact with the client, sensitizes the client to the need for estate planning, and motivates the client to become involved in the process. This sequence of contact is partly because both the life underwriter and the financial planner can advertise their services and otherwise solicit business. Attorneys and accountants may engage in advertising only in a limited and regulated manner.

Financial planning is a discipline of relatively recent origin. The financial planner may be an independent businessperson or may be affiliated with a large investment, insurance, accounting, or other institution. The financial planner may provide services solely for a fee or, if permitted by state law, the fees for planning may be offset, in whole or in part, by commissions on the sale of financial products. Financial planning is a process for arriving at comprehensive solutions to a client's personal, business, and financial problems and concerns. The term covers a wide range of financial services and products. It is the ability of financial planners to cooperate with other members of various disciplines to develop an overall plan for the client that is one of their most significant contributions to client service and to the estate planning team.

The Estate Planning Team

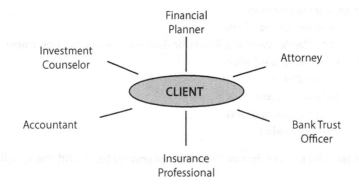

The next member of the estate planning team, the accountant, is the advisor most likely to have annual contact with the client through preparation of the client's tax returns. This gives the accountant the opportunity to be familiar with the size, amount, and nature of the client's estate. The accountant may be the person who provides valuations for assets in the estate. Valuation might be particularly crucial if one recommendation in the estate plan is a buy-sell agreement to provide for a transfer of a business interest upon death or disability. The accountant may also be of help in preparing a final estate tax return. Accountants who possess a CPA are typically the best choice for team members.

The trust officer is the next member of the team. This may be the person to whom the client has initially turned for information and estate planning services if professional management is desired in the administration of a trust. A good trust officer will be familiar with the field of estate planning and the various estate planning tools that can be used. As executors or trustees, trust officers have primary responsibility for settling the estate, investing estate assets during the administration period, and making distributions—as necessary—to the estate or trust beneficiaries. The bank trust department may also be responsible for filing estate and fiduciary income tax returns.

The insurance specialist plays an important role on the estate planning team because he or she can provide products that give the estate the necessary cash to pay the estate tax and other liabilities as well as to fund the income needs of the surviving family. Life insurance may be the primary asset of some estates and, consequently, the major source for family income after an estate owner dies. Life insurance agents who have become CLU®s are knowledgeable in the fields of insurance, as well as estate planning and taxation, and can provide an invaluable service as an informed member of the team.

The next member of the team is the attorney. The attorney is a crucial member because planning cannot be accomplished nor can a plan be executed without an attorney's knowledge of the law. Typically, the attorney is the professional who drafts all of the legal documents necessary to implement the plan. These documents virtually always include wills and may include trusts, buy-sell agreements, or other documents if a more sophisticated estate plan is elected. The attorney is responsible for assuring that the intentions of the client are expressed in legally enforceable documents that serve as the basis for carrying out the client's postmortem plan.

The creation of an estate plan is a highly rewarding experience for the estate planning practitioner regardless of the discipline from which he or she comes. Although there may be a different emphasis in various estate plans stemming from the knowledge and background of the practitioner, the primary objective of a good planner is to effectuate and implement both the desires and objectives of the individual for whom the plan is created. The client is the director of the plan. The professionals are the producers. An estate plan reflects the personality of the client. It may evidence the client's cares and concerns for other human beings as well as for himself or herself. On the contrary, the plan may reflect or focus on the client's own self-interest, grievances, and grudges. Much is revealed about the client's character, philosophy of life, and attitudes by the types of planning options he or she selects and the reasons for which they are selected.

Estate planning has become vastly more complicated and challenging as a field of practice. In order to be an effective estate planner, one must be familiar with applicable local and federal law. One must also have a working knowledge of subject matter pertaining to property, probate, wills and trusts, federal and state taxation, corporations, partnerships, business, insurance, and divorce. An estate planner must be able to explain to a client relevant portions of these subjects in plain language. If the client is spoken down to or expected to deal with technical jargon, the client will not feel confident and may well abandon the project. A client has an absolute right to fully understand all the options and make his or her own decisions.

CHAPTER REVIEW

Key Terms and Concepts

estate planning	intestate
life estate	will
estate in fee simple absolute	equitable apportionment
forced heirship	digital assets
intestate-succession	tax bracket creep
escheat	

Chapter 1: Review Questions

1. Identify the different kinds of taxes within the transfer tax system. [1]

2. What is the meaning of the term estate planning in its broadest sense? [1]

3. Briefly describe the historical development of estate planning. [2]

4. All state intestacy statutes share common characteristics as to the distribution of a decedent's property.

    a. What principles do the intestacy statutes follow in the statutory distribution of a decedent's property?

    b. Which individuals and organizations typically cannot inherit through intestate succession? [2]

5. To what extent does a valid will displace the statutes of intestate succession? [2]

6. Why is it important for an estate plan to be revised periodically? [3]

7. What provisions in a will or trust are sometimes overlooked? [4]

8. Explain why tax planning objectives should be subordinate to the primary objectives of estate planning. [1]

9. Why is the form of property ownership an important consideration in estate planning? [2]

10. Why are medical expense insurance and disability income insurance important concerns in estate planning? [4]

11. How is inflation an impediment to effective estate planning? [4]

12. Identify the factors that are important in assessing an estate's liquidity needs. [4]

13. Why is estate liquidity analysis particularly important for a closely held business owner? [4]

14. Explain how psychological impediments may be a barrier to proper estate planning. [4]

15. Describe the stages in the estate planning process. [3]

16. Identify the various types of professionals on the estate planning team, and explain how their respective functions complement one another. [5]

Chapter 1: Review Answers

1. Gift tax, estate tax, generation-skipping transfer tax, and qualified domestic trust taxation are all types of transfer taxation.

2. In its broadest sense, estate planning is the accumulation, conservation, management, and distribution of an estate.

3. Throughout history, various cultures have recognized the need for postmortem transfers of property to meet family or individual needs. For example, the Code of Hammurabi indicates that the culture had a plan of intestate succession. Both the Greek and Roman civilizations allowed testamentary disposition of property. The Romans developed a system of forced heirship that is still in use today in Louisiana.

   The most widespread influence on modern statutes, however, is the English common law, which developed after 1066. In that feudal society—in which the only property that a person could transfer at death was his interest in the land—conflicts developed between tenants in possession of land, the presumptive heirs, and the overlord. Although conflicts were eventually resolved in favor of the tenants, it was not until 1540 that a testamentary right of disposition over property—the Statute of Wills—enabled property owners to dispose of most of their property via written instrument.

   The English common law became the foundation for American law in most legal areas, including estate planning. As the estate planning process evolved, various legislatures in the United States enacted state inheritance taxes in the late 19th century, and the federal government enacted laws taxing gratuitous transfers of property (property passing at death) in 1915 and lifetime gifts in 1932.

4. a. Intestacy statutes follow a standardized line of succession that controls who will succeed to ownership of a deceased person's property. The statutes are based on spousal and blood relationships to the decedent, rather than on the decedent's intentions or desires.

    b. Friends and charitable organizations typically cannot inherit any of the deceased's property through intestate succession.

5. A valid will largely—but not entirely—displaces the statutes of intestate succession. In order to avoid the financial dependence of the deceased's spouse and minor children on the state, most states have either common-law rules or statutory provisions that protect a portion of the deceased's property for a surviving spouse, regardless of the provisions in the will. Although such laws vary from state-to-state, they are all a form of intestate succession.

6. An estate plan should be revised periodically to ensure that it keeps pace with the estate owner's most recent intentions. For example, the birth of new children or grand-children, a family member's illness or disability, shifts in the estate owner's objectives, or changes in tax laws are all reasons to review the estate plan and make sure that it continues to meet the estate owner's goals.

7. The following provisions are often overlooked in an estate plan, will, or trust: guard-ianship, simultaneous death, the residuary estate, tax apportionment, and contingent beneficiaries.

8. Tax relief should not be the primary objective of estate planning. A plan that reduces the client's tax liability to zero but does not meet his or her personal objectives is a poor plan and a disservice to the client. The best estate plan reflects the client's wishes, needs, and objectives *and* reduces the potential tax liability to the lowest possible level.

9. The form of property ownership is an important consideration in estate planning because it often predetermines the estate tax liability and even the ultimate owner-ship of that asset upon the asset owner's death.

10. Medical expense insurance and disability income insurance are important concerns in estate planning because the costs of a protracted period of disability or a prolonged illness may erode an estate to the point that there will be nothing—except debt—to leave beneficiaries.

11. The effects of inflation will have a direct impact on an estate. As the value of the dollar is eroded, the adequacy of the estate diminishes. Failure to take inflation into account when projecting the adequacy of an estate 10 to 30 years in the future will probably make it impossible to carry out the estate owner's intentions.

12. The four factors that are important in assessing an estate's liquidity needs are (1) the amount and terms of the estate owner's debt, (2) the projected estate tax liability, (3) the type of assets in the estate, and (4) the marital status of the testator.

13. When a closely held business is the primary asset and source of income to the decedent and family, the financial consequences to the family when the decedent's salary and bonuses cease can be enormous. With adequate planning, salary continuation plans, retirement plans, and life insurance proceeds can ease the financial burden and provide liquidity.

14. Many people are afraid to deal with the fact of their own mortality or are so overwhelmed by the magnitude of estate planning that they delay the process. Inability to confront their own mortality and procrastination are both impediments to proper estate planning.

15. The stages in the estate planning process are as follows:

    - Data is obtained.

    - The existing estate plan is evaluated for potential impediments.

    - The plan is designed, reviewed, and approved by the client.

    - The plan is implemented.

    - The plan is reviewed periodically to make sure it continues to meet the client's objectives as they evolve.

16. The types of professionals who make up the estate planning team are as follows: an attorney, an insurance specialist, a bank trust officer, an accountant, an investment specialist, and a financial planner. Their respective functions complement on another by enabling the client to achieve total financial planning. Combining the expertise of advisors in a variety of disciplines offers comprehensive solutions to the client's personal, business, and financial concerns.

Chapter 2:

Ethics for the Estate Planner

Learning Objectives

An understanding of the material in this chapter should enable the student to

LO 2.1 **Define the three purposes of ethics.**

LO 2. 2 **Distinguish between ethics and compliance.**

LO 2. 3 **Explain how moral perception and moral imagination facilitate ethical decision making.**

LO 2. 4 **Describe the six moral characteristics of a profession.**

LO 2. 5 **Explain the relationship between giving estate planning advice and the unauthorized practice of law.**

LO 2. 6 **Discuss the issues of working with clients who may be experiencing declining mental competency.**

INTRODUCTION

Among other things, ethics deals with the question of how individuals fulfill their personal and professional responsibilities. Included among such responsibilities are the keeping of commitments and the fair, respectful treatment of others. The best way to determine those responsibilities is to consider a professional's underlying objective or purpose. It is that objective or purpose that determines what actions are necessary and appropriate for that goal or purpose to be accomplished.

The function of the estate planner is to preserve and enhance the client's estate. Because the provision of such a service requires competence, certain expertise, and primary concern for the good of the client, estate planning exhibits all of the characteristics of a profession. Inherent in estate planning, therefore, are all of the ethical responsibilities that accrue to professionals. In this chapter, we are going to consider the question of ethical behavior as it relates specifically to the estate planning professional. Let's begin with the question of how to distinguish ethics from compliance.

LO 2.1   Define the three purposes of ethics.

WHAT IS ETHICS?

ethics

Ethics is defined as a set of principles which reflect the shared beliefs and values of a given society or culture. Ethical principles are needed to accomplish three tasks:

1. To govern behavior which is not appropriately regulated by the law. Consider the example of a gossiping friend or a chronically late dinner guest. Most agree these behaviors are unethical, but most would also agree that it would not be appropriate to criminally sanction these sorts of behavior.

2. To supplement legal condemnation with moral disapproval. The spheres of law and ethics frequently overlap. For example, an attorney who violated attorney-client privilege for personal gain would not only be subject to legal sanction, but would also be subject to ethical sanctions as well.

3. To encourage behavior that goes beyond what the law requires. Often, what it takes to meet our ethical obligations goes beyond what the letter of the law requires. For example, while the law requires that we disclose certain information to our clients, an ethical obligation may require us to make sure that this disclosure is meaningful and the client is able to effectively and efficiently incorporate this information into a plan.

In other words, the sphere of ethics both supplements and reinforces the sphere of legal obligations. At times, ethics requires us to go above and beyond our legal duties. However, there are other distinctions we can make between ethics and the law and ethics and compliance.

LO 2. 2   Distinguish between ethics and compliance.

compliance

The first distinction is that ethical choices are supposed to be freely chosen in a way that **compliance** (or legally compelled) choices are not. The argument is that when people choose to be ethical they do not do so because they are compelled by a fear of punishment or fear of consequences. In this sense, ethical choices are properly free to reflect our beliefs and values.

The second distinction is that just as ethical actions should not be chosen out of fear of the consequences, they should also not be chosen solely for the hope of additional gain or reward. Plato, an ancient Greek philosopher, distinguishes between two types of actions: (1) action which is thought to be good for itself and its consequences, and (2) action which is only good for its consequences. Health is an example of the first type since we value being healthy for its own sake (it feels good to be healthy) as well as for its consequences (if we are healthy we can pursue other activities we value). Going to the dentist or to the doctor may be an example of the second type of good action. We don't particularly enjoy our time in the dentist's chair; the activity is only worthwhile because of its consequences—absence of pain and disfigurement. The question is, which class of goods does ethical behavior belong to? Plato—and most moral philosophers—believe that ethical behavior falls into the first category, which contains the highest and best good, something which is good for itself and good for its consequences.

Plato's distinction gets at an important point, which is that it is not appropriate to treat ethical behavior as a mere means to another goal. To treat ethical behavior as a mere strategy for promoting one's self interest is to miss the point. Imagine a company which embarks on an environmentally friendly renovation of their manufacturing facilities for the sole purpose of being able to brand themselves in the community as the "company that cares." Depending on if members of the community will appreciate their efforts and respond to the company in the desired ways, this may or may not be a sound business strategy. However, it is not an ethical one. The company's decision makers are looking at the activity of environmentally focused renovation with the same enthusiasm that most of us view an overdue trip to the dentist. They do not see that the activity of protecting the environment is a good that is valuable and choice-worthy in itself as well as yielding financially beneficial consequences.

The good news is that acting ethically does not require us to have entirely pure motives—we can certainly value the decision to go ahead with the renovation both because it is in our financial interest (consequences) and because it respects our commitment to the community and the environment and, therefore, is good in itself. However, both components have to be present. In short, we have to be motivated not only by the chance for personal gain, but also by the desire to act well.

LO 2. 3   **Explain how moral perception and moral imagination facilitate ethical decision making.**

MORAL PERCEPTION AND MORAL IMAGINATION

moral perception

Ethical decision making is the ability to determine which course of action or decision is morally right. However, before a decision can be made and action taken, another crucial step is necessary. This step is called moral perception. **Moral perception** enables us to perceive the morally relevant details and facts in a particular situation. Consider the following example:

EXAMPLE

Your firm is looking to hire a new office manager. You have knowledge that one of the top candidates for the position has a history of substance abuse. You wonder whether to disclose this information to the head of the hiring committee.

When I ask people how they would respond if faced with such a dilemma, they often respond that they don't have enough information to answer the question. When I inquire further into what they would like to know, I usually receive the following questions:

- How do I know about the substance abuse? Is it firsthand information, or is it second-hand information? If secondhand, is the information from a reliable source?

- How long did the abuse continue? When did the abuse stop?

- Are there any potential liability issues for me personally if I share this information?

- What role does the office manager play in interacting with clients and other staff?

These are all very good questions. In fact, the point of the exercise is to enable people to identify the information they need to know in order make a good decision. For example, some students believe that there is a morally relevant difference in the situation of a sober alcoholic who has been a member of AA for 15 years and a candidate who recently stopped drinking. It seems that these cases should be treated differently.

moral imagination

It is also important to ask, "Who will be affected by this decision? And, how will they be affected?" In answering these questions, we use a capacity called moral imagination. **Moral imagination** allows us to speculate as to how the possible consequences of our decisions will affect other people around us, both in the short term and the long term. Both moral perception and moral imagination allow us to be sure that we are not missing any important facts about the case.

ETHICAL DECISION MAKING

ethical decision making

In **ethical decision making**, we take the information we are able to glean from our acts of moral perception and moral imagination and make a decision. Let's return to the example we just discussed. It is possible you may develop a chart that looks like this:

List of Stakeholders	
Who is affected?	**How are they affected?**
Candidate	• Might not get the job • Might have difficulty finding a job on account of previous history • Might take legal action if she discovers your role in disclosing information
Company	• Might be exposed to harm if the candidate returns to previous substance abuse • Might be exposed to legal action if candidate sues for libel • Coworkers and others who work directly with the office manager might be harmed if the candidate is hired and returns to substance abuse
You	• Might be blamed by the company if they find out you withheld information about the candidate • Might be the subject of legal action by the candidate if you disclose information

There is a conflict of values at stake in this situation as well:

- **Compassion:** Most people believe in second chances. Depending on the circumstances of the case, it may be seen as unjust to deprive the candidate of her chance for redemption. This is especially true if she has difficulty finding a position with her background. Compassion dictates that we show empathy and understanding when confronted with the suffering and failings of other people.

- **Respect for Privacy:** Most people believe that we have a right to keep certain information about ourselves private.

- **Loyalty to Employer:** Most people believe that they have an obligation to look out for the best interests of their employer. If you possess information that your employer would deem materially relevant to decision making, it would be unjust for you to withhold this information.

- **Loyalty to Self:** This value encompasses your loyalty to your own self-interest and your commitment to other obligations you have undertaken, such as financial support of your family or friends. If disclosing (or not disclosing) this information will place you in legal or financial jeopardy, this should be taken into account.

You could probably think of additional values or perhaps you could name them in different ways, but the main point is that ethical judgment is always a matter of deciding among different values. At times, this can be a relatively simple exercise, but on other occasions it can be incredibly difficult.

IN SEARCH OF A STANDARD

In order to decide how to act, it is necessary for us to adopt a moral standard which will allow us to weigh the relative merits of each of the competing stakeholders and groups we referred to above. Without a standard, we would have no way of knowing which stakeholder or which value should be prioritized in this situation.

Different philosophical systems offer different ethical standards. A great amount of debate in philosophical ethics concerns which one of these standards is correct. Philosophers who write about these matters claim that their ethical standards apply universally, that is, they apply to all people facing ethical dilemmas no matter where or in what time period they live. These are interesting debates, but it is important here to focus on the ethical standards that apply specifically to estate planners and other financial services professionals. Since in addition to the ethical standards that apply to us all, certain professionals, including estate planners, are subject to additional ethical standards and guidance.

WHAT IS A PROFESSION?

Solomon Huebner, the founder of The American College of Financial Services, claims that a profession is defined by the possession of four characteristics. The first is that professions engage in a vocation that is useful and noble. Professional activities contribute value to society through providing a needed service. For example, doctors provide for the health and comfort of our bodies, and accountants allow for the free market of shares by validating the financial reports and the overall health of corporations. In general, the financial services industry is useful to society because its practitioners help people manage their financial risks and provide for their financial futures.

It is instructive to consider Huebner's use of the term "vocation." According to Lawrence Blum, the concept of a vocation includes a specific place and a designated purpose within society. Vocation carries with it certain values, standards, and ideals. "Vocation implies that the ideals that it embodies are ones that speak specifically to the individual in question. There is a personal identification with the vocation, with its values and ideals and a sense of personal engagement that helps to sustain the individual in her carrying out the activities of the vocation."[1] Huebner's use of the term "vocation" points to his belief that an attachment to a vocation results in a personal transformation. For Huebner, it is impossible to become a professional without adopting these professional values. Blum affirms Huebner's insistence on professional values by saying, "An individual with a vocation must believe deeply in the values and ideals of the vocation and must in some way choose or at least affirm them for herself."[2]

The second characteristic noted by Huebner is that the professions require the possession of expert knowledge. For example, a professional not only understands that he or she possesses a moral obligation to act in the best interest of the client but also understands which course of action in this particular situation actually promotes the best interests of the client. The true professional needs to be competent, and so it is a responsibility of the true professional to stay abreast of the latest developments, not only learning latest practices but also understanding why they are beneficial.

The third characteristic of Huebner's definition is that to be a professional means to "abandon the strictly selfish commercial view and ever keep in mind the advantage of the client in the application of that knowledge." The strictly commercial view, according to Huebner, is defined as pursuing one's self-interest to the exclusion of everyone else. The strictly commercial view, then, is extreme in that it promotes unfettered selfishness.

In the English language, the words "self-interest" and "selfishness" have very different meanings. It is important and natural for people to look out for their own interests. In fact, if people are not self-interested, or if they do not have a healthy self-love, they do both their neighbors and themselves a disservice. However, if we pursue our self-interest at the expense of another, we go too far and are selfish.

The fourth characteristic of a professional according to Huebner is a spirit of loyalty to other professionals. We have an obligation to refrain from engaging in malicious gossip about fellow professionals and are also obliged to help other professionals in the carrying out of their responsibilities when it is appropriate. Professionals are also directed to work to maintain the positive reputation of the industry in general by not engaging in unethical behavior. This

---

1. Lawrence Blum, *Moral Perception and Particularity* (Cambridge: Cambridge University Press, 1994), 104.
2. Blum, 104.

includes monitoring and policing fellow professionals who engage in unethical behavior or calling to task those who engage in unethical behavior. The obligation of loyalty to the profession is grounded in the fact that the profession is larger than the sum of its members. The important service to society performed by the profession transcends the individual contributions of its members. This obligation goes beyond loyalty to individuals and requires professionals to defend and protect the integrity of the profession itself.

LO 2. 4   Describe the six moral characteristics of a profession.

MORAL DUTIES OF PROFESSIONALS

moral duties

Unlike moral standards which apply to all persons equally, professionals take on additional **moral duties** by virtue of their status as professionals. A moral duty is an action we are obliged to perform or an action we are obliged to refrain from performing. This is the case for two reasons: the first is that professionals possess expert knowledge, which enables their clients to depend upon them for reliable guidance. The client's dependence upon the professional opens the client up to harm through the professional's intentional or unintentional disregard of the client's interests. It is important to note that many financial transactions require specialist knowledge, which means that the client is, in many cases, entirely dependent upon the expertise of the professional. As financial products have become more complex, it is necessary for people to seek the aid of a professional to ensure their financial future. Hence, the professional has a heightened duty of care on the basis of the vulnerability of the client and the asymmetry of the information.

The second reason is that professionals undertake their role as an expert adviser on a voluntary basis. They offer guidance and advice of their own free will and consequently accept additional moral and legal responsibilities. In addition, professionals are compensated well for taking on these duties which render them particularly binding.

THE PROFESSIONAL'S MORAL STANDARD

In 1984, The American College adopted a code of ethics which serves as the ethical standard for the behavior of its designees.

The Professional Pledge reads:

> *"In all of my professional relationships, I pledge myself to the following rule of ethical conduct: I shall, in light of all conditions surrounding those I serve, which I shall make every conscientious effort to ascertain and understand, render that service which, in the same circumstances, I would apply to myself."*

In short, the ethical standard requires the designee to treat the client as he or she would like to be treated in similar circumstances. This an example of the Golden Rule, which demands that we "do unto others as you would have them do unto you." You often hear people say, "Well, how would you like to be treated in this situation?" This question clarifies your obligations since unless you can find a relevant difference between yourself and someone else in the very same situation, it seems you are required to treat this person as you would want to be treated. Another reason this question is helpful is that we usually see those things which are in our own best interests in a much clearer manner than we recognize the interests of others. This is because our perception of our own advantage is not muddled by prejudice or bias which is often the problem when we consider the interests of others.

As we analyze how we would really like to be treated in a similar situation, I think it is possible to come up with the following principles.

Integrity

integrity

Most of us want our financial services professional to act with **integrity**. Most interpretations of integrity tie it to honesty. Nevertheless, honesty and integrity are not correlative terms since to have integrity requires more than simply telling the truth. Lying is a symptom of the lack of integrity and does not quite get to the core meaning. For another, more basic meaning, we need to get to the word's origin as a mathematical concept. It comes from the word *integer*, which refers to *whole* numbers. This definition of integrity is the quality or state of being complete or undivided. Integrity demands the professional to act according to the same principles in both her personal life and her business life. Integrity means wholeness, the kind of wholeness referred to when people are praised for "having themselves together."

What does it mean for someone to have it all together? Daryl Koehn characterizes the person of integrity as someone who is introspective and is able to give an honest reckoning of his or her strengths and weaknesses. This self-knowledge allows people of integrity to be comfortable with others. "People of integrity can dwell comfortably anywhere in the world. As long as they can live with themselves, they are satisfied."[3]

Objectivity

objectivity

Objectivity is dealing with the facts in a way that is not distorted by personal feelings, prejudices or interests. In short, it means not to be partial to one's own perspective or advantage. Most clients would prefer financial services professionals to act in accordance with objectivity.

The ideal of objectivity is grounded in the professional's obligation to subordinate his or her own interests to the needs and interests of the client. This is particularly important since the professional functions as an advice-giver and is trusted to give sound counsel that is in the interest of the client. Threats to objectivity cluster around problems which arise from conflicts of interests that can distort the professional's advice and recommendations.

Fairness

fairness

The principle of **fairness** revolves around the idea that like things should be treated in like ways. Any deviation from this principle requires an explanation to the affected parties that demonstrates the differences which justify the unequal treatment. For example, consider a financial service professional who charges one of his clients significantly lower fees for service than he charges another client. Differential pricing, on its face, is not necessarily a violation of the principle of equality. It is possible the clients concerned warrant different treatment. Perhaps working with one client demands more of the professional's time and attention because his financial plan is much more complex, while the other client is relatively low maintenance and does not require much in terms of the professional's resources.

However, a differential pricing policy may appear unjust if it was discovered that the professional charged his clients varying rates based on their race or ethnicity. This pricing policy raises troubling moral questions since the policy is based on characteristics that are irrelevant to the value of the services provided.

---

3.   Daryl Koehn, "Integrity as a Business Asset", *Journal of Business Ethics*, 58 (2008): 131.

What factors are relevant in determining a fair pricing policy? We tend to think that if the professional is providing greater value to the client, it is reasonable to expect the client to compensate the professional accordingly. Many professionals with more experience or education demand more in terms of compensation than their colleagues with relatively less experience or education. This practice strikes most people as appropriate on the assumption that increased education and experience translate into greater value for the client. However, the professional is not required to provide any additional value to the client based on the client's race. In the same way, a professional's race does not contribute or detract from the value they are able to provide to a client. Quite simply, racial status does not factor into the value proposition at all.

Another interpretation of fairness requires that the financial services professional take the legitimate interests of all parties involved into consideration and give each person or constituency what is owed to them. All professionals, because of the different constituencies they serve, as well as their obligations to consider the public interest, are forced to consider what is fairly owed to all the stakeholders affected by their decisions. In brief, professionals have additional obligations besides the ones owed to their clients. It is certainly the case that professionals are obliged to help their clients within the boundaries of the law and regulation. Maintaining healthy and viable financial services corporations and an efficient and stable regulatory environment ultimately promotes the good of the client.

Competence

competence

We obviously want our financial advisor to be competent. **Competence** refers to the expert knowledge a professional maintains and builds upon through continued education and experience. The principle of competence also includes the manner in which professionals handle situations where they lack the requisite knowledge to provide acceptable service to their clients. The competent professional is obliged to admit what he or she does not know. In short, the competent professional should act only within his or her area of expertise and defer to outside experts when situations call for such consultation.

Competence is important to most people because they don't have the expertise or information necessary to make a decision in their best interest. This lack of information is what encouraged them to seek the counsel of a financial services professional. Clients depend on financial services professionals as expert advice-givers and trust these professionals to help them make good decisions to secure their financial future. Although the client (principal) can observe the actions and behavior of the professional (agent), he or she is not capable of assessing whether the professional is acting in the client's best interests.

In short, the client cannot be sure whether the professional is doing a good job in protecting his or her interests. Professional organizations, such as the American Medical Association and the American Bar Association, were founded, in part, to vouch for the competence of their members and provide assurance to the public that they could put their faith in the expertise of their members. In order for the professions to flourish, the public must have faith in the competence of financial services professionals to provide them with the tools necessary to meet their financial goals and objectives.

Diligence

diligence

It is possible to interpret this principle in three different ways. The first interpretation is that **diligence** requires providing services in a reasonably prompt and thorough manner. One of the ways in which professionals respect their clients is through fulfilling their commitments and obligations within an appropriate time frame. An important aspect of diligence in this sense is making sure clients have suitable expectations of when work will be completed. Failure of a professional to meet the legitimate expectations of his or her client creates disappointment and undermines the trust necessary to build a successful client relationship.

A second requirement of the principle of diligence is that professionals provide services with "due care". Due care requires undertaking one's duties in a painstaking manner. The term "painstaking" implies both a close attention to detail and persistent focus and effort over the course of time. Given the complexity and diversity involved in the activity of financial planning, it is difficult to enumerate specific behaviors that are either diligent or negligent, but it is obvious that diligence demands that the financial services professional act with care and attention at each stage of the planning process.

Finally, diligence requires professionals to carefully gather information about a client's background, long-term goals, and sophistication regarding financial markets and products. A one-size-fits-all approach is not legally or morally appropriate for a professional who is compensated on the basis of his or her ability to apply general principles to a specific individual case. Not only are professionals required to carefully gather information in order to understand the particular situation and needs of each individual client, they are also required to exercise due care when giving financial advice and making recommendations to their clients.

Confidentiality

confidentiality

Confidentiality of client information is a requirement based on a promise made to the client not to divulge personal information. Clients not only provide information about the state of their finances and financial goals, but also often reveal sensitive information regarding their family dynamics. Moreover, it is necessary for them to do so in order that a financial services provider is able to offer useful guidance and work with them to achieve their financial goals. It is important that the only reason this information was revealed to the advisor in the first place was to aid the agent in helping the principal achieve his or her financial goals and objectives. Using this information to achieve other purposes violates the conditions under which the information was revealed in the first place and is a manipulation of the client's trust in the advisor.

People often have excellent reasons for not wanting their neighbors, employers, and even certain family members to know about their financial situation and objectives. Consequently, the obligation of confidentiality owed by financial services professionals to their clients is the foundation of a lasting and trusting relationship.

LO 2. 5   Explain the relationship between giving estate planning advice and the unauthorized practice of law.

UNAUTHORIZED PRACTICE OF LAW

Because much of the knowledge necessary for estate planning deals with legal concepts, there is often concern over whether one is practicing law without a license. Indeed, the line between unauthorized practice and other advice is sometimes a fine one.

What is the unauthorized practice of law? There is no definitive answer to that question. The American Bar Association's Model Rules of Professional Conduct takes the position that the definition of the practice of law is established by the law of the different jurisdictions. This seems to imply that what constitutes the unauthorized practice of law could vary from jurisdiction to jurisdiction. The Model Code's predecessor, the ABA's Code of Professional Responsibility, took the position that "it is neither necessary nor desirable to attempt the formulation of a single, specific definition of what constitutes the practice of law. Functionally, the practice of law relates to the rendition of services to others that call for the professional judgment of a lawyer. The essence of the professional judgment of the lawyer is his educated ability to relate the general body and philosophy of law to a specific legal problem of a client. . . ."

Neither expertise in a particular subject matter area nor knowledge of the law is sufficient to allow anyone other than a lawyer to give legal advice. Giving such advice is clearly reserved to those who are licensed to practice law.

Even with the Bar Association's ambiguous definition of the unauthorized practice of law, there are activities that are universally recognized as the practice of law; therefore, they are to be engaged in only by lawyers. Drafting legal documents is one such activity. Lawyers themselves, however, can also be engaged in the unauthorized practice of law. If an attorney practices in a jurisdiction in which he or she does not have a license to practice law, it is unauthorized practice. This situation can easily and unintentionally occur when estate planning involves an entire family, members of which reside in several jurisdictions, or for clients who plan to move or retire to another state. To further complicate matters, the definition of the practice of law is established on a state-by-state basis; therefore, what constitutes the unauthorized practice of law may differ from state to state. An attorney must examine the relevant state law definition.

The area of giving advice is even more problematic. For example, when does giving advice about the taxation of a particular trust arrangement that is properly within the province of the CPA or trust officer become *legal advice* and thereby solely within the province of the attorney? This is the crucial question in this difficult area. Some general guidelines are available, however, to assist the nonlawyer. If the advice is generally informational (that is, if the general principles of a proposal or technique are outlined for the client's information), there should not be a problem. Even if the advice is specifically related to the client's situation, there is no unauthorized practice violation if the advice is given on a settled area of law that is a matter of common knowledge in the estate planning field.

Because this problem is so difficult to resolve and penalties can be severe, the early and continuous involvement of an attorney in the estate planning process is perhaps the best way to deal with the unauthorized practice issue.

General Boundaries for Authorized Practice of Law
- attorney—legal advice/drafting documents
- bank trust officer—trust tax advice
- accountant—tax advice/estate planning
- insurance professional—advice on estate planning/estate liquidity
- investment specialist—estate liquidity/taxation of investments

Note: There is no precise definition of what constitutes the unauthorized practice of law.

LO 2. 6   Discuss the issues of working with clients who may be experiencing declining mental competency.

WORKING WITH ELDERLY CLIENTS

The standard professional model for working with clients is a model of autonomous decision making. The goal as an advisor is to provide the client with the tools and information to make informed decisions. The advisor should not supplant the client's judgment with his or her own decisions. While clients do often want the advisor to make decisions, it's really up to the client.

Despite its noble goals, this standard model can create ethical dilemmas and conflicts of interest, especially when working with elderly clients or other individuals with diminishing mental competencies. As your clients age, their decision-making abilities will likely decrease. This occurs naturally and can also occur due to disease or disability. Diseases like Alzheimer's are much more prevalent and have more impact in older clients. As America and the baby boomers continue to age, mental diseases like Alzheimer's will have a growing impact on our nation. Once an elderly client's mental capacity becomes compromised, it might not be in their best interests to have autonomous decision making anymore. However, this creates real challenges for the advisor. The advisor will need to watch out for warning signs that the client could be experiencing diminishing mental competency but at the same time still be respectful and protect the client's privacy. At some point, it might become warranted to bring other family members into the fold. It is better if the client agrees to this process while they are still healthy and aware. Planning for declining mental competency is all a part of estate planning. So a proper estate plan will have preempted many of these issues.

Members of the financial services industry play a crucial role in assisting their clients plan for and maintain their financial security. Clients and potential clients rely on the guidance and advice provided by their financial services professionals to make good decisions about their financial needs, goals and future. Society depends on the work of financial services professionals to ensure that its citizens are able to maintain healthy and independent lives even in times of economic hardship, uncertainty, and loss. This dependence on the profession as a whole, and individual financial services professionals in particular, is based on the belief that their trust is well-placed and they can have confidence in the integrity of the professionals with whom they work and the organizations charged with regulating their behavior.

Most financial services professionals recognize both the vulnerability of their clients and their dependence on the products, services and advice they provide. Many strive to be worthy of the trust that is placed in them. These professionals seek to move beyond acting in accordance with the letter of the law and strive to fulfill the spirit of the law in their actions, just as Solomon Huebner would have wished.

ETHICAL DILEMMA

The ethical dilemmas presented in this text illustrate common scenarios that could present a financial or estate planner with an ethical predicament. The resolution of any dilemma, of course, depends on how one applies ethical codes, rules, and principles to the specific situation. The comments are meant to provide thought about these issues and not give a definitive resolution to them.

Marcie is an estate planner who works for a multidisciplinary firm called Everything, Inc. She and her colleagues at Everything work together as a team for their clients who often simultaneously make demands on multiple firm members.

Marcie has a particular client who needs an expert in international taxation and business. Although Everything has a very knowledgeable and competent CPA and business planner, Marcie knows her client's interests would probably be better served by one or two individuals who work at other firms.

The client asks Marcie, "Whom would you recommend I go to for advice regarding my international taxation and business situation?"

> » ***Does Marcie have an ethical dilemma?***

A Possible Resolution

What recommendation should Marcie make? Should she refer the client to the external experts or send the client to someone in her firm, which is what the firm expects? Marcie's dilemma involves the concern for serving the best interests of the client which conflicts with her concern to be loyal to her firm.

It is important to keep in mind that financial and estate planning is about relationships. Marcie owes the client reliable, honest advice. At the same time, the firm relies on Marcie to maintain business.

Marcie could refer the client to the external experts, but in doing so she deprives the firm of business and jeopardizes its long-term sustainability. If the client likes the external expert, that client might decide to take all his or her business there. On the other hand, Marcie should realize that it is simply bad business—for herself and for the firm—to jeopardize the relationship with the client by not providing the expert advice the client expects and is entitled to.

This need not be an either/or decision. Marcie could simply suggest to the client that there likely are people outside the firm who have more expertise; but she could also suggest that it might be better for the client to stay inside the firm to take advantage of the team-based approach.

Another alternative would be to inform the firm's manager about what is happening. He or she might actually support an external recommendation. Many firms have discovered this potential conflict and the more sensitive ones have made provisions, or are willing to make exceptions, for these circumstances.

Finally, the level of expertise might not matter. While most clients need good advice, they do not necessarily need the best advice. However, if Marcie believes that this client does need someone with a particular expertise, it is her responsibility not to mislead the client into believing he or she is getting that level of advice when that is not the case if the client remains with the firm. While there is no single "right" answer for what Marcie should do, she must remember that there are guidelines she needs to explore in order to make a responsible decision.

CHAPTER REVIEW

Key Terms and Concepts

ethics   integrity
compliance   objectivity
moral perception   fairness
moral imagination   competence
ethical decision making   diligence
moral duties   confidentiality

Chapter 2: Review Questions

1. What are the three purposes of ethics? [LO 2.1]

2. What is the difference between ethics and compliance? [LO 2.2]

3. Define moral imagination and explain its role in ethical decision making. [LO 2.3]

4. Describe moral perception and explain its role in ethical decision making. [LO 2.3]

5. What is the difference between self-interest and selfishness? [LO 2.4]

6. How does Blum define vocation? Why is the financial services industry a vocation? [LO 2.4]

7. Why do professionals take on additional ethical responsibilities? [LO 2.4]

8. List the six ethical principles which follow from the application of the Professional Pledge. Can you think of additional principles which should apply? [LO 2.4]

9. What guidelines are available to the estate planner in determining whether an activity may constitute the unauthorized practice of law? [LO 2. 5]

Chapter 2: Review Answers

1. The three purposes of ethics are:

    - To govern behavior which is not appropriately regulated by the law.

    - To supplement legal condemnation with moral disapproval.

    - To encourage behavior which goes beyond what the law requires.

2. The first difference is that ethical choices are supposed to be freely chosen in a way that compliance (or legally compelled) choices are not. The second is that ethical actions should not be chosen out of fear of the consequences.

3. Moral imagination allows us to speculate as to how the possible consequences of our decisions will affect other people, both in the short term and the long term.

4. Moral perception allows us to determine when a situation may require an ethical response.

5. While it is important and natural for people to look out for their own interests (self-interest), if we pursue our self-interest at the expense of another, we go too far and are selfish.

6. According to Lawrence Blum, the concept of a vocation includes a designated purpose within society. Vocation carries with it certain values, standards, and ideals. The financial services industry is a vocation insofar as it serves society by helping people protect against risk, efficiently allocate resources, and promote their future financial security.

7. Professionals take on additional ethical responsibilities for the following reasons:

    - Professionals possess expert knowledge, which enables their clients to depend upon them for reliable guidance.

    - Professionals undertake their role as an expert adviser on a voluntary basis.

8. The six ethical principles which follow from the application of the Professional Pledge are as follows:

    1. Integrity
    2. Objectivity
    3. Fairness
    4. Competence
    5. Diligence
    6. Confidentiality

9. While there are activities that are universally recognized as the practice of law (drafting legal documents, for example) and, therefore, must be practiced only by lawyers, there are other areas that are not as clearly defined. An example is giving advice about taxation of a trust arrangement. Is that advice solely within the province of an attorney, or can a trust officer give such advice?

    As a guideline, if the advice is generally informational, giving it does not constitute the unauthorized practice of law. Even if the advice specifically relates to a client's situation, there is no unauthorized use if it is given on a settled area of the law that is common knowledge in estate planning. Nevertheless, because this issue is complex, it is wise to involve an attorney in the estate planning process as early as possible.

Chapter 3:

Ownership of Property

Learning Objectives

An understanding of the material in this chapter should enable the student to

LO 3.1   **Differentiate between the characteristics of real and personal property.**

LO 3. 2   **Differentiate between the various types of ownership interests in property.**

LO 3. 3   **Explain the importance of property situs and the owner's domicile.**

LO 3. 4   **Explain the different ways in which property can be owned concurrently, as well as the advantages and disadvantages of each form.**

LO 3. 5   **Describe the nature and legal complexities of community property.**

property

Before financial services professionals can fully develop an estate plan, they must familiarize themselves with the property of clients. This includes information about the extent of the client's ownership interests as well as the form in which various assets are held. The term **property**, as used here, encompasses anything capable of being owned. It includes actual outright ownership of material objects as well as a right to possess, enjoy, use, consume, or transfer something. The limited ability to direct who will enjoy or possess some object may also be considered a property right.

One may own property or something of value whether there is present possession or merely the right to come into possession at some designated time in the future. One can own the entire property or a limited portion of it in conjunction with others.

Property can be owned absolutely with no restrictions. It can also be owned subject to a variety of conditions or limitations-such as time duration or use restrictions—whether future or present.

Within the parameters imposed by law, one's imagination sets the bounds of the intricacies of ownership rights. The more common types of property ownership are discussed herein.

LO 3.1   Differentiate between the characteristics of real and personal

property.

Real Property

All property falls within two broad categories—it is either real or personal (see figure below).

real property

Real property is land and anything on the land that has been permanently attached or affixed to it. Land refers to the ground and everything attached or growing on it, or otherwise intended to be regarded as going with the ground, such as trees, shrubs, and growing crops.

Real property includes buildings and fixtures that are permanently attached to and go with the land. However, it does not include such things as a mobile home if it is left in a readily movable condition. For example, a mobile home with unremoved wheels will generally be regarded as personal property. In short, real property is all property other than personal property.

Types of Property

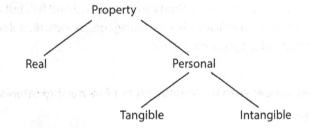

PERSONAL PROPERTY

All property other than land or any interest in land is personal property. Personal property is further characterized as either tangible or intangible.

Tangible Personal Property

tangible personal property

Tangible personal property is easy to identify. Stated simply, **tangible personal property** is anything that can be touched, seen, and felt. The property actually represents itself and is the actual object. For example, a chair has the look, feel, substance, and function of a chair. Tangible personal property has intrinsic value.

Property Categories

Real Property	Personal Property
• land	• tangible
• permanent attachments to land	- furniture
- trees	- jewelry
- buildings	- cars
- house	
	• intangible
	- bonds
	- life insurance
	- stock certificates

Intangible Personal Property

intangible personal property

Other forms of personal property are known as intangibles. **Intangible personal property** has no intrinsic value in itself. The real value of intangibles exceeds the value of the physical object that represents the property. The representation can be touched and felt, but it is not the thing itself. Some examples are stock certificates, leases, mortgages, bonds, digital property and other such representations of property ownership.

LO 3. 2   Differentiate between the various types of ownership interests in property.

MAJOR TYPES OF OWNERSHIP INTERESTS

estate

As explained earlier, at common law, the term estate historically referred to all manner of interests in real property only. An **estate** is defined in the *Restatement of Property* as an interest in land that "is or may become possessory" or "ownership measured in terms of duration." Today, estates in property refer to personal property as well as real property. It is possible to have absolute ownership of property without any limitations. It is also possible to own or have the right to use or possess something for a specified time, such as "use of my vacation house for 10 years." One can also receive an interest in property that will take effect only after a period of time, such as after 10 years, or after the person presently in possession dies. An individual who owns property subject to time limitations possesses an ownership right that is not perpetual or infinite. While these rights are subject to limitations, the property owner may enforce them to the extent of this individual's ownership rights. Although restricted, these rights can be presently valued by taking the limitations into consideration. For example, it is possible to use actuarial tables to place a present value on the absolute right to receive a property interest at a specified future time or when the present owner's interest ends.

Fee Simple Estates

fee simple estate

The largest, most complete interest in real estate that one can own is referred to as a **fee simple estate** or *estate in fee simple absolute*. It is an interest that belongs absolutely to an individual. It is potentially infinite in time. Most individually owned property falls into this category. Someone who owns land, a farm, or a house outright possesses a fee simple estate in that property. The owner has the absolute right to keep it during his or her lifetime and pass it on to his or her heirs (or anyone else) at the owner's death. If the owner wishes, he or she can sell the property or give it away while alive.

Most property ownership falls into the category of the fee simple estate. Generally, people who own their residences possess a fee simple interest in the real estate.

Although the fee simple absolute form of ownership provides the most complete interest in property to the owner, it is incorrect to assume that no restrictions exist as to the property rights. Virtually all property interests in modern society are subject to restrictions. For example, zoning laws limit the use of property to specific functions. Also, a property owner cannot use the property for illegal purposes or to create a public nuisance. Finally, all property is subject to being taken by the government, with just compensation to the owner, by the constitutional powers of eminent domain.

Split-Ownership Interests

Life Estates

life estate

A more limited, but common, form of property ownership is a life estate in the property. A **life estate** can be measured by the life tenant's life or by the term of someone else's life, if another person's life has been designated as the measuring life. A life estate gives the owner the absolute right to possess, enjoy, or derive income from the property for the span of the measuring life, at which time the interest terminates.

EXAMPLE 1

Under his father's will, Alan Abel has been given the exclusive use and possession of his father's residence for Alan's lifetime. When Alan dies, the residence will be transferred to the beneficiary named under his father's will. Alan can live in the house until he dies, allow others to live in it, or rent it. He can also sell his interest. But his interest (or his buyer's interest) in the property will end at his death. The duration of this type of possessory interest is limited by the life of the life tenant (Alan).

EXAMPLE 2

Alan's father's will could have given Alan the exclusive use, possession, and enjoyment of the property for the life of Alan's brother, Bob. This type of transfer would still be a life estate in the property but it would be measured by the life of a person other than Alan, the life tenant. Alan's interest in the property would end when the individual who was the measuring life (Bob) died.

In contrast to an owner in fee simple, the owner of a life estate for his or her own life has no interest in the property to transfer at death. However, if the life estate is for the life of another (not the life tenant), the estate continues until the end of the measuring life and that interest can be transferred.

Although the holder of a life estate has the current rights to income from the property, the life tenant has certain duties to the remainderperson. The life tenant is bound not to waste the property. Examples of waste include: (1) failure to pay property taxes, (2) failure to insure the property against foreseeable losses, and (3) destruction of the property's income-providing source. The waste of the property creates a legal right of action by the remainder persons against the life tenant.

Estate for Term of Years

estate for a term of years

Another type of estate that may or may not outlast a life estate is one created for a definite, limited period of time. An interest in property established for a specific duration is called an **estate for a term of years**. The period of time involved may be as short as one month or last for many years. It may extend beyond the lifetime of the tenant. The important thing to remember is that it is a right to possess and enjoy property as an owner for a definite period of time.

EXAMPLE

Suppose that Alan (in the prior two examples) instead of receiving a life estate was given exclusive rights to the residence for 10 years, after which the property would go to Bob. Thus, Alan would possess an estate for a specified time period or a term of years, instead of a life estate.

If the tenant dies before the end of the term of years, the right to possess the property for the remainder of the term will be determined by the tenant's will or the laws of intestacy. However, the tenant in possession of an estate for a term of years does not have the right to transfer the property at the end of the term of his or her property interest. This is because someone else has retained or has been granted an interest in the property that will commence when the estate for a term of years expires. Perhaps the most common modern example of an estate for a term of years is a leasehold; however, leaseholds may contain certain restrictions (for example, on assignability) that were not part of these estates at common law.

Property Ownership Interests—Present Interests
- fee simple estate
  - largest, most complete ownership
- split ownership
  - life estate
    - ◊ duration measured by a life
  - estate for a term of years
    - ◊ specific duration period

OTHER TYPES OF PROPERTY INTERESTS

Other types of property interests that can have significance for estate planners are future interests in property. The term future interest may be misleading because a future interest is a present right to possess or enjoy property in the future. Some examples of future interests are remainder interests and reversionary interests.

Remainder Interests

remainder interest

A **remainder interest** in property is a present right to future enjoyment as distinguished from a present interest in property that gives an absolute, immediate right to use and enjoy the property. The remainder interest must take effect immediately upon the expiration of another estate remainder. It may ripen or take effect at a designated future time or on the occurrence of an event, such as the death of the present life tenant.

EXAMPLE

Don is given property for his life. After that, it passes to Tom absolutely. Don possesses a life estate and Tom is the remainderperson. Tom's right to the use and possession of the property begins when Don's interest expires. In this situation, Tom has a present absolute right to take possession of the property at Don's death.

Vested or Contingent Remainders

indefeasibly vested remainder

To further complicate this type of ownership right, remainders may be either vested or contingent. A vested interest in property is an absolute and presently fixed right to possess and enjoy the property either now or in the future. Postponement of actual possession to a future time does not prevent the interest from being presently vested. When an individual's remainder interest is vested, he or she owns a present legally enforceable right to possess and enjoy that property when the interest comes into being. Note that it is a presently determined right although enjoyment may not occur until a future date. A vested absolute right to receive the entire property at some future time after the present interest ceases is known as an **indefeasibly vested remainder**. Should the remainderperson die before that time, the vested remainder interest he or she possessed at death becomes enforceable by the estate or heirs at the moment the present interest ceases.

On the other hand, a contingent property right is a more uncertain one. It may never become a possessory interest. A contingency is usually dependent on the occurrence or nonoccurrence of an event or condition. Only time will tell if the necessary contingencies occur that determine whether the right to possess and enjoy the property will actually be obtained. If the contingency does not occur, the anticipated property right dependent on the happening would not become a possessory one. On the other hand, if all conditions are met, the interest would vest and become absolute.

EXAMPLE

Suppose Tom (in the prior example) will receive his interest in property only by surviving Don, who has a life estate. If Tom dies before Don, the property will go to Ed at Don's death. Tom is a remainderperson but, in this case, he is a contingent rather than a vested remainderperson. The contingency is whether Tom will survive beyond Don's interest in the property. Ed's interest is also a contingent remainder because he will inherit the property only if Tom predeceases Don.

Reversionary Interests

reversionary interest

Another kind of interest in property is called a **reversionary interest**, or a *reversion interest*. This type of interest occurs when the owner of an estate transfers a lesser estate to another. A reversionary interest gives the owner (grantor) the right to have all or part of the property that he or she originally owned returned to the owner or the owner's estate.

The fact that the grantor retained a reversionary interest by transferring less than the total estate does not mean that the grantor retained a present right to possess and enjoy the property concurrently with the present estate owner. In fact, a reversion is only a present retained right to future enjoyment. Reversions are always vested.

> **EXAMPLE**
>
> James owns Blackacre in fee simple absolute. He conveys Blackacre to Ellen for her life. Ellen has a life estate in Blackacre. But because James conveyed less than his total interest, he retained a reversionary interest in Blackacre. Because of the reversionary interest, at Ellen's death Blackacre reverts to James, if he is living, or to his estate.

The method for determining whether a reversionary interest has been retained can be ascertained by applying the following formula: If the estate (that is, property value) transferred is less than the estate owned, then a reversionary interest exists.

Both remainder and reversionary interests are fraught with income and estate tax consequences that may create tax traps for the unwary. Essentially, these are incomplete transfers that may cause the property transferred or the income generated to be taxed to the original grantor or the grantor's estate as if the grantor was still an owner in possession. It is important to have property transfers structured so the desired tax consequences are achieved.

Property Ownership Interests—Future Interests
- remainder interest
  - vested/contingent
  - future enjoyment
- reversionary interest
  - future return to the grantor

Legal and Equitable Ownership

It is possible to have different types of rights in the same property held by different parties. One may be the legal owner without the right to the beneficial enjoyment from the property, and vice versa.

The legal owner is the one who holds legal title to the property. As a rule, the legal owner is the absolute owner and has all the rights and obligations connected with property ownership. The person with legal title is generally the one in possession. He or she has the full rights of use, enjoyment, and control over the property. Technically, an absolute owner holds both legal and equitable title.

There are certain circumstances, however, in which legal and equitable ownership are split between different parties. A common example of this division of title occurs when property is held in trust. By definition, under our trust laws, legal and equitable title are separated between parties. The trustee is the party who holds legal title. According to the terms of the trust, the trustee must invest and manage the property under the fiduciary standards established by state law. However, the income generated by the trustee's efforts is then distributed to or held for the benefit of others (the beneficiaries) who hold equitable title.

The person with equitable title to property is the one who is entitled to all of the benefits from the property. This refers to such benefits as the right to use, possess, or enjoy the property, as well as the right to have income from the property.

Equitable ownership and beneficial ownership mean the same thing and are sometimes used interchangeably. The equitable owner of a trust is the beneficiary of a trust for whose benefit the property is being managed. As long as the trust continues, the trustee will hold legal title (with all the attendant fiduciary responsibilities), and the beneficiaries will be the equitable or beneficial owners only. Upon termination of the trust and final distribution of the trust property to the ultimate beneficiaries, both titles are united in the beneficiaries who become absolute owners.

Legal Versus Equitable (Beneficial) Ownership

Legal Title	Equitable Title
• fiduciary (trustee/guardian of property)	• beneficiary
- has possession of property	- is entitled to property benefits
- has right to invest/manage property	

LO 3.3   **Explain the importance of property situs and the owner's domicile.**

SITUS

situs

Situs refers to the place where property is located or kept. Because each state has an interest in the welfare of its residents as well as in the protection of property located within its borders, all transfers of real and personal property are subject to state law. Under both state statute and local ordinances, state and local governmental authorities regulate and tax all real estate within their jurisdiction. The state has this power over real property within its borders, irrespective of where the property owner actually lives. The situs or location of real property is particularly important to the estate planner because all real property, as well as tangible personal property, is subject to the laws and taxing powers of the jurisdiction in which it is located.

Situs—Location of Property
- real estate (taxable only by state of location)
- tangible personal property (taxable generally by state of location)
- intangible personal property (may be taxable by any state having a reasonable connection to the property)

DOMICILE

domicile

Another important factor to consider when developing an estate plan is the domicile of an individual. **Domicile** is the place individuals consider to be their permanent residence and to which they intend to return if they have temporarily left. Individuals may have personal residences in more than one state. While it was once thought that people could have only one domicile, the U.S. Supreme Court has decided otherwise as shown later in this chapter under the heading "Multiple Taxation." Generally, a husband and wife are presumed to have the same domicile.

Domicile—Property Owner's Primary Residence
tangible personal property (taxable by state of location; typically owner's domicile)
intangible personal property (possibly also taxable by state of owner's domicile)

When a person dies, the estate is usually probated, distributed, and taxed under the laws of the state in which he or she is domiciled. One's domicile becomes significant because there is great variation among state death tax laws. Simply put, inheritance and estate tax laws imposed by different states are not uniform. A state has an interest in claiming that an individual is domiciled within its borders in order to collect tax revenue.

Depending on the nature of a person's property, it may be taxed (1) by the state of domicile, (2) by the state of location, or (3) by both. Specific types of property are discussed below.

Real Estate

Real estate is taxed solely by the state where the property is located. This results from the principle that one state does not have jurisdiction to take action on real property located in another state. Courts have consistently followed this principle and prevented states from taxing real property located in other states. Another example of this principle is that succession of real property is also determined by the laws of the situs state.

EXAMPLE

Ted was domiciled in state X at the time of his death but owned real property in state Y. Ted's will is invalid under the laws of state X but valid under the laws of Y. The real property in Y passes under the provisions of Ted's will, but Ted's other property passes under the intestate succession laws of X.

Tangible Personal Property

While it is simple to determine the situs of real estate, tangible personal property may be another matter because it is transportable. Generally, tangible personal property is taxed by the state where the property is kept. Depending on the local law, it may be taxed also by the state of domicile. The situs of tangible personal property is the place where its use is fixed for a reasonable time for ordinary and customary use purposes. Under the theory that all property belonging to a domiciliary is taxable by the state of domicile, that state may also attempt to tax tangible personal property of a decedent located elsewhere.

Intangible Personal Property

In some instances, local jurisdictions also have an interest in the taxation of the intangible personal property of their residents as well as nonresidents. Intangibles are generally taxed by the state of domicile, regardless of their location or connection with another state. It makes no difference where intangibles are kept. Any state with a reasonable connection or nexus to the property may impose a tax on its value.

> **EXAMPLE**
>
> If an individual is a resident of Pennsylvania but owns stock in a corporation in Delaware, the state of the corporate domicile (in this case, Delaware) can impose a tax on the transfer of shares of a nonresident stockholder, if its laws so provide. Some states, such as Pennsylvania, exempt intangible personal property of nonresidents from taxation when the property is transferred at death. However, many states (such as Pennsylvania) will tax the intangibles of a resident although the property is situated outside the state.

Establishing Domicile

There are a number of things an individual can do to establish domicile in a particular state.

Some examples that indicate intent to establish domicile are voter registration, automobile registration, driver's license, location of bank accounts and safe-deposit boxes, situs of principal residence, passport, reference to domicile in will, address listed with the Social Security Administration, and payment of property as well as income taxes. In some states, a special form may be filed as a declaration of domicile to establish primary residence. The place where financial and legal advisers are located will assist in determining the state of domicile.

While an individual ideally should sever ties with a former state of domicile, many individuals (particularly those who spend winter months in a warmer climate) may retain residences and other connections in their former states. If so, it may be prudent to reside in the state of intended domicile for more than half of the year or at least for more time than in any other state. An individual may also establish memberships in social clubs and religious organizations in a particular state to indicate intent of domicile.

Multiple Taxation

Because each state has its own revenue laws and public policy, state death taxation is locally determined. There is no simple way to predict the likelihood of double taxation of property passing at death. It is conceivable that more than one state will attempt to tax the same property. In a well-known Supreme Court case, *In re Dorrance Estate*, the Supreme Court held that it was legal for more than one state to have an interest in the property of an individual.

The statutes of the states involved should be carefully researched when an individual owns property in more than one state, which would subject the property to taxation under that state's jurisdiction. If the courts of two different states have each made a lawful finding of domicile, there is no constitutional barrier to taxation by both states.

Individuals who split their residences between two states should take a definitive position as to the state where they wish their property to be taxed at death. Knowledge of state death tax laws is critical for proper premortem planning. In some instances, the only death taxes due will be state taxes because the federal estate tax deductions and the increased basic credit amount will eliminate estate taxation at the federal level for all but larger estates.

LO 3. 4　　**Explain the different ways in which property can be owned concurrently, as well as the advantages and disadvantages of each form.**

CONCURRENT OWNERSHIP

Property can be owned entirely by one individual, thereby making that individual the sole owner. A person may also own a portion of the property. Partial interests either may be segregated and delineated or may consist of an undivided interest in the entire property.

EXAMPLE

A person can own an undivided one-third interest in real estate. Likewise, a person can own 50 percent of the stock of corporation X. In both cases, the value of the interest owned is measured as a percentage of the whole.

There are several ways to own property in conjunction with other individuals. A discussion of the more common types of co-ownership follows.

In most common-law states, there are generally three possible ways to own property in conjunction with others. They are (1) tenancies in common, (2) joint tenancies with right of survivorship, and (3) tenancies by the entirety. Each of these categories has distinguishing features. The rights of the co-owners vary depending on the form of co-ownership. Each form of concurrent ownership is governed by local law. In addition, there may be federal, estate, gift, or income tax consequences flowing from the transfer of a co-owner's interest either during lifetime or at death.

Understanding and properly structuring ownership of property interests is critical to the establishment of a carefully designed estate plan for an individual client. At best, there is both mystery and misunderstanding regarding the rights as well as the limitations of various forms of co-ownership.

Tenancies in Common

tenancy in common

Property owned concurrently by two or more persons who may be, but are not necessarily, related is generally called a **tenancy in common**. There may be any number of owners who hold property as tenants in common. Each tenant's share is an undivided part of the entire property. However, each tenant need not own an equal share with the other cotenants—ownership interests may or may not be equally divided. Each tenant's share may be based on an allocation that was agreed on by the cotenants. A common method for division of shares may be the percentage contribution that each tenant in common made to the purchase price of the property.

Unless restricted by contract or agreement with the other co-owners, each tenant is free to sell or dispose of his or her interest in the property to whomever the tenant wishes. The tenant does not require the consent or even the knowledge of the other cotenants. In other words, each cotenant is free to be divested of his or her property interest by sale, gift, or will. If the cotenant holds an interest in a tenancy in common and dies without a will, that individual's interest will be distributed to his or her heirs under the intestate laws of the state in which the cotenant resides. In legal parlance, the interest of a tenant in common as described above is said to be freely alienable (capable of being transferred), descendible (capable of being passed by descent or inherited), and devisable (capable of being bequeathed).

Concurrent Ownership—Tenancy in Common

- Ownership is by two or more related or unrelated parties.
- Ownership interests may be unequal.
- Property can be real or personal.
- Each ownership portion is an undivided part of the whole property.
- The owner has the freedom to sell, dispose, exchange, gift, or will his or her interest.

A cotenant is generally treated as a separate owner of his or her share of the property for income tax purposes. Each cotenant is entitled to his or her share of any income generated by the property. If the cotenant's interest is sold, gain or loss will be realized as though the cotenant had owned the property individually. A tenant in common will have a certain basis in the property depending on his or her proportionate interest in and contribution to the property.

To the extent that one tenant has received a greater proportionate interest than his or her contribution to the tenancy, a gift has been made from the cotenant who contributed a greater proportionate amount to the cotenancy at its creation. A gift may also occur if the property is sold and a cotenant receives a greater share of the proceeds than his or her contribution represents.

Generally, all tenants are obligated to pay expenses for maintaining or operating the property in proportion to their respective interests. In addition, state law may provide that the cotenant not in possession may be entitled to receive a proportionate amount of rent from the cotenant in possession of the property.

One of the most important characteristics of the tenancy in common is that there are no survivorship rights. Each tenant's interest in the property may be left to the tenant's heirs, and at death, the tenant's gross estate will include the fair market value of his or her proportionate interest.

When a cotenant sells or otherwise disposes of his or her interest in a tenancy in common, the new owner will become a tenant in common with the remaining cotenants. At the time of sale, the cotenant will realize gain or loss on his or her share that will be treated as if it was separate property. If a property is indivisible, a tenant in common may cause the entire property to be sold by a partition sale under local law. In that case, the sale proceeds will be distributed in accordance with the respective interests owned by each cotenant. Use of a forced sale to partition the property at auction will probably not generate a price equal to the true market value of the property potentially obtainable in a private sale.

A tenancy in common may also be created by operation of law when a joint tenancy is severed by agreement of the parties, by divorce of the joint tenants, or by the sale of a joint tenant's interest.

Joint Tenancies with Right of Survivorship

joint tenancy with right of survivorship

Individuals are often intrigued by ownership as joint tenants with right of survivorship because they have heard that joint tenancies are nonprobate property. **Joint tenancy with right of survivorship** is a joint ownership interest that gives the surviving owner a nonprobate right to the deceased owner's share by operation of law. When one owner dies, his or her share of the property passes in equal shares to the other surviving joint-owners. There is a common belief that no tax consequences stem from such jointly held property. Some people think that the elimination of probate fees, including executors' commissions and lawyers' fees, outweighs other considerations. In truth, there are some positive aspects of joint ownership with survivorship rights, especially convenience. In addition, some married couples may derive a sense of unity and partnership from owning some or all of their property in this form of joint ownership. However, as will be seen, joint ownership with survivorship rights also involves giving up some rights in the property and forgoing flexibility in estate planning.

qualified joint interests

nonqualified joint interests

Joint tenancy with right of survivorship is similar to tenancies in common in that there may be two or more joint tenants. Joint tenants may or may not be related to one another.. Spousal joint tenancies with right of survivorship and tenancies by the entireties are referred to as **qualified joint interests** under Internal Revenue Code Sec. 2040(b). However, if a third party (nonspouse) is a joint tenant, all of the joint interests are **nonqualified joint interests**. Each joint tenant is considered to be an owner of the entire property subject to the rights of the other joint owners. Therefore, all joint tenants with right of survivorship must have equal rights and obligations with respect to the property. Unlike tenancies in common, there cannot be disproportionate ownership; that is, one joint tenant with right of survivorship cannot have a two-thirds interest while another has a one-third interest.

During life, each joint tenant may sell his or her interest in the property without the other joint tenants joining in the conveyance, but such a transaction will sever the joint tenancy with right of survivorship. One joint tenant may also sell his or her interest in the property to the other joint owners. On severance, the form of ownership may change to another form of joint ownership—generally tenants in common—or the property itself may be divided among the joint tenants. If the property is equitably divisible, a joint owner may receive his or her share of the property free of the other joint owners by physically partitioning the property. However, if the property is not equitably divisible, it must be sold and the proceeds divided.

The primary difference between tenancies in common and jointly held property with right of survivorship is that jointly held property passes to the surviving joint tenants at the death of one of the joint owners. When there are more than two joint tenants, the property ultimately passes to the last-surviving joint tenant, who, as the sole surviving owner, has all rights in the property. The last-surviving joint tenant is free to hold or dispose of it in whatever way desirable. If the last-surviving joint tenant owns it at death, the full value will be included in his or her gross estate. Jointly held property is not transferred by will. It passes to the surviving joint tenants by operation of law outside of the will. That is what is meant by the phrase *right of survivorship*. Beneficiaries of a deceased joint tenant other than the surviving joint tenant(s) have no rights in the property. An advantage of a joint tenancy with right of survivorship is that the property passes free of probate in many states. If so, the expenses connected with probate, such as executor's commissions or attorney's fees, may be eliminated. Jointly held property will be includible in the gross estate of the deceased joint tenant for federal and state estate tax purposes to the extent of that tenant's contribution to or interest for state death tax purposes. Some states exempt a joint tenant's interest from state death taxes when the joint tenants are married.

Concurrent Ownership—Joint Tenancy with Right of Survivorship

- Ownership is by two or more related or unrelated parties.
- Property can be real or personal.
- Ownership interests must be equal.
- At death, interest passes to surviving tenant(s).
- Ownership can be severed.

Sometimes it is difficult to determine whether a co-ownership of property is a tenancy in common or a joint tenancy with right of survivorship. Local law generally favors tenancies in common over joint tenancies with right of survivorship. Any ambiguity in the form of ownership will be construed as a tenancy in common rather than as a joint tenancy. A jointly owned tenancy should include in the title the phrase *with right of survivorship* to make the intent clear. When a married couple is divorced, their jointly held property will generally be converted to a tenancy in common, unless they decide, by agreement, to hold the property as joint tenants with right of survivorship on a nonrelated basis.

When a joint tenancy is created and one of the joint tenants contributes more than his or her share of personal funds to acquire the jointly held property, that joint tenant makes a gift to the other joint tenant. Also, if one of the joint owners pays more than his or her share of either mortgage payments or the cost of maintenance and operation of the property, that joint owner is making a gift to the other joint tenants. This is true only if the contributing joint tenant cannot regain the property without the other joint tenant participating in the transfer. If the contributing joint tenant has full right of unilateral withdrawal, such as from a joint bank account, no gift is made at the creation of such a joint tenancy. It is only when the donee-joint tenant withdraws the jointly held property that a gift is made.

EXAMPLE

If Ms. Jones deposits money in a joint savings account that she opens in both her name and her son's name, she has not made a gift until her son withdraws some of the money for his own use. The donee-joint tenant must receive some benefit from the property before a completed gift is made.

Bank Accounts

Each state has its own laws with regard to the legal relationship between joint tenants with right of survivorship who own bank accounts, savings bonds, or securities. If a joint bank account is created, each joint owner owns a proportionate part of the account balance and is entitled to receive his or her proportionate amount of the interest income, on which he or she is taxed (unless it is tax-exempt income). Of course, if the account is owned by spouses who file a joint return, there are no income-splitting advantages. With other types of accounts, the interest should be reportable by each joint tenant in proportion to the amount the joint tenant contributed to the account. Banks usually report the income as taxable to the joint tenant whose Social Security number is on the account. The most common joint tenancy bank account is often called a revocable account. There is no gift if a person uses personal funds to open a joint bank account. A gift is considered made only when the other joint owner (the donee) makes withdrawals. However, there are also joint tenant bank accounts that vest immediately. The accounts provide the joint tenants with equal interests at the time the account is established.

Government Savings Bonds

When a Series EE (or E) or Series HH (or H) government savings bond is held in joint ownership, there is no gift when the bond is purchased because the joint owner who contributed the funds can cash in the bond at any time and get his or her money back. As with joint bank accounts, a gift occurs when the donee-joint tenant redeems the bond and retains a greater share of the proceeds than he or she had contributed to the purchase price. At that time, a gift is made from the contributing joint tenant to the donee-joint tenant equal to the redemption value of the bond reduced by the percentage contribution to the purchase price that the donee-joint tenant made.

Safe-Deposit Boxes

When a safe-deposit box is held in joint ownership, both joint tenants have access to the contents of the box. This does not mean that the contents of the box would be considered owned in equal shares by each joint tenant. The contents of the box remain the property of the joint tenant who deposited them. Joint tenants of a safe-deposit box must comply with the joint-ownership requirements of local law with regard to the ownership of the box contents. Depending on the nature of the contents, there should be a written document specifying that a legal transfer from the sole owner to the other joint lessee of the box has occurred if they intend to own the contents equally as joint owners. If true joint ownership with right of survivorship is created, the income and gift tax consequences will depend on the type of property that has been thus transferred in writing.

Securities

Basically, the above types of joint ownership (bank accounts and government savings bonds) are revocable creations that do not invoke gift tax ramifications at the inception of the joint tenancy. However, the treatment for joint ownership of securities is different, because there is a formal agreement between the joint owners of securities and the broker.

If the securities are registered in the names of the co-owners as joint tenants with right of survivorship and not as tenants in common, a gift occurs from the contributing joint tenant to the donee-joint tenant when the securities are transferred to the account or purchased for the account. However, the result is not the same if the account has been registered in street name. The term *street name* describes securities held in the name of a broker or another party rather than in the name of the owner(s). An IRS ruling holds that no gift occurs on the creation of a joint street-name account when one of the joint tenants has furnished more than half of the consideration. A gift occurs when the other party withdraws from the account more than his or her proportionate contribution to the account because securities registered in individuals' names as joint tenants require the signatures of both to sell the securities. However, the signatures of both are not required when the account is in street name.

As to income tax consequences, if securities are registered in joint names, each joint tenant is entitled to a proportionate share of the interest income under local law. Again, if the joint tenants are husband and wife, it is likely that they will file a joint return that would make allocation of income irrelevant.

To summarize, the financial services professional should keep in mind that joint tenancies may have gift tax ramifications depending on the nature of the property held as joint tenants with right of survivorship, when there has been a disproportionate contribution to the property by one of the joint owners. No gift will occur if the contributing tenant can, at any time, withdraw the property contributed and regain sole possession of it, because the transfer is incomplete as long as the contributing joint tenant retains dominion and control over the property. A gift will occur when the noncontributing or donee-joint tenant withdraws from the joint tenancy a greater proportion than the amount contributed. At that time, the gift becomes irrevocable and complete. However, in the case of joint tenancies that require both signatures to sell or transfer property, a gift will be made at the time the property is transferred to a joint tenancy.

If the joint tenants are husband and wife, there is no gift tax liability, although one spouse may have contributed more than half of the property to the joint tenancy. This is so because the Economic Recovery Tax Act (ERTA) of 1981 defines a married couple as a single economic unit. Although a gift has been made from one spouse to another, the unlimited gift tax marital deduction applies so that there will be no tax to pay. Furthermore, no gift tax return is required for transfers from one spouse to a joint-ownership arrangement with the other spouse.

Tenancies by the Entirety

tenancy by the entirety

A **tenancy by the entirety** is similar to a joint tenancy with right of survivorship although it is more restrictive. It is limited to co-ownership of property held by a husband and wife. By definition, a tenancy by the entirety exists only during marriage and will be terminated upon divorce of the spouses. Local law will determine some of the features of a tenancy by the entirety. For example, in most states each tenant is entitled to half of the income from the property. However, in those states still governed by common law, the husband may be entitled to all the net income from the property. Presently, about half the states and Washington, D.C. have some type of tenancy by the entirety property interest.

The primary difference between a tenancy by the entirety and jointly held property with right of survivorship is that neither spouse may unilaterally terminate the tenancy by conveying his or her interest to a third party during lifetime. In contrast to the types of ownership previously described, a tenancy by the entirety cannot be severed by selling either party's undivided interest without the consent of the other tenant. Husband and wife must join in a sale or other conveyance to third parties.

Because there are variations under local law with regard to each of these forms of co-ownership, the financial services professional must review the local law before advising clients regarding the rights and obligations of each form of co-ownership. Generally, it is presumed that the form of ownership is a tenancy in common if co-owners are not married. However, if they are a married couple, a tenancy by the entirety may be presumed. Some jurisdictions insist that the words *right of survivorship* are necessary in order to construe the co-ownership as a joint tenancy or tenancy by the entirety. Tenancies by the entirety are essentially limited to co-ownership of real estate by a husband and wife. Some states have completely abolished the tenancy by the entirety form of ownership.

Concurrent Ownership—Tenancy by the Entirety
- Ownership can be only by married couples.
- Property can be real or personal property.
- At death, interest passes to the surviving spouse.
- Ownership cannot be severed without the consent of both spouses.

Advantages and Disadvantages of Joint Tenancies and Tenancies by the Entirety

There are both advantages and disadvantages (beyond tax considerations) of joint tenancies with right of survivorship and tenancies by the entirety. Advantages of these forms of joint ownership include the following:

- Under most state laws, property owned as tenants by the entirety generally cannot be reached by creditors of one of the tenants. Such property can be reached only by joint creditors. (**Note**, *however, that in a U.S. Supreme Court case, a federal tax lien against one tenant by the entirety was held to attach to the entirety property* [United States v. Craft, *122 S. Ct. 1414, 2002*].)

- These forms of ownership are convenient for certain types of assets, such as bank accounts, because either tenant has access to the account.

- Joint tenancies and tenancies by the entirety may give one or both of the tenants a feeling of security. This is especially true when the owners are spouses and one spouse has contributed most of the funds.

- When one tenant dies, the property passes directly to the surviving joint tenant. There are no probate delays. There may be little or no administrative and transfer costs. The property will remain fully accessible to the surviving owner.

- In many states, these forms of property ownership between spouses pass free of state death taxes.

- Because such property passes by operation of law and not under will, it is a private arrangement and not open for public scrutiny.

Joint Tenancies with Right of Survivorship and Tenancies by the Entirety

General Advantages
- limited access by creditors of one tenant by the entirety
- convenience
- feeling of security
- avoidance of probate delay
- reduction in administrative and transfer costs
- possible avoidance of state death taxes
- privacy
- full control by survivor

General Disadvantages
- access by creditors of one joint tenant with right of survivorship
- gift tax potential
- additional estate tax potential
- full control by survivor
- insufficient liquidity potential

There are also disadvantages inherent in these jointly held property arrangements. Some of the disadvantages of these forms of joint ownership include:

- Under most state laws, property owned as joint tenants with right of survivorship can be reached by creditors of an individual joint tenant.

- There are potential gift taxes at the creation of some of these property ownership interests. (**Note**: Transfers may qualify for the unlimited marital gift tax deduction.)

- There may be additional federal estate taxation. The entire value of property held jointly with right of survivorship, except for spousal joint tenancies created after

December 31, 1976, may be in the estate of the first joint owner to die. The entire property will then be owned by the surviving tenant and will be fully subject to estate taxation again at the survivor's death. (**Note**: Transfers may qualify for the unlimited estate tax marital deduction.)

- The surviving tenant will gain full control over the property and may ultimately dispose of it in any way desired. The decedent's will, trust, or other dispositive documents will have no effect on the disposition of the jointly held property.

- The decedent's estate may be faced with a liquidity problem. Property passing directly to the surviving tenant may not be made available to the decedent's estate for the payment of taxes, debts, or expenses.

While these forms of ownership may be both convenient and psychologically comforting, they may not constitute the best estate plan for all persons and may severely impair an appropriate estate plan when used improperly. As an individual's estate increases, a review and analysis of such property should be made to determine if it is the best form of ownership for the individual's needs.

It has been stressed that there are both tax and nontax reasons to create different forms of property ownership when held by more than one individual concurrently. There is no one answer with regard to arrangements of property. Generally, a combination of different ownership arrangements will provide the best results in good estate planning. One important factor to examine is the size of the relative estates of potential co-owners of property.

Property Ownership	Tenancy in Common	Joint Tenancy with Right of Survivorship	Tenancy by the Entirety
Permitted number of owners?	*Ownership by two or more individuals.*	*Ownership by two or more individuals.*	*Ownership only by two married individuals.*
Must owners be related?	*No.*	*No.*	*Yes, must be married.*
Can ownership be unequal?	*Yes, ownership may be equal or unequal.*	*No. Contribution can be unequal, but each has equal ownership rights.*	*No. Each has equal ownership rights.*
Kind of property—real or personal?	*Either real or personal.*	*Either real or personal.*	*Either real or personal. Some states real property only.*
Can owner sell or make a gift of the property without other owner's consent?	*Yes, owner can dispose of his/her share without the consent of the other joint owners.*	*Yes, owner can dispose of his/her share without the consent of the other joint owners, but the joint tenancy is severed.*	*No. Both must consent.*
Can owner transfer his/her share by will?	*Yes.*	*No. Share automatically passes to the survivor(s) by operation of law.*	*No. Survivor automatically becomes sole owner by operation of law.*
Is property reachable by an individual owner's creditors?	*Yes, to the extent of his/her contribution to the property.*	*Yes, to the extent of his/her contribution to the property.*	*Only creditors of both owners can reach the property.*

Transfer on Death Arrangements and Deeds

Some property owners do not wish to own property concurrently, but they do wish to transfer the property automatically at death to their loved ones without incurring the costs and hassles of probate. A growing number of jurisdictions are making this possible by enacting legislation which allows the owner to enter a transfer on death (TOD) arrangement. For example, many banks and financial institutions permit bank accounts and investment accounts to be transferred at the owner's death to another person or persons if the appropriate paperwork is completed. Beneficiary designations on retirement accounts are essentially TOD arrangements.

If the property is real estate, such as a personal residence or a commercial building, a state's law may permit counties to record transfer on death deeds which automatically transfer the real estate to another person after the death of the owner.

TOD arrangements differ from state to state. In general, the advantages are: low cost to prepare, the transfer is not a gift, and probate avoidance. The main disadvantages of TODs, compared to trusts, are: (1) TODs are only effective after the owner dies; and (2) the owner has no control over where the property is transferred if the person designated in the TOD is deceased when the owner dies or after the person designated in the TOD dies. With trusts, property managers can be named in the event the owner becomes incapacitated before death, and successor beneficiaries can be named to ensure the property is transferred according to the owner's wishes. Despite these drawbacks, many clients are using TODs to transfer property after they die.

LO 3. 5   Describe the nature of community property.

Community Property

Community property is another form of co-ownership limited to interests held between husband and wife that has particular significance today because of our mobile society. Only nine of the 50 states are community-property states. The laws of the particular community-property state in which a married couple resides must be examined to determine accurately the specific effect on a married couple's property ownership. Each state has developed its own special variations that make it difficult to generalize about community-property laws for all nine states.

Historical Origins

The community-property system currently in use in nine states is based on Spanish and French civil law pertaining to marital property rights. Brought to America by Spanish and French colonists, the ancient concept was grounded in a precept of equality. Because a marriage is a community consisting of two marital partners who, through their joint labors, industry, and efforts, contribute to the prosperity of the marriage, both spouses possess an equal right to the property and its benefits.

The planner must be aware that, while the community-property states share some common features and definitions, there is no one uniform community-property system. Although the fundamental aspects of community-property law are similar in the different states, many differences have evolved because of refinements by state legislatures. The estate planner should guard against the expectation that specific aspects of one community-property state carry over to another community-system state.

Arizona, California, Idaho, Louisiana, Nevada, New Mexico, Texas, and Washington are the traditional eight community-property states. Wisconsin is recognized as the ninth community-property state since its version of the Uniform Marital Property Act (UMPA), incorporating many community-property concepts, became effective in January 1986. Instead of the term *community property*, Wisconsin uses the term *marital property*. While Louisiana still closely follows the civil law, the other states have adopted some traditional American common-law principles to meet changes in societal and economic needs. In addition to the above-mentioned nine community-property states, Alaska allows a statutory election for certain property to be treated as community property. In other words, Alaska has statutory provisions allowing Alaskan residents to elect community-property status to the extent provided in a community-property agreement or a community-property trust. In 1998, Alaska passed a statute permitting nonresidents of Alaska to transfer property into a trust, referred to as a community-property trust. If the trust has one or more Alaskan trustees, any portion or all of the trust property is treated for tax purposes as community property. Generally, these trusts are created so that some or all of the trust property receives a step-up in basis (discussed in a later chapter) at the death of the first spouse.

Nature of Community Property

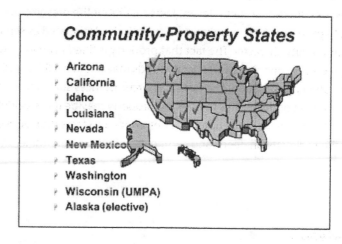

Community-Property States

- Arizona
- California
- Idaho
- Louisiana
- Nevada
- New Mexico
- Texas
- Washington
- Wisconsin (UMPA)
- Alaska (elective)

community property

separate property

In **community-property** states, property interests acquired during marriage are presumed to be owned equally by spouses. The community-property principle recognizes the existence of community ownership of property by husband and wife. In essence, each spouse is deemed to own a one-half interest in property acquired during the marriage regardless of which spouse actually acquired, earned, gained, or is otherwise responsible for ownership of the property. This is not to say that all property belonging to a married couple is necessarily community property. A husband and wife can own property separately in their own individual rights. For instance, property owned by either spouse prior to the marriage continues to be the spouse's separately owned property during the marriage (unless affirmative steps are taken by the owner spouse to change the ownership status of the **separate property**). Property inherited by or gifted to an individual spouse during marriage also retains separate property characterization. Wisconsin uses the terminology of the UMPA and refers to separate property as individual property.[1] For purposes of this chapter, the general terms *community property* and *separate property* are used.

Presumptions as to Marital Property

Generally speaking, the underlying community-property presumption is that property owned by a husband and a wife belongs to both of them in equal shares, except for that property that can be proven to belong to a spouse separately. Concerning certain issues such as termination of a marriage by death or divorce, the rights of creditors, tort liability, and tax treatment, the community-property system generally presumes that all property owned during a marriage is community property. This presumption is not conclusive, however, if separate status of property can be proven or if there are other relevant facts that rebut the presumption. In other words, the separate property of a spouse must be specifically designated as separate property to retain its noncommunity character. The fact that property is titled in an individual spouse's name or was acquired with one spouse's separate funds may not in itself be sufficient evidence to rebut the community presumption. The facts and circumstances surrounding the use of the property and the conduct of the parties toward the property may be more evidentiary than the title or the source of funds for its initial purchase. Common-law states (that is, non-community-property states) rely directly on deeds and certificates of title to determine ownership.

---

1.   Wis. Stat. 1985–86, § 766.31.

transmutation

In addition, practically all the community-property states grant spouses the power to determine or change the character of their property as community or separate. For instance, Texas
previously only allowed community property to be transmuted to separate property. Currently,
Texas law permits separate property to be transmuted to community property.[2] Therefore,
spouses may change community property to separate property and vice versa. Changing the
source or nature of property in community-property states by transmutation is often done
for the purpose of achieving tax savings. The legal term for voluntarily changing the nature
of property is **transmutation** (in Wisconsin, classification or reclassification). Depending on
the type of property and particular circumstances, transmutation may result from contract
(bilaterally) or gifts (unilaterally). There are two important transmutation restrictions, however.
First, federal law obligations cannot be circumvented by transmuting property; and, second, a
transmutation that is effective between spouses may not be effective against third parties like
creditors.

The best way to overcome the general presumption favoring community property is for
married partners who reside in or move in and out of community-property states to keep
complete, organized, and accurate records of their personal financial matters. Another way to
secure property ownership is for couples to file an inventory of assets at the time of marriage
to serve as an official record of separate identity. Note that in some community-property states,
especially California, the general presumption is less difficult to rebut when the marriage is of
relatively short duration. In some states it is possible for individuals to waive their rights in community property in a prenuptial agreement. Although the general community presumption in
and of itself is quite straightforward, different circumstances readily lend themselves to more
involved issues.

EXAMPLE

Mary and Anthony became engaged and planned to marry the following spring. They
made purchases for their new home and their future together. Although Mary wanted
to furnish their home with antiques, Anthony felt that antiques were too expensive and
impractical. Before the wedding Mary, the wealthier of the two, decided to purchase the
antiques with her own separate funds, and she arranged for delivery to take place after
the wedding. In this case, arguments could be made both that the furniture is separate
property and that it is community property. Was the furniture acquired before or after
the marriage? Although in this scenario the presumption of community property could
easily be rebutted, Mary may have intended the property to be community marital

---

2.   Tex. Fam. Code Secs. 4.201–4.206 (2003).

property. If the antiques were partially paid for with Mary's separate funds prior to the marriage and the balance paid with community funds after the wedding, are the antiques still Mary's separate property? If the antiques appreciate in value and are later sold at a gain, are the profits community property or separate property?

Separate Property
- property acquired prior to marriage
- property acquired by gift
- property acquired by inheritance, bequest, or devise
- property acquired in a court award
- property transmuted into separate property

While earnings from the labor of a husband and a wife are nearly always community property, community-property states are almost evenly divided in how they treat "rents, issues, or profits" of separate property realized during marriage. Idaho, Louisiana, Texas, and Wisconsin generally treat the rents, issues, and profits generated by separate property acquired during a marriage as community property but hold that natural increases in the size or value, that is, appreciation, of separate property due to market changes and inflation continue to be separate property. Therefore, if the separate property of community spouses is sold, the gain on the sale continues to be separate property. If the gain is used to acquire other property, the newly acquired property is separate property. In the remaining states, rents, issues, and profits of separate property retain a separate-property identity, but increases in value resulting from community labor and effort belong to the community. In all community-property jurisdictions, however, income and earnings generated by separate property prior to marriage remain separate, and income and earnings produced by community property constitute community property. It is not difficult to imagine the problems that can arise with regard to the benefits flowing from community property. The spouse claiming the separate nature of property has the burden to overcome the community presumption with adequate proof. Evidence of separate ownership is difficult to provide if adequate records are not kept, particularly when there has been commingling of separate and community funds and other assets over the years. Tracing the property's separate identity may be virtually impossible in such cases.

Joint Tenancy

Property may be held concurrently by two or more individuals with a right of survivorship. The concept of joint tenancy with right of survivorship is embraced by all common-law states. At the time of one spouse's death, the jointly held property passes automatically, by operation of law, to the surviving spouse. Administrative delay is avoided and, because the property does not go through the probate process, probate costs are reduced. The majority of married partners in common-law states own their family residences as joint tenants with right of survivorship or, similarly, as tenants by the entireties.

None of the community-property states recognize the tenancy-by-the-entireties form of ownership, and joint tenancy with right of survivorship is restricted. Some community-property states, however, statutorily create a right of survivorship in the family homestead so that a surviving spouse is not left homeless.

Generally, a survivorship component is not present with community property. This is not to say that married couples in community states cannot hold property as joint tenants with right of survivorship. About half the states permit a survivorship provision with community ownership of property. Some community-property states—Arizona, Idaho, Nevada, and Washington, for instance,—have laws permitting residents to own property titled as community property with right of survivorship. In these states, this form of titling overrides a community spouse's disposition of the particular property by will. The property, because it passes by operation of law, is not subject to probate. Generally, community property is probate property except in some community states. In these states, if the decedent-spouse's community share passes to the surviving spouse, it does not pass through probate. In other community states, it is strictly an either-or ownership; couples have the choice of owning property in the community sense, jointly with right of survivorship, or as tenants in common.

Married partners who have acquired property during marriage in a community state and do not want it to be community property have to take affirmative steps to override the community identity with their chosen form of ownership. In most of the community states it is the form of property expressed in the title document that controls. If one of the spouses claims that ownership is other than what is stated in the deed, bank account, certificate, or title, that individual has the burden of proving the alleged form of ownership. For joint ownership to supersede the community presumption, a number of the states require an express reference in the title that the particular property is held as joint tenants with right of survivorship. When community property is titled or retitled in joint tenancy with right of survivorship, a transmutation of the community property into separate property results.

Classification Rules

time-of-acquisition rule

inception-of-title rule

The general classification rule is known as the **time-of-acquisition rule** or the **inception-of-title rule**. This rule provides that the character of an asset, separate or community, is established at the time the asset is acquired, and once established, the character is not altered by later events. So, if prior to a marriage one of the parties acquires property, it is and remains the acquiring spouse's separate property. If during the marriage the property is improved using community funds, the property is still the acquiring spouse's asset, but the nonacquiring spouse may have a right to reimbursement for one-half of the community funds spent on the improvements.

EXAMPLE 1

At the time of H and W's marriage, H owned several acres of unimproved land valued at $15,000. Using community funds, H and W built a home for $175,000 and later improved the residence by adding several bedrooms, bathrooms, and an in-ground pool with bathhouse for $50,000. The value of the home is $350,000 at the time H and W divorce. Although the land remains H's separate property, W has a community claim for reimbursement of her half of the community funds expended to improve H's separate property. Alternatively, H has a claim for the value of the land.

EXAMPLE 2

Using the facts of the previous example, assume the $50,000 of home improvements came from W's separate funds, which W inherited at her uncle's death. W has to affirmatively prove that the $50,000 was her separate property in order to overcome the community presumption.

A claim to reimbursement, however, may fail when there is evidence of one spouse's intention to make a gift of a community interest to improve the other spouse's separate property.

To establish that property acquired during a marriage is one spouse's separate property, the claiming spouse may show that the asset was acquired in one of the following ways:

- by gift or inheritance
- by purchase with separate property or by separate credit
- by recovery for personal injuries

In keeping with the lack of uniformity among the community-property states, states vary in applying the time-of-acquisition rule. For instance, Louisiana law provides that the character of personal property is established when title passes but that the title for real estate is determined at the time the property is actually conveyed.

PROPERTY CHARACTER

The character of property is determined by the character of the property used to acquire it initially. For instance, if solely separate property is used to acquire other property during marriage, the newly acquired property is also separate property, and when entirely community property is exchanged for other property, the new property retains a community character (absent an agreement of the spouses to treat the property otherwise).

EXAMPLE

John spends his separate funds to make a down payment on a cottage in the mountains to be used as a family vacation home. It is titled in the names of both John and his wife, Jane, since the intention is for the cottage to be community property. It is likely the cottage will be characterized as a community asset, based on the parties' intent.

Commingling

commingling

Although the rule that property has the same character of the property with which it was acquired seems straightforward, it is not that simple. The characterization of property may become very complex when there has been a commingling of marital property. **Commingling** occurs when properties of different characters are mixed, blended, and jumbled up. In these situations, the community presumption typically prevails over the parties' conflicting claims. Even if the character of the property can be traced, other issues may arise: Do the spouses share the commingled property in percentages proportionate to their separate contributions, or is the commingled property the separate property of one spouse with the other spouse then having the legal right of a creditor for reimbursement of contributions made? Furthermore, some states restrict tracing in certain circumstances.

EXAMPLE

Shortly after their marriage, Dave and Betsy open bank accounts in both their names. Each places separate funds in the accounts and over time makes additional deposits using community funds. In the course of the marriage there are withdrawals, purchases, sales, and exchanges of assets with commingled bank funds. If Dave and Betsy should later decide to divorce, they are likely to disagree as to what constitutes community and separate property.

Life Insurance

The principles governing the classification of life insurance policies are somewhat different in the community-property states. The treatment of life insurance is an important consideration for estate planners and policy owners because of the impact it may have on a decedent's estate taxes and because it is an asset that is often overlooked by a migrating couple. Fortunately, all of the information needed to classify an insurance policy is written in the policy. To determine and separate policy-ownership interests in community-property states, three basic doctrines are used.

The proration or apportionment doctrine concept is favored in California and Washington to establish policy ownership interests. This method views the separate and community components of policy proceeds proportionately to the separate and community funds applied to the premiums paid. In other words, the proration theory looks to the source of the payment of the policy premiums.[3]

The inception-of-the-title doctrine has been adopted in Texas, Louisiana, and New Mexico in many life insurance cases. This approach looks to the character of the funds used to purchase the policy, whether the purchase occurs before or after the marriage. The original funds used to purchase the policy establish its character. If community funds are used for other premium payments, the surviving spouse has a right to reimbursement for his or her share of community funds used for the payments but does not share in the growth in the policy's value.

The third doctrine classifies life insurance ownership according to the nature of the funds used for the final or last premium payment and has been relied upon in Arizona and Idaho in some group life insurance cases.[4] This approach views all but the final payment as voluntary install-ment payments and the final premium payment as completing the purchase of the policy. Whole life insurance cases, at least in Arizona, follow a reimbursement theory.[5]

Simply stated, each of the doctrines described above seeks to trace the source of the money applied to the premium payments to determine the character of the policy and the proceeds, and each approach may give rise to some inequities.

---

3. *Coffey's Estate*, 81 P.2d 283 (1980).
4. *Gaethje v. Gaethje*, 442, P.2d 870 (1968); *Travelers Insurance Co. v. Johnson*, 544, P.2d (1975).
5. *Everson v. Everson*, 537 P.2d 624 (1975); *Honnas v. Honnas*, 648 P.2d 1045 (1982).

Business

If a business is started during the marriage with community property and labor, allocation disputes upon termination of the community are normally easier to resolve than if a premarital business is started with separate property and increases in value after marriage are due at least partially to community capital and labor. An increase in business value during marriage because of improved market conditions does not in and of itself change the original separate character of the business.

EXAMPLE

Prior to marriage Martha started an interior decorating business. The business-owned realty was valued at $75,000 at the time of Martha's marriage. At the time of Martha's divorce, which occurred 8 years later, the realty had increased in value to $130,000, due solely to favorable market conditions. The $55,000 increase in value is Martha's separate property.

However, when income is generated by separate property acquired during marriage, approximately half the states consider that the rents, issues, and profits belong to the community, while the remaining states hold that these retain their separate character. Increases in business value attributable to the labor efforts of either or both spouses are frequently held to belong to the community. The issue of labor contributions may be at least somewhat resolved if one or both spouses withdraw a salary from the business. On the whole, the courts appear to be more restrictive in applying commingling concepts to businesses than to bank accounts.

Debts, Obligations, and Liabilities

Although it may seem logical to assume that community principles apply similarly to assets and liabilities, this is not the case. The states are in much greater accord in the treatment of community assets than of community liabilities. The widest differences among the nine sets of community-property statutes and case law occur in the treatment of liabilities. (The term liabilities is typically used in a broad sense to encompass debts, expenses, and obligations.)

There are some areas of relative agreement: (1) a spouse's separate property is usually subject to the claims of the spouse's creditors for the spouse's separate debts; (2) generally, one spouse's separate property cannot be reached by the creditors of the other spouse's separately created debts; and (3) the separate property of both spouses may be available if both partners contracted for the liability.

Differences are more likely to arise when creditors of separately created debt seek to collect from community assets or from one spouse's half of community assets, or regarding the following questions:

- the degree to which community assets are available to satisfy premarital debt
- the order in which assets become available to satisfy liabilities
- the exclusion of specific community assets from the claims of creditors
- the availability of community and/or separate property for liabilities created by one spouse for the benefit of the community
- the use of community property of a later marriage to satisfy alimony and support obligations generated by a spouse's previous marriage and children
- the use of community assets to satisfy one spouse's tort claims

Complexities, problems, and inconsistencies involving community liabilities abound.

Community Property and Transfer Taxes

Federal estate tax law[6] requires a decedent's gross estate to include the value of all property in which the decedent had an interest at the date of death. Property rights, however, are determined under state law. In certain situations this means that federal estate and gift tax provisions are applied to a decedent's property in accordance with state property law provisions. Although it is not explicitly stated in the Internal Revenue Code, case law has traditionally recognized that a decedent-spouse's gross estate includes only the decedent's half interest in community property, even if the community property is titled solely in the decedent's name. On the other hand, in a common-law state, if all the marital property were titled in the decedent-spouse's name alone, the spouse's gross estate would include the value of the entire property. Basically, common-law property is identified by the person who owns or has title to the property. If, however, spouses in a common-law state hold property titled as joint tenants or as tenants by the entireties, only half the property value is included in the decedent-spouse's gross estate.

EXAMPLE

Harvey and Joan, a married couple, have always lived in a community-property state. At the time of Harvey's recent death, they owned $12,800,000 of community property, all of which was titled solely in Harvey's name. Harvey's adjusted gross estate will include $6,400,000 of community assets. However, if Harvey and Joan lived in a common-law state, the full $12,800,000 would be included in Harvey's adjusted gross estate.

---

6. IRC Sec. 2033.

Thus, a decedent-spouse in a community-property state will, in many instances, have a smaller gross estate than the same decedent-spouse in a non-community-property jurisdiction. Of course, after the Economic Recovery Tax Act (ERTA) of 2001 and the unlimited marital gift and estate tax deduction became effective in 1982, the transfer tax discrepancies for spouses between community and common-law states became moot.

EXAMPLE 1

Harvey and Joan have always lived in a community-property state. Harvey dies owning $12,800,000 of community property.

Harvey's adjusted gross estate	$6,400,000
Allowable marital deduction	(6,400,000)
Harvey's taxable estate	0

EXAMPLE 2

Harvey and Joan have lived all of their lives in a common-law state. Harvey dies owning $12,800,000 of noncommunity property.

Harvey's adjusted gross estate	$12,800,000
Allowable marital deduction	(12,800,000)
Harvey's taxable estate	0

EXAMPLE 3

Harvey and Joan have lived all of their lives in a community-property state. Harvey dies when there is $12,800,000 of community property. Harvey leaves his community-property share to his son.

Harvey's adjusted gross estate	$6,400,000
Allowable marital deduction	0
Harvey's taxable estate	$6,400,000

Although the unlimited marital estate and gift tax deduction serves to equalize the transfer tax results between community- and noncommunity-property states when the surviving spouse is the beneficiary of the decedent spouse's estate (as in the preceding examples), if someone other than the surviving spouse receives the decedent's property, transfer tax differences between community and noncommunity jurisdictions are more likely.

Clients on the Move

Mobility is a common aspect of modern life in the United States. Whether for employment or for personal or other reasons, a significant number of Americans move from one state to another each year. Unfortunately, mobility is often overlooked by planners. Clearly, changing domicile between common-law and community-property states and even between community-property states can pose some complicated estate planning problems. Often, questions are not raised about the legal implications of family moves until there is a death or divorce. Once a marriage dissolves, a determination of the parties' individual legal rights regarding their assets may be formidable or, worse, impossible unless adequate records have been kept over the years.

Moving from a community-property state to a common-law state does not change the character of marital property acquired in the community jurisdiction unless the parties take steps to expressly change the property to a character other than its community identity. The Uniform Disposition of Community Property Rights at Death Act has been enacted by many common-law states. This act provides for the recognition of community property as retaining its community-property identity at death when spouses move from a community-property state to a common-law state and when community-property funds are used for the purchase of real property in a common-law state.[7] As is the case with many uniform acts, however, the Uniform Disposition of Community Property Rights at Death Act has not been enacted by the adopting states uniformly. Therefore, the act varies within the adopting jurisdictions. Estate planners of migrant couples also need to be aware of the likelihood that judges and lawyers practicing in one system are probably not familiar with the legal issues of the other system.

Clearly, addressing all the legalities of the community-property systems is beyond the scope of this chapter. However, regardless of the state in which an estate planner practices or a married couple presently resides, a planner should understand that there are two different legal systems affecting marital property. The planner must be aware of the many implications of client mobility and must recognize that wills, trusts, disclaimers, antenuptial agreements, buy-sell plans, and so forth, that are drafted in one jurisdiction have to be reviewed to make sure they are effective in the current jurisdiction.

---

7.   Unif. Disp. of Comm. Prop. Rts. at Death Act Sec. 2 (1995).

CHAPTER REVIEW

Key Terms and Concepts

property
real property
tangible personal property
intangible personal property
estate
fee simple estate
life estate
estate for a term of years
remainder interest
indefeasibly vested remainder
reversionary interest
situs
domicile

tenancy in common
joint tenancy with right of
  survivorship
qualified joint interests
nonqualified joint interests
tenancy by the entirety
community property
separate property
transmutation
time-of-acquisition rule
inception-of-title rule
commingling

Chapter 3: Review Questions

1. Explain what is meant by the real value of intangible personal property. [LO 3.1]

2. There are many types of estates and interests in real property. In each of the following instances, state briefly the type of estate or interest in real property that is created:

    a. Alex grants land to Ben and his heirs forever.

    b. Alex grants land to Ben for life and, upon Ben's death, to Chris and his heirs forever.

    c. Alex gives Ben the right to use his land for 10 years. [LO 3.2]

3. Assume John gives Sally the absolute right to use his beach house for her life. Upon Sally's death, all rights in the beach house will be returned to John or his estate. What type of property interests do John and Sally each have? [LO 3.2]

4. Explain how a person can hold legal title to property but not possess an equitable interest in the property. Give an example of this type of ownership. [LO 3.2]

5. Differentiate between domicile and situs, indicating the steps an individual can take to establish domicile. [LO 3.3]

6. Gloria Gershwin was domiciled in Alabama. She also owned real property in Florida, tangible personal property in New Hampshire, and intangible personal property in Texas. Which states have an interest in taxing these various properties at her death? [LO 3.3]

7. What rights does a co-owner of property held as tenants in common have with respect to:

   a. selling one's interest to a third party,

   b. giving it away to a third party,

   c. leaving it to beneficiaries at death? [LO 3.4]

8. At the death of a cotenant in a tenancy in common, what is the relationship of the cotenant's heirs and the surviving cotenant? [LO 3.4]

9. How does jointly owned property with rights of survivorship differ from a tenancy by the entirety with regard to a:

   a. sale of the property during lifetime,

   b. gift to a third person,

   c. transfer on the death of one of the tenants? [LO 3.4]

10. Explain the ramifications of having each of the following types of property owned jointly with right of survivorship:

    a. bank accounts,

    b. government savings bonds,

    c. securities. [LO 3.4]

11. What are the advantages and disadvantages of owning property jointly with right of survivorship? [LO 3.4]

12. Identify the community-property states. [LO 3.5]

13. Distinguish between separate property and community property in a community-property state. [LO 3.5]

14. Describe the best way for overcoming the general presumption favoring community property. [LO 3.5]

15. What kinds of property are characterized as separate property? [LO 3.5]

16. Explain why the transfer tax results between community- and non-community-property states would be similar when the surviving spouse is the beneficiary of the decedent spouse's estate. [LO 3.5]

17. Why should the estate planner in a common-law state have a working understanding of community-property laws? [LO 3.5]

Chapter 3: Review Answers

1. The real value of intangibles is in excess of the value of the physical object that represents the property. The representation can be touched and felt, but it is not the thing itself. Some examples are stock certificates, leases, mortgages, bonds, and other such representations of property ownership.

2. The type of estate or real property that is created is as follows:

   a.   a fee simple estate

   b.   a life estate to Ben and a remainder interest to Chris

   c.   an interest for a term of years

3. John has a reversionary interest and Sally has a life estate.

4. Under some circumstances, the legal owner of property (the person who holds legal title to the property) and the equitable owner (the person with the right to beneficial enjoyment of that property) are different parties. An example of this division of ownership is property held in trust. Here, the trustee, who invests and manages trust property, is the party who holds legal title to the trust. The trust beneficiaries, however, hold equitable title to trust property since they are entitled to the income generated by the trustee's efforts.

5. Domicile is the place that individuals consider to be their permanent residence and to which they intend to return if they temporarily leave. Situs is the place where property is located.

   Some indications of an individual's intent to establish domicile are as follows: voter registration, automobile registration, driver's license, passport, location of a bank account or safe-deposit box, situs of a principal residence, reference to domicile in a will, address listed with the Social Security Administration, and payment of property and income taxes. In certain states, there is a special form to file as a declaration of domicile to establish primary residence.

6. Gloria's state of domicile, Alabama, would have a right to tax all her property except the real estate located in Florida. Since real estate is always taxed in the state where it is located, the state of Florida has the right to tax real estate located there. Her tangible personal property may be taxed by the state where taxable situs exists. This means New Hampshire may have jurisdiction to tax the personal property located there. The intangible personal property is subject to tax by the domiciliary state, Alabama. Texas may also tax her intangible personal property, unless Texas exempts the intangible personal property of a nonresident from taxation.

7. Subject to the terms of the tenancy-in-common agreement, if applicable, a co-owner of property held as tenants in common has the following rights:

    a. Each co-owner is free to sell his or her interest to whomever the tenant wishes without the consent or knowledge of the other co-owners.

    b. Each co-owner can give away his or her interest to a third party without the other co-owner's consent or knowledge.

    c. Through the co-owner's will, each co-owner can freely dispose of his or her interest to beneficiaries at the co-owner's death.

8. There are no survivorship rights. Each tenant's interest in the property can be left to the tenant's heirs, and the tenant's gross estate will include the fair market value of his or her proportionate interest at death.

9. a. Joint tenants can sell their interests during lifetime to third parties. This action generally severs the joint tenancy, causing partitioning of the property. Tenants by the entireties may transfer their interests only with the consent of the spouse-cotenant.

    b. See answer (a) above.

    c. Under both forms of ownership, the property transfers by right of survivorship to the survivor at the death of one of the tenants.

10. a. With a joint bank account, each joint owner owns a proportionate part of the account balance and is entitled to receive one-half of the interest income. There is no gift if a person uses personal funds to open a joint bank account. A gift is considered to have been made only when the other joint owner (the donee) makes withdrawals.

    b. When government bonds are held in joint ownership with right of survivorship, there is no gift when the savings bond is purchased because the joint owner who contributed the funds can cash the bond in at any time and get his or her money back. A gift occurs only when the other joint tenant (the donee) redeems the bond and retains a greater share of the proceeds than he or she contributed to the purchase price.

c. If securities are registered in the names of the co-owners as joint tenants with right of survivorship, a gift occurs from the contributing joint tenant to the donee-joint tenant when the securities are transferred to or purchased for the account. The results are not the same, however, if the securities are registered in street name; no gift occurs when a joint street-name account is created even if one of the joint tenants furnishes more than one-half of the consideration. A gift occurs only when the other party withdraws more than his or her proportionate amount from the account.

11. The advantages of owning property jointly with right of survivorship are as follows:

- Joint ownership is convenient for certain types of assets because either tenant has access to the account.

- Joint ownership may offer one or both of the tenants a feeling of security, especially if the owners are spouses and one of them has contributed most of the funds.

- When one tenant dies, property passes directly to the other tenant without probate delay and with little or no administrative or transfer cost.

- In many states, joint property ownership between spouses passes free of state death taxes.

- Since such property passes by operation of law and not under a will, it is not subject to public scrutiny.

Disadvantages are as follows:

- At the creation of some of these types of property ownership interests, there are potential gift taxes.

- There may be additional federal estate taxation.

- The survivor will gain full control of the property and can dispose of it in any way he or she desires. The decedent-tenant, therefore, loses all control of the property.

- Under most state laws, property owned as joint tenants with right of survivorship can be reached by creditors of an individual account.

12. There are nine community-property states. The eight traditional community-property states include Arizona, California, Idaho, Louisiana, Nevada, New Mexico, Texas, and Washington. Wisconsin is recognized as the ninth community-property state since its version of the Uniform Marital Property Act, incorporating many community-property concepts, became effective in 1986.

13. Generally, property acquired by a husband and wife during their marriage belongs to them both in equal shares; it is community property. Property that can be proven to belong to a spouse separately is separate property. It may not be sufficient to rebut the community-property assumptions by simply having certain property titled in one spouse's name or acquired with one spouse's separate funds. The facts and circumstances concerning the property's use and the spouses' conduct toward the property may carry more evidentiary weight in determining ownership.

14. The best way to overcome the general presumption favoring community property is for married partners who reside in or move in and out of community-property states to keep complete, organized, and accurate records of their personal financial matters.

15. Property that was acquired during marriage by one spouse as a gift, by inheritance, as a result of a judgment award for personal injuries, or from purchase with a spouse's separate money or credit retains its separate identity.

16. The unlimited marital estate and gift tax deduction serves to equalize the transfer tax results between community- and non-community-property states when the surviving spouse is the beneficiary of the decedent spouse's estate. If someone other than the surviving spouse is the recipient of the decedent's property, transfer tax differences are more likely.

17. Because of the increasing mobility of today's families, estate planners need to understand the legalities in both common-law and community-property states even if their practice is in a common-law state. Changing domicile or moving from one jurisdiction to another can complicate clients' property ownership issues and pose estate planning problems. Planners need to be aware that legal agreements drafted in one jurisdiction may not be effective in the current jurisdiction.

Chapter 4:

Trusts, Trustees, and Other Fiduciaries and Powers of Appointment

Learning Objectives

An understanding of the material in this chapter should enable the student to

LO 4.1   **Describe the history and origin of trusts.**

LO 4. 2   **Explain the fundamentals and elements of trusts and the various purposes that trusts serve.**

LO 4. 3   **Describe the basic types of trusts and their nontax characteristics.**

LO 4. 4   **Explain how powers of appointment may be used to provide flexibility in dispositive planning.**

LO 4. 5   **Explain what a fiduciary is and describe the sources of fiduciary powers.**

LO 4. 6   **Identify the duties and powers of a fiduciary.**

LO 4. 7   **Explain how a fiduciary is selected.**

LO 4. 8   **Describe how and when trustees are removed.**

Perhaps the best-known and most widely used estate planning device is the trust. Trusts, like people, come in all shapes and sizes. That is, there are many types of trusts and they perform a variety of functions. The purpose for which a trust is created usually influences the type used. Trusts can be designed to accomplish one or many goals. Within the parameters established by state law, the uses of trusts are limited only by the imagination of the creator. The trust device enables an individual to accomplish goals with respect to family and property that would be difficult, if not impossible, to attain otherwise.

There are many types of trusts in existence today, and not all were created by natural persons. In addition to trusts created by individuals, there are corporate trusts, employee benefit trusts, government trusts, and others. Trusts can be created for personal, business, social, or charitable purposes. Basically, any group or organization (whether a business, charitable, or social group) that can legally own property can create a trust. Only living persons, however, can create a testamentary trust (a trust under a will), because wills are made solely by natural persons. This discussion is limited to those trusts created by individuals for personal use. The rule against perpetuities and the subject of powers of appointment are also examined.

LO 4.1   Describe the history and origin of trusts.

Origin of Trusts

The use of trusts originated in England during feudal times. At that time, there were many burdens associated with the legal ownership of property. By separating legal title from the benefits and use of property, a way was found to remove the burdens from the life tenant. In early times, the words *use* and *trust* were applied synonymously and interchangeably, although there were some differences between them. Both terms were first introduced into England shortly after the Norman Conquest in 1066. The fiduciary relationship represented by the trust form of ownership was formalized in 1536 when the Statute of Uses was adopted in England.

In essence, the trust represents a split ownership of property. Legal title is held by one party while equitable ownership rests in another. Originally, trusts were used principally

- to avoid the burdens of holding legal title to property, including being subject to rights of creditors as well as rights of dower and curtesy

- to allow religious houses to obtain profits from land, although they were prohibited under the law from owning land

- to provide greater freedom in conveying land during life

In early times, trusts were unknown in countries that followed Roman or civil law. With time, however, substitutes for the trust form of ownership evolved. In recent years, the trust form of ownership has been adopted by statute in some civil-law countries.

LO 4. 2   Explain the fundamentals and elements of trusts and the various purposes that trusts serve.

FUNDAMENTALS OF TRUSTS

trust

trustee

What is this unique and versatile estate planning vehicle called a trust? By definition, a **trust** is a legal relationship in which one acts in a fiduciary capacity with respect to the property of another. Fiduciary capacity requires that a person (the fiduciary) receive and hold title to property that is held for the benefit of another person (a beneficiary), to whom the fiduciary owes the highest duty of good faith. When a fiduciary relationship exists, there is a legally enforceable obligation imposed on the person who holds legal title to the property to keep or use it, as well as to deal with the property objectively and solely for the benefit of another. The holder of the legal title is called a **trustee**. The party for whom the property is managed is the equitable titleholder and is known as the beneficiary. The trust is thus a fiduciary relationship concerned with certain persons and property to which various rights and duties are attached.

Purposes of Trusts

The purposes for which trusts are created are as varied as their creators. One of the primary reasons for setting up a trust is to obtain competent and professional management as well as investment of trust property. Another purpose is to protect the property for the beneficiaries, thereby providing them with income and asset security.

A trust may supply a missing element or skill in the abilities of the settlor (grantor) or the beneficiaries. For example, the beneficiary may not have the necessary character, knowledge, skill, judgment, or business acumen to properly manage and invest the trust property. If a grantor is concerned that one or more of these characteristics are missing in the heirs, this individual may find that the creation of a trust is an ideal way to substitute for the missing elements.

Ultimately, the grantor wants to be assured that after his or her death, there is some way of achieving a measure of security and protection for the family as well as preserving the property that the grantor had worked so hard to accumulate. Creating a trust may be an ideal way to relieve the grantor's concerns by providing the knowledge that his or her beneficiaries will receive appropriate care.

Another reason to use a trust is to protect the interests of children from an earlier marriage. Also, trust assets may be beyond the reach of a spouse's right of election at the grantor's death. The creation of a revocable or an irrevocable trust while the grantor is alive (also referred to as an inter vivos or living trust) helps the grantor leave property to whomever he or she wishes. Today, marital problems are common. There may be multiple parents and multiple children from more than one marriage with whom to contend. Use of trusts can enable the grantor to arrange his or her property so it is channeled to the intended beneficiaries and protected from others.

A trust may also be established for the benefit of the grantor or for the grantor's spouse. If it is a living trust, it can free the grantor to do other things. There will be continuous management of the grantor's property during a trip or disability. A trust can protect one's assets from the reach of creditors if one is involved in a new business venture, particularly a risky one. A living trust also gives the grantor the opportunity to see the trust in operation while alive to make sure that it is being managed appropriately.

Although not directly stated, the trust can give the creator an opportunity to continue to manage after death. By specifying in the trust instrument the conditions and timing of distributions of income, principal, or both, the grantor can control the availability of assets for the beneficiaries after death. If the trust is an inter vivos trust that is in operation before the testator's death, the continuous management of the testator's assets forms a bridge between life and death.

A trust offers an excellent method of handling and consolidating accumulations of wealth. If it is an irrevocable trust, and the trust instrument provides for accumulation of income, the trust will function as a separate taxpayer, possibly at a lower tax bracket than the grantor's. If there are multiple beneficiaries or multiple trusts, income tax savings may possibly be obtained through allocation of income among the beneficiaries and the trust. For example, the trustee may be given discretionary powers with regard to sprinkling income and/or principal among one or more beneficiaries according to their needs. Or the trust instrument may be more restrictive by providing that income or principal is to be used to provide only such things as medical care, education, the purchase of a primary residence, or entry into a new business.

Trusts can also afford opportunities to save estate taxes. Any appreciation in the value of property transferred to an irrevocable trust escapes taxation in the grantor's estate provided that he or she does not retain certain powers. Should the property's value appreciate greatly after being transferred to the trust, considerable estate tax savings result. Trusts can be structured so that the beneficiaries have broad access to both income and principal, and yet the trust principal is not included in their estates for estate tax purposes. As noted earlier, the judicious use of trusts and their beneficiaries as multiple taxpayers also provides an opportunity to have trust income divided among more than one beneficiary in potentially lower tax brackets.

In addition, if a corporate trustee is used and the trust assets are invested in common-trust funds, an individual with a relatively modest estate of $50,000 to $300,000 benefits from the advantages of diversification and regular investment advice that otherwise would not be affordable.

In summary, trusts can be set up to provide management services, income and estate tax savings, and other benefits. However, the greatest benefit of many trusts is the flexibility they afford that enables beneficiaries to have the use of both trust income and principal to achieve the grantor's objectives.

Elements of Trusts

There are five elements common to all trusts:

- the creator

- the trustee
- the property
- the beneficiaries
- the terms of the trust (generally contained in a written document)

Creator

grantor

The creator of the trust is the one who intentionally causes the trust to come into existence and is also variously known as the **grantor**, settlor, trustor, or testator (in the case of a testamentary trust). The creator of the trust is the individual who transfers his or her property to another, the trustee, who agrees to hold and manage the property for the benefit of yet another party, the beneficiary. Unless the grantor retains certain powers over the trust or serves as a cotrustee, his or her role in relation to the trust ceases once the transfers have been completed and the trust becomes operative. Of course, the grantor may continue to be involved with the trust as a beneficiary or trustee. (See the figure.)

Trust Concept

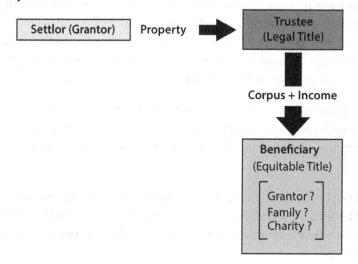

Unless the grantor falls afoul of the grantor-trust rules (which are discussed later in this book and which can make trust income taxable to the grantor), the grantor's continuing relationship, if any, to the trust is generally nominal.

Terms for an Individual Creating a Trust
- trustor
- settlor
- grantor
- creator

Trustee

It was stated earlier that a trust is a fiduciary arrangement with respect to property. The fiduciary relationship remains between the trustee and the beneficiary, not between the grantor and the trustee. Also, after a trust is established, no fiduciary relationship remains between the grantor and the trust beneficiaries.

A trustee may be a living person or persons. The trustee may also be a corporate institution, such as a bank, or a combination of one or more individuals and a financial institution legally empowered to act in a fiduciary capacity. While every trust requires a trustee, the trust will not fail if the original trustee resigns, becomes incapacitated, or declines to serve. If no provision is made for designation of a successor trustee, the court of the jurisdiction where the trust is administered (the situs of the trust) may be petitioned to appoint a new trustee. If an interim period exists between appointment of trustees, the trust remains temporarily inactive.

Despite the fact that a successor trustee can be appointed by a court of competent jurisdiction, the trust document should always designate at least one successor trustee. In the event that both the original trustee and the successor are individuals, it is a prudent idea to provide a corporate trustee as an ultimate successor if neither of the individual trustees can or will serve. This avoids the necessity for legal proceedings and costs.

Trust Property

The next essential element in the trust is the trust property. This is also called the trust corpus, res, or principal. Almost anything capable of legal ownership (real, personal, or even an enforceable contract right, such as the ownership of a life insurance policy) may be transferred to and held in a trust. This does not mean, however, that all property is suitable for placement in a trust.

Beneficiaries

beneficiary

The fourth necessary element is the **beneficiary**. This is the person for whom the trust is created. Beneficiaries hold equitable or beneficial title to the property. The beneficiaries have legally enforceable rights that they may defend and protect in the event that the trust is managed improperly.

In addition to primary beneficiaries, contingent beneficiaries also may be named and provided for in a contingent beneficiaries clause. The trust may also provide separately for beneficiaries who are to receive only income and for remainderpersons to whom the trust principal will be released when the trust terminates (or at an earlier time when distributions of principal are permitted). Note that beneficiaries must be legal persons (that is, persons or institutions who can enforce their rights in a court). Under common law, trusts for the benefit of pets could not be established. Today, however, many states have enacted pet trust statutes that permit pets to be trust beneficiaries for the pets' lives.

This is not to say that trusts cannot be set up to benefit an individual who is legally incompetent. In such a situation, a guardian is appointed to enforce the incapacitated person's rights.

It should be noted that a trust will be held invalid if the sole trustee is also the sole beneficiary under the common-law doctrine of merger. When legal and equitable (beneficial) title are merged in one individual, he or she is considered the outright owner and the trust ceases to exist. However, a trustee may also be a beneficiary provided that there are either cotrustees or other beneficiaries of the same trust.

Trust Terms

trust terms

Trust Term Provisions. The last element necessary for a trust consists of the **trust terms**. Usually, the trust terms are embodied in a written instrument called the trust instrument, deed of trust, or indenture of trust. The trust terms or powers are derived from those specified in the trust instrument as well as from the law of the jurisdiction in which the trust is situated and under which it is governed.

The trust terms include a set of powers, usually administrative, that may establish the scope of both the responsibilities and duties of the respective parties. The trust terms may also place limitations and restrictions on the trustee's powers. The grantor may designate the types of investments permitted by the trustee, or the grantor may give the trustee broad discretion in making investments. This discretion is limited only by the standard for investments by a fiduciary set forth by the local jurisdiction under which the trust is governed. Clearly, in constructing the trust, the grantor has the original power to give the trustee exclusive, discretionary, or limited powers regarding investing and managing the trust property as well as distributing property to the beneficiaries.

The trustee is guided in the investment and management of trust property as well as in the administration of his or her duties by the above-mentioned sources—the terms of the trust instrument itself and governing state law. To the extent the trust instrument contains explicit directions and mandatory responsibilities, the trustee has an obligation to fulfill these acts with undivided loyalty for the beneficiary. The trustee must act in accordance with the grantor's directions, but only as long as there is no impermissible conflict with state law. It may happen that the trust is silent with respect to certain administrative powers and duties. In that case, state law controls.

The trust may contain a spendthrift provision, which provides a restriction against attachment by creditors of trust assets, whether they are creditors of the beneficiary or the grantor. In this way, the trust protects beneficiaries from their own indiscretion and poor judgment. In essence, a spendthrift clause restricts beneficiaries from assigning their trust income or principal interests prior to receiving the interests themselves. Therefore, such a clause guarantees the beneficiary will not lose the income before receiving it.

EXAMPLE

"The purpose of this trust is to protect Sam Spender from his own financial mismanagement and to provide him with a reasonable means of support, free from the claims or interests of others. Any and all distributions from the trust shall be paid directly to the beneficiary, Sam Spender, and to no other person or entity. The beneficiary shall not have the power to transfer, assign, or pledge his interest in the principal or income of this trust prior to receipt."

For instance, typically a spendthrift provision would prevent beneficiaries from using their trust interest as security for a loan or from selling the beneficial future interest in the property. All jurisdictions, however, enforce beneficiary predistribution agreements to transfer property passing under a will or from a trust to creditors when it is received by the beneficiary. Clearly, once trust income or principal has been distributed to a beneficiary, the interest is accessible to creditors.

A trust may also contain a savings clause with respect to the rule against perpetuities or state law that limits the duration of trusts. In effect, the provision may provide that, notwithstanding any other provision to the contrary, the trust terminates within the time allowed under the rule against perpetuities or comparable law.

Other standard provisions of a trust may provide instructions for appointment of a successor trustee in the event that the present trustee resigns, is incapacitated, or fails to serve. Grounds for removal of a trustee and instructions for the replacement of one may be found in the trust instrument. The trust may also contain a provision pertaining to the trustee's fee. Generally, a corporate trustee requests that a provision be inserted in the trust stating that the institution be compensated in accordance with its standard schedule of fees in effect at any particular time.

Trust Elements
- creator (grantor/settlor/trustor)
- trustee (legal title)
- property (corpus/principal)
- beneficiaries (beneficial title)
- provisions/terms

Legal Limitations on Trust Duration

rule against perpetuities

There are two limitations pertaining to the duration of private, noncharitable trusts that affect the trust's validity as well as the exercise of any power of appointment created by the trust or will. These limitations were enacted to prevent property from being held in trust indefinitely. The objectives of the law are of the law is that property should be alienable and should eventually take its place within the stream of commerce. (Alienation is the right to sell, give away, or dispose of property at will.) A perpetuity is any limitation or condition that takes away or suspends a person's power to alienate property for an extensive or infinite time period. Therefore, the **rule against perpetuities** regulated the creation of future interests in trusts and requires that for the trust to be valid, an interest in property has to take effect within a prescribed time period. Historically, the rule against perpetuities is a common-law rule providing that no interest in property is valid unless the interest must vest (take effect) no later than 21 years plus 9 months (in the case of a posthumous child, the period of gestation) after some life or lives in being (after the life of a named living person) when the interest was created.

EXAMPLE

A grantor of property who has no children cannot create a trust for his grandchildren because there is no "life in being" (no children or children's children have been born yet) when the trust is created. The trust is held to be void under the rule. On the other hand, suppose the grantor has a son when he creates a trust that, by its terms, passes property at death in trust to the son and, on the son's death, to the son's children. The trust does not violate the rule against perpetuities because the trust duration can be measured by the life of the son, a person in being, at the creation of the trust.

The date on which the interest is considered to be created is different for revocable and irrevocable trusts. If the trust is irrevocable when created, the date of the trust's creation starts the period within which the interest must vest. If the trust is revocable, the time period begins if and when the trust becomes irrevocable. If the interest is created by will, the date of the testator's death is the initial measuring point for a will or a testamentary trust, since the instrument does not become effective or irrevocable until then. The common-law rule against perpetuities has been enacted into law by statute in many states, and almost half the states have repealed it. Some state legislatures have also shortened the time period for vesting.

In 1986, the National Conference of Commissioners on Uniform State Laws approved The Uniform Statutory Rule against Perpetuities. The Uniform Act was amended in 1990 and is now being adopted by different states. The act takes a wait-and-see approach to vesting. It allows a 90-year period (as opposed to 21 years and 9 months from lives in being) from the date an interest is created for the interest to vest. Only if an interest does not in fact vest within the 90 years does the disposition become invalid. Consequently, the Uniform Act applies solely to interests that under the common-law rule would be invalid only because of uncertainty as to whether the interests would vest within the common-law time period. Under the new act, interests are not considered invalid unless vesting does not actually occur within the 90-year period. Currently, an increasing number of states are statutorily adopting or are considering amendments to the traditional common-law rule against perpetuities.

For states in which the traditional common-law rule applies, the proposed distribution plan should be analyzed to determine that no interest will vest so remotely that the rule against perpetuities would be violated before a trust is drafted. In this analysis, it is crucial to remember the different dates of creation.

EXAMPLE

A direction in a trust specifies that it shall be held for the life of the grantor's wife, and that on her death an equal share for each of the grantor's children shall be set aside and continued in trust for the child's life. At the death of the last of the grantor's children, the corpus is to be distributed to their children (the grantor's grandchildren) or their heirs. If the trust is a testamentary trust, there is no violation of the rule against perpetuities because the corpus beneficiaries (the grantor's grandchildren) will be ascertainable and the interest will vest within a life or lives in being (the grantor's children) at the time the interest is created (the death of the grantor).

However, if the trust is an irrevocable inter vivos trust, it will violate the rule against perpetuities. This results because the interest comes into being at the time the trust is created, and it is possible that the last child of the grantor will not have been born at that time. (For purposes of the rule against perpetuities, the grantor and the grantor's

> spouse are presumed to be able to have children until they die.) Because distribution of the corpus is not to take place until the death of the last of the grantor's children, there is a chance that the interests will not vest within the prescribed period.

Note that under the traditional rule against perpetuities there is a violation of the rule if even a *possibility* exists when the interest is created that the interest will not vest absolutely within the required time. This means that in many states, the operation of this rule does not wait to see what actually happens, but rather invalidates the interest prospectively. Drafters of trust instruments should be careful to see that shares for any individual not in being at the creation of the trust are made payable to such persons outright or held only during the lives of persons who are living when the trust is created.

A common testamentary scheme is to skip the tax on the primary beneficiary's death and to make a distribution of principal at that time. For example, an older brother may give his younger brother a life estate in property. At the younger brother's death, any of the brother's children surviving him will receive the corpus. If a child is deceased, that child's issue would take his or her parent's share. In this arrangement, there are no problems with the rule against perpetuities, because all interests will vest indefeasibly at the expiration of a life in being at the creation of the interest. In other words, when the interest is created at the death of the older brother (the effective date of his testamentary disposition), all the interests must vest at the expiration of a life in being at the time the interest was created (the younger brother's). This result can be ascertained because, at the death of the measuring life in being (the younger brother's), all of his children will be ascertainable and the trust corpus under the terms of the example would belong to them absolutely if they are living. In the event a child of the younger brother is deceased, the deceased child's portion belongs absolutely to his or her issue.

The common-law rule against perpetuities is extremely complex in application. Consequently, most wills and trusts contain a perpetuities-savings clause to eliminate possible perpetuities problems. For testamentary trusts, the following is a typical savings clause:

> Notwithstanding the directions given my trustee above as to the distribution of income and principal, every trust established by this Will shall terminate, if it is not already terminated, 21 years after the death of the last survivor of my wife, my children, and any lineal descendant of mine alive *on the date of my death*. At the termination of such trust or trusts, my trustee shall immediately transfer, convey, and pay over the principal of each of the trusts to the lineal descendants then living of the child of mine on whose account the trust was established, per stirpes. If there are no such individuals living, to my lineal descendants then living, per stirpes, and if none, to the American Heart Association.

If the trust is an inter vivos trust, the italicized phrase (above) should be replaced with a phrase such as "on the date of the creation of this trust."

rule against accumulations

Another historic common-law rule, called the **rule against accumulations**, states the period during which income may accumulate. It was enacted using the same principle as the rule against perpetuities, and, in most cases, the permissible period during which the interest must vest is the same as under the rule against perpetuities. There are a few states that have shortened the period for accumulations. Certain states permit accumulations today only for charitable purposes or during a child's minority.

Trust Situs

Because a trust can be established anywhere, the grantor has some flexibility in establishing a situs for the trust. It need not be the grantor's domicile. A trust generally can be established subject to the laws of another state by stating that fact in the instrument. There may be tax or other advantages to setting up a trust outside of the grantor's domicile.

Flexibility Through Trustee Discretion

Most modern trusts allow trustees broad latitude and discretion in their investment and management decisions. Trustees may also be given absolute discretion regarding distributions of income or principal to named beneficiaries. The trustee may have the power to distribute income or principal unequally among the beneficiaries, depending on their individual needs. Or there may be specific guidelines for allowing special expenditures for such expenses as undergraduate or postgraduate education, purchase of a principal residence, or investment in a new business. The more flexibility the trustee has, the better he or she may be able to serve and provide for the true needs of the beneficiaries as they arise, just as the grantor would have done if the grantor had retained control of his or her own property. Flexibility is especially important since, within the general framework established by the grantor, the trustee generally is required to continue to fulfill the grantor's objectives regarding his or her property and loved ones long after the grantor is incapacitated or deceased. In fact, a trust may continue to exist through several generations of beneficiaries. In this case, however, there may be additional generation-skipping transfer taxes with which to contend if the trust benefits more than one generation of income beneficiaries.

LO 4. 3　　Describe the basic types of trusts and their nontax characteristics.

TYPES OF TRUSTS

The use of trusts for estate, gift, and income tax planning is discussed at length later. At this time, we will discuss some of the various types of trust arrangements commonly used today. The purpose of this discussion is to help students become familiar with some basic types of trusts and their nontax characteristics.

Living Trusts

Revocable Trusts

living trust

revocable living trust

A **living trust** (*inter vivos trust*) is created and operates before the death of the settlor. A **revocable living trust** is created when the grantor transfers the trust property to the trustee but reserves the power to alter or terminate the arrangement and reclaim the trust property. (See the figure below.) As discussed later, a transfer to a truly revocable trust does not change the grantor's federal estate, gift, and income tax picture. Essentially, the transfer is treated as an incomplete gift. Obviously, there must be nontax reasons to create the revocable living trust. The advantages of this arrangement include the following:

- The grantor may not have the ability or time to manage the property to the maximum benefit of the beneficiaries.

- The grantor may be able to enjoy the psychological benefits of gifting property in trust for the trust beneficiaries while retaining the ability to reclaim the property.

- The grantor has the ability to observe the operation of the trust under the current trustee. This also gives the trustee the opportunity to become familiar with the grantor's dispositive intentions before the trust becomes irrevocable.

- The revocable trust becomes irrevocable at the death of the grantor and passes by operation of law to the beneficiary. This avoids probate costs and provides for a transfer with less publicity.

- Ancillary jurisdiction for out-of-state property can be avoided if the grantor's out-of-state intangibles are transferred to revocable trusts in the grantor's state of domicile.

- A grantor who is a sole proprietor of, or partner in, an ongoing business may transfer the business to a revocable trust to avoid termination of the business at the grantor's death.

Types of Trusts

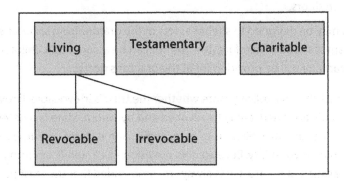

Irrevocable Trusts

irrevocable trust

A living trust may also be established as an **irrevocable trust** by the grantor. In this case, the property is transferred to the trust permanently, and the grantor cannot terminate the trust and reclaim the property before the trust terminates by its terms. As we will discuss later, a truly irrevocable trust is treated as a completed gift for gift, estate, and income tax purposes. Irrevocable trusts provide tax advantages, such as estate reduction and income shifting. Unfortunately, transfers to an irrevocable trust are completed gifts and may result in gift tax liability to the grantor.

Many grantors are reluctant to permanently lose possession and control over the trust property. Only extremely wealthy individuals with superfluous assets will typically feel comfortable with a permanent transfer of substantial assets to an irrevocable trust. However, besides the tax advantages mentioned above, there are several nontax objectives that are satisfied by the living irrevocable trust transfer.

Among these objectives are the following:

- The grantor can establish the trust to manage property for a needy dependent. The trustee in this arrangement can provide a valuable service to the grantor. That is, the beneficiary has to deal with the trustee rather than the grantor for the needed funds.

This can prevent a continuing undesirable conflict between the grantor and the dependent.

- The trustee may possess investment and accumulation skills not held by the grantor to manage the trust property.

- The trust property avoids probate at the death of the grantor.

- The trust property provides for the beneficiaries and is not subject to claims of the grantor's creditors.

- The trust may be designed to shelter assets of the grantor from spousal-election rights at the grantor's death. Therefore, the grantor can be assured that children from a former marriage will be provided for at the grantor's death.

The terms of the trust should explicitly state whether the trust is irrevocable. If revocable, the trust terms should indicate when it may be revoked and by whom. State law determines this provision if the trust document is silent as to revocability. Some states presume revocability, while others presume irrevocability. Because this provision has a significant impact on both federal and state taxation of the trust, it is always recommended that the trust provisions be clearly stated.

Testamentary Trusts

testamentary trust

A **testamentary trust** is created under the will of a testator. As such, it is never irrevocable until the testator's death or permanent legal incapacity.

Charitable Trusts

charitable trust

Charitable trusts have a long history of development under the common law of England and are valid under the laws of all states of the United States. In a later chapter, we will discuss the estate planning uses for specific types of charitable trusts. However, it is probably true that most gifts in trusts to charity are motivated by benevolent rather than tax-saving objectives.

Characteristics of Charitable Trusts

Charitable trusts have several elements in common with regular trusts. There is the normal requirement that the trust creator have an intention to create the trust and transfer the property to the trust. The legal title to the trust property is held by the trustee, who administers the trust according to the trust terms.

The charitable trust is a type of public trust and has some special characteristics not existing in a truly private trust. First, the trust must be for a specific charitable purpose. Generally, the objective of the charitable trust is to improve society in some manner. Charitable purposes include governmental improvement, advancement of religion, educational or scientific advancement, relief of poverty, and other purposes of community advancement. For tax purposes, the Internal Revenue Code is more specific in defining a charitable purpose.

The terms of a charitable trust must not provide a benefit for a definite individual among the class of potential beneficiaries. However, the charitable trust must have a definite class of beneficiaries. For example, a charitable trust could be created to fund estate planning research at The American College. However, it is not permissible to create a charitable trust to fund a travel budget for your favorite estate planning professor.

cy pres

A charitable trust, as opposed to a private trust, may be created for an unlimited duration. We discussed the rule of perpetuities earlier, which provides that a trust cannot have an indefinite life. This rule does not apply to a charitable trust, and there is generally no legal time limit on the length of the trust. The trust continues until it terminates by its terms or fails for some other reason. In fact, it is not necessary for a charitable trust to fail even when its intended purpose becomes impossible. A doctrine of law known as cy pres (pronounced see-pray) was developed to prevent the failure of trusts that cannot be applied to their original charitable purpose. A court may enforce a trust that has a general charitable intent. When applying **cy pres**, the court attempts to find another charitable purpose similar to the initial charitable intention of the trust settlor. Cy pres may be applied when the initial charitable trust does not provide enough property to meet its purpose, or when the trust purpose has already been accomplished or becomes impossible, and additional funds remain in the trust.

It is the intended beneficiary who enforces a private trust in the courts. This is one reason for the requirement that a private trust have specific beneficiaries. Because a charitable trust cannot have specific beneficiaries, there is no logical individual to enforce the terms. Typically, the attorney general of the state is empowered to enforce charitable trusts.

LO 4. 4 **Explain how powers of appointment may be used to provide flexibility in dispositive planning.**

POWERS OF APPOINTMENT

Basic Terminology

donee of the power

lapse

appointees

A power of appointment is an interest held in property by an individual known as the holder, or **donee of the power**. The property interest is a right given to another to designate the disposition of property subject to the power. The act of designating the property by the donee is known as the *exercise* of the power. The possible recipients of the property after the exercise of the power depend on the terms of the power of appointment. Failure to exercise a power is known as **lapse** of the power. A power of appointment is created when the owner of the property, known as the donor of the power, creates the power in a donee to designate the donor's property that is subject to the power. The recipients of the property after the donee exercises the power are known as the **appointees**. Powers of appointment come into existence in various forms and are often gleaned from the provisions, for example, in trusts and powers of attorney. Rarely are the words "power of appointment" contained in the document; rather the phrase and attendant ramifications are inferred from the powers, rights, and control an individual is given under the terms of the document. Note that for gift tax purposes the term donee refers to the recipient of the gift property.

For *power-of-appointment* purposes, however, the term *donee* refers to the recipient of the power. It is the *appointees* who receive the property itself. Depending on the type of power of appointment, a donee may also be an appointee.

EXAMPLE

Tom Tuttle placed an apartment building he owns in trust under the following terms. The income from the trust is to be provided for Tom's wife, Tina, for life, and Tina is given the power to appoint the property at her death to any of Tom and Tina's children then living. In this case, Tom is the donor of the power and Tina is the donee. Any of their children living at Tina's death are possible appointees. If Tina designates in her will which of the children is to receive the property, the power will be exercised at her death. If Tina fails to make this provision, the power will lapse and the property will pass under these circumstances to Tom's heirs at law.

Types of Powers of Appointment

general power

A power of appointment that gives the donee a right at any time to designate the property to parties that include the donee or the donee's estate or creditors is known as a **general power** of appointment. The donee of a general power essentially has all rights to the property at the time the power becomes exercisable. We will learn later that the donee who possesses a general power at the time of death has the property subject to the power included in his or her gross estate.

> ## General Power of Appointment
>
> There is an unlimited right to appoint property to:
> - yourself
> - your creditors
> - your estate
> - your estate creditors

special (limited) power

A **special (limited) power** of appointment restricts the donee's right to designate the property to a specific class of appointees. The power held by Tina Tuttle in the previous example is a special power because she may appoint the apartment building only to any of the children living at the time of her death. With a special power of appointment, the donee of the power cannot be a direct appointee of the property.

The time that a power may be exercised may also be restricted by the donor. That is, the donee may be permitted to designate the property to an appointee at any time, or there may be only a specific time when the power can be exercised. One type of power that is important for estate planning is a testamentary power. This type of power is exercisable only at the death of the donee through the provisions of the donee's will. The power held by Tina Tuttle in the prior example is a testamentary special power of appointment.

Special Power of Appointment

Property may <u>not</u> be appointed to:

- yourself
- your creditors
- your estate
- your estate creditors

Purposes of Powers of Appointment

There are some estate and gift tax consequences to planning powers of appointment. A discussion of these is reserved for future chapters. However, the power of appointment is an obviously flexible and useful dispositive device for nontax reasons. The primary reason for using a power of appointment is to delegate a dispositive decision and/or postpone the time at which the dispositive decision is made. The various types of powers, and the restrictions that can be imposed on the powers, create a flexible transfer mechanism. The donor of the power can retain some control over the property and the dispositive decision while delegating the actual decision to another. For example, the donor chooses the property made subject to the power. The donor can choose when the property will be transferred and restrict its ultimate receipt to a limited class.

The donor may have important reasons for delegating the dispositive powers to another. First, this removes the dispositive decision and any discontent resulting from the decision from the original owner of the property. For example, benevolent grandparents may want to transfer property to their grandchildren. By creating a power to be held by the grandchildren's parents, the grandparents place the decision in the hands of the parents, who best know the needs, worthiness, or goals of the grandchildren.

Furthermore, the donor may wish to postpone the time the transfer of property is to be made. For example, parents may not want to transfer property to their children until they reach majority. To prepare for the contingency that the donor will not survive the period of postponement of the transfer, it is necessary to delegate the decision to another. Often a parent donates the power to the other parent to make the property transfer. Many powers are created by will for this purpose. By both delaying and delegating the ultimate transfer, the donor can take a wait-and-see approach for transferring property. By using this technique, the donee of the power is able to exercise the power at the time the donor actually desires to transfer the property. The donee of the power can make the appropriate designation in light of the circumstances existing at that time.

LO 4. 5 **Explain what a fiduciary is and describe the sources of fiduciary powers.**

WHAT IS A FIDUCIARY?

No study of trusts would be complete without an understanding of the role of trustees and other estate planning fiduciaries. Under the common-law system predominant in English-speaking countries, a form of property ownership has evolved in which legal title to property is held by one person or entity separate from the beneficial or equitable ownership interest held by another person or entity. When this arrangement exists, the individual or institution that holds bare legal title has the duty to manage the property for the benefit of the equitable (beneficial) owner. The equitable owner (or beneficiary) is entitled to possess and enjoy the property as well as to receive income generated by the property. The person or institution that holds and manages property for the benefit of another is called a fiduciary.

fiduciary

Fiduciary is a broad term that applies to several types of relationships. By definition, a **fiduciary** is an individual or institution charged with the duty to act exclusively for the benefit of another party as to matters within the scope of the relationship between them. The relationship created between the one who manages the property and the other party (beneficiary) who receives the income as well as other benefits of ownership is called a fiduciary relationship.

All fiduciaries, whether individuals or institutions, are required to manage the property in their care according to strict fiduciary principles and standards established by state law. In accepting the responsibility for management of another's property, a fiduciary holds a special position of trust in relation to the beneficiaries. Because fiduciaries are entrusted with legal responsibility for the property of others, it is important to understand the role of fiduciaries as well as the scope of their duties and powers. The types of fiduciaries discussed in this chapter are trustees, guardians, and personal representatives of estates (executors and administrators).

Fiduciary relationships are created in different ways depending on the type of fiduciary relationship involved. Differences and similarities among trustees, guardians, and personal representatives of estates exist as to the source of their powers, the duration of their position, and the nature and extent of their duties and responsibilities.

A person named to a fiduciary position does not have an obligation to accept the appointment. However, once the person accepts the position, he or she is under a legal duty to fulfill all the obligations inherent in the relationship until he or she is relieved of the fiduciary duties or resigns.

Fiduciary Arrangements
- trustee
  - duties exist until the trust terminates according to the trust terms (may last for many years)
- guardian
  - duties exist until legal disability or minority of the ward ends
- personal representative of estate (executor/administrator)
  - duties exist until the estate is settled and property is distributed (usually 1–3 years)

Sources of Powers

Fiduciaries receive their power from different sources. When an individual dies, the state has a particular interest in the orderly transfer of the decedent's property to the beneficiaries as well as in seeing that the estate is settled and closed within a reasonably short time, usually no more than one to 2 years. It is in the best interest of the state that beneficiaries be self-sustaining during the administration of an estate and that the decedent's property is transferred as expeditiously as possible. Laws have been enacted that prescribe the procedures for settling estates and managing property during the period of estate administration or guardianship. Likewise, the state has an interest in the protection of the property of minors and incompetents.

Because of the state's concerns noted above, the personal representatives of estates (executors or administrators) and guardians of persons and/or properties all derive their powers from the statutory law. All these types of fiduciaries are appointed by the courts and must make an accounting to the court, either at regular intervals or in order to be discharged from their duties, or both. Upon satisfactory completion of their responsibilities, these fiduciaries may apply to the appropriate court to be discharged from their duties. The court that oversees these fiduciary relationships may be called a probate court, surrogate court, or orphans' court, depending on the designation used by a particular jurisdiction.

On the other hand, trusts are not usually regulated by the court. Generally, trusts are private arrangements established by a trust settlor (grantor) who appoints another person or entity to manage the individual's property for the benefit of others (possibly including the settlor). The trustee's powers, therefore, are generally derived from the trust instrument.

Duration of Fiduciary Powers and Duties

The average estate exists for a relatively short period, usually only one or 2 years, and in any event, not beyond the time that administration is completed and the decedent's property is transferred to the intended beneficiaries. An executor's (or administrator's) powers and duties generally terminate when the estate assets are distributed to the beneficiaries, and the estate is closed. A trust, on the other hand, can last for many years. It is not unusual for a trust to be in existence for 20 or 30 years, or longer. The trustee's duties and powers do not end until the termination of the trust. After a guardian is appointed, the guardianship lasts until the legal disability of the ward, be it the ward's minority or incompetency, terminates.

Both guardians and personal representatives are empowered to function as soon as they are appointed by the court. However, trustees do not assume their duties until property is actually transferred to the trust.

Accountability of Various Fiduciaries

A personal representative of an estate or a guardian will file an accounting with the court when his or her task is completed. If everything is in order, the estate is closed or the guardianship terminated, and the personal representative or guardian discharged. By contrast, a trustee is not required to make an accounting to the court. A trustee may, however, be required to account regularly to the beneficiaries. As noted earlier, the trustee is appointed by a grantor (creator of the trust) and receives powers and limitations under the terms of the trust instrument itself.

LO 4. 6   **Identify the duties and powers of a fiduciary.**

DUTIES OF A FIDUCIARY

Loyalty

The most fundamental duty owed by a fiduciary to the beneficiaries is undivided loyalty regarding all matters within the scope of the relationship. A fiduciary can be held accountable to the beneficiaries if he or she does not conform with those standards.

A fundamental doctrine or statement of fiduciary principles has evolved that governs the conduct of all fiduciaries under the common law (now generally codified by state legislatures).

The Restatement of the Law of Trusts[1] contains a list of the following fiduciary principles:

- Trustees must be loyal to the beneficiaries.

---

1.   The Restatements are a series of treatises setting out general legal principles.

- Traditionally they must not delegate their responsibilities to others if they can be performed by the trustees themselves.
- They must keep and render accounts of the trust or estate.
- They must furnish information to the beneficiaries (make full disclosure);
- They must administer the trusts or estates with reasonable care, skill, and diligence in the fiduciary performance of their duties.

Trustees must also

- keep control of the property
- preserve the property
- enforce claims and defend actions against the property
- keep the property separate and segregated from their own property and from the property of others
- make the property productive
- pay income to beneficiaries
- deal impartially with beneficiaries if more than one exists

Trustees have a duty to communicate with other trustees, if any, as well as to act in concert with them. The trust instrument may require the unanimous consent of all trustees (if more than one), or may stipulate that a majority vote of trustees is sufficient. The instrument may also state that a beneficiary-trustee may not take part in decisions involving his or her beneficial share.

A fiduciary generally is said to be held to standards of a person of ordinary prudence, care, and skill. A trustee must exercise that same degree of care and skill that a person of ordinary prudence would exercise in dealing with his or her own property. There is a different interpretation of this standard of conduct for the lay fiduciary than there is for the professional fiduciary. If trustees are professionals, they are held to higher standards than lay persons and are generally held to the prudent-person standard with regard to investment and management of trust property. The professional fiduciary or the corporate trustee is held to a still higher standard because he or she is considered an expert.

Duty Not to Self-Deal

The fiduciary also has a duty not to self-deal or profit at the expense of the beneficiaries. The duty of loyalty is violated if the trustee sells trust assets to himself or herself as an individual, even if acquired at fair market value. However, if the trustee makes full disclosure of all the pertinent facts to all beneficiaries and they are competent to approve the transaction, it might be acceptable. Alternatively, if the appropriate court is made aware of the transaction and orders or approves the sale, the trustee is exculpated from liability for self-dealing. Certainly, a trustee should never sell trust assets to himself or herself at a bargain price, because the beneficiaries could hold the trustee accountable for the difference. The trustee should not permit self-interest to interfere with the duty of loyalty to the beneficiaries. Any sale of trust property to the trustee is voidable (reversible) by the beneficiaries, unless they are advised of all pertinent facts and consent.

Some questions arise regarding the duty against self-dealing when the transaction is profitable for the beneficiary. What if a trustee sold personal securities to the trust at fair market value or even at a better price than the marketplace offered? It might be to the financial advantage of the trust or estate to purchase these assets. If the securities are obtained by the trust at a good price and are a proper investment for trust assets, should a trustee be allowed to transact such a sale?

Clearly, unless the trustee obtains the consent and approval of all beneficiaries who are of legal age and competent, the trustee's property should not be sold to the trust, and the trustee should not purchase trust property for himself or herself. If any of the beneficiaries are minors or legally incompetent, they do not have the capacity to consent to a sale; thus, it is not binding on them. If the sale is improper, a trustee can be held personally responsible to the beneficiaries for any loss incurred.

On the other hand, if these same securities were acquired from a stranger and then plummeted in value because the stock market declined, the trustee would have no obligation to restore the loss to the beneficiaries, provided the trustee had acted diligently and with reasonable care when purchasing the securities for the trust. Although there are times when it is to the bona fide financial advantage of everyone concerned for the fiduciary to personally acquire trust property or sell property to the trust, it should not be attempted if there is any appearance of self-dealing or personal profit gained by the trustee. The best practice is to fully inform all beneficiaries, get written consent, and then get court approval to move forward with any self-dealing situations. The situation is less troublesome when the trust is a revocable living trust and the beneficiary is also the trustee. In same cases, depending on your state, you can also add an exoneration clause into the trust to limit some of the concerns about self-dealing. However, check in your specific state to see if these exoneration clauses are allowed.

Duty to Preserve Property and to Make It Productive

A fiduciary is also under a statutory duty to protect and preserve property as well as to make it productive. The fiduciary has a duty to keep trust property invested so it produces income for the beneficiaries. Otherwise, the fiduciary may be personally surcharged for leaving money idle. In one case, an executor left cash in a checking account for almost 2 years at no interest. The executor was personally surcharged and made to pay to the beneficiaries the amount of interest this money would have earned if invested at current rates.

Duty of Impartiality Toward Beneficiaries

A trustee also has a duty to deal impartially with beneficiaries, which can be a difficult task if the income beneficiaries and remainderpersons are different. Investing in capital assets with high current yields but little chance of appreciation could increase the income beneficiary's share at the expense of the remainderperson. This is sometimes a difficult matter to resolve. Certainly, the trustee must try to act as impartially and objectively as possible regarding the interests of the various beneficiaries.

Other duties of trustees generally pertain to investing and managing the property prudently, taking care of trust administration expenses, paying all necessary taxes, keeping records and accounting to the beneficiaries when required to do so, and making payments of income and principal as required under the terms of the trust instrument. The trustee must follow all directions given in the trust instrument (except those that would be either illegal if fulfilled or impossible to fulfill), dealing impartially with beneficiaries and exercising discretion when applicable, according to instructions.

Special Responsibilities of Corporate Trustees

The corporate fiduciary must be particularly careful not to profit or benefit from the relationship. Therefore, when a bank serves as trustee, the deposit of the trust funds into its own bank departments would be equivalent to making an unsecured loan from the trust to itself. There is conflicting authority regarding the deposit by a bank of fiduciary funds into its own banking department. This issue is covered by statute in some states. In other states, the issue has been resolved by the courts.

The Restatement of Trusts provides that a bank depositing trust funds into its own bank department commits a breach of trust, unless it is authorized to do so under the terms of the trust. National banks are not permitted to deposit trust funds in their bank departments, unless collateral security equal to the amount of the deposit is delivered to their trust department. Since FDIC insurance is currently $250,000 (in 2019, per depositor/per ownership category), this issue is not as significant as previously. As a general rule, a bank fiduciary is not disloyal to the beneficiaries of trusts if the bank is managing the trust funds in a prudent and reasonable way.

What about a corporate trustee who manages two trusts and sells the stock of one trust to the other? There is a conflict of loyalty if the assets from one trust are sold to the other, even at a fair price. Neither should a corporate fiduciary sell property belonging to the estate or trust to any director, officer, employer, or affiliate of the institution by which he or she is employed. National banks are prohibited by regulation from participating in such transactions, except under certain circumstances that do not actually weaken this restriction.

Fiduciary Duties

- Be loyal to the beneficiary.
- Act for the benefit of the beneficiary.
- Do not delegate responsibilities that the fiduciary is able to perform (Uniform Prudent Investor Act allows delegation).
- Disclose facts affecting any transaction.
- Preserve investment assets for the beneficiary.
- Make assets productive.
- Do not self-deal.
- Be impartial toward income beneficiaries and remainderpersons.

common trust funds

proprietary mutual funds

Today, most banks and trust companies do have authority to establish and operate common or collective investment funds for their trust accounts. This means that the assets of many small trusts, guardianships, and estates may be pooled, invested, and managed as a single fund, which is particularly important where small trusts are concerned. It permits the corporate trustee to make sound investments at reduced costs and gives the trust the advantage of expert advice as well as diversification that might not be possible if the trust were invested and managed separately. These commingled or collected investments have come to be known as **common trust funds**. They are allowed by the federal government without becoming taxable entities themselves. A bank or trust company may establish a common trust fund that is not subject to income taxes, provided that the trust accords with the regulations promulgated by the Federal Reserve System and such a fund is allowable under state law. Common trust funds have been proven to provide good investment services for small trusts and guardianships at reduced administration expenses. In recent years, a number of financial institution trustees have replaced common trust funds with **proprietary mutual funds** (a mutual fund created by the bank or trust company under the regulated investment company regulations) to achieve certain tax advantages.

FIDUCIARY POWERS

Some common powers of fiduciaries include the power to retain or sell investments, mortgage property, borrow money, and mortgage or pledge property as collateral. Other general powers include: the power to compromise claims; employ attorneys, investment advisors, accountants, or other agents; and distribute property in cash or kind or both, and in divided interests at such values as an executor or trustee deems appropriate. Corporate trustees usually desire a power in the trust instrument allowing them to invest and reinvest in common trust funds, irrespective of any local law requiring diversification.

Other powers include leasing property and giving options to buy. Making loans from the trust to third parties is often not allowed under state law, even if secured, unless the instrument specifically authorizes them. Trust instruments may require the unanimous action of trustees or, alternatively, a majority vote to act on a specific matter. The trust instrument can also insulate trust or estate assets from the reach of the beneficiaries' creditors. It may also contain a clause that frees the trustee from all statutory restrictions in investments. A donor or testator generally has wide latitude in the powers given to the trustee or executor.

Investment Powers

prudent-person rule

In the absence of investment provisions in the trust instrument, the sources of investment restrictions on the trustee are: the common law, the statutes, and the courts. Typically, states follow the common-law **prudent-person rule**, or a statutory legal list of qualified investments is prescribed.

A useful legal description of the prudent-person rule is as follows:

> In making investments of trust funds, the trustee is under a duty to the beneficiary (a) in the absence of provisions in the terms of the trust or a statute otherwise providing, to make such investments and only such investments as a prudent person would make of his own property having primarily in view the preservation of the estate and the amount and regularity of the income to be derived; (b) in the absence of provisions in the terms of the trust, to conform to statutes, if any, governing investments by trustees; and (c) to conform to the terms of the trust (except under certain specified conditions).

The statement of the prudent-person rule in the model statute is as follows:[2]

> In acquiring, investing, reinvesting, exchanging, retaining, selling, and managing property for the benefit of another, a fiduciary shall exercise the judgment and care under the circumstances then prevailing, which men of prudence, discretion, and intelligence exercise in the management of their own affairs, not in regard to speculation but in regard to the permanent disposition of their funds, considering the probable income as well as the probable safety of their capital.

Uniform Prudent Investor Act. The Uniform Prudent Investor Act (UPIA) was introduced in 1992. This act has been adopted in some form by a great majority of states and Washington, D.C. It presents new rules to guide trustees in investing trust assets. The act embodies a "modern portfolio theory" and "total return" approach to the exercise of fiduciary investment discretion, as well as risk versus return analysis. The performance of a fiduciary is measured according to the total portfolio instead of separate, individual investments. Investments must be chosen based on the investment's suitability for the beneficiaries of each account. A trustee is permitted to make any appropriate investments in order to achieve the trust's risk/return objectives and to meet the other requirements of prudent investing. The UPIA is in direct contrast to several aspects of the prudent-person rule.

Standards of the prudent-person or prudent-investor rules judged trustees on individual investment performance, which was to be accomplished with due care and prudence in their selection of investments. Under this standard, it was essentially inappropriate to delegate investment responsibilities. However, the UPIA mandates that trustees delegate investment management and other duties to professionals when necessary. Another major way in which the UPIA differs from the prudent-person standard is the requirement that a prudent fiduciary has a duty of income and investment diversification.

One ramification of the Uniform Act is that existing trusts may need to be amended to conform to its standards.

Legal-List States

legal-list states

Legal-list states are states which prescribe the investments that fiduciaries must make, unless the terms of the instrument or relationship permit otherwise. Except for conservatorship and

---

2.   Model statutes are attempts by legal scholars to produce uniform laws and standards that will be adopted in all states.

guardianship accounts, states that have enacted the Uniform Prudent Investor Act are expected to have repealed their legal-list statutes. Legal-list states are either mandatory or permissive. A legal-list state is said to be mandatory if there is a prescribed list of investments in which the fiduciary must invest. Any investment that the fiduciary makes outside the list is considered a breach of trust, thus making the fiduciary liable to the beneficiaries for any loss suffered. In other words, any investment not specifically named in the list is considered a nonlegal investment. Other legal-list states are said to be permissive. Those states print a list with prescribed investments or classes of investments in which the fiduciary may invest. If the fiduciary invests in a property named in the list, there is no breach of duty to the trust. However, the fiduciary may invest in property not stated on the list and take the chance of a beneficiary objecting to the investment. If any objection is made, it is the fiduciary's burden to show that the investment was proper.

State Investment Powers

- prudent-person rule
- mandatory legal list
  - Trustee investments are limited to a state-prescribed list.
  - Nonlist investment is a breach of trust.
  - The trustee is liable to beneficiaries.
- permissive legal list
  - The trustee may invest in nonlist investments.
  - The burden is on the trustee to show proper investment.
  - There is no breach of trust for listed investments.
- Uniform Prudent Investor Act

Waiving Statutory Limitations

In addition to the standard of investment delineated under the law, there are authorizations and limitations for investments that are stated in the trust instrument. Since most trust instruments expressly provide the powers of the trustee with regard to investments, the use of legal lists is rare. If directed otherwise by the trust instrument, a trustee may invest outside the scope of the standards set by state statute or common law. Some trusts give the trustee broad discretion, not only regarding the type of investments the trustee makes but also with the manner as well as type of distribution that is made to the beneficiaries. One of the advantages of creating a trust is the flexibility that it can provide. To obtain maximum flexibility, care should be taken that broad powers are given to the trustee to manage the trust according to the intentions of the grantor.

Breach of Fiduciary Duties

As already noted, the trustee is subject to statutory duties to protect and preserve trust property as well as to make that property productive. The trustee has a responsibility to keep the property invested and may be held liable for breach of that duty; an example is leaving money idle. All fiduciaries are answerable to the beneficiaries for whom they act if they commit any breach of their responsibilities or duties as trustees, executors, or guardians. Occasionally, trustees entrusted with large or small sums of money have been tempted to divert it to their personal use.

EXAMPLE

A trustee borrowed trust assets for his personal use. He converted these funds and never repaid the trust. When this was later discovered, the beneficiaries had a right of action against him both civilly and criminally.

The foregoing was a clear case of a breach of duty. More frequently, the breach is not as evident.

EXAMPLE

A trustee keeps funds in bank savings accounts secured by the Federal Deposit Insurance Corporation. These accounts are earning only a relatively low percentage of interest annually.

Because other liquid investments yield a higher return, is the trustee in the second example breaching fiduciary duty to keep the money invested properly? The trustee walks a fine line in this area. All decisions made by the trustee are fraught with some degree of potential liability. In addition, impartiality among different classes of beneficiaries as well as among beneficiaries of the same class must always be maintained. Can the trustee invest in assets that will increase the income to the income beneficiaries at the expense of safety of principal? The answer is no. Sometimes the investment that produces the highest yield is also acquired at the greatest risk. However, if there are two investments approximately equal in safety, the trustee has a duty to invest in the one that produces the higher yield.

Conflict Between Trustee and Beneficiary

Not only must there be impartiality among different classes of beneficiaries, there must also be no conflicts of interest between the trustee and the beneficiary. The trustee cannot profit at the expense of the trust. For example, a corporate trustee may retain its own shares of stock in an account when its shares were held as an original investment by the grantor of the trust.

However, in dealing with its own stock, a corporate trustee must exhibit undivided loyalty to the trust. When a trust first comes into existence, there may be shares of the corporate trustee's own stock that were investments originally owned by the settlor and are then transferred to the trust. In that case, a corporate trustee in a prudent-person state may retain its own shares of stock in the trust account. However, if the trust did not already contain the corporate trustee's own stock, a corporate trustee has a duty not to purchase this stock unless the trust instrument authorizes or instructs it to do so. If the trustee is operating in a legal-list state, he or she might have to sell the corporate trustee's stock transferred to the trust within a reasonable time if the stock does not qualify as a legal investment in that state. Of course, the trustee does have a duty to sell the stock at a fair price. Statutory authority generally does not encourage retention of original investments that might create a divided loyalty. The only time a trustee can retain stock owned by the creator of the trust, regardless of whether these stocks have been prudent investments or are qualified under the legal list of a state, is when the trust instrument specifically authorizes or directs the trustee to retain those investments.

The trustee has an obligation to look first to the trust instrument and then to the state's statute for guidance as to the trustee's responsibility. If the trust instrument contains a provision authorizing the trustee to retain original investments without liability to the trustee (except for loss or depreciation resulting from improper retention), the trustee may be permitted to do so without liability. However, in all cases regarding new investments, the trustee's duty is to invest trust assets in such a way that the intent of the trust is carried out and the interest of the beneficiary is best served.

LO 4. 7   Explain how a fiduciary is selected.

SELECTION OF A FIDUCIARY

What qualities are valuable in a fiduciary? In addition to the quality of loyalty, which is essential, a fiduciary should be honest, should have a high degree of integrity, should be responsible, and should have an interest in the welfare of the beneficiaries. It is also important for a fiduciary to have experience in the management of property and the investment of assets. The fiduciary should be willing to serve and be available to make the appropriate investments as well as to devote sufficient time to the management of the trust. The fiduciary should also be available to communicate with the beneficiaries, should stay in contact with them as necessary, and should also be understanding to the beneficiaries and sympathetic to their needs.

Trustees

One of the most difficult decisions that grantors must make is the selection of appropriate trustees. Sometimes grantors name themselves trustees. In other situations, grantors name their spouses, siblings, trusted employees, or business associates as trustees. The problem that such a nomination presents is that if the grantor or a related or subordinate trustee is named, many (if not most or all) of the usual discretionary powers that create the flexibility in a trust must be forgone to achieve favorable tax consequences. On the other hand, much of the important flexibility inherent in a trust is lost if the grantor chooses not to forgo favorable tax benefits.

Flexibility is extremely important. Typically, a grantor is primarily interested in the financial welfare of the life tenant (usually a spouse or other close relative) and is only secondarily interested in the security of the remainderpersons. Quite often a remainderperson is named in a trust merely to avoid the estate tax that would occur at the life tenant's death. However, trust law favors preservation of capital for the remainderpersons—even at the expense of the life tenant. For this reason, a trustee typically hesitates to act in a way that might seem to unduly favor the income beneficiary. Without discretionary powers, the trustee cannot serve the life tenant's best interests.

Would a related or subordinate trustee be deterred from liberally exercising discretionary powers in spite of the existence of substantial objective standards? In other words, would the trustee go along with the suggestions of the grantor and the beneficiaries, even at the risk of assuming liabilities for the remainderpersons? Is the use of a related or subordinate trustee a way to achieve flexibility, while at the same time protecting the tax favorability of a trust?

There are at least five factors that ought to be considered in selecting trustees as well as in deciding between a corporate (and therefore independent) trustee and an individual (often related and/or subordinate) trustee.

- For tax reasons, if a beneficiary is also named as a trustee, that individual may not participate in any discretionary decision that may be personally beneficial. The income tax law treats an individual who can spread the income among a class of which he or she is a member as being in constructive receipt of all such income, no matter how it is actually distributed. Likewise, if an individual, as trustee, can decide how corpus (principal) is to be distributed among a class of beneficiaries of which that individual is a member, that power over the corpus may cause the entire trust property to be part of the trustee's estate because the power to allocate corpus is considered the equivalent of a general power of appointment. Furthermore, if either of these powers is exercised in favor of others, the trustee-beneficiary may be treated as if he or she has made a transfer subject to the gift tax.

- Individuals can die or become incapacitated. Certainly, substantial physical changes are possible (and even likely) over the long period that most trusts run. If an individual trustee is about the same age as a mature grantor, it is likely that the benefits of having an individual trustee would be at best temporary.

- If an individual who is also a family member is selected as trustee, that person is often placed in an uncomfortable and perhaps untenable position. The possibility for a conflict of interest is great. Family discord and bitterness may arise when the trustee must refuse the request of one or more of the beneficiaries for what may be perfectly valid reasons. Most grantors probably prefer not to place a son or daughter in the middle of such a family dispute.

- Regardless of the size of the trust fund, individual trustees are not audited and consistently checked to the same degree as corporate fiduciaries. Temptations and pressures make individual trustees even more vulnerable to breaches of trust through arbitrary action, ignorance of obligations, or embezzlements of agents. Unfortunately, lawsuits are generally meaningless, even where *temporary borrowing* of trust funds by individual trustees is discovered. Since their personal fortunes are usually not adequate to compensate the beneficiaries, judgments against them are worthless. Conversely, if an employee of a corporate trustee makes an error or is guilty of embezzlement, the bank almost always has the financial ability to replace the loss.

- The incredible complexity of a rapidly changing tax law coupled with the investment, management, and other responsibilities of a trustee make that position a highly specialized and formidable task.

These five reasons all indicate that the use of an independent corporate trustee (often together with one or more individuals) is indicated where the grantor desires favorable tax treatment as well as flexibility with regard to investment, management, and beneficiary need.

Selecting Trustees
- individual/related/subordinate trustee
  - beneficiary trustee—discretionary powers over trust income or corpus may cause tax ownership
    - ◊ death or incompetence potential
  - family member trustee—possible conflicts of interest and family discord
    - ◊ little regulatory supervision—opportunities for breach of trust
    - ◊ tax law complexities/changes—difficult to stay current
- corporate/independent trustee (bank)

- holds legal title only—no personal tax ownership
- fiduciary relationship not affected by employee death or incapacity
- conflicts of interest avoided
- regular auditing
- expectancy of tax expertise

Executors

executor

The only legal requirements in choosing an **executor** are that this person be a mentally competent adult who has not been convicted of a felony. This individual may have to furnish a bond by purchasing an insurance product from a surety who will pay the heirs for their losses if the executor does not perform his or her duties under the will. As already noted, this latter requirement can be waived by will. However, a court-appointed administrator or an out-of-state executor is required to post a bond. In view of this requirement, it is prudent, if possible, to name at least one coexecutor who resides in the state where the will is to be probated.

Choosing the right executor, however, requires some additional, careful consideration. In order to choose the best executor, one must look for qualities in an individual or institution that will best carry out the task with which an executor is charged. At first blush, one may consider an individual who is closest to the family. Yet that individual may have no expertise either in managing assets or in dealing with the court system. Because an executor assumes his or her role at a time when a family may be under great stress after the decedent's death, it is wise to choose someone who is competent in managing property as well as honest and loyal; an executor must also be sensitive to the needs of the beneficiaries. Like other fiduciaries, the executor must adhere to fiduciary principles and exercise reasonable care, skill, diligence, and prudence in performing his or her duties.

When considering whom to name as an executor, one might ask some of the following questions:

- Does the prospective executor have the necessary business, financial, and administrative ability to assemble, conserve, and transfer the assets of an estate?

- Does the individual have the time and effort necessary to carry out an executor's duties, and will he or she be willing to devote energy to estate matters? Particularly when a business is a major estate asset, the executor may find that many more hours must be put in than anticipated when he or she accepted the responsibility.

- Does the individual have knowledge of the testator's business, personal affairs, and family relationships?

- Is the individual likely to have a conflict of interest with other beneficiaries?

If one is writing a will, it is wise to designate a successor executor in the event the original executor is unavailable, unwilling, or unable to serve in that capacity when called upon. Another decision that must be made is whether to name an individual, a corporate fiduciary, or both as coexecutors. A corporate fiduciary has expertise and experience in handling estate or trust property. Presumably, it is objective and impartial in carrying out its responsibilities. A corporate institution is expected to afford a measure of continuity and financial responsibility. There is no danger of a corporate trustee or executor dying or becoming incompetent. However, a corporate fiduciary may not have the same concern or personal interest in the beneficiaries. A corporate fiduciary also may not be as accessible to communicate with the beneficiaries on personal matters of concern to them. On the other hand, an individual executor might find the duties burdensome and unfamiliar. Without using professional services, an individual executor may also be incompetent. If all tasks are performed by the executor alone, including the filing of necessary tax returns, the best tax or financial results may not be achieved for the beneficiaries. The corporate executor always charges a fee that is printed on an established fee schedule and may be changed from time to time. An individual may also be allowed an executor fee for services; however, that fee might be voluntarily waived or reduced to a lesser amount if the executor is also a beneficiary under the will.

Perhaps the best of both worlds is to name a corporate executor (who takes primary responsibility for the investment and management of assets as well as the preparation of probate forms and tax returns) and an individual executor (who may be consulted on matters of distribution and who will attend to the personal needs of the beneficiaries). A combination of corporate and individual coexecutors offers checks and balances, thus ultimately providing greater service to beneficiaries.

Another consideration is the size of an estate. A small, liquid estate does not require the same attention or expertise as a complex, large estate. In small estates, an individual executor might be a perfectly acceptable choice.

Guardians

guardian

A **guardian** is someone appointed by the court who is responsible for caring for another. The individual who requires a guardian is either a minor or a person who is mentally or physically incompetent to care for his or her personal needs or property. The individual for whom the guardian is appointed is known as a ward. In some states, a guardian, unlike a trustee, does not necessarily have legal title to the property administered for the incompetent individual. Guardians are appointed by the court and must be discharged by the court when the term of the guardianship ends. The guardian's source of authority is the statutory and judicial law of the state in which he or she serves. This differs from the trustee, whose authority comes from both state law and from the trust instrument specifying the trustee's powers. Guardianship lasts only for the period of minority or incompetency. In actuality, a guardianship may last for the ward's lifetime. In contrast, a trustee may serve succeeding generations of beneficiaries. Like an executor, a guardian may be required to post a bond. Once the court is satisfied that the guardian is competent to serve, the court issues letters of guardianship as evidence of the guardian's authority to take responsibility for the ward's property as well as to care for the ward personally. A guardian's duties may be as varied as those of a parent.

guardian ad litem

There are several types of guardianships. The most common are the guardian of the property and guardian of the person. The guardian of the property pertains to the care and management of the ward's property, it is purely a business relationship for which the guardian generally receives a fee for services. A guardian of the person usually is given funds from the guardian of the property to take care of the minor or incompetent individual. The guardian of the person might live with the incompetent individual and provide food, clothing, shelter, and education for the minor. Another type of guardian, called a **guardian ad litem**, is appointed by the court for a particular purpose, generally to defend a specific lawsuit or legal proceeding in which the minor is a party. This type of special guardian is discharged by the court when the legal issue is resolved.

testamentary guardian

guardian de son tort

A parent may name a guardian of his or her minor children in a will. Unless there is good reason to override this choice, the court usually honors it and appoints that person, called a **testamentary guardian**. The natural guardians of a child are the parents. However, courts in many states may not name the natural parent as guardian of the property of a minor. If the minor is old enough, a guardian may also be elected by the minor child. In some states, a minor over age 14 or 15 may choose his or her own guardian, who will be appointed unless there are reasons not to do so. Occasionally, a person assumes a guardianship of a minor or incompetent individual without seeking or obtaining court approval. This type of guardian is called a **guardian de son tort** (of his or her own wrong). Because this type of guardian assumes these responsibilities, he or she is held fully responsible for all acts performed as a guardian.

Because a guardian is a fiduciary, he or she is held to the same standards as trustees or executors. One should not accept a position as guardian unless one intends to devote the attention required by the scope of the relationship.

LO 4. 8   Describe how and when trustees are removed.

REMOVAL OF TRUSTEES

Authorities differ on whether to give trust beneficiaries the power to remove a corporate trustee and substitute a new one. There are valid arguments on both sides of the debate.

Among the reasons why powers should be provided to remove the trustee and substitute a new one are the following:

- The trust department personnel may change, and a beneficiary may not be able to get along with the new bank contact.
- It may be desirable to shift the situs of a trust from one jurisdiction to another because of changes in trust or local tax law.
- The residence of the beneficiary may change. If the beneficiaries have moved a substantial distance, it may be inconvenient and inefficient to have a trustee in one state manage the property of a beneficiary in another state. Personal interest may wane due to lack of contact between the trust officer handling the account and the beneficiary.

Serious tax hazards exist if the beneficiary who has the power to remove a trustee can appoint himself or herself as successor. This might subject the property and the trust to inclusion in that beneficiary's estate. If the power to remove the trustee is desired, generally it should be specified that another corporate trustee must be designated as successor. For example, the adult income beneficiaries could be given the power to remove the corporate trustee and designate its successor; however "such successor must be another corporate trustee with paid-in capital and retained earnings of at least $_____." (Insert dollar amount, for example, $100,000,000.)

Removal of Trustees
- beneficiary and trustee conflict
- changes in state trust law
- changes in state tax law
- inconvenience—beneficiary has moved

Ethical Dilemma

The ethical dilemmas presented in this text illustrate common scenarios that could present a financial or estate planner with an ethical predicament. The resolution of any dilemma, of course, depends on how one applies ethical codes, rules, and principles to the specific situation. The comments are meant to provide thought about these issues and not give a definitive resolution to them.

Mr. Samuels, a professional financial and estate planner, is the independent trustee for certain members of the Reynolds family. Edwin Reynolds, the senior family member, recently established an irrevocable trust that was funded with a significant amount of cash and marketable securities. Although Edwin is 80 years old, he is quite fit physically and mentally.

Three of Edwin's four adult children are beneficiaries of the trust. For reasons personal to Edwin, his youngest son, Ralph, who is 40 years old, is not named as a trust beneficiary. In fact, Edwin has not left anything to Ralph in his will. While all four of the Reynolds children are aware of their father's trust, no one is aware that Ralph in not a beneficiary. In order to keep family discord to a minimum, Edwin has chosen not to tell his wife or their children that he is not bequeathing anything to Ralph in his will.

Ralph is also a client of Mr. Samuels. During several conversations, Ralph made it very clear that he is relying on the inheritance from his father and is making decisions based on the expectation of receiving a sizable sum from his father's trust.

In another discussion, Mr. Samuels points out to Ralph that his expenses are increasing without adequate income to cover them for much longer. Ralph replies, "That's not a problem. My father might be in good health now, but he's not going to live forever—not more than another 10 years at the most, I would say. And when he dies. . . ." As Ralph's voice drifts off, Mr. Samuels knows he is thinking about the inheritance he is expecting—which Mr. Samuels knows he is not going to receive.

>> ***What is Mr. Samuels' ethical dilemma?***

A Possible Resolution

The dilemma for Mr. Samuels is whether to tell Ralph about his father's trust or continue to advise him as if he knows nothing about it. Mr. Samuels is faced with a conflict of obligations. He has confidential information that he learned from one client (Edwin) that directly impacts the financial affairs of another client (Ralph).

Not revealing this information to Ralph will affect Ralph's financial plans because Mr. Samuels knows that Ralph is relying on expected income that he is not going to receive.

It seems Mr. Samuels should not tell Ralph, because informing Ralph of his father's decision is a breach of confidentiality against Edwin. However, if Mr. Samuels does not inform Ralph, his financial future might be seriously damaged.

There may be a way to resolve this without breaching confidentiality against Edwin and still offering sound advice to Ralph.

It is important to keep in mind the tremendous uncertainty surrounding this situation—the many events that have not yet occurred and might not occur in the predicted manner or order. Edwin could live longer than the 10 years Ralph predicts or, even if Edwin dies within that period, Ralph could die before him. Another possibility is that circumstances could change Edwin's mind, and he could at some point bequeath Ralph some sort of financial inheritance. Yet another possibility is that Ralph's siblings could decide to share their inheritance with him despite their father's refusal to bequeath it.

More importantly, while the information Mr. Samuels has about Edwin's estate might inherently change the specific advice that a good financial planner would give to Ralph, the presence of all sorts of uncertainty should influence a financial planner to advise Ralph to keep his expenses in check until the anticipated windfall becomes a reality. The fact that Mr. Samuels knows that Ralph is unlikely to receive the windfall he anticipates merely strengthens the argument—it is not new information. So without breaching confidentiality, Mr. Samuels could strongly encourage Ralph against decisions based on uncertain (and perhaps improbable) outcomes. Mr. Samuels must keep in mind that he is the advisor, not the decision maker. That Ralph might make a decision that goes against the planner's advice is not Mr. Samuels' responsibility.

Another point to ponder is that Edwin and Ralph might not be aware they both have independent relationships with Mr. Samuels. For Mr. Samuels to indicate uncertainty regarding Ralph's future inheritance does not, therefore, constitute an inherent breach. Even if Ralph does know that Mr. Samuels is his father's financial planner, he might not make the connection. If he does, Mr. Samuels can honestly say that his advice is not based on his relationship with Edwin, but on basic principles that would guide his counsel to any client.

Another possibility is that Mr. Samuels suggest to Edwin that he inform his children of his plans. It is likely that Edwin has already thought through the consequences of his choices, and it is therefore unlikely that he would want to change his decision now. Mr. Samuels must be careful not to reveal anything about his relationship with Ralph because, even though he is looking out for Ralph's interests, any communication exchanged as part of that relationship would also constitute a breach of a client's confidentiality. Ralph might not want his father to know anything about his financial condition—particularly that he is relying on an expected inheritance.

If all else fails, Mr. Samuels could refer Ralph to another financial planner. This, however, seems to run counter to his specific goals—that is, to maintain a growing business and to provide the best advice for his clients. Even without being able to reveal privileged information, Mr. Samuels is providing worthwhile advice to Ralph, and it is not certain that another planner would be positioned to do the same. It could be argued that to refer Ralph to someone else would be the same as abandoning a client.

This is a difficult situation. As in most predicaments, there is no perfect resolution. It is always painful to watch a client make poor decisions. In this case, where Mr. Samuels has specific knowledge that he cannot share without breaching a confidence, it is particularly difficult. He must keep in mind that his responsibility is merely to provide advice; sometimes that means watching clients make poor decisions in spite of his advice. He is not responsible for those decisions but rather for the quality of the advice he offers.

A financial planner's best response is preparation: Be proactive, anticipate these conflicts, and determine ways to cope with them if they do arise.

CHAPTER REVIEW

Key Terms and Concepts

fiduciary	trust terms
common trust funds	rule against perpetuities
proprietary mutual funds	rule against accumulations
prudent-person rule	living trust
legal-list states	revocable living trust
executor	irrevocable trust
guardian	testamentary trust
guardian ad litem	charitable trust
testamentary guardian	cy pres
guardian de son tort	donee of the power
trust	lapse
trustee	appointees
	general power

Chapter 4: Review Questions

1. What is the historical origin of trusts? [LO 4.1]

2. Identify the elements common to all trusts. [LO 4.2]

3. Explain whether each of the following trust arrangements is valid:

   a. A trust is created for the benefit of the settlor's son. The settlor is the sole trustee of the trust.

   b. A trust is created in which the settlor is the sole trustee. The settlor and his son are the beneficiaries during the settlor's lifetime, and the son is the sole beneficiary after the settlor's death.

   c. A trust is created for the sole benefit of the settlor. The settlor is also the sole trustee. [LO 4.2]

4. Describe the legal limitation imposed to prevent a property interest from being left either in trust or in the form of successive life estates forever. [LO 4.2]

5. Explain why the grantor of a trust might provide the trustee with broad discretion in administration of the trust. [LO 4.2]

6. Describe the possible nontax advantages for the establishment of revocable living trusts. [LO 4.3]

7. What differences exist between the creation and the effective dates of living and testamentary trusts? [LO 4.3]

8. Why might a grantor transfer property to an irrevocable trust? [LO 4.3]

9. Briefly describe the process of creation and exercise of a power of appointment. [LO 4.4]

10. Who are the potential recipients of property held by a trustee under a general power of appointment? [LO 4.4]

11. Mary Planner and her husband, Tom, have three children, aged 5, 3, and 1. Mary transfers property to a trust for the benefit of her children with Tom as trustee. Mary hopes the trust will be used for the children's college educations. Describe how a limited power of appointment, donated to Tom, may be used to meet this goal. [LO 4.4]

12. Explain what is meant by a fiduciary relationship. [LO 4.5]

13. Identify the sources of powers of the following: (a) trustees, (b) executors, (c) administrators, (d) guardians. [LO 4.5]

14. Describe (a) the duration of the powers and duties and (b) the accountability of trustees, personal representatives of estates, and guardians. [LO 4.5]

15. What are the principal duties common to all fiduciary relationships? [LO 4.6]

16. Explain what is meant by the statement that "a trustee has a duty to deal impartially as among the beneficiaries." [LO 4.6]

17. Explain the difference between states that follow the prudent-person rule and legal-list states, and differentiate further between permissive and mandatory legal-list states. [LO 4.6]

18. Describe two examples of a breach of fiduciary duties and the remedy that is available to the beneficiaries when a breach has been committed. [LO 4.6]

19. What factors should be considered in selecting a fiduciary? [LO 4.7]

20. What characteristics are important for an executor to possess? [LO 4.7]

21. Describe the different types of guardians, and explain how they differ from trustees. [LO 4.7]

22. What are potential reasons for including trust provisions concerning the removal of trustees? [LO 4.8]

Chapter 4: Review Answers

1. Trust arrangements originated in feudal England. The separation of legal and equitable ownerships removed the burdens of legal ownership from life tenants.

2. These five elements are common to all trusts:
   - the creator
   - the trustee
   - the property
   - the beneficiaries
   - the terms of the trust

3. a. The grantor may name himself as trustee of a trust that he creates for the benefit of someone else—in this case, his son. However, he must function in the role of trustee according to fiduciary principles solely for the benefit of the beneficiary. Depending on the kind of trust (revocable or irrevocable) and whether the trust income is used for the support of a minor son, there may be undesired tax consequences.

   b. A trust in which the grantor names himself as trustee and beneficiary is valid if there is another beneficiary. The son is a beneficiary with an adverse interest to the grantor. Here, the grantor would have to act impartially as trustee on behalf of both beneficiaries of the trust.

   c. This trust will be held invalid because the settlor is the sole trustee and also the sole beneficiary. He is actually dealing by and for himself as an individual. Legal and equitable title are said to merge and there is, in fact, no trust.

4. There are two limitations on trust duration: the common-law rule against perpetuities, and the common-law rule against accumulations.

The traditional rule against perpetuities provides that no interest in property is valid unless the interest must vest no later than 21 years plus 9 months after some life or lives in being when the trust was created.

The traditional rule against accumulations stipulates the period during which income may accumulate. In most cases, the period during which the interest must vest is the same as it is in the rule against perpetuities.

5. The more flexibility the trustee has, the better he or she will be able to meet the beneficiaries' needs as they arise, according to the grantor's intentions.

6. Some nontax reasons to establish revocable trusts are as follows:

   - The grantor does not have the time or the ability to manage the property for the beneficiaries' maximum benefit.
   - The grantor can enjoy the psychological benefits of gifting the property in trust while still being able to reclaim the property.
   - The grantor can see how the trust operates under the current trustee and discern the trustee's dispositive intentions before the trust becomes irrevocable.
   - At the grantor's death, the revocable trust will become irrevocable and pass to the beneficiaries without probate costs or publicity.
   - If the grantor's out-of-state intangible property is transferred to revocable trusts in the grantor's state of domicile, ancillary jurisdiction for out-of-state property can be avoided.
   - If the grantor is the sole proprietor of or partner in a business, he or she can transfer the business to a revocable trust to avoid the business's termination at the grantor's death.

7. A living trust is created and becomes effective before the death of the settlor. A testamentary trust is created under a testator's will and becomes effective upon his or her death.

8. The reasons why a grantor might transfer property to an irrevocable trust are as follows:

   - If the grantor wants to manage property for a needy dependent, he or she can establish an irrevocable trust, naming the dependent as beneficiary.

The beneficiary will have to deal with the trustee instead of the grantor for funds, which can prevent any potential conflict between the grantor and the dependent.

- The trustee has investment and accumulation skills that the grantor does not have.

- At the grantor's death, the trust will avoid probate.

- Trust property is not subject to claims by the grantor's creditors.

- The trust can shelter the grantor's assets from spousal-election rights and thereby provide for the grantor's children from a former marriage at the grantor's death.

9. A power of appointment is created when the owner of the property (the donor) creates the power in a donee to designate the donor's property that is subject to the power. The donee's act of designating the property is the exercise of a power of appointment.

10. The potential recipients of property under a general power of appointment are the donee, the donee's estate, and/or the donee's creditors.

11. Mary has transferred property to the trust held by her husband, Tom, as trustee. Mary may be concerned about her premature death and desires to delegate the dispositive control to Tom. Since Mary does not know which of her children will survive to college age, or actually go to college, she wants to delay the distribution decision. Mary could create a special power of appointment in Tom, exercisable when the children reach age 18, to appoint a portion of the property to any of her children then living. With this planning technique, Tom can provide the college funds at the time each child enters college.

12. A person or institution that holds or manages property for the benefit of another party is a fiduciary. The relationship between that individual or institution and the other party (the beneficiary) is a fiduciary relationship.

13. Executors, administrators, and guardians derive their power from state law and are appointed by a state court with competent jurisdiction. If an executor or guardian is named in a will, the court will often affirm that choice but is not bound to do so.

Trusts are private agreements. The trustee derives his or her power from the trust document and is *not* court appointed.

14. Because a trust can be in existence for 20 or 30 years and sometimes even longer and a trustee's powers and duties do not end until the termination of the trust, a trustee's powers and duties can last for many years. The powers and duties of personal representatives of the estate, on the other hand, generally last for a relatively short period because the average estate exists for only one or 2 years. A guardian's powers and duties last until the ward's incompetency ends or the ward reaches the age of majority.

Personal representatives of the estate and guardians file an accounting with the court when their tasks are complete. They are discharged and the estate is then closed. A trustee, however, is not required to make an accounting to the court but is regularly accountable to beneficiaries.

15. Common to all fiduciary relationships are the duties to

   • be loyal to the beneficiaries—to act for the beneficiaries in matters within the scope of the fiduciary relationship, not to delegate fiduciary responsibilities to others if they can be performed by the fiduciary, and to make full disclosure of all facts known to the fiduciary when entering into a personal transaction with the beneficiaries

   • not self-deal or profit at the expense of the beneficiaries

   • preserve and protect property to make it productive

   • be impartial toward beneficiaries

16. The trustee must try to act as objectively as possible regarding the various beneficiaries' interests—that is, not to invest or manage trust property so that it increases one beneficiary's share at the expense of another.

17. Under the prudent-person rule, the trustee, in making investments of trust funds, is required to (1) make only investments that a prudent person would make of his or her own property, with the goal of preserving the estate and income derived from it, (2) conform to all statutes governing investments by trustees, and (3) conform to the terms of the trust.

Legal-list states dictate the investments that fiduciaries must make, unless the terms of the trust or the fiduciary relationship permit otherwise. A legal-list state is mandatory if there is a prescribed list of investments in which the fiduciary must invest. Any investment made outside of the list is not legal. Permissive legal-list states print a list of investments (or classes of investments) in which fiduciaries must invest. There is no breach of duty if fiduciaries invest in property named on the list. They may also invest in property not stated on the list, however, and take the chance of having a beneficiary object to the investment.

18. Two examples of a breach of fiduciary duties are: (1) diverting money from the trust for the fiduciary's personal use, or (2) letting trust funds remain idle. All fiduciaries are answerable to the beneficiaries for whom they act if a breach is committed.

19. In selecting a fiduciary, the following must be considered:

    - the advisability of naming a beneficiary as a trustee
    - the possibility that the trustee will die or become incapacitated while the trust is still in existence
    - the wisdom of appointing a family member as a trustee
    - the extent of auditing the trustee will undergo (individual trustees are not audited or consistently checked to the same degree as corporate trustees)
    - the complexity of the trustee's responsibilities

20. An executor should have the following characteristics:

    - the business, financial, and administrative ability to assemble, conserve, and transfer estate assets
    - the time and effort required to fulfill the executor's duties
    - knowledge of the testator's business, personal affairs, and family relationships
    - no conflict of interest with any of the beneficiaries

21. There are several types of guardians, as follows:

    - guardian of the person, who cares for the ward
    - guardian of the property, who cares for and manages the ward's property
    - guardian *ad litem*, who is appointed by the court to perform a particular purpose on the ward's behalf and is discharged when the issue is resolved
    - testamentary guardian, who is named in the testator's will as guardian of the minor children
    - guardian *de son tort*, who assumes guardianship without seeking or obtaining court approval

Unlike trustees, guardians do not have legal title to trust property. They are appointed by the court (except for the guardian *de son tort*) and must be discharged by the court when the term of guardianship ends. Thus, the guardian's authority derives from the statutory and judicial law of the state in which he or she serves. The trustee, on the other hand, derives authority from state law and from the trust instrument.

Guardians serve for the period of the ward's minority or incompetency. Trustees may serve succeeding generations of beneficiaries.

22. Reasons why trust provisions concerning the removal of trustees should be considered

- significant incompatibility of trustee and beneficiary
- future changes in trust law
- future changes in tax law
- geographic inconvenience

Chapter 5:

Lifetime Transfers by Gift—An Overview

Learning Objectives

An understanding of the material in this chapter should enable the student to

LO 5.1   Explain what constitutes a gift, and identify the types of gifts.

LO 5. 2   Describe the types of gratuitous transfers that are not gifts.

LO 5. 3   Explain the requirements for a completed gift.

LO 5. 4   Identify the nontax advantages of lifetime gifts.

LO 5. 5   Explain how property may be valued for gift tax purposes.

The subject of lifetime transfers by gift is presented in two chapters to enable the student to better understand all aspects and elements of gratuitous lifetime transfers before studying the system of gift and estate taxation. Chapter 5 discusses the reasons (other than tax advantages) for making gifts, what constitutes a gift, the various types of gifts, how to distinguish between gifts and other gratuitous transfers that are not gifts, gifts that are exempt, requirements for a completed gift, and valuation of gifts for gift tax purposes.

LO 5.1   Explain what constitutes a gift, and identify the types of gifts.

TECHNICAL DEFINITION OF A GIFT

Elements of a Gift

gift

Under common law, a **gift** is defined simply as a voluntary transfer without equal consideration. For tax law purposes, neither the Code nor the Regulations specifically define what is meant by the term gift.

However, the regulations dealing with the valuation of gifts provide that in cases where property is transferred for less than adequate and full consideration in money or money's worth, the

$$\text{Value of property transferred} - \text{Consideration received} = \text{Gift}$$

Note that this definition focuses on whether the property was transferred for adequate and full consideration in money or the equivalent of money, rather than whether the transferor intended to make a gift. This is because Congress did not want to force the IRS to prove something as intangible and subjective as the transferor's state of mind. In fact, the regulations state that donative intent is not an essential element of the transfer for *gift tax* purposes. However, donative intent is required for a gift to be tax exempt for *income tax* purposes. The IRS, however, may show the lack of donative intent to establish that a transfer was in the ordinary course of business and not, in fact, a gift. For gift tax purposes, the key factors are: (1) the objective facts of the transfer (adequacy of consideration); and (2) the circumstances surrounding the transfer, not the subjective state of mind of the transferor. The donative intent may become important in the investigation of the circumstances of the transfer.

donor

donee

The courts examine certain factors to determine if a taxable gift was made:

- Was the **donor** (maker of the gift) competent to make a gift?
- Was the **donee** (person to whom the gift is made) capable of accepting the gift?
- Was there a clear and unmistakable intention on the part of the donor to absolutely, irrevocably, and currently be divested of dominion and control over the gift property?

Assuming that these three objective criteria are met, three other elements must be present. There must be

- an irrevocable transfer of the present legal title to the donee so that the donor no longer has dominion and control over the property in question
- delivery of the gift to the donee (or the most effective way to command dominion and control of the gift)
- acceptance of the gift by the donee

All these requirements must be met before a gift is subject to tax. The essence of these tests can be distilled into the following factors (state law is examined to determine the presence or absence of these elements):

- a transfer of property for less-than-adequate consideration by a donor competent to make a gift
- delivery of the gift property by a donor, which absolutely, irrevocably, and presently divests the donor of dominion and control over the gift property
- acceptance of the gift property by a donee

Adequate and Full Consideration in Money or Money's Worth Defined

Sufficiency-of-Consideration Test

Because the measure of a gift is the difference between the value of the property transferred and the consideration received by the transferor, a $100,000 building that is transferred from a mother to her daughter for $100,000 in cash clearly does not constitute a gift. However, the mere fact that consideration has been given does not pull a transaction out of the gift tax realm. To be exempt from tax, the consideration received by the transferor must be equal in value to the property transferred. This is known as the sufficiency-of-consideration test. If the daughter in the example above pays $60,000, the excess value of the building—$40,000—is within the scope of the gift tax. To escape potential gift taxation, there must be adequate and full consideration equal in value to that of the property transferred.

Effect of Moral, Past, or Nonbeneficial Consideration

Consideration is not in money or money's worth when the consideration is moral consideration, past consideration, or consideration in the form of a detriment to the transferee that does not benefit the transferor. The classic example of non-monetary consideration is a man who transferred $100,000 to a widow when she promised to marry him. (Upon remarriage she would forfeit a $100,000 interest in a trust established for her by her deceased husband; the $100,000 from her fiancé was to compensate her for the loss.) The Supreme Court held that the widow's promise to marry her fiancé was not sufficient consideration because it was incapable of being valued in money or money's worth. Nor was her forfeiture of $100,000 in the trust sufficient consideration, because the benefit of that value did not go to the transferor, her fiancé, although the widow did in fact give up something of value.

Consideration in Marital Rights and Support Rights Situations

Two issues often arise in connection with the consideration question: (1) Does the relinquishment of marital rights constitute consideration in money or money's worth? (2) Does the relinquishment of support rights constitute consideration in money or money's worth?

The Code is specific in the case of certain property settlements. IRC Sec. 2516 provides that transfers of property or property interests made under the terms of a written agreement between spouses in settlement of marital or property rights are deemed to be for an adequate and full consideration. Such transfers are, therefore, exempt from the gift tax—whether or not the agreement is approved by or incorporated into a divorce decree—if the divorce and the agreement occur within a specific 3-year period in relation to each other. For example, if a husband agrees to give his wife $100,000 as a lump-sum settlement in exchange for her release of all marital rights that she has in his estate, the $100,000 transfer is not subject to the gift tax if the requirements stated above are met.

A spouse's relinquishment of the right to support constitutes consideration that can be measured in money or money's worth. Likewise, a transfer in satisfaction of the right to support of the transferor's minor children is made for money's worth. (But most transfers to or for the benefit of adult children are generally treated as gifts, unless state law requires the transferor to support that child for some reason.)

Transfers Pursuant to Compromises or Court Orders

Consideration is an important factor when a transfer is made pursuant to compromises of bona fide disputes or court orders. Such transfers are not considered taxable gifts because they are deemed to be made for adequate and full consideration. For example, if a mother and daughter are in litigation and the daughter is claiming a large sum of money, a compromise payment by the mother to the daughter is not a gift. However, in an intrafamily situation in which the court is not convinced that there is a bona fide arm's-length adversarial proceeding, the gift tax will be imposed. For example, in a case where a widow settled with a son who threatened to break his father's will, the gift tax was levied.

Likewise, the gift tax can be applied even in the case of a transfer made pursuant to (or approved by) a court decree if there is not an adversary proceeding. For example, when an incompetent's property was transferred by the incompetent's guardian to another, the transfer has been held to be a gift even though it was approved or mandated by a court decree, assuming the incompetent had no legal duty to transfer the property. (Note, however, that if one who was declared incompetent in appropriate legal proceedings attempts to personally give away property—that is, without the guardian's consent—a gift may not result if the local law requires legal capacity as an essential element of a valid gift.)

Types of Gifts

direct gifts

Direct gifts—cash or tangible personal property—is the subject of most transfers affected by the gift tax law. Delivery of the property itself generally effectuates the gift. Real property is typically given by the delivery of an executed deed. If a person purchases a U.S. savings bond but has the bond registered in someone else's name and delivers the bond to that person, a gift has been made. (If the bonds are titled jointly between the purchaser and another, no gift occurs until the other person cashes in the bond or has the bond reissued in his or her name only.)

Income that will be earned in the future can constitute a gift presently subject to tax. For example, an author can give a right to future royalties to a daughter or son. Such a gift is valued according to its present value; that is, the gift is not considered to be a series of year-by-year gifts valued as the income is paid, but rather a single gift valued on the date the right to future income is assigned. Current valuation is made even if, for some reason, the payments are reduced substantially or cease altogether. In other words, no adjustment is required—or allowed—if the actual income paid to the donee is more or less than the valuation.

Forgiving a debt constitutes a gift in nonbusiness situations. For example, if a father lends his son $100,000 and later cancels the note, the forgiveness constitutes a $100,000 gift.

Some forgiveness of indebtedness, however, constitutes income to the benefited party. If a creditor tears up a debtor's note in return for services rendered by the debtor, the result is the same as if the creditor compensates the debtor for the services rendered and the debtor then uses the cash to satisfy the debt. The debtor realizes income and does not receive a gift.

Payments in excess of obligations can be gifts. Clearly a person does not make a gift when he or she pays the bills. Therefore, when a person pays bills or purchases food or clothing for a spouse or minor children, that person is not making gifts. Courts have allowed considerable latitude in this area. But if a father gives his minor daughter a $50,000 ring, the IRS may claim the transfer goes beyond his obligation of support. Payments made on behalf of adult children are often considered gifts. For example, if a mother pays her adult son's living expenses and mortgage payments, or gives an adult child a monthly allowance, the transfer is a gift subject to tax.

taxable gift

In another situation the taxpayer, pursuant to an agreement incorporated in a divorce decree, created two trusts for the support of his minor children. He put a substantial amount of money in the trusts, which provided that after the children reached age 21 they, were to receive the corpus. The court measured the economic value of the father's support obligation and held that the excess of the trust corpus over that value was a **taxable gift**. Only the portion of the transfer required to support the children during their minority was not subject to the gift tax.

Is the Transfer a Taxable Gift?

The factors used to make the determination if a transfer is a **taxable gift** include whether the

- donor and donee were respectively competent to make and accept the gift
- donor *fully* gave up all ownership and control of the property
- property was transferred for less than its value in money or money's worth
- property value exceeded the federal annual exclusion amount ($15,000 for 2019)
- delivery of the gift is made to the donee

indirect gifts

Indirect gifts, such as the payment of another's expenses, are subject to the gift tax. For instance, if a father makes payments on an adult son's car or pays premiums on a life insurance policy his wife owns on his life, such payments are gifts.

The shifting of property rights alone can trigger gift tax consequences. In one case, an employee gave up his vested rights to employer contributions in a profit-sharing plan. He was deemed to have made a gift to the remaining participants in the plan. Similarly, an employee who has a vested right to an annuity is making a gift if the choice is made to take—irrevocably—a lesser annuity coupled with an agreement that payments are continued to the designated beneficiary. No gift occurs until the time that the employee's selection of the survivor annuity becomes irrevocable.

Third-party transfers may be the medium for a taxable gift. For example, if a father gives his son $100,000 in consideration of his son's promise to provide a lifetime income to the father's sister, the father has made an indirect gift to his sister. Furthermore, if the cost of providing a lifetime annuity for the sister is less than $100,000, the father also has made a gift to his son.

The creation of a family partnership may involve an indirect gift. The mere creation or existence of a family partnership (which is often useful in shifting and spreading income among family members and in reducing estate taxes) does not, per se, mean a gift has been made. But if the value of a family member's services is nil or minimal and earnings are primarily due to assets other than those contributed by the partners in question, the creation of the partnership (or another partner's contribution of assets) may constitute a gift.

At the other extreme, if new partners contribute valuable services in exchange for their share of the partnership's earnings, and the business does not own a significant amount of capital assets, the formation of a family partnership does not constitute a gift.

Transfers by and to corporations are often forms of indirect gifts. Technically, the gift tax is not imposed upon corporations, but transfers by or to a corporation are often considered to be made by or to corporate shareholders. The regulations state that if a corporation makes a transfer to an individual for inadequate consideration, the difference between the value of the money or other property transferred and the consideration paid is a gift to the transferee from the corporation's stockholders. For example, a gratuitous transfer of property by a family-owned corporation to the father of the shareholders of a corporation could be treated as a gift from the children to their father.

Generally, a transfer to a corporation for inadequate consideration is a gift from the transferor to the corporation's other shareholders. A gift to a corporation (that is, shareholders) is usually treated as a future-interest gift because shareholders do not have present and immediate access to the gift. For example, a transfer by a mother to a corporation that she and her children own is treated as a gift from the mother to the children. (The amount of such a gift is computed after subtracting the percentage of the gift equal to the percentage of the transferor's ownership.)

A double danger lies in corporate gifts. The IRS may argue that: (1) in reality the corporation made a distribution taxable as a dividend to its stockholders; and (2) the shareholders in turn made a gift to the recipient of the transfer. Because any distribution from a corporation to a shareholder generally constitutes a dividend to the extent of corporate earnings and profits, the IRS could claim that a transfer was first a constructive dividend to the shareholders and then a constructive gift by them to the donee. For example, if a family-owned corporation sold property with a fair market value of $450,000 for $350,000 to the son of its shareholders, the transaction could be considered a $100,000 constructive dividend to the shareholder-parents, followed by a $100,000 constructive gift by them to their son.

There are exceptions to the general rule that transfers to or from corporations are contraindicated. A transfer may be deemed to be a charitable contribution from the corporation, not from the shareholders, and a contribution to a corporation for inadequate consideration may be deemed to be a contribution to capital rather than a gift. For example, a corporation may make a contribution to the Boy Scouts of America and take a deduction of up to 10 percent of its taxable income, with certain adjustments (IRC Sec. 170(b)(2)). Furthermore, if there is a legitimate business motive, the transfer may not be a gift even if adequate consideration is lacking. Generally, gift tax problems arise only when the corporation is family-owned and closely held.

Life insurance—or life insurance premiums—can be the subject of an indirect gift in three types of situations: (1) the purchase of a policy for another person's benefit, (2) the assignment of an existing policy, and (3) payment of premiums.

The insured has made a gift measurable by the cost of the policy if the insured purchases a policy on his or her life and

- names a beneficiary or beneficiaries other than his or her estate
- does not retain the right to regain the policy or the proceeds or revest the economic benefits of the policy (that is, retains no reversionary interest in himself or herself or the estate)
- does not retain the power to change the beneficiaries or their proportionate interests (that is, makes the beneficiary designation irrevocable)

All three of these requirements must be met, however, before the insured is deemed to have made a taxable gift.

If an insured makes an absolute assignment of a policy, or in some other way relinquishes all rights and powers in a previously issued policy, a gift is made. It is measurable by its replacement cost (which, in the case of a whole life policy, equals the interpolated terminal reserve plus the unearned premium at the date of the gift).

This can lead to an insidious tax trap. Assume a wife owns a policy on the life of her husband. She names her children as revocable beneficiaries. At her husband's death, the IRS could argue that the wife has made a constructive gift to the children equal to the entire amount of the death proceeds. It is as if the wife received the proceeds to which she was entitled and then gave that money to her children.

An extension of this reasoning, which was actually (and successfully) applied by the IRS, is a case in which the owner of policies on the life of her husband placed the policies in trust for the benefit of her children. Because she reserved the right to revoke the trust at any time before her husband died, she did not make a completed gift—until his death. It was not until his death that she relinquished all her powers over the policy. When her husband died, the trust became irrevocable, and the gift therefore became complete. The value of the gift was the full value of the death proceeds rather than the replacement value of the policy when it was placed in trust.

LO 5. 2   Describe the types of gratuitous transfers that are not gifts.

GRATUITOUS TRANSFERS THAT ARE NOT GIFTS

A number of common situations incur no gift tax because they do not involve gifts in the tax sense. These situations fall into three basic categories: (1) property or an interest in property that has not been transferred, (2) certain transfers in the ordinary course of business, and (3) sham gifts.

Requirement That Property or Interest in Property Be Transferred

Gratuitous Services Rendered

gratuitous service

The gift tax is imposed only on the transfer of *property* or an *interest in property*. Although the term *property* is given the broadest possible meaning, it does not include services that are rendered gratuitously (in other words, it is a **gratuitous service**). Regardless of how valuable the services are that one person renders for the benefit of another, those services do not constitute the transfer of property rights, and therefore do not fall within the scope of the gift tax (Rev. Rul. 56–472, 1956–2 C.B. 21).

Difficult questions often arise in this area. For example, if an executor performs the multiple services required to administer a large and complex estate, the services are clearly of economic benefit to the estate's beneficiaries. Yet, because services are just that, they do not constitute a transfer of property rights. If the executor formally waives the fee (within 6 months of appointment as executor) or fails to claim the fees or commissions by the time of filing, and indicates through action (or inaction) that he or she intends to serve without charge, no property is transferred. Conversely, once fees are taken (or if the fees are deducted on an estate, inheritance, or income tax return), the executor has received taxable income. If the executor then chooses not to (or neglects to) actually receive that money and it goes to the estate's beneficiaries, an indirect (and possibly taxable) gift is made to those individuals.

Disclaimers (Renunciations)

disclaimer

Generally, a potential donee is deemed to have accepted a valuable gift unless it is expressly refused. However, in some cases, an intended donee may decide (for whatever reason) that he or she does not want or need the gift. If the donee disclaims the right to the gift (that is, refuses to take it), it will usually go to someone else as the result of that renunciation.

By disclaiming, the intended transferee is in effect making a transfer to the new recipient that is subject to the gift tax—unless the **disclaimer** meets the IRC disclaimer requirements.

qualified disclaimer

A disclaimer that does meet those requirements is called a **qualified disclaimer** and is treated for gift tax purposes as if the property interest passes directly from the original transferor to the person who receives it because of the disclaimer. In other words, the disclaimant is treated as if no transfer of property or interest in property was made to the person to whom the interest passes because of the disclaimer. The property is treated as though it passed directly from the original donor to the eventual recipient. This makes the qualified disclaimer an important estate planning tool.

There are a number of requirements for a qualified disclaimer of gifted property under federal law:

- The refusal must be in writing.
- The refusal must be irrevocable.
- The writing must be received by the transferor, or the transferor's legal representative, or the holder of the legal title to the property no later than 9 months after the later of: (1) the date on which the transfer creating the interest is made (date of death); or (2) the date the person disclaiming becomes 21.
- The person disclaiming must not have accepted the interest or any of its benefits.
- Because of the refusal, someone other than the person disclaiming must receive the property interest. The person making the disclaimer cannot in any way influence the selection of who will be the recipient of the disclaimed property.

Note that state law requirements for disclaimers may vary from federal law, so that what constitutes a qualified disclaimer under federal law may not be valid for state law disclaimer purposes.

EXAMPLE

Jamie creates a trust on April 1, 2019, in which Jamie's favorite child John is to receive the income from the trust for life. Upon John's death, the corpus of the trust is to pass to John's child, Katie. If either John or Katie wishes to make a qualified disclaimer, it must be made no later than 9 months after April 1, 2019.

Reasons to Engage in a Qualified Disclaimer

If you are about to inherit property, but you are having creditor issues or going through bankruptcy, it might be best to disclaim the benefits and have them go to a family member instead. Remember you cannot control where they go, but as a practical matter you will likely know the next person in line for the property. Sometimes, it can be helpful to take full advantage of the marital deduction or for generation-skipping-transfer tax issues. Sometimes the disclaimer can be used to fix an issue with the will in the event the will was out of date and did not really match the decedent's intentions. In other cases, the property could impact government benefits so it might be beneficial to turn down the property. In some cases, it might be as simple as the parent not needing the property and not wanting to have to re-gift to the children.

The Promise to Make a Gift

Although income that will be earned in the future can be the subject of a gift, the Tax Court holds that the promise to make a gift in the future is not taxable—even if the promise is enforceable. This is because a mere promise to make a transfer in the future is not itself a transfer. The IRS agrees, as long as the gift cannot be valued. But if the promise is enforceable under state law, the IRS will attempt to subject it to the gift tax when it becomes capable of valuation.

Transfers in Ordinary Course of Business

Compensation for Personal Services

Situations often arise in business settings that purport to be gifts from corporate employers to individuals. The IRS often claims that such transfers are, in fact, compensation for personal services rather than gifts and argues that the property transfer constitutes income to the transferee rather than a gift by the transferor. In these cases, the focus is on the effect to the transferee; did the transferee receive taxable income or a tax-free gift?

ordinary business transaction

A payment may be taken out of the normal gift tax rules (and thus be considered taxable income to the recipient) by the regulations, which state that "the gift tax is not applicable to . . . ordinary business transactions." An **ordinary business transaction**, defined as a sale, exchange, or other transfer of property (a transaction that is bona fide, at arm's length, and free from donative intent) made in the ordinary course of business is considered as if made for an adequate and full consideration in money or money's worth.

A situation is considered an ordinary business transaction and is not classified as a tax-free gift to the recipient if it is "free from donative intent." This means that donative intent becomes quite important. The taxpayer-recipient, of course, likes to have the transaction considered an income-tax-free gift, while the IRS reaps larger revenues if the transfer is considered compensation, and is therefore taxable income. A payment is considered a tax-free gift to the recipient (the donor must still pay any gift taxes) rather than taxable income if the donor's dominant reason for making the transfer is detached and disinterested generosity rather than consideration for past, present, or future services. An example is an employer who makes flood-relief payments to employees from a feeling of affection, charity, or similar impulses. It is not a gift if the primary impetus for the payment is: (1) the constraining force of any legal or moral duty; or (2) an anticipated economic benefit.

Among the factors typically studied in examining the donor's intent are

- the length and value of the employee's services
- the manner in which the employer determined the amount of the reputed gift
- the way the employer treated the payment in the corporate books and on tax returns; that is, whether the payment is deducted as a business expense

The corporation's characterization of payment is often persuasive when the corporation makes a payment or series of payments to the widow or widower of a deceased employee. The employer generally prefers to have such payments taxed as compensation to the employee's survivors so the corporation can deduct payments as compensation for the employee's past services.

In one case, a business friend gave a car to the recipient after the recipient had furnished him with the names of potential customers. The car was not a gift but was intended as payment for past services as well as an inducement for the taxpayer to supply additional names in the future. In another case, however, an employer made a payment of $20,000 to a retiring executive when he resigned. After examining the employer's esteem and kindness as well as the appreciation of the retiring officer, the court stated that the transfer was a gift and not taxable income. In a similar case, another court came to the same conclusion when it found payments were made "from generosity or charity rather than from the incentive of anticipated economic benefit."[1]

This type of issue—whether the transfer is a gift or compensation—is settled on a case-by-case basis after an analysis of the circumstances evidencing motive or intent. Generally, an intrafamily transfer is considered a gift even if the recipient rendered past services, while transfers to persons outside the family are usually considered compensation.

Bad Bargains

bad bargain

A **bad bargain** is another ordinary-course-of-business situation. A sale, exchange, or other property transfer made in the ordinary course of business is treated as if it was made in return for adequate and full consideration in money or money's worth. This assumes the transaction is bona fide, at arm's length, and not donative in intent.

There are a number of court-decided examples of bad bargains that have not resulted in gift tax treatment. In one case, certain senior executive shareholders sold stock to junior executives at less than fair market value, as part of a plan to give the younger executives a larger stake in business profits. The court noted that the transfers were for less-than-adequate consideration but stated that "the pertinent inquiry for gift tax purposes is whether the transaction is a genuine business transaction, as distinguished, for example, from the marital or family type of transaction." Bad bargains (transfers for less-than-adequate money's worth) are made every day in the business world for one reason or another, but no one would think for a minute that any gift is involved, even in the broadest sense of the term *gift*.

Another example of a no-gift situation is a group of businesspeople conveying real estate to an unrelated business corporation with the expectation of doing business with that corporation in the future.

But the ordinary-course-of-business exception has its limits; there is no protection from the gift tax law if the transferor's motive is to pass on the family fortune to the following generation. In one case, a father transferred property to his children at a price below the fair market value. In return, he received non-interest-bearing notes rather than cash and continued to make certain payments on the children's behalf with respect to the property. The court ruled these actions showed that, in reality, he was not dealing with his children at arm's length. That same

---

1.   https://en.wikipedia.org/wiki/Commissioner_v._Duberstei

result could occur if the father employs the son at a wage of $50,000 a year, but the son renders services worth only $20,000 a year. The IRS could claim that the $30,000 difference constitutes a gift.

What Is *Not* a Taxable Gift?
- transfer in which transferor receives consideration equal to transferred property's value
- transfers made due to court orders
- transfers made due to dispute compromises
- promises to make a gift
- gratuitous services
- qualified disclaimed property
- transfers in ordinary course of business
- transfers within the annual exclusion amount
- certain transfers between spouses pursuant to divorce
- transfers to providers of educational or medical services
- transfers to political organizations
- incomplete gifts

Sham Gifts

It is often advantageous—for income or estate tax purposes—to characterize a transaction as a gift. The taxpayer's goal is to shift the burden of income taxes from a high- to a relatively low-bracket taxpayer and yet keep the income within the same family unit. But if the transfer has no real economic significance other than the hoped-for tax savings, it is disregarded for tax purposes. That is, if the transaction does not have meaning—apart from its tax sense—it is not considered a gift by the IRS or by the courts, and therefore does not shift the incidence of taxation.

For example, a well-known golfer contracted with a motion-picture company to make a series of films depicting his form and golf style. In return, the golfer was to receive a lump sum of $120,000 plus a 50-percent royalty on the earnings from the picture. But before any pictures were made, he sold his father the right to his services for $1. The father, in turn, transferred the rights in the contract to a trust for his son's three children. The court held that the entire series of transactions had no tax effect and the income was completely taxable to the golfer.

Assignment-of-income questions are among the most common and confusing in tax law because they often involve inconsistent property, gift, and income tax results. For example, a mother could agree to give her son one-half of every dollar she earned in the following year. The agreement might be effective for property law purposes, and the son could have an enforceable legal right to one-half of his mother's income. Gift tax law might also recognize the transfer of a property right, and the present value of a mother's future income could be subject to the gift tax. Yet, for income tax purposes, the mother remains liable for taxes on the entire earnings.

A general agent for a life insurance company assigned renewal commissions to his wife. Although the wife had a property-law right to the commissions, and the present worth of the renewals the wife would receive was treated as a gift, the general agent was subject to income tax on the commissions as they were paid. In a similar case, a doctor transferred the right to accounts receivable from his practice to a trust for his daughter. Again, the court held that as the trustee received payments from the doctor's patients, those sums were taxable to the doctor even though he had made an irrevocable and taxable gift.

Gifts of income from property meet a similar fate. For example, if a woman assigns the right to next year's rent from a building to her daughter or next year's dividends from specified stock to her grandson, the transfers are effective for property-law purposes and generate gift taxes, but the income is taxable to the donor for income-tax purposes.

Gifts of the income-producing property, however, produce a more satisfactory result for donors; if the tree (property), the source of the income generated, is given away, the fruit (income) it bears is taxable to the tree's new owner. Thus, if the donor in the examples above had given both the building and the stock, gifts equal to the value of those properties would have been made, and the income produced by those assets would be taxed to her daughter and grandson, respectively. Likewise, if stock that cost the donor $1,000 is transferred to a donee when it is worth $2,500 and is later sold by the donee for $3,500, the donee takes the donor's cost ($1,000) as basis (with adjustments for any gift taxes paid) and pays income tax on the gain ($2,500).

Exempt Gifts

A few types of gratuitous transfers are statutorily exempted from the gift tax. A qualified disclaimer, described above, is a good example (IRC Sec. 2518(a)). Certain transfers of property between spouses upon divorce (IRC Sec. 2516) are other examples.

Tuition paid to an educational institution for the education or training of an individual is exempt from the gift tax, regardless of the amount paid or the relationship of the parties (IRC Sec. 2503(e)). It is not required that the donor and donee be related for the gift to be exempt. This means parents, grandparents, or even friends can pay private school or college tuition for an individual without fear of incurring a gift tax.

Still another exempt transfer is the payment of medical-care expenses. A donor can pay for the medical care of a donee without making a gift. This allows children or other relatives—or friends—to pay the medical expenses of needy individuals (or anyone else) without worrying about incurring a gift tax (IRC Sec. 2503(e)).

Also, transfers of money or other property to a political organization (as defined in IRC Sec. 527(e)(1)) are exempt from the gift tax if the transfer is for the use of the political organization (IRC Sec. 2501(a)(5)). But contributions to individuals do not come within the exemption.

Exempt Gifts
- qualified disclaimer
- educational tuition
- medical care
- political organization contributions

LO 5. 3   Explain the requirements for a completed gift.

REQUIREMENTS FOR A COMPLETED GIFT

completed transfer

A *completed transfer* is necessary before the gift tax can be applied. The phrase **completed transfer** implies that the subject of the gift is beyond the donor's recall; that is, the donor has irrevocably parted with dominion and control over the gift (see 26 CFR 25.2511-2 - Cessation of donor's dominion and control). There is no completed gift if the donor has the power to change the disposition of the gift and thus alter the identity of the donee(s) or the amount of the gift. Technically stated, if the donor can revoke the gift (either alone or in conjunction with a party who does not have a substantial amount to lose by the revocation), it is not a completed gift.

Parting with dominion and control is a good test of completeness, but in a number of cases it is difficult to ascertain just when that event occurs. Some of the more common problem areas are: (1) incomplete delivery situations, (2) cancellation of notes, and (3) incomplete transfers to trusts.

Incomplete Delivery

There is incomplete delivery when certain technical details are omitted or a stage in the transfer process is left uncompleted. For example, no gift is made at the moment the donor gives the donee a personal check or note. The transfer of a personal check is not complete and taxable until it is paid (or certified or accepted) by the drawee, or until it is negotiated for value to a third person. For instance, depending on the particular circumstances, if a check is mailed in December, received in late December, but not cashed until January of the following year, it may be treated for gift tax purposes as though no gift is made until that later year. This is because the maker of a check typically is under no legal obligation to honor the check until it is cashed (presented for payment or negotiated to a third person for value). Likewise, a gift of a negotiable note is not complete until it is paid.

gift causa mortis

An individual on his or her deathbed will sometimes make a gift in anticipation of imminent death from a specific illness, indicating that he or she wishes the donee to have the gifted property at the donor's death. Such a gift is called a **gift causa mortis**. It is a gift conditional upon the donor's dying as he or she anticipates. What happens if the donor recovers? Assuming the facts indicate that the gift was indeed a *gift causa mortis* (that is, the transfer was made in anticipation of death from a specific illness, and the gift was contingent on the occurrence of the donor's death), neither the original conveyance nor the return of the property to the donor is subject to the gift tax if the transferor recovers and the transferee returns the property. A *gift causa mortis* is a conditional gift that becomes complete only at the donor's death and is, therefore, incomplete as long as the donor is alive.

A gift of stock is completed on the date that properly endorsed stock certificates are delivered to the donee or the donee's agent by the donor. If the donor instead delivers the stock to his or her agent or broker, or to the issuing corporation or its transfer agent, for the purpose of having the stock certificates transferred into the name of the donee, the gift is complete on the date the stock is transferred to the donee on the books of the corporation (Treas. Reg. 25.2511–2(h)).

The transfer of U.S. government bonds is governed by federal law rather than state law. Even if state law requirements for a valid gift are met, for tax purposes no completed gift is made until the registration is changed in accordance with federal regulations. For example, if a grandmother purchases a U.S. savings bond registered as payable to her and her two grandchildren as co-owners, no gift is made to the grandchildren until one of them surrenders the bond for cash.

The creation of a revocable joint bank account (checking or savings) constitutes a common example of an incomplete transfer. Typically, the person making a deposit can withdraw all the funds or any portion of them. Therefore, the donor retains a power to revoke the gift, and it is not complete. When the donee makes a withdrawal of funds from the account (and thereby eliminates the donor's dominion and control), a gift of the funds occurs. A determination should be made to ascertain the particular state's presumption regarding survivorship for joint accounts. Some states presume that accounts have no survivorship rights unless the parties expressly include language stating a survivorship element at the creation of the account. Conversely, other states presume that joint accounts automatically provide survivorship rights unless otherwise specified. A joint account without a survivorship feature may be referred to as a convenience account or agency account. Often, the depositing party to an agency account does not intend for the other joint tenant(s) to receive any remaining funds at the death of the depositor.

A similar situation exists in the case of a joint brokerage account. The creation and contribution to a joint brokerage account held in street name is not a gift until the joint owner makes a withdrawal for personal benefit. At that time, the donee acquires indefeasible rights, and the donor parts irrevocably with the funds. Conversely, if a person calls a broker and says, "Buy 100 shares of Texas Oil and Gas and title them in joint names—mine and my spouse's—with rights of survivorship," the purchase constitutes a gift to the spouse. The spouse acquires rights that he or she did not have to a portion of the stock. No gift tax is due in this case owing to the unlimited gift tax marital deduction (discussed in a later chapter).

Totten trusts

pay-on-death (POD) account

Totten trusts (bank accounts in which the donor who is the named "trustee" makes a deposit for the donee—"Joanne Q. Donor in trust for James P. Donee"—and retains possession of the savings book) are typical revocable transfers. Because the donor retains the right of withdrawal until death (when the balance passes to the beneficiary), no gift occurs at the creation of the account, and the named donee is not generally entitled to the property until the donor's death. This type of nonprobate arrangement is also called a **pay-on-death (POD) account**. Generally, a Totten trust or pay-on-death account may be in the form of a checking account, savings account, money market account, or certificate of deposit.

Some property cannot be delivered conveniently to the intended donee; farm property is a good example. When it would be difficult or impossible to make physical delivery of the gift, a gift is usually considered completed when the delivery is as complete as possible. In one case, a father owned cattle he wished to give to his minor children. The court held that the gift was complete when he branded the livestock with each child's initials, even though he kept the cattle with others he owned. The court held that the father was acting as the natural guardian of the children and had done everything necessary to make a completed gift.

Real estate is transferred through the execution of a deed in favor of the donee. But if the donor retains the deed, does not record it, makes no attempt to inform the donee of the transfer, and continues to treat the property as his or her own, no transfer occurs.

Cancellation of Notes

In many cases, a transfer of property is made, and then the transferor takes back notes from the donee. The transaction is not characterized as a sale until the transferee pays off the notes. But if the transferor forgives the notes, the forgiveness is a gift.

Cancellation of notes is a frequently used technique for two reasons. First, it provides a simple means of giving to a number of donees certain property that is not readily divisible. Second, by forgiving the notes over a period of years, the donor can maximize the use of the federal gift tax annual exclusion and basic credit amount (discussed in a later chapter). A good example is a donor who deeds real estate to her sons and takes back notes payable serially on an annual basis. Each son is required to pay his mother $10,000 per year. But when the notes come due, the donor marks the notes "canceled by." The gift occurs in the year each note is canceled—as long as there is no preestablished plan for the donor to forgive notes on a systematic basis in future years.

Incomplete Gifts in Trust

Donors sometimes transfer property to a trust but retain the right to revoke the transfer. When property is transferred to such a revocable trust, that transfer is not a completed gift. Only when the donor relinquishes all retained control over the transferred property, that is when the trust becomes irrevocable, is a completed gift made.

Tax liability is measured by the value at the moment the gift becomes complete rather than at the time of the transfer. This can have harsh tax consequences. For example, if the donor retains the power to alter the interests of the trust beneficiaries, even if no powers can be exercised for the donor's own benefit, the transfer is not complete. For instance, assume that a father transfers stock to a trust for his two children and three grandchildren. The income of the trust is payable to the donor's children for as long as they live, and then the remainder is payable to his grandchildren or their estates. If the donor retains the power to vary the amount of income his children receive or to reach into corpus to enhance their security, the gift is incomplete. But the gift becomes complete when the donor relinquishes control. If that happens when the stock has substantially increased in value, as is often the case, the gift tax payable by the donor also substantially increases.

Incomplete Transfers for Gift Tax Purposes

- checks (incomplete until paid/certified/accepted)
- anticipation of imminent death (causa mortis)
- stock (incomplete until endorsed and delivered to donee or titled in donee's name on corporate books)
- U.S. government bonds (incomplete until federal registration requirements are met or bonds are surrendered by donee for cash)
- joint bank accounts (incomplete until donee withdraws funds)
- deeds (incomplete until delivered to donee/recorded in donee's name)
- forgiveness/cancellation of debt (incomplete until debt on property is canceled)
- incomplete gifts (incomplete as long as donor/grantor retains rights in transferred property)

LO 5. 4   Identify the nontax advantages of lifetime gifts.

Nontax Advantages of Lifetime Gifts

Individuals give property away during their lifetimes for many reasons. Although a detailed discussion of the nontax motivations for lifetime giving is beyond the scope of this chapter, some of the reasons include the following:

- privacy that would be impossible to obtain through a testamentary gift

- potential reduction of probate and administrative costs

- protection from the claims of creditors

- vicarious enjoyment of seeing the donee use and enjoy the gift

- opportunity for the donor to see how well—or how poorly—the donee manages business or other property

- provision for the donee's education, support, and financial well-being

LO 5. 5   Explain how property may be valued for gift tax purposes.

VALUATION OF PROPERTY FOR GIFT TAX PURPOSES

Valuation is the first step in the computation of the gift tax. Only after the property is valued can the annual exclusion and various deductions be applied in arriving at the amount of the taxable gift and the ultimate gift tax.

The amount of the gift is the fair market value of the property on the date the gift becomes complete. For gift tax purposes, value is defined as "the price at which the property would change hands between a willing buyer and a willing seller, neither being under any compulsion to buy or to sell, and both having reasonable knowledge of relevant facts." According to the IRS, there are a number of factors to consider when determining the fair market value of property. The IRS states that all factors impacting the value are relevant and must be considered. However, the IRS does stress four main factors: 1) the cost or selling price of the item, 2) sales of comparable properties, 3) replacement cost, and 4) expert opinions (appraisals).

Another factor that impacts the FMV is determining the date of the transfer. Certain property rights take time to transfer. For instance, an option must be exercised before it changes hands as a completed transfer. If you give someone an option to purchase your house today for $500,000 when your house is worth $500,000, but they do not exercise this option until your house is worth $600,000. At that point, they would transfer to you $500,000 and you would have transfered the house with a FMV of $600,000. The remaining $100,000 would be a gift and, if the donee is a qualified charity it would be a charitable contribution of $100,000.

What Is Fair Market Value?

Fair market value is the amount a willing buyer and a willing seller would accept and pay with neither being obliged to buy or sell and both having knowledge of relevant facts.

Sales of comparable properties is one of the best ways to determine the FMV of your own property. However, you do need to pay attention to the degree of similarity between your property and the comparable piece of property. Additionally, pay attention to the timing of both sales - how far apart were they, has something happened to the market between these two sales, and the circumstances of each sale.

While replacement cost (the cost to purchase or build a new property) can help when determining the starting point for the fair market valuation of property, the replacement cost new of an item often has no similarity to the fair market value today due to depreciation and other factors. However, the replacement cost new can give a good starting point that can then be modified for use, wear and tear, depreciation, obsolescence of the item, and other factors to arrive at a more reasonable valuation. Although the provisions of the gift tax law on valuation parallel the estate tax law in many respects, there is one major difference—property transferred during lifetime is valued for gift tax purposes on the date the gift is made. No alternate valuation date is allowed.

There are certain valuation problems unique to the gift tax law. These include problems associated with: (1) indebtedness with respect to transferred property, (2) restrictions on the use or disposition of property, (3) transfers of large blocks of stock, and (4) valuation of life insurance and annuity contracts.

Indebtedness With Respect to Transferred Property

Generally, when the subject of a gift is encumbered or otherwise subject to an obligation, only the net value of the gift—the value of the property less the amount of the obligation—is subject to the gift tax. Under this rule, which assumes the donor is *not* personally liable for the debt, the amount of the gift is the donor's equity in the property.

However, if the donor is personally liable for the indebtedness—which is secured by a mortgage on the gift property—a different result occurs. In this case, the amount of the gift may be the entire value of the property, undiminished by the debt. The reason for the difference is that, if a solvent donor makes a gift subject to a debt and the creditor proceeds against the pledged property, the donee is, in effect, paying the donor's personal debt. In some cases, this makes the donee a creditor of the donor. If the donee can then collect from the donor the amount paid to the donor's creditor, the donee has received the entire value of the gift rather than merely the equity.

For example, assume a donor transfers a $100,000 building subject to a $40,000 mortgage on which the donor is personally liable. If the donor's creditors collect the $40,000 by proceeding against the pledged building, and the donee is subrogated to that creditor's rights against the donor-debtor (that is, the donee now stands in the shoes of the creditor), the donee can collect an additional $40,000 from the donor.

A third possibility is that the donor-debtor is personally liable for the indebtedness secured by a mortgage on the gifted property, but the donee has no right to step into the creditor's shoes and recover the debt from the donor. In this case, the amount of the gift is merely the amount of the donor's equity in the property. In this example, that amount would be $60,000 ($100,000 fair market value minus $40,000 of indebtedness).

If the donee has no right to proceed against the donor and recover the debt, the actual facts determine the result. If the donor in fact pays off the liability after transferring the mortgaged property to the donee, the donor makes an additional gift. But if the donee pays off the liability (or if the mortgagee forecloses), the gift is only the donor's equity.

net gift

One of the obligations that can be imposed upon a donee is a requirement that the donee pay the gift tax. The donor has the primary liability to pay the gift tax, and the donee is only secondarily liable. The donor can—expressly or by implication—require the donee to pay the donor's gift tax liability. If the donee is required to pay the gift tax imposed on the transfer (or if the tax is payable out of the transferred property), the gift is referred to as a **net gift**. With a net gift, the value of the donated property is reduced by the amount of the gift tax.

Obviously, the two figures—net amount transferred and tax payable on the transfer—are interdependent. Fortunately, there is a revenue ruling formula for making the computation when such interdependent variables are involved.

It is important to note that, for income tax purposes, there are cases that state the donor must recognize gain if the donee pays the tax or if payment is made from the gifted property. Gain is realized by the donor for income tax purposes to the extent the gift tax paid by the donee exceeds the donor's basis in the property.

Restrictions on Use or Disposition of Property

Value is affected by restrictions placed on the donee's use or ability to dispose of the property received. The general rule is that most restrictive agreements do not fix the value of such property but often have a persuasive effect on price.

For example, a donor gives stock to his daughter subject to an agreement between the corporation and its shareholders. Under that agreement, the corporation is entitled to purchase those shares at their book value, $30 per share, upon the retirement or death of the stockholder. Does the existence of such an agreement fix the value of the shares at book value? After all, no buyer would pay more than $30 a share while the restriction is operative. But if the stock has *use values* other than sale values (for example, if it pays dividends of $10 a year), it may have a fair market value exceeding $30 a share.

On the one hand, the corporation's option right to purchase the stock at $30 a share limits the fair market value; on the other hand, use values, such as the right to receive dividends, increase the fair market value. How much the use values increase the fair market value is largely dependent on how much time is likely to pass before the corporation has an opportunity to exercise its option, and also on the probability that the corporation will exercise its option at that time.

In the example above, a court would probably state that the existence of a restrictive agreement would not fix the purchase price, because the circumstances requiring purchase (retirement or death) do not exist at the date of the gift. However, the existence of the agreement itself is likely to have a depressing effect on the market value of the stock and result in a discounted gift tax value.

Transfers of Large Blocks of Stock

blockage discount

A principle that applies to the valuation of both lifetime gifts and testamentary transfers is the so-called **blockage discount**. This blockage rule may allow the taxpayer the benefit of a discount below the actual listed market value of transferred stock. The rule applies if the taxable transfer consists of a block of stock large enough to depress the market value of each share if the entire block is sold at once. The discount is allowed for the hypothetical reduction in value of the shares, assuming a sale of the entire block over a reasonable period of time. However, the transferor may diminish or remove the advantage of the blockage discount if the block of stock to be transferred is divided among several donees or the transfer is spread over a number of tax years.

Valuation of Life Insurance and Annuity Contracts

When a life insurance policy is the subject of a gift, the value is the policy's replacement value: the cost of similar or comparable policies issued by the same company.

If the policy is transferred immediately (within the first year) after its purchase, the gift is equal in value to the gross premium paid to the insurer.

If the policy is paid up at the time it is assigned (or is a single-premium policy), the amount of the gift is the amount of premium the issuing company would charge for the same type of single-premium policy of equal face amount on the insured's life, based on the insured's age at the transfer date. (The impaired health of the insured is not considered by the regulations, but the IRS might argue that the adverse health of the insured at the time of the gift affects valuation.)

If the policy is in a premium-paying stage at the time it is transferred, the value of the gift is generally equal to: (1) the interpolated terminal reserve plus (2) unearned premiums on the date of the gift.

Except in the early years of most contracts, the interpolated terminal reserve is roughly equivalent to the policy's cash value. In special conditions, such as when the interpolated terminal reserve does not approximate the policy's true value, the value of a premium-paying policy may be more than the sum of the interpolated terminal reserve plus unearned premiums as of the date of the gift. (An example is the insured donor who is terminally ill and has only one or 2 months to live.) Unearned premiums are defined as the proportionate part of the last premium paid that is attributable to the remainder of the period for which the premium was paid.

EXAMPLE

Todd transferred a whole life insurance policy to his son Otto on January 1, of this year. The policy terminal reserve was $18,000 on July 1, of last year and $21,000 on July 1, of this year. If Todd paid the full $1,400 annual premium on July 1, of this year, the value of the policy for gift tax purposes is $20,200. The interpolated reserve was $19,500 on January 1, of this year, because this is the midpoint of the year during which the reserve increases by $3,000. Half the premium ($700) is unearned at the time of the gift. Therefore, the policy value was $20,200 ($19,500 + $700) on January 1, of this year.

Premiums paid by (or on behalf of) the donor after the transfer are also gifts. Therefore, when an owner of a life insurance policy irrevocably assigns that policy to another person or a trust, each premium the owner pays subsequent to the transfer is considered a gift to the new policyowner (or the beneficial owner or owners of the trust's assets).

Usually the premium payer and the donor are the same. However, the IRS has stated that if an employee assigns his or her group life insurance policy to an irrevocable trust established for the employee's family, a cash premium paid by the employer is deemed to be a gift in the amount of the premium. Generally, therefore, the deemed gift is from the employee to the beneficiaries of the trust.

Inclusion Value of Policies Owned on Life of Another	
Policy	**Value**
• new	• gross premium paid
• paid-up or single-premium	• replacement cost
• premium-paying whole life	• unearned portion of last premium plus interpolated terminal reserve
• term	• unused premium

Editor's Note: In certain circumstances for income tax purposes under final Treasury regulations and Revenue Procedure 2005-25 concerning the valuation of life insurance after August 28, 2005, life insurance policies are valued at fair market value and may not necessarily be valued solely on an interpolated terminal reserve plus unearned premiums basis.

Gift Tax Property Valuation Problem Areas

- encumbrance of debt or obligation
  - fair market value diminished by debt amount (unless donor has personal liability for debt)
- restrictions in use or disposition
  - fair market value diminished by limitations
- transfers of large blocks of stock
  - valuation discount may apply
- patents
  - sales of comparable properties
  - replacement costs
- life insurance
  - replacement value of similar policy

CHAPTER REVIEW

Key Terms and Concepts

gift

donor

donee

taxable gift

direct gifts

indirect gift

gratuitous service

disclaimer

qualified disclaimer

ordinary business transaction

bad bargain

completed transfer

gift causa mortis

Totten trust

pay-on-death (POD) account

net gift

blockage discount

Chapter 5: Review Questions

1. Describe the factors that **must** be present for a transfer to be considered a taxable gift for gift tax purposes. [LO 5.1]

2. Steven agrees to give his wife, Ellen, $100,000 as a lump-sum settlement upon their divorce. In turn, she agrees to give up all the marital rights she may have had in his estate. What requirements must be met for Steven's transfer to escape gift tax liability? [LO 5.1]

3. Mr. John Powers lends his adult son, Eric, $15,000 with interest at the rate of 10 percent. Mr. Powers cancels the note his son gave him. Explain the gift tax implications, if any, involved in this transaction. [LO 5.1]

4. George pays the rent for his 24-year-old daughter who is an aspiring actress living in New York. Has George made a gift? [LO 5.1]

5. Marty gives Mary, his daughter, $15,000 with the requirement that she must transfer an automobile she owns to her brother, Mark. The car is worth $11,000. Has a gift been made? To whom? Explain. (Ignore the annual exclusion.) [LO 5.1]

6. Steve is the sole proprietor of a small firm with a net worth of $300,000. He makes his 12-year-old daughter, Lara, a one-third partner.

   a. Has a gift been made in this transaction?

   b. Has a gift been made to Lara if she is an adult and performs bookkeeping services for the firm without a salary? [LO 5.1]

7. Alan and his wife, Sally, are the only stockholders in the AB Corporation, a real estate development company that owns various small parcels of undeveloped real estate. Alan is thinking of having the AB Corporation transfer certain individual parcels of real estate to his children for a price well below their true market value. What tax problems do you see in this proposed plan? Explain. [LO 5.1]

8. Joan Bolton owns a policy on the life of her husband, Jim. She names her children as beneficiaries because she has a large estate. Explain the potential problems of this arrangement. [LO 5.1]

9. Mr. Caruthers, a retired executive, takes over and manages the business owned by his son during his son's illness. The son would have had to pay $10,000 for a comparable replacement, but his father makes no charge for the services. Has a gift been made? Explain. [LO 5.2]

10. Describe the requirements necessary to have a qualified disclaimer of gifted property. [LO 5.2]

11. List the factors you would examine to determine whether property transferred to an employee is a gift or compensation for personal services. [LO 5.2]

12. A general agent for Wildlife of Arkansas assigns all his renewal commissions to his daughter. Explain the
    a. gift tax effect of the transaction,
    b. income tax effect of the transaction. [LO 5.2]

13. Identify the types of gifts that are exempt from the gift tax. [LO 5.2]

14. Explain whether the following transactions are completed gifts: [LO 5.3]
    a. Ed Smith gave his son a check in October of last year. As of February of this year, the son had not yet cashed it.
    b. Jim Johnson, who thought he was dying of a rare disease, transferred title to his $200,000 home in Ocean City, Maryland, to his sister. Miraculously, Jim survived, and his sister deeded the house back to him after his complete recovery.
    c. Jenny Moore purchased a $10,000 U.S. savings bond and had the bond titled in Jenny's name as well as the names of her three adult grandchildren as co-owners. She has just told them of the gift.

d. The tennis pro, Harry Hathaway, placed his summer earnings in a joint bank account with his brother, Stewart. Stewart withdrew $8,000 of the $10,000 Harry had placed in the account.

15. Gloria Gordon established an irrevocable trust for her son, Brian, and her daughter, Jamie. Gloria placed $100,000 of common stock into the trust.

   a. Explain the gift tax effect of the transfer of stock to the trust if Gloria retained the power to alter the amount of income and principal for each of her children.

   b. Describe the potential result if Gloria relinquished the right to allocate income to her beneficiaries at some future date. [LO 5.3]

16. What are the nontax advantages of making lifetime gifts? [LO 5.4]

17. Drew Mazino owns land worth $60,000 with a mortgage of $20,000 against it. Drew is not personally liable for the debt. Drew gives the property to his daughter.

   a. Compute the amount of the gift.

   b. Describe how your answer would change if Drew were personally liable for the debt in a state where the donee is subrogated to the rights of Drew's creditors.

   c. Would your answer to 17 b. differ if the donee had no right to proceed against Drew to recover the debt? [LO 5.5]

18. Describe the effect of *blockage* on gift taxation. [LO 5.5]

19. Ben Huggins plans to transfer the ownership of three policies on his life to his four adult children. Explain how the following types of policies are valued for gift tax purposes:

   a. a 20-pay life policy in its 21st year (a whole life policy that becomes paid up after 20 years of premium payments),

   b. a 10-year-old whole life policy on which Ben pays premiums annually,

   c. a newly purchased policy. [LO 5.5]

20. Alec transferred a whole life insurance policy to his son on July 1, of last year. The policy terminal reserve was $25,000 on January 1, of last year, and $28,000 on January 1, of this year. If Alec paid the full $2,500 annual premium on January 1, of this year, what is the value of the policy at the time of the gift? [LO 5.5]

Chapter 5: Review Answers

1. The transfer of property must be completed. That is, a competent donor must transfer the property in a manner that divests the donor of dominion and control and places property within the control of the donee. A competent donee must accept the gift. The transfer must be for less than full and adequate consideration.

2. The transfer must be pursuant to a written agreement between Steven and Ellen in settlement of marital rights. The divorce must occur within a period beginning one year prior to and ending 2 years after the agreement.

3. In nonbusiness situations, forgiving a debt constitutes a gift. Thus, in this case, ignoring the annual exclusion, Mr. Powers will have made a gift of $15,000 to his son.

4. Because George's daughter is an adult, payment of the rent is not George's legal obligation. Consequently, it constitutes a gift.

5. Ignoring the annual exclusion, Marty has given his daughter a direct gift of $4,000, which is the excess of $15,000 over the value of her car. Marty has also given his son an indirect gift of $11,000.

6. a. A gift has been made because Lara is performing no services for the partnership and has contributed no capital to its formation.

   b. If a new partner contributes capital or valuable services in exchange for a share of the business, there normally would not be a gift. However, a gift is likely to exist in this case since the bookkeeping service would have a value of less than $100,000. The gift value will be the $100,000 less the value of the services.

7. Alan and his wife may be considered by the IRS to have received a taxable dividend (equal to the value of the transferred real estate, less the price paid by the children). In addition, Alan and his wife would then be considered to have made a gift to their children (equal to the amount of the dividend).

8. When Jim dies, the IRS could argue that Joan has made a constructive gift to her children equal to the full amount of the life insurance policy's death proceeds—as if she received the proceeds and then gave the money to her children.

9. The rendering of services is not considered to be a gift.

10. The requirements for a qualified disclaimer of gifted property are as follows:

- The refusal must be in writing.

- The writing must be received by the transferor, the transferor's legal representative, or the holder of the legal title to the property no later than 9 months after the later of: (1) the date on which the transfer is made or (2) the date the person who is disclaiming reaches age 21.

- The person disclaiming must not have accepted the interest or any of its benefits.

- Someone other than the disclaimant must receive the property, and the disclaimant cannot influence the selection of the recipient of the disclaimed property.

11. The factors to examine to determine whether property transferred is a gift or compensation are as follows:

- the length and value of the employee's services

- the way the employer determined the amount of the reputed gift

- how the employer treated the payment in the corporate books and tax returns

12. a. The renewal commissions are treated as a gift from the general agent to his daughter.

    b. The general agent is subject to income tax on the commissions.

13. The following types of gifts are exempt from gift tax: qualified disclaimers, some transfers of property between spouses upon divorce, tuition paid to an educational institution, payment of medical care, and transfers of property or money to a political organization for that organization's use.

14. a. There is no completed gift until the son cashes the check.

    b. Neither the conveyance nor the return of the property is treated as a completed gift because the transfer of title was conditioned on Jim Johnson's death. A gift made in anticipation of death—a gift causa mortis—becomes complete only at the donor's death.

    c. There is no completed gift until one of the grandchildren surrenders the bond for cash.

d. A completed gift was made when Stewart Hathaway withdrew funds from the joint account that Harry had established.

15. a. Gift tax liability is measured at the time the gift becomes complete. There is no completed gift until Gloria relinquishes the power to alter the trust beneficiaries' interests. If that happens when the stock has increased in value significantly, the gift tax that Gloria must pay will also substantially increase.

b. Once Gloria relinquishes the right to allocate income to Brian and Jamie, she has made a completed gift. Her tax liability is measured at that time.

16. The nontax advantages of making lifetime gifts are as follows:

- Making a lifetime gift offers the donor privacy, which is impossible to obtain through a testamentary gift.

- Probate and administrative costs may be reduced by making a lifetime gift.

- A lifetime gift is protected from creditors' claims.

- The donor can enjoy seeing the donee use the gift.

- There is an opportunity for the donor to assess how well or how poorly the donee manages the gifted property.

- The gift can provide for the donee's education, support, and financial well-being.

17. a. Because the donor is not personally liable for the debt, the amount of the gift is the property's net value, or $40,000.

b. Under these circumstances, the amount of the gift is the value of the property unreduced by the debt, or $60,000.

c. In this situation, the amount of the gift is merely the amount of the donor's equity in the property, or $40,000. However, if Drew later decides to pay the mortgage debt, his daughter will have an additional gift of $20,000.

18. If a transfer consists of a block of stock large enough to depress the market value of each share if the entire block of stock is sold at once, a blockage discount may apply. This gives the taxpayer a discount below the stock's actual listed market value for determining the gift tax.

19. a.   Since this policy is paid up at the time of the transfer, the value for gift tax purposes is the amount of premium the issuing insurer would charge for the same type of policy of equal face amount on Ben's life (based on his age at the time of transfer).

     b.   The value of this policy, which is in the premium-paying stage at the time Ben makes the transfer, is the interpolated terminal reserve plus the unearned premiums on the date of the gift.

     c.   The value of the newly purchased policy on Ben's life for gift tax purposes is the gross premium paid to the insurer.

20. The value of the policy is the interpolated terminal reserve plus the unearned premium at the time of the gift. The interpolated terminal reserve was $26,500 on July 1 of last year since this is the midpoint of the year during which the reserve increases $3,000. Half the premium ($1,250) is unearned at this time. Therefore, the policy value was $27,750 on July 1 of last year when the gift was made.

Chapter 6:

Lifetime Transfers by Gift—An Overview of Federal Gift Taxation

Learning Objectives

An understanding of the material in this chapter should enable the student to

LO 6.1   **Describe the purpose, nature, and scope of the federal gift tax.**

LO 6. 2   **Describe several tax-related advantages of making lifetime gifts.**

LO 6. 3   **Describe the allowable reductions that can be used in determining taxable gifts.**

LO 6. 4   **Review the issues and strategies related to gifting property to minors.**

LO 6. 5   **Explain the procedure for computing the federal gift tax.**

LO 6. 6   **Explain the requirements for reporting and paying the federal gift tax.**

LO 6. 7   **Explain how the basis of gifted property is determined.**

LO 6. 8   **Identify the various strategies and factors that must be examined in selecting property for gifts.**

LO 6.1   **Describe the purpose, nature, and scope of the federal gift tax.**

PURPOSE, NATURE, AND SCOPE OF GIFT TAX LAW

Purpose

If individuals could give away their entire estate during lifetime without the imposition of any tax, rational people would arrange their affairs so that at death nothing would be subject to the federal estate tax. Likewise, if individuals could give income-producing securities or other property to members of their families, freely and without tax cost, the burden of income taxes could be shifted back and forth to lower brackets, and income taxes would be saved.

Originally, the federal gift tax was designed to equalize the transfer tax treatment between taxpayers who make inter vivos (lifetime) transfers and those who transfer their assets at death. Prior to the Economic Growth and Tax Relief Reconciliation Act of 2001 (EGTRRA 2001), the nature of the federal estate and gift tax system combined both tax systems, and a common set of tax rates was applicable to both inter vivos and after-death transfers. Although the gift and estate tax system shared many commonalities under EGTRRA 2001, beginning in 2002, there were distinctions. After passage of the Tax Relief, Unemployment Insurance Reauthorization, and Job Creation Act of 2010 (TRA 2010), however, the federal gift and estate tax systems once again became unified.

Nature

The gift tax is an excise tax. An excise tax may be any of various taxes, duties, or fees upon certain privileges like the privilege to transfer property. It is not levied directly on the gift itself or on the right to receive the property, but rather on the right of an individual to transfer money or other property to another for less than full and adequate consideration. (The tax is imposed only on transfers by individuals, but certain transfers involving corporations are treated as indirect transfers by corporate stockholders.)

The gift tax is based on the value of the property transferred. It is computed on a progressive schedule based on cumulative lifetime gifts. In other words, the tax rates are applied to total lifetime taxable gifts (all gifts less the exclusions and deductions) rather than only to taxable gifts made in the current calendar year.

Scope

The Treasury regulations summarize the comprehensive scope of the gift tax law by stating that "all transactions whereby property or interests are gratuitously passed or conferred upon another, regardless of the means or device employed, constitute gifts subject to tax." Almost any transfer or shifting of property or an interest in property can subject the donor (the person transferring the property or shifting the interest) to potential gift tax liability to the extent that the transfer is not supported by adequate and full consideration in money or money's worth—that is, to the extent that the transfer is gratuitous. Direct and indirect gifts, gifts made outright, and gifts in trust (of both real and personal property) can be subject to gift tax. The gift tax is imposed on the shifting of property rights, regardless of whether the property is tangible or intangible. It can be applied even if the property transferred (such as a municipal bond) is exempt from federal income or other taxes.

This broad definition of gifts includes transfers of life insurance, partnership interests, royalty rights, checks, or notes of third parties. Forgiving a note or canceling a debt may also constitute a gift.

Almost any party can be the donee (recipient) of a gift subject to tax. The donee can be an individual, partnership, corporation, foundation, trust, or other "person." A gift to a corporation is typically considered a gift to the other shareholders in proportion to their proprietary interests.

Similarly, a gift to a trust is usually considered to be a gift to the beneficiary or beneficiaries in proportion to their interests.

In fact, a gift can be subject to the tax (assuming the gift is complete) even if the identity of the donee is not known at the date of the transfer and cannot be ascertained.

2019 Estate Tax Rates		
For Taxable Estates in this Range	**You'll Pay this Base Amount of Tax**	**Plus This Rate on the Excess Above the Lower End of the Range**
$0 to $10,000	$0	18%
$10,000 to $20,000	$1,800	20%
$20,000 to $40,000	$3,800	22%
$40,000 to $60,000	$8,200	24%
$60,000 to $80,000	$13,000	26%
$80,000 to $100,000	$18,200	28%
$100,000 to $150,000	$23,800	30%
$150,000 to $250,000	$38,800	32%
$250,000 to $500,000	$70,800	34%
$500,000 to $750,000	$155,800	37%
$750,000 to $1 million	$248,300	39%
$1 million and up	$345,800	40%
Source: https://www.fool.com/taxes/2019/01/10/2019-estate-tax-rates.aspx		

LO 6. 2   Describe several tax-related advantages of making lifetime gifts.

Tax Advantages of Lifetime Gifts

estate and gift tax systems

appreciation

The unification of the **estate and gift tax systems** in 1976 was an attempt to impose the same tax burden on transfers made during life as on those made at death. The disparity of treatment between lifetime and testamentary gifts is minimized through the adoption of a single unified estate and gift tax rate schedule. Both lifetime and testamentary gifts are subject to the same rate schedule and are taxed cumulatively, so that gifts made during a lifetime increase the rate at which gifts made at death will be taxed. Some significant benefits of inter vivos gifts are the following:

- First, an individual can give up to $15,000 (indexed amount for 2019) gift tax free every year to each of an unlimited number of donees. This means that in 2019 a father desiring to make a $15,000 gift to each of his four children and four grandchildren could give a total of $120,000 in 2019 without gift tax liability. (The annual gift tax exclusion is discussed in greater detail later.) Because an individual's spouse can also make such gifts, up to $30,000 per year of money or other property—multiplied by an unlimited number of donees—can be transferred gift tax free. In the example above, the donor and spouse together could give up to $240,000 in 2019 on a gift-tax-free basis. In fact, one spouse can make the entire gift if the other spouse consents; the transaction can then be treated as if both spouses made gifts. This is known as *gift splitting*. (Provisions are covered in detail later.)

- A second tax incentive for making an inter vivos gift, as opposed to a testamentary gift, is that if a gift is made more than 3 years prior to a decedent's death, the amount of any gift tax paid on the transfer is not brought back into the computation of the gross estate. In the case of a sizable gift, avoidance of the gross-up rule can result in meaningful tax savings. The gross-up rule means that all gift tax payable on taxable gifts made within 3 years of the donor's death is included in calculating the value of the gross estate, even if the gift itself is not added back. For example, if an individual makes a *taxable* gift and has not previously used his or her basic credit for gift tax, the gift tax payable or paid on the value of the gift in excess of the gift tax basic exclusion amount will not be brought back into the estate tax computation if the gift was made more than 3 years before the donor died.

- Third, when a gift is made during lifetime, any appreciation accruing between the time of the gift and the date of the donor's death escapes estate taxation. This may result in a considerable estate tax (as well as probate and inheritance tax) savings. Ignoring the annual exclusion, if a father gives his daughter stock worth $100,000 and it appreciates to $600,000 by the date of the father's death 5 years later, only the $100,000 value of the stock at the time of the gift enters into the estate tax computation as an adjusted taxable gift. The $500,000 of appreciation does not enter into the computation as an adjusted taxable gift and, thus, does not increase the decedent's marginal estate tax bracket. An excellent example of both advantages is a gift of life insurance made more than 3 years prior to the insured's death. A substantial death benefit could be removed from a donor's estate at the cost of only the gift tax, if any, on the value of the policy at the time of the transfer. In the case of a whole life policy, this is usually roughly equivalent to the policy cash value plus unearned premiums at the date of the gift. If the insured lives for more than 3 years after the transfer and the premiums are present-interest gifts of the annual gift tax exclusion amount per year or less, there is no estate tax inclusion, and none of the **appreciation** (the difference between the death benefit payable and the adjusted taxable gift, if any, at the time the policy was transferred) is included in the insured's estate.

- Fourth, there are often strong income tax incentives for making an inter vivos gift. This advantage derives from moving taxable income from a high-bracket donor to a lower-bracket donee. Of course, this advantage is limited by the tax rules related to unearned income of children under age 19 (or age 24 for a full-time student whose unearned income does not exceed one-half of his or her support for the taxable year).

- Fifth, gifts of the proper type of assets may enable a decedent's estate to meet the mathematical tests for an IRC Sec. 303 stock redemption, an IRC Sec. 6166 installment payout of taxes, and the IRC Sec. 2032A special use valuation of farms and certain other business real property.

- Sixth, no gift taxes have to be paid until the transferor makes cumulative *taxable* gifts in excess of the basic exclusion amount (credit exemption equivalent amount) in the year of the gift. The basic exclusion amount as indexed in 2019 is $11,400,000 and the tax rate above this amount is 40 percent.

The Advantages of Gifting

- $15,000 federal gift tax annual exclusion (2019) ($30,000 if gift splitting)
- gross up rule—gift tax paid at least 3 years before donor's death avoids gross estate
- appreciation in property not subject to estate tax
- income tax savings—transfer of property from high-income-tax-bracket donor to lower-bracket donee
- achievement of other favorable tax treatment
  - IRC Sec. 303 stock redemption
  - IRC Sec. 6166 estate tax installment payouts
  - IRC Sec. 2032A special-use valuation
- basic credit amount leverage

LO 6. 3   **Describe the allowable reductions that can be used in determining taxable gifts.**

ALLOWABLE REDUCTIONS FOR GIFT TAX

Gift tax rates are applied to a net figure—taxable gifts. Before the tax on a transfer is computed, certain reductions are allowed. These reductions may include the following:

- gift splitting
- an annual exclusion

- a marital deduction
- a charitable deduction

Gift Splitting

The tax law permits a married donor—with the consent of the nondonor spouse—to elect to treat a gift to a third party as though each spouse has made one-half of the gift. The election must be made on the applicable gift tax return of the donor spouse.

gift splitting

Gift splitting is an artificial mechanism; even if one spouse makes the entire gift, for tax-computation purposes the single transfer is treated as though each spouse made only one-half of the gift. This means that the rate of tax that each will pay is calculated separately by reference to each spouse's prior gifts.

Furthermore, if a nondonor spouse agrees to gift splitting, it has a direct effect on the future gift tax and estate tax that the nondonor spouse may eventually have to pay if the gift exceeds the annual exclusion. Even though the nondonor spouse did not *actually* make one-half of the gift, to the extent it exceeds the annual gift tax exclusion it becomes an *adjusted taxable gift* to be added: (1) to all other gifts deemed to have been made for purposes of calculating the future gift tax bracket, and (2) to the taxable estate at the nondonor spouse's death.[1]

Gift splitting applies only to gifts that are made by a married donor to a third party and only with respect to noncommunity property. It was introduced into the tax law to equate the tax treatment of common-law taxpayers with that of community property residents. When one spouse earns a dollar in a community-property state, 50 cents is automatically and immediately deemed to be owned by the other spouse. Therefore, if the couple gives that dollar to their daughter, each spouse is treated as giving only 50 cents.

Gift splitting places the resident of a common-law state in the same position. For example, if a married individual in a common-law state gives her son a gift worth $30,000 and the requisite gift-splitting election is made, this individual is considered to have given only $15,000 for purposes of the gift tax computation. Her spouse is treated as if he has given the other $15,000—even if none of the gift was his property.

If the spouses elect to split gifts to third parties, all gifts made by either spouse during that reporting period must be split.

---

1.   This occurs unless the gift has already been included as an adjusted taxable gift in computing the estate tax of the donor spouse.

The privilege of gift splitting applies only to gifts made while the couple is married. Therefore, gifts made by the couple before they were married may not be split, even if they were married later during the same calendar year. Likewise, gifts made after the spouses are legally divorced or after one spouse dies may not be split. But gifts made before one spouse dies may be split even if that spouse dies before signing the appropriate consent or election; the deceased spouse's executor can make the appropriate election or consent.

Annual Exclusion

Purpose of the Exclusion

A *de minimis* rule is instituted primarily to avoid and lessen administrative record keeping. The annual gift tax exclusion (as indexed for inflation after 1998—Taxpayer Relief Act of 1997 (TRA 1997)) is a classic example of such a rule. It was instituted to eliminate the need for a taxpayer to keep an account of or report numerous small gifts. Congress intended that the amount of the annual exclusion be set large enough so that no reporting is required in the case of wedding gifts or other occasional gifts of relatively small amounts.

Effect of Gift Splitting Coupled With the Exclusion

Generally, the annual exclusion allows the donor to make up to $15,000 (2019) worth of gifts (other than future-interest gifts, defined below) tax free to any number of persons each year. Because an exclusion of up to $15,000 is allowed per donee per year, the total maximum excludible amount is determined by multiplying the number of persons to whom gifts are made by $15,000. For example, if an unmarried man makes cash gifts in 2019 of $2,000, $8,000, and $16,000 to his brother, father, and son, respectively, the $2,000 and the $8,000 gifts are fully excludible; $15,000 of the $16,000 gift to his son is excludible.

If the same individual is married and his spouse consents to split the gift, each spouse is deemed to have made one-half of the gift. This means both spouses can maximize the use of their annual exclusions. Assuming the nondonor spouse makes no gifts, the table below shows that none of the $26,000 is subject to tax.

Effect of Gift Splitting With Annual Exclusion							
Donee	Amount of Gift to Donee	Treated as if Donor Gave	Exclusion	Subject to Tax	Treated as if Nondonor Spouse Gave	Exclusion	Subject to Tax
Brother	$ 2,000	$1,000	$ 1,000	0	$ 1,000	$ 1,000	0
Father	8,000	4,000	4,000	0	4,000	4,000	0
Son	16,000	8,000	8,000	0	8,000	8,000	0
Totals	$26,000	$13,000	$13,000	0	$13,000	$13,000	0

Present-Interest Versus Future-Interest Gifts

present-interest gifts

An annual exclusion is allowed only for **present-interest gifts** and is denied to *gifts of a future interest*. A present interest is one in which the donee's use, possession, or enjoyment begins at the time the gift is made. Stated technically, a present interest is an immediate, unfettered, and ascertainable right of the donee to use, possess, or enjoy the gift.

future-interest gift

A **future-interest gift** refers to any interest or estate in which the donee's possession or enjoyment will not commence until some period of time after the gift is made. Technically, "future interest" is a legal term, and "includes reversions, remainders, and other interests or estates, whether vested or contingent, and whether or not supported by a particular interest or estate, which are limited to commence in use, possession, or enjoyment at some future date or time." (Treas. Reg. Sec. 2503-3(a))

Present and Future Interest

- present interest—immediate, unrestricted, and ascertainable right to use, possess, or enjoy the gift
- future interest—commencement of the donee's possession or enjoyment will be at some period in time after the gift is made

Clearly, the outright and unrestricted gift of property to a donee (even a minor) that passes legal and equitable title qualifies as a present-interest gift.

A single gift can be split into two parts: One is a present interest that qualifies for the annual exclusion; the other is a future interest that does not.

EXAMPLE

A widowed donor creates a trust and places income-producing property in the trust. The income is payable annually to the donor's son for life, and at the son's death the remainder is payable to the donor's grandson. The gift to the son of the right to receive income annually for life is a present-interest gift because he has an unrestricted right to its immediate use, possession, or enjoyment. If the son is 30 years old at the time of the gift and $100,000 is placed into the trust, the present value of that gift is $92,681 ($100,000 times .92681, which is the present value of an income stream payable for the life of a 30-year-old based on a principal amount of $100,000. The factor for the life interest [.92681] is based on a hypothetical interest rate of 6.6 percent and current mortality. The valuation of life estates, term interests, and remainder interests is based on an interest rate adjusted monthly as mandated in IRC Sec. 7520.) The present value of the life income interest gift ($92,681) may then be further reduced by the annual exclusion amount.

If the donor in the above example is married and the appropriate election and consent are filed, each spouse can claim an annual exclusion even though only the donor places property in the trust. No exclusion is allowed with respect to the ultimate gift of the corpus to the grandson, because his possession or enjoyment may not commence until sometime in the future.

If the donor provides that her son is to receive income for 10 years and then the principal is to pass to her grandson, and the donor places only $1,000 in the trust, the exclusion for the gift of the income interest is $472.25 ($1,000 times .47225, the value of a 10-year term interest at a hypothetical interest rate of 6.6 percent). Gift splitting with a spouse does not increase the amount of the exclusion, and each spouse is allowed a $236.12 exclusion. Again, no exclusion is allowed for the gift of the future interest (remainder) that passes to the grandson at the end of 10 years, even though he has an interest that cannot be forfeited. This is because he does not have the right to immediate possession or enjoyment; any delay in the absolute and immediate right of use, possession, or enjoyment of the property or the income therefrom is fatal to the gift tax annual exclusion.

Note that if the trustee in either situation above is given the power or discretion to accumulate the income, rather than distribute it, the donor's son would not receive the unfettered and immediate use of the income, and it would be impossible to ascertain the present value of the income interest. For example, assume the trustee is directed to pay the net income to the son for as long as the son lives but is authorized to withhold payments of income during any period the trustee deems advisable and to add such payments to corpus. In this case, even the income interest is a gift of a future interest, and no annual exclusion is allowed.

When the trust agreement requires the trustee to accumulate income for a time (or until the occurrence of a specified event), the income interest is also a future interest.

Crummey powers

Crummey Powers. The present-interest requirement for annual-exclusion purposes indicates that a gift in trust has to currently provide the donees with an unfettered right to use, possess, and benefit from the trust. The benefit could be a current disposition of income or corpus, or the beneficiaries could be provided with current withdrawal rights or powers. Tax rules provide that if each trust beneficiary has, at a minimum, the so-called **Crummey powers** (demand powers), the transfer to the trust qualifies as a present-interest gift for the beneficiaries. Because there is an interrelationship between Crummey powers and the exception for lapses of general powers of appointment, to avoid having the beneficiary treated as having a general power of appointment, the demand powers held by the beneficiary should allow the beneficiary the noncumulative right to demand the lesser of: (1) the beneficiary's share of the annual addition to the trust, or (2) the maximum annual exclusion for the year of the gift. When there is more than one beneficiary, the Crummey powers should be given ratably to each.

Since there is no chance that the beneficiaries can request an amount greater than the grantor's annual addition to corpus, an insurance policy will not be stripped by the beneficiaries. In actual practice, the beneficiaries cooperate since they realize that the long-term benefit of the trust is more important than the current demand rights. For the irrevocable life insurance trust with Crummey powers to qualify as a present-interest gift, the trustee must notify each beneficiary of the right to exercise the powers. This right must exist for a reasonable period of time each year (such as 30 days). If each beneficiary's demand power is limited to the amounts specified above, the annual lapse of this power is not treated as a taxable gift that lapsing beneficiaries make to other trust beneficiaries.

The 5-and-5 power is a special exception under Sec. 2514 that allows the lapse of general powers taking place during the life of the holder to avoid being treated as a taxable gift. The exception is limited to the extent the lapse does not exceed the *greater of* $5,000 or 5 percent of the value of the property from which the appointment would have been satisfied. In other words, if what could have been transferred but was not transferred due to the lapse does not exceed $5,000 or 5 percent of the value of the property, that de minimus amount is not treated as the exercise of a general power of appointment. Consequently, the holder is permitted to appoint trust corpus up to the greater of $5,000 or 5 percent without any gift tax consequences.

If the powerholder has the power to appoint an amount or percentage in excess of the greater of $5,000 or 5 percent, the excess over said amount is treated as gift for gift tax purposes.

EXAMPLE

Suppose Franny was a beneficiary of a trust established by her mother many years ago. The trust provided income to Franny for life and a noncumulative, annual general power of appointment over the greater of $5,000 or 5 percent of the trust corpus. Under the trust Franny was given the power to appoint 12 percent (7 percent more than 5 percent under the 5-and-5 power) of the trust. If the value of the trust remains at all times at $800,000, each lapsing year Franny will be treated for gift tax purposes as if she made a gift of 7 percent of the value of the trust, or $56,000.

The 5-and-5 power exception, however, does not apply to lapses that take place in the year of the holder's death. This means that the annually lapsing power to claim or appoint $5,000, or up to and including $5,000, of trust corpus each year that was not exercised during the holder's year of death will be included in his or her estate.

EXAMPLE

Franny was a beneficiary of a trust established by her mother many years ago. The trust provided income to Franny for life and a noncumulative, annual general power of appointment over the greater of $5,000 or 5 percent of the trust corpus. When Franny dies, the trust terminates and the remainder passes to Franny's cousin, Wade, or to Wade's estate. If the value of the trust remains at all times at $800,000 and Franny died this year without exercising her 5-and-5 power, $40,000 (5 percent of $800,000) will be included in her estate.

In the example in which Franny was provided with the power to appoint 12 percent of trust corpus, in the year of Franny's death $96,000 (12 percent of $800,000) will be included in her estate (in addition to inclusion of a previously lapsed amount in excess of the 5-and-5 power, which is beyond the scope of this course).

Planning Point: Drafting powers of appointment to utilize the 5-and-5 exception power is a common estate and gift planning device. Generally, the right is given so that it can be exercised each year. However, the 5-and-5 power is a noncumulative right; therefore, the failure (or lapse) to exercise the right each year does not increase the percentage or dollar amount for the following year. In many cases, the 5-and-5 power is not expected or intended to be exercised. It is granted in combination with a Crummey withdrawal power. After a specified Crummy demand period, the power lapses and the lapsed value remains within the trust.

Identity of Donees

The number and amount (or availability) of annual exclusions depend on the identity of the donee(s), the type of asset involved, and the restrictions, if any, placed on the asset. When a gift is made in trust, the beneficiaries of the trust (and not the trust itself) are considered the donees. For instance, if there are three life-income beneficiaries, up to three annual exclusions could be obtained. Conversely, if five trusts are established for the same beneficiary, only one exclusion is allowed. (Technically, the actuarial value of each gift in trust to that beneficiary is totaled and added to direct gifts the donor made to that beneficiary to ascertain whether and to what extent an annual exclusion remains and is allowable for the present transfer.)

Transfers to two or more persons as joint tenants with right of survivorship, tenants by the entirety, tenants in common, or tenants in partnership are considered multiple gifts. Each tenant is deemed to receive an amount equal to the actuarial value of his or her interest in the tenancy. If, for example, one person has a one-half interest in a tenancy in common, a cash gift of $6,000 to the tenancy is treated as a $3,000 gift to that person. This amount is added to other gifts made directly to the donee by the same donor to determine how much of the exclusion is allowed. (However, note that a tenancy by the entirety, where neither spouse can sever an interest without the other's consent, is considered a future-interest gift and does not qualify for the annual exclusion.)

In all probability, gifts to partnerships should follow the same rules as other tenancies: A gift to a partnership should be treated as if made to each partner in proportion to his or her partnership interest. Because a partnership is a special form of property ownership, it is referred to as a tenancy in partnership and the parties to a partnership are called tenants in partnership.

LO 6. 4   **Review the issues and strategies related to gifting property to minors.**

Gifts to Minors

Outright gifts to minors pose no particular qualification problem concerning the annual exclusion. The IRS states in a revenue ruling that "an unqualified and unrestricted gift to a minor, with or without the appointment of a guardian, is a gift of a present interest." But there are, of course, practical problems involved, especially with larger gifts. Although minors can buy, sell, and deal with some limited types of property, such as U.S. savings bonds, gifts of other types of property create difficulties. For example, some states do not give minors the legal capacity to purchase their own property, care for it, or sell or transfer it. Some states forbid the registration of securities in a minor's name, and a broker may be reluctant to deal in securities titled in a minor's name. In many states, a minor has the legal ability to disaffirm a sale of stock sold at a low price that later rises in value. Furthermore, a buyer receives no assurance of permanent title when a minor signs a real estate deed. Legal guardianship of the minor is not a viable answer in many situations. Because guardianship laws are rigid, a guardian must generally post bond, and periodic and expensive court accounting is often required. Most important, a parent may not want to give a minor control over a large amount of cash or other property.

To minimize these and other practical problems involved with most large gifts to minors, such transfers are generally made in trust or under some type of guardianship or custodian arrangement. An incredible amount of litigation developed over whether such gifts qualified for the annual exclusion. Sec. 2503 of the Internal Revenue Code provides clear and precise methods of qualifying gifts to minors for the annual exclusion. There are three basic means of qualifying *cared-for gifts* to minors under Sec. 2503:

- a Sec. 2503(b) trust
- a Sec. 2503(c) trust
- the Uniform Transfers (Gifts) to Minors Act

Sec. 2503(b) trust

Sec. 2503(b) Trust. To obtain an annual exclusion for gifts to a trust, the individual can establish a trust that *requires* income to be distributed at least annually to (or for the use of) the minor beneficiary. Income is the actual accounting income of the trust as determined by the trust agreement and state law. The trust agreement states how income is to be used and gives the trustee no discretion as to its use. The minor receives possession of the trust principal whenever the trust agreement specifies. A distribution does not have to be made by age 21; corpus may be held for as long as the beneficiary lives—or for any shorter period of time. In fact, the principal can actually bypass the income beneficiary and go directly to the individuals whom the grantor—or even the named beneficiary—specifies. The trust agreement can also control the dispositive scheme if the minor dies before receiving trust corpus. This is a **Sec. 2503(b) trust**. Trust assets do not have to be paid to the minor's estate or appointees.

In reality, the mandatory payment of income to (or in behalf of) beneficiaries seems onerous—especially while the beneficiary is a minor. But such income can be deposited in a custodial account and used for the minor's benefit or left to accumulate in a custodial account until the minor reaches majority (at which time the unexpended amount is turned over to the beneficiary).

Although the entire amount of property placed in a 2503(b) trust (also referred to as a mandatory income trust or MIT) is considered to be a gift, for exclusion purposes it is split into two parts: the income interest and the remainder or reversion interest. It is the present interest of the income stream that qualifies for the annual exclusion present-interest requirement. The value of the income interest qualifying for the annual exclusion is discounted. The value of the income—measured by multiplying the amount of the gift by a factor that considers both the duration over which the income interest will be paid and the discounted worth of $1 payable over the appropriate number of years—is eligible for the annual exclusion. The balance of the gift (principal) does not qualify for the annual exclusion.

For example, assume a donor places $10,000 into a Sec. 2503(b) trust that is required to pay her 10-year-old daughter all income until she reaches age 25. Assume, too, that the present value of the income the daughter receives over those 15 years is $7,793.66. If the income is payable for her entire life, the present value jumps to $9,894.90.

It is important to note that, according to at least one revenue ruling, the annual exclusion is denied for a 2503(b) trust that permits the principal to be invested in non-income-producing securities, real estate, or life insurance policies.

Sec. 2503(c) trust

Sec. 2503(c) Trust. The Sec. 2503(b) trust described above has the advantage of not requiring distribution of principal when the minor reaches age 21, but it does require a current (annual) distribution of income. The **Sec. 2503(c) trust**, on the other hand, requires that income and principal be distributed when the minor reaches age 21 but does not require the trustee to distribute income currently. Special tax treatment under Sec. 2503(c) was created to allow parents to make annual exclusion gifts without giving their minor children actual control of the gifted property. Under Sec. 2503(c) a gift in trust is not treated as a gift of a future interest (although it actually *is* a future interest transfer) for gift tax purposes if certain requirements are met.

The requirements that make it possible for a donor to obtain the annual exclusion for a gift to a minor under Sec. 2503(c) are: the trust must provide that (1) income and principal are expended by or in behalf of the beneficiary, and (2) to the extent not so expended, income and principal pass to the beneficiary at age 21, or (3) if the beneficiary dies prior to that time, income and principal go to the beneficiary's estate or appointees under a general power of appointment. (The annual exclusion is not lost merely because local law prevents a minor from exercising a general power of appointment.)

A substantial amount of flexibility can be built into the 2503(c) trust. Income that has been accumulated, as well as any principal in the trust, can be paid to the donee when the donee reaches age 21. This approach may be indicated if the sums involved are not substantial. However, the donor may want the trust to continue to age 25 or some other age as long as the beneficiary can request complete distribution at age 21, and he or she is informed of the right to distribution. It is possible to provide continued management of the trust assets and, at the same time, avoid forfeiting the annual exclusion by giving the donee, at age 21, a right for a limited period of time to require immediate distribution by giving written notice to the trustee. If the beneficiary fails to give written notice, the trust can continue automatically for whatever period the donor provided when the donor established the trust. Alternatively, some states have lowered the age of majority from 21 to 18, or some in-between age. A trust can provide that the distribution be made between the age of majority and age 21 without jeopardizing the Sec. 2503(c) exclusion. (The rule is that 21 is the maximum, rather than the minimum, age at which the trust assets must be made available.)

A 2503(c) trust has a number of advantages over the type of custodianship found in the Uniform Gifts to Minors Act (UGMA) or Uniform Transfers to Minors Act (UTMA) arrangements described below, and as shown in the table below.

UTMA/UGMA

Uniform Transfers (Gifts) to Minors Act (UTMA/UGMA). The Uniform Transfers (Gifts) to Minors Act (or comparable laws, such as the Model Gifts to Minors Act) provides an alternative to the Sec. 2503(c) trust. The Uniform Transfers to Minors and Uniform Gifts to Minors Acts (**UTMA/UGMA**) are a simple way to make fiduciary gifts to minors. These custodial arrangements are frequently utilized for smaller gifts not only because of their simplicity but also because they offer the benefits of management, income and estate tax shifting, and the investment characteristics of a trust with little or none of the document drafting costs. There is no court supervision of UGMA and UTMA accounts.

All states and the District of Columbia have enacted laws that simplify making gifts to minors and permitting adults to make gifts of property to minors with the property registered in a custodian's name. The custodian, who may be the donor, holds the property for the minor. The initial forms of UGMA statutes included restrictive limits on the categories of investments permitted for an UGMA transfer. UGMA accounts are permitted to hold cash, life insurance, securities, and annuities, but not real property. UTMA accounts, on the other hand, in addition to UGMA property interests, can hold any type of transferable property interests such as intellectual property, real property, patents, partnership interests, and so forth. Transfers to UTMA accounts are treated as completed gifts. Under both the UGMA and UTMA, custodial property is distributed at age 21 unless the jurisdiction has modified the age of majority. Some states allow a donor to select ages past age 21.

Although UTMA custodial accounts are similar to trusts, they are more restrictive than trusts. Some of the following limitations apply to custodial accounts that do not apply to trust arrangements:

1. Custodial accounts are not separate tax-paying entities. All income is taxed to the minor. Irrevocable trusts, on the other hand, are considered separate tax-paying entities, and the trust is taxed on an accumulated income.

2. Custodial accounts exist for one person whereas trusts may have numerous beneficiaries.

3. Custodial accounts do not have spendthrift provisions that are often included in trusts.

4. If a donor serves as custodian of an UTMA account (in most instances, a parent serves as custodian of the child's account), and the donor-custodian dies during the minor's lifetime, the principal is included in the custodian's gross estate. This gross estate inclusion is the result of Secs. 2036 and 2038 retained life interests that in turn result from the donor-custodian's power to distribute income and principal to the minor.

5. Custodial property generally must be distributed to UTMA beneficiaries at age 21. Distributions of trust corpus to beneficiaries may be provided for at later ages.

Gifts to Minors

Factor	Trust	UGMA or UTMA
Type of Property	Donor can make gifts of almost any type of property.	Type of property must be permitted by appropriate statute. Gifts of real estate may not be permitted.
Dispositive Provisions	Donor can provide for disposition of trust assets if the donee dies without having made disposition.	Disposition must follow statutory guidelines.
Investment Powers	Trustee may be given broad, virtually unlimited investment powers.	Custodian limited to investment powers specified by statute.
Time of Distribution of Assets	Trust can continue automatically even after beneficiary reaches age 21. Trustee can make distribution between state law age of majority and age 21.	Custodial assets must be paid to beneficiary upon reaching majority. (Note: Some states have extended the distribution age requirement past age 21.)
Format	Multiple beneficiaries and unequal distributions permitted.	Only one minor for each account.
Income Taxation	Irrevocable trust is a separate tax-paying entity.	Custodial account is not a separate tax-paying entity; minor is the taxpayer.
Special Provisions	Spendthrift and simultaneous death clauses permissible.	No spendthrift clause allowed; simultaneous death not relevant.
Other	Irrevocable trust property avoids inclusion in decedent trustee-grantor's estate. Property may be used to satisfy obligations of minor's support.	The death of the donor custodian causes inclusion of custodial property in donor-custodian's estate. Property may not be used to satisfy support obligations to minors, including obligations under a divorce decree.

Most states, however, amended their statutes to include broader investment powers. Today, practically all states have adopted UTMA. (When UTMA was adopted in 1983, it essentially replaced UGMA.) The UTMA statutes generally permit any type of property transfer.

For example, in Pennsylvania the UTMA gift may be made as follows:

- if the subject of the gift is a security in registered form, by registering it in the name of the transferor, other adult person, or trust company, followed in substance by the words, "as custodian for (<u>name of minor</u>) under the Pennsylvania Uniform Transfers to Minors Act"

- if the subject of the gift is a security not in registered form, by delivering it to an adult other than the transferor or to a trust company, accompanied by a statement of gift in the following form or substance, signed by the donor and the person designated as custodian:

  I, (name of transferor or name and representative capacity if a fiduciary), hereby transfer to (name of custodian), as custodian for (name of minor) under the Pennsylvania Uniform Transfers to Minors Act, the following: (Insert a description of the custodial property sufficient to identify it.)

  Dated:_____

  (Signature) _____

  (name of custodian) acknowledges receipt of the property described above as custodian for the minor named above under the Pennsylvania Uniform Transfers to Minors Act.

  Dated:_____

  (Signature of custodian) _____

- if the subject of the gift is money, by paying or delivering it to a broker or financial institution for credit to an account in the name of the transferor, an adult other than the transferor, or a trust company followed in substance by the words "as custodian for (<u>name of minor</u>) under the Pennsylvania Uniform Transfers to Minors Act"

- if the subject of the gift is a life or endowment insurance policy or annuity contract, by causing the ownership of such policy or contract to be recorded on a form satisfactory to the insurance company or fraternal benefit society, in the name of the transferor, an adult other than the transferor, or a trust company, followed in substance by the words, "as custodian for (name of minor) under the Pennsylvania Uniform Transfers to Minors Act," and having the policy or contract delivered to the person in whose name it is thus registered as custodian

Planning Point: When using Secs. 2503(b) and 2503(c) trusts, a grantor must choose between two frequently undesirable consequences to obtain the annual exclusion: an arrangement requiring the annual distribution of all trust income to the minor, or an arrangement requiring the distribution of trust principal at age 21. Crummey demand powers in non-2503(b) and (c) trusts resolve this predicament. By providing the minor with the right to withdraw a small amount from the trust each year, the Crummey provision in the trust avoids mandatory distributions of income during minority and of corpus at age 21.

Ways to Transfer Gifts to Minors

Sec. 2503(b) trust

- The present value of income for the term of the trust qualifies for the annual exclusion.
- Trust income must be distributed for the minor's benefit at least annually.
- Trust corpus may be held after the age of majority or for the benefit of others.

Sec. 2503(c) trust

- Trust income can be accumulated.
- Income and principal must be distributed by age 21.
- Income and principal must be distributed to a deceased minor's estate.

Uniform Transfers/Gifts to Minors Act (UTMA/UGMA)

- A custodial account is created.
- Property is registered in the custodian's name for the benefit of the minor.
- Requirements are set by state law.
- UGMA restricts types of property the account holds.
- Income and principal must be distributed at majority (or later in some states).

529 plan

529 Plans As A Transfer For Minors. In addition to the three basic means of qualifying cared-for gifts to minors under Sec. 2503, a 529 plan can also be an effective estate planning tool in order to transfer assets out of the estate for the benefit of a minor. A **529 plan** is a tax-advantaged savings plan designed to encourage saving for future college costs. 529 plans are sponsored by states, state agencies, or educational institutions. There are a variety of benefits in a typical 529 plan including the fact that earnings are not subject to Federal tax and generally are not subject to state tax as long as the funds are used for qualified education expenses for a designated beneficiary, such as tuition, fees, books, room, or board. Remember, contributions to a 529 plan are not deductible on your federal income tax return, but may be deductible on your state income tax return. 529 plans can now be used to help pay for a computer, Internet access for educational purposes, and primary and secondary education up to $10,000 per year.

Anyone can set up a 529 plan and name anyone as a beneficiary. You can name family members, friends, or even yourself. You are able to change the designated beneficiary to another family member, but there can be some restrictions on changing beneficiaries. There are no income restrictions to setting up a 529 plan and no limit on the number of plans you can set up. However, there are contribution limitations on the plan. First, contributions cannot exceed the amount necessary to provide for the qualified education expenses of the beneficiary. 529 plans are controlled by a custodian who controls the funds until they are withdrawn.

Contributions to a 529 plan can have gift tax issues. For instance, you are still subject to the $15,000 annual exclusion for 2019. However, if you make a contribution to a 529 plan over $15,000 and under $75,000 you can elect to treat the contribution as made over a five-cal-ender-year period for determining gift taxes. You can also engage in gift splitting if you are married and put up to $150,000 in a 529 plan excluded from gift taxes in one year by electing to treat it as spread over 5 years. You can gift more, but it will be a taxable gift. The maximum contribution to a 529 plan depends on your state, but can often reach into the mid $500,000 range in 2019. Some research suggests that almost 25 percent of all college savings are found in 529 plans. 529 plans can go to the student, account owner, or the school. There are benefits and drawbacks to each option.

How Type of Asset Affects the Exclusion. The type of asset given and the restrictions placed on that asset may prevent the donor from obtaining the annual exclusion.

Clearly, an outright gift of non-income-producing property qualifies for the gift tax exclusion. Does the same property qualify if placed in a trust? The IRS uses three arguments to disallow annual exclusions:

- The right to income (which is the only current right given to a life beneficiary) from a gift of non-income-producing property is a future interest because its worth is contin-gent on the trustee's converting it to income-producing property.

- It is impossible to ascertain the value of an income interest in property that is not income-producing at the time of the gift.

- If a gift tax exclusion is allowable, the exclusion must be limited to the actual income produced by the property (or expected to be produced) multiplied by the number of years over which the income beneficiary is expected to receive the income—dis-counted to its present value according to tables in government regulations.

Non-dividend-paying stock held in trust is a good example of property that may not qualify for the gift tax exclusion. In a number of cases, the IRS has been successful in disallowing an exclu-sion for gifts in trust that consisted of stock in closely held corporations paying no dividends. Gifts in trust of life insurance policies pose the same problem: a mother assigns policies on her life to a trust created to provide financial protection for her daughter. The trust provisions do not provide the daughter with Crummey withdrawal powers. At the mother's death, the policy proceeds will be reinvested and the daughter will receive the net income of the trust for life. Is the mother allowed the exclusion for the present value of her daughter's income interest? The regulations say no, since the daughter will not receive income payments until her mother dies.

Summary of Rules for Ascertaining the Amount and Availability of the Gift Tax Annual Exclusion. The rules regarding the annual exclusion can be summarized as follows:

- A gift in trust is a gift to a trust's beneficiaries and not to the trust for determining the number of annual exclusions to which a donor is entitled.

- The value of an income interest in a trust qualifies for the exclusion if the trustee is required to distribute trust income at least annually—even if the value of the remainder interest does not qualify.

- The gift of an interest that is contingent upon survivorship is a gift of a future interest. (If a gift in trust is made with income going to the grantor's son for life and then to the grantor's daughter for life, the gift to the son will qualify but the daughter's interest will not.)

- A gift is one of a future interest if enjoyment depends on the trustee's discretion. (The nature of the interest must be present as of the date of the gift and is not, for example, determined by what the trustee may subsequently do or not do in the exercise of a discretionary power.)

- A gift must have an ascertainable value to qualify for the exclusion. (The exclusion is denied if the donor or anyone else can divert the income from the beneficiary.)

Exclusion of Transfers for Educational and Medical Expenses

For public-policy reasons, Congress provided another exclusion for specific qualified transfers. A gratuitous transfer is excluded from taxable gifts if made on behalf of an individual: (1) for tuition to an educational institution for the education or training of the individual or (2) to a provider of medical services for medical care received by the individual. These exclusions are not limited in amount and are independent of the annual exclusion. However, it is important to note that the payments must be made directly to the provider of services to qualify for the exclusion. Payments made directly to an individual as reimbursement for educational or medical expenses incurred are taxable gifts, unless such gifts are eligible for an annual exclusion.

Gift Tax Marital Deduction

gift tax marital deduction

An individual who transfers property to a spouse is allowed an unlimited deduction (subject to certain conditions) known as the **gift tax marital deduction**. The purpose of the gift tax marital deduction is to enable spouses to be treated as a single economic unit.

Requirements to Qualify for Gift Tax Marital Deduction

For a gift to qualify for the gift tax marital deduction, the following conditions must be satisfied:

- The recipient of the gift must be the spouse of the donor at the time the gift is made.
- The recipient spouse must be a U.S. citizen.
- The property transferred to the donee spouse must not be a terminable interest that disqualifies the gift for the marital deduction.

Most of the qualifications above are self-explanatory. The terminable-interest rule for marital-deduction gifts is similar to the rule employed for estate tax purposes. The effect of these rules is that generally no marital deduction is allowed if the donee spouse's interest in the transferred property terminates after a lapse of time or on the occurrence or nonoccurrence of a specified contingency.

The exception is for a gift of *qualifying terminable interest in property* (QTIP) assets. (In the past, a gift or bequest of a terminable interest in property—one that could end at a spouse's death, for example, and would therefore escape taxation—was not eligible for the gift or estate tax marital deduction.)

Current law provides that if a donor spouse gives a donee spouse a *qualifying income interest for life*, it qualifies for the gift (or estate) tax marital deduction. To qualify for QTIP treatment, the following requirements must be met:

- The spouse must be entitled to all the income from the property (and it must be payable annually or more frequently).
- No person can have a power to appoint any part of the property to any person other than the spouse.
- The property must be taxable at the donee spouse's death. (In the case of a bequest, the first decedent's executor makes an irrevocable election that the property remaining at the surviving spouse's death is taxable in the survivor's estate.)

Terminable Interest Rule
- disallows gift tax marital deduction when the donee-spouse's interest in the gifted property will end
  - after a specified period of time or
  - on the happening or not happening of a specified contingency

Exception: qualifying terminable interest property (QTIP)
- allows terminable interest to qualify for marital deduction if
  - spouse is entitled to income from property
  - power to appoint property is limited to spouse
  - unconsumed property is included in spouse's estate

Lifetime Gifts to an Alien Spouse

alien spouse

The marital deduction is denied for gifts to a spouse who is not a U.S. citizen (an **alien spouse**). Presumably, the purpose of this limitation is to prevent the avoidance of the federal estate and gift tax system by permitting deductible transfers to an alien spouse who could, conceivably, avoid the transfer tax system entirely by leaving the country with the gifted assets.

super-annual exclusion

However, a special provision was enacted to permit significant nontaxable transfers to an alien spouse as an exception to the rule. Transfers to an alien spouse qualify for a basic **super-annual exclusion** amount of $100,000 ($155,000 in 2019 as indexed for inflation) each year if

- the gift otherwise qualifies as an annual-exclusion gift
- the gift meets the requirements for a gift tax marital deduction (except for the requirement that the donee is a U.S. citizen)

Gift Tax Charitable Deduction

gift tax charitable deduction

A donor making a transfer of property to a qualified charity may receive a charitable deduction equal to the value of the gift (to the extent not already covered by the annual exclusion). The net effect of the **gift tax charitable deduction**—together with the annual exclusion—is to avoid gift tax liability on gifts to qualified charities. There is no limit on the amount that can pass gift tax free to a qualified charity.

The gift tax deduction is allowed for all gifts made during the calendar year by U.S. citizens or residents if the gift is to a qualified charity. A qualified charity is defined as:

- the United States, a state, territory, any political subdivision, or the District of Columbia, if the gift is to be used exclusively for public purposes
- certain religious, scientific, or charitable organizations (IRS Code Section 2522)
- certain fraternal societies, orders, or associations (IRS Code Section 2522)
- certain veterans' associations, organizations, or societies (IRS Code Section 2522)

Technically, the charitable deduction is limited and is allowable only to the extent that the gift is included in the total amount of gifts that are made during the year. The phrase *total amount of gifts* refers to gifts in excess of the annual exclusion.

EXAMPLE

In 2019 a single client makes total gifts of $52,000: $20,000 to his daughter and $32,000 to The American College of Financial Services. After taking annual exclusions, the client's gross gifts are $5,000 (the gift of $20,000 to the daughter, less the $15,000 exclusion) and $17,000 (the $32,000 gift to The American College of Financial, less the $15,000 annual exclusion). Therefore, the client's charitable deduction is limited to $17,000. The total taxable gifts are just $5,000 (the amount to the daughter over the annual exclusion).

The reason for the rule that the annual exclusion is taken first is obviously to prevent the allowance of a charitable deduction equal to the total amount of the gift, which, in turn, when added to the allowable annual exclusion, would result in an extra annual gift tax exclusion.

In certain cases, a donor transfers a remainder interest to a qualified charity. A noncharitable beneficiary is given all or part of the income interest in the transferred property, and the charity receives the remainder at the termination of the income interest. When a charitable remainder is given to a qualified charity, a gift tax deduction is allowable for the present interest value of the remainder interest only if at least one of the following four conditions is satisfied:

- The property that was transferred was either a personal residence or a farm.
- The transfer was made to a charitable remainder annuity trust.
- The transfer was made to a charitable remainder unitrust.
- The transfer was made to a pooled-income fund.

The terms *charitable remainder annuity trust, charitable remainder unitrust*, and *pooled-income fund* are defined in essentially the same manner as they are for estate and income tax purposes.

Net Gifts

Sometimes a donor gratuitously transfers property to a donee that is subject to some form of obligation. In some cases, a donee voluntarily agrees to pay the gift tax on the value of the donor's gift. In other instances, the donor makes the gift with the understanding that the donee must pay the gift tax. The gross value of the gift is reduced by the amount of the gift tax paid by the donee, and the gift tax is then calculated on the remaining (net) amount of the gift. Net gifts may also have income tax ramifications to the extent the donee's payment of gift tax is greater than the donor's basis in the property.

LO 6. 5   **Explain the procedure for computing the federal gift tax.**

CALCULATING GIFT TAX PAYABLE

Computing the gift tax payable begins with ascertaining the amount of taxable gifts in the current reporting calendar year. To find the amount of taxable gifts, all gifts are valued first. If appropriate, the gift is then split, and annual exclusions as well as the marital and charitable deductions are applied. Note that the gift and estate tax credit and the issue of whether gift tax actually has to be paid are irrelevant for the limited purpose of computing taxable gifts.

Examples and the accompanying computation formats illustrate the process.

EXAMPLE 1

Assume a single donor makes certain outright gifts in the last month of 2019: $70,000 to his son, $2,500 to his daughter, $4,000 to his grandson, and $5,000 to The American College of Financial Services (a total of $81,500).

Computing Taxable Gifts

Step 1:	**List** total gifts for year		$81,500
Step 2:	**Subtract** one-half of gift deemed to be made by donor's spouse (split gifts)	0	
	Gifts deemed to be made by donor		81,500
Step 3:	**Subtract** annual exclusion(s)	(26,500)	
	Gifts after subtracting exclusion(s)		55,000
Step 4:	**Subtract** marital deduction	0	
Step 5:	**Subtract** charitable deduction	0	
	Taxable gifts		$55,000

Although there were four donees, the annual exclusion is $26,500 and does not total four times $15,000. This is because the annual exclusion is the lower of: (1) the annual exclusion or (2) the actual net value of the property transferred. In this example, the annual exclusion for the $70,000 gift to the son is $15,000, and the $2,500, $4,000, and $5,000 gifts are limited to the actual value of each gift, for the sum of $26,500.

EXAMPLE 2

A slight change in the facts in the example above illustrates the computation when the donor is married and his wife consents to splitting their gifts to third parties. In this case, only one-half of the gifts made by the donor is taxable to the donor (one-half of the gifts made by the donor's wife to third parties is also included in computing the donor's total gifts). A separate (but essentially identical) computation is made for the donor's wife. That computation would show (a) the other half of the husband's gifts to third parties plus (b) one-half of the wife's actual gifts to third parties (since all gifts must be split if any gifts are split).

Computing Taxable Gifts

Step 1	List total gifts for year		$81,500
Step 2	Subtract one-half of gift deemed to be made by donor's spouse (split gifts)	(40,750)	
	Gifts deemed to be made by donor		40,750
Step 3	Subtract annual exclusion(s)	(20,750)	
	Gifts after subtracting exclusion(s)		20,000
Step 4	Subtract marital deduction	0	
Step 5	Subtract charitable deduction	0	
	Taxable gifts		$15,750

(The calculation on the wife's return parallels this return.)

Note that in this example the annual exclusions are computed after the split, and each donor's exclusions are

gift to son	$15,000
gift to daughter	1,250
gift to grandson	2,000
gift to The American College of Financial Services	2,500
	$20,750

EXAMPLE 3

If the married donor in this example also makes an outright spousal gift of $110,000, the computation is as follows:

	Computing Taxable Gifts		
Step 1	*List* total gifts for year		$191,500
Step 2	*Subtract* one-half of gift deemed to be made by donor's spouse (split gifts)	(405,750)	
	Gifts deemed to be made by donor		150,750
Step 3	*Subtract* annual exclusion(s)	(35,750)	
	Gifts after subtracting exclusion(s)		115,000
Step 4	*Subtract* marital deduction	(95,000)	
Step 5	*Subtract* charitable deduction	0	
	Taxable gifts		$20,000

Credits

The Tax Reform Act of 1976 unified the gift and estate tax systems and created a credit against gifts made either during lifetime or at death. The gift tax credit, which provides a dollar-for-dollar reduction of the tax otherwise payable. Under EGTRRA 2001, the credit amount for gifts is $345,800 after 2001. Under the Tax Relief, Unemployment Insurance Reauthorization, and Job Creation Act (TRA 2010) the gift, estate, and generation-skipping tax credit and exclusion amounts became unified once again for the three transfer tax systems. Under TRA 2010 the credit and exclusion amounts are referred to as the basic credit amount and the basic exclusion amount. For 2019, the basic exclusion amount is $11.4 million (2019) and the basic credit amount is $4,505,800 (2019).

EXAMPLE 4

When the total value of taxable gifts for the reporting period is found, the actual tax payable is computed using the following method:

Computing Taxable Gifts

Step 1	*Compute* gift tax on *taxable* gifts regardless of when made (use rate schedule)	$
Step 2	*Compute* gift tax on all *taxable* gifts made prior to the present gift(s) (use rate schedule)	$
Step 3	*Subtract* step 2 result from step 1 result	$
Step 4	*Enter* gift tax credit remaining	$
Step 5	*Subtract* step 4 result from step 3 result to obtain *gift tax payable*	$

EXAMPLE 5

For instance, a widow gives $200,000 to her daughter and $25,000 to The American College in the last month of 2019. Both transfers are present-interest gifts. If she has made no previous taxable gifts in prior years, the computation is as follows:

Computing Taxable Gifts

Step 1	*List* total gifts for year		$225,000
Step 2	*Subtract* one-half of gift deemed to be made by donor's spouse (split gifts)	0	
	Gifts deemed to be made by donor		225,000
Step 3	*Subtract* annual exclusion(s)	(30,000)	
	Gifts after subtracting exclusion(s)		195,000
Step 4	*Subtract* marital deduction	0	
Step 5	*Subtract* charitable deduction	(10,000)	
	Taxable gifts		$185,000

To find the gift tax payable on this amount, the procedure is as follows:

Computing Taxable Gifts

Step 1	Compute gift tax on taxable gifts regardless of when made (use rate schedule)	$ 50,000
Step 2	Compute gift tax on all taxable gifts made prior to the present gift(s) (use gift and estate rate schedule)	$ 0
Step 3	Subtract step 2 result from step 1 result	$ 50,000
Step 4	Enter gift tax credit remaining (2019)	$4,505,800
Step 5	Subtract step 4 result from step 3 result to obtain gift tax payable	$ 0

The step 1 entry—$50,000—is found by using the rate schedule for estate and gift taxes, which shows that the tax on $150,000 is $38,800 and that there is a 32 percent tax on the remaining $35,000, which comes to $11,200 ($38,800 + $11,200 = $50,000). The gift tax credit of $4,505,800 corresponds to the $11,400,000 gift and estate tax exclusion in 2019. This amount is derived as follows. From the estate and gift tax rate schedule, the tax on $1,000,000 is $345,800. The tax rate on gifts in excess of $1,000,000 is 40%. Thus, the tax on the $11,400,000 exclusion is $4,505,800 (($11,400,000 - 1,000,000) x .40) + $345,800). When the $4,505,800 gift tax credit exceeds the tax, there is no tax. In other words, until an individual's aggregate lifetime taxable gifts exceed $11,400,000 in 2019, no gift tax is owed.

Note that the rate table is used regardless of when the gifts were made.

LO 6. 6   **Explain the requirements for reporting and paying the federal gift tax.**

REPORTING GIFTS AND PAYING TAX

Future-Interest Gifts

A gift tax return (Form 709) is required for a gift of a future interest regardless of the amount of the gift. For example, if a grantor transfers $100,000 to an irrevocable trust payable to the grantor's spouse for life and then to the grantor's son, a gift tax return is required regardless of the value of the son's remainder interest. The term *future interest* is defined in the same manner as for annual exclusion purposes: a gift in which the donee does not have the unrestricted right to the immediate use, possession, or enjoyment of the property or the income from the property.

Present-Interest Gifts

Because of the annual exclusion, no gift tax return is due until present-interest gifts made to one individual exceed the current exclusion amount. At that point, a return must be filed on an annual basis when a gift to one person in one year exceeds the current allowable annual exclusion amount, even if no gift tax is due (such as when gift-splitting provisions eliminate the tax). For example, in 2019 if a married woman gives $15,001 to her son, the transfer is tax free, assuming she never used any of her lifetime exclusion. However, a gift tax return is required, because the gift exceeds the annual-exclusion limit by $1. Also, remember that a return must be filed when a couple elects to split gifts.

A gift tax return must be filed and the gift tax, if any is due, must be paid by April 15 of the year following the year in which the taxable gifts were made. If an extension is granted for filing the income tax return, the time limit for filing the gift tax return is automatically extended also.

Gifts to a spouse that qualify for the marital deduction do not require the filing of a gift tax return. However, a 709 gift tax return must be filed when one spouse makes a marital deduction gift to a donee spouse and elects to have the transfer treated as qualifying terminable interest property (QTIP).

Gifts to Charities

Currently, gift tax returns are not required for charitable contributions made to domestic (U.S.) charities (Taxpayer Relief Act of 1997) of a donor's entire interest in the property transferred, that is, the donor has not transferred any of the interest to a noncharitable donee). In the case of a noncharitable donee, the charitable transfer must be reported at the same time the noncharitable gift is noted on a gift tax return.

If a split-interest gift is made to a charity (when there are charitable and noncharitable donees of the same gift), the donor cannot claim a charitable deduction for the entire value of the transfer. In this case, the donor must file and report the transfer subject to the filing requirements discussed above. For example, if an individual establishes a charitable remainder trust with the income payable to the individual's daughter for life and the remainder payable to a charity at her death, a gift tax return must be filed.

Qualified Charities
- U.S. states, territories, any political subdivision, District of Columbia
- certain religious, scientific, or charitable organizations
- certain fraternal societies, orders, or associations
- certain veterans' associations, organizations, or societies

Liability for Payment

The donor of the gift is primarily liable for the gift tax (Sec. 2502(c)). However, if the donor for any reason fails to pay the tax when it falls due, the donee becomes liable to the extent of the value of the gift (Sec. 6324(b)). This liability begins as soon as the donor fails to pay the tax when due.

Generally, the tax must be paid at the time the return is filed. However, reasonable extensions of time for payment of the tax can be granted by the IRS—but only on a showing of *undue hardship*. This condition means more than inconvenience. It must appear that the party liable to pay the tax will suffer a *substantial financial loss* unless an extension is granted. (A forced sale of property at a sacrifice price is an example of a substantial financial loss.)

LO 6. 7   Explain how the basis of gifted property is determined.

Determination of Basis of Gifted Property

carryover of donor's basis

When property is transferred from a donor to a donee and the donee later disposes of it through a sale or other taxable disposition, gain or loss depends on the donee's basis. In return, the donee's basis is carried over from the donor. **Carryover of donor's basis** means the *donor's* basis for the gift property immediately prior to the gift becomes the *donee's* basis for that property.

For example, if an individual pays $10 per share for stock and transfers it when it is worth $20, and the donee sells it when it is worth $30, the donee's basis for that property is the donor's $10 cost. The gain, therefore, is the difference between the amount realized by the donee, $30, and the donee's adjusted basis, $10.

An addition to basis is allowed for a portion of any gift tax paid on the transfer from the donor to the donee. The addition to basis is for that portion of the tax attributable to the appreciation in the gift property (the excess of the property's gift tax value over the donor's adjusted basis determined immediately before the gift). This increase in basis may be added to the donee's carryover basis for the property.

Stated as a formula, the basis of gifted property is the donor's basis increased as follows:

$$(\text{Net appreciation in value of gift} \div \text{Amount of gift}) \times \text{Gift tax paid}$$

This means that the basis carried over from the donor is increased only by the gift tax on the net appreciation in the value of the gift. For example, ignoring the annual exclusion, an individual bought stock worth $40,000 and gave it to his daughter when it was worth $100,000. If the donor paid $23,800 in gift taxes at the time of the gift, the daughter's basis is as follows:

Donor's basis $40,000

plus

Gift tax on *net appreciation in value* (here, the difference between the $100,000 value of the gift at the time of transfer and the donor's cost, $40,000)

($60,000 ÷ $100,000) × $23,800 = 14,280

equals

Daughter's basis $54,280

LO 6. 8   **Identify the various strategies and factors that must be examined in selecting property for gifts.**

Gift-Selection Factors

Gift tax strategy must be part of a well-planned and carefully coordinated estate planning effort. This, in turn, requires careful consideration of the type of property to gift. With any gifting plan, the selection of assets for gifting depends on the donor's particular goals and circumstances. There are a number of strategies and factors that must be examined in selecting the types of property that are appropriate for gifts. Some of the general considerations in planning gift tax property are as follows:

- Is the property likely to appreciate in value? Other things being equal, planners generally try to pick property that will appreciate substantially in value after the time of the transfer. Removal of the appreciation in the property (as well as the income generated by the transferred property) from the donor's estate should save a meaningful amount of estate taxes. These transfers will remove the anticipated future appreciation from the donor's estate at a time when the property value for gift tax is lower than the later estate tax value. Real estate, certain securities, artwork, collectibles, and life insurance are common examples of assets likely to appreciate. Life insurance, for example, is property with a low present value but a high appreciation potential. If held until the date the insured dies, its appreciation in value is guaranteed. Furthermore, because there are no carryover-basis problems, the proceeds are exempt from income tax. However, if the death of the donor is imminent, gifts of donor-owned life insurance are not recommended. The 3-year rule under IRC Sec. 2035 will cause inclusion of the policy proceeds in the decedent-donor's estate if the policy is gifted within 3 years of death. Even if a donor's property item has already appreciated by the time the donor considers gifting it, the asset may still be a good transfer choice. This could be the case if the property is expected to be sold and the donee is in a lower income tax bracket than the donor.

- Is the donee in a lower income tax bracket than the donor? Income splitting between the donor and the donee may be obtained by transferring high-income-producing property to a family member in a lower bracket. Naturally, high-income-producing property is best for this purpose. Generally, though, high-income-producing property should not be gifted to children under the age of 19 (or 24 if a full-time student) because of the kiddie-tax rules. High-dividend participating preferred stock in a closely held business or stock in a successful S corporation is a good example of high-income-producing property. (Note: S corporation stock should not be gifted if the transfer will terminate S status.) Conversely, if the donor is in a lower bracket than the donee (for instance, if the parent who is retired makes a gift to a financially successful, middle-aged child), the use of low-yield, growth-type property may be indicated.

- Is the property subject to indebtedness? A gift of property subject to indebtedness that is greater than its cost to the donor may result in a taxable gain. A gift of such property causes the donor to realize capital gain on the excess of the debt over basis.

- Does the property have a sale price lower than the donor's basis in the property? If so, the donor should consider selling the property to take advantage of the loss deduction for income tax purposes and either gift the sale proceeds or select other gift property.

EXAMPLE

The gift of a building that cost the donor $10,000, appreciated to $100,000, and was mortgaged to $70,000 results in an income tax gain to the donor on the difference between the debt outstanding at the time of the transfer and the donor's basis (assume $70,000 for the debt outstanding and the donor's basis of $10,000). In this example, the gain is $60,000. It is realized at the time the gift becomes complete.

- Is the donor likely to need or want to use the property in the future? If there is a reasonable possibility the donor may want the property, such as a residence, at some later time, other gift property should be selected.

- Is the property necessary for qualification of favorable tax benefits under Secs. 303 (special provision for capital gains for redemptions), 6166 (installment payment of estate taxes), and 2032A (special use valuation)? To qualify under these Internal Revenue sections, a decedent's estate must include specified percentages of certain businesses or farm property. Therefore, if a donor is considering making gifts of business interests or closely held stock, the donor needs to consider whether or not the transfer(s) will disqualify the donor's estate from obtaining the favorable tax treatment allowed to farms and small businesses under Code Secs. 303 (redemption of stock for death taxes), 6166 (installment payments of estate tax), and 2032A (special-use valuation).

- Is the gift property's basis above, below, or approximately the same as the property's fair market value? As stated above, income tax law forbids the recognition of a capital loss if the subject matter of the gift has a basis above the property's present fair market value. Neither the donor nor the donee can recognize a capital loss with respect to such property. Furthermore, if the gift property's basis is above present fair market value, there is no gift tax addition to basis because that addition depends on appreciation at the time of the transfer. Since there is no appreciation, no gift tax addition is allowed. Factored into any gratuitous transfer arrangement, whether it is an occasional transfer or a structured gifting plan, is that the donor and donee must be mindful of the general rule that the donor's basis in gifted property carries over to the donee.

Conversely, if the donor's basis for income tax purposes is very low relative to the fair market value of the property, it might be advantageous to retain the property until death because of the *stepped-up-basis-at-death rules*. (This is especially true if inclusion of the property will generate little or no estate tax because it will pass to a surviving spouse and qualify for a marital deduction, or if the asset owner is sheltered by the basic credit amount.) The result of the stepped-up-basis provision is that a portion of the future capital gain is avoided in the event the property is later sold by the estate or heir. But if the property should be sold, it may pay to transfer it to a low-bracket family member by gift; that individual could then sell it and realize a lower capital-gains tax.

Another possibility is that the donor's basis is approximately the same as or only slightly below fair market value. Again, the rules providing for a gift tax addition to basis are of little help, since the addition to basis is limited to the gift tax allocable to appreciation in the property at the time of the gift.

There are also numerous nontax subjective issues that donors making sizable gifts should address:

- Is the gift likely to cause the donor any financial concerns or reduce the donor's customary standard of living?

- Does the donor have expectations or concerns with respect to the donee's ability to manage or invest the gift?

- Is the donor concerned about equalizing the value or nature of gifts to donees such as children or grandchildren?

- Is conflict likely among donees if more than one potential donee wants the same property subject to gifting?

- Is the donor concerned about the stability of the donees' marriages or the potential for future divorce?

- Is the donor worried about the donees having creditors' claims?

Factors in Gift Selection
- property's likelihood of appreciating in value
- unlikelihood of donor's needing the property in the future
- property's not being subject to indebtedness (greater than basis)
- the income tax brackets of the donor and donee
- carryover of basis to donee
- possible estate disqualification from other favorable tax treatment Code sections

CHAPTER REVIEW

Key Terms and Concepts

estate and gift tax systems
appreciation
gift splitting
present-interest gifts
future-interest gift
Crummey powers
Sec. 2503(b) trust
Sec. 2503(c) trust

UTMA/UGMA
529 plan
gift tax marital deduction
alien spouse
super-annual exclusion
gift tax charitable deduction
carryover of donor's basis

Chapter 6: Review Questions

1. What is the nature of the gift tax, and what is its objective? [LO 6.1]

2. What is the effect of the estate and gift tax system? [LO 6.1]

3. What are the tax-related incentives for making lifetime gifts? [LO 6.2]

4. Larry and Louise Longfellow are considering giving $16,000 to each of their three children in 2019.

    a. Can Louise make the entire gift from her own funds and still split the gift with Larry?

    b. How much is each spouse deemed to be giving after the split?

    c. Explain whether the consent for the split gift can be made after Larry's death. [LO 6.3]

5. Explain the purpose of the annual gift tax exclusion. [LO 6.3]

6. Cecelia and Henry Hunt have seven children. Henry would like to give each child as much money as possible in 2019 without exceeding the annual exclusion limits. Assume Cecelia will join in the gifts. Compute the maximum total amount Henry can give the children in 2019 within the limits he has established. [LO 6.3]

7. Will the following transfers qualify for the annual exclusion in 2019? Explain.

    a. Bill Nagle gives his son, Bill, Jr., an outright gift of $16,000.

    b. Bill transfers $14,000 in cash to a trustee. Income from the trust is to be paid to Bill's daughter annually, and the remainder is to go to Bill's son upon the daughter's death.

    c. Same facts as in 7b. above, but the trustee is given the discretion to accumulate rather than distribute income.

    d. Bill transfers $14,000 in cash to a trust, but the trustee is required to accumulate all trust income until Bill, Jr., is 21, at which time the entire principal is to be distributed to him. [LO 6.4]

8. Mrs. Martin is considering the gratuitous transfer of $50,000 to her daughter, Nancy, in trust for Nancy's lifetime, with remainder to Nancy's children. The trustee has discretion to distribute income. Explain whether this gift qualifies as one of a present interest, future interest, or both, if trust income is distributable to Nancy at the discretion of the trustee only. [LO 6.4]

9. For what reasons might a donor consider making large and/or recurring gifts to minors in a form other than as outright gifts? [LO 6.4]

10. Gifting money into a 529 plan can be a good way to fund a child or grandchild's college and graduate school costs. However, there are some gift tax issues and funding limitations. Explain. [LO 6.4]

11. Explain if and when the following types of property may qualify for the annual exclusion:

    a. an outright gift of life insurance,

    b. life insurance transferred to a trust with no Crummey demand powers,

    c. premium payments on life insurance owned by a trust where the beneficiary has Crummey demand powers,

    d. gifts in trust of closely held non-dividend-paying stock [LO 6.4]

12. Distinguish between an IRC Sec. 2503(b) trust and a Sec. 2503(c) trust regarding:

    a.   distribution of income,

    b.   discretion of trustee in accumulating income,

    c.   time by which trust principal is required to be distributed,

    d.   payment of trust assets if minor dies [LO 6.4]

13. Compare an IRC Sec. 2503(c) trust to the Uniform Gifts to Minors Act regarding:

    a.   type of property that can be used,

    b.   allowable dispositive provisions for gift assets,

    c.   investment flexibility that can be given to the trustee,

    d.   time by which assets must be distributed [LO 6.4]

14. Josephine Carmeron gave her husband, Thomas, $210,000. How is this gift treated for gift tax purposes? [LO 6.3]

15. Mr. Fisher is married and has made gifts of his own property in 2019. Neither Mr. Fisher nor his wife has made any prior gifts. Mrs. Fisher joined in making all gifts to the following third parties: $36,000 in cash to their son; $54,000 (market value) of common stock, which cost $35,000, to Mr. Fisher's brother; $32,000 (market value) of common stock, which cost $5,000, to the XYZ Hospital, a nonprofit public charitable institution; and a gift to Mrs. Fisher of $52,000 (market value) of corporate bonds, which cost $60,000.

    a.   What would be the total taxable gifts, if any, made by Mr. Fisher in 2019 after taking into account all available exclusions and deductions? Explain each step in your answer.

    b.   What would be the total taxable gifts, if any, made by Mrs. Fisher in 2019? Explain each step in your answer. [LO 6.3]

16. Assume that Paul Gaffney, an unmarried donor, gave $60,000 to his friend, Ellen, and $25,000 to the American Red Cross in 2019.

    a.   Compute the gift tax payable, assuming Paul had made no prior gifts. Use the tax rate schedule for computing the estate and gift taxes. (Refer to table on 6.4)

    b.   Compute the gift tax payable, assuming instead that Paul had made $100,000 of taxable gifts back in 2008. (Refer to table on 6.4) [LO 6.3]

17. Explain if and when a gift tax return would be required in the following situations in 2019:

    a. Marvin Jackson gives his niece a $2,000 charm bracelet for her birthday.

    b. Jessie Rotelli gives her husband a Mercedes-Benz valued at $60,000.

    c. Pat Cressito places $15,000 in trust for her niece. The trustee has the discretion to accumulate income until Pat's niece is 21. After that, all principal and income will be distributed to the niece. [LO 6.5]

18. Compute the donee's basis for income tax purposes in the following situation: Lee Rostler bought stock for $50,000. He gave it to his son when it was worth $150,000. Lee paid $38,800 in gift taxes on the transfer. Assume Lee had already used his basic credit amount for gift tax purposes and his annual exclusion amount for the year of the gift to his son. [LO 6.7]

19. You have been discussing the use of a gift-giving program with a client. Explain to her in general terms what characteristics the ideal subject of a gift would have. [LO 6.8]

Chapter 6: Review Answers

1. The gift tax is an excise tax. As such, it is not levied on the gift itself or the right to receive it but on an individual's right to transfer property to another for less than full consideration. The objective of the tax is to equalize the transfer tax treatment between taxpayers who make lifetime gifts and those who transfer their assets at death.

2. The nature of the estate and gift tax system reflects the fact that the tax is imposed on all property transferred in a taxable manner regardless of when the transfers occur. The tax is imposed at one set of rates, regardless of whether the transfer takes place during the donor's lifetime or is testamentary. Thus, transfers should move the donor up the progressive rate structure as they occur. For this reason, current gifts are added to prior gifts to determine the tax bracket applicable to such gifts. (As we will learn later, life-time gifts made after 1976 are added to the taxable estate of a decedent to determine the estate tax bracket applicable to testamentary transfers.)

3. The tax advantages of making lifetime gifts are as follows:

    •   An individual can give tax free up to $15,000 (2019) per donee per year ($30,000 if he or she is married and uses gift splitting).

    •   If a gift is made more than 3 years before the donor's death, the amount of any gift tax paid is not brought back into the donor's estate and, thus, avoids the gross-up rule.

    •   Any appreciation in the gift escapes estate taxation.

    •   There may be income tax advantages if the amount of taxable income moves from a high-tax-bracket donor to a low-tax-bracket donee.

    •   Gifts of the right type of assets may enable the donor's estate to meet the tests for an IRC Sec. 303 redemption, a Sec. 6166 installment payout of taxes, or a Sec. 2032A special-use valuation.

    •   No gift taxes have to be paid until the donor makes cumulative taxable gifts in excess of the basic (gift tax) exclusion amount of $11.4 million in 2019.

4. a. Louise can make the entire gift herself and still split the gift with Larry as long as he consents to gift splitting.

    b. Each spouse is deemed to have given $8,000.

    c. Gifts made while both Louise and Larry were alive, even if Larry dies before signing the consent, can still be split as long as Larry's executor makes that election.

5. The purpose of the annual gift tax exclusion is to eliminate the need for a taxpayer to report numerous small gifts and, thus, to lessen administrative record keeping.

6. Henry can give each child $30,000 and elect to treat it as a split gift with Cecelia. Therefore, he will file a gift tax return and make the election to have Cecelia split the gift with him. Although a gift tax return must be filed in order to make this election, no tax will be due. This is because when a person makes a gift and splits it with his or her spouse, it is treated as if $15,000 was given to the donee by each spouse, although, in fact, the gift was made by the donor-spouse. Therefore, Henry can give a total of $210,000 to his children in 2019 without exceeding the annual exclusion.

7. a. Yes. An outright gift of $16,000 is a present-interest gift. Since an annual exclusion of $15,000 may be taken in 2019, Bill has made a taxable gift of $1,000 to his son, Bill, Jr.

   b. Bill has made two gifts in this case. The gift of income to his daughter (which can be measured as the right to receive income for life based on her life expectancy) qualifies for the annual exclusion. The gift of the remainder interest to Bill's son is a future-interest gift and, although it can be valued actuarially at the time of the gift, no annual exclusion will be allowed since the son cannot enjoy and possess the property until his sister dies.

   c. Since the trustee can accumulate income and is not required to distribute it, such income may be added to the principal to increase the remainderman's interest. Since this is the case, no annual exclusion will be allowed for either the gift to the income beneficiary or the gift to the remainderman.

   d. This transfer will qualify for the annual exclusion as a transfer to a Sec. 2503(c) trust. Although the trustee may accumulate trust income until the beneficiary reaches age 21, the entire principal must be distributed to him at that time. Sec. 2503(c) permits an exception to the general rule denying an annual exclusion when income is accumulated. However, the principal must become distributable when the beneficiary attains age 21.

8. In this situation, neither the gift of the trust income to Nancy nor the gift of the remainder or corpus to Nancy's children is eligible for the annual exclusion. A present-interest gift that qualifies for the annual exclusion generally transfers an immediate right to possession or enjoyment of the property or property interest to the donee. When a restriction or postponement is placed on the donee's right to the use, possession, or enjoyment of the property or interest therein, the gift is one of a future interest.

In this situation, the income is distributable only at the discretion of the trustee, which means that the income may be accumulated if the trustee so desires. Thus Nancy has no immediate right to the use and enjoyment of the income; therefore the income interest is a gift of a future interest. Likewise, the use and enjoyment of the remainder by Nancy's children is postponed until Nancy's death, making it a gift of a future interest.

9. Although minors can buy, sell, and deal with limited types of property (U.S. savings bonds, for example), outright gifts of other property can create problems. For example, in some states, minors cannot purchase, care for, sell, or transfer their own property. Some states do not allow securities to be registered in a minor's name. In many states, a minor can disaffirm a sale of stock sold at a low price that later rises in value. Similarly, a buyer receives no assurance of permanent title when a minor signs a real estate deed. And perhaps most important, a parent may not want to give a minor control over a large amount of cash or other property.

10. A 529 plan qualifies for the present interest annual exclusion amount of $15,000 in 2019. You can also gift up to $75,000 in a single year and elect to treat it as if you contributed over a five-year period. Additionally, you can engage in gift splitting for up to $150,000 per beneficiary. However, remember that there are maximum caps on 529 plans depending on the state in which it is set up in—with the top contribution limits being in the $500,000 range in 2019.

11. a. An outright gift of life insurance qualifies for the annual exclusion.

    b. For the annual exclusion to apply, trust beneficiaries must receive a present interest. Simply transferring life insurance to the trust does not meet the present-interest requirement.

    c. Premium payments on life insurance owned by a trust qualify for the annual exclusion if beneficiaries have Crummey demand powers. Crummey demand powers give beneficiaries a present interest.

    d. Non-dividend-paying stock held in trust may not qualify for the annual exclusion. In many cases, the IRS has held that the exclusion does not apply because the stock does not represent a present interest.

12. a. A Sec. 2503(b) trust requires a current (annual) distribution of income. A Sec. 2503(c) trust does not require income to be distributed currently.

    b. The trustee is given no discretion regarding income accumulation in a Sec. 2503(b) trust. In a Sec. 2503(c) trust, the trustee can be given broad discretion.

c. In a Sec. 2503(b) trust, principal can be distributed whenever the agreement speci-fies. It can be paid when the donee reaches 21, or corpus can be held for as long as the beneficiary lives or for a shorter period. Principal can also bypass the income beneficiary entirely and go to individuals the grantor or beneficiary selects.

A Sec. 2503(c) trust requires that principal be distributed when the donee reaches age 21 (or at a later age if the donor so stipulates, depending on the donee's nonexercise of the right to immediate distribution at age 21).

d. A Sec. 2503(b) trust can control disposition of trust assets if the minor dies before receiving the trust corpus; assets do not have to be paid to the minor's estate or appointees. With a Sec. 2503(c) trust, income and principal go to the beneficiary's estate or appointees if the minor dies before age 21.

13. a. Almost any type of property can be used in a Sec. 2503(c) trust. The type of prop-erty gifted under the UGMA must be permitted by statute.

b. With a Sec. 2503(c) trust, the donor can provide for disposition of trust assets. Disposition of trust assets must follow statutory guidelines under the UGMA.

c. The trustee can be given broad investment powers under a Sec. 2503(c) trust. Under the UGMA, investment powers are limited by statute.

d. A Sec. 2503(c) trust can continue even after the beneficiary is 21; furthermore, the trustee can distribute assets between the state's lawful age of majority and age 21. Trust assets must be paid to the beneficiary when he or she reaches majority under the UGMA.

14. There is no gift tax. A person who transfers property to his or her spouse is allowed an unlimited gift tax marital deduction.

15. a. and b. The total taxable gifts made by Mr. Fisher and Mrs. Fisher in 2019 would amount to $15,000 each, as shown below:

		Recipient	Mr. Fisher's Taxable Gifts	Mrs. Fisher's Taxable Gifts
Value of gift	$36,000	Son	$18,000	$18,000
Less annual exclusion			(15,000)	(15,000)
Taxable (net) gift			$3,000	$3,000
Value of gift	$54,000	Brother	$27,000	$27,000
Less annual exclusion			(15,000)	(15,000)

	Recipient	Mr. Fisher's Taxable Gifts	Mrs. Fisher's Taxable Gifts
Taxable (net) gift		$12,000	$12,000
Value of gift	$32,000 XYZ Hospital	$16,000	$16,000
Less annual exclusion		(15,000)	(15,000)
Less charitable deduction		(1,000)	(1,000)
Taxable (net) gift		0	0
Value of gift	$52,000 Mrs. Fisher	$52,000	
Less annual exclusion		(15,000)	
Less marital deduction		(37,000)	
Taxable (net) gift		0	

First, for federal gift tax purposes, Mr. Fisher could split the $36,000 cash gift to his son in half, reducing it to $18,000. A gift made by one spouse to any person (other than the other spouse) can be treated as though one-half was made by the donor and one-half was made by the donor's spouse, provided the spouse consents to the gift. In this case, Mrs. Fisher did join in the gift.

In addition, each donor is entitled to an annual exclusion for gifts of a present interest to each donee. The cash gift is a gift of a present interest, and Mr. Fisher made no other gifts to his son this year.

Second, for federal gift tax purposes, the value of the gift of stock to Mr. Fisher's brother is its market value of $54,000. Again, Mr. Fisher could split the gift with his wife, reducing the amount given from each spouse to $27,000. Mr. Fisher could deduct the 2019 $15,000 annual exclusion, leaving a balance of $12,000.

Third, there would be no federal gift tax on the gift of stock to the XYZ Hospital. In computing his taxable gifts, a donor may take an annual exclusion and deduct in full the balance of all gifts to qualified charitable institutions.

Fourth, lifetime gifts between spouses are not taxable because there is an unlimited gift tax marital deduction. It is no longer necessary to file a gift tax return when one spouse makes an otherwise taxable gift to the other one.

Mrs. Fisher would have taxable gifts of $15,000 during 2019.

Mrs. Fisher's share of the $36,000 cash gift to her son is $18,000. From this $18,000, Mrs. Fisher may deduct her $15,000 annual exclusion, leaving a net gift of $3,000.

Mrs. Fisher's share of the $54,000 gift of stock to Mr. Fisher's brother is $27,000. From this amount, Mrs. Fisher may deduct her $15,000 annual exclusion; $12,000 is her net gift.

Since all gifts to third parties must be split between the spouses, if any one gift is to be so split, one-half of the gift to XYZ Hospital would be considered a gift made by Mrs. Fisher. However, all gifts to qualified charities are fully deductible for gift tax purposes.

16. a.

i.	Total gifts for 2019	$ 85,000
ii.	Subtract annual exclusion(s)	(30,000)
iii.	Gifts after subtracting exclusion(s)	55,000
iv.	Subtract charitable deduction	(10,000)
	Taxable gifts	$ 45,000

Compute Gift Tax Payable

v.	Gift tax on all taxable gifts	$ 9,400
vi.	Gift tax credit (2019)	$4,505,800
	Gift tax payable	0

b.

i.	Gift tax on all taxable gifts regardless of when made	$ 37,300
ii.	Gift tax on all taxable gifts made prior to present gifts	(23,800)
iii.	Subtract b(ii) from b(i)	$ 13,500
iv.	Enter remaining basic credit amount ($4,505,800 – $23,800)	$4,482,000
v.	Subtract b(iv) from b(iii) to obtain gift tax payable	If the result is a negative number, zero gift tax is owed.

17. a. No gift tax return is required because the gift is under the annual exclusion amount.

b. No gift tax return is required because Jesse's gift qualifies for the marital deduction.

c. A gift tax return is required because the $15,000 in trust is a future-interest gift.

18.

$$\begin{array}{ll}
\$150,000 & \text{Gift value} \\
-50,000 & \text{Donor's basis} \\
\hline
\$100,000 & \text{Appreciation}
\end{array}$$

$$\$100,000 \div \$150,000 \times \$38,800 = \$25,866.66 \text{ Gift tax on net appreciation}$$

$$\begin{array}{ll}
\$50,000.00 & \text{Donor's basis} \\
\$25,866.66 & \text{Gift tax on net appreciation} \\
\hline
\$75,866.66 & \text{Basis of gift to Lee's son}
\end{array}$$

19. Some of the characteristics of an ideal gift are as follows:

- The property is likely to appreciate in value.

- The donee is in a lower-income-tax bracket than the donor.

- The property is not subject to indebtedness.

- The donor is not likely to want or need the property in the future.

- It is not necessary for the donor to keep the property in order for his or her estate to qualify for advantageous tax benefits under Secs. 303, 6166, or 2032A.

- The property's basis is approximately the same as its fair market value.

Chapter 7:

Transfers at Death

Learning Objectives

An understanding of the material in this chapter should enable the student to

LO 7.1   **Explain what a will is.**

LO 7. 2   **Describe the advantages of a will, and explain the requirements for a valid will.**

LO 7. 3   **Describe the two common modes of distribution under wills, and explain what types of provisions are found in wills.**

LO 7. 4   **Describe other types of wills.**

LO 7. 5   **Explain how a will may be amended or revoked.**

LO 7. 6   **Explain the spouse's right of election against a will**

LO 7. 7   **Describe the grounds for contesting a will.**

LO 7. 8   **Describe the use of testamentary trusts and pour-over trusts in wills.**

LO 7. 9   **Explain how property can be transferred at death by contract.**

LO 7. 10   **Explain how property can be transferred at death by operation of law.**

Property is transferred at death by one of several methods. It can pass under the terms of a validly drawn will. Property may also be transferred or assigned by contract designations in, for example, life insurance policies; and prenuptial and postnuptial agreements. Finally, property may pass by operation of law. Jointly owned property with right of survivorship falls into this category, as does property passing by intestate succession.

LO 7.1   **Explain what a will is.**

TRANSFERS BY WILL

Introduction

A *will* is a personal declaration of one's intentions regarding the disposition of property at death. It describes matters to be taken care of after death. It becomes legally enforceable at death and is not operative until that time. Prior to one's death, a will may be amended, revoked, or destroyed by the maker at any time.

If an individual dies without a valid will, he or she is referred to as dying intestate. If you die without a valid will your property will still transfer to someone else. Your property will transfer by contract, trust, or operation of law. Any property not covered by a will, contract, trust, or other operation of law mechanism (like survivorship interests) will pass by way of the state's succession laws. State succession laws vary dramatically and they determine how property passes to your heirs when you die intestate. Lastly, to die testate means to die with a valid will.

Wills
- intestate—dying *without* a valid will
- testate—dying *with* a valid will

executor/executrix

Wills are not a one-trick pony. In fact, wills can accomplish a tremendous number of goals. Wills can help you manage, dispose, and control your property after your death. A properly drawn will can assure the orderly and sound distribution of an estate. Because all property not transferred by contract or operation of law must be transferred through probate, the will becomes the estate plan for all probate property. Writing a will allows the decedent to name a personal representative of his or her choice, who is called an **executor/executrix**. If an executor or executrix is not named, the probate court will appoint a personal representative called an administrator to handle your estate. There is usually a security bond requirement, often called a surety bond or executor bond. The surety bond can help the value of the estate avoid loss due to the wrongful actions of the executor. The price of the bond can vary depending on the value of the estate, credit worthiness of the executor, and state requirements. However, many wills waive the requirement of the bond, reducing the cost and burden of acting as an executor. However, in a very large and complex estate, it could be a good idea to keep the bond requirement or even plan for further insurance coverage through the will. The decedent also has the flexibility through the will to name a successor executor should the named executor be unable or unwilling to serve. Those matters can be attended to privately without court intervention. The will should also discuss the authority and power of the executor, a process for removal of an executor, a successor executor, and the compensation of the executor.

Fiduciaries of Estates
- executor/executrix
- personal representative
- personal administrator

A carefully drawn will contains positive directions and instructions to the executor. An executor is someone chosen by the decedent who is responsible for administering the estate. The executor should be an individual or corporate fiduciary who is competent to perform the required duties and who is trusted by the testator. The testator can give the executor broad powers and discretion with respect to the management and distribution of the estate. It is as if the executor steps into the decedent's shoes during the estate administration period. The executor is charged with the following duties:

- gathering the assets of the estate
- probating the will
- filing tax returns
- paying taxes and other debts of the estate
- providing interim support for the beneficiaries
- settling the decedent's business interests
- collecting benefits and income due to the estate
- filing an accounting with the probate court (also referred to as orphans' court or surrogate's court in some states)
- distributing property to intended beneficiaries
- closing the estate

While form documents can be used to help develop a will, no two wills should be exactly the same. People often have different planning objectives, needs, desires, and assets. Additionally, the requirements for wills vary from state to state. If you relocate in retirement or at any point in your life you should have an attorney review your will to make sure it is still valid and enforceable in your new state.

Contents of Wills

exordium clause

A will is a legal declaration of a person's intended disposition of property. The beginning usually includes a statement by the testator regarding the testator's intention of domicile. This is often referred to as an exordium clause. An **exordium clause** identifies the testator, his or her location, and desire to create a valid will. The statement usually reads: "I, John Jones of Marion County, Indiana, declare this to be my last will, hereby revoking all former wills and codicils." Thus, John Jones has declared himself to be a resident of the state of Indiana. The statement implies that he wishes his property to be governed by Indiana law. This statement is particularly important if the testator owns residential real estate in more than one state. Additionally, it is usually helpful to have a clause revoking all prior wills even if you did not actually draft another will at any point. This can help cut down on fraud and other issues. A will should contain clear, positive directions. A will is usually looked to for guidance as if the testator were present directing the disposition of the property.

Contents of a Will:
1. Statement of ownership (i.e., it's your will)
2. Statement of domicile
3. Revocation of all prior wills
4. Establishment of an executor
5. Alternate or successor executors
6. Executor bond requirements
7. Executor compensation clause
8. Statement of executor powers
9. Survivorship clause
10. General and specific property bequests
11. Residuary bequests
12. Guardianships
13. Payments of debts and taxes
14. No-contest clause
15. Savings clause
16. Burial directions

precatory language

bequest

A will may contain directions regarding burial or cremation, perpetual care of a gravesite, and payment for a tombstone or memorial plaque. However, these burial decisions should also be placed elsewhere since the will is often not consulted until after an individual is buried or cremated. If there are specific bequests, they are usually made early in the will. These bequests may be made to individuals or charities in specific amounts or of specific objects. When a testator wants some possessions to pass to specific persons but realizes that his or her current wishes may change, the use of precatory language in the will may solve matters. **Precatory language** is a written expression of the testator's wishes regarding specific matters. Precatory language in a will usually states that the testator has preferences and wishes concerning his or her personal effects. The will may even mention a separate list or letter that identifies particular items and desired distributions. Although the separate writing is not part of the will, it is kept with the will. The testator is then able to alter the list or letter as necessary. Although the executor is not bound to carry out the specific preferences, the separate writing provides guidance. Alternatively, a testator may create a list of certain personal property items and name the intended beneficiaries. If the testator's state of domicile permits, the will may dispose of the personal property by reference to the list. If nothing more, such a list may, in a sense, serve as moral direction to the beneficiaries and reduce disputes by explanation of the testator's wishes. State law should always be reviewed prior to using precatory language. Property passing to others under a will may be referred to as a **bequest**.

Bequests may be made in one of four ways:

- bequests of specific property
- bequests of cash
- bequests of cash to be paid from a special source
- bequests that are paid out of the residue or from what remains after all other legacies and expenses have been paid

EXAMPLE

An unmarried individual with several friends may make many specific bequests of cherished objects, cash, and intangible personal property. The testator may then direct that the residue of the estate be given to several charities after payment of all expenses and taxes. In other words, the charities will get what is left rather than receiving specific gifts. A will may also be written the other way, with a specific gift to a charity made before the residue is distributed.

Also found in the early part of the will is a paragraph directing the disposition of the decedent's tangible personal property, including the transfer of automobiles and automobile insurance. An executor is usually given broad discretion either to dispose of tangible personal property that is not usable or to allocate such property among the beneficiaries at the executor's sole discretion if agreement cannot be reached among them. You will also want to make sure you have a survivorship clause in the will that ensures your bequests only go to those individuals that survive you. In some cases, you might not want this and will want the property to transfer to your brother's family even if he died. So, if that is the case, make sure the will fits your individual bequest needs.

ademption

It may happen that the decedent does not have sufficient assets to make all the bequests provided for in the will. The state statute provides the order in which bequests are to be abated or satisfied if there are insufficient assets for all of them. In addition, if the decedent disposed of a particular piece of property that was the subject of a specific bequest, the issue of **ademption** arises. The legatees of that bequest get nothing unless the will contains a provision to substitute other property.

After taking care of specific bequests and tangible personal property, the residue of the estate is distributed. This provision may or may not include the disposition of specific real estate or of a business interest that may be treated separately. If the residue of the estate is made payable to a trust, the direction is contained in the residuary clause.

In a will, the testator designates an executor, a successor executor, or coexecutors. A will usually contains clauses that give the executor specific and general powers, such as the power to pay the taxes and debts of the decedent as well as the taxes and debts of the estate, the power to collect life insurance proceeds payable to the estate, and all other powers that an executor must have over the property to make the appropriate transfers and distributions. As noted elsewhere, it is customary for the will to contain a clause stating that the executor may serve without bond.

A will may also contain a clause stating that the testator either exercises or declines to exercise a power of appointment, if such a power of appointment has been granted to him or her. Carefully drafted powers of appointment often require that they be specifically exercised or waived within the donee's will. However, if a testator is the holder of a power of appointment, his or her wishes in regard to this power should be expressly set out in the will. This prevents an inadvertent exercise of the power if the will is imperfectly drafted.

Another useful type of provision is one directing that the executor hold any assets for the benefit of minors or incompetents—or transfer these assets to the individuals responsible for caring for such disabled persons.

There is no question that having a valid will has many advantages in comparison to intestacy. However, a will rarely provides all the guidance the decedent's executor and surviving relatives may need. Typically, there are many questions to be resolved that are not addressed in the will. To help solve this problem, a testator can also leave additional written instructions to help answer anticipated questions.

One area that is sometimes in doubt involves funeral arrangements. It is not uncommon for surviving loved ones to differ as to what the deceased wanted in terms of burial. Did the decedent want a memorial service, cremation or burial, open casket or closed casket?

These are just some of the questions that routinely arise. If the decedent had the foresight to prepare a separate document stating the desired funeral arrangements, there would be no doubt or decision making for grieving relatives. The instructions could include the names of the individual(s) the decedent would like to speak at a service, the clothing the decedent wishes to be buried in, the amount of money to be spent, the name of the funeral home, type of religious service, and so forth.

It is also useful for the instructions to include the names and phone numbers of the decedent's lawyer, doctors, accountant, broker, insurance agent, veterinarian, plumber, electrician, and lawn care service, as well as insurance and pension plan information. A written inventory of assets, location of assets, value of each asset, length of time owned, and instructions regarding the assets (such as directions about investments or family business) is certain to help the executor and family.

For instance, a decedent may have owned some furniture or artwork that only he or she knew was quite valuable. The article may be gifted, thrown away, or sold for far below its true value by an unknowledgeable family member or executor. An inventory and instructions relieve the burden on the survivors to guess what the decedent would have wanted and help to preserve family harmony during an often stressful time.

If you are concerned about heirs challenging your will, you can add a no-contest clause. The no-contest clause basically removes the heir from any inheritance or gives them a nominal amount, even sometimes $1, if they challenge the validity of the will or their share of the property. No-contest wills do not work well if you leave someone out entirely as there is no downside to the challenge. However, they can work well for someone who stands to lose money if they challenge the will and fail. Some states have restrictions on no-contest clauses, allowing for contests in good faith and under other circumstances.

Make sure you also have a residuary clause which catches any assets that were not distributed elsewhere in your estate or will. Sometimes you can use this residuary amount to pay estate costs or taxes. Additionally, you could roll this money into a testamentary pour-over trust in order to manage and distribute the property. At the same time, you should make mention of where and how you want debts, taxes, and creditors paid from your estate.

In addition to distribution of property, the will can also be an appropriate place to name a guardian and successor guardian for your minor children. While the court is not bound by your recommendation, the will carries a lot of weight in determining the guardian for your minor children.

A savings clause can also be useful, depending on the state, to eliminate any language and fix the will if there is a defective portion without destroying the validity of the entire will.

LO 7. 2   **Describe the advantages of a will, and explain the requirements for a valid will.**

Advantages of a Will

It is only by will that an executor of choice can be named. The will also may provide that an executor shall serve without posting a bond or other security in order to perform his or her duties. Under a will, a decedent may transfer real estate, stock, or business interests as he or she wishes. The decedent can direct disposition of tangible personal property separately from the residue (the part of the estate that remains after all other gifts have been made). The decedent can also assure the maximum marital deduction desired for property passing to a spouse. The estate's share of the tax burden can be specified. In the absence of an instruction regarding payment of taxes, state statutes will generally allocate the expenses of the estate, including federal estate taxes, to the residuary share of the estate—that is, the residuary beneficiaries—in proportion to their respective inheritances. This means that the beneficiaries bear the tax burden proportionately. For example, both federal and state law could empower an executor to collect federal estate taxes from the named beneficiaries of life insurance policies included in a decedent's gross estate. Alternatively, by inserting a tax apportionment clause in the will, the decedent has the power to direct the source of tax money. A direction could also be given that taxes are to be paid from the residue of the estate to relieve the marital share or specific bequests of the tax burden.

A guardian may also be designated to care for minor children or other legally incompetent dependents. A will may contain trust provisions to protect the interests of beneficiaries from their creditors. Trusts under a will can be created to control the management and timing of the distribution of income and principal from the estate. Executors and trustees can be given broad powers to invest and manage property.

Wills give testators the ability to leave their property as they choose and not as the state dictates. Testators have the ability to name charitable beneficiaries in their wills. They can make gifts to anyone they choose regardless of the relationship. In writing wills, testators may also disinherit someone who would otherwise take under the intestacy laws.

Advantages of a Valid Will

- avoid intestacy laws
- control
- choice of executor
- waiver of executor requirement to post bond
- distribution of property to chosen beneficiaries

- transfer of property to charity
- maximum advantage of marital deduction
- direct source of property to pay death taxes
- designation of guardian for minor children

Testators can designate orders of survival of themselves and their spouses in the event of a common disaster. This prevents the loss of the marital deduction and avoids potential additional taxation. Of course, it must be assumed that a will has been validly drawn and executed to obtain the above advantages.

REQUIREMENTS OF A TYPICAL WILL

While most wills are professionally drafted and executed under the guidance of an attorney, other types of wills may be acceptable as valid under state law if they conform to certain formalities and statutory requirements. Other kinds of wills are *holographic* and *nuncupative* wills, and the requirements for them are discussed later in this chapter. A primary requirement of all written wills is that the instrument be signed at the end. All writing after the testator's signature or mark, other than the acknowledgment of witnesses or a self-proving provision, is not recognized as part of the body of the will. In addition to the testator's signature, a will should be dated. Many states require witnessing the signing of the will by two or three competent people. To prevent the possible voiding of an inheritance, a beneficiary with a financial interest should not be a witness to the signing of a will. Most, but not all, states require a will to be witnessed at the time of execution. However, all states require some attestation by witnesses when the will is admitted to probate. The attesting witnesses must swear that they are familiar with the testator's signature and that the signature at the end of the document is the testator's true signature. The date, testator's signature, and witnesses are the three most common will requirements by states. However, some states will require more information like a clause distributing property or a clause stating that it is your will.

General Will Requirements
signature of testator at end of document
- date
- witnesses
- testamentary/legal capacity of testator at time will is executed (not at death)
    - age of state majority
    - mental competence

self-proving provision

Many states have passed laws that permit self-proving provisions at the end of wills. A **self-proving provision** eliminates the need to locate attesting witnesses at the time of probate. At the time of execution, the witnesses sign a notarized acknowledgment that they saw the testator sign the will and that the testator was of sound mind as well as competent to execute a will at that time. However, remember that just because a will has been notarized does not mean that the will is a valid will. Notarization indicates that the will is self-proving.

Testamentary Capacity

testamentary capacity

State laws strictly prescribe the conditions necessary for a valid will. The maker or testator (another name for the maker) must have the legal capacity to make a will. Legal capacity pertains to age and mental competence. In some states, the person making a will must have reached the age of majority. In other states, the age may be considerably younger. The testator must be of sound mind, which means that he or she understands what is being done. In other words, the testator knows that he or she is writing a will. The testator must have both recognition and knowledge of the property that he or she possesses and intends to dispose of by a will. The testator must recognize relatives and friends who are the natural objects of his or her love and affection. Lastly, the testator must understand how and to whom the property is being distributed. All of these combined attributes, called **testamentary capacity**, are measured as of the time the will is written. The document is considered valid if the testator understood what he or she was doing when it was written, even if the testator is mentally incompetent at the time of death.

Pre-Will Considerations

- Use your full name even if you are generally known by one or more nicknames. Nicknames can be mentioned in parentheses after your legal name.
- Name the person to be nominated as your executor. Ask the nominee if he or she is willing to be your executor prior to creating your will.
- Name at least one alternate executor in case your original nominee is unable or unwilling to serve at the time of your death.
- Decide if your executor should post bond or whether the bond requirement is waived.
- List your assets that will pass by the terms of your will. (Note that property that passes by operation of law—for example, property titled jointly with right of survivorship—or by contract—for example, property having beneficiary designations such as life

insurance policies—cannot pass under your will.

- Decide if there are specific assets you wish to leave to specific beneficiaries.
- List the names and relationships of beneficiaries of your assets. Decide to whom your property passes if one or more named beneficiaries predeceases you

LO 7. 3   Describe the two common modes of distribution under wills, and explain what types of provisions are found in wills.

Modes of Distribution Under Wills

There are two common forms of distribution for the property of a decedent. Distributions may be made *per stirpes*, which means "by roots or stock," or *per capita*, which means "by the heads." This distinction becomes particularly important when an individual bequeaths property to children and one or more of those children dies survived by children. However, per stirpes, per capita, and with representation are only important when a class beneficiary group was used and one or more members of the class predeceased the testator. If all members of the class are alive, you just split up the assets equally among the class. However, if one or more members die, you need to determine how to split up the assets and if you want any assets to go to the deceased class member's heirs.

per stirpes distribution

per capita distribution

per capita with representation distribution

Per stirpes distribution provides that members of a designated class, including deceased members, inherit as members of the class. Per stirpes comes from Latin, meaning "by or through the roots." Representatives (heirs) of a deceased member take the decedent's share by representation of the deceased ancestor, not as individuals. **Per capita distribution** provides that members of a class, including heirs of deceased members, share in the inheritance as individuals. Essentially per capita treats all surviving beneficiaries as equals. **Per capita with representation distribution** (12 states use) requires the surviving lineage of a deceased beneficiary to split up equally the deceased beneficiary's share. However, if the entire class is gone (all children dead) the grandchildren would split the entire pool of assets equally. Intestacy laws will define the heirs and usually do not fit the client's estate plan.

EXAMPLE

Suppose Adam had four children, three of whom are alive and one of whom is deceased but survived by two children at the time of Adam's death. If distribution is to be made per stirpes, the estate is divided equally into four parts. Each of the three living children receives a one-quarter interest and the two surviving children of the deceased child equally share that deceased child's one-fourth interest.

On the other hand, if distribution is to be made on a strict per capita basis, each lineal descendant, regardless of the degree of relationship to the decedent, inherits the property. Thus, the estate is divided equally among the three living children and the two children of the deceased child. This results in each of Adam's children and grandchildren taking one-fifth of the property.

The interpretation of the terms per stirpes and per capita differs under the various state laws. In the absence of a specification in the will, the applicable method is determined by local law. The majority of states adopt per stirpes distribution in the absence of the testator's clear intent to distribute per capita. To avoid confusion and to guarantee that the intent of the testator is fulfilled, the preferred method is to provide for the desired distribution in the will.

Will Distribution Methods
- per stirpes (by the roots/class)
- per capita (by the heads/persons)
- per capita with representation

OTHER TYPES OF WILLS

LO 7. 4   Describe other types of wills.

Holographic Wills

holographic will

Slightly more than one-third of the states allow a will that is totally handwritten by the testator to be accepted for probate. This type of will is called a **holographic will**. It must be signed at the end but need not be witnessed. Some states require that a holographic will be dated by the testator, and at least one state requires that it be found among the valuable papers of the testator to be accepted as a valid will. Interestingly, even if a holographic will is written on numerous pieces of paper, the writings are not required to be fastened together.

Nuncupative Wills

nuncupative wills

Nuncupative wills are oral wills made by the testator, in the presence of witnesses, during a final illness shortly before death when it is impossible to write a will. Where such wills are permitted, the witnesses must submit an affidavit declaring the testator's final wishes. In other words, the testator's verbal declaration must be reduced to writing within a few days after the oral will is made. Some states allow nuncupative wills. Execution formalities for the written version of the testator's nuncupative will, such as the number of witnesses, are usually the same requirements a state imposes for traditional written wills.

Joint and Mutual Wills

joint will

Joint wills and mutual wills are sometimes called love wills. Two related persons may decide to execute a single joint will if they have a common scheme for the disposition of their property. Most often, a **joint will** is written by a husband and a wife. Both parties sign the one document. As a practical matter, joint wills may create a problem upon probate. The original will for both parties is admitted to probate at the death of the first party. Consequently, if the surviving party does not write a later will, it is cumbersome and possibly costly to search for the original will that was filed with the probate court and made part of the probate record of the first decedent. A question may also arise as to whether the living individual is, in some way, contractually bound when the original will is filed because the parties have bound themselves, morally if not legally, to deal with their property according to a prearranged plan. After the death of one of the parties, it is questionable whether the second party is bound to the preexisting plan or is free to change the will. In many situations, the courts have held that a binding contract existed between the parties that became irrevocable upon the death of the first party to a mutual will arrangement.

Joint wills are rarely drafted because most testators want to be able to change their will provisions after one spouse dies. Even if the spousal testators did not intend to create a contractual arrangement when their joint will was executed, a court could interpret this to be an irrevocable agreement on the intent of the spouses at the time of creation.

mutual will

A joint will should be distinguished from a **mutual will**, also referred to as a mirror, reciprocal, or "sweetheart" will. Mutual wills exist when two or more parties agree to have their property distributed in a particular fashion upon their death. They execute separate wills that have reciprocal provisions. Mutual wills could also be signed jointly, which makes them both mutual and joint wills.

Both joint and mutual types of will arrangements are cumbersome. They should not be entered into without objective advice regarding the ramifications. For instance, one consequence of joint and mutual wills is a possible loss of the marital deduction. Many disputes among beneficiaries of contrary wills arise from writing such agreements. An example of an agreement to write a mutual will may be part of a property-settlement agreement pursuant to a divorce.

EXAMPLE

Both parties may agree that no one but the offspring of their marriage will inherit any of their property. As part of the agreement, each party executes a reciprocal will leaving all their property to the children born of their marriage. There is some question of whether the parties can legally be contractually bound not to revise or revoke their wills. Such an agreement is contrary to the law of wills and the general principles providing that a will is a unilateral declaration that can be voluntarily altered, amended, or revoked at any time during the testator's life.

LO 7. 5   Explain how a will may be amended or revoked.

Amending or Revoking a Will

codicil

Wills are a unilateral declaration of intention and may be amended or revoked at any time. They are legally enforceable only if they meet the qualifications for validity and are still in effect at the time of death. Sometimes a will requires minor changes that may be made by writing a codicil. A **codicil** is a modification of the will. One or more paragraphs may be revoked or amended, leaving the rest of the will intact. A codicil must be signed with the same requirements and formality as the original will.

A will may be revoked in its entirety in one of several ways. Most commonly, a more recent will is written declaring that all prior wills are revoked. Revocation can also occur by making a codicil that specifically invalidates the will. Not all subsequent wills or codicils have the effect of revoking a former will. To effect total revocation, a new will must state that it is intended to revoke the former document. In the absence of such a declaration, it is a matter for construction and interpretation by the courts as to whether the new will revokes the earlier one or merely modifies it. A modification may be accepted if there is a partial inconsistency. Making a later, valid will that is totally inconsistent with an earlier one can also constitute a revocation of the former will.

Alternatively, a will can be revoked by the maker if he or she intentionally destroys it or mutilates it by tearing. However, inadvertent or unintentional destruction of an original will would not cause a revocation if there is some way of proving its existence and validity. A copy that is certified as the last will is usually accepted as such if it can be shown conclusively that the original was inadvertently destroyed.

In some states, wills may also be totally or partially revoked by an act that causes invalidation under state law. If a divorce occurs that is not contemplated in the will, in some states the entire will is revoked. In other states, only the provisions of the will that pertain to the former spouse are revoked by operation of law.

When a testator marries subsequent to the writing of a will, the will may be revoked entirely unless it specifically contemplates the marriage, or the new spouse is entitled to the equivalent of an intestate share. Similarly, after-born or after-adopted children not contemplated in the will may cause the will to be revoked, or these children may be entitled to an intestate share unless the property in question passes to a surviving spouse or the omission of the after-born or after-adopted child is intentional.

Furthermore, a murderer of the testator cannot inherit under the will. States do not allow these individuals to profit from such an act.

Revocation of a Will
- subsequent will expressly revoking prior wills
- codicil expressly revoking prior wills
- subsequent will totally inconsistent with prior will
- intentional destruction or mutilation of prior will
- certain acts (divorce, marriage, murder, after-born or after-adopted children)

LO 7. 6   Explain the spouse's right of election against a will.

Spouse's Right of Election Against a Will

spousal right of election against the will

The right of election against the will is an elective right of a spouse to receive a specific portion or percentage of the decedent-spouse's estate in spite of the will. A spouse who is legally married to the testator at the time of death cannot be totally disinherited under most state laws.

Even though a will can disinherit a spouse totally, the spouse can generally assert a statutory right to claim a certain share of the estate (for example, a surviving spouse may have a right to 30 percent of the estate). In many states, property subject to the **spousal right of election against the will** includes not only property owned by the testator at death, but also certain property that the testator gave away during lifetime—as long as he or she retained the right to the income or other use of the property until death. In some states, life insurance paid to a named beneficiary avoids the right of election. The exercise of a right of election can also be avoided by a valid, properly drafted antenuptial agreement.

LO 7.7   Describe the grounds for contesting a will.

CONTESTING A WILL

Disappointed heirs, entirely or partially overlooked in the will, may attempt to have the will set aside through legal channels. After a will is admitted to probate, any interested parties may file an action to contest the will's validity. An interested party is one who stands to benefit if the will is overturned. There are six grounds on which a will may be contested. One or more of them may be alleged in an attempt to have the will invalidated.

- The first ground is improper execution. In other words, some ingredient essential to the valid execution of a will is missing, such as the fact that the requisite number of witnesses did not sign the declaration.

- It may be claimed that the testator was not legally competent to make a will at the time of execution.

- A third ground commonly alleged is that the testator was under duress or unduly influenced by another to make the will as he or she did. This has sinister implications. The accusation is that the testator was not functioning as a free agent in expressing personal intentions but was following the advice of another party (usually someone with a financial interest in the outcome).

- The fourth ground for contesting a will is fraud. Someone defrauded the decedent into making a particular will by outright lies or otherwise misleading him or her.

- The will is alleged to be a forgery. That means it is not the true will of the testator, and the testator did not sign it.

- A will may be contested on the grounds that the one admitted to probate had been revoked by an act of the testator before death.

will contest

Some of the warning signs that indicate an increased likelihood of a **will contest** include the following:

- a will that is created, arranged, and/or paid for by a primary beneficiary
- a will that has bequests that are very different from prior wills
- a will that disinherits one or more natural heirs
- a will disposing of great wealth
- a will created and signed by a testator without the benefit of an attorney
- a will with unusual dispositions
- a will by a physically or mentally weak person
- a will passing significant property to other than lineal heirs who represent the estate

A will may also be wholly or partially revoked by operation of law. In other words, the provisions of the will are not legally enforceable in that the directions or bequests would not be legal if made.

Note that contesting a will is very different from a spouse's election to take against the will. Contesting a will is aimed at destroying the entire will's validity, while the statutory election only gives a spouse a certain share of the estate while leaving the will otherwise intact.

LO 7. 8   Describe the use of testamentary trusts and pour-over trusts in wills.

TESTAMENTARY TRUSTS

testamentary trust

A **testamentary trust** is one created within a will as a part of the will. It becomes both effective and irrevocable at the time of death. Because a testamentary trust is contained in the body of the will, it becomes a matter of public record when the will is probated. Thus, it is open to public scrutiny. By definition, a testamentary trust generally becomes part of the probate estate. The trust is created under the will when the testator uses language indicating an intent to have some of the property held in trust. Frequently, a trust under a will is a contingent trust. An example of such a provision is the testator who bequeaths all the property outright to a surviving spouse. However, in the event that the spouse predeceases the testator, he or she gives the property to the minor children in trust until they reach majority or other suitable age for distribution. The testamentary trust must contain the same elements as a living trust. There must be an intention to create the trust and trust property, as well as a method to determine beneficiaries.

A testamentary trust may be a trust that provides a lifetime income to the surviving spouse with the remainder passing to other beneficiaries at the spouse's death. If a testator creates this type of trust, the trustee manages and invests property to provide income for the income beneficiary (surviving spouse). At the death of the income beneficiary, the trust principal is distributed to the remainderperson in accordance with the terms of the trust. As with living trusts, the trustee holds legal title to the property with the beneficiaries holding equitable title. The testator may direct that principal be distributed either on the happening of an event, such as the death of an income beneficiary or upon a remainder beneficiary reaching a stated age. A testator may also direct that the remainder beneficiary or beneficiaries receive partial distributions of principal at specific ages. It is also possible to accumulate income until the beneficiary attains a certain age, at which time it is distributed. The testamentary trust may contain a power-of-appointment provision giving the donee of the power (for example, the surviving spouse) the ability to apportion assets among proposed remainderpersons at some future time when distribution is to be made. This power provides flexibility in making sure that assets are distributed according to need as opposed to a fixed-share division determined when the trust is executed. As long as this power is limited so that the person who holds the power can only appoint to the remainderperson, it does not cause the testamentary trust to be included in the power holder's estate for estate tax purposes.

Because the testamentary trust is created under a will and becomes part of the probate estate, there are no savings in estate taxes or income taxes during the testator's lifetime. Moreover, there is no protection from probate costs. A testamentary trust is frequently used when the testator does not wish to part with property during lifetime but recognizes the need for a disposition in trust for the benefit of one or more family members after his or her death. While there is no estate tax saving in the testator's estate by creating a life estate for the first generation of beneficiaries, the property can be available to provide income and possible distributions of principal as needs arise during the beneficiaries' lives without passing through their estates at their death. Testamentary trusts can have built-in flexibility with discretion in the trustee to sprinkle income and possibly principal among various beneficiaries in different income and estate tax brackets whose needs may differ.

Tax savings may also be accomplished with the establishment of separate trusts. Trusts can be divided into separate shares when the youngest or oldest remainder beneficiary attains a specific age, thereby creating additional tax-paying entities. The trustee may also be given discretionary powers to accumulate or pay out income, again taking into consideration the relative tax brackets of the beneficiaries and trusts as well as their income needs in any taxable year. Furthermore, the trustee may be given authority to purchase life insurance on the life of a life-income beneficiary that provides security for that beneficiary's family at the beneficiary's death. For example, a life-income beneficiary who receives $50,000 of income per year from a trust is a good illustration. At that individual's death, a substantial change in his or her family's living conditions may result when the income from the trust ends. The life insurance proceeds can be used to replace that income. Payment of life insurance premiums on the life of a beneficiary is not taxable income to the beneficiary. Compared with the beneficiary's purchasing his or her own life insurance with after-tax dollars, more tax savings can result if the trust is in a lower income tax bracket than the beneficiary.

To summarize, a testamentary trust functions similarly to any other kind of trust after the testator's death. Because it is part of a will, the testamentary trust is revocable until death, at which time it becomes irrevocable. The trust can provide security and professional management for beneficiaries after the testator is gone. It also gives the testator some control even after death with regard to the intermediate and final distributions of property. While no estate taxes are saved at the testator's death, the trust may provide for life-income beneficiaries so that assets escape taxation at the death of the income beneficiaries. Because the trust is irrevocable once it is operative, it can provide tax savings through income splitting and accumulation of income.

The testator may provide for any one or more of a variety of methods for the distribution of principal from a testamentary trust. For instance, the trust terms may provide that the principal is to be distributed at the discretion of the trust beneficiary. The discretion amounts to giving the trust beneficiary complete control over the trust principal. Another possibility is to provide for trust principal to be distributed at the sole discretion of the trustee. This arrangement gives the beneficiary no control over when principal may be received. A variation of this arrangement is to provide that trust principal be distributed at the discretion of a designated third party, other than the trustee or the trust beneficiary. Under either of these last two methods, trust principal can be distributed at any time but requires the approval of someone other than the trust beneficiary. The testator may specify when trust principal is to be distributed. For example, the trust may provide that determined percentages of trust principal are to be distributed as one or more beneficiaries attain a specific age. Alternatively, there may be directions for a certain percentage of trust principal to be distributed each year or every second, third, or fourth year. A third possibility is to provide for no distributions of trust principal until termination of the trust itself. Here, postponement of distribution of trust principal is limited only by the rule against perpetuities. There are numerous choices available to the testator other than those previously mentioned. Generally, a testator has complete flexibility to determine the method of the distribution of trust principal, subject only to limitations on accumulations for an unreasonably long period of time.

Pour-over Trusts

pour-over trusts

Pouring over refers to a dispositive device that has come into use in recent years. **Pour-over trusts** simply mean that property is transferred or poured over from an estate, trust, retirement plan, or life insurance policy into a preexisting estate or trust. It may occur in one of several ways. An individual may create a living trust executed prior to a will that provides that, at the individual's death, the residue of his or her estate is payable to a preexisting trust to be administered with the other trust assets. Pour overs can also take place the opposite way. A preexisting living trust may be poured into the estate and administered and distributed under the terms of the will as part of the residuary estate. By either means, the pour-over device can be used to consolidate the grantor's assets, thereby simplifying administration. Another benefit is that administrative costs are reduced.

If the pouring over is from a will into a living trust, a legal question arises concerning the pre-existence of the trust. For example, a will cannot be made stating that assets are to be poured over into a trust that is not executed until the following year because the named trust was not in existence at the time the will was written. To have legal effect, pouring over must be done into existing instruments. Therefore, the trust must be executed prior to a will if that is the type of pour-over arrangement in question. Also, a question arises if the preexisting trust is amended or terminated after the will is executed. Because the amendment was not within the contemplation of the testator when the testator's will was written, does the pour-over device also refer to the amendment to the trust agreement? This problem has been resolved by statute in many states by authorizing the pouring over into an amended trust agreement, if the original trust agreement was in existence at the time the will was executed. The financial services professional should consult the statutes of the jurisdiction(s) in which a client resides to determine whether an amended trust will have validity for pouring over under a preexisting will. Otherwise, a new will should be drafted after the amendments to the trust are made. There is an act called the Uniform Testamentary Additions to Trust Act that has been adopted by a number of states. In those states that have adopted the act, amendments to a living trust enacted subsequent to the execution of a will from which assets will pour over to the trust are deemed valid.

LO 7. 9   **Explain how property can be transferred at death by contract.**

TRANSFERS BY CONTRACT

Property may also be transferred at death by contract. The most usual situation involves life insurance contracts. In addition, antenuptial and postnuptial agreements are becoming more common.

Life Insurance and Other Contracts

Life insurance proceeds payable to a named beneficiary pass outside the will to the beneficiary, be it an individual or a trust. Policy proceeds are always distributed according to the beneficiary designation on the policy. Directions for distribution in the will have no effect, unless no designated beneficiary is named or the policy is made payable to the estate. Likewise, death benefits from retirement plans pass to named beneficiaries outside the will unless they are made payable to the estate or the executor in his or her capacity as personal representative of the estate.

Antenuptial and Postnuptial Agreements

antenuptial (prenuptial) agreement

It is not uncommon today for persons to make prenuptial or antenuptial agreements with their intended spouse. An **antenuptial (prenuptial) agreement** (the terms "antenuptial" and "prenuptial" are synonymous) is a legally binding agreement between two parties in anticipation of marriage. The agreement provides for limitations on transfers of property between them in relinquishment of their marital rights to each other's property. These agreements can be very useful when it is not a first marriage for one or both spouses. Either spouse may wish to protect property accumulated before the present marriage for children of a prior marriage. An alternate way of preserving property for children is through the use of trusts. However, antenuptial agreements may serve a variety of purposes. The agreement may provide for certain transfers from one party to the other before the marriage as an inducement to enter the legal relationship. Antenuptial agreements may also substitute for statutory elections and other inheritance rights of a spouse at death. The agreement may provide that when one spouse dies, the other spouse will receive a fixed sum in full satisfaction of his or her rights to share in the deceased spouse's estate. The spouse who accepts the terms of an antenuptial agreement will receive that property on the death of the decedent in lieu of a statutory share that is the right of a surviving spouse. As stated earlier, the antenuptial agreement has the full force and effect of an arm's-length contract. Unless duress, fraud, and similar wrongs were involved, false information was supplied, or information was hidden regarding the extent of assets and size of the estate of either party when the agreement was reached, a court of law generally upholds its terms. Aside from trusts, antenuptial agreements can provide full protection of one's estate for one's intended beneficiaries.

Postnuptial agreements may be entered into between spouses in settlement of marital rights and property usually pursuant to a divorce. Typically, in such an agreement, each spouse gives up all rights in the other spouse's estate. These agreements may or may not provide for postdeath support benefits. To the extent that payments cease upon the death of either spouse, the other spouse gives up all rights as a creditor of the estate. However, if the benefits of a postnuptial or property settlement agreement survive death, the other party has rights against the decedent's estate as a creditor.

Transfers at Death by Contract
- life insurance proceeds
- retirement plan death benefits
- antenuptial and postnuptial agreements

LO 7. 10   **Explain how property can be transferred at death by operation of law.**

TRANSFERS BY OPERATION OF LAW

operation of law

Property not passing by will or contract may pass by what is called **operation of law**. An example of property passing by operation of law is the transfer of jointly held property to the surviving joint tenant. In addition, certain property may pass to survivors under laws pertaining to family allowances and homestead allowances. Another type of transfer in this category is intestate succession.

Transfers of Property at Death
- by will
- by contract
- by operation of law

Joint Tenants with Right of Survivorship

Property held jointly with right of survivorship (including tenancies by the entirety) automatically passes to the surviving joint tenant. In addition, a bank account held in trust for a named individual passes automatically to the beneficiary. This type of account is called a Totten trust or a pay-on-death account. The term is somewhat of a misnomer because it is not a legal trust. Totten trusts and pay-on-death accounts are payable-on-death arrangements. The decedent retains the right to control the assets in the account until death, at which time it passes automatically to the named beneficiary outside the will. The survivorship form of ownership takes precedence over provisions in a will.

Family Allowance

family allowance

One of the first distributions from a decedent's estate permitted by all states is called a **family allowance**. It is a small, specified amount set aside for the interim support of a surviving spouse and minor children during the period of estate administration. This special allowance provides the surviving family members with immediate funds, consequently avoiding the delay usually associated with distributions from a decedent's estate until after all debts have been paid. The amount of the allowance varies by state and by the size of the decedent's estate and family needs. It is property the family may keep. It is not considered part of the distributable estate and is usually exempt from state death taxation. The funds are paid to the family despite unsecured creditor and tax claims.

Homestead Allowance

homestead

Another amount set aside in most states is the homestead allowance or rights. Basically, the homestead allowance is an exemption that keeps a specified amount of real property and, in some states, personal property of the decedent out of the reach of unsecured creditors. Its fundamental purpose is to keep the family from being dispossessed of its home and being impoverished as a result of the decedent spouse's death. It prevails over a disposition of the family home under the decedent's will. The so-called **homestead** pertains to the home the family lives in and the property surrounding the home, subject to acreage limitations that vary greatly by state. In addition to a homestead allowance consisting of real and sometimes personal property, many states also grant monetary homestead allowance amounts to the surviving spouse and to minor children.

Intestacy

All property not passing by contract, will, or operation of law passes under the laws of intestate succession (called *laws of descent and distribution* in some states). Intestate means "without making a will." A person who dies without a will or with a will that has been revoked, annulled, or in some other way declared invalid is said to die intestate. A decedent can also die partially intestate. Partial intestacy occurs when a testator has a valid will, but the document does not dispose of all of the testator's property. There are intestate laws of each jurisdiction that prescribe the way an intestate's (the word as used frequently signifies the decedent) property is to be distributed. The law of the state where the person is domiciled controls the distribution of all the person's property located within the state. The intestate distribution of the decedent's real property, or tangible personal property, located outside of the state of domicile, is determined by the laws of the state where the property is located.

No distinction is usually made between real and personal property with respect to distribution under the laws of intestate descent. To provide for all property not otherwise transferred, each state has established laws of intestate succession. There is a prescribed order for disposition to the heirs of the deceased person. Intestate succession refers to the specified order of distribution by the state of the property of persons who die without leaving a valid will.

EXAMPLE

Henry dies, leaving $900,000 worth of property. He does not have a will; $300,000 passes to Henry's wife. The remaining $600,000 is divided equally among his three adult children despite the fact that he was very close to his sister and planned to leave her a significant amount of assets at his death.

There are variations among the states with respect to the descent and distribution of an intestate's property. Usually, the person given primary consideration is the surviving spouse. That is not to say that the surviving spouse takes all. Generally, a surviving spouse receives from one-third to one-half of the decedent's estate if there are living children or parents of the decedent. One scheme of intestate succession provides that a share first be set aside for the surviving spouse. An example is a provision for the first (some stated amount) dollars plus half of the estate to go to the surviving spouse. The remaining half is then divided equally among all children of the decedent. If there is no surviving spouse, surviving children may inherit the entire estate in equal shares. Next in line of lineal heirs are parents of the decedent. If a spouse survives but there are no children, the parents generally share the probate estate with the surviving spouse. Brothers and sisters usually come next in line, and so on. The order is a rigid one.

State intestacy statutes do not provide for inheritances for friends, business associates, or charities. Nor do they always make adequate provision for surviving spouses. Relatives of an individual who died intestate are frequently shocked, angered, and financially hurt by the controls put on the decedent's assets by the court. No amount of persuasion can alter the statutory scheme or convince the court that the decedent intended the property to pass to other persons.

escheats

If there are no living relatives, the property **escheats** to the state. Escheat means that property reverts to the state for lack of any individual competent to inherit the property. In other words, there are no heirs or next of kin to whom the property can pass by way of intestate succession. The state is the ultimate owner and taker of the estate. Usually, some state institution is designated to receive the property.

> **Transfers at Death by Operation of Law**
> - joint tenants with right of survivorship
> - family allowance
> - homestead allowance
> - intestacy

Ethical Dilemma

The ethical dilemmas presented in this text illustrate common scenarios that could present a financial or estate planner with an ethical predicament. The resolution of any dilemma, of course, depends on how one applies ethical codes, rules, and principles to the specific situation. The comments are meant to provide thought about these issues and not give a definitive resolution to them.

> Maria Gonzales is an estate planning attorney who, 2 years ago, drafted and supervised the execution of mirror wills for her longtime, wealthy, married clients, Frank and Carole Bogard. The primary objective of their wills was to benefit their three adult children and six grandchildren.
>
> Recently, however, Maria received a phone call from Carole Bogard to make an appointment to change her will. Carole told Maria she did not want her husband to know of the appointment or of her intention to revoke her current will. When the appointment took place, Carole informed Maria that she needed a new will because she has a special relationship with someone whom she wishes to provide for at her death. The relationship, she assured Maria, was quite established as it had been going on for years. Carole said that if for some remote reason the

relationship ended, she would simply execute a new will. When Carole saw that Maria was reluctant to carry out her wishes, she said that, as her attorney, Maria was obligated to draft a new will for her. She also stated that she would take the Bogard's lucrative business elsewhere if Maria did not comply.

> ### *What should Maria do?*

A Possible Resolution

The dilemma that Maria confronts is particularly troublesome. There is no easy answer to such a situation. It is not at all uncommon for attorneys to represent both a husband and wife, and sometimes other family members as well. It is the attorney's responsibility to provide counsel to his or her clients within the context with which they seek advice.

Maria was initially hired to assist Frank and Carole Bogard in their joint endeavor, which she did. Carole's current request is construed as separate from that. Any communication she has with Maria regarding this matter is considered confidential and protected by the long-standing principle of attorney-client privilege. Professional rules bar her from saying or doing anything that might jeopardize that confidentiality.

Considering all of this, Maria could choose to dissuade Carole and risk turning away her business. But this does not seem to make sense for either one of them. They have a preexisting relationship and, if Maria does not comply, someone else will. Her responsibility is to guide clients, not to make decisions for them or judge the decisions they make.

A suggested course of action is for Maria to do what Carole asks. She can encourage Carole to inform her husband of her changes from their prior mirror wills, and she can urge her to make sure accommodations are included for her children. However, there is no guarantee that Maria will feel good about this resolution or any other one. What she must remember is that, as an attorney, she serves her clients by enabling them to achieve their goals. It is not her job to judge what those goals are.

At the same time, even though Maria's behavior is in line with legal rules and ethical principles, she needs to be prepared for potential challenges. She should make certain she has malpractice insurance and that she maintains it. Should Frank discover Carole's new will, he will likely feel betrayed and might accuse

Maria of behaving inappropriately. While Maria might want to avoid this unpleasantness—and she could by turning Carole away—she is not, in fact, acting inappropriately by representing Carole. She might not feel comfortable about Carole's choices, but that is not her responsibility. Her responsibility is to translate Carole's wishes into a legally binding instrument.

CHAPTER REVIEW

Key Terms and Concepts

executor/executrix
exordium clause
precatory language
bequest
ademption
self-proving provision
testamentary capacity
per stirpes distribution
per capita distribution
per capita with representation
  distribution
holographic will
nuncupative will

joint will
mutual will
codicil
spousal right of election against the
  will
will contest
testamentary trust
pour-over trust
antenuptial (prenuptial) agreement
operation of law
family allowance
homestead
escheat

Chapter 7: Review Questions

1. Describe what a will document is and its purpose. [LO 7.1]

2. What are the advantages of having a will? [LO 7.2]

3. What are the requirements for a valid will? [LO 7.2]

4. What are the elements of testamentary capacity with respect to a valid will? [LO 7.2]

5. What are the typical provisions that a person can make in a will? [LO 7.3]

6. Identify the different types of wills. [LO 7.4]

7. Explain how a person may revoke or amend his or her will. [LO 7.5]

8. Distinguish between:

    a. a wife exercising her spousal right of election against the will [LO 7.6]

    b. a wife contesting her husband's will [LO 7.7]

9. What are the grounds for contesting a will? [LO 7.7]

10. What property disposition planning purposes can a testamentary trust accomplish? [LO 7.8]

11. Describe the various methods of distributing principal from a testamentary trust. [LO 7.8]

12. When would life insurance proceeds be distributed under the provisions of a will? [LO 7.9]

13. Under what circumstances is a person considered to have died intestate? [LO 7.9]

14. Explain how property can be transferred at death by operation of law {LO 7.10]

Chapter 7: Review Answers

1. A will is an individual's declaration of how he or she wishes his or her property to pass at death. The purpose of a will is to assure the orderly and sound distribution of a decedent's probate estate.

2. Advantages of having a will include the following:

    • An executor of choice can only be named by will.

    • Under a will, a decedent can transfer real estate, stock, or business interests as he or she wishes (not as the state dictates).

    • The decedent can ensure the maximum marital deduction for property passing to his or her spouse.

    • A will can specify the estate's share of the tax burden.

    • A will can designate a guardian.

    • Trusts created under a will can control the management and timing of distribution and principal from the estate; trust provisions can give executors and trustees broad powers to invest and manage property and can protect beneficiaries' interests from creditors.

3. The requirements for a valid will are as follows:

    • The instrument must be signed at the end.

    • The will must be dated.

    • In many states, the will must be witnessed by competent witnesses at the time it is executed.

    • Competent witnesses must be able to swear that the signature at the end of the will is the testator's when the will is admitted to probate.

4. To meet the elements of testamentary capacity, the testator must

    - be of legal age (which can vary by state) to make a will

    - be mentally competent at the time the will is written

    - recognize and know the property he or she intends to dispose of by will

    - recognize family and friends who are the natural objects of his or her love and affection

    - understand how and to whom his or her property is to be distributed

5. Typically, a will includes

    - a statement by the testator regarding his or her intention of domicile

    - a direction for the executor to pay all debts, as well as the expenses of the testator's last illness and funeral, from the estate

    - directions regarding burial or cremation

    - bequests, written either in specific or precatory language

    - directions regarding disposition of the testator's tangible personal property

    - designation of executor, successor executor, or coexecutors, with clauses defining specific and general powers

    - a clause stating that the testator either exercises or declines to exercise a power of appointment

    - if there are minors or incompetents, a clause directing the executor to hold any assets for their benefit

6. The different types of wills are holographic wills, nuncupative wills, and joint and mutual wills.

7. The most common way to revoke or amend a will is to make a more recent one that declares all prior wills are revoked. A codicil may also specifically invalidate a will. In addition, a will can be revoked if the maker of the will intentionally destroys or mutilates it.

    In some states, an act that causes invalidation under state law will revoke a will. A divorce may revoke an entire will, or it may revoke only the provisions that pertain to the former spouse. The will may also be revoked if the testator remarries, or if children are born or adopted after the will is drafted.

8. a. A spousal election against the will does not question the validity of the will. It is simply an election by the surviving spouse to take his or her statutory elective share of the decedent's property in lieu of what was left to the surviving spouse in the will. The remainder passes according to the will.

    b. The will contest by the wife is an attack on the actual validity of the will. For example, the survivor could claim that the will was a forgery, or that the testator was unduly influenced or legally incompetent when it was formed. If the will contest is successful, the will is invalid (or partially invalid) and the property will pass by the terms of a prior will or, if none, by the laws of intestacy of the relevant state.

9. The grounds for contesting a will are

    *   improper execution

    *   legal incompetence of the testator

    *   duress or undue influence on the testator to make the will

    *   fraud

    *   forgery

    *   revocation

10. A testamentary trust provides security and professional management of trust property after the testator is gone. It also gives the testator some control regarding both the immediate and final distribution of his or her property.

11. Principal from a testamentary trust can be distributed at the discretion of the trust beneficiary, the trustee, or a designated third party. The testator may also specify when trust principal is to be distributed, and he or she generally has complete flexibility— that is, the method of distribution is subject only to the rule against accumulations.

12. Life insurance proceeds are distributed under the provisions of a will only if no designated beneficiary is named or the policy is made payable to the estate.

13. A person is considered to have died intestate if he or she dies without a will or with a will that has been revoked or declared invalid in some other way.

14. Property not passing by will or contract may pass by operation of law. An example of this would be property held jointly with rights of survivorship automatically passing to the surviving joint tenant. Another example would be a family allowance to provide the family of the deceased with immediate funds to avoid delays while the estate is administered or the homestead allowance to keep a specified property out of the reach of unsecured creditors.

Chapter 8:

Administration of the Estate

Learning Objectives

An understanding of the material in this chapter should enable the student to

> **LO 8.1**   **Explain the probate process.**
>
> **LO 8. 2**   **Describe the appointment of an executor or an administrator.**
>
> **LO 8. 3**   **Explain what is involved in assembling and managing the estate property.**
>
> **LO 8. 4**   **Review the settlement and wrapping up of an estate.**

Death does not always forewarn. It sometimes strikes suddenly and when it is least expected. The business affairs and personal obligations of an individual may be in order or, alternatively, when one's life is cut short, there may be many entanglements to unravel. After death, a process begins called estate administration. The purpose of estate administration is to resolve all outstanding responsibilities, obligations, and rights of the decedent as well as the transfer of all property to intended beneficiaries. Before the final transfers can be accomplished, the decedent's unfinished business and personal obligations must be resolved. These include payment of debts and taxes, transfers of any business interests, and collection of all amounts owed to the decedent while living, as well as amounts that would be payable to beneficiaries or the estate because of the individual's death, such as life insurance proceeds, veteran or employee death benefits, and so forth. The funeral director must be paid as well as the medical and hospital bills resulting from the last illness. In addition, cash must be made available for the immediate living needs of the family and others for whom the decedent had some financial responsibility.

Basically, whether the decedent died testate (with a will) or intestate (without a will), the estate settlement process is similar. There are several stages in the settlement process:

- initial responsibilities
- probating the will
- appointing an executor or administrator
- assembling property
- managing the estate
- paying debts and taxes
- distributing the estate

Initial Responsibilities

Even before a personal representative is appointed, there are matters that require attention. They may involve arranging the funeral, notifying relatives and close friends, and making arrangements for distant relatives to come to the funeral. Action may be necessary temporarily to protect and preserve estate assets. If the decedent was a professional person, someone must temporarily assume these professional duties. If the decedent was the owner of a closely held business or farm, responsibility for business activity may have to be delegated so that the business or farm may remain in operation. Once the funeral is over, a determination must be made as to the existence of a will.

LO 8.1 **Explain the probate process.**

PROBATING THE WILL

probate

The probate process begins when the original will is deposited with the probate court of the county where the decedent resided. By definition, **probate** is the legal act or process of proving a will. To probate the will means to prove to the court that the instrument presented is the last valid will of the deceased person. The proof must be made before a duly authorized person that the document presented as the last will and testament of a deceased person is, in fact, the document it purports to be. The term probate has come to refer to all matters over which probate courts have jurisdiction, including settlement of decedents' estates, appointment and supervision of guardianships, and resolution of will contests. The jurisdiction of the probate, surrogate, or orphans' court extends to the probate assets of the decedent. Probate assets are the property that passes under, and is subject to the terms of the will or, if no will exists, the property subject to administration by the court due to intestacy.

When a will is admitted to probate, the signature of the testator (the individual leaving a will in force at death) must be verified. This is done by calling the subscribing witnesses (witnesses who were present at the signing of the will). If there were no witnesses to the signing or the subscribing witnesses cannot be found, attesting witnesses must be summoned to verify the decedent's signature. These are persons who can attest to the fact that the signature on the will is the decedent's true signature, and they are familiar with the signature as they have seen it written on various occasions. Fortunately, self-proving wills are now widely accepted. Self-proving wills contain a notarized acknowledgment by the witnesses that they saw the testator, being of sound mind, voluntarily sign the will. A self-proving will can be admitted to probate without calling witnesses to the signing. The self-proving will saves the executor the time, expense, and inconvenience of locating subscribing witnesses.

Once the will is validated, the executor or administrator is sworn in and formally appointed. Letters testamentary or letters of administration (as they are called if an administrator is appointed) are then issued.

Probate and Nonprobate Assets

A decedent's estate consists of all property owned outright, in conjunction with others, or in which the decedent possessed certain rights at the time of death. This property is characterized as either real estate or tangible and intangible personal property. Intangibles are such items as stock certificates, corporate or government bonds, bank accounts, bank certificates, mutual fund shares, or money market trust assets.

Other intangible assets and rights (such as Social Security benefits, veteran benefits, proceeds of life insurance, benefits under private or government pension plans, benefits under state workers' compensation acts, and survivors' interests in joint and survivor annuity contracts) may represent the bulk of the estate assets. These amounts may be payable to a decedent's survivors by operation of law or under the terms of a contract. If these assets are payable to named beneficiaries, they pass directly to the beneficiary and not under the will. They are not subject to probate. Therefore, they are nonprobate assets unless they are made payable to the estate. If payable to the estate, they become probate property subject to estate administration.

While they pass outside the will, nonprobate assets may still be taxable for either or both federal and state estate and inheritance tax purposes. An example of a nonprobate asset that may be taxable for state inheritance purposes is a bank account owned by the decedent but held in trust for a named individual, that is, a Totten trust. The proceeds of such an account are transferred to the named beneficiary by operation of law. However, because this account was owned by the decedent alone but in trust for another (as opposed to joint ownership with rights of survivorship, which is exempt from *state* death taxes in some states), the account may be taxable under state law for estate or inheritance tax purposes. The administrator has a duty to include this property in the inventory submitted to the court and pay any death taxes resulting from inclusion of such property in the estate.

It should be remembered that the probate process is not automatic. Someone (either the executor named in the will or another interested party) must present the will for probate if letters testamentary are to be granted to the executor.

Advantages and Disadvantages of Probate

There are both advantages and disadvantages to probate. The primary advantages of probate include the following:

- The will is validated.
- The executor's actions are supervised.
- A dispute-resolution forum is provided for estate issues, including the guardianship of minors and conservatorship of incapacitated parties.
- The inventory and valuation of the decedent's assets and liabilities are carried out.
- Proof of legal title to real property is established.
- A time frame is set for creditors' claims to be presented prior to the distribution of assets to the estate beneficiaries.
- Philanthropic bequests receive public recognition.

The primary disadvantages of probate include the following:

- There is a lack of privacy in that the decedent's will, beneficiary information, and the claims of creditors are a matter of public record.
- Property distribution may be time-consuming, depending on the complexity of the estate, will disputes, and the jurisdiction.
- There is inflexibility because probate must be carried out according to state statute.
- Costs result from court supervision according to state statute.
- Executor commissions and attorney fees are generated.
- Property owned in nondomiciliary states or countries may be subject to ancillary probate.

Methods to Avoid Probate

If, after weighing the pros and cons of probate, an individual wants to avoid probate for some or all property, there are several possible avoidance methods or will substitutes, some of which are discussed below.

Joint Tenancy

Property that is titled as joint tenants with right of survivorship or property that is titled as tenants by the entireties is not subject to probate at the death of the first joint tenant.

Property Passing by Contract at Death

Property passing to a beneficiary (other than the decedent's estate) under the terms of a contract is also considered nonprobate property. These assets may include, for example, the proceeds of life insurance, Social Security benefits, pension plan proceeds, IRAs, and survivors' interests in annuities. Generally, property passing to beneficiaries by small-estate administration also avoids the probate process.

Government Savings Bonds

When an individual purchases Series EE and Series H U.S. savings bonds and designates someone else to be paid at the purchaser's death, the proceeds are not included in probate.

Totten Trusts and Payable-on-Death Accounts

Certain types of accounts established at financial institutions become payable to the named beneficiary at the death of the individual who established the account. The depositor has sole control and access to the account during lifetime.

Deeds

deed

Deeds are another will-substitution device. To be a completed transfer, the **deed** must be irrevocably delivered to the transferee or to an escrow agent. If the deed is transferred to an escrow agent, the agent holds the deed for an established period of time or until the transferor's death, at which time it is delivered to the eventual intended recipient. When an escrow agent holds a deed for future delivery, any income tax liability with regard to the property subject to the deed remains the responsibility of the transferor. Recording the deed is not necessary until delivery is made to the transferee-owner.

Living Trusts

Another probate-avoidance method is the living (revocable) trust. Property that is transferred to a trust during an individual's lifetime is distributed according to the terms of the trust. Because the trustee rather than the grantor owns and manages the trust assets, at the time of the grantor's death, the probate court has no authority (except in limited circumstances) over the property.

The living trust is often a favored probate-avoidance technique because there are many other benefits to holding property in this way. The decedent continues to control the property after death through the trust terms; trust assets receive a full-basis step up at the decedent's death; transfers to the trust are not subject to public knowledge; the grantor is able to observe the operation of the trust during lifetime; and out-of-state property held by a trust can avoid ancillary probate.

Small Estate Administration

Most states exempt an estate from probate if the decedent's total estate or real property does not exceed a specific dollar amount. In some states an estate might qualify for special settlement procedures that can actually avoid probate altogether if the estate meets certain gross value limits. For example, in Pennsylvania an estate qualifies as a small estate when the total gross value does not exceed $50,000. This allows the property to be disturbed faster and without much court oversight.

Methods to Avoid Probate

- Title property in joint tenancy with right of survivorship or tenancy by the entirety
- Pass property by contract (such as life insurance, IRAs, pension plan benefits, and so on)
- Create Totten trusts and payable-on-death accounts, which are nonprobate
- Transfer property by deed
- Establish living trusts (property in a living trust is nonprobate)
- Small estate administration

Ancillary Probate

ancillary probate

If the decedent owned property in other states, the executor has a duty to locate the property and make all necessary transfers, either by taking possession of the property or by selling it on behalf of the estate. Typically, an estate administration proceeding has to be conducted in each state in which a nondomiciled decedent owned real property. The court in the county where the property is situated appoints an ancillary administrator to oversee the transfer of these assets. Multiple proceedings result in added expense and inconvenience. If the owner transfers the properties to a trust during lifetime, however, the additional expenses and inconvenience of **ancillary probate** can be avoided. Ancillary administration of assets is avoided because the trustee holds title to the property, and the property is administered according to the terms of the trust.

LO 8. 2　　Describe the appointment of an executor or an administrator.

APPOINTMENT OF EXECUTOR OR ADMINISTRATOR

If the decedent had a will, an executor was probably named to whom authority was given for settlement of the estate. An executor is also known as the personal representative of an estate. Broadly speaking, a personal representative is the individual or institution charged with responsibility for management of the estate, including: gathering all assets; collecting all amounts owed the decedent; paying debts, expenses, and taxes; and distributing assets to the beneficiaries. The position requires a high degree of responsibility and involves many duties. Although named in the will, an executor must petition the probate court for formal appointment to be recognized by all persons dealing with the estate as the estate's personal representative.

If a valid will is not found, a petition must be filed in the probate court of the county where the decedent resided to have an administrator appointed. Procedures for appointment of an executor or an administrator are prescribed by state statute and vary according to local law.

If the decedent did not name an executor, state law prescribes the order of persons entitled to be appointed as administrator. This order is based on degree of relationship to the decedent. To qualify for the position of executor, one must be legally competent and have reached legal age—18 years in most states.

If a corporation is chosen, it must be one authorized to act as a fiduciary in that state. In some states, courts will not appoint an individual who is a nonresident. A court is usually influenced by the wishes and recommendations of the family. As to the choice of a competent administrator, sometimes a family member who is eligible to be an administrator may not feel qualified to serve. The appointment may be renounced in favor of other persons or an institution better suited for the position. Also, the court may exercise its discretion in the appointment of an appropriate administrator so that, in its judgment, the estate will be settled properly. It is not bound to follow the order prescribed by state statute.

Posting Bond

posting bond

Individuals may state in their wills that named executors may serve without **posting bond** as security. The courts will honor this direction provided that an executor is competent to serve. A bond or surety bond is a certificate in which a person or insurance company, the "surety," agrees to pay up to and including the bond amount to the court if the personal representative does not perform, or improperly performs, the duties of administering the estate. Bonds protect the interests of beneficiaries, heirs, tax collectors, and creditors from suffering losses as a result of the representative's improper or even negligent management of the decedent's estate. When a corporate entity is appointed to represent the estate, bond is not required.

The amount of a bond is based on the estate value, the assets comprising the estate, the relationship of the personal representative to the decedent, and other aspects of the particular estate. As bond and surety requirements vary from state to state, the amount required may, for instance, be the same as the estimated value of the decedent's personal property or up to double that amount. The bond premium is paid on an annual basis. Because the cost of a bond is paid with estate funds, it should be canceled as soon as the estate is closed. Today, most estate planning practitioners consider a bond to be unnecessary.

Some states, however, require a bond to be posted despite the testator's waiver of the bond. If an individual administrator is appointed by the court, a bond with surety (secured by cash or other collateral) is required to protect the estate's beneficiaries and creditors. In most states, if an institution is named as administrator, a bond may still be required but usually without surety.

The amount of the bond varies depending on the approximate size of the estate and the fee schedule prescribed by state statute. Generally, bonds are posted in amounts up to twice the value of the probate estate. Because the exact size of the estate is unknown at this early stage, it may be necessary to post an additional bond at a later date when the full value of the estate has been determined.

Letters Testamentary

letters testamentary

After the bond is obtained, **letters testamentary** or letters of administration are issued by the court. These letters are certifications by the court that the named personal representative was granted authority to act on behalf of the estate during the administration period until he or she is discharged by the court, at which time the estate may be closed.

Advertising

advertising

The personal representative has an obligation to publicize the existence of the estate, thereby notifying all interested parties (including creditors and debtors of the decedent) that this personal representative has authority to act as the estate's representative for all purposes. This is done by advertising in a local newspaper of general circulation and in a legal periodical in the county in which the estate is being probated.

Advertising provides notice to all creditors and debtors that the decedent has died and creditors and debtors may settle their accounts with the decedent's personal representative. Advertising starts the statute of limitations running. If creditors do not notify the executor of their claim within a fixed period set by local law (generally 3 to 6 months but certainly within one year of the advertisement), they will be barred from collecting any amounts owed to them by the decedent.

LO 8. 3   Explain what is involved in assembling and managing the estate property.

ASSEMBLING ESTATE PROPERTY

One of the first tasks of the personal representative is to assemble the property belonging to the estate. All estate assets must be gathered, safeguarded, and managed during this interim period of estate administration. This task ranges from a relatively simple one to an extremely complex, time-consuming, and expensive project. Executors should make every reasonable effort to collect all accounts receivable due to decedents from their business or profession. They may find themselves involved in the sale or continued operation of a decedent's business.

Complications may arise if the decedent owned property or partial interests in property in conjunction with others, such as interests in limited partnerships. These may be based in states other than the state of domicile (where the will is usually probated) or abroad. The decedent may also have possessed assets or business interests in foreign countries. The decedent may have been the beneficiary of one or more trusts or the custodian of another's assets. The estate may be entitled to death benefits under an employment contract. The decedent may have possessed or retained remainder interests in property. There are many involved property rights.

The executor is the one with the responsibility to take possession of and make all appropriate transfers of a decedent's property. In addition to assembling the assets, the executor has a duty to make certain that valuables are safeguarded and insured, if necessary, during the administration period. This might involve the use of safe-deposit boxes and storage vaults.

The executor may find it necessary to possess the instincts of a sleuth and the patience of a saint if the estate was left in a disorganized condition. Whether a simple or complex matter, it is the personal representative who has the legal responsibility to gather all estate property, wherever situated, making the transfers necessary to do so.

Safe-Deposit Boxes

One of the first places to look for information and valuable papers is the decedent's safe-deposit box. Once an individual passes away, a safe-deposit box titled in the decedent's own name is closed, except for limited purposes. Usually a representative of the bank is present when the box is opened for the first time after death. The will may be found in a safe-deposit box, which is not necessarily a good location for a will as one of the first things to find out is who has been named executor.

A will itself has no intrinsic value. If possible, for simplicity's sake, it should be kept among the valuable papers of the decedent or with the decedent's attorney rather than in a safe-deposit box. The personal representative should make a diligent search for more than one safe-deposit box to assure that all safe-deposit boxes in the name of the decedent have been located. In some states, the safe-deposit box cannot be opened except in the presence of a representative of the state taxing authority in addition to a representative of the bank. If the box contains possessions belonging to someone other than the decedent, the personal representative should not surrender this property without obtaining a receipt from the person taking possession of the property.

Proceeds of Life Insurance and Qualified Plans

Life insurance policies should be located and a claim made for all life insurance benefits. The insurance company will provide the executor with Form 712, to be filed with the federal estate tax return. There are optional modes of payment of life insurance proceeds. These various settlement options should be discussed with the beneficiaries. An appropriate settlement option should be chosen, unless the insurance is made payable to the estate or to a trust, in which case the insurance is usually paid in a lump sum. If the decedent had a right to receive death benefits from pension or profit-sharing plans, these proceeds should be applied for. Here, again, there may be a choice of payment plan. The mode of payment may have significant income tax consequences and should be reviewed carefully.

Surviving spouses may also apply for lump-sum Social Security death benefits and any Veterans Administration survivor benefits to which they are entitled.

MANAGING THE ESTATE

digital assets

nontransferable

Once the estate is assembled, the executor is obligated to properly manage the assets of the estate. This includes: managing cash, securities, and business interests; valuing assets; and obtaining necessary legal and accounting services. Remember that certain assets can be extremely difficult to find and access. For example, **digital assets**, which are properties stored electronically such as online bank accounts, Bitcoin, software programs, and websites, can be **nontransferable** upon death, meaning that the heirs cannot receive the property. It can also be difficult to access the digital assets because of username and passwords that are unknown to the estate. Even just tracking down all of the assets can be difficult after a person's death due to the lack of a paper trail or physical storage location. Searching through email accounts and combing online credit card statements often becomes necessary to find all of a deceased person's digital assets.

Estate Accounts

Any cash belonging to the decedent should be deposited in an estate checking account as soon as assets are released to the estate. Checks should be ordered for payment of the estate's debts. Although funds necessary to pay bills should be kept in a checking account, the executor has an obligation to keep other reasonable sums of money producing interest income during the estate-administration period. Therefore, a savings account or money market trust account in the name of the estate should also be opened. If the decedent had a personal-brokerage account, it should be closed and the securities or cash should be transferred to an estate account, unless the decedent's will specifically directed the executor to keep that account open for a specific time or purpose.

Valuation of Assets

Besides locating and taking possession of the decedent's property, the executor must determine the value of all estate assets as of the date of death. These values fix the value of assets in the estate for both estate and inheritance tax purposes. All banks in which the decedent had accounts must be contacted to obtain the date-of-death values, including all accrued interest for the short-tax year ending with the decedent's death. Real property and unique personal property of any special value (such as art objects or coins) may require appraisal by an independent appraiser. Copies of the decedent's income tax returns and canceled checks for the past 3 years should be obtained. They provide a record of the time of financial transactions as well as their cost. It will also be necessary to learn of any valuable rights the decedent may have owned, such as patent rights, royalties, or contract rights, and to determine the fair market value of these rights on the date of death. If the decedent was a professional or a sole proprietor, the value of the decedent's business or profession must be appraised for estate tax purposes.

After all assets have been located and appraised, an inventory listing all the assets and their values is filed with the probate court.

Legal and Accounting Work

If the executor is inexperienced in financial, business, and tax matters, or if the estate is complicated, administrative duties may be delegated to others. For example, the executor may hire an attorney specializing in estate matters as well as an appraiser to obtain reasonable values for the estate property. The decedent's accountant may be consulted about tax and business matters. An attorney specializing in estate planning may be called in by the executor to perform all legal work and assist with some of the financial matters as well. This is often the same attorney who drafted the will. Today, many banks, although not named as a fiduciary under the will, are willing to offer estate-settlement services on a fee-for-service basis. The trust department of a bank handles these matters routinely. A bank's trust department has the capacity to perform all administrative tasks for the estate, including the preparation of all tax returns.

Management or Sale of Business

In addition to the foregoing responsibilities, an administrator or executor may have to sell assets of the estate by personal sale or auction to raise the necessary cash to pay the debts, taxes, and administration expenses of the estate. This may involve sale of a personal residence or all or part of a business interest. The executor must decide whether the business interest or professional practice of the decedent must be sold or whether it can be maintained to provide a source of income for the family. The executor may become intimately involved in making decisions regarding the business until such time as it may be liquidated, sold, or transferred to the heirs. The executor is responsible for the interim management and investment of all assets of the estate.

LO 8. 4   **Review the settlement and wrapping up of an estate.**

PAYMENT OF DEBTS AND TAXES

It is the executor's responsibility to pay all bills and debts of the decedent and to keep records of all costs of administering the estate. The administrator or executor is also responsible for payment of any court costs, attorney fees, administrator or executor fees, as well as fees for appraisals of property, and probate costs. Executors may also have some out-of-pocket expenses for which they may reimburse themselves.

Order of Payment of Claims

The executor has to establish the validity of all claims against the estate. A creditor must present a claim within a statutory time period. As stated previously, this time varies from state to state and may be as much as one year, but in recent years the time period has been short-ened by many states to 9 or 6 months. There is a prescribed order of priority for payment of claims. If there are insufficient assets to pay all the claims in full, then the primary classes are paid in full first, with lower priority claims remaining unpaid entirely. Within a class of claims, each debt must be paid pro rata. While each state establishes its own order of preference for payment of debts, the following is a typical order: (1) debts that have a special lien on property not exceeding the value of the property; (2) funeral expenses; (3) taxes; (4) debts owed to the United States government and to the state; (5) judgments of any court of competent jurisdic-tion to the extent that they are a lien against the property of the decedent at death; (6) wages due to any domestic servant or mechanical or agricultural laborer for the year immediately prior to the decedent's death; (7) medical expenses and services provided during the year pre-ceding the death; and (8) all other debts and claims.

Filing of Tax Returns and Payment of Taxes

Records of any federal gift tax returns (Form 709) must be obtained; gift tax returns for any tax-able gifts made in the year of death must also be filed. If the gross estate plus adjusted taxable gifts exceed a statutory amount equal to the basic exclusion amount (exemption equivalent of the basic credit amount), the executor must file a federal estate tax return within 9 months after the decedent's death. Also, any elections must be made by the time the estate tax return is filed, including extensions. Some states also impose a gift tax on lifetime gratuitous transfers and/or an estate tax on transfers at death.

In addition to payment of federal estate taxes, the estate may be liable for taxes on real property, personal property, and possibly intangible personal property located in the state. Federal and state income taxes will also need to be paid, both for the short taxable year prior to the decedent's death and the remaining period of that tax year after death. This may include filing a joint return with the surviving spouse for the year of death. State inheritance or estate taxes must be paid if any tax is due. If there is a discount for early payment of state inheritance tax, the executor must decide when to pay the inheritance tax and weigh the advantages or disadvantages of paying it early. Sometimes, early payment is impossible because there are no liquid assets in the estate that can be used for this purpose. For example, the major asset of an estate may be real estate. Prior to the sale of such property, the estate will not have cash to pay many of its obligations. In that case, early payment of inheritance taxes is not possible and the discount is, of necessity, lost. If a trust has been established, some taxes may be payable by the trust.

A determination must be made as to who the taxpayer is and how the taxes will be allocated among the estate, any trust, or the beneficiaries of each. Frequently, a will contains a tax clause that directs the way taxes are to be apportioned. If there is no tax clause in the will, taxes are allocated according to the state statutory scheme.

There are still other decisions that an executor should make with regard to payment of taxes. A choice must be made whether to have all assets valued on the date of death or the alternate valuation date, which is 6 months from the date of death. For decedents dying after July 18, 1984, the alternate valuation date can be used only if both the value of the gross estate and the amount of federal estate tax will decrease by using the alternate valuation date (IRC Sec. 2032(c)). An example of an estate that could still use the alternate valuation date is one that has substantial amounts of stocks and bonds whose prices have dropped significantly within the 6-month period between the date of death and the alternate valuation date. In that case, the executor may select the alternate valuation date to reduce taxes. Also, if more than 35 percent of the adjusted gross estate consists of a closely held business or farm, the executor should consider the advisability of electing a 14-year, 9-month payment of the estate tax attributable to the value of that closely held business or farm included in the estate. An extension of time to pay the tax may also be requested based on reasonable cause.

There is also a provision in the Internal Revenue Code for special valuation of a farm or business real estate. Any election to specially value these properties at their current-use value rather than at their highest and best use must be made when the federal estate return is filed. If the estate contains qualified terminable interest property (QTIP), the executor must also decide whether to elect to qualify this property for the marital deduction. There may be some credits or deductions that can be taken for taxes previously paid on the estate of a person whose property was inherited by the decedent within 10 years of the decedent's death. Also, the executor may be given discretion in the will to take deductions either on the federal estate tax return or the decedent's income tax return to achieve the lowest tax liability. All of the above decisions fall within the scope of the executor's discretion and responsibilities.

DISTRIBUTING THE ESTATE

As the estate administration process draws to a close, the executor will prepare an accounting for the court and the beneficiaries. This procedure varies from state to state. An accounting is filed in the county where the will was probated. It may be a formal proceeding with notice to interested parties, or it may be an informal proceeding. At this time, any interested parties have the right to object to the accounting and to have any matters at issue resolved by the judge with whom the accounting is filed.

If there is no objection to the accounting, the executor or administrator then proceeds to make final distribution of the estate assets. When the executor makes distributions, it is important that releases and receipts be obtained from the beneficiaries to relieve the executor from further liability to each beneficiary because of the property transferred to him or her. When that has been accomplished, the administrator or executor may be discharged by the court, at which time the estate can be closed. If any property is found after that, it may be necessary to reopen the estate on a limited basis to have this property probated.

Disclaimers

The possibility may arise that a beneficiary does not wish to accept either a bequest under the decedent's will or an intestate share of the estate that he or she is entitled to receive. A reason may be that the beneficiary's own estate is substantial. The beneficiary may not want to further burden his or her own estate with additional estate taxes. Alternatively, it may be a way of releasing an inheritance so that it will go to other beneficiaries in greater need than himself or herself. If a beneficiary does not wish to accept an inheritance, it is possible to refuse this legacy by making a *qualified disclaimer*. If the requirements of a qualified disclaimer are met, the property will be treated as if it had never passed to that individual. There are several requirements under the Internal Revenue Code to qualify a disclaimer for federal estate tax or gift tax purposes: (1) there must be an unqualified refusal by the beneficiary to accept the bequest or the gift; (2) this refusal must be written; (3) the disclaimer must be received by the donor, the donor's legal representative, or the legal titleholder of the property within 9 months of the decedent's death, 9 months from the date of the gift or, if later, within 9 months after the beneficiary becomes 21 years of age; (4) the beneficiary must not have accepted the interest or any of its benefits; and (5) the interest must then pass to someone other than the person making the disclaimer or to the spouse of the decedent without the beneficiary's direction.

The law provides that a disclaimer complying with the requirements of the federal tax statute is considered to qualify for federal estate and gift tax purposes, regardless of qualification under local law. The law provides some uniformity in the application of the federal disclaimer statute, although state law may still hold the disclaimer ineffective to pass title directly to the later beneficiary without gift tax considerations.

All or part of an interest in property may be disclaimed. However, the disclaimed part must represent an undivided portion of the interest. The beneficiary of an estate has 9 months following the decedent's death in which to make this disclaimer. It must be received by the executor or administrator of the estate in writing. If a federal estate tax return is filed, a copy of the disclaimer must be filed with the return. It is also possible to disclaim a power of appointment over property if the requirements previously stated are met.

CHAPTER REVIEW

Key Terms and Concepts

probate   letters testamentary
deed   advertising
ancillary probate   digital assets
posting bond   nontransferable

Chapter 8: Review Questions

1. What property in a decedent's estate is subject to probate? [1]

2. What are the advantages and disadvantages of probate? [1]

3. What are the responsibilities of an executor? [2]

4. What is the problem associated with having a will located in a safe-deposit box? [3]

5. What functions must an executor or administrator perform in managing an estate? [3]

6. Describe some of the challenges of the estate settlement process when digital assets are involved. [3]

7. Describe the general priority for paying claims if an estate has insufficient assets to pay all claims in full. [4]

8. Describe the responsibilities of an executor or administrator with respect to filing tax returns and paying taxes. [4]

9. For what reasons might a beneficiary disclaim an inheritance? [4]

Chapter 8: Review Answers

1. All property that passes under and is subject to the terms of the will is admitted to probate. If there is no will, all property subject to the administration of the court due to intestacy is admitted to probate.

2. The main advantages of probate are that it provides a process for the validation of a decedent's will and provides for the appointment of a personal representative of the estate. It permits court supervision of an executor's activities concerning the decedent's estate and grants a forum for the resolution of will contests and other matters concerning the estate. Probate oversees the inventory, valuation, and distribution of estate property. It also establishes a time period prior to distribution of estate assets during which the decedent's creditors must come forward to present their claims to the estate.

   Disadvantages of probate typically are the delays and inflexibilities concerning estate matters and distribution of estate property to the beneficiaries. The procedures necessitated by the probate process are according to statute and may be more time-consuming than is desired. Other negative aspects are expenses and lack of privacy. The will, creditors' claims, and other personal matters involving the decedent's estate are a matter of public record. There are costs for court supervision of the estate plus executor and attorney fees.

3. The executor is responsible for managing the testator's estate—gathering all assets; collecting all amounts owed the decedent; paying debts, expenses, and taxes; and distributing assets to the beneficiaries.

4. If the will is located in a safe-deposit box titled in the decedent's own name, the box is closed once that person dies. Gaining immediate access to the will can therefore be a problem.

5. The functions an executor must perform to manage an estate are as follows:

   - Establish an estate checking account and savings or money market account.
   - Locate, take possession of, and determine the value of estate assets as of the date of death; file an inventory of assets with the probate court.
   - Hire financial, business, tax, and estate specialists, as necessary.
   - File necessary tax returns, make sure elections and disclaimers are made on time, and pay taxes due.

6. Digital assets can be difficult to locate due to the lack of a paper trail. Access to the assets can be difficult because of passwords and usernames. Digital assets are often nontransferable assets - meaning that no one can inherit the asset. All of these factors can create challenges for an otherwise well-planned estate.

7. The order for payment of claims is typically as follows: (1) debts that have a special lien on property not exceeding the property's value, (2) funeral expenses, (3) taxes, (4) debts owed the United States government and the state, (5) court judgments, (6) wages due any servant or laborer for the year prior to the decedent's death, (7) medical expenses for the year preceding death, and (8) all other debts and claims.

8. The executor must get records of prior gift tax returns (and must file a return for gifts in the year of death) and determine whether the taxable estate plus adjusted taxable gifts (post-1976 lifetime taxable transfers not included in the decedent's gross estate) exceed the basic exclusion amount.

    In addition, the executor should pay property taxes, state inheritance (or state) taxes, and relevant income tax returns. For example, the executor should file the decedent's final income tax return and an estate income tax return for each year the estate is open.

9. A beneficiary might want to disclaim an inheritance because his or her own estate is substantial, and the beneficiary does not want the estate to incur additional estate taxes. The beneficiary might also disclaim in order to release the inheritance to other beneficiaries whose needs are greater.

Chapter 9:

Valuation of Assets for Federal Estate and Gift Taxation

Learning Objectives

An understanding of the material in this chapter should enable the student to

LO 9.1   **Explain why it is important to value assets for estate planning purposes.**

LO 9. 2   **Determine the general rules that need to be followed in the valuation process.**

LO 9. 3   **Identify problems that may occur in the valuation process.**

LO 9. 4   **Explain how certain types of assets are valued.**

LO 9. 5   **Identify the general methods used to value closely held businesses.**

LO 9. 6   **Explain how various types of lifetime transfers with retained interests are valued.**

LO 9.1   **Explain why it is important to value assets for estate planning purposes.**

IMPORTANCE OF VALUING ASSETS

One of the most complex and uncertain aspects of the estate planning process is the valuation of property for federal estate and gift tax purposes. Frequently, the taxpayer's representative values property at one amount; the IRS attempts a second figure; and, if the issue cannot be settled between the taxpayer and the IRS, the courts generally settle on some middle ground. Thus, value is a variable upon which reasonable minds can and will differ. Value is not determined merely by flipping a coin. There are techniques to substantiate values. These devices include careful and thorough appraisals by qualified experts, documentation of sales of similar property recently sold, and well-drawn, arm's-length restrictive agreements, such as buy-sell arrangements.

The estate planning professional must be keenly aware of the problems and costs associated with the lack of pre-death valuation planning. There are a number of reasons why valuation is of particular importance in the estate planning process.

First, it is impossible to determine potential liquidity needs that an executor may experience unless values are placed on the various assets owned by the client. A hypothetical probate of the estate is impossible until values are assigned to various assets. Qualification for stock redemptions under Sec. 303 or installment payments of taxes attributable to business interests under Sec. 6166 depend on the value of the decedent's stock relative to the value of the decedent's other assets. If the appropriate test(s) cannot be met, neither technique for paying estate taxes is available. For planning purposes, this means that both the value of a client's stock and the worth of other assets must be estimated with reasonable accuracy.

In addition, many estate owners are thinking about establishing gift programs or have already done so. Because of the income and estate tax advantages still inherent in gifts, gratuitous transfers of property may be meaningful when they are subject to minimal gift tax costs. Furthermore, inter vivos gifts to charity can yield large, immediate income tax deductions. But to properly consider the various ramifications and potential advantages involved in a lifetime transfer, a knowledge of valuation is essential.

The third reason that valuing assets is an important technique for the estate planner relates to the funding of buy-sell agreements. For example, if a client is one of several owners of a business, quite often a buy-sell agreement is advisable. The first step in arranging such an agreement is to arrive at a fair market value for the business. Obviously, it is impossible to assure each costockholder (or partner) that beneficiaries will receive an equitable price on death or disability unless the current worth of each person's business interest is ascertained.

Why the Lowest Value Is Not Always the Best

Because both federal estate and gift taxes are based on the value of property interests transferred, at first glance it makes sense to attempt to value property at the lowest reasonable figure. However, achieving the lowest possible valuation for an asset is not always the most appropriate objective.

One example in which a higher valuation might be advantageous is the formula for a buy-sell agreement. Especially from the point of view of the decedent's survivors, where alternative liquidity funding is impractical, it may be better to set a formula in a buy-sell agreement that puts a higher value on the stock in a closely held business (and thereby provides more cash for the decedent's survivors) than to establish a formula that provides a lower estate tax value (yielding a lower price for the decedent's business interest).

When closely held stock is valued high relative to other estate assets, the disadvantage of the additional tax payable due to the higher valuation may be more than offset by the advantages of qualifying for a Sec. 303 stock redemption or a Sec. 6166 election to pay federal estate taxes attributable to a business interest in installments.

LO 9. 2 Determine the general rules that need to be followed in the valuation process.

Date Assets Are Valued

alternate valuation date

Generally, federal estate taxes are based either on the fair market value of the transferred property as of the date the decedent died or, if applicable, on the value of the property 6 months after the date of the decedent's death (**alternate valuation date**). Once the date-of-death valuation or the alternate valuation date is selected, that date applies to all assets in the estate, subject to the exceptions noted below.

If the alternate valuation date is selected and property is distributed, sold, exchanged, or otherwise disposed of within the 6-month period after the decedent's death, that property is valued as of the date of distribution, sale, exchange, or other disposition, not as of the 6-month date.

Certain types of property diminish in value as time goes on. Any property interest which is affected by the mere passing of time, such as an annuity, patent, or remainder interest, is valued as of the date the decedent died, even if the alternate valuation date applies to other estate assets.

Federal Estate Tax—Asset Valuation Dates
- date of death (earliest date)
- date of sale, exchange, distribution, disposition
- alternate valuation date (6 months after death)

General Valuation Rules

fair market value

There is very little in the Internal Revenue Code about how to value items for federal estate tax purposes. Although the value of the gross estate is mentioned in the Code, the word value is not defined. The estate and gift tax regulations provide that value is meant to be **fair market value**, which is defined as

> the price at which the property would change hands between a willing buyer and a willing seller, neither being under any compulsion to buy or to sell, and both having reasonable knowledge of relevant facts.

By this definition, the value that may be placed on property can vary substantially, depending on who is valuing the item and what factors are being used. The regulations state that it is not necessary to have either an established market for an item or a willing buyer and seller as mentioned above. In the absence of an actual sale, the value of an asset is based on a hypothetical sale.

Generally, the following external factors are examined in deciding the extent to which sales price is indicative of value:

- the frequency of sales (Courts tend to disregard isolated or sporadic sales.)

- the relationship between the seller and the buyer (Sales between parents and children or employers and employees are seldom given great weight in light of their almost inherently unequal bargaining positions.)

- options to purchase or sell (Offers, as opposed to options, present little evidence of value.)

Once all these value-affecting factors are considered, each factor must be given a relative weight.

LO 9. 3   Identify problems that may occur in the valuation process.

Specific Problems in Valuation

Some items present minimal valuation problems. If there is an established market for identical property, value is basically a question of fact. But evidential proof—and often opinion—is necessary when the following occurs:

- There are different markets for the same property, such as in the case of a property with both wholesale and retail markets.

- The appraisal of worth must be made on the basis of comparison with somewhat similar property. (Which comparable property should be selected? How comparable is it?) In such a case, what is derived is at best an opinion based on fact.

- The property in question is unique, such as a patent or copyright, in which case the data must be analyzed (Is the examiner capable of making an adequate analysis?), and an opinion must be formulated as to how much the potential anticipated benefits are worth.

In practice, valuation problems are frequently viewed by the IRS and the courts as problems of negotiation and compromise. An appraiser's objective is to derive a fair and sound value that, if litigated, would likely be sustained in court.

LO 9. 4 **Explain how certain types of assets are valued.**

VALUATION OF REAL PROPERTY

This chapter will not examine the valuation process for all types of property. However, the valuation of real property, as well as stocks of closely held corporations, provide good examples of the essential gift and estate tax valuation process.

Valuation of Land and Property Affixed to Land

Land is unique. Therefore, the value of any real property (land or property affixed to land) on a given date may be subject to widely differing opinions. If there is no market for such property, a controlling factor is the greater of: (1) the highest price available, and (2) the *salvage* value, which is the disposal value of the property at the end of its useful life. When there is a market for real property, the basic factors that affect valuation are

- the size, shape, and location of the property
- the nature and condition of the property, its physical qualities and defects, and the adequacy or inadequacy of its improvements
- the actual and potential use of the property and how the trends of development and economic conditions (such as population growth) affect it
- the suitability of the property for its actual or intended use
- zoning restrictions
- the age, size, and condition of the buildings (degree of deterioration and obsolescence)
- the market value of other properties in the area in which the property is located
- environmental factors such as the presence of or nearness to hazardous materials and wetlands laws' restrictions
- the value of net income received from the property (Rentals are often capitalized at a rate of between 6 and 12 percent and then adjusted for depreciation; the same principle can be applied to gross rents after adjustment for operating cost.)
- prices at which comparable property in the same area was sold at a time near the applicable valuation date—providing the sale was an arm's-length transaction for the best price available
- the cost to duplicate the property after taking depreciation into account

- the value accepted by state probate courts for purposes of state death taxes, if based on appraisals made by qualified real estate experts
- unusual facts

In the event of a sale of real property within a reasonable period of time after the decedent's death in such a manner as to ensure the highest possible price, the amount received is usually accepted as its value. Unaccepted offers to purchase the property are also considered. What about a sale at auction? Usually, this price is accepted only if it appears there was no other method to obtain a higher price.

Land does not have to produce income or have an active market to attain substantial value. When land is in or adjacent to a settled community, owners frequently hold such land in anticipation of realizing its true value from future sales. For example, a home at the edge of an expanding shopping center might be worth far more to the shopping center developer than it would be to a potential home buyer.

Special-Use (Current-Use) Valuation for Certain Real Property (IRC Sec. 2032A)

special-use valuation (2032A)

The test of fair market value described above is the *highest and best price* that would be agreed upon between a willing buyer and a willing seller. This has often caused farm or business real estate to be valued at the price at which it might have been valued if it was going to be used for residential or industrial development rather than at the price it is worth according to its current use. For special-use valuation purposes, a "farm" includes stock, dairy, fruit, fur-bearing animals, truck farms and dairy farms, nurseries, ranches, woodlands, orchards, plantations, greenhouses, and other horticultural or agricultural commodity structures. An executor (if certain conditions are met) can elect to use a **special-use valuation** approach (*current-use valuation approach*). That is, the real estate is valued taking into consideration how it is currently being utilized instead of how it *might* be used if placed in its most profitable use.

The special-use valuation provided by this method cannot be used to reduce a decedent's gross estate by more than $1,140,000 (2018).

EXAMPLE

At the time Stuart Sims died in 2019, his estate included qualifying real property that had a highest- and best-use value of $6,500,000. The special-use value of the property is $5,480,000. The difference between the highest and best-use value and the special-use value is $1,020,000 ($6,500,000 – $5,480,000). Therefore, Stuart's estate is allowed a reduction of $1,020,000 in 2018 when the maximum reduction allowed is $1,160,000 in 2018.

Requirements for Special-Use Valuation. The following conditions must be satisfied before current-use valuation is allowed for estate tax purposes:

- The decedent must have been a U.S. citizen or resident.
- The farm or other closely held business (real and personal property qualifying for the special use) must constitute at least 50 percent of the decedent's gross estate (after certain adjustments for mortgages and liens).
- The net value of real property qualifying for the special use must constitute at least 25 percent of the adjusted gross estate value.
- The real property in question must pass to a *qualified heir* (essentially, a lineal descendant of the decedent's grandfather).
- Either the decedent or a family member must have owned the real property—and used it as a farm or in a closely held business—for at least 5 of the 8 years immediately prior to the date the decedent died.
- Either the decedent or a member of the decedent's family must have materially participated in the operation of the farm or business for at least 5 out of the 8 years immediately prior to the decedent's death.
- The property must continue in its special use by qualified heirs for 10 years after the decedent's death.

A special tax lien is placed on all real property valued according to current use until the conditions for special-use valuation are met. If the special-use valuation requirements are not fulfilled, the lien remains on the property until a recapture tax is paid. The heirs remain personally liable to pay that tax.

Furthermore, a written agreement must be filed with the estate tax return. It must be signed by everyone who has an interest in the real property qualifying for special valuation. Each of these individuals must consent to the imposition of the recapture tax described below.

Interestingly, if the qualified heir dies during the 10-year recapture period, the recapture requirements die, too.

farm-method formula of valuation

Special-Use Methods Available. There are a number of methods allowed for valuing real estate of closely held businesses or farms. The **farm-method formula of valuation** is illustrated in the following example.

> ### EXAMPLE
>
> Farmer Jones owns 300 acres of farmland in Swedesboro, New Jersey. Nearby farm-land of about the same acreage produces an average annual gross rental of $172,000. Average annual state and local real estate taxes are $16,000. Assume the interest rate for loans from the Federal Land Bank is 8 percent.
>
> The average annual computations are made on the basis of the 5 most recent calendar years before the farmer's death.
>
> Under the *farm-method formula of valuation*, valuation of the farmer's land is computed as shown below:
>
> $$(\$172{,}000 - \$16{,}000) \div .08 = \$1{,}950{,}000$$

This formula for valuing farmland is not used if there is no comparable land from which the average rentals can be determined. In that case, an executor might elect to value the farmland in the same manner that closely held business real property is valued (through a capitalization method, comparable sales prices, or any other factor that fairly values the farm or other closely held business).

recapture

Recapture of the Special-use Tax Benefit. As previously stated, if the property is disposed of to nonfamily members within 10 years after the death of the decedent, there is an additional estate tax or **recapture** tax imposed on the qualified heir. If the heir or a member of the heir's family fails to participate materially in the business operation for 10 years after the decedent's death, it is treated as a cessation of the qualified use, also causing recapture.

Recapture of the difference in tax between the current-use and highest-and-best-use methods of valuation occurs when the real estate is sold, disposed of, or no longer used for the same qualified use within the 10-year period. Also, the eligible qualified heir must be engaged in the active management of the farm or business during the recapture period. If during this period the heir is under age 21, disabled, a full-time student, or the surviving spouse, a fiduciary may qualify in providing active management for the heir. Leasing arrangements may be entered into when the decedent or heirs are unable to or do not wish to meet the qualified-use restrictions themselves.

If recapture occurs and results in additional estate taxes, the real estate receives a new basis stepped up to what the basis would be if special-use valuation had not been elected. Otherwise, the basis upon a subsequent sale of the property by the qualified heir(s) is the current-use valuation. However, the increased basis obtained if recapture occurs does not include retroactive changes in depreciation, other deductions, or credits reflecting the increased basis.

Exceptions to the recapture rules are loss of the property through involuntary conversion or exchange of the real estate in a like-kind exchange. No recapture is triggered generally under these circumstances. There are also special rules for woodlands and a limited right of judicial review.

Planning Point 1: With proper advance planning, an estate owner can assure the qualification of his or her estate for the 50 percent and 25 percent mathematical tests of Sec. 2032A. For instance, lifetime gifts of nonbusiness property to others will increase the ratio of the closely held business or farm to the adjusted gross estate. Note, however, that for the sole purpose of calculating the mathematical tests under Sec. 2032A (as well as other favorable tax treatment Code sections such as Secs. 6166 and 303), the 3-year rule under Sec. 2035 requires the inclusion of the value of transfers the decedent made within 3 years of death.

Planning Point 2: Qualified heirs and advisors must weigh the estate tax savings against the restrictions on the qualifying property's use and disposition for the 10-year period after the decedent's death versus the potential for higher capital gains tax resulting from a sale of the qualifying property after the decedent's death.

VALUATION OF PERSONAL PROPERTY

Valuation of Household and Personal Effects

willing buyer-willing seller rule

The general rule for valuing household property and personal effects, such as watches, rings, and so forth, can be called the **willing buyer-willing seller rule**. A room-by-room itemization is typical, especially when household goods include articles of artistic or intrinsic value, such as jewelry, furs, silverware, paintings, engravings, antiques, books, statuary, oriental rugs, and coin or stamp collections.

In non-community-property states, *household goods* and the like personally acquired by and used by husband and wife during marriage are generally presumed to be the marital property.

Therefore, in the absence of sufficient evidence to rebut this presumption, household goods and personal effects are includible in the estate of the first spouse who dies.

Valuation of Listed Stocks

Where a stock has an established market and quotations are available to value the stock as of the date in question, the fair market value (FMV) per share on the applicable valuation date governs for both gift and estate tax purposes.

The FMV is based on selling prices when there is a market for the stock or bond. This is the mean between the highest and lowest quoted selling price on the valuation date. If there were no sales on the valuation date, but there were sales on dates within a reasonable period both before and after the valuation date, the FMV is determined by taking a weighted average of the means between the highest and lowest sales on the nearest date before and the nearest date after the valuation. The average is then weighted inversely by the respective number of trading days between the selling date and the valuation date.

When a large block of stock cannot be marketed in an orderly manner, the block might depress the market because it cannot be converted to cash as readily as a few shares could be. Therefore, selling prices and bid-and-asked prices may not reflect fair market value. Sometimes it may be necessary to value this type of stock as if it were closely held and not actively traded. If this can be established, a reasonable modification of the normal basis for determining FMV can be made. In some cases, a *blockage discount* is determined by the effect that block would have had on the market if it were sold over a reasonable period of time and in a prudent manner. A similar situation occurs when sales at or near the date of death are either few or of a sporadic nature and may not indicate a fair market value.

The converse of the blockage situation above occurs when the block of stock to be valued represents a controlling interest (either actual or effective) in an ongoing business. Here the price of normally traded shares may have little relation to the true value of the controlling lot. The large block can have the effect of increasing value because of its element of control.

Valuation of Corporate Bonds

Valuation of bonds is similar to valuation of listed common stock. The means of the selling prices on or near the applicable valuation date (or—if there were no sales—the means of bona fide asked prices weighted inversely to the number of trading days from the valuation date) determine the fair market value of the bonds.

In the absence of sales or bid-and-asked prices, the value must be determined by

- ascertaining the soundness of the security

- comparing the interest on the bond in question to yields on similar bonds

- examining the date of maturity

- comparing prices for listed bonds of corporations engaged in similar types of business

- checking the extent to which the bond is secured

- weighing all other relevant factors, including the opinion of experts, the goodwill of the business, the industry's economic outlook, and the company's position in the industry as well as its management

Valuation of U.S. Government Bonds

Series EE (or E) bonds are valued at their redemption price (market value) as of the date of death, since they are neither negotiable nor transferable and the only definitely ascertainable value is the amount at which the Treasury will redeem them.

Certain U.S. Treasury bonds (*flower bonds*) owned by a decedent at the date of death and forming part of the gross estate may be redeemed at par value if used to pay federal estate taxes. These bonds are valued at the higher of the market price and par value. Flower bonds were fixed-income bonds that were originally purchased at a discount in anticipation of federal estate taxes. When the bondholder died, the bonds matured at par value and were used to pay the decedent's estate taxes. Sometimes flower bonds were referred to as "estate tax anticipation bonds." The last of this type of bond matured in 1998.

Even if such bonds are not used to pay estate taxes, the courts have often held that, when the bonds could be used for the payment of estate taxes, they are valued at the higher of market and par value. When the bonds could not be applied to pay the estate tax, their value is market (the mean quoted selling price value).

Valuation of Life Insurance

Proceeds of life insurance on the life of the decedent receivable by or for the benefit of the decedent's estate are taxed in the decedent-insured's estate. In addition, when the decedent held incidents of ownership, such ownership invokes taxation. The amount includible is the amount receivable by the beneficiary. This includes dividends and premium refunds. In determining how much is includible, no distinction is made between an ordinary life policy, a term policy, group insurance, or an accidental death benefit.

If a settlement option is elected, the amount that is payable as a lump sum is the amount includible. If the policy did not provide for a lump-sum payment, the amount includible is the commuted amount used by the insurance company to compute the settlement option payments.

The value of an unmatured policy owned by a decedent on the life of another is included in the policyowner's gross estate (when the policyowner predeceases the insured) according to the following:

- If a new life insurance policy is involved, the gross premium paid is the value.
- If the policy is a paid-up or a single-premium policy, its value is its replacement cost—that is, the single premium that company would have charged for a comparable contract of equal face value on the life of a person who was the insured's age (at the time the decedent-policyholder died).
- If the policy is a premium-paying whole life policy, the value is found by adding any unearned portion of the last premium to the interpolated terminal reserve.
- If the policy is a term policy, the value is the unused premium.

The IRS issued Treasury regulations (Treas. Reg. Secs. 1.402; 1.79; 1.83) and Revenue Procedure 2005-25, which offer new guidance for the valuation of certain life insurance contracts for income tax purposes.

LO 9. 5   Identify the general methods used to value closely held businesses.

VALUATION OF STOCK OF CLOSELY HELD CORPORATIONS

The valuation of closely held corporate stock is often one of the most difficult and time-consuming problems faced by the executor of a decedent's estate. By definition, closely held stock is incapable of valuation solely by recourse to an established market (that is, closely held stock is seldom traded). In fact, the criteria used to define closely held stock include: (1) a limited number of stockholders, (2) restrictions imposed upon a shareholder's ability to transfer the stock, (3) the absence of an exchange listing or regular quotation in the over-the-counter market, and (4) an irregular and limited history of sales or exchanges.

There is no formula provided by the Internal Revenue Code or the regulations that is applicable to every closely held stock valuation situation. However, there are guidelines that should be considered in every valuation case. The key IRS ruling on point, Rev. Rul. 59–60, suggests that the following factors be considered:

- the nature of the business and the entire history of the enterprise
- the economic outlook in general as well as the condition and outlook of the specific industry
- the book value of the stock and the financial condition of the business (The Tax Court considers this factor in almost every case.)
- the company's earning capacity (For many businesses—especially those that do depend heavily on capital to produce profits—this will be the most important valuation factor.)
- the company's dividend-paying capacity

goodwill

- the existence of goodwill (**goodwill** can be defined as the economic advantage or benefit that is acquired by a business *beyond* the mere value of the capital invested in it because of the patronage it receives from constant or habitual customers, its local position, its reputation for skill or punctuality, other accidental circumstances or necessities, or public partialities or prejudices. In short, goodwill is a broad term implying that a company has a purchase value exceeding the worth of its tangible assets. *Note: A business may have goodwill value even if no amount for goodwill is shown on its accounting statements.*)
- prior stock sales and size of the block of stock to be valued
- fair market value of stock of comparable corporations engaged in the same or similar type of business where the stock is actively traded in an established market

Rev. Rul. 59–60 reaffirms that no fixed formula of valuation can be devised that is applicable to all situations and that, ultimately, the fair market value of closely held stock must be determined on an individual basis.

When faced with a gift or estate tax valuation question, courts sift through innumerable elements—besides the eight basic factors mentioned in Rev. Rul. 59–60. Some of the valuation factors used by the courts (but given varying weight depending on the circumstances) are

- the values accepted by the IRS when other estates held the same stock
- the price for the stock in the decedent's will
- the values as determined by expert witnesses
- the relationships between prices, earnings, and book values

- the degree of control of the business represented by the block of stock to be valued
- the value of the services of the key individual who has died

Valuation Methods Used by the IRS

Although the Internal Revenue Service incorporates many factors into most valuations of closely held businesses, the two methods consistently used as starting points are: (1) adjusted book value and (2) capitalization of adjusted earnings.

Adjusted Book Value

book value

Book value (stated assets less liabilities, divided by the number of outstanding shares) is particularly applicable in the following instances:

- when the business in question is primarily an asset-holding company, such as an investment company
- when the company is in the real estate development business and assets, rather than earnings, are the key to valuation
- when the company is a one-person corporation, which is generally worth only its liquidation value
- if the corporation is being liquidated at the valuation date or it is likely that it will be liquidated in the near future (It is important also to consider the impact of sacrifice sales and capital-gains taxation, since the true value of a liquidating corporation is the amount that is actually available to the shareholders after the liquidation.)
- when the industry is highly competitive but the business is only marginally profitable (Adjusted book value is particularly useful in these cases, because past earnings are probably an unreliable tool in the measurement of potential future profits.)

adjusted-book-value method

The **adjusted-book-value method** involves adjusting the asset components of a business to an approximate fair market value for each such component. An adjustment is necessary, since most accounting statements carry assets at some figure other than fair market value. Adjustments are necessary to reflect the difference between true market value and book figures when

- assets are valued at cost (Most accounting statements carry land, for example, on the balance sheet of a company at an amount far less than what it is worth on the open market. The result is a book value bearing little or no relationship to present worth.)

- assets have been depreciated at a rate in excess of their true decline in value (For instance, equipment may have been purchased for $500,000 and depreciated to $200,000. Although it is carried on the firm's books at $200,000, the asset may really be worth a lot more or a lot less than the amount shown on the balance sheet.)

- mention of items such as potential future lawsuits or unfavorable long-term leases has been omitted or not clearly noted in the footnotes or body of the firm's balance sheets

- assets have been completely written off even though they possess substantial value, resulting in a book value far below reality

- assets such as franchises and goodwill are shown on accounting statements at nominal cost or not shown at all

- there are difficulties in collecting accounts receivable

- a firm's inventory includes items that have become obsolete or are not readily marketable

There are still other factors that indicate the need for adjustment of pure book value. For instance, a downward adjustment from pure book value is indicated when the business's liquidity position is poor (the business has low current assets relative to its current liabilities), the firm is experiencing a shortage of adequate working capital, or it is burdened with sizable long-term debt. If large selling expenses and capital-gains taxes are likely in the event of liquidation, downward adjustments from book value are indicated.

Another factor that is difficult to ascertain but quite important is the need, if any, to adjust book value because of retained earnings. The book value of a business might appear to be high because of the retention of earnings over a number of years. This might be deceptive, since the company's current earnings may be low and the outlook for increased earnings in the future may be poor. Since valuation is an attempt to ascertain what a hypothetical willing buyer would pay, such a situation indicates the need to reduce book value.

After these adjustments to book value are made, the adjusted book value is then divided by the number of shares outstanding to determine the per-share value of the stock.

Capitalization of Adjusted Earnings

capitalization-of-adjusted-earnings method

The second of the two basic starting-point methods is the **capitalization-of-adjusted-earnings method**. Here the IRS multiplies adjusted earnings by a factor appropriate for the specific industry at the predetermined valuation date. The capitalization rate varies inversely with the degree of risk and the rate of return, as illustrated in the table below.

Capitalization-of-Adjusted-Earnings Method			
Risk	**Categories**	**Rate of Return**	**Capitalization Rate**
Low to medium	Old, established businesses with large capital assets and established goodwill (Few businesses are in this category.)	8%	12
Medium to high	Established businesses of competitive character needing highly competitive management (such as factories manufacturing products under patents and trademarks)	10% to 15%	7 to 10
High	Businesses requiring skill in management but no special or rare type of knowledge; earnings constantly present under highly competitive conditions; large capital not required to enter field	18% and above	6
High	Small businesses—highly competitive—requiring small capital	18% and above	5
High	Businesses depending on special skills of one person or a small group of individuals; highly competitive; small capital required; high mortality	18% and above	2 to 4
High	Personal businesses involving minute amount of capital and depending on the skill of one person	18% and above	1 to 2

With the capitalization-of-earnings method, a closely held business is valued according to a projected amount of sustainable earnings, which is then "capitalized" by a rate of return that has been adjusted for risk. In simple terms, a money-making machine generating $_____ amount of earnings is being valued for a potential buyer. The fundamental steps of the capitalization method of valuation are as follows:

- Select a capitalization rate appropriate for the business.

- Project sustainable earnings for the business.

- Multiply the capitalization rate by the projected sustainable income to determine the business's operating value.

- Add the amount of operating value and the value of the business's nonoperating assets.

The investment return on capital invested in a well-established business with minimal risk is relatively low. Another way of stating this same principle is that it takes a long time to recover the capital invested in such a business. However, the low-risk factor coupled with a yield in excess of the amount possible from alternative investments encourages potential buyers to offer relatively high prices. Conversely, an individual investing in a business with a higher risk factor demands a higher rate of return, wants to receive capital back more quickly, and therefore is willing to pay less for the business. A comparison of two companies might be helpful in illustrating this point. Assume that both companies earn $100,000 a year after taxes.

> **Company A:** The Goforit Company is relatively small and is in a highly competitive industry. It is likely that a buyer would desire a return of 20 percent per year on his or her money (in other words, for this level of risk, the buyer wants to recover capital fairly quickly) to warrant the risk of purchasing this company. So the less paid for the business, the faster the recovery of capital. A buyer who thought he or she could receive 20 percent per year on his or her money would be willing to pay no more than, for example, five times the annual after-tax earnings: $500,000 ($100,000 x 5). This is essentially the procedure the IRS uses to value the firm; it multiplies after-tax earnings by an appropriate capitalization rate.

> **Company B:** Assume the Solid Company is an older corporation with a proven record of profits; it has a strong management team, high-profit potential, and a substantial average annual earnings growth rate. The same investor might be willing to settle for a much lower rate of return given this level of risk. In other words, an investor would value the business at a higher amount because of its safety-of-principal factor—say, a total of $800,000 (8 years' after-tax earnings).

It is important to note that the previous table is only a guideline. The return a potential buyer would demand varies from time to time depending on: (1) the specified level of risk; and (2) the earning rates of comparable alternative investments. There are no correct capitalization rates; there are different rates used at different times and under different circumstances by the IRS and the courts.

Another factor that must be considered even before applying the capitalization rate to the after-tax earnings is that in many cases the earnings themselves must be adjusted. A realistic appraisal of the earning power of a company can sometimes be obtained only through first adjusting earnings by

- adding back bonuses paid to stockholders or their families
- adding back salaries that were excessive, or reducing earnings when salaries paid were inordinately low
- adding back excessive rents paid to stockholders, or subtracting nominal and unrealistically low rents paid to stockholders
- eliminating nonrecurring income items
- adjusting for excess depreciation

- adjusting earnings to take into consideration nonrecurring expenses, a major change in accounting procedures, widely fluctuating or cyclical profits, abnormally inflated or deflated earnings, or strong upward to downward earning trends. (Sometimes the IRS averages earnings over a 3- to 5-year period and then weights the average so that an upward earnings trend is given greater weight.)

The total capitalization result is then divided by the number of shares outstanding to ascertain the per-share value.

The reasonableness of the final result obtained by capitalization can be checked by a method once officially used (and still unofficially used) by many IRS agents. This is known as the ARM (Appeals and Review Memorandum) 34 method. Basically, under ARM 34 a five-step process is used:

1. Figure a reasonable rate of return on the tangible assets of the business.

2. Subtract that return from the annual earnings figure used. The difference is the portion of earnings generated by intangibles.

3. Capitalize profits generated by those intangibles to determine their value.

4. Add the results of the above computation to the net worth of tangibles. The total is the value of the corporation.

5. Divide the total value of the corporation by the number of shares outstanding for the per-share value of the corporation.

Effect of Minority or Controlling Interest

When the shares that are being valued represent a minority interest in a business, a reduction in value is often allowed. This minority-interest discount arises because, by definition, minority shares have no power to force dividends, compel liquidation, or control corporate policy. This makes the stock less appealing and narrows the potential market to the remaining (and usually controlling) shareholders. It, therefore, reduces the price at which each share might be purchased. Discounts of from 10 to 30 percent are often allowed.

The opposite result occurs when the shares in question represent a controlling interest. In this case, the IRS generally seeks to substantiate a higher value. In other words, the size of the block of stock itself is a relevant factor. Although it is true that a minority interest in an unlisted corporation's stock is more difficult to sell than a similar block of listed stock, by the same token the controlling interest of a corporation represents an added element of value. It, therefore, justifies a higher valuation for a specific block of stock.

Valuation of Specific Property

- publicly traded stock/corporate bonds (date of death/alternate valuation date fair market value [FMV] per share on established market/exchange)
- U.S. government bonds (date-of-death redemption price)
- closely held corporation stock
  - adjusted-book-value method
  - capitalization-of-adjusted-earnings method

More than 50 percent of the voting shares constitutes a controlling interest, while less than 50 percent constitutes a minority interest.

Note that if a father leaves two shares to his son who already has 49 shares (assume that only 100 shares are outstanding), the two shares represent in value more than a mere 1/50 of the value of the outstanding stock. Together with the interest that the son already owns, those two shares represent control of the corporation.

Use of Restrictive Agreements

Although a closely held corporation has a limited market by definition, most shareholders restrict the marketability of coshareholders' stock even further through purchase options or mandatory buy-sell agreements. If the terms of such an agreement definitely fix the value of the shares in question, it is not necessary to examine either book value or earnings. The price fixed in the restrictive agreement generally serves as the fair market value of the shares if the agreement was formed by *unrelated parties*. However, to peg the value of *family* corporation stock for federal estate tax purposes, the following three requirements must be met:

1. **the bona fide business arrangement rule.** The agreement must be part of a bona fide business arrangement.

2. **the device rule.** The agreement must not be a device to transfer the property to members of decedent's family for less than full and adequate consideration in money or money's worth.

3. **the comparability rule.** The terms of the agreement must be comparable to similar arrangements entered into by persons in an arm's-length transaction.

Treasury regulations indicate that tests are presumed satisfied if the parties are not family members (or natural objects of the bounty) of the transferor. For these purposes, the terms *family members (or natural objects of the transferor's bounty)* pertain to the transferor's spouse, the transferor's or spouse's lineal descendants, and the spouses of the lineal descendants.

The valuation of a closely held business interest continues to be a critical component in any estate planning. The ability to establish the value of a business interest serves to quantify the liquidity needs of the estate and make planning predictable. Restrictions on the sale of business interests usually tend to depress the value of the business interests. Frequently, the restrictions serve one or more legitimate business objectives by imposing important limitations on the transfer and use of property. Appropriately drafted restrictions can, in certain situations, minimize the taxation of gifts or transfers especially in a family-setting context. It was due to this reduced tax effect that Congress enacted Code Sec. 2703(a) to prohibit the consideration of restrictions for valuation purposes in agreements created or significantly modified after October 8, 1990. Code Sec. 2703(b) however, provides an exception by allowing taxpayers to establish valuation based on stated restrictions contained in the buy-sell agreement. For a taxpayer to have restrictions considered for valuation purposes under the exception of Sec. 2703(b), the taxpayer must satisfy the three-part test consisting of the bona fide business arrangement, the device rule, and the comparability rule mentioned above. If all three parts of the test are not met, valuation restrictions on the business interests will be disregarded. Consequently, the value for gift tax purposes to the transferor will be greater than the lower value allowed when the stated restrictions meet the required three tests. When buy-sell restrictions and price provisions are not recognized for gift, estate, or generation-skipping transfer tax purposes, many estates will find themselves embroiled in expensive and time-consuming valuation disputes with the IRS and faced with potentially major liquidity shortfalls. Thus, planning must be aimed either at meeting the requirements so that provisions and prices in agreements are given validity in establishing the value of the closely held business interest or at obtaining greater life insurance to fund the additional liquidity needs. The regulations indicate that all three requirement tests must be satisfied independently.

Bona Fide Business Purpose Test

The desire to retain control of the business within the current closely held group (the family) and provide for the successful transition after the departure of an owner has generally been found to be a bona fide business purpose. The terms of the agreement should clearly state this purpose.

Device Test

Planners must now carefully document facts that indicate the arrangement was not a device to pass the property to members of the decedent's family (the natural object of the decedent's bounty) at a bargain price. Presumably, this means the agreement should provide a fair price when executed and be expected to provide a fair market value price at any time in the future.

Proving this is both expensive and time consuming since appraisal reports and expert testimony will probably be required if a dispute arises.

Comparability Test

The requirement of comparability is also likely to prove difficult to satisfy. In order to fix estate tax value, it must be shown that the arrangement is one that could have been obtained in an arm's-length transaction. Would the decedent have entered into such an arrangement with an unrelated third person? This requirement of comparability applies not only to price but also to all the other terms of the contract between the parties.

Factors to be taken into account for comparability include: (a) the expected term of the agreement, (b) the present value of the property, (c) the expected value of the property at the time of exercise, and (d) the consideration, if any, offered for the option.

The four different types of restrictive agreements that have been successful in pegging the value of stock for federal estate tax purposes are the following:

- reciprocal options among stockholders, during life and death. Under an option a specified person is given the right to purchase the stock at a designated price for a fixed period of time. Here, the buyer controls the event.

- options granted to one stockholder only (but the price must be fair and arrived at by arm's-length bargaining). Intrafamily arrangements in this category are suspect.

- options granted to the corporation

- mandatory buy-sell (cross-purchase and stock-redemption) agreements under which the estate of a deceased stockholder must sell and the corporation (or other stockholders) must buy at a predetermined price or according to a predetermined formula. The obligation to sell at the agreed-upon price, however, must be binding not only upon the decedent's executor at the decedent's death but also upon the stockholder himself or herself during lifetime. The price at death does not control if a shareholder is free during lifetime to realize a higher price. Likewise, restrictions that are binding only during the decedent's lifetime but not at death are equally ineffective. In a mandatory buy-sell agreement, neither party controls the event.

A mere right of first refusal, which requires that any shares offered for sale must first be offered to the corporation (or other shareholders) at the proposed transfer price, does not conclusively peg the value of the stock. However, a first-offer commitment may have the effect of depressing the value of the stock.

While restrictions on the transfer of closely held shares are never conclusive regarding value for gift tax purposes, they are a factor to be considered in arriving at valuation.

LO 9. 6 **Explain how various types of lifetime transfers with retained interests are valued.**

VALUATION OF LIFETIME TRANSFERS WITH RETAINED INTERESTS

The Estate Freeze

estate freeze

An **estate freeze** is an estate planning technique designed to meet several goals. The primary goal is estate tax reduction. An estate freeze can be defined as any method designed to restrict the value of property or property interest to its current value in an individual's eventual taxable estate. Following an estate-freeze transaction, the appreciation in property subject to the freeze accrues to someone other than the original owner (presumably the original owner's heirs). However, an individual considering an estate freeze generally has a second goal—to retain enough wealth to provide for his or her needs until death.

Under prior transfer tax law, elaborate schemes were employed to provide the transferor with an effective estate freeze through the transfer of appreciation rights in property to the next generation heirs, while at the same time leaving the transferor with enough strings attached to the property to provide a substantial current income stream. Thus, an estate freeze can be distinguished from an outright gift by the fact that the transferor does not transfer all interests in the property during his or her lifetime.

subtraction method

Under previous tax law, the freeze was often accomplished mainly through techniques that took advantage of valuation manipulations. Because some portion of the freeze property was actually transferred, the gift tax value of the transfer had to be determined. Valuation of transfers with retained interests was normally accomplished for gift, estate, and generation-skipping purposes through the subtraction method of valuation. The **subtraction method** of valuation determines the value of the transferred interest as the difference between: (a) the value of the entire property interest, and (b) the value of all interests in the property that continue to be held by the donor and are not transferred.

Stated simply:

The value of the whole less the value of what is kept equals the gift tax value of what is given away.

In 1990, Congress, through the Revenue Reconciliation Act, established gift tax Secs. 2701–2704 in IRC Chapter 14 Special Valuation Rules to deal with the perceived valuation abuses.

These Code Sections focus on the valuation of assets at the time of transfer for the purposes of determining a gift tax. In essence, the general rule under Sec. 2701 provides a harsh result for taxpayers attempting to freeze the value of their family business for transfer-tax purposes. For the purposes of determining

1. whether the transfer of an interest in a *controlled* corporation or partnership to or for the benefit of a *member of the family* of the transferor is a gift and

2. what the gift tax value of such gifts is,

the value of certain *retained rights* with respect to an *applicable retained interest* held by the transferor or an *applicable family member* immediately after the transfer is generally deemed to be zero. In essence, no valuation credit is given for the value of rights that are retained, and the subtraction method of valuation cannot be used except in limited situations. The gift tax value of the stock transferred is equal to the value of the transferor's entire interest prior to such transfer.

EXAMPLE

A, the sole owner of ACO, Inc., owns 100 shares of common stock valued at $100,000. ACO recapitalizes and issues $90,000 (valued under traditional (prior) valuation rules) of 10 percent noncumulative preferred stock to A in exchange for 90 shares of common stock. A then gifts 10 shares of ACO common stock to A's child. A believes the gift of common stock is entirely sheltered by the gift tax annual exclusion. However, Sec. 2701 applies, since A transfers an interest in a controlled corporation to a family member and retains rights (the preferred stock) after such transfer. The value of the gift is, in fact, $100,000, since A's retained preferred stock must be given a zero value under Sec. 2701.

The following definitions are necessary for an understanding of Secs. 2701–2704.

- **member of the family.** For these purposes, *member of the family* means only the transferor's spouse, the lineal descendants of the transferor or transferor's spouse, and a spouse of any such descendant. Thus, the statute is applicable only if a transfer is made to the transferor's spouse or to junior-generation issue (and spouses) of the transferor. This makes sense, since the estate freeze implies a transfer of the growth interests to future generations for discounted transfer tax cost.

- **applicable family member.** *Applicable family member* means only the transferor's spouse, an ancestor of the transferor or transferor's spouse, and the spouse of any such ancestor. Thus, the retained interest must be held by the transferor, his or her spouse, or senior-generation family members (and spouses) for the statute to apply. Again, this is logical, since the freeze involves the retention of frozen rights by the generation whose estate tax concerns are more immediate.

- **applicable retained rights.** Retained rights for Sec. 2701 purposes include certain distribution (dividend) rights but only if the transferor and all applicable family members control the corporation or partnership. In determining whether sufficient interest is held within the family, the transferor and any applicable family member are deemed to hold any interest held by a brother, sister, or lineal descendant. Retained rights also include "extraordinary payment rights" such as a liquidation, put, call, or conversion rights. These applicable retained rights are valued at zero, unless they are qualified payment rights (described later), for the purposes of determining the gift tax value of a transferred interest.

- **retained rights not treated as "applicable retained rights."** The harsh rule provided to applicable retained rights does not apply to any right that must be exercised at a specific time and at a specific amount. It also does not generally apply to a right to convert into a fixed number (or a fixed percentage) of shares of the same class of stock in a corporation as the transferred stock (or which would be of the same class but for nonlapsing differences in voting power). In other words, if a retained interest carries rights that are not valued at zero under Sec. 2701, the value of these rights is their fair market value determined under traditional valuation methodology.

- **controlled entity.** An entity is controlled if, immediately before the transfer, the transferor, applicable members, and any lineal descendants of the parent of the transferor (or parents of the transferor's spouse) hold at least 50 percent (by vote or value) of the stock of a corporation or at least 50 percent of the capital or profits interests in a partnership.

So the general rule of Sec. 2701 is that an estate freeze involving the intrafamily transfer of corporate stock or partnership interests results in an immediate gift tax based on the entire value of the business held by the senior family member. The transferor gets no credit for the value of the senior business interest retained upon a gift (or sale) of a junior interest to a family member.

The Sec. 2701 rules do not apply to the following retained interests, which can be accorded full fair market value for gift tax purposes:

- **marketable transferred interests.** Sec. 2701 does not apply if there are readily available market quotations on an established securities market for the value of the transferred interest.

- **marketable retained interests.** Similarly, these rules do not apply to any applicable retained interest if there are readily available market quotations on an established securities market for the value of the applicable retained interest.

- **interests of the same class.** Sec. 2701 does not apply if the retained interest is of the same class of equity as the transferred interest. For this purpose, nonvoting common stock is treated as the same class as voting common.

- **proportionate transfers.** Sec. 2701 does not apply to a transfer by an individual of equity interests if the transfer results in a proportionate reduction of each class of equity interest held by the transferor.

Qualified Payments Exception

Although the general rule is that applicable retained rights are valued at zero (which under the subtraction method means that the value of what was given away or sold is assigned a value equal to the entire worth of the business), retained rights to *qualified payments* are valued under general valuation principles.

Qualified payments are dividends payable on a periodic basis under cumulative preferred stock (or comparable payment under a partnership interest) to the extent that such dividend (or comparable partnership payment) is determined at a fixed rate. A payment is treated as having a fixed rate if it is in fact fixed once and for all, or if it is determined at a rate that bears a fixed relationship to a specified market interest rate.

EXAMPLE

Parent (P) holds all the outstanding stock of X Corporation. Assume the fair market value of X is $1.5 million. X is recapitalized so that P holds 1,000 shares of $1,000 par value preferred stock bearing an annual cumulative dividend of $100 per share (the aggregate fair market value of which is assumed to be $1 million) and 1,000 shares of voting common stock. P transfers the common stock to P's child. Sec. 2701 applies to the transfer because P has transferred an equity interest (the common stock) to a member of P's family and immediately thereafter holds an applicable retained interest (the preferred stock with its distribution and other rights). P's right to receive annual cumulative dividends is a qualified payment right and is valued for purposes of Sec. 2701 at its fair market value of $1,000,000. The amount of P's gift, determined using the subtraction method of valuation is $500,000 ($1,500,000 – $1,000,000).

The Minimum-Value Rule

Congress wanted to be sure that at least some minimum value was assigned to an equity interest transferred to a family member in an estate freeze. Even if there are actual or deemed qualified payments (or other rights valued under traditional methods), the Code now specifies a minimum valuation for any junior equity interest transferred by gift or sale to a family member. Examples of junior equity interests include common stock or partnership interests with rights to capital and profits junior to other partnership interests.

For example, if a father gives common stock to his son while retaining cumulative preferred stock, the minimum-value rule requires that the total common stock of the corporation may not be valued at less than 10 percent of the sum of the total value of all stock interests in the corporation *plus* the total indebtedness of the corporation to the transferor or an applicable family member. What this means is that the gift tax value of common stock that is gifted to a family member must be at least 10 percent of the total value of stock that is held by the transferor. A similar minimum-value rule applies in the partnership context.

Additional Gift Taxes

These rules also prevent parents from shifting growth to the next generation by failing to make distributions on the retained preferred interest. Any payments that are not made accrue to the transferred growth interest. If the qualified payments are not in fact made at the times and in the amounts used in valuing the retained right to the qualified payments, the transferor's taxable gifts (or the transferor's estate if appropriate) may be increased to reflect the value of the preferred stock based on the actual distributions made.

Valuation of Transfers in Trust with Retained Interests

Before Sec. 2702, estate freezes were often created using trusts to hold the property. A classic example was the grantor-retained income trust (GRIT).

EXAMPLE

A 63-year-old mother contributed $100,000 to a trust that would provide income to herself for the shorter of 10 years or her life, and then pay the remainder to her daughter. The mother made two transfers: first, an income interest for the shorter of 10 years or the life of a 63-year-old (which she retains the value of) and, second, a gift of the remainder interest following the retained income interest. The total transfer-tax cost (under prior law) would be the value of the remainder at the time the trust was created. Thus, the subtraction method of valuation resulted in a gift equal to the total value of the property less the value of the retained income interest. The appreciation on the property while held by the trust completely escapes transfer taxes, which is, of course, the purpose of the freeze.

Prior Law

In general, prior to the creation of Sec. 2702, transfers to trusts with retained interests by the transferor or family member were valued using actuarial tables described under the general valuation rules of Sec. 7520 (described below). These mathematical tables show the worth of a stream of dollars at various discount rate assumptions using the government's life expectancy tables. Typically, the value of a remainder interest was determined (under the subtraction valuation concept) as the difference between: (a) the value of entire amount contributed to the trust, and (b) the actuarial value of the retained interest (as determined under the Sec. 7520 tables). The actual income generated by the trust's assets might have been significantly more or less than the table values, but actual income was not considered in the gift tax valuation of contributions made to a trust.

IRC Sec. 2702

In keeping with the IRS concern about the potential for abuse associated with intrafamily transfers of wealth, Congress enacted Sec. 2702 to thwart practices by which taxpayers tried to shift significant value in trust and then, by playing actuarial games, claim the value of the transfer was appreciatively less than the amount actually transferred. Therefore, to halt taxpayers from setting up trusts benefiting family that allowed for the overvaluation of retained interests and the undervaluation of remainder interests (the taxable gift portion), Sec. 2702 requires that for individuals to receive the actuarial value of the trust's annuity interest, retained interests have to be "qualified interests" that can be valued with reasonable certainty. As long as the retained interests are "qualified," the value can be subtracted from the total value of the transfers to obtain the transferor's gift tax liability. If the retained interests are not "qualified," the transferor cannot reduce the transfer by the full actuarial value of what is retained.

In other words, under the IRC Sec. 2702 rules, for the purpose of determining: (a) whether a transfer in trust to or for the benefit of a member of the family of the transferor is a gift, and (b) the value of the gift, the value of any interest in the trust retained by the transferor or any applicable family member is generally treated as zero. If an individual makes a transfer to a trust benefiting a member of her family, she is deemed to have retained none of the cash or other assets and is treated as if she had given away the entire amount she transferred to the trust. In the preceding example, the mother would be treated as having gifted the full $100,000 and would not be able to deduct the value of her retained income rights for the 10 years of trust income.

As stated above, there are exceptions. Some retained interests in trust are given "subtraction" value effect for determining the gift tax value of transfers in trust.

Qualified Interests. A retained *qualified interest* in the trust by the transferor or applicable family member is valued at its full Sec. 7520 table value. A qualified interest is either

- a right to receive fixed amounts payable at least annually (a GRAT, or grantor-retained annuity trust interest), or

- a right to receive amounts payable at least annually that are a fixed percentage of the trust's assets determined annually (a GRUT, or grantor-retained unitrust interest), or

- any noncontingent remainder interest if all other interests in the trust are GRATs or GRUTs

GRAT

A **GRAT** is an irrevocable trust in which the grantor retains a right to receive fixed payments (just like a fixed annuity) payable at least annually for his or her life (or the joint lives of the grantor and one or more life tenants) or for a term of years (actuarially identical to a charitable remainder annuity trust). At the end of the term or life interest, the remaining trust corpus is paid to designated beneficiaries. The annuity interest is valued under Sec. 7520 rules, and the gift value of the remainder is determined by subtracting the value of the annuity interest from the total value of the principal placed in trust.

GRUT

A grantor-retained unitrust, or **GRUT**, is an irrevocable trust in which the grantor retains the right to receive amounts payable, at least annually, that are a fixed percentage of the trust's assets as revalued annually (just like a variable annuity). The GRUT is actuarially identical to a charitable remainder unitrust. The term of the trust may be based on the life of the annuitant (or joint lives of two or more annuitants) or a specified term of years. At the end of the term of the trust, all remaining trust assets pass to the designated remainderpersons. The gift tax value of the GRUT may be subtracted from the value of the property transferred to the trust to determine the gift tax value of the remainder interest.

Thus, a grantor-retained income trust (GRIT), which provides the actual trust income, and other retained interests are valued at zero and are generally ineffective for estate planning purposes unless other exceptions (discussed below) apply.

Personal Residences and Tangible Personal Property. Regular (Sec. 7520) valuation rules also apply in cases where

- the property is a property to be used as the personal residence of the person holding a term interest in the trust (referred to as a Qualified Personal Residence Trust (QPRT)), or
- the exercise or nonexercise of the holder of a *term interest* in tangible property does not affect the valuation of the remainder interests in such property

GRITs are effective for estate planning if the property is used as the personal residence of the person holding the term interest. In this situation, the remainder interest is valued in the subtraction valuation manner, even if the remainder interest is held by a family member. Second, where the exercise or nonexercise of rights by the holder of a term interest in tangible property (such as artwork) does not affect the valuation of the remainder interest in such property, the term interest is not valued at zero for gift tax purposes, even if the remainder interests are held by family members.

If the trust corpus consists of the property described in this exception, retained interests—not limited to GRATs or GRUTs—are valued under normal valuation rules. Thus, the subtraction method of valuation results in a reduced gift tax cost of transferring the remainder interest.

Valuation of Partial Nonconcurrent Property Interests

It is sometimes necessary to value partial interests in property such as annuities, term interests, and life estates, since these property rights are often transferred to heirs and become subject to either estate or gift taxes. In addition, certain charitable transfer techniques, such as charitable remainder and lead trusts, must be valued to determine the estate, gift, and/or income tax deductions. Congress revamped the tax valuation methodology for such partial interests and added to the complexity of the process in an effort to stamp out perceived abuses in the old methods.

Sec. 7520 of the Internal Revenue Code now mandates that the current mortality rates and the current interest rate (revised monthly) must be used to determine the actuarial present value of annuity, term, remainder, and life interests in property. The more recent mortality rates are based on the most current census data and gender-neutral tables.[1] The interest rate used to discount the partial interests to present value is 120 percent of the applicable federal midterm rate (AFMR) for the month in which the valuation is made.[2] The actual factor used to determine

---

1. The actuarial tables are presented in the *Actuarial Tables Alpha and Actuarial Tables Beta* available by writing to the Superintendent of Documents, United States Government Printing Office, Washington, DC 20404.
2. The applicable federal rates are published monthly in the *Internal Revenue Bulletin* and are reprinted in numerous

the value of a partial nonconcurrent interest involves several calculations and varies month to month according to changes in the AFMR.

The nature of the calculation for determining such valuations requires a significant degree of mathematics acumen and creates a high possibility for error. As a result, most practitioners rely on software for making such calculations.

An additional problem with using these rules is the monthly variation in the interest rate. The tax value of such partial interests must be determined at a specific point in time. For example, gift tax calculations must be made at the time of the transfer. Thus, the gift tax imposed on the inter vivos transfer of a partial nonconcurrent interest is based on the value of the interest using the applicable rate for the month in which a completed transfer is made. The same rule holds true when determining the income or gift tax deduction for a charitable remainder or lead interest donation. The applicable rate for the month in which the decedent dies is used to value the testamentary transfer of such partial interests. Therefore, the tax benefits or detriments of the transfer of remainder, term, annuity, or life interests in property depend on the month of the transfer.

loose-leaf services on tax and financial planning. The actual rate used for Sec. 7520 purposes is 120 percent of the AFMR rounded to the nearest two-tenths of one percent. For example, 6.56 percent is 6.6 percent for the purposes of valuing remainder, term, annuity, or life interests.

CHAPTER REVIEW

Key Terms and Concepts

alternate valuation date
fair market value
special-use valuation (2032A)
farm-method formula of valuation
recapture
willing buyer-willing seller rule
goodwill
book value

adjusted-book-value method
capitalization-of-adjusted-earnings
  method
estate freeze
subtraction method
GRAT
GRUT

Chapter 9: Review Questions

1. Why is it important to establish a reasonably accurate valuation of assets for estate tax purposes? [LO 9.1]

2. Explain why the lowest possible valuation for an asset may not be the price an executor would place on property for federal estate tax purposes. [LO 9.1]

3. When is property usually valued for estate tax purposes? [LO 9.2]

4. What are the general rules for valuing property? [LO 9.2]

5. What are some of the problems that may occur in the valuation process? [LO 9.3]

6. George Smith died in 2019 and his estate consists primarily of a 2,000-acre family farm. Farms of this size rent for $400,000 annually in the area near the Smith farm. Local real estate taxes are $80,000 and the average federal land bank loan interest rate is 8 percent. Under the farm-method valuation formula, what is the special-use valuation of the Smith farm? [LO 9.4]

7. In general terms, describe the events that could cause a recapture of the special-use valuation tax benefit. [LO 9.4]

8. Explain how the following assets are valued for estate or gift tax purposes:
    a. household and personal effects,
    b. listed stocks,
    c. corporate bonds,

    d.   U.S. government bonds,

    e.   life insurance. [LO 9.5]

9. Explain why it is difficult to evaluate stock in closely held corporations. [LO 9.5]

10. In what situations is the use of the adjusted-book-value method applicable for valuing closely held businesses? [LO 9.5]

11. Why does the book value of business assets often differ from their fair market value? [LO 9.5]

12. What adjustments to earnings must often be made to appraise a company's earning power realistically? [LO 9.5]

13. Distinguish between the effect of a minority interest and that of a controlling interest on the valuation of closely held stock. [LO 9.5]

14. Under what conditions will the price established under a buy-sell agreement for the stock of a deceased stockholder normally fix the value of the decedent's stock for federal estate tax purposes? [LO 9.5]

15. Explain how the subtraction method of valuation is used to value transfers with retained interests. [LO 9.6]

16. Explain the significance of the minimum-value rule in the context of an estate freeze. [LO 9.6]

Chapter 9: Review Answers

1. There are a number of reasons why accurate asset valuation is important to the estate planning process. First, it is impossible to determine potential liquidity needs that an executor may experience unless proper values are placed on the owner's assets during life. Qualification for a Sec. 303 stock redemption or the installment payment of estate taxes under Sec. 6166 depend on the value of the decedent's stock relative to the value of the decedent's other assets. If the appropriate test(s) cannot be met, neither technique for paying estate taxes is available.

    Second, because of the income and estate tax advantages inherent in gifts, gratuitous transfers of property may be meaningful when they are subject to minimal gift tax costs. However, to properly consider the various ramifications and potential advantages involved in a lifetime transfer, a knowledge of valuation is essential. A third reason valuing assets is important relates to the funding of buy-sell agreements. The first step in arranging such an agreement is to arrive at a fair market value for the business. Obviously, it is impossible to assure each costockholder (or partner) that beneficiaries will receive an equitable price on death or disability unless the current worth of each person's business interest is ascertained.

2. A higher valuation of a business interest might be advantageous in the formula for a buy-sell agreement. From the point of view of the decedent's survivors, where alternative liquidity funding is impractical, it may be better to set a formula in a buy-sell agreement that puts a higher value on the business interest (and thereby provides more cash for the decedent's survivors) than to establish a formula that provides a lower estate tax value (yielding a lower price for the decedent's business interest). Moreover, when a business interest is valued high relative to other estate assets, the disadvantage of the additional tax payable due to the higher valuation may be more than offset by the advantages of qualifying for a Sec. 303 stock redemption or a Sec. 6166 election to pay federal estate taxes attributable to a business interest in installments.

3. The general rule is that a decedent's property is valued at its date-of-death value.

4. There is very little in the Internal Revenue Code about how to value items for federal estate tax purposes. Although the *value* of the gross estate is mentioned in the Code, the word value is not defined. The estate and gift tax regulations provide that value is meant to be *fair market value*, which is defined as follows: the price at which the property would change hands between a willing buyer and a willing seller, neither

being under any compulsion to buy or to sell and both having reasonable knowledge of relevant facts.

By this definition, the value that may be placed on property can vary substantially, depending on who is valuing the item and which factors are used. The regulations state that it is not necessary to have either an established market for an item or a willing buyer and seller as mentioned above. In the absence of an actual sale, the value of an asset is based on a hypothetical sale.

Generally, the following external factors are examined in deciding the extent to which the sales price is indicative of value:

- the frequency of sales (Courts tend to disregard isolated or sporadic sales.)
- the relationship between the seller and the buyer (Sales that are between parents and children or employers and employees are seldom given great weight in light of their almost inherently unequal bargaining position.)
- options to purchase or sell (Offers, as opposed to options, present little evidence of value.)

Once all these value-affecting factors are considered, each factor must be given a relative weight.

5. Some items present more difficult valuation problems when the following occurs:
   - There are different markets for the same property.
   - The appraisal of worth must be made on the basis of comparable property, which is a subjective standard.
   - The property in question is unique.

   In practice, valuation problems are frequently viewed by the IRS and the courts as problems of negotiation and compromise. An appraiser's objective is to derive a fair and sound value that, if litigated, would likely be sustained in court.

6. Under the farm-method formula, the comparable net rental is capitalized at the federal land bank loan rate to determine the special-use valuation of farmland. For the Smith farm, the value is ($400,000 − $80,000) ÷ .08 = $4,000,000.

7. The tax benefit from special-use (current-use) valuation of real property may be recaptured under certain circumstances. If the property is disposed of to nonfamily members within 10 years after the death of the decedent, there is an additional estate tax or recaptured tax imposed on the qualified heir. If the heir or a member of the

heir's family fails to participate materially in the business operation for 5 or more years during an 8-year period ending within 10 years after the decedent's death, it is treated as a cessation of the qualified use, causing recapture. There is a 2-year grace period following the decedent's death before the heir must commence the qualified use without risking recapture.

Recapture of the difference in tax between the current-use and highest-and-best-use methods of valuation occurs when the real estate is sold, disposed of, or no longer used for the same qualified use within the 10-year period. Also, the eligible qualified heir must be engaged in the active management of the farm or business during the recapture period. If during this period the heir is under age 21, disabled, a full-time student, or the surviving spouse, a fiduciary may qualify in providing active management for the heir.

8.   a.   The general rule for valuing household property and personal effects, such as watches, rings, and so forth, can be called the *willing buyer-willing seller rule*. In non-community-property states, household goods and the like personally acquired by and used by husband and wife during marriage are generally presumed to be the property of the husband. Therefore, in the absence of sufficient evidence to rebut this presumption, household goods and personal effects are includible in the husband's estate.

     b.   When a stock has an established market and quotations are available to value the stock as of the date in question, the fair market value (FMV) per share on the applicable valuation date governs for both gift and estate tax purposes.

          The FMV is based on selling prices when there is a market for the stock or bond. This is the mean between the highest and lowest quoted selling price on the valuation date. If there were no sales on the valuation date, but there were sales on dates within a reasonable period both before and after the valuation date, the FMV is determined by taking a weighted average of the means between the highest and lowest sales on the nearest date before and the nearest date after the valuation. The average is then weighted inversely by the respective number of trading days between the selling date and the valuation date.

          When a large block of stock cannot be marketed in an orderly manner, the block might depress the market because it cannot be converted to cash as readily as a few shares could be. Therefore, selling prices and bid-and-asked prices may not reflect fair market value. Sometimes, it may be necessary to value this type of stock as if it were closely held and not actively traded. If this can be established, a reasonable modification of the normal basis for determining FMV can be made.

In some cases a blockage discount is determined by the effect that block would have had on the market if it were sold over a reasonable period of time and in a prudent manner. A similar situation occurs when sales at or near the date of death are either few or sporadic and may not indicate a fair market value.

The converse of the blockage situation above occurs when the block of stock to be valued represents a controlling interest (either actual or effective) in a going business. Here the price of normally traded shares may have little relation to the true value of the controlling lot. The large block can have the effect of increasing value because of its element of control.

c. The valuation of bonds is similar to the valuation of listed common stock. The means of the selling prices on or near the applicable valuation date (or—if there were no sales—the means of bona fide asked prices weighted inversely to the number of trading days from the valuation date) determine the fair market value of the bonds.

In the absence of sales or bid-and-asked prices, the value must be determined by

- ascertaining the soundness of the security
- comparing the interest on the bond in question to yields on similar bonds
- examining the date of maturity
- comparing prices for listed bonds of corporations engaged in similar types of business
- checking the extent to which the bond is secured
- weighing all other relevant factors, including the opinion of experts, the goodwill of the business, the industry's economic outlook, and the company's position in the industry as well as its management

d. Series E (EE) bonds are valued at their redemption price (market value) as of the date of death, since they are neither negotiable nor transferable and the only definitely ascertainable value is the amount at which the Treasury will redeem them.

Certain U.S. Treasury bonds (so-called flower bonds) owned by a decedent at the date of death and forming part of the gross estate may be redeemed at par value if used to pay federal estate taxes. These bonds are valued at the higher of the market price and par value.

Even if such bonds are not used to pay estate taxes, the courts have often held that when the bonds could be used for the payment of estate taxes, they are valued at the higher of market and par value. When the bonds could not be applied to pay the estate tax, their value is market (the mean quoted selling price value).

e. Proceeds of life insurance on the life of the decedent receivable by or for the benefit of the decedent's estate are taxed in the decedent-insured's estate. In addition, when the decedent held incidents of ownership, such ownership invokes taxation. The amount includible is the amount receivable by the beneficiary. This includes dividends and premium refunds. In determining how much is includible, no distinction is made between an ordinary life policy, a term policy, group insurance, or an accidental death benefit.

If a settlement option is elected, the amount that is payable as a lump sum is the amount includible. If the policy did not provide for a lump-sum payment, the amount includible is the commuted amount used by the insurance company to compute the settlement option payments.

The value of an unmatured policy owned by a decedent on the life of another is included in the policyowner's gross estate (when the policyowner predeceases the insured) according to the following:

- If a new life insurance policy is involved, the gross premium paid is the value.

- If the policy is a paid-up or a single-premium policy, its value is its replacement cost—that is, the single premium that company would have charged for a comparable contract of equal face value on the life of a person who was the insured's age (at the time the decedent-policyholder died).

- If the policy is a premium-paying whole life policy, the value is found by adding any unearned portion of the last premium to the interpolated terminal reserve.

- If the policy is a term policy, the value is the unused premium.

9. The valuation of closely held corporate stock is often one of the most difficult and time-consuming problems faced by the executor of a decedent's estate. By definition, closely held stock is incapable of valuation solely by recourse to an established market (that is, closely held stock is seldom traded). In fact, the criteria used to define closely held stock include: (1) a limited number of stockholders, (2) restrictions imposed upon a shareholder's ability to transfer the stock, (3) the absence of an exchange listing or regular quotation in the over-the-counter market, and (4) an irregular and limited history of sales or exchanges.

There is no formula provided by the Internal Revenue Code or the regulations that is applicable to every closely held stock valuation situation. However, there are guidelines that should be considered in every valuation case. The key IRS ruling on point, Rev. Rul. 59–60, suggests that the following factors be considered:

- the nature of the business and the entire history of the enterprise

- the economic outlook in general as well as the condition and outlook of the specific industry

- the book value of the stock and the financial condition of the business (The Tax Court considers this factor in almost every case.)

- the company's earning capacity (For many businesses—especially those that do depend heavily on capital to produce profits—this will be the most important valuation factor.)

- the company's dividend-paying capacity

- the existence of goodwill (Goodwill can be defined as the economic advantage or benefit that is acquired by a business beyond the mere value of the capital invested in it because of the patronage it receives from constant or habitual customers, its local position, its reputation for skill or punctuality, other accidental circumstances or necessities, or public partialities or prejudices. In short, goodwill is a broad term implying that a company has a purchase value exceeding the worth of its tangible assets. Note: A business may have goodwill value even if no amount for goodwill is shown on its accounting statements.)

- prior stock sales and the size of the block of stock to be valued

- fair market value of stock of comparable corporations engaged in the same or similar type of business where the stock is actively traded in an established market

  Rev. Rul. 59–60 reaffirms that no fixed formula of valuation can be devised that is applicable to all situations and that, ultimately, the fair market value of closely held stock must be determined on an individual basis.

10. Adjusted book value is particularly applicable in the following instances:

- when the business in question is primarily an asset-holding company, such as an investment company

- when the company is in the real estate development business and assets, rather than earnings, are the key to valuation

- when the company is a one-person corporation, which is generally worth only its liquidation value

- if the corporation is being liquidated at the valuation date or it is likely that it will be liquidated in the near future (It is important also to consider the impact of sacrifice sales and capital-gains taxation, since the true value of a liquidating corporation is the amount that is actually available to the shareholders after the liquidation.)

- when the industry is highly competitive but the business is only marginally profitable (Adjusted book value is particularly useful in these cases, because past earnings are probably an unreliable tool in the measurement of potential future profits.)

The adjusted-book-value method involves adjusting the asset components of a business to an approximate fair market value for each such component. An adjustment is necessary, since most accounting statements carry assets at some figure other than fair market value.

11. The book value of business assets often differs from fair market value because for book purposes

- assets are valued at cost (Most accounting statements carry land, for example, on the balance sheet of a company at an amount far less than what it is worth on the open market. The result is a book value bearing little or no relationship to present worth.)

- assets have been depreciated at a rate in excess of their true decline in value (For instance, equipment may have been purchased for $500,000 and depreciated to $200,000. Although it is carried on the firm's books at $200,000, the asset may really be worth a lot more or a lot less than its cost, or the $200,000 used on the balance sheet.)

- mention of items such as potential lawsuits or unfavorable long-term leases has been omitted or not clearly noted in the footnotes or body of the firm's balance sheets

- assets have been completely written off even though they possess substantial value, resulting in a book value far below reality

- assets such as franchises and goodwill are shown on accounting statements at nominal cost or not shown at all

- there are difficulties in collecting accounts receivable

- a firm's inventory includes items that have become obsolete or are not readily marketable

There are still other factors that indicate the need for adjustment of pure book value. For instance, a downward adjustment from pure book value is indicated when the business's liquidity position is poor (the business has low current assets relative to its current liabilities), the firm is experiencing a shortage of adequate working capital, or it is burdened with sizable long-term debt. If large selling expenses and capital-gains taxes are likely in the event of liquidation, downward adjustments from book value are indicated.

12. A realistic appraisal of the earning power of a company can sometimes be obtained only through first adjusting earnings by

- adding back bonuses paid to stockholders or their families

- adding back salaries that were excessive, or reducing earnings when salaries paid were inordinately low

- adding back excessive rents paid to stockholders, or subtracting nominal and unrealistically low rents paid to stockholders

- eliminating nonrecurring income items

- adjusting for excess depreciation

- adjusting earnings to take into consideration nonrecurring expenses, a major change in accounting procedures, widely fluctuating or cyclical profits, abnormally inflated or deflated earnings, or strong upward to downward earning trends. (Sometimes the IRS averages earnings over a 3- to 5-year period and then weights the average so that an upward earnings trend is given greater weight.)

13. When the shares being valued represent a minority interest in a business, a reduction in value is often allowed. This minority-interest discount arises because, by definition, minority shares have no power to force dividends, compel liquidation, or control corporate policy. This makes the stock less appealing and narrows the potential market to the remaining (and usually controlling) shareholders. It, therefore, reduces the price at which each share might be purchased. Discounts of from 10 percent to 30 percent are often allowed.

The opposite result occurs when the shares in question represent a controlling interest. In this case, the IRS generally seeks to substantiate a higher value. In other words, the size of the block of stock itself is a relevant factor. Although it is true that a minority interest in an unlisted corporation's stock is more difficult to sell than a similar block of listed stock, by the same token the controlling interest of a corporation represents an added element of value. It, therefore, justifies a higher valuation for a specific block of stock. More than 50 percent of the voting shares constitutes a controlling interest, while less than 50 percent constitutes a minority interest.

Note that if a father leaves two shares to his son who already has 49 shares (assume that only 100 shares are outstanding), the two shares represent in value more than a mere 1/50 of the value of the outstanding stock. Together with the interest that the son already owns, those two shares represent control of the corporation.

14. In the case of buy-sell agreements, a mandatory buy-sell (either a cross-purchase or a stock redemption) agreement will normally peg the value of a decedent's stock for federal estate tax purposes. Under this type of agreement, the estate of the deceased stockholder must sell and the corporation or other stockholders must buy at a predetermined price or according to a predetermined formula. The obligation to sell at the agreed-upon price, however, must be binding not only upon the decedent's executor at the decedent's death but also upon the stockholder himself or herself during lifetime. The price at death does not control if a shareholder is free during lifetime to realize a higher price. Likewise, restrictions that are binding only during the decedent's lifetime but not at death are equally ineffective. In a mandatory buy-sell agreement neither party controls the event.

A mere right of first refusal, which requires that any shares offered for sale must first be offered to the corporation (or other shareholders) at the proposed transfer price, does not conclusively peg the value of the stock. However, a first-offer commitment may have the effect of depressing the value of the stock.

15. The valuation of certain transfers with retained interests may be accomplished using the subtraction method of valuation. The subtraction method of valuation determines the value of the transferred interest as the difference between: (a) the value of the entire property interest, and (b) the value of all interests in the property that continue to be held by the donor and are not transferred.

Stated simply: *The value of the whole less the value of what is kept equals the gift tax value of what is given away.*

16. Congress wanted to be sure that at least some minimum value was assigned to an equity interest transferred to a family member in an estate freeze. Even if there are actual or deemed qualified payments (or other rights valued under traditional methods), the Code now specifies a minimum valuation for any junior equity interest transferred by gift or sale to a family member. Examples of junior equity interests include common stock or partnership interests with rights to capital and profits junior to other partnership interests.

Chapter 10:
Buy-Sell Agreements

Learning Objectives

An understanding of the material in this chapter should enable the student to

LO 10.1 **Describe the purposes served by buy-sell agreements, and identify their advantages.**

LO 10. 2 **Identify the common provisions found in most types of buy-sell agreements.**

LO 10. 3 **Describe the various types of buy-sell agreements used in business entities.**

LO 10. 4 **Describe how each type of price-setting mechanism used in buy-sell agreements works.**

LO 10.1 **Describe the purposes served by buy-sell agreements, and identify their advantages.**

buy-sell agreements

Buy-sell agreements are the most common planning method used for the disposition and continuation of small business interests. The goal of any business-continuation arrangement is the acquisition of a decedent business owner's interest by one or more business survivors or by the entity itself. Another purpose of a buy-sell agreement is to provide cash to the decedent's heirs for the sale of the business interest. Because an owner's death is typically disruptive, the business often fails. When a business owner dies, his or her executor's fiduciary role is to collect, preserve, and distribute the decedent's assets. The business interest presents numerous difficulties for the executor unless the decedent had a business-continuation plan prior to his or her death. Buy-sell agreements also cover, disability and divorce situations.

A properly designed buy-sell agreement assures that the estate's interest in the business can be sold for a reasonable price. The business purchasers, usually the surviving co-owners, will then obtain the decedent's business interest according to the terms of the agreement and avoid the difficulties associated with probate. Remember that a buy-sell agreement will avoid probate as the property will not pass under the will nor will the business interest pass under state succession laws. Instead, the business interest will be transferred by way of contract upon the decedent's death. If no business-continuation plan is in place, the executor may be compelled to sell the decedent's business interest to pay the estate's settlement costs and death transfer taxes within 9 months (or less) after death. These circumstances may result in a forced sale of the business for less than fair market value. Without a buy-sell contract the survivors face significant uncertainty: Will the executor or heirs sell the decedent's interest to outsiders? Will the other owners' interests be greatly devalued?

Advantages of a Buy-Sell Agreement

The benefits of a buy-sell agreement can be summarized as follows:

- It guarantees a market for the business interest.
- It provides liquidity for the payment of death taxes and other estate settlement needs.
- It makes the estate planning process more reliable for the owners because it helps to peg the estate tax value of the decedent's business interest.
- It provides for the continuation of the business in the hands of the surviving owners and/or employees.
- It makes the business more attractive to creditors since a plan to continue the business is in place.
- It prevents transfers to unrelated parties.
- It avoids the need for expensive appraisals to establish a purchase price.

LO 10. 2   Identify the common provisions found in most types of buy-sell agreements.

General Format of Buy-Sell Agreements

Most properly drafted buy-sell agreements have several common provisions, regardless of the specific type of agreement. Common terms of a typical buy-sell agreement include the following:

- *parties involved.* All buy-sell agreements should contain a provision clearly identifying the parties to the agreement.
- *purpose.* All agreements should have a statement indicating the agreement's purpose. This provision serves to document the intent of the parties should a later dispute occur.
- *commitments.* The agreement should state the obligations of all parties to the agreement (for example, that the decedent-business owner's estate will sell the decedent's interests to the surviving owners according to the terms of the agreement).
- *business interest description.* The document should contain a description of the business interests subject to the agreement.
- *transfer restrictions during lifetime.* Most buy-sell agreements should include a clause, which is referred to as a first-offer or right-of-first-refusal provision, that prevents the parties from disposing of the business interest to outsiders while the parties are living.

- *purchase price.* The agreement should specify a fixed purchase price or a method for determining a price at which the business interest is to be bought and sold.

- *funding.* The document should specify how the purchase price is to be funded. In most instances, life insurance is used for funding. It is uniquely suited for funding buy-sell agreements, since the very event that creates the need for cash provides the cash. If life insurance is selected as the funding method, the agreement should indicate the type of policies being used, who are the owners and beneficiaries of the policies, and who is responsible for paying their premiums.

- *transfer details.* The agreement should describe the actual specifics of the business transfer. For instance, when and where the settlement is to occur are important aspects of the agreement.

- *modification/termination.* There should be provisions for modification or termination of the buy-sell agreement if the parties later determine that the form of the current agreement no longer achieves the parties' objectives.

All parties to a buy-sell agreement should obtain competent legal counsel in creating the agreement.

LO 10. 3   Describe the various types of buy-sell agreements used in business entities.

BUSINESS-CONTINUATION AGREEMENTS

business-continuation agreement

Buy-sell agreements can be entered into for a variety of reasons. If the primary purpose is to maintain the business after the decedent's death, this type of agreement is often referred to as a **business-continuation agreement**. However, any buy-sell agreement should be coordinated with all other business and personal estate plans. There are three main types of buy-sell agreements, which can be broken down further into other categories depending on the type of business. First, there is a mandatory buy-sell agreement in which the company or buyers are required to purchase the decedent's interest. This type of buy sell is primarily for business-continuation purposes. The second type is an agreement that requires the decedent to offer his or her interest to the company first, a right of first refusal. The third one allows the decedent to offer his or her business interest to his or her heirs first. All of these can be used, but it must match up with the specific company's goals and the decedent's needs.

Sole Proprietorships

A sole proprietorship is a business that has only one individual owner. It is distinct from other forms of business ownership in many ways. Most important, this type of business is not treated as a business entity separate unto itself. There is no legal distinction between the business's and the owner's personal assets. This means that when the sole proprietor dies or loses legal capacity to operate the business, the sole proprietorship must terminate. Planning for this contingency is vital if the proprietor's family expects to get full value for the business.

Often, a buy-sell agreement is used to ensure a definite sale and purchase when the time comes. The agreement binds the proprietor's estate to sell and the purchasers to buy the business interest.

Determining a Purchaser

In some cases, there may be an obvious successor to the sole proprietorship, such as an adult child or other family member who is willing and capable to take over. Sometimes the potential purchaser is a key employee or group of employees. Employees may be willing to enter into a buy-sell agreement to protect their own future employment. If there are no key employees or natural successors to the sole proprietor, it is often recommended that the sole proprietor hire an employee who has the potential to take over the business and provide a training program for that employee.

Characteristics of Proprietorship:
Buy-Sell Agreements
- one owner
- potential purchaser(s)
  - key employee
  - group of employees

Life Insurance Arrangements for Sole Proprietorships. The life insurance arrangements for a sole proprietorship buy-sell agreement are relatively simple. The purchasing party is obligated to provide sale proceeds to the decedent-proprietor's estate. The applicant, owner, and premium payer of the life insurance on the proprietor's life should be the purchasing party. The coverage on the proprietor's life should be sufficient to make the required payments to the estate. In addition, the insurance funding the agreement should be reviewed periodically. It may be necessary for the future purchaser to obtain additional coverage later because of increases in the value of the proprietorship.

Partnerships

By operation of law, a general partnership terminates at the death of the partner unless the partnership agreement provides for continuation. If there has been no lifetime planning, a decedent partner's business interest will have to be liquidated by the surviving partner(s). The surviving partners are required to provide a fair liquidation price to a decedent partner's estate. However, it is often difficult for the surviving partners to make these payments without imposing a tremendous burden on the future partnership income.

The goal of the surviving partners is to continue the partnership business without interruption. Obviously, they would like to keep liquidation payments to a minimum. Therefore, the surviving partners' goals are incongruent with those of the decedent partner's estate. Unless there is a prearranged plan, a dispute between the heirs and the remaining partners is likely.

The solution is a binding partnership buy-sell agreement. Since a partnership has more than one business owner, the buy-sell agreement must address the possibility that any of the partners will be the next to die. Consequently, the partnership agreement should contain mutual promises between the partners that provide for different purchasers and sellers depending on the circumstances. Each partner binds his or her estate to sell if he or she is the first to die. Each partner also agrees to purchase the partnership interest held by the decedent-partner's estate if he or she is among the surviving partners.

Types of Partnership Buy-Sell Agreements

entity-purchase agreement

Entity-Purchase Agreement. Under the **entity-purchase agreement**, it is the partnership entity that becomes the purchaser in the buy-sell agreement. Technically, the partnership liquidates the interest held by the decedent-partner's estate. In other words, the partnership makes payments to the estate that liquidate the interest held by the estate. Under an entity buy-sell agreement, both the partners and partnership are parties to the contract that provides for continuation of the partnership business by the surviving partners.

cross-purchase buy-sell agreement

Cross-Purchase Agreement. With a **cross-purchase buy-sell agreement**, the individual partners are the sellers and purchasers. The partners make mutual promises to be a buyer or seller depending on the circumstances. Each partner agrees to purchase a share of any decedent partner's interest and to bind his or her estate to sell its partnership interest to the surviving partners.

The choice between the entity and cross-purchase approach is complex. Factors such as the number of partners, differences in income tax treatment, cost basis of the different partners, and financial considerations of the partnership will dictate the appropriate choice.

Types of Partnership Buy-Sell Agreements
- entity-purchase agreement
  - partnership makes payments to the estate to liquidate the decedent-partner's interest
- cross-purchase agreement
  - surviving partners purchase the decedent-partner's interest

Insurance Arrangements for Partnership Buy-Sells

entity (liquidation) agreement

Entity (Liquidation) Agreement. The entity buy-sell approach, or **entity (liquidation) agreement**, provides that the partnership will liquidate the interest of a decedent-partner at death. If life insurance is used to fund the agreement, the partnership is the applicant, owner, and beneficiary of the policies on the lives of each partner who is a party to the agreement. Ideally, the partnership strives to maintain face amounts of coverage equal to its obligations under the agreement. Generally, the partnership should adopt the entity approach if it is in a better financial position to make the premium payments than the individuals themselves, or if there are a large number of partners entering into the agreement.

Cross-Purchase Agreement. The cross-purchase agreement provides that the surviving partners are obligated to buy a prearranged share of a decedent-partner's interest from the decedent's estate. The agreement is usually funded by life insurance policies owned by the individual partners. Each partner should purchase life insurance policies on the lives of the other partners whose deaths obligate the policyowner to purchase the decedent's partnership interest. Thus, the individual partners become owners, beneficiaries, and premium payers for life insurance policies covering the lives of the other partners. Assuming "N" represents the number of business owners, the formula used for determining the number of policies needed is $N \times (N - 1)$. Therefore, four partners would require 12 (4×3) life insurance policies. When a partner dies, the surviving partners receive the policy proceeds that are transferred to the decedent's estate in exchange for the partnership interest. Ideally, each partner acquires a policy with a death benefit equal to his or her share of the purchase price of a decedent-partner's interest.

Closely Held Corporations

A corporation is a legal entity separate from its shareholders. It provides limited liability to its shareholders and is treated as a separate taxpayer with tax rates and rules quite different from those applicable to individual taxpayers. In a closely held corporation, the key individuals usually include the shareholders. Because of this situation, the death, retirement, or disability of these key individuals threatens the future of the corporation. Therefore, it is reasonable for the corporation and its shareholders to adopt a buy-sell agreement.

Types of Corporate Buy-Sell Agreements

stock-redemption buy-sell agreement

Entity (Stock-Redemption) Purchase Agreement. With a **stock-redemption buy-sell agreement**, the corporation is the purchaser of the stock at the death of a shareholder. Each shareholder-party to the agreement binds his or her estate to transfer the stock to the corporation in exchange for the required purchase price. The corporation redeems a decedent-shareholder's stock in exchange for a redemption distribution. The corporation either retires the stock or holds it as treasury stock. From the surviving shareholders' standpoint, the practical effect of a stock redemption is that the percentage ownership held by each surviving shareholder increases proportionately when a decedent-shareholder's stock is redeemed.

Entity-Purchase Buy-Sell Agreement

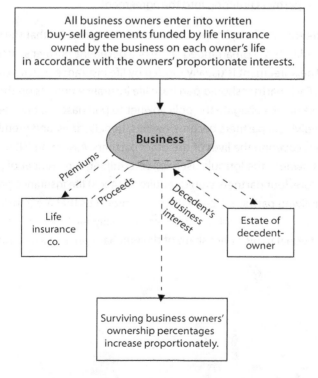

The tax treatment of a stock redemption is extremely complex and beyond the scope of this book. Traditionally, a stock redemption is treated as a distribution of cash or property from the corporation to a shareholder and constitutes a taxable dividend to the redeemed shareholder. Under certain exceptions, a redemption may be treated as a sale or exchange subject to capital gains. It is essential to qualify the stock redemption as a sale or exchange to avoid harsh tax consequences to the redeemed shareholder's estate. Generally speaking, a stock-redemption plan does not qualify for the favorable sale-or-exchange tax treatment if family members of the decedent own stock in the corporation and plan to be the decedent's successors in the corporation. Other tax issues associated with a stock-redemption agreement concern income tax cost-basis problems for the surviving shareholders.

Corporate Cross-Purchase Agreement. The corporate cross-purchase agreement is similar to the partnership agreement. Each shareholder agrees to purchase a specified percentage of the decedent-shareholder's stock at the time of death. Although the corporation is not a direct party to the agreement, the stock certificates it issues should be endorsed with a statement that the stock is subject to the terms of the buy-sell agreement.

Cross-Purchase Buy-Sell Agreement

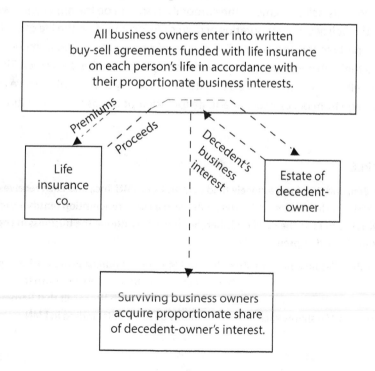

If only a few corporate shareholders are involved, there are two primary tax advantages to a cross-purchase agreement:

- The sale of stock by a decedent-shareholder's estate is treated as a sale or exchange, allowing the estate favorable capital-gains treatment.

- Because the surviving shareholders are direct purchasers, each receives an income tax cost basis in his or her stock equal to the amount of the purchase price paid.

Types of Closely Held Corporation Buy-Sell Agreements

- entity (stock-redemption) purchase agreement
  - corporation purchases decedent-shareholder's interest
- corporate cross-purchase agreement
  - surviving shareholder(s) purchase(s) decedent-partner's interest

Insurance Arrangements for Corporate Buy-Sells

Stock-Redemption Agreements. If life insurance is chosen as the funding mechanism for a stock-redemption buy-sell agreement, the corporation should be the applicant, owner, and beneficiary of the policies. The corporation acquires life insurance on the life of each shareholder who is a party to the agreement. The receipt of policy proceeds at a shareholder's death provides the cash necessary to redeem the decedent-shareholder's stock. The stock-redemption buy-sell agreement should be updated periodically to prevent the face amounts of insurance coverage from becoming inadequate for redemptions as the corporation increases in value.

EXAMPLE

Barney, Ben, and Bart form a closely held corporation, LMN, Inc., and each receives 100 shares of stock. The three shareholders enter into a stock-redemption (entity-purchase) buy-sell agreement so the surviving shareholders can continue the business in coequal ownership if one dies prematurely.

Suppose Ben dies first. Ben's death obligates LMN, Inc., to purchase his stock at a prearranged price. Corporate funds are then transferred to Ben's estate in return for his 100 shares of stock. This stock is retired by the corporation, with the result that Barney and Bart now own 100 shares each of the 200 shares of stock outstanding in LMN.

Cross-Purchase Agreements. If life insurance is used to fund a cross-purchase agreement, each shareholder should purchase adequate life insurance on the lives of the other shareholders. Each individual shareholder then becomes owner, beneficiary, and premium payer for the life insurance policies covering the lives of the other shareholders. As with the partnership cross-purchase agreement, the formula for determining the number of policies needed is N x (N − 1). If there are three parties to the contract, six (3 × 2) insurance policies are necessary.

At a shareholder's death, the surviving shareholders receive the death benefits from the policies and transfer the proceeds to the decedent-shareholder's estate in exchange for the appropriate amount of his or her stock. Because individual shareholders must be relied upon to maintain the funding for the agreement, there is often the concern that some parties will not live up to the terms of the contract. To ensure that the cross-purchase agreement is carried out, a trustee is often used as an overseer to hold the policies and consummate the purchase and sale of stock at a shareholder's death.

EXAMPLE

Mannie, Mo, and Mac form a closely held corporation, XYZ, Inc., and receive 100 shares of stock each at the time of incorporation. The three shareholders also enter into a cross-purchase buy-sell agreement at this time. The premise of the agreement is for the surviving shareholders to continue the business in equal ownership. In the contract Mannie, Mo, and Mac execute the buy-sell agreement to bind their estates to sell their shares of stock to the surviving shareholders. Each shareholder agrees to purchase one-half of the shares of stock held by the estate of a deceased shareholder.

Suppose Mannie is the first to die. When the agreement is carried out, Mo and Mac each purchase 50 shares of stock in XYZ, Inc., from Mannie's estate. Mannie's estate will then have liquid funds to meet expenses and distribution requirements. Mo and Mac will continue to operate XYZ after the buyout. Each will hold 150 shares of stock out of the 300 shares outstanding in XYZ.

Clearly, the tax and nontax implications of buy-sell agreements are complex and unique to each business arrangement. The specifics of any buy-sell contract should be hammered out only after careful deliberation by all the parties to the contract and with the advice of experts in this area.

Funding Buy-Sell Agreements With Life Insurance

- entity purchase/stock redemption
  - entity is applicant, owner, premium payer, and beneficiary of the policies on lives of business owners (partners/shareholders)
- cross-purchase
  - each business owner is applicant, owner, premium payer, and beneficiary of policies on the other business owner's lives

LO 10. 4   Describe how each type of price-setting mechanism used in buy-sell agreements works.

SETTING A PRICE IN A BUY-SELL AGREEMENT

In general, the first decision that must be made in developing a buy-sell agreement is establishing a price. This problem is unusually difficult because so many factors (such as the time of death, the condition of the business on the date of the buyout, and the influence of economic conditions) pose a multitude of variables that are not only unknown and unknowable but also interdependent. In spite of these problems, it is necessary to arrive at a price-of-valuation formula. Obviously, there is no *right* method, and every method has its problems.

Determining a pricing method and a price in a buy-sell agreement is crucial for accepting the value of the partnership or corporation interests for federal estate tax purposes. For instance, if the IRS determines that the agreement is a testamentary device rather than serving a legitimate business purpose, the price will be upheld among business owners but not necessarily for estate tax purposes. Therefore, the estate will be obligated to honor the agreement price but the estate tax value could be significantly more. Consequently, what the estate receives for the sale of the decedent's interest could be significantly less than the value on which the transfer tax is predicated.

In order for the price in a buy-sell agreement to be binding for tax purposes, especially with family buy-sells, the transaction must represent an arm's-length agreement among the parties. It must be one that reasonably recognizes the different and usually competing interests of all parties. In other words, the price must be the same as one reached by unrelated parties.

Courts may employ the following factors to determine whether a buy-sell agreement is a testamentary device:

- the manner in which the price was chosen
- whether there was an independent appraisal and/or independent professional advice

- whether the beneficiary of the agreement is the object of the decedent's bounty

- the decedent's health when establishing the agreement

- the decedent's age at the time of the agreement

- whether all the parties to the agreement were equally and consistently bound by its terms

- whether there was any negotiation involved concerning the terms of the agreement

- the type of relationship that existed between the parties to the agreement

There are essentially four methods that business individuals use as a price-setting mechanism in a buy-sell agreement:

- fixed price

- formula-determined price

- appraisal-determined price

- combination of the above mechanisms

Fixed Price

Setting a price and stating it in the agreement has the advantage of being simple and clear. If Steve, Robert, and Lee are all parties to the agreement, each person knows exactly what his family would receive upon his death as well as what he would receive in the event of disability. For example, if they use a fixed price of $900,000 and each individual owns a one-third interest, each person's interest would be worth one-third of $900,000, or $300,000.

There are drawbacks to a fixed-price mechanism. The main disadvantage is that the agreement will likely fail the tests to peg the value of stock in a family corporation. Because a fixed price does not adequately reflect fluctuations in market value, it is likely that the IRS will find the agreement to be either: (1) a device to pass the stock to family for less than full consideration, or (2) inconsistent with the terms of an agreement reached at arm's length. Even if the parties are unrelated, the fixed-price provision generally provides an inaccurate result.

Can the drawback of the fixed-price mechanism be alleviated by a requirement that the parties revalue the business each year and that the value as of the last revaluation stands? In theory, the solution seems sound. However, as a practical matter, the parties to a buy-sell agreement seldom actually make their intended annual revaluation. If the value of the business increases substantially from the time the fixed price is set, the survivors of the deceased business owner will receive an amount that does not accurately reflect the true value of the business. Likewise, if one of the business owners becomes ill, he or she will want to readjust the price upward to provide more cash for the family in return for the business owner's business interest. But the interest of the healthy business owners is diametrically opposed to that of the sick colleague. The result is that the equal bargaining position contemplated by the agreement no longer exists.

It may make sense to set a fixed price (using one or more of the valuation methods discussed above that are used by the IRS and the courts) and then provide in the contract for yearly revaluations, plus an additional provision that if no revaluation has been made within X months of the date of death, then the price shall be the average of the valuations rendered by two qualified appraisers (or some similar technique).

Formula-Pricing Mechanism

The main disadvantage of a fixed-price mechanism for valuing a business interest is definitional (that is, the price is fixed by agreement while the value of the business interest may fluctuate widely). What is indicated is a pricing mechanism based on a formula. The formula itself may take a number of factors into consideration. For example, the formula may be an adaptation of an ARM 34 or some other method that considers various, easily ascertained, objective factors.

The most common formula approach uses some type of capitalization-of-earnings method. Often, the parties take other value-affecting factors into consideration by the multiple used. For example, one business may be valued at 10 times average earnings for the past 5 years, while another might be valued at 3 times average earnings for the past 8 years. Obviously, the greater the risk and the lower the stability of a business, the lower the earnings multiple is. Industry studies by statistical analysis companies can be used to discover the multiple for any given type of industry. Adjustments may have to be made for specific facts or abnormalities with regard to a particular business. Many of these adjustments are discussed above. The multiple itself may vary from time to time as economic conditions change. In some cases, the formula gives more weight to the earnings of those years immediately preceding the decedent-business owner's death than to the earnings of prior years. If family members are parties, it is imperative that the formula chosen be consistent with similar arm's-length agreements.

Appraisal

Many authorities feel that the fairest means of ascertaining the value of a business is to state in the buy-sell agreement that two appraisers should be employed. One appraiser is hired by the surviving shareholders, while the other represents the decedent's interest. The two appraisers would come to an agreement on an appropriate valuation, or in the absence of agreement, a third appraiser would be appointed by the first two to make a final binding determination of value.

The parties can give the appraisers carte blanche in their appraisal process, or they can instruct them to take into consideration certain factors and ignore others. For example, the buy-sell agreement can specify that the appraisers are to ignore goodwill or value it in a certain way.

The Uniform Standards of Professional Appraisal Practice (USPAP) contain the rules of valuation followed by many appraisers.

Combination Mechanism

A fixed-price mechanism coupled with an appraisal and a formula method, which begins with a fixed price as a floor and enhances that amount if earnings or book values reach a certain level, are other ways to solve the difficult and perplexing problem of providing variable but realistic prices for a business owner's interest.

CHAPTER REVIEW

Key Terms and Concepts

buy-sell agreements
business-continuation agreement
entity-purchase agreement

cross-purchase buy-sell agreement
entity (liquidation) agreement
stock-redemption buy-sell agreement

Chapter 10: Review Questions

1. What are the advantages of entering into a buy-sell agreement? [LO 10.1]

2. Identify some of the provisions that all buy-sell agreements typically contain. [LO 10.2]

3. Explain why life insurance is the preferred method for funding buy-sell agreements. [LO 10.3]

4. Why might a business-continuation agreement be necessary for a sole proprietorship? [LO 10.3]

5. Describe the two basic types of buy-sell agreements for:

    a. partnerships

    b. corporations [LO 10.3]

6. Describe four methods for specifying or determining the purchase price in a buy-sell agreement. [LO 10.4]

Chapter 10: Review Answers

1. The advantages of a buy-sell agreement can be summarized as follows:

   - It guarantees a market for the business interest.

   - It provides liquidity for the payment of death taxes and other estate settlement needs.

   - It makes the estate planning process more reliable for the owners because it helps to peg the estate tax value of the decedent's business interest.

   - It provides for the continuation of the business in the hands of the surviving owners and/or employees.

   - It makes the business more attractive to creditors since a plan to continue the business is in place.

2. Most properly drafted buy-sell agreements have several common provisions, regardless of the specific type of agreement. Common terms of a typical buy-sell agreement include the following:

   - **parties involved.** All buy-sell agreements should have a provision clearly identifying the parties to the agreement.

   - **purpose.** All agreements should have a statement indicating the agreement's purpose.

   - **commitments.** The agreement should state the obligations of all parties to it (for example, that the decedent-business owner's estate will sell the decedent's interests to the surviving owners according to the terms of the agreement).

   - **business interest description.** The document should contain a description of the business interests subject to the agreement.

   - **transfer restrictions during lifetime.** Most buy-sell agreements should include a clause, which is referred to as a first-offer or right-of-first-refusal provision, that prevents the parties to the agreement from disposing of the business interest to outsiders while the parties are living.

   - **purchase price.** The agreement should specify a fixed purchase price or a method for determining a price at which the business interest is to be bought and sold.

   - **funding.** The document should specify how the purchase price is to be funded.

- **transfer details.** The agreement should describe the actual specifics of the business transfer.

- **modification/termination.** There should be provisions for modification or termination of the buy-sell agreement if the parties later determine that the form of the current agreement no longer achieves the parties' objectives.

3. Life insurance is uniquely suited for funding buy-sell agreements, since the very event that creates the need for cash provides the cash.

4. A sole proprietorship is a business that has only one individual owner. It is distinct from other forms of business ownership in many ways. Most important, this type of business is not treated as a business entity separate unto itself. There is no legal distinction between the business's and the owner's personal assets. This means that when the sole proprietor dies or loses legal capacity to operate the business, the sole proprietorship must terminate. Planning for this contingency is vital if the proprietor's family expects to get full value for the business.

    Often a buy-sell agreement is used to ensure a definite sale and purchase when the time comes. The agreement binds the proprietor's estate to sell and the purchaser(s) to buy the business interest.

5. a. **Types of Partnership Buy-Sell Agreements**

    Entity-Purchase Agreement. Under the entity approach, it is the partnership entity that becomes the purchaser in the buy-sell agreement. Technically, the partnership liquidates the interest held by the decedent-partner's estate. In other words, the partnership makes payments to the estate that liquidate the interest held by the estate. Under an entity buy-sell agreement both the partners and partnership are parties to the contract that provides for continuation of the partnership business by the surviving partners.

    Cross-Purchase Agreement. With a cross-purchase buy-sell agreement, the individual partners are the sellers and purchasers. The partners make mutual promises to be a buyer or seller depending on the circumstances. Each partner agrees to purchase a share of any decedent partner's interest and to bind his or her estate to sell its partnership interest to the surviving partners.

    b. **Types of Corporate Buy-Sell Agreements**

    Entity (Stock Redemption) Purchase Agreements. With a stock-redemption agreement, the corporation is the purchaser of the stock at the death of a shareholder. Each shareholder-party to the agreement binds his or her estate to transfer the stock to the corporation in exchange for the required purchase price. The corporation redeems a decedent-shareholder's stock in exchange for a redemption distribution. The corporation either retires the stock or holds it as treasury stock. From the surviving shareholders' standpoint, the practical effect of a stock redemption is that the percentage ownership held by each surviving shareholder increases proportionately when a decedent-shareholder's stock is redeemed.

Corporate Cross-Purchase Agreements. The corporate cross-purchase agreement is similar to the partnership agreement. Each shareholder agrees to purchase a specified percentage of the decedent-shareholder's stock at the time of death. Although the corporation is not a direct party to the agreement, the stock certificates it issues should be endorsed with a statement that the stock is subject to the terms of the buy-sell agreement.

6.   There are essentially four methods that business individuals use as a price-setting mechanism in a buy-sell agreement. These price-setting mechanisms are

- fixed price

- formula-determined price

- appraisal-determined price

- combination of the above mechanisms

Fixed Price

Under this method, a final price is set and stated in the agreement. This method has the advantage of being simple and clear, although frequently the agreement provides for yearly reevaluations of the price to keep it up-to-date.

Formula Mechanism

The most common formula approach uses some type of capitalization-of-adjusted-earnings method. Often, the parties take other value-affecting factors into consideration by the multiple used. For example, one business may be valued at 10 times average earnings for the past 5 years, while another might be valued at 3 times average earnings for the past 8 years. Obviously, the greater the risk and the lower the stability of a business, the lower the earnings multiple is. Adjustments for specific facts or abnormalities with regard to a particular business may have to be made. The multiple itself may vary from time to time as economic conditions change. In some cases, the formula gives more weight to the earnings of those years immediately preceding the decedent-business owner's death than to the earnings of prior years. If family members are parties, it is imperative that the formula chosen be consistent with similar arm's-length agreements.

Appraisal

Many authorities feel that the fairest means of ascertaining the value of a business is to state in the buy-sell agreement that two appraisers should be employed. One appraiser is hired by the surviving shareholders, while the other represents the decedent's interest. The two appraisers would come to an agreement on an appropriate valuation or, in the absence of agreement, a third appraiser would be appointed by the first two to make a final binding determination of value.

Combination Mechanism

A fixed-price mechanism coupled with an appraisal and a formula method, which begins with a fixed price as a floor and enhances that amount if earnings or book values reach a certain level, are other ways to solve the difficult and perplexing problem of providing variable but realistic prices for a business owner's interest.

Chapter 11:

Federal Estate Taxation: The Gross Estate— Part I

Learning Objectives

An understanding of the material in this chapter should enable the student to

- **LO 11.1** **Describe the concept of gross estate.**

- **LO 11.2** **Distinguish between the federal estate tax and other death taxes.**

- **LO 11.3** **Describe the general rule for inclusion of property under sections 2031 and 2033 in the gross estate of a decedent.**

- **LO 11.4** **Explain the various types of property that are includible in the gross estate under section 2035 if transferred or disposed of within 3 years of death.**

- **LO 11.5** **Explain how transfers of property with retained life interests and powers under sections 2036, 2037, and 2038 may be treated for federal estate tax purposes.**

LO 11.1　　　**Describe the concept of gross estate.**

INTRODUCTION—GROSS ESTATE

If a meaningful estate plan is to be written, a clear understanding of the size of the client's gross estate is essential. The concept of the *federal gross estate*, as it is called, is crucial because its size and the types of assets it includes directly determine what planning techniques the financial planner should employ.

This clear understanding of the federal gross estate begins with the Internal Revenue Code. The Internal Revenue Code divides the manner in which a gross estate is to be constructed into two broad categories: (1) what the estate owner actually owned at the date of death, and (2) what the estate owner is deemed to have owned at the date of death. The first of these categories is simple, the second quite complex.

The concept of the *actual estate* is logical. The doctrine requires all property interests the decedent owned at the date of death to be included in the gross estate. This inclusion results in estate taxation. The legal requirement that such property be included as part of the gross estate is logical: If a decedent owned the property at the date of death, he or she should be taxed on that ownership interest for federal estate tax purposes.

There is a second, more complex tier to our twofold system of federal estate taxation. We have labeled this second element the *constructive estate*. There are several provisions in the estate tax portion of the Internal Revenue Code that result in the pulling back of former property interests into the decedent's gross estate so that the fair market value of those interests, either at the date of death or on the alternate valuation date, becomes taxable as part of the estate. A statutory framework does exist that may result in a significant amount of federal estate tax being imposed on the constructive estate.

A two-tiered system of inclusion exists because the IRS convinced Congress that there are many actual and potential situations when estate owners, bent on estate tax avoidance, transfer property interests so that the value of that property will not *actually* be owned by the estate owners at the date of death. If the statutory framework were such that only interests *actually* owned by decedents could be subjected to federal estate taxation, a transfer of property interests would successfully defeat the tax. But often, the IRS concluded, estate owners want the best of both worlds. That is, they will transfer property interests to others so that as a matter of property law they no longer own the property, but as a matter of practicality they continue to enjoy the property as if they still owned it.

One primary objective of estate planning traditionally has been to obtain the maximum savings in federal and local death taxes as well as other transfer costs. Most clients want to transfer their property to family members and other beneficiaries at a minimum cost with the least shrinkage to the estate. For many persons with small- and medium-sized estates, the basic credit amount shelters the estate from tax.

In addition, there is now an unlimited maximum marital deduction that allows married individuals to pass their entire estate to their surviving spouses free of federal estate tax. In spite of these benefits, under current law the federal estate tax must be taken into consideration in planning an estate for the following reasons:

- The basic credit amount shelters up to $22.4 million from tax per married couple in 2018. Basic credit is $4,505,800 per person in 2019.

- The marital deduction is available only at the first death of a married couple (presuming the survivor does not remarry).

- Inflation may cause certain estates to exceed the basic credit amount.

- The size of the federal deficit might in the future cause Congress to look for increased revenue from the estate and gift tax system.

As a cautionary word, the financial planner must determine the unique objectives of a client in the estate planning process. Overall objectives must be planned. The effect of taxes on the estate is only one consideration in preparing an estate plan. While no plan should be implemented without an analysis of the tax consequences, federal estate taxes should not be the controlling factor, regardless of the size of the estate. The field of tax law is a dynamic and constantly shifting area, based on tax statutes as well as regulations and further supported by interpretations through case law and revenue rulings. This chapter and subsequent ones on the federal estate tax laws review general principles in the field that will enable the financial planner both to understand and to explain to a client the impact of federal estate taxation. These chapters, however, provide only an introduction to a complex, continually changing area of tax law.

LO 11. 2   Distinguish between the federal estate tax and other death taxes.

THE FEDERAL ESTATE TAX

The federal estate tax is imposed on the transferor or the transferor's estate and is based on the privilege to transfer property. Congress recognized that a tax limited to property transferred at death would have been an open invitation to tax-avoidance schemes to dispose of property during lifetime. Therefore, under the Tax Reform Act of 1976, a unified estate and gift tax system was enacted to prevent lifetime dispositions from escaping taxation or being taxed at lower rates. The 1976 act provided a unified, cumulative system for taxation of certain transfers by gift during lifetime and transfers at death at the same tax rates. Since January 1, 1977, adjusted taxable gifts (as they are called) are taken into consideration and added to the taxable estate in computing any federal estate tax due at death.

The Economic Growth and Tax Relief Reconciliation Act (EGTRRA) of 2001, however, enacted some provisions that changed the unified system of the 1976 act.

Under EGTRRA 2001 beginning January 1, 2002, the gift tax exclusion became $1,000,000 even though the estate tax exclusion increased to $1.5 million in 2004 and 2005; $2 million in 2006, 2007, and 2008; $3.5 million in 2009; and was scheduled to be repealed for 2010 only to be followed by EGTRRA sunset provisions that called for a return to pre-EGTRRA rules unless Congress acted and legislated new law. The gift tax was not repealed, however, and the exclusion remained at $1 million through 2010. In addition, the gift tax rate decreased each year in conjunction with the top estate tax rate. For 2010, the top gift and income tax rate was 35 percent. In December 2010 Congress passed the Tax Relief, Unemployment Insurance Reauthorization, and Job Creation Act of 2010 (TRA 2010). Amongst other provisions, TRA 2010 allowed for a $5 million exclusion for gift, estate, and generation-skipping taxes for 2011. Congress passed the American Taxpayer Relief Act of 2012 extending the basic exclusion amount of $5 million and continued indexing this amount for inflation. The Tax Cuts and Jobs Act of 2017 (TCJA) doubled the exclusion for gift, estate, and generation-skipping taxes to $11.18 million per person ($22.36 million per couple) in 2018 through 2025, when the exclusion reverts to the 2017 level indexed for inflation. The lifetime exclusion is currently $11.4 million in 2019 as indexed for inflation.

Congress also addressed situations where the donor transferred property to another but continued to retain powers, controls, or interests over the transferred property for his or her lifetime under certain sections of the federal estate tax law. Congress perceived these incomplete lifetime dispositions as the equivalent of testamentary transfers at death, since the donor still had some control over or enjoyment from the property during lifetime or power over the property at death. These types of rights or powers, if held by a decedent at death, may cause the property to be included in the decedent's gross estate.

federal estate tax

All property, either owned directly by the decedent at the time of death or subject to the decedent's control in a manner sufficient to cause that property to be included in the gross estate under one of the federal estate tax rules, is included in the estate for federal estate tax purposes. The **federal estate tax** applies to the entire estate and is imposed on the estate itself, which is primarily liable for payment of the tax. The way in which property is transferred is irrelevant in this regard. In other words, the property may be transferred by will, intestacy, contract, or operation of law. To the extent that there are assets in the estate, the estate is responsible for the tax liability. However, if the estate does not contain sufficient assets to pay the tax liability, beneficiaries of the estate may be charged with the tax liability to the extent of the value of property they inherit.

Estate Taxation of Residents, Citizens, and Nonresident Aliens

gross estate

All property owned by citizens or residents of the United States at the time of their death is subject to the federal estate tax, regardless of where the property is located or where they reside. The **gross estate** includes all property owned by a citizen or resident of the United States at death valued at its fair market value on the date of death or alternate valuation date (6 months after death). The tax is a progressive tax similar to the federal income tax. It is based on a graduated rate schedule that increases with the size of the estate.

The federal estate tax is applied differently to those who are considered nonresident noncitizens (nonresident aliens). As for nonresident noncitizens, only the value of their property located in the United States and owned by them at the time of their death is subject to federal estate tax. Note that the property owned by noncitizens may also be subject to foreign death taxes, as may foreign property held by U.S. citizens. The federal taxation of such individuals and their property often depends on the terms of the estate tax treaty (if any) between the United States and the relevant foreign nation.

LO 11. 3   Describe the general rule for inclusion of property under sections 2031 and 2033 in the gross estate of a decedent.

IRC Sec. 2031: Basic Includibility

Our system of federal taxation is controlled by statute. Because the federal estate tax is no exception, our starting point in studying the concept of the gross estate is to look to the specific Internal Revenue Code section defining the gross estate. Sec. 2031 provides, in very vague fashion, that the gross estate shall include "the value of all property, real or personal, tangible or intangible, to the extent provided by Secs. 2033 through 2046." Obviously, Sec. 2031 is an empty provision, devoid of much substance, because it merely cites other Internal Revenue Code sections for justification of inclusion of assets. Unless a particular property interest is covered by Secs. 2033-2046, there is no gross estate inclusion. Sec. 2031 may be thought of as a road map, telling us where else to look in the Internal Revenue Code to determine whether property has to be included as part of a decedent's gross estate.

Because of the vague nature of Sec. 2031, it is important to treat the subsequent provisions of the estate tax sections in detail.

THE CATCHALL PROVISION (IRC SEC. 2033)

Section 2033 of the Internal Revenue Code states the general rule that the gross estate includes the value of all property interests, real or personal, tangible or intangible, of an individual on the date of death to the extent of his or her interest in the property. Sec. 2033 is designed as nothing more than a catchall provision. Subsequent Code provisions provide the fine-tuning.

In order to include a property or a property interest under this section, the decedent's interest must rise to the level of an *interest in property*. This is broader than merely stating that property *owned* by the decedent at the time of death is to be included. It requires the inclusion of property interests to the extent of any interest in such property.

Once we know that property in which the decedent possessed an *interest* will be required to be included as part of the decedent's gross estate, the question arises, what is an *interest*? The answer lies in *state* law.

Types of Property Interests Includible Under Sec. 2033

State law creates legal interests and rights. This Code section has been interpreted to mean that federal taxation is to be applied based on locally determined rights and interests. Accordingly, if under state law a decedent is considered to own property or possess an interest in such property, then Sec. 2033 will apply to that particular property and its value will be pulled into the federal gross estate.

For situations in which there is a factual or legal question about a decedent's property interest, the federal courts rule on such questions, but they are required to apply principles of state property law.

The regulations are not particularly helpful in this regard as they say only that the property interest must be one that was a beneficial interest (Treas. Reg. Sec. 20.2033–1(a)). That is to say that, for purposes of IRC Sec. 2033, a mere legal interest—such as holding title purely as a fiduciary—is not an interest that rises to the level of a property interest in which the decedent had a beneficial interest. Therefore, the interest is not includible in the decedent's gross estate.

Property and property interests that are includible under Sec. 2033 are those that are "owned" by the decedent. While this ownership concept may provide a convenient shorthand way of describing the property interests includible in a decedent's gross estate under this Code section, it is not always precise. Other limitations may cause property or property interests owned by a decedent to be excluded from this particular section. However, the same property or property interests may be specifically included in the gross estate under other sections of the federal estate tax law.

For example, the right to borrow money against the cash value of an insurance policy may not be a property interest sufficient to include the policy proceeds in the decedent's gross estate under Sec. 2033. But the proceeds are included because of another section that specifically requires their inclusion. (Those types of interests in property that are specifically includible in the decedent's gross estate are discussed later in this and the following chapter.)

Limitations on Property Interests Includible Under Sec. 2033

The federal estate tax is levied on the right to transfer property at death. Therefore, if the decedent had no right to transfer property or a property interest to another at death, either by will or under the intestacy laws, the value of those property interests is not includible in the gross estate under this section no matter how great the decedent's interests were during lifetime. An example of an interest in which the decedent possessed no right to pass the property at death is a life estate created by another. Any interest in property that was given to the decedent by another, the transfer of which the decedent cannot control and that ceases at the decedent's death, is not included in his or her gross estate. Only inheritable interests (interests that can be transmitted to another by the decedent at death) are subject to the tax.

Three factors apply to all property in determining whether it is includible in the decedent's gross estate under Sec. 2033. First, what types of property are includible under state or federal law? Second, was the decedent's interest in the property large enough to warrant its inclusion in the estate? Third, did the decedent possess this interest at the time of death, and to what extent?

Specific Types of Property Includible Under Sec. 2033

Under Sec. 2033, the decedent's estate includes any interest in real estate, whether the property comes into the possession of the personal representative or passes directly to the heirs. The decedent's estate also includes cash or money equivalents, whether kept in a bank, savings or checking account, certificates of deposit, money market funds, or a safe-deposit box. The gross estate includes any stocks, bonds (including tax-exempt bonds), notes, and mortgages owned by the decedent, as well as the value of any outstanding loans the decedent made to others. His or her estate also includes the value of income tax refunds not yet paid, patents, and copyrights.

Property subject to indebtedness is also includible in the decedent's gross estate. If the decedent is personally liable for the indebtedness, the full value of the property is included in the gross estate and the estate is allowed a deduction for the amount of the debt. If the decedent is not personally liable for the indebtedness (for example, a nonrecourse note), only the value of the decedent's equity in the property is included in the gross estate and no deduction is allowed for the debt.

Under Sec. 2033, the gross estate also includes any amount to which the decedent was entitled before he or she died. For example, a claim for damages for pain and suffering as a result of someone else's negligent act is includible in the decedent's estate because it could have been recovered by him or her before death. On the other hand, the proceeds of a wrongful death claim, although brought by the decedent's personal representative on behalf of his or her heirs, are not included in the gross estate because the decedent had no right of action or interest in the proceeds at any time before death. It is not relevant that the decedent's death was instrumental in someone else's acquiring an interest in the property. The relevant test is whether there was anything the decedent had a right to own or receive while alive that passes to another by reason of the decedent's death.

If the decedent was entitled to a refund because of an income tax overpayment, this income tax refund is an asset includible in the gross estate under Sec. 2033. The same is true if the decedent and the decedent's spouse had filed a joint return. In the case of a joint return in which an income tax refund is due, the amount includible in the decedent's gross estate is the amount by which his or her contribution toward payment of the income tax exceeds the decedent's income tax liability. Any medical insurance reimbursements due to the decedent at the time of death are also includible in the gross estate.

Outstanding dividends declared and payable to the stockholders of record on or before the date of the decedent's death are included in the decedent's gross estate (Treas. Reg. § 20.2033–1(b)). Thus, if a shareholder dies after the record date but before the dividend is paid, the dividend is the shareholder's property and is included in the decedent-shareholder's estate. The critical date is the ownership on the record date of the dividend. If the decedent dies after the dividend is declared but before the record date, he or she did not own the right to the dividend at death. Therefore, the value is not included in the decedent's gross estate. Of course, if the dividend is declared after the date of death, it is not included in the gross estate because the decedent's right to receive the dividend did not accrue while the decedent was alive.

Sec. 2033 has sufficient scope to include in a decedent's gross estate not only tangible and intangible assets actually owned by the decedent at death but also assets that were due the decedent but not yet received by him or her. Income items that have already been earned by a decedent but not collected as of the date of death are *income in respect of a decedent (IRD)*. Even though such items are taxed for federal income tax purposes, the items may also be required to be included as part of the gross estate. They may, therefore, be subject to federal estate tax as well.

Examples of income in respect of a decedent include the following:

- fees earned by a decedent but not yet paid and collected as of the time of death
- royalties earned by the decedent but not yet paid
- rents accrued up to the date of the decedent's death on property the decedent owned
- bonuses, unpaid salary, and the like previously earned by the decedent but not yet paid
- dividends on shares of stock the decedent owned at the time of death but payable subsequent to death
- IRA accounts (in excess of basis)
- business accounts receivable
- vested amounts in qualified retirement plans

Although such items trigger both income tax and estate tax liability, Sec. 691(c) of the Internal Revenue Code allows an income tax deduction for the amount of estate tax to the party who receives and reports the income for federal income tax purposes. Furthermore, an income tax deduction is also permitted for any generation-skipping tax attributed to IRD assets included in a taxable termination, or a direct skip resulting from the decedent's death. The deduction must be allocated among IRD recipients according to their proportionate share of the amount of gross IRD.

EXAMPLE

Becky is the beneficiary of her Uncle Pete's IRA. In 2019, Uncle Pete died with a taxable estate of $18 million and an IRA valued at $2 million. The tentative federal estate tax in 2019 is $7,945,800 and the net estate tax is $3,440,000 ($7,945,800 - 4,505,800) with the inclusion of the IRA in the estate. Without inclusion of the IRA in the gross estate, the tentative estate tax is $7,145,800 and the net estate tax is $2,640,000 ($7,145,800 - 4,505,800). The tax difference with and without inclusion of Uncle Pete's IRA is $800,000 ($3,440,000 - 2,640,000). Therefore, $800,000 (the additional amount of estate tax liability resulting from inclusion of the IRA in the decedent's estate) can be used to reduce Becky's income tax liability as the IRA is distributed to her. (See the table below.)

Difference in Estate Tax Between Inclusion and Exclusion of IRA			
Estate Tax With IRA Inclusion		**Estate Tax Without IRA Inclusion**	
Year of death	2018	Year of death	2018
Adjusted gross estate	$20,000,000	Adjusted gross estate	$18,000,000
Taxable estate	$20,000,000	Taxable estate	$18,000,000
Adjusted taxable gifts	$0	Adjusted taxable gifts	$0
Tentative tax base	$20,000,000	Tentative tax base	$18,000,000
Tentative tax	$7,945,800	Tentative tax	$7,145,800
Gift tax paid	$0	Gift tax paid	$0
Gross federal estate tax	$7,945,800	Gross federal estate tax	$7,145,800
Allowable basic credit amount (2018)	$4,505,800	Allowable basic credit amount (2019)	$4,417,800
Net federal estate tax	$3,440,000	Net federal estate tax	$2,640,000

Also included in the decedent's estate is miscellaneous property, such as interests in partnerships and unincorporated businesses. These interests are listed in the estate tax return on a separate schedule from stock that a decedent might own in either a publicly held or a closely held corporation. All the decedent's tangible personal property—including furniture, jewelry, and household items—is includible in the gross estate. Frequently, however, household items and wedding gifts are considered to be the wife's property if acquired at or near the time of the marriage. In such cases, the value of these items is not included in the decedent husband's gross estate; however, documentation may be necessary to successfully support the exclusion of such items.

Under Sec., the decedent's estate also includes any vested rights to receive property in the future. These future interests in property include reversionary interests as well as remainder interests and are includible at their values on the date of death as computed actuarially according to IRS tables.

EXAMPLE

If Stephen creates a trust for the benefit of his divorced wife, Betty, and gives Betty income for life with the property to revert to Stephen or his estate upon her death, his reversionary interest is an includible asset. Because the property reverts to Stephen if he survives her or to his estate should he predecease her, his estate and heirs have an absolute right to receive the trust property at some future time. Therefore, a value for this reversionary interest will be determined at Stephen's death.

Includible future rights also include fixed ascertainable rights to receive income from the property as well as remainder interests in the corpus either at some future time or upon the occurrence of some future event. These future interests are also includible. Examples include postdeath partnership profits. Entitlement to future income (such as renewal commissions) is another example of property rights owned outright by the decedent that must be included in the gross estate. Property representing future income will, of course, be income taxable to the estate or beneficiaries when it is actually received. As already noted, to the extent that estate tax was attributable to the inclusion of these items in the estate, a special income tax deduction for the amount of estate tax allocated to these items is allowed to the property recipient in the year the item is includible in income.

Sec. 2033 includes in the decedent's gross estate the value of his or her share of property held in conjunction with others. Thus, if the decedent owns property as a tenant in common with others, the decedent's tenancy share is includible in the gross estate. If disproportionate shares as tenants in common are not specified, the interests are presumed to be equal. For example, if there are three tenants, they are each presumed to own a one-third interest. The value of the decedent's share of community property is included in the estate. As stated before, if the decedent's interests are limited to lifetime enjoyment and there is no property interest to pass on at death (for example, a life estate given to the decedent by another), the value of that right is not included in the gross estate. This results because the decedent never possessed rights in the property that could be transferred at death, and the estate tax is levied on transfers of property. However, an interest in property is includible in the gross estate although it is limited, contingent, or remote, provided that it does not end with the decedent's death. Of course, the contingency or remoteness of the interest affects its valuation.

incidents of ownership

Sec. 2033 may also apply to inclusion of life insurance. If a decedent owns a life insurance policy on his or her own life at the date of death, the face amount of that policy must be included in the gross estate pursuant to Sec. 2042(2). This section establishes a standard regarding **incidents of ownership** whereby the owner of a life policy is required to include the proceeds in the gross estate in the event that he or she possessed any incidents of ownership.

If, however, the decedent at the time of death owns a life insurance policy on the life of another person, such as the decedent's spouse, child, or business associate, Sec. 2042 has no application because the decedent possesses no incidents of ownership over a policy on his or her own life. But such a life insurance policy is property for Sec. 2033 purposes, and as such, the value of the decedent's interest is included as part of the decedent's gross estate. In other words, when one spouse dies, the cash value and unexpired premium of the life insurance policy owned by that spouse on the life of the other spouse will be drawn into the gross estate. Because of this, it is felt that "cross-ownership" of life insurance policies between husband and wife is not always a prudent choice.

Sec. 2033 Inclusion

- real property
- cash/money equivalents
- stocks/bonds
- notes
- mortgages
- outstanding loans by decedent to others
- income tax refunds due
- patents/copyrights

- damages owed to decedent
- dividends declared and payable
- income in respect of decedent (IRD)
- partnership/unincorporated business interests
- tangible personal property
- vested future rights
- decedent's share of property held with others
- insurance owned on life of another

As already emphasized, the estate tax imposed under Sec. 2033 is predicated upon the extent of the decedent's ownership interest at death. This can raise difficult questions as to whether any property transferred by the decedent was void or voidable as well as whether the decedent disposed of any interest before death by a gift or sale. Transfers, sales, loans, partnership, or business ventures—especially those involving spouses and intrafamily arrangements where legal formalities have not been meticulously observed—present particularly difficult problems that must be resolved on an individual basis.

While the IRS still has Sec. 2034 on dower and curtesy, these two concepts have been all but abolished.

LO 11. 4 **Explain the various types of property that are includible in the gross estate under section 2035 if transferred or disposed of within 3 years of death.**

INCLUSION OF CERTAIN GIFTS, TRANSFERS, AND GIFT TAXES (IRC SEC. 2035)

As a general rule, gifts made within 3 years of death are not included in the gross estates of decedents dying after December 31, 1981, except for certain limited purposes. The following are some exceptions to the general rule:

- transfers with retained interests for life
- transfers taking effect at death
- transfers in which the decedent reserves the right to alter, amend, revoke, or terminate the transfer or the power to affect the beneficial interest in the transferred property
- transfers of life insurance policies by the insured
- gift taxes paid

Note that Sec. 2035 does not cause inclusion of the transfers noted above if the decedent retains the interest until the time of death. Sec. 2035 deals only with a disposition of the interest by the decedent during the 3 years preceding death. A disposition may be a gift of, or the exercise or release of, a right or power. Except for gifts of life insurance and gift taxes paid, the initial transfer of property need not be made within the 3-year period preceding the decedent's death, for it is the date of the disposition of *the retained interest* that is determinative.

Transfers with Retained Interests for Life

The first exception to the general rule that lifetime gifts are not includible in the gross estate pertains to property transferred by the decedent during lifetime in which the decedent retained certain rights or powers for his or her lifetime. It is the giving up, releasing, or exercising of these retained rights or powers within 3 years of death that causes the property to which the retained rights applied to be includible in the decedent's gross estate under this Code Section. Therefore, includible in the decedent's gross estate are those lifetime transfers in which the decedent reserved: (1) the right to receive or determine who receives income from the property, or (2) the right to designate who is entitled to possession or enjoyment of the property (including himself or herself) either (a) for life, (b) for a period that did not actually end before death, or (c) for a period that cannot be determined without reference to the decedent's death. If the decedent gave up the retained rights pertaining to the property more than 3 years before death, such property is not includible in the gross estate. Transfers of retained rights by the decedent within 3 years of death that effect inclusion under Sec. 2035 include the use, possession, income, or other enjoyment of the transferred property for himself or herself, or the right to name other persons who may possess or enjoy the transferred property or income from the property. It makes no difference whether the decedent either retains this right alone or can exercise the right only with another. Furthermore, it is insignificant as to whether or not the person with whom the decedent has to act possesses an adverse interest in the property (meaning that the other person is a beneficiary or potential beneficiary of the property).

EXAMPLE

Ten years ago, Tom Smith transferred, for no consideration, ownership in his farm to his three daughters. He retained the right to live on the property rent free. Two years ago, Tom moved to another state and relinquished any and all rights over the farm property, including the right to live there. He died a few months after moving. The fair market value of the farm property at the date of death (or alternate valuation date) will be drawn into his gross estate because he gave up the retained right over the asset within 3 years of the date of his death.

More of the specific rules and some examples of transfers under this exception are included later in a full discussion of IRC Sec. 2036.

Transfers Effective at Death

Other rights that cause the property to be includible in the gross estate are transfers that become effective at death. These are transfers to others that can be obtained only by surviving the decedent, provided that the decedent retained a reversionary interest in the property and the reversionary interest exceeds 5 percent of the value of the property at the date of death. This type of transfer is includible in the decedent's estate under Sec. 2035 if he or she either exercised the power or transferred it within the 3 years prior to death. If the decedent retained the power until death, the transferred property is includible in the estate under IRC Sec. 2037.

EXAMPLE

Lois Forbes transferred a portfolio of marketable securities to her sister, Joan, several years ago. Under the terms of the transfer, if Joan predeceases Lois, the portfolio of securities is to be returned to Lois. Actuarial tables reflect the fact that this reversionary interest exceeds 5 percent of the value of the property. Two years ago, Lois modified the arrangement by relinquishing the right to receive the marketable securities back if Joan dies before her, and instead arranged for the property to pass to Lois's brother, Ronald, if Joan dies before Lois. If Lois dies within 3 years of relinquishing the right to receive the marketable securities back, the fair market value of the securities portfolio on the date of Lois's death (or on the alternate valuation date) will be included in Lois's gross estate under Sec. 2035.

Transfers in Which Decedent Reserves Certain Rights

If a decedent disposes of any of the retained rights to alter, amend, revoke, or terminate the transfer, or to affect the beneficial interest in the transferred property within the 3 years preceding death, the value of the property is includible in the decedent's gross estate under Sec. 2035. If the interests are retained until his or her death, the value of the transferred property is includible under IRC Sec. 2038.

EXAMPLE

Bob created a trust into which he transferred $110,000 worth of marketable securities. The trust was irrevocable, but Bob had the power to amend the instrument, including the right to add beneficiaries and the right to change what existing beneficiaries were to receive. The trust had originally been created 7 years ago. Bob amended the document so he could no longer make any changes, alterations, or revisions to the trust 2 years ago, and died this month. The fair market value of the corpus of the trust on the date of death or the alternate valuation date would be included in Bob's gross estate under Sec. 2035 because he relinquished a Sec. 2038 power within 3 years of his death. Had no such relinquishment been made, Sec. 2038 would have applied to pull the property in the trust into Bob's gross estate.

Gifts of Life Insurance within 3 Years of Death

The next type of inclusion under Sec. 2035 pertains to gratuitous transfers of life insurance made by the insured within 3 years of death. Gifts of life insurance policies made within 3 years of death are includible in the gross estate whether or not a gift tax return was required to be filed. Life insurance is an unusual product because its value as a gift for gift tax purposes may easily fall below the level of the annual exclusion amount necessary to file a gift tax return or to make a taxable gift. However, the value of the proceeds may far exceed the gift tax value.

Therefore, gratuitous transfers of life insurance by the insured made within 3 years of death are included in the gross estate at the full value of the proceeds.

Gift Taxes on Gifts within 3 Years of Death

The *gross estate* of a decedent includes any gift taxes paid by either the decedent or the decedent's estate on any gift made by the decedent or the decedent's spouse within 3 years of the decedent's death. This provision prevents a reduction in the size of a decedent's gross estate because of dollars that were previously spent to satisfy the federal gift tax obligation. The amount of tax subject to this rule is the tax paid on gifts made after 1976 and within 3 years ending on the date of the donor's death.

gross-up rule

This **gross-up rule** also includes any taxes attributable to the decedent's consent to split a gift made by the decedent's spouse within 3 years of the decedent's death. The decedent's share of the gift tax paid on a gift split with a spouse is the amount of tax attributable to the decedent's share of the gift. Gift taxes paid by the spouse of the decedent on gifts split with the decedent are not includible in the gross estate of the decedent under this rule. The effect of this rule is to discourage deathbed gifts that would otherwise remove the amount of gift taxes paid from the donor's estate.

> ### EXAMPLE
>
> Suppose the decedent made a taxable gift of $1 million to an individual on which a gift tax of $345,800 was payable, and the donor died 2 years later. The $1 million is excluded from his or her gross estate. (It is brought back as an adjusted taxable gift in computing the estate tax liability.) However, the amount of gift tax, $345,800, is includible in the decedent's gross estate under the gross-up rule of Sec. 2035.

Exceptions to the 3-Year Rule

Note that current law provides that no transfer made within 3 years of death need be included in the gross estate if no gift tax return was required to be filed. This refers to present-interest gifts worth less than the annual gift tax exclusion. The annual exclusion, as indexed for inflation, allows gifts of present-interest property to be transferred by a donor to an unlimited number of donees per year. Therefore, no gifts worth less than the amount of the annual exclusion are included in the gross estate, since no gift tax return need be filed. The value of these transfers is includible only for the limited purposes of determining qualification for certain tax benefits.

Also, since ERTA '81, the value of all property effectively transferred within 3 years of death is includible in the gross estate for the limited purpose of determining whether the estate qualifies for

- deferral of estate tax under Sec. 6166

- redemption of stock to pay administrative and funeral expenses and estate taxes under Sec. 303

- special-use valuation under Sec. 2032A

- determining the amount of property subject to federal estate tax liens

This exception has been added to the law to prevent a decedent from making deathbed transfers solely to facilitate qualification for the foregoing favorable tax benefits under Secs. 303 (special provision for capital gains for redemptions), 6166 (installment payment of estate taxes), or 2032A (special-use valuation). Otherwise, a decedent could easily gift nonbusiness or nonfarm property, thus increasing the relative percentage value of the closely held business or farm in the estate so that the estate may qualify for special tax treatment.

EXAMPLE

Mr. Murray is gravely ill. From his deathbed, he arranges to transfer the stock in his closely held business to his son, John. Mr. Murray dies 2 weeks later. For estate tax purposes, the fair market value of the transferred stock does *not* return to the *gross* estate because the Sec. 2035 3-year rule does not apply in this situation. However, to determine whether the estate qualifies for the installment payout provisions of Sec. 6166, the value of the stock will be considered to be part of the gross estate.

The same exception to the rule applies to gratuitous transfers made to a spouse within 3 years of death. Although no gift tax return has to be filed because of the unlimited gift tax marital deduction, the law provides that the value of gifts between spouses made within 3 years of one spouse's death is includible in the gross estate for the limited purpose of determining the qualification for the above-mentioned tax benefits.

LO 11. 5   **Explain how transfers of property with retained life interests and powers under sections 2036, 2037, and 2038 may be treated for federal estate tax purposes.**

TRANSFERS WITH RETENTION OF LIFE INTEREST (IRC SEC. 2036)

A decedent's gross estate includes the value of all property transferred gratuitously by the decedent during lifetime in which he or she retained or reserved: (1) the right to use, possess, or enjoy the property or the right to receive the income from the property; or, alternatively, (2) the right, either alone or in conjunction with any other person, to designate the persons who should possess or enjoy the property or the income from the property. In order for the property to be included in a decedent's gross estate under this Code section, the rights must be retained or reserved for

- the decedent's life, or
- for a period not ascertainable without reference to the decedent's death, or
- for any period that does not, in fact, end before the decedent's death

Remember that retained life interests when transferred to family members are subject to Sec. 2702, which requires a grantor-retained annuity trust (GRAT), grantor-retained unitrust (GRUT), or qualified personal residence trust (QPRT) in order to subtract the retained interest from the total gift.

Thus, whereas Sec. 2035 speaks to the transfer of retained rights (held in previously transferred property) within 3 years of death, Sec. 2036 addresses retained rights (in previously transferred property) that the decedent held for life, or for a time period not determinable without reference to the decedent's death, or for a time period that did not end before the decedent's death.

Retention or reservation by the decedent of any of these rights or interests in the property causes the entire value of the property transferred to be includible in the decedent's gross estate under this Code section. The value, however, is reduced by the value of any income interest that: (1) is not subject to the decedent's interest and power, and (2) is actually being enjoyed by another person at the time of the decedent's death. Therefore, if the decedent retained income from only part of the property transferred, the amount includible in the gross estate corresponds proportionately to the value of the entire property.

EXAMPLE

Sheila Gordon transfers 1,000 shares of AT&T stock to her daughter but retains the right to receive income from one-half of the shares. The value of 500 shares at the time of Sheila's death is includible in her gross estate, since she reserved the right to receive the income from 500 shares for her life.

Retention of Rights for Benefit of Transferor for Decedent's Lifetime

A transfer with retained interests is taxable in the gross estate when the transferor retains either the possession of, enjoyment of, or the right to the income from the transferred property for indicated periods. It is not necessary that the transferor retain all rights.

An example of the retention of rights for the decedent's lifetime follows:

EXAMPLE

If Michael makes a gift to Rachael of a Renoir painting but reserves the right to keep the painting in his home for his lifetime, the value of the painting is includible in his estate.

The retained life estate need not be legally enforceable as long as the donor has retained a substantial economic benefit.

EXAMPLE

If Michael conveys his personal residence to Rachael but reserves the right (either expressly or by implication) to occupy the premises rent free during his lifetime, the value of the property at the time of his death is includible in his gross estate.

Thus, in the above example, Michael actually did transfer the residence to Rachael by deed. She was the legal titleholder. However, there was an implied understanding that he was entitled to continue living there until his death, although he could not have legally enforced that understanding. The retained interest or powers that result in the inclusion of property in a decedent's gross estate need not be expressly provided for in the instrument of transfer, but may be inferred from the conduct of the parties.

Furthermore, a decedent will be considered to have retained the right to income to the extent that the income is to be used to discharge the decedent's legal obligations, such as the support of dependent children.

Another type of situation in which property may be includible in the estate of the decedent is the following example.

EXAMPLE

A decedent, Katherine, is the life income beneficiary of a testamentary trust created by someone else. She did not retain a life estate, because she had never possessed the original trust property. However, she was allowed to transfer additional property to the trust under the terms of the trust. During her lifetime, she added $100,000 to the existing trust principal of $200,000. At her death, all trust property passed to her heirs. Assuming that no other property was contributed to the trust, the proportionate share of the principal she contributed from which she received income for life is treated as a retained interest and is includible in her estate when she dies. Thus, if the trust was required to distribute all income currently, and the value of the principal passing at Katherine's death was $300,000, $100,000 (representing her contribution to the trust, from which she retained income for life) is includible in her estate.

In one Tax Court case, a decedent transferred bonds to a trust for the benefit of her grandchildren. She did not retain any interest in the bonds. However, she detached the interest coupons and kept them as her own at the time of the creation of the trust. The value of the bonds was included in her gross estate because she indirectly kept control over and retained the income from the trust property.

reciprocal trusts

Reciprocal Trusts. Another type of plan that is legally unenforceable but from which there is a course of conduct implying agreement to provide income for life involves the use of **reciprocal trusts**. If irrevocable reciprocal trusts are created (such as those created by a husband and wife for each other as life beneficiaries), the property of each trust is includible in the life beneficiary's estate if the arrangement leaves both grantors in approximately the same economic circumstances in which they would have been had they created trusts naming themselves as life income beneficiaries.

The reciprocal-trust doctrine can best be illustrated by the following example.

EXAMPLE

Adam creates a trust for the benefit of Bette, and simultaneously Bette creates a trust of equal value for the benefit of Adam. The trust Adam has created has a corpus of $400,000 and provides that any income generated by the trust corpus is to be paid to Bette for Bette's life with a remainder interest to Bette's children. The trust Bette has created also has a corpus of $400,000 and provides that any income generated by that trust corpus is to be paid to Adam for Adam's life with a remainder interest to Adam's children.

In this example, neither Adam nor Bette has technically retained a life interest. But, as a practical matter, both Adam and Bette are in the same situation, as though nothing had ever been transferred into any trust.

Because such an arrangement was perceived to be an unfair loophole in Sec. 2036, the courts have developed what has come to be referred to as the reciprocal-trust doctrine. The trusts created by Adam and Bette are disregarded for tax purposes. Each grantor is treated as having created a trust under which he or she retains a life interest for himself or herself. Under the reciprocal-trust doctrine, the trusts are "uncrossed," and the court will deem each beneficiary to be the grantor of the trust that was created for the beneficiary's benefit for purposes of estate tax liability (*U.S. v. Estate of Grace*, 395 U.S. 316). This approach results in inclusion of the corpus in the gross estate. Therefore, in the example above, the $400,000 corpus in the trust created by Adam will be included in Bette's gross estate, and the $400,000 corpus in the trust created by Bette will be included in Adam's gross estate.

There are, however, some planning methods that may prevent IRS challenges based on the reciprocal trust doctrine in some instances: (1) varying the terms of the two trusts so that they are not substantially identical, (2) funding each trust with different assets, and (3) creating the trusts at different times, possibly even a few years apart. Using these techniques will be important under the Tax Cuts and Jobs Act (TCJA) with regard to spousal lifetime access trusts (SLATs) from 2018 to 2025.

Right to Vote Stock in a Closely Held Corporation. Another danger for the unwary planner may occur when an individual transfers stock of a controlled corporation but retains the right to vote the shares (either directly or indirectly). This retention of voting rights is considered a retention of the enjoyment of the transferred property. The value of the transferred stock will be included in the gross estate of the decedent. A controlled corporation is one in which the decedent directly or indirectly owned or had the right, either alone or with any other person, to vote stock having at least 20 percent of the total combined voting power of all classes of stock. This rule pertains to persons who have irrevocably transferred stock for less than full consideration after June 22, 1976. If the stock is not in a controlled corporation, it is not includible in the decedent's gross estate although the decedent did hold the power to vote the transferred shares.

In one case, an individual transferred 19 shares of a closely held corporation's stock to a trust and gave the trustee sole authority to vote the shares. However, it was agreed at the time of the transfer that the trustee would consult with the grantor with respect to voting and that the trustee would vote only with the grantor's consent. It was held that the grantor-decedent indirectly retained the right to vote the transferred shares, although they were transferred to an irrevocable trust. The full value of the shares at the time of death was includible in the grantor's gross estate.

Retention or Reservation by the Decedent of Property for a Period Not Determinable Without Reference to the Decedent's Death

This test involves a situation where the retained interest is tied to the time of the decedent's death. If the facts and circumstances are such that the lifetime test discussed above is not met but this second test is met, Sec. 2036 will still apply.

This concept can be illustrated by the example that follows:

EXAMPLE

Mr. Harris transfers property to a trust with the provision that he receive quarterly installments of income. However, there is a condition that no part of the income accruing during the quarter in which he dies is to be paid to him or to his estate. Because the trust is set up in this way—that the transferor is not to receive income up until the time of his death—the lifetime test is not met. Clearly, this appears to be an attempt to thwart the rule regarding retained interests. Because the last payment cannot be ascertained without reference to his death, however, the value of the trust property is includible in his estate.

Retention or Reservation by the Decedent for a Period That Does Not, in Fact, End before the Decedent's Death

This third test makes Sec. 2036 relevant when the transferor has retained an interest for a period of time not phrased in terms of his or her life or death, but only in the event that this time period does not end prior to the death of the transferor. Because of this third test, there does not have to be any reference to the decedent's life or death in the transfer agreement.

This concept can be illustrated by the following example:

EXAMPLE

Samantha Connors transfers Blackacre to her son, Henry, reserving the right to the income from the property for 10 years. Samantha dies in the eighth year. Based on these facts, the entire value of Blackacre is includible in Samantha's estate because she reserved an income interest not for her lifetime but for a period that did not, in fact, end before her death.

Right to Designate Who Shall Possess or Enjoy the Property

Even though a decedent did not retain the right to enjoy or possess the property, Sec. 2036 requires that the gross estate also include the value of all property over which the decedent retained the right to designate (alone or with any other person) who may enjoy or possess the property as well as the right to vary beneficial interests. Thus, if a grantor creates an irrevocable trust for beneficiaries other than himself or herself, but is named as trustee and has the power to accumulate or distribute income, the value of the trust property is included in the grantor's gross estate. The reason for inclusion is that the grantor had power to withhold income from the beneficiaries, thereby denying them possession and enjoyment of that income. This power to accumulate income is a retention of the right to designate who may enjoy the property. Retention of certain administrative and management powers over the trust also may cause the value of the trust property to be included in the grantor-trustee's estate.

In another case, the grantor created an irrevocable trust giving the trustee power to vary beneficial interests. She reserved for herself the right to fill vacancies for the position of trustee. There was no prohibition against the grantor appointing herself as trustee. The court held that in reserving this right the grantor retained an interest sufficient to cause the trust property to be includible in her estate.

As a general rule, property placed in an irrevocable trust is not included in the grantor's gross estate if the grantor merely retained the right to appoint a successor-trustee other than himself or herself upon resignation of the original trustee. In *Estate of Helen S. Wall,*[1] the Tax Court reasoned that, because independent commercial trustees are under a fiduciary obligation to beneficiaries, the retained power to substitute an independent corporate trustee was not sufficient to cause inclusion of the trust property in the decedent's gross estate under Secs. 2036 or 2038. In 1995, as a result of the *Wall* case and other cases, the IRS issued Revenue Ruling 95–58,[2] which provides that a grantor's power to remove a trustee and appoint a corporate trustee or a person other than the grantor who is not related or subordinate to the grantor is not, in and of itself, equivalent to the grantor's retention of control over the trust. In essence, Rev. Rul. 95–58 means that a grantor's mere right to remove and replace a trustee with an independent trustee will not cause inclusion of the trust in the grantor's gross estate under Secs. 2036 or 2038.

Also, the Internal Revenue Service has attempted to include trust property in situations where the grantor-trustee retained only certain administrative and managerial powers over the trust but not the power to accumulate or distribute income. Most courts have held that the existence

---

1. *Estate of Helen S. Wall*, 101 T.C. 300 (1993).
2. Revenue Ruling 95-58, IRB 1995–36, 16 (Sept. 5, 1995).

of these "boilerplate" powers does not give a decedent the right to designate persons who shall possess or enjoy the transferred property such that it is includible in the gross estate.

A frequently used estate planning device involves the irrevocable assignment of life insurance policies to a trust by the insured during the insured's lifetime. Proceeds of life insurance are not taxable in the insured's gross estate if the insured was totally divested of all incidents of ownership in the policy more than 3 years prior to death, and the proceeds are not payable to the estate. Under current law, the result is not changed even if the insured continues to pay premiums on the policy assigned. However, suppose rather than continuing to pay the premiums directly, the insured funds the trust with income-producing property. Any income is to be applied first to the payment of premiums. The regulations under this section of the Internal Revenue Code provide that, if the income from property transferred by the decedent is required to be applied by the transferee for the decedent's pecuniary benefit, the decedent is considered to have retained the right to income or enjoyment of the transferred property. Whether payment of premiums by the trustee with trust income is a *pecuniary benefit* that requires the value of the property to be included in the decedent's gross estate depends on the irrevocability of the assignment.

If policies of life insurance are irrevocably assigned and the decedent is divested of all incidents of ownership in favor of the trust, the value of property transferred by the decedent to fund that trust should not be included in the decedent's estate merely because the income from the property was used to pay premiums. It is the trust and the beneficiaries who have benefited from the premium payments, not the decedent. Alternatively, if the decedent retained any incidents of ownership in the policies, the payment of premiums from the trust income can certainly be regarded as having been for the decedent's pecuniary or economic benefit. Therefore, the value of the policies is includible in the decedent's gross estate.

If an individual transfers property to an insurance company in exchange for a commercial annuity, this section has no application upon the transferor's death. The transfer is free and clear. It was made for full and adequate consideration in money or money's worth, and the insurance company is obligated to pay the annuity without regard to the income or principal of the property transferred. Whether this section has application in the case of a private annuity depends upon the transfer and the circumstances surrounding it. It has been held that a transfer of property by the decedent to an individual in return for a promise to make periodic payments to the decedent during lifetime is not an includible transfer, provided that the transferee is under an absolute obligation to make the payments and the amount of the payments is not determined by reference to the actual or estimated income from the property transferred.

EXAMPLE

Alex transfers property to Bruce in consideration of Bruce's promise to support Alex for the rest of Alex's life. If Bruce is free to use the property transferred in any manner that Bruce wishes, and if Bruce discharges the obligation to support Alex irrespective of the amount of income from the transferred property, there is no inclusion. An opposite result was reached when a decedent transferred property to her children in return for their promise to pay her a stipulated amount of income for her life. At the time of the transfer, the estimated annual income from the property was equal to the amount of the annuity, but the income averaged less than the amount of the annuity after the transfer. Her children made no attempt to make up the difference. The Tax Court held that the value of the property was includible in the decedent's gross estate.

Amount Includible in the Gross Estate

Under Sec. 2036 pertaining to retained interests for life, the amount that is includible in the decedent's gross estate is not the value of the interest retained or controlled by him or her but the value of the entire property transferred, valued on the date of death. The lifetime transfer is treated as if the decedent had retained the entire property and not just the right to income or beneficial enjoyment for life. It should be remembered that if retained rights are subject to a definite external standard, the property subject to the rights is not includible.

Transfers That Take Effect at Death (IRC Sec. 2037)

Sec. 2037 is the includibility section of the Code that pulls transfers of reversionary interests taking effect at death into the decedent's gross estate. The decedent's gross estate includes the value of property transferred by him or her for less than full and adequate consideration, if the possession or enjoyment of the transferred property can be obtained only by the beneficiary surviving the decedent *and* the decedent having retained a reversionary interest (an ability to have the property returned to him or her) that was worth more than 5 percent of the value of the transferred property immediately before death.

Under the first condition, any beneficiary must survive the decedent in order to obtain possession or enjoyment of the property through ownership. In other words, the possession or enjoyment of the transferred property is conditional on surviving the decedent-transferor.

EXAMPLE 1

Sam Smith transfers property irrevocably in trust for the benefit of his wife, Barbara. Barbara is to receive income for life. The remainder is to go back to Sam, if living, at her death. If he is not living, the property goes to their children, Michael and Rachael. If Sam predeceases his wife, the interest to Michael and Rachael is includible in Sam's gross estate, because it is contingent upon Sam's death. In this case, Sam possesses a reversionary interest (assumed to be worth more than 5 percent of the value of the property transferred). The entire value of the transferred property subject to the reversion, less the actuarial value of the outstanding income interest possessed by his wife, is included.

EXAMPLE 2

A decedent, Harvey, transferred property to a trust that was to pay income to his daughter for life. At his daughter's death, the trust terminates and the property passes to his daughter's surviving child or, if there is no surviving child, to the decedent or to his estate. Each beneficiary can possess or enjoy the property without surviving the decedent. Therefore, the property is not includible in the decedent's gross estate as a transfer taking effect at death, no matter how great the value of the decedent's reversionary interest.

A reversionary interest includes the possibility that the transferred property either may return to the decedent or the decedent's estate or may be subject to the decedent's power of disposition. It does not apply to the reservation of a life estate or to the possibility of receiving income solely from the transferred property only after the death of another individual. The term *reversionary interest* also does not include the possibility that the decedent may receive an interest in the transferred property by inheriting the property through the estate of another person.

EXAMPLE

A transferor is not considered to retain a reversion in an outright gift to a spouse merely because of the possibility that the spouse will give the property back to the transferor, or that the transferor will inherit the property back from his or her spouse by will. If some alternate event (such as the expiration of a term of years or the exercise of a power of appointment) triggers a transferee's possession or enjoyment of the property, such property generally is not included in the decedent's gross estate under this section. This is because the transferee could possibly obtain possession and enjoyment of the property while the transferor was still alive.

Caution is necessary in creating irrevocable transfers to make certain that no interest or power with respect to income is retained. Although it appears that no reversionary interests exist, there may be an oversight if the grantor unintentionally neglects to provide for all contingencies. Under local law, the result might be that the property reverts to the decedent or the decedent's estate if no designated beneficiary survives him or her (implied reversion). Included under this provision is the common situation of using a short-term trust to provide temporarily for the support of another individual.

EXAMPLE

A father creates an irrevocable trust for the benefit of his son. The son receives income for 11 years, after which time the trust corpus is returned to the father, if living, otherwise to the father's issue. Should the father die before the expiration of the trust term, his reversionary interest in the property calculated actuarially is includible in his estate.

The reversionary-interest requirement is met not only if the decedent or the decedent's estate might have reacquired the transferred property, but also if there exists, immediately prior to death, a possibility that the property would be disposed of by the decedent.

EXAMPLE

Anne transfers property in trust for Barbara during Anne's lifetime, with remainder to Carol, but if Carol dies without issue, Carol's estate is limited to a life interest and the property passes to the individual(s) designated to inherit under Anne's will. Carol's interest is contingent upon surviving Anne. The property is includible in Anne's estate, although it might not become known until well after Anne's death whether said power of disposition actually comes into effect.

For the value of the property subject to the reversionary interest to be includible in the decedent's estate, it must be worth more than 5 percent of the value of the property transferred as of the moment preceding the decedent's death. Furthermore, for the property to be included in the decedent's gross estate under this section, all of the conditions that are described in this section must be met.

Revocable Transfers (IRC Sec. 2038)

Sec. 2038 presents one more method to draw transferred property back into the gross estate. If property transferred gratuitously by the decedent during lifetime is subject to any change through the exercise of a power to alter, amend, revoke, or terminate, or to affect beneficial enjoyment either by the decedent alone or in conjunction with any other person, and these powers exist at the decedent's death, the value of the property subject to the power is includible in the decedent's gross estate under Sec. 2038. This is true if the power is exercisable by the decedent alone or in conjunction with anyone (including beneficiaries who would have an adverse interest). The language is all-encompassing and causes taxation in the decedent's estate. Thus, if a grantor-trustee has the power to distribute principal to an income beneficiary prior to the date the beneficiary is entitled to receive principal, the value of the property subject to the power is includible in the grantor-trustee's estate. It does not matter that the prohibited power is not exercisable in favor of the decedent or is exercisable only in conjunction with persons having adverse interests; nor does it matter in what capacity the power is exercisable. Neither is it essential that the decedent did not retain the power but acquired it from another source (IRC Sec. 2038(a)(1)). The critical factor is that the decedent possessed the power at the time of death.

Examples of the types of powers addressed by this section of the Internal Revenue Code include the power: (1) to change the beneficiaries, (2) to hasten the time that the beneficiary can receive the property, or (3) to increase or decrease the amount of property allocated to any beneficiary.

As stated before, the decedent—either alone or with others—must have possessed one of the prohibited powers at the time of death to cause inclusion under this section. If, however, there was a condition beyond the decedent's control that limited the use of the power, and that condition did not occur before the decedent died, the property is not included in the decedent's gross estate as a transfer subject to the power to revoke.

It makes no difference in what capacity the decedent could have exercised this power. For example, if the decedent transferred property to a trust naming himself or herself trustee and then gave the trustee the power to revoke the trust, the property is included in the decedent's estate. Similarly, if the decedent appointed another person as trustee but retained the power to appoint a successor-trustee upon the resignation of the original trustee (including naming himself or herself as trustee), the property is also included in the estate. Reserving a power to remove a trustee at will and appoint another trustee causes a similar result. However, if any rights to revoke, alter, amend, or terminate the trust or change trustees are given to another person, and the decedent reserves no rights whatsoever with regard to these powers, the value of the property in the trust is not included in the decedent's gross estate.

While the property is included in the decedent's gross estate, whether he or she had the power to change or terminate the property interest either alone or with others, regardless of their capacity or interests, there are two exceptions to this rule: (1) if the decedent's power can be exercised only with the consent of all parties having an interest (either vested or contingent) in the transferred property, and (2) if this power adds nothing to the rights of the parties under local law, the property is not included in the decedent's estate. Note that this exception applies only if all parties must consent to the exercise of a power to change or end the property interest.

The following powers have been determined to be powers to alter, amend, revoke, or terminate that cause the property subject to the power to be included in the decedent's gross estate. Note that only the part of the transferred property that is subject to the decedent's power as described above is included in the gross estate under this provision of the Code. Powers to alter, amend, revoke, or terminate include the: (1) power to revoke or terminate a trust to which the property is transferred, whether this power results in a return of corpus to the grantor or acceleration of enjoyment by the beneficiaries; (2) power to control and manage the trust property, except where this power is limited to administrative or mechanical details only, such as designation of funds as income or principal, investment policy, issuance of voting proxies, or other matters that do not alter the rights or interests of the beneficiaries; (3) power to change beneficiaries or to vary the amounts distributable; (4) power to appoint by will or change shares of beneficiaries by will; (5) power to revoke, which exists by virtue of state law; (6) power to invade a trust created by another for whose benefit the decedent created a similar trust (reciprocal trusts); and (7) power to replace without cause the trustee with another.

Sec. 2038 Inclusion Powers
- Change beneficiaries for income or corpus.
- Increase/decrease a beneficiary's share.
- Terminate the trust.
- Revoke the trust.
- Manage/control trust property.
- Replace the trustee with self/spouse.

The following powers have been determined *not* to constitute powers sufficient to cause taxation in the decedent's estate under Sec. 2038:

- power in others than the grantor to revoke the transfer or return part of it to the grantor (but such transfers may be taxed under another section discussed earlier as transfers intended to take effect at death)

- certain powers contingent on the occurrence of a particular event

- powers as to mechanics or details only, such as powers to direct issuance of voting proxies, to help determine investment policies, and to direct investment and reinvestment of funds

- power to add to corpus

- power over trusts created by others with funds not derived from the decedent and not supported by similar trusts created by others. An example of this last power is the power in the decedent as trustee over another's trust in which the decedent has no beneficial interest.

Sec. 2038 Noninclusion Powers
- Add to trust corpus.
- Help determine investment policies.
- Direct the issuance of voting proxies.

An example of retained powers under Sec. 2038 is shown in the following situation.

EXAMPLE

The decedent, Mr. Jones, creates a trust that provides income to Mark for life with the remainder going to Sandra or her heirs. The decedent retains the power to invade principal for Sandra's benefit during Mark's lifetime. The entire property is included in the decedent's gross estate under this Code provision. The decedent, by exercise of his power to invade, can affect the time when Sandra receives enjoyment of the property as well as the amount of income Mark receives. If, however, the decedent retains only the power to accumulate income and add it to corpus, the only interest the decedent can affect is that of Mark, the income beneficiary. Therefore, it is only the value of Mark's income interest that will be included in the decedent's gross estate under this provision.

Remember that this provision sometimes overlaps and can operate in conjunction with the provision discussed earlier where the decedent retains powers to possess, enjoy, or receive income for life, or designate who is to receive or possess the property. That section (Sec. 2036) brings the entire value of the property on the date of death into the decedent's gross estate. Sec. 2038 includes only the value of the interest in property subject to the powers to alter, amend, revoke, or terminate.

EXAMPLE

Ed Smith transfers property to a trust for the benefit of his 20-year-old son, Sandy. The trust provides that Sandy is entitled to all the income from the trust until he is 40, when he is to receive the corpus. Ed retains the right to terminate the trust at any time, with corpus to be distributed to Sandy upon termination. Ed dies when Sandy is 30. The amount includible in Ed's estate under Sec. 2038 is the amount of the trust corpus less the value of the income interest (over which Ed had no power). The value of the income interest is determined actuarially at the time of Ed's death.

ascertainable standard

There are cases in which transferred property otherwise subject to Sec. 2038 escapes gross estate inclusion. Such a situation involves the presence of an **ascertainable standard**. In other words, although the decedent possessed prohibited powers, the property interest subject to the powers is not included in the decedent's gross estate if the power is subject to an ascertainable standard. This refers to an external standard imposed upon the decedent limiting the exercise of the power strictly to provide for the support, maintenance, health, or education of a beneficiary.

EXAMPLE

A decedent transfers property in trust to provide income to Ken for life, remainder to Don or his heirs. The decedent retains the power to invade corpus for Ken's benefit but only for his health, maintenance, support, or education. Because the decedent's power to invade corpus is subject to a standard that may be reviewed by the court, the situation is as if the decedent really holds no power at all. Note that if the decedent's power was not governed by an *ascertainable standard*, the fact that he or she could exercise this power only with the consent of the beneficiary whose interest would be adversely affected would not prevent the value of the property subject to this power from being included in the decedent's gross estate.

It is obvious from the discussion above that there are many potential problems to consider in planning gratuitous lifetime transfers of property in order to avoid inclusion of the property in a decedent's gross estate. Careful drafting of trust instruments can allow the decedent to retain some degree of control without triggering estate taxation under one of the Code sections. If the decedent wishes to retain some powers over property transferred during lifetime, he or she would be wise to consult a planner experienced in these areas. With good planning, the decedent can accomplish personal objectives, yet avoid inclusion of transferred property interests in the gross estate.

CHAPTER REVIEW

Key Terms and Concepts

federal estate tax   gross-up rule
gross estate   reciprocal trusts
incidents of ownership   ascertainable standard

Chapter 11: Review Questions

1. Explain the concept of gross estate. [LO 11.1]

2. Describe the theories underlying the federal estate tax. [LO 11.2]

3. Who is primarily responsible for payment of the estate tax? [LO 11.2]

4. Mr. Jones transferred $60,000 to a trust that was to last for 11 years. During that time, all income was to be distributed to his two children who were beneficiaries of the trust. At the end of 11 years, the trust was to terminate and all principal was to be returned to Mr. Jones or his estate. The trust was irrevocable. Mr. Jones died 7 years after the trust was created. What, if anything, will be includible in his gross estate? [LO 11.3]

5. Explain whether and why the following items an individual owned at the time of his death will be included in his gross estate for federal estate tax purposes. At what value, if any, will the property be included?

    a. real estate in Atlantic City valued at $200,000 where the decedent had a right to live rent free for life. This property had been given to the decedent by his father for his life, after which it was to pass to his son under the terms of his father's will

    b. $160,000 par value of municipal bonds due the year after the decedent's death

    c. 10 acres of undeveloped land in Arizona owned by the decedent and his two brothers as tenants in common

    d. IBM stock valued at $30,000 owned by the decedent individually

    e. proceeds of a wrongful death claim brought by the decedent's personal representative after his death in an automobile accident

    f. $5,000 in dividends declared and of record but not paid at the time of the decedent's death

g. a claim for damages arising from a car accident in which the decedent was involved prior to his death

h. commission income that the decedent had earned for the month prior to his death but that had not yet been paid to him

i. a Matisse painting hanging in his home

j. property in a trust established by his brother for the benefit of his brother's son of which the decedent was the sole trustee. The property in the trust is valued at $50,000 [LO 11.3]

6. Jennifer Johnson, a business owner, died 2 years ago with uncollected accounts receivable of $94,000. She was also holder of a note from her brother for $25,000 due last year, and she owned rental real estate. The present tenants had executed a 5-year lease agreeing to pay $7,000 in rent annually for the entire lease term.

a. Explain which of these items will be includible in her gross estate and at what values.

b. To whom will the income be taxable when received? [LO 11.3]

7. Richard Ricardo, CLU, a life insurance agent, had $128,000 of renewal commissions payable to him over the next 3 years. After his death, they were payable by contract to his surviving spouse. He died last year.

a. Explain whether the rights to this future income are includible in Ricardo's estate.

b. What is the rationale behind the allowance of an income tax deduction to the recipient on future income items that have been subject to tax in a decedent's estate? [LO 11.3]

8. Sandra Taylor dies this year and is survived by her husband and two minor daughters. Explain which of the following items will be included in her gross estate and at what values:

a. a $100,000 certificate of deposit that Sandra gave to her husband last year

b. a life insurance policy on her life for $200,000 that she transferred to an irrevocable trust for the benefit of her children last year

c. a $50,000 amount that she placed in a custodial account for each of her daughters 10 years ago. She is the custodian of the account

d. a condominium in Florida that she transferred to her brother 10 years ago while she still retained the right to use it for life

    e.   an inter vivos irrevocable trust established by Sandra in which she retained only the power to allocate the income distributions between her two daughters who are the named beneficiaries of both income and corpus

    f.   an inter vivos irrevocable trust established by Sandra 10 years ago. Her husband is to receive income for his life after which the corpus would be returned to Sandra if living and, if not, it would pass to her two daughters

    g.   a revocable trust containing $150,000 of securities that Sandra established for the benefit of her mother. Sandra was to receive income for life and, at her death, the property was to be held in further trust for her mother for life. At her mother's death, the corpus was to be distributed to Sandra's two daughters [LO 11.4]

9.   Bobby Block transferred a life insurance policy to a trust 5 years ago. At this time, Bobby had already used his entire gift tax basic exemption amount with prior gifts. Assume it was a paid-up policy with a gift tax value of $1 million, and that he paid a gift tax in the amount of $345,800. He died this year. How much, if anything, is includible in his gross estate? [LO 11.4]

10. John Jamison transferred $200,000 of tax-exempt bonds to a trust for the benefit of his grandchildren 2 years ago. He died this year. Assume the gift tax paid was approximately $60,000.

    a.   What amount, if any, is includible in his gross estate and why?

    b.   Would your answer to 11.a. be different if the transfer was made to his spouse? [LO 11.4]

11. Assume Arthur gave property worth $53,000 to his nephew 10 years ago and paid a gift tax of $16,000 on a $40,000 ($50,000 - 13,000 (the annual gift tax exclusion amount at that time)) taxable gift. Arthur had exhausted his basic credit amount. At the time of Arthur's death last year, the property had appreciated in value to $130,000. What amount, if any, is includible in Arthur's gross estate? [LO 11.4]

12. A donor gratuitously transferred property worth $250,000 12 years ago. However, the donor retained the right to income from the property for life. Upon the donor's death this year, the property was worth $475,000. What amount, if any, is includible in the decedent's gross estate? [LO 11.5]

13. Mr. Johnson established a trust for the benefit of his minor children. The trust income was $10,000 annually, $2,500 of which was used to pay for the support and maintenance of the children. The remainder of the income was accumulated in the trust for distribution to the children at age 21. Mr. Johnson died before either of his children reached maturity. What amount, if any, will be includible in his estate? [LO 11.5]

14. Mitchell Mellen gave his niece, Margaret, his townhouse in New York City. By unwritten understanding, he continued to live in the house until his death 5 years later. Is any of the property includible in his gross estate? If so, under what theory is it includible? [LO 11.5]

15. Karen created a trust naming her brother, Michael, as life income beneficiary. At his death, the corpus was to go to Michael's children. At the same time, Michael created a trust and named his sister, Karen, as life income beneficiary with the corpus to go to Karen's children at her death. Each trust was funded with $75,000. All income was to be distributed at least annually. Karen died 6 years later. How would these trusts be treated for federal estate tax purposes? [LO 11.5]

16. Watson Howard gratuitously transferred all of his stock in Safe Aircraft to his daughter. He had owned 35 percent of the total voting stock of Safe Aircraft. Mr. Howard retained no right to income from the trust; however, he kept the right to vote the stock he had transferred. One year before his death, he transferred his voting rights to his daughter. What, if anything, is includible in his gross estate? [LO 11.5]

17. Alan Anderson owned a ranch in Colorado that he placed in trust for the benefit of his adult children, Pamela and Arthur. Under the terms of the trust, he retained the right to determine each year what percentage of the income would go to each child and what amount would be retained in the trust. He could make this decision only in conjunction with the Turner Trust Company, an independent trustee. He died 4 years after the property was placed in trust. At the time of his death, the ranch was worth $700,000. At the time of the transfer, the ranch was valued at $450,000. What amount, if any, is includible in his gross estate? [LO 11.5]

18. Richard Allison created a trust that provided income to his son, Roger, for life. At Roger's death, the trust principal is to be distributed to Roger's children. However, Mr. Allison retained the right to distribute principal to his grandchildren during Roger's lifetime. Two years before his death, he distributed one-half of the principal to his grandchildren. What amount, if any, is includible in Mr. Allison's estate? [LO 11.5]

Chapter 11: Review Answers

1. The term *gross estate* refers to the property or interests a decedent actually owned at death and the property or interests a decedent is deemed to own at date of death.

2. The federal estate tax is based on the privilege to transfer property, recognizing that a tax limited to transfers at death would invite tax-avoidance schemes to transfer property during lifetime. Therefore, a cumulative estate and gift tax system was enacted for taxation of certain transfers of property during lifetime and at death at the same tax rates. Incomplete lifetime dispositions—transfers of property over which the donor retains control—are equivalent to testamentary transfers at death, which causes the property to be included in the decedent's gross estate for tax purposes.

3. The decedent's estate is primarily responsible for payment of estate taxes, but if the estate does not contain enough assets to pay the taxes, the estate beneficiaries may be liable to the extent of the value of the property they inherit.

4. The trust principal is includible in Mr. Jones's gross estate because it is a reversionary interest to which Mr. Jones or his estate has an absolute right.

5. a. This property is not included as it is a life estate conferred by another person that the decedent could not transfer at his death.

    b. The full fair market value of the bonds is includible. The value may be less than the par value of the bonds and will be determined either at the date of death or on the alternate valuation date as the executor elects.

    c. One-third of the value of the Arizona land is includible.

    d. The IBM stock is totally includible.

    e. No part of the wrongful death claim is includible in the decedent's gross estate because the decedent must be dead before a wrongful death action can be brought. The right to bring a wrongful death claim belongs to the decedent's personal representative or to his heirs, and not to the decedent.

    f. The $5,000 in dividends declared and of record at the time of the decedent's death is includible because he had an absolute right to receive the dividends in the future.

    g. The claim for damages is includible in the decedent's estate because he could have recovered them during his life. Valuation may be difficult as it is a contingent claim.

h. The full amount of the commission income is includible as income in respect of a decedent because the decedent had an absolute right to receive it.

i. The full fair market value of the Matisse painting is includible unless it can be proved that the property belongs to his spouse.

j. No part of the trust property is includible in the decedent's estate as he held only bare legal title and had no beneficial interest in the trust.

6. a. The $94,000 in uncollected accounts and the $25,000 note are includible in Jennifer's gross estate because both are income in respect of a decedent—that is, income earned by the decedent but not yet received at the time of death. The rental income accrued up to the date of Jennifer's death is also includible in her gross estate.

   b. The recipient of the income—the estate or the beneficiaries—will be liable for the income tax but can deduct from the income tax the amount of the estate tax attributable to that income item.

7. a. The $128,000 in renewal commissions is includible in Richard Ricardo's estate because it is income in respect of a decedent.

   b. Without the special income tax deduction, there would be an overpayment of taxes without allowing the recipient of the property to deduct the amount of estate tax already paid.

8. a. No amount of the $100,000 certificate of deposit is includible in Sandra's gross estate because it is a completed gift.

   b. All the life insurance proceeds are includible because the transfer to the irrevocable trust was less than 3 years prior to her death.

   c. The entire balance of the custodial accounts ($100,000) is includible because as custodian she retained the power to distribute or withhold income and principal (that is, to affect the beneficial enjoyment of the property).

   d. The full value of the condominium is includible because she retained the right to use the property for her life.

   e. The value of the income interests will be includible as Sandra retained the right to affect beneficial enjoyment *of the income* by shifting the proportionate interests.

   f. Sandra has retained a contingent reversionary interest that will be includible in her gross estate if the value of the reversionary interest computed actuarially just prior to her death exceeds 5 percent of the transferred property (Sec. 2037).

   g. The full value of the trust property is includible in Sandra's estate since she retained the power to revoke the trust.

9. Nothing is includible in Bobby Block's gross estate because he paid the gift tax 5 years ago and retained no interest in the policy. The $345,800 amount would have been includible in his estate if the gift tax had been paid within 3 years of his death.

10. a. The $60,000 gift tax paid within 3 years of death is includible in Jamison's gross estate.

    b. Nothing is includible as the gift qualified for the gift tax marital deduction and no gift taxes were paid.

11. Nothing is includible in Arthur's gross estate. Since he had retained no rights to the property, the fact that it appreciated in value is irrelevant. That amount is not brought back into Arthur's estate. Nor is the gift tax he paid includible because it was not within 3 years of his death. The $40,000 taxable gift will be added back as an adjusted taxable gift made after 1976.

12. Because the donor retained the right to income from the property for life, the full amount of the property at the donor's death ($475,000) is includible in the donor's estate.

13. If the trust was funded with income-producing property, one-fourth of which was used to satisfy the support obligation of the decedent, his gross estate will include the value of the property that generated the income used to satisfy his legal obligations. Therefore, one-fourth of the trust principal valued at the time of the decedent's death will be included in his estate.

14. The value of the property at the time of Mitchell's death is includible in his gross estate. Even though the agreement that Mitchell could continue to live in the house was not in writing, the implied understanding is a retained interest in the property, which causes the townhouse to be included in Mitchell's estate.

15. This is clearly a case of reciprocal trusts. Michael and Karen could just as easily have placed property in trust for the benefit of their own children, reserving a life income interest for themselves. Use of the reciprocal trust arrangement will be ignored by the IRS since each grantor was left in exactly the same position as if he had created a trust with income for life to himself and the remainder to his children. Therefore, the entire value of the trust corpus that each created will be included in Michael's or Karen's gross estate.

16. Since Watson retained the right to vote all his stock and he was a more-than-20-percent shareholder (indirectly) at the time of his death, the stock is includible in his gross estate as a transfer within 3 years of death. This is so despite the fact that he released

all voting rights one year before his death. It does not matter that he created the trust and gave away the stock earlier in time.

17. The amount of $700,000 is includible in Alan Anderson's gross estate. Retaining the right to determine what percentage of income would go to each child—even if it is in conjunction with an independent trustee—is enough to cause the value of the ranch at Alan's death to be included in his gross estate.

18. The entire value of the property in the trust on the date of Mr. Allison's death is includible in his gross estate because he retained the power to invade corpus for the benefit of the remainderman during the life of the income beneficiary. This constitutes a power to alter the beneficial enjoyment of the property both of the income beneficiary and the remainderman. Therefore, the entire amount is includible in Mr. Allison's gross estate. If Mr. Allison had not retained the power to distribute principal but only to accumulate the income (that is, add it to the principal), the only interest that he could affect would have been Roger's, the income beneficiary. In that case, the amount includible in his estate would be the value of Roger's income interest at the time of his death.

Chapter 12:

Federal Estate Taxation: The Gross Estate— Part II

Learning Objectives

An understanding of the material in this chapter should enable the student to

> **LO 12.1   Describe estate taxation of annuities.**
>
> **LO 12.2   Explain the rules for inclusion of jointly held property in the gross estate.**
>
> **LO 12.3   Explain the estate taxation of general powers of appointment, and differentiate between general powers and special powers with respect to inclusion in the gross estate.**
>
> **LO 12.4   Explain the general rules concerning the inclusion of life insurance in the gross estate, and describe some ways in which life insurance can avoid estate taxation.**

LO 12.1   Describe estate taxation of annuities.

ANNUITIES (IRC SEC. 2039)

Sec. 2039 of the Internal Revenue Code concerns the federal estate taxation of annuity products. With certain limited exceptions, a decedent's gross estate includes the present value of an annuity or other payment receivable by any beneficiary as a result of having survived the decedent. Included under this section are any agreements, commercial or private annuities, and employee retirement annuities (including all proceeds from qualified plans generally for decedents dying after December 31, 1984). Annuities or payments under certain contracts included in the gross estate are those that were payable to or receivable by the decedent

- for his or her lifetime
- for a period that did not, in fact, end before the decedent's death
- for a period that cannot be ascertained without referring to the decedent's death

A decedent's right to a payment is sufficient. The decedent need not have actually received or be receiving payments by the date of death, nor must the time at which payments would commence have passed by the date of death. However, those annuities that end at the decedent's death and do not provide payments to any beneficiary afterward are not subject to inclusion in the decedent's gross estate. Thus, contracts under an annuity for life that provide payments to the decedent and end at his or her death are not included in the gross estate, because there is nothing that the decedent can transfer or pass on to another at death. In other words, nothing is included in the decedent's gross estate because the decedent possessed no transferable interest.

Definition of Terms

The provisions of Sec. 2039 concerning estate tax inclusion of annuities are complicated. It may be helpful to define some of the terms so the student understands the types of arrangements and rights to payment that may or may not cause their inclusion in the decedent's gross estate. As used under this Internal Revenue Code section, the term *annuity or other payment* refers to one or more payments extending over any period of time. That means there may be several payments or a single lump-sum payment to be made to a beneficiary after the decedent's death. There is no requirement that these payments be equal, unconditional, or periodic. Stated differently, the amount as well as the timing of each payment may vary.

The meaning of the term *contract* or *agreement* is very broad and includes any arrangement, agreement, understanding, plan, or combination of them arising from the decedent's employment. An includible annuity may be a bona fide contract between the employer and the employee or it may be a plan for salary continuation, such as one that was established unilaterally by the decedent's employer. It may even include an unwritten arrangement for payments to an employee's beneficiary pursuant to a practice consistently followed by the employer.

The statutory term *was payable to the decedent* refers to annuity payments or other payments that the decedent was actually receiving at the time of death, regardless of whether he or she had an enforceable right to have these payments continued. Furthermore, an annuity is considered *receivable* by the decedent, although it may be forfeitable on the occurrence or nonoccurrence of a particular event, such as the recipient's remarriage. However, if the annuity agreement contains a provision that certain occurrences or nonoccurrences make it forfeitable, the possibility of forfeitability has an effect on the value of the annuity in the gross estate. In addition, an annuity is included in the gross estate if the decedent, immediately before death, had a right to receive payments in the future. In other words, as long as the decedent had an enforceable right to receive payments at some time, these payments need not have been immediately payable before death. If the decedent was in compliance with the obligations under the contract or agreement up to the time of his or her death, the decedent is considered to have had an enforceable right to receive future payments under a contract.

annuity

joint and survivor annuity

As stated earlier, the term **annuity** includes periodic payments for a specific time. There may be a single agreement or a combination of several agreements between the parties. Examples of contracts or agreements for payments that constitute annuities or other payments included in the gross estate are the following:

- contract under which the decedent was receiving or was entitled to receive an annuity or other payment immediately before death and for the duration of his or her life. The contract provides that payments are to continue after the decedent's death to a beneficiary named by him or her if the beneficiary survives the decedent.

- a contract under which the decedent was receiving payments before death together with another person for their joint lives. Payments would continue to the survivor after the death of either individual. This type of contract is called a **joint and survivor annuity**.

- a contract or agreement between the decedent and his or her employer under which the decedent was receiving or entitled to receive an annuity or other stipulated payment after retirement for the duration of the decedent's life, with payments to a designated beneficiary upon the decedent's death, if such beneficiaries survive the decedent. It makes no difference whether the payments to the survivor were fixed by contract, or subject to any options or elections exercisable by the decedent.

- a contract or agreement between the decedent and the decedent's employer that provided for an annuity or other payments to a designated surviving beneficiary, if the decedent died prior to retirement or before the expiration of a specific time.

- a contract or agreement under which the decedent, immediately before death, was receiving or entitled to receive an annuity or other payment for a specified time period, with payments to continue to a named beneficiary if the decedent died prior to the expiration of the specified time period

As previously mentioned, the value of an annuity contract is includible in the decedent's gross estate although payments are not to begin until after the death of the purchaser and primary annuitant (generally the same individual). A key factor is whether the decedent had an enforceable right to receive payments from a plan or combination of plans during lifetime had he or she lived. For example, a right to receive disability income in the event of disability prior to retirement causes a salary continuation plan to the employee's surviving spouse to be includible in the employee's gross estate if the employee dies before retirement. This is true even if the employee was never disabled. In other words, the value of a surviving beneficiary's annuity or other payment is includible in the gross estate only if the contract or agreement (or combination) under which payments are to be made to the survivor also gave the decedent a payment or a right to payment. It is the right to the payment that controls inclusion in the gross estate, not whether the decedent actually received any amount under the annuity before death. Also, any combination of arrangements or plans arising out of the decedent's employment may be includible under this section. Such contributions are treated as if they were made by the decedent. Payments are includible whether they are paid to the estate or to a named beneficiary.

Amount Includible

The amount includible in the decedent's gross estate is the value of the payments to the surviving beneficiary that represents the proportionate part of the purchase price of the contract contributed by the decedent. This includes contributions made by the decedent's employer, if they were made by reason of the decedent's employment. However, to the extent that the surviving beneficiary or anyone other than the decedent furnished part of the original purchase price, that portion is not included in the decedent's gross estate.

> **EXAMPLE**
>
> Tom Taylor purchased a joint and survivor annuity for himself and his sister, Ann. If he paid the total purchase price, the entire value of Ann's survivorship interest will be included in Tom's gross estate if he predeceases Ann. On the other hand, if Tom contributed 60 percent of the money to purchase the annuity and 40 percent of the contribution came from Ann's separate funds, only 60 percent of the value of the survivor's income interest would be includible in Tom's estate. It should be noted that if the decedent's employer or former employer contributed to the purchase price of the contract, the employer's contribution will be treated as if it was made by the decedent. Therefore, if Tom's employer purchased an annuity for him as a key employee and contributed the entire purchase price, the employer's contribution will be treated as if it was made by Tom, the decedent. Thus, any survivorship interest will be fully includible in Tom's estate.

Specifically *excluded* from taxation under this Code section are all amounts paid "as insurance under policies on the life of the decedent." This is not to say that proceeds of life insurance will not be included in the decedent's gross estate. Proceeds of life insurance on the decedent's life are includible in the gross estate under another Code section (IRC Sec. 2042), if certain conditions exist. If a single contract contains or has contained both life insurance and annuity elements, the amount, if any, that is includible under this section is based on whether or not there was any insurance element in the contract at the moment of death.

Only those contracts that contain no life insurance elements are includible under Sec. 2039. The amount of insurance a contract contains, if any, may be determined by the relationship of the policy's reserve value to the value of the death benefit at the time of the decedent's death. If the decedent dies before the reserve value equals the death benefit, an insurance element exists under the contract, and the contract is considered to be an insurance policy for estate tax purposes. Alternatively, if the decedent dies after the reserve value equals the death benefit, no insurance element exists any longer under the contract, and the agreement is considered to be solely a contract for an annuity. Notwithstanding the above, if a death benefit under a contractual arrangement can never exceed the total premiums paid plus interest, there is no insurance element present (Treas. Reg. Sec. 20.2039-1(d)).

The following situation is adapted from the aforementioned regulations section.

EXAMPLE

Under a nonqualified retirement plan, an employer, Marge, purchased a contract from a life insurance company that would provide her employee, Sam, with an annuity of $100 per month for life upon the employee's retirement at age 65. Under the contract, a beneficiary named by the employee would receive a similar annuity for life upon the employee's death after retirement. In addition, the contract provided for a lump-sum payment of $20,000 to the designated beneficiary instead of the annuity described above if the employee died before he reached retirement age. Assume that the reserve value of the contract would be $20,000 when the employee reaches age 65. Thus, if the employee died after reaching retirement age, the death benefit to the beneficiary would be considered an annuity, includible in the employee's gross estate. On the other hand, if the employee dies before reaching age 65, the death benefit would constitute insurance under a policy on the life of the decedent because the reserve value would be less than the death benefit. Therefore, the includibility in the gross estate would be determined under the estate tax section dealing with insurance (IRC Sec. 2042) and not under Sec. 2039.

Income in Respect of a Decedent (IRD)

Amounts paid on annuity contracts are treated as income in respect of a decedent (IRD) for tax purposes. The amounts are IRD to the extent the payments exceed the decedent's investment in the annuity. Payments are considered to be IRD whether they are paid in a lump sum or paid as a series of payments. Although IRD property is included in a decedent's gross estate, it does not receive a step up in basis.

EXAMPLE

Wainwright purchases a deferred annuity for $10,000 providing for payments to him to commence in 10 years. Baxter is the beneficiary of the contract. Five years after purchasing the annuity, Wainwright dies and Baxter receives the contract. The value of the annuity account was $15,000 at the time of Wainwright's death. The increase in the contract's value ($5,000) is IRD. Baxter will have income taxation on $5,000 of income. The value of the contract included in Wainwright's estate under Sec. 2039 is the fair market value of $15,000. Baxter is allowed an income tax deduction for the amount of estate tax attributed to the IRD portion of the contract being included in Wainwright's estate.

Valuation

Commercial annuity contracts (those issued by companies regularly engaged in the sale of annuities) are valued differently from others. A commercial contract is valued based on the cost of comparable contracts sold by the issuing company as of the date of the decedent's death. Therefore, referring to an earlier example, if Tom had purchased a commercial annuity for himself and Ann, the value in Tom's estate would be the cost of a single life annuity on Ann's life at the time of his death if he had contributed the entire purchase price (Treas. Reg. Sec. 20.2031-8(a)). If, however, the annuity was payable under a private contract, it would be valued for estate tax purposes according to the actuarial tables found in the federal estate and gift tax regulations (Treas. Reg. Secs. 20.2031–10; 25.2512–9).

Valuation Date

Date-of-Death Value

reduction in value by mere lapse of time

The value of benefits under an annuity contract is determined on the primary annuitant's date of death. Because an annuity is an asset that experiences a **reduction in value by mere lapse of time** (mortgages and notes receivable are examples of other "wasting assets"), the alternate valuation date does not apply to any annuity included in the gross estate (IRC Sec. 2032(a)(3)), even though the estate qualifies for and elects the alternate valuation date for other assets.

Benefits under an annuity contract are always valued on the date of death. Therefore, when the alternate valuation date applies to an estate, the benefits paid out during the 6-month period between the date of death and the alternate valuation date cannot be used to reduce the value of the annuity for estate tax purposes. Also, if the benefits are payable in a lump sum, the amount payable becomes the date-of-death value that is used on the estate tax return.

However, as stated earlier, the amount included in the decedent's gross estate is proportionately reduced if the decedent did not pay the full cost of the annuity contract.

Value of Annuity Reduced by Other Than Mere Lapse of Time

A different value may apply, however, if a reduction in value occurs for a reason other than mere lapse of time.

EXAMPLE

Suppose a husband had purchased a joint and survivor annuity for himself and his wife. The husband dies, and after his death his wife is entitled to receive payments for the remainder of her life. Unfortunately, the wife dies 4 months after the husband. In this case, an event other than mere lapse of time occurred during the period between the date of death and the alternate valuation date that reduced the value of the annuity to zero. If the husband elects the alternate valuation date, the only amount includible in the husband's estate is the value, as of his death, of the payments received by his widow during the 4-month postdeath period. It is determined by finding the difference between the value of an annuity for her life determined as of the husband's death and the actual value of the annuity determined as of the date of her death.

Lump-Sum Payments

lump-sum payments

As will be seen later, **lump-sum payments** are included at full value. When payments are made in installments, whether for a fixed period, in a fixed amount, or for the life of the beneficiary, the valuation is made on a commuted basis (the present value of the right to receive future income).

Annuities Receivable From Qualified Employee Retirement Plans

The Deficit Reduction Act of 1984 generally repealed all estate tax exclusion of qualified plan proceeds for decedents dying after December 31, 1984. There are two exceptions:

1. A nonemployee-spouse's interest in qualified plan proceeds that arise solely as a result of the application of community-property laws is totally excluded from his or her gross estate provided that the nonemployee-spouse predeceases the employee plan participant (IRC Sec. 2039(c)).

2. If the proceeds of a qualified plan were in pay status on December 31, 1984, and prior to the date of enactment of the Deficit Reduction Act of 1984 (July 18, 1984), the participant had irrevocably elected a beneficiary designation that would have qualified the plan proceeds for estate tax exclusion, the $100,000 exclusion amount is still available (DRA '84 Secs. 525(b)(2); (b)(3)).

LO 12.2   **Explain the rules for inclusion of jointly held property in the gross estate.**

JOINTLY HELD PROPERTY WITH RIGHT OF SURVIVORSHIP (IRC SEC. 2040)

Sec. 2040 covers the way jointly titled property is included in a decedent's gross estate.

Joint Tenancies Held by Married Couples (Qualified Joint Interests)

A special rule has been enacted that controls the estate taxation of joint property with right of survivorship held solely by a married couple (qualified joint interests) as well as property held as tenants by the entirety. Section 2040(b)(1) was created under the Tax Reform Act of 1976 (TRA '76). This section pertains to the one-half inclusion rule for spouses. As a result of TRA '76, after December 31, 1976, the rule is that one-half the value of such property, regardless of which spouse furnished all or part of the consideration, is included in the gross estate of the first spouse to die. This is an automatic rule. The actual contribution of each spouse is irrelevant. For some spousal joint tenancies with right of survivorship created prior to January 1, 1977, however, the percentage-of-contribution rule applies.

Percentage-of-Contribution (or Consideration-Furnished) Rule (Nonqualified Joint Interests)

percentage-of-contribution rule

All property held in joint tenancy with right of survivorship by joint tenants other than spouses alone (nonqualified joint interests) is treated under a different rule. The property is included in a deceased joint tenant's estate according to a **percentage-of-contribution rule**. Property held as joint tenants with right of survivorship by a decedent is included in the decedent's estate to the extent of the decedent's interest (the fractional share of the joint tenancy) at the time of death. However, any part of the decedent's interest in the joint tenancy is not included in the decedent's gross estate if it can be proved that the joint tenancy originally belonged to a surviving joint tenant or was purchased by funds contributed by the surviving joint tenant. The percentage-of-contribution rule pertains to all nonqualified joint interests, including joint tenancies in which spouses and one or more nonspousal parties are joint tenants.

In addition, if it can be shown that the surviving joint tenant's interest in the property was received from the decedent for less than full and adequate consideration, that portion of the joint tenancy is included in the decedent's estate. In this case, the amount included in the decedent's gross estate is the value of the actual gift of property itself or the amount of funds transferred to the donee joint tenant for the purpose of purchasing property to be held in joint tenancy.

EXAMPLE

Ted and Carol are siblings who hope to purchase a vacation home at the New Jersey shore. Because Ted is currently short on funds, Carol provides the entire purchase price. Ted dies tragically 3 years after the purchase of the property, when the vacation home is worth $350,000. The general rule is that Ted's interest in the property, valued at $175,000 at the time of his death, is included in his gross estate. However, Ted's estate is capable of rebutting the general rule by proving that Carol provided all of the original purchase price. If such evidence can be established, no amount of the joint tenancy will be included in Ted's estate at the time of his death.

Thus, if one joint tenant gave income-producing property to another joint tenant, and if the posttransfer income was contributed toward the purchase of jointly held property, the amounts attributable to such income are not deemed to have been received from the other joint tenant.

EXAMPLE

Father (F) made numerous $10,000 gifts of cash to Son (S) over the past years. S invested the gifts and earned $12,000 of interest. This year F and S purchased unimproved land for $36,000 and titled the property in joint tenancy. S used the $12,000 interest toward the purchase price, and F contributed the balance. If F predeceases S, for F's estate tax purposes S will be treated as contributing $12,000 of the land's purchase price and $24,000 will be included in F's gross estate.

Burden of Proof

Under the percentage-of-contribution rule, the burden of proof to demonstrate that the surviving joint tenant made some contribution to the acquisition of the joint tenancy is on the surviving joint tenant or the decedent's estate. If successful, that portion representing the percentage of contribution made by the surviving joint tenant is excluded from the gross estate.

Joint Property Acquired by Gift or Inheritance

Jointly held property that is acquired by gift, bequest, or inheritance is treated in a slightly different way. If the decedent and the decedent's spouse acquired the property by gift or inheritance, one-half of the value is included in the decedent's estate. However, if the decedent acquired the property as joint tenants with right of survivorship as a gift or inheritance with persons other than a spouse, the value representing his or her fractional interest is includible in the estate. To determine the decedent's fractional share, the value of the property is divided by the number of joint tenants with right of survivorship, presuming that each joint tenant owns an undivided interest in the entire property.

EXAMPLE

If a decedent, James, inherited a farm from his father in equal shares with his three sisters and a brother, and he is the first joint tenant to die, one-fifth of the value of the property is included in his gross estate.

Advisability of Marital Joint Tenancies with Right of Survivorship

Advantages

There are still advantages in holding property jointly with right of survivorship by spouses. Jointly held property between spouses is generally nonprobate property. This means that the property is not subject to estate administration. All benefits of ownership remain available to the surviving joint tenant without interruption during the administration period. Because the property does not pass through probate, total administration expenses and attorney fees may be reduced. One-half of the property attributed to the decedent's interest included in the decedent's gross estate is entitled to the full benefit of the unlimited marital deduction. Therefore, there is no estate tax liability because of the property's inclusion. Another benefit of joint ownership is the comfort and feeling of harmony and security that it creates between spouses.

Disadvantages

A disadvantage may be that the surviving joint tenant obtains full control over the future disposition of the property. This may defeat a portion of the original estate plan of the first joint tenant to die. Should the survivor remarry, the property becomes subject to a spouse's right of election by the survivor's second spouse.

In addition, only one-half of the property receives a step up in basis at the first joint tenant's death. As mentioned earlier, the savings in estate tax and probate costs may possibly be worth less than the potential savings in capital-gains tax had the property been fully included in the decedent's gross estate and acquired a fully stepped-up basis.

basis

As you may recall from a previous assignment, **basis** is a term used for income tax purposes. There are special rules concerning the basis of property transferred at death. Property that is included in a decedent's gross estate acquires a new basis. The new basis is either an increase to or a decrease from the fair market value of property on the date of death.

Characteristics of Joint Tenancies

- nonprobate property
- passage of property by operation of law
- partial basis step up at first death
- uninterrupted ownership for survivor
- full control and ownership for survivor

Alternatives

Alternate solutions involve keeping the property in sole ownership, as illustrated in the following example.

EXAMPLE

If a decedent-husband held the property in his name alone and left the property outright to his wife as a special bequest in his will, the entire property, although included in the gross estate, is also eligible for the marital deduction. Therefore, no estate tax results from inclusion of the property in his estate. In addition, the basis in the hands of the surviving wife becomes the fair market value on the date of the husband's death or alternate valuation date, if applicable. Of course, the property is then probate property, which may generate additional costs to the estate. There also may be a delay in formally transferring the property to the surviving spouse. Furthermore, if the husband retains ownership of the property with the intention of passing it to his surviving spouse using the unlimited marital deduction and his wife predeceases him, he loses the benefit of the marital deduction for the property passing through his estate. However, when he dies, the entire property receives a stepped-up basis in the hands of his beneficiaries. Remember that even if the husband dies first, at his spouse's death the entire value of the property is taxable for federal estate tax purposes in the second estate. In other words, to the extent that either spouse does not dispose of the property during their lifetimes, it is included at full value in the estate of the second spouse to die. Of course, the next tier of beneficiaries will obtain another step-up in basis to fair market value at the second death.

Other factors to consider when arranging property ownership are the relative sizes of the parties' estates as well as the variation in their ages and health factors. Likewise, the quality of the parties' relationship is significant. Although no-fault divorce laws and equitable distribution statutes now apply to some extent in almost all states, jointly held personal property is freely accessible to either spouse whether together or separated. Possession by the donee may defeat the interest of the donor's spouse temporarily or permanently, to the extent the asset is converted or consumed.

Because of one or more of the above considerations, the estate planner may recommend the termination of a joint tenancy between spouses, thereby transferring the entire interest to one of the spouses. Keep in mind that the unlimited marital deduction for gift-tax purposes now makes it possible to transfer property back and forth between spouses without the gift tax ramifications that previously existed. For example, if the decedent's estate includes a closely held business that qualifies for special-use valuation, the deferral of estate tax payments, or a Sec. 303 stock redemption, and the business was in the decedent's own name alone, the value of the business in relation to the decedent's adjusted gross estate would be increased if he or she had transferred some *nonbusiness* joint assets to the decedent's spouse as sole owner. The proportionate increase in the value of the business interest in relation to the decedent's estate may enable the estate to qualify for any of these potentially desirable tax benefits by meeting the percentage tests for eligibility. Alternatively, if the property under consideration is solely owned nonbusiness property, placing it in joint names removes one-half of the date-of-death value from the decedent's estate, thereby making it easier to qualify for a Sec. 303 redemption, Sec. 6166 deferral to pay estate tax, or special-use valuation under Sec. 2032A.

The following example illustrates how ownership of property in joint names as opposed to sole ownership affects the ability to qualify for one of the tax benefits mentioned above where qualification is based on a percentage test.

EXAMPLE

Mr. Jones is the sole shareholder of a closely held business that has a fair market value of $2 million. His gross estate is valued at $8 million. He desires to leave approximately one-half of his estate to his second wife, with the net balance after payment of taxes and expenses bequethed to his two sons from a prior marriage, who work with him in the business. Debts and expenses of the estate will probably be about $75,000. Under such a plan, the estate would not qualify for the tax relief provided by either Sec. 6166 (providing for installment payments of estate tax over 14 years) or a Sec. 303 redemption (providing for a redemption of stock to pay estate taxes and funeral and administrative costs). This is because the value of the business interest equals only 25 percent of this adjusted gross estate, not greater than 35 percent required by Secs. 303 and 6166. Considering the division of property described above, his sons would have difficulty meeting the estate tax liability payable from the residue unless the closely held business had significant amounts of cash.

As an alternative plan, if Mr. Jones desires to maintain the flexibility to qualify for the tax benefits described, he can transfer a sufficient portion of nonbusiness property to joint ownership with his spouse. This transfer, in turn, reduces his adjusted gross estate by an amount that enables the estate to qualify under the 35-percent-of-adjusted-gross-estate test under Sec. 6166 and Sec. 303. Bear in mind that if he does not survive more than 3 years after making the transfer to a joint tenancy with his spouse, the property transferred will be included in his estate for purposes of qualification under Sec. 6166 and Sec. 303. However, the use of joint tenancies for this purpose can lead to beneficial results.

LO 12.3   **Explain the estate taxation of general powers of appointment, and differentiate between general powers and special powers with respect to inclusion in the gross estate.**

POWERS OF APPOINTMENT (IRC SEC. 2041)

power of appointment

Sec. 2041 concerns the way a power of appointment is included in a decedent's gross estate. A **power of appointment** over property is the right of the holder of the power to specify who will become the recipient or owner of the property. Depending on the type of power of appointment, the holder of the power may or may not be able to designate himself or herself as the property owner. Powers of appointment are usually created within trust documents. The grantor of the trust is typically the donor and the trustee is the donee. Actual or permissible appointees are the trust beneficiaries.

Power of Appointment Terminology

- donor—grantor of power over property
- donee—holder of power
- permissible appointee—individuals, class, or group of possible recipients of property
- appointee—recipient of property
- taker in default—recipient of property as a result of a lapse or release

Historically, according to common law and property law, property subject to a power of appointment is not treated as being owned by the powerholder. The holder is merely held to be an agent or proxy for the donor. For gift and estate tax purposes, however, general powers of appointment are subject to transfer tax. When a power of appointment is originally created during the donor's lifetime, the donor makes a gift to the donee-powerholder. If the donee-powerholder then exercises the power to benefit someone other than himself or herself or his or her creditors, the donee-powerholder likewise has made a gift of the (same) property. No gift for gift tax purposes occurs if the donee exercises the power in favor of himself or herself. In turn, when a general power is created by will or by trust as a result of the donor's death, the transfer is subject to estate tax liability. And, following this pattern, if a general power is exercised by the donee-powerholder at death, the holder is subject to estate taxation on the (same property) transfer. Naturally, the annual exclusion (in the case of a gift), the marital deduction, and/or the basic credit amount may eliminate or reduce the tax on transfers.

During the general powerholder's lifetime there are three times when the gift tax is applicable to a general power of appointment:

- when the powerholder exercises the power in favor of someone else
- when there is a *release* of the power
- when there is a *lapse* of the power

release

lapse

A **release** takes place when the donee affirmatively gives up the right to exercise the power. The power then passes to the taker by default. A **lapse** occurs when the powerholder merely does not exercise the power, in which case it also passes to whoever is the taker by default.

General Powers

general power of appointment

A decedent's general power of appointment over property has value for federal estate tax purposes under Code Sec. 2041. The gross estate includes the value of all property subject to a **general power of appointment** possessed by the decedent at the time of death. When an individual is given a legal right to appoint (direct the disposition of) property that is not his or hers, that right is called a power of appointment. A general power is a power over property so broad that it approaches actual ownership or control over the property subject to the power. Property subject to such a power will be includible in the estate of a person who holds that power, the so-called donee of the power. If the decedent has been given a power by another person (called the donor of the power), and this power allows the decedent to appoint the property to himself or herself, his or her creditors, the estate, or the estate's creditors, it is considered a general power of appointment. Note that the decedent need not have the power to appoint property to all four categories. The power to appoint to one of the four is sufficient for a power to be a general power of appointment for estate tax purposes (*Estate of Edelman v. Comm'r*, 38 T.C. 972 (1976)). Again, the person who possesses the power and has the right to exercise it is called the donee or holder of the power.

General Power of Appointment

| Donor | Power over Donor's Property ➡ | Donee |

Donor's Property

Appointees:

Anyone, including
Donee
Donee's creditors
Donee's estate
Donee's estate creditors

As long as the decedent holds the power, it makes no difference whether the power is exercisable by him or her only during lifetime, only at death, or both during life and at death (*Snyder v. U.S.*, 203 F.Supp. 195 (W.D. Ky. 1962); *Jenkins v. U.S.*, 428 F.2d 538 (5th Cir. 1970)).

General Power of Appointment

You have an unlimited right to appoint property to

- yourself
- your creditors
- your estate
- your estate creditors

A general power includes the unlimited right of the decedent-donee to use the corpus of a trust for the decedent's own benefit.

EXAMPLE

If the decedent, Herman, was given the power in a trust to distribute or appoint trust principal to or among any of four beneficiaries not including himself, this would not be a general power of appointment. However, if the trust contained an additional power in the decedent to invade corpus without limitation for his own benefit at any time, the power would be a general power of appointment since he had the power to deplete corpus partially or totally for his own benefit, thereby defeating the rights of the other beneficiaries. It is immaterial for estate tax inclusion whether or not he actually exercised this power in his favor.

Because a general power over property is, by definition, so closely akin to actual ownership, a formal surrender of the power (a release) or failure to use the power (a lapse) may be treated similarly to a transfer of the property itself. Therefore, if the release or lapse is coupled with a lifetime retention of the income produced by the property subject to the power (as is typically the case when a grantor gives the same person a lifetime income interest and a withdrawal power), or if the transfer is conditioned on surviving the decedent or subject to the former holder's power to alter, amend, revoke, or terminate the transfer, the property subject to the power may have to be included in the gross estate.

This type of transfer is includible because it is considered the tax equivalent of a transfer of property actually owned by the decedent.

Special Powers

special (limited) power of appointment

A general power of appointment is to be distinguished from a limited or special power. A **special (limited) power of appointment** is one in which the donor of the power limits the donee with respect to the persons to whom the donee may appoint the property. It does not qualify as a general power if the power is: (a) exercisable only in favor of one or more persons (or all other persons) not including the decedent, the decedent's creditors, the estate, or the creditors of the estate, or (b) if it is specifically not exercisable in favor of the decedent, the decedent's creditors, the estate, or the creditors of the estate.

Special Power of Appointment

Special Power of Appointment

Property may *not* be appointed to

- **yourself**
- **your creditors**
- **your estate**
- **your estate creditors**

As previously stated, a donee's ability to appoint property subject to a power of appointment to himself or herself causes the power to be a general power. There are, however, three additional exceptions to the general-power-of-appointment basic rule: when the donee's invasion of corpus is limited to (1) an ascertainable standard, (2) when an exercise of power requires the consent of either the donor of the power or an adverse party, or (3) an annual, noncumulative right to the greater of $5,000 or 5 percent of trust corpus. If a donee's power is restricted to these exceptions, the donee will be considered to hold a special power of appointment rather than a general one for gift or estate tax purposes.

EXAMPLE

Courtney died recently. Under her will, Courtney provided for some of her property to be placed in trust for the benefit of her adult children. A local bank is trustee. Trust provisions grant the bank a special (limited) power of appointment over distributions of trust principal to the children at specified ages and events.

Property over which the decedent has a special or limited power is not includible in his or her gross estate. However, if the decedent had a power over property that he or she exercised in favor of someone else, but the decedent retained an interest in the property for life, the value of the property will be includible in the decedent's gross estate.

EXAMPLE

A decedent, Franklin, was given a lifetime general power of appointment by his sister to designate who would receive a lakefront vacation home. The decedent exercised this power in favor of his daughter but retained the right to use the property for his life. The right to use the property for life brings the value of the property subject to the power into his gross estate, although he had previously exercised the power and disposed of the property.

Limitations by Ascertainable Standard

ascertainable standard

If the decedent possesses the power to consume or invade for his or her own benefit, but the power is limited by an **ascertainable standard** (such that the property may be used or invaded only for reasons of the decedent's health, education, support, or maintenance), the power of appointment is considered a special, not a general, power. Support and maintenance are generally construed in accordance with the standard of living to which the decedent was accustomed. The ascertainable standard, often used in discretionary trusts, is often referred to as the Health, Education, Maintenance, and Support (HEMS) standard.

EXAMPLE

If Mr. Smith creates a trust and gives his son, Walter, the right to invade corpus for Walter's health, education, support, or maintenance, Walter has a special power of appointment that will not cause the corpus subject to the power to be included in his gross estate (IRC Sec. 2041(b)(1)(A)).

Ascertainable Standard

- health
- education
- maintenance
- support

Powers Exercisable Only with the Consent of Others

A power of appointment, that otherwise causes the value of property subject to the power to be includible in the estate of the donee of the power, may escape inclusion wholly or partially if the power can be exercised only with the consent of others.

Powers Exercisable Only with the Consent of the Donor of Power

A power created after October 21, 1942, that can be exercised only with the consent or joinder of the creator (donor) of the power is not considered a general power of appointment for federal estate tax purposes (IRC Sec. 2041(b) (1)(C)(i)).

Powers Exercisable Only with the Consent of a Person Having a Substantial Adverse Interest

Similarly, a power created after October 21, 1942, that can be exercised only with the consent or joinder of a person having a substantial adverse interest is not treated as a general power, and the property subject to the power is not includible in the estate of the donee (IRC Sec. 2041(b)(1)(C)(ii)).

EXAMPLE

Assume that Albert grants John and Betty the unrestricted power to appoint property to Betty during her lifetime. In default of the appointment, the property will pass to John at Betty's death. At her death, if the property has not been appointed to her, no portion of the value of the property is includible in her gross estate. She is not deemed to have a general power of appointment since John had a substantial adverse interest.

If the consent of the person without an adverse interest is required, the value of the property subject to the power is fully includible in the donee's estate.

EXAMPLE

Assume that Albert grants John and Betty the unrestricted power to appoint property in favor of Betty during her lifetime. In default of appointment, the property passes to Carol on Betty's death. When Betty predeceases John, Betty is deemed to possess a general power of appointment because John does not have a substantial adverse interest in the property subject to the power. In no event could John have been the beneficiary of the property. The entire value of the property subject to the power is included in Betty's gross estate at her death. This is so because Betty and John could have appointed the property to Betty during her lifetime, and she was not limited to exercising the power only in conjunction with the creator of the power or someone having an adverse interest in the property.

Note that a trustee whose only powers are administrative ones exercisable in a fiduciary capacity is not a person who has an adverse interest in the property.

If a power created *before* October 21, 1942, is exercisable by the decedent only in conjunction with *any other person*, it is not treated as a general power (IRC Sec. 2042(b)(1)(B)). For general powers created before October 21, 1942, it is irrelevant that the party whose consent was required had no interest, adverse or otherwise, in the property. The mere requirement of the consent of another person is sufficient to defeat inclusion of property subject to such powers in the decedent-donee's estate.

Powers Exercisable Only with the Consent of Others in Whose Favor Power Could Be Exercised

If a person is given a power that can be exercised only in conjunction with others in whose favor the power could be exercised, only a fractional part of the property is includible in the donee's estate. The fractional portion is determined by dividing the value of the property by the number of persons in whose favor the power could be exercised (IRC Sec. 2041(b)(1)(C)(iii)).

EXAMPLE

Assume that Albert grants John and Betty the unrestricted right to appoint property to either of them (with the consent of the other) during their lifetimes. In default of an appointment, the property passes to Myrna. At Betty's death, one-half of the value of the property is includible in her gross estate.

Other Limitations on Powers

5-and-5 power

Although the decedent is given what is otherwise a general power of appointment, it is not included in the gross estate if the decedent's power is limited to a noncumulative right to withdraw the greater of $5,000 or 5 percent of the aggregate value of the property each year. This power is sometimes referred to as a **5-and-5 power**. For gift and estate tax purposes, only *general* powers of appointment are subject to transfer tax. When a power of appointment is originally created during the donor's lifetime, the donor makes a gift to the donee-powerholder. If the donee-powerholder then exercises the power to benefit someone other than himself or herself or his or her creditors, he or she also has made a gift of the (same) property. No gift for gift tax purposes occurs if the donee exercises the power in favor of himself or herself. In turn, when a general power is created by will or by trust as a result of the donor's death, the transfer is subject to estate tax liability. And, following this pattern, if a general power is exercised by the donee-powerholder at death, the holder is subject to estate taxation on the (same property) transfer. Naturally, the annual exclusion (in the case of a gift), the marital deduction, and/or the basic credit amount may eliminate or reduce the tax on transfers.

During the general powerholder's lifetime there are three times when transfer taxes are applicable to general powers of appointment:

- when the powerholder exercises the power in favor of someone else
- when there is a release of the power
- when there is a lapse of the power

Failure to withdraw the money each year is said to be a lapse constituting a release of the power. If the decedent dies possessing this power, the amount includible in the estate is only the amount that the decedent could have appointed in favor of himself or herself in the year of death. To the extent that the power to appoint the property exceeds the greater of $5,000 or 5 percent of the value of the assets subject to the power, there is a taxable disposition by the decedent's failure to exercise the power of withdrawal. In other words, the decedent is deemed to have made a gift to the remainderperson of the excess property that is not withdrawn each year. The gift tax effect is exactly the same as if the decedent had appointed the property to himself or herself and gifted it to the remainder portion of the trust.

EXAMPLE

A trust established by Mr. Ford was funded with $500,000 worth of securities. His son, Frank, is to receive all income for life with the remainder going to Frank's children. Frank was given a noncumulative right to withdraw $40,000 per year from the trust. Because this is a noncumulative right, he releases those funds each year that he does not withdraw all or part of the $40,000. Releasing the excess of the greater of $5,000 or 5 percent of the trust corpus is treated as a taxable transfer (it is a gift to the trust, that is, the trust beneficiaries). In this example, 5 percent of the trust corpus equals $25,000. The excess distribution equals $15,000 ($40,000 minus $25,000). It is a taxable transfer with a reserved right to income from the portion remaining in the trust. Because he is the life-income beneficiary, a portion of the trust valued at the date of his death will be included in his gross estate. The ratio for inclusion is determined by dividing the excess distribution ($15,000) by the total current value of the trust ($500,000—assumed for the purpose of this example). In this case, $15,000 ÷ $50,000, 3 ÷ 100, or 3 percent of the value of the trust corpus, at Frank's death will be includible in his gross estate.

If failure to exercise a power of withdrawal occurs in more than one year, the proportionate amount of property over which the power lapses that is treated as a taxable disposition is determined separately for each year. It is the aggregate of all taxable portions for all years (not to exceed 100 percent) that is includible in the decedent's gross estate. Remember that the value of the 5-and-5 power in the year of death is also includible.

5-and-5 Power

Noncumulative right to withdraw the *greater* of

$5,000

or

5% of the aggregate value of property annually

Disclaiming a Power

If a decedent refuses to accept a power of appointment in a manner consistent with the requirements of a qualified disclaimer under the federal disclaimer statute (IRC Sec. 2518), the decedent is considered to have disclaimed or renounced the power of appointment. Although the power was a general power, nothing will be included in the decedent's gross estate because that power was never accepted by the decedent. A disclaimer is invalid once the power over the property has been accepted. Also, a qualified disclaimer does not result in a taxable gift if the necessary federal requirements are met.

If the donee of a power does not wish it to be included in his or her gross estate, the donee must release or exercise the power during lifetime. Also, the donee must not exercise the power and retain any rights or power over the property that would cause it to be included under IRC Secs. 2036, 2037, or 2038 (for example, the right to income for life). Otherwise, the property will still be included in the donee's gross estate unless he or she releases these impermissible retained rights more than 3 years prior to death (IRC Sec. 2041(a)(2)).

Time and Method of the Creation of a Power

A power of appointment created by will is considered to be created on the date of the testator's death. A power of appointment created by deed or other instrument during the creator's lifetime is deemed to be created on the day the instrument becomes effective.

The use of the words *general power of appointment* is not essential. Determination of the existence of a power is based on what it purports to accomplish rather than on either the wording used by the creator or local property law connotations. Therefore, a right given to a person with a life estate in a trust to withdraw or consume the trust principal may rightly be considered a general power of appointment over the property.

Effect of Legal Competence to Exercise a Power

Property subject to a general power of appointment is includible in the decedent's estate even though the decedent could not exercise the power because he was legally incompetent or a minor (Rev. Rul. 75-351, 1975-2 C.B. 368; Rev. Rul. 55-518, 1955-2 C.B. 384). Numerous U.S. Circuit Court of Appeals decisions support this conclusion, and there no longer appears to be any doubt about this issue. (See *Estate of Gilchrist v. Comm'r*, 630 F.2d 340 (5th Cir. 1980); *Pennsylvania Bank & Trust Co. v. U.S.*, 597 F.2d 382 (3d Cir.), cert. denied, 444 U.S. 930 (1979).)

It has even been held that the possession of a general power at death is sufficient to cause inclusion of the property subject to the power in the decedent's estate, even though the decedent was not aware of the existence of the power (*Estate of Freeman v. Comm'r*, 67 T.C. 202 (1976)).

LO 12.4   **Explain the general rules concerning the inclusion of life insurance in the gross estate, and describe some ways in which life insurance can avoid estate taxation.**

LIFE INSURANCE (IRC SEC. 2042)

Sec. 2042 defines when the proceeds of life insurance are included in the gross estate of the insured for federal estate tax purposes.

Types of Contracts Included

Life insurance as used in this section refers to all types of policies. It includes whole life policies, term insurance, group life insurance, limited-payment life, endowment contracts (prior to being paid up), retired lives reserves insurance, and death benefits paid by fraternal societies operating under the lodge system. In addition, the proceeds of certain other types of insurance policies (such as accident insurance and flight insurance available at air terminals) are considered proceeds of life insurance for estate tax purposes. Likewise, proceeds of war-risk insurance and national service life insurance are included in the gross estate, as well as insurance paid under double indemnity clauses by reason of the accidental death of an insured.

To be considered an insurance contract, there must be an actuarially determined element of risk on which the premium cost of the contract is based. There must be risk sharing between the insured and the insurer so that the insurer stands to sustain a loss if the insured does not live for the intended life expectancy.

Another element inherent in insurance policies is that the original purchaser must have an insurable interest in the policy.

Proceeds of life insurance on the decedent's life are included in the gross estate under this Code section if: (1) the decedent possessed any incidents of ownership in the policy, (2) the proceeds are receivable by the estate, or (3) the proceeds are receivable by another for the benefit of the estate.

The term *incidents of ownership* refers to a number of rights of the insured or the insured's estate in the economic benefits of the policy. It is not limited to ownership in a technical sense. Rights that are considered incidents of ownership include the following:

- the power to name or change beneficiaries or beneficial interests
- the right to assign the policy
- the right to revoke an assignment

- the right to surrender or cancel the policy

- the right to pledge the policy for a loan

- the right to obtain a loan against the surrender value of the policy

- the power to change the beneficiary when the policy is owned by a closely held corporation of which the decedent is a sole or controlling shareholder. (However, to the extent that proceeds are payable to the corporation or a third party for a valid business purpose, such as payment of a corporate debt, the corporate-owned policy on the life of the sole or controlling shareholder will not be attributed to the shareholder and will not be includible in his or her estate.)

- the right to prevent cancellation of an insurance policy owned by the decedent's employer by purchasing the policy for its cash surrender value

- the power to change the beneficial ownership in a policy or its proceeds, or to change the time or manner of enjoyment of the policy or its proceeds should the policy of life insurance on the insured's life be owned by a trust

- the reservation of rights to deal with the policy even if the policy is physically transferred to another

- the power to require the nominal owner of the policy to exercise an incident of ownership, thereby having control over the actions of the owner of record

- the right to a reversionary interest worth more than 5 percent of the value of the insurance policy immediately before the insured's death. (In other words, there must be more than a 5 percent chance based on the value of the policy immediately before the death of the insured that the right or rights will return to him or her.)

Avoidance of Sec. 2042 Inclusion
- **no responsibility for insured's estate expenses**
- **no incidents of ownership**

If the insured possesses any of the above rights, the full proceeds of life insurance will be included in the gross estate even if the insured cannot exercise these rights without the consent of some other person. Inclusion in the estate occurs regardless of the decedent's ability to exercise the right at death. For example, the decedent might have been in flight or incompetent at the time of death. If the insured retains rights of ownership while acting in a fiduciary capacity, the policy proceeds will be included in the estate if any rights of incidents of ownership can be exercised for the insured's personal benefit.

Decedent as Trustee

In general, if the decedent-insured has no beneficial interest in the insurance policies while acting as a trustee, he or she is not considered to have powers equivalent to a testamentary disposition that would bring the proceeds of life insurance into the estate. There is at least one court case that rejected this differentiation and included proceeds in the decedent's estate when a mere incident of ownership was possessed, regardless of the manner in which the decedent acquired it and the capacity in which he or she possessed it (as trustee). In this case, the decedent-insured was the owner and beneficiary of life insurance policies as sole trustee of three trusts created by his brother. As trustee, he had the power to change the time and manner of enjoyment of the policies and proceeds by his power to withdraw dividends, to obtain loans, and to convert the policies from whole life insurance to endowment life insurance (*Rose v. U.S.*, 511 F.2d 259 (5th Cir. 1975)).

In essence, planners should be cognizant that there have been numerous cases involving a decedent's possession of similar rights that have reached contrary outcomes. Without question, a financial services professional should make a client aware that any meaningful rights in the policy held by the client at the time of death may cause the entire proceeds to be includible in the client's gross estate. It is irrelevant how the decedent obtained these ownership attributes or whether exercise of these rights or powers would directly or indirectly benefit him or her. The distinguishing factor that causes inclusion of the policy in the decedent's estate is whether that individual possessed the right at his or her death and not whether the decedent had the capacity or ability to exercise it.

Proceeds Payable to or for the Benefit of an Estate

proceeds payable to or for the benefit of an estate

The full proceeds of life insurance are also included in the decedent's estate if they are "**proceeds payable to or for the benefit of an estate**." This phrase is operative if the life insurance is receivable by the estate, the executor, or any other person who has the power to act on behalf of the estate. It is immaterial that the policy was purchased and owned by someone other than the decedent, and the owner retained complete control over the policy during the decedent-insured's lifetime (IRC Sec. 2046(1)).

Similarly, the proceeds are included in the decedent's estate if they are made payable to a trust that is required to use the proceeds for the payment of death taxes, claims, and administrative expenses of the decedent or the estate. However, if the trustee is merely given a discretionary power to pay these expenses and is not required to use trust assets to satisfy estate obligations, the proceeds will not be included in the estate except to the extent they are actually used to satisfy estate obligations.

If proceeds were used as collateral security for a loan held by a corporation, they are considered receivable for the benefit of the estate since the corporation is a creditor of the estate. However, the value of the unpaid balance at the date of the decedent's death with interest accrued is deductible from the gross estate as a debt of the estate.

If the proceeds of life insurance made payable to the decedent's estate are community assets in community-property states, only one-half belongs to the decedent. Therefore, only one-half is included in the decedent's gross estate as proceeds receivable by or for the benefit of the estate (Treas. Reg. Sec. 20.2042-1(b) (2) *Estate of Madsen v. Comm'r*, 690 F.2d 164 (9th Cir. 1982)).

Proceeds Used to Pay Estate Taxes

As noted in the preceding example, insurance proceeds are also includible in the decedent's gross estate as insurance receivable by the personal representative when the proceeds are actually used to pay estate taxes. Also, if proceeds are receivable by an individual beneficiary but the beneficiary is legally obliged to pay taxes, debts, and other expenses of the estate, the proceeds are includible in the estate to the extent of the beneficiary's obligation to use the proceeds for these purposes.

Life insurance proceeds paid directly to a divorced spouse are includible in the decedent's gross estate if the decedent was required to name the former spouse as beneficiary of the insurance proceeds on his or her life and if the decedent was required to maintain the policies, unless the former spouse died or remarried. However, the above is an arm's-length, bargained-for agreement; as such, a deduction in the amount of the proceeds is allowed from the gross estate as a debt of the estate.

Group Life Insurance

Group life insurance is treated similarly to other types of life insurance. A group life insurance policy taken out by an employer is included in the decedent employee's estate if the decedent had the right to change beneficiaries, terminate the insurance policy, or prevent cancellation of the contract by purchasing the policy.

However, if the employee's power to terminate the policy is limited to terminating employment, that is not an incident of ownership sufficient to bring the policy proceeds into the employee's gross estate. Also, a right to convert the group policy to an individual policy when the decedent's employment ends is not a right sufficient to bring the policy proceeds into the estate if this right is transferable and the decedent irrevocably assigns the policy as well as the conversion privilege to another. In such a case, the decedent has no control over the assignee's right to the proceeds and no incidents of ownership over the policy.

Proceeds From the Estate of Another

The terms *incidents of ownership* and *reversionary interest* do not apply to either a life insurance policy or to the proceeds a decedent receives by inheritance through the estate of another person (such as a surviving spouse under a statutory right of election).

Inclusion of Life Insurance
- proceeds received by decedent-insured's estate (Sec. 2042)
- decedent-insured's incidents of ownership in policy (Sec. 2042)
- proceeds received by another for the benefit of decedent-insured's estate (Sec. 2042)
- decedent's ownership of policy on life of another (Sec. 2033)
- insured's gift of policy within 3 years of death (Sec. 2035)

Insurance on the Life of Another

Policies of life insurance that the decedent owns on the life of another are not included under this section. However, the value of these policies is included in the decedent's gross estate as property that is owned at death under Sec. 2033, the general inclusion section. If the decedent owns a policy on someone else's life, the amount that is includible in the decedent's estate is determined as follows:

- If the policy is new, the gross premium paid is the value.

- If the policy is a paid-up or single-premium policy, its value is its replacement cost—that is, the single premium that the issuing company would have charged for a comparable contract of equal face value on the life of a person who was the insured's age (at the time the decedent policyholder died).

- If the policy is a premium-paying whole life policy, the value is found by adding any unearned portion of the last premium to the interpolated terminal reserve.

- If the policy is a term life insurance policy, the value is the unused premium.

Relationship to Marital Deduction

If insurance is payable to the spouse or the spouse's estate in a lump sum or in the form of an annuity only if the spouse survives the decedent by up to 6 months, the proceeds qualify for the marital deduction assuming they have been included in the gross estate. If proceeds are left at the interest option for the life of the surviving spouse, they qualify for the marital deduction if they are payable to the spouse's estate or to persons to whom the spouse appoints the property at death. If the spouse fails to exercise this power of appointment over the proceeds, they may still qualify for the marital deduction if the proceeds are received by named contingent beneficiaries as a result of the spouse's failure to appoint them. Likewise, if proceeds are to be paid in installments for a definite period of time or if there is a refund feature, the proceeds qualify if payments following the death of the surviving spouse are payable to those beneficiaries whom the surviving spouse has designated to receive the remaining payments. Proceeds also qualify for the marital deduction if the spouse receives all the interest for life and proceeds pass to a trust or named beneficiary at the spouse's death under the qualified terminable interest rules. Note that if life insurance is payable to a surviving spouse but is not includible in the decedent's gross estate because he or she retains no incidents of ownership, the marital deduction does not apply.

Transfers of Life Insurance within 3 Years of Death

Any gratuitous transfer of a life insurance policy by an insured made after 1976 and within 3 years of a decedent's death is includible in the decedent's gross estate as a transfer made within 3 years of death. In these circumstances, however, the proceeds are not reportable on the life insurance schedule as proceeds owned at death, but are reportable on the schedule provided for lifetime transfers. Motivation or intention in making the transfer is irrelevant. Although other completed gifts made within 3 years of death are excluded from the gross estate by the Economic Recovery Tax Act of 1981 (ERTA '81), effective for decedents dying on or after January 1, 1982, there is a specific exception for gratuitous transfers by the insured of life insurance policies on the insured's life within 3 years of death. The full value of life insurance proceeds from policies on the decedent's life transferred by the decedent within 3 years of death is included in the gross estate (IRC Sec. 2035(d)(2)).

All insurance on the decedent's life, whether or not owned by the decedent, is reported on Schedule D of the federal estate return. If proceeds are received in a lump sum, the value reported is the net proceeds received, but if policy proceeds are paid other than in a lump sum, the value listed is the value of proceeds as of the date of the decedent's death. Insurance proceeds on the life of a nonresident noncitizen (nonresident alien) are not taxable for federal estate tax purposes and need not be reported. Along with the schedule on the estate tax return, the personal representative must file a Form 712 Life Insurance Statement for each life insurance policy listed in the schedule that is included in the gross estate. These statements may be obtained from the insurance company that issued the policy.

The following table summarizes the estate tax inclusion sections.

Gross Estate Inclusion Section	
IRC Section Number	**Inclusion Section Description**
2031	Broad, nonspecific provision for inclusion to the extent provided by Secs. 2033 through 2046
2033	General miscellaneous ("catch all") inclusion of any property in which the decedent had an interest: any interest in real estate, cash and cash equivalents, stocks, bonds, notes, mortgages, the value of outstanding loans, the value of tax refunds due to the deceased, tangible personal property, outstanding dividends that have been declared and are payable, income receivable, interests in unincorporated businesses, and/or cash value of life insurance owned by the decedent on the lives of others
2034	Dower/curtesy interests (replaced by statutory law in most states)
2035	Certain interests transferred within 3 years of death
2036	Interests in previously transferred property that were retained at death
2037	Reversionary interests in previously transferred property that are obtained by surviving decedent
2038	Interests in previously transferred property that are subject to potential alteration, change, amendment, revocation, termination, or effectuation of beneficial enjoyment
2039	Annuities and/or payments under certain contracts if the decedent had the right to the payments during his or her lifetime and payments continue beyond his or her death
2040	Joint tenancies with right of survivorship and/or tenancies by the entireties
2041	Value of property subject to a general power of appointment held by the decedent at the time of his or her death
2042	Proceeds of a life insurance policy if: the decedent had any incidents of ownership in the policy; the proceeds are payable to the estate; or the proceeds are receivable by another for the benefit of the estate

MINI-CASE

Based on the following fact pattern and assuming Mr. Smith died in 2019, predeceasing Mrs. Smith, indicate, with reasons, the assets and their values that would be included in Mr. Smith's gross estate for federal estate tax purposes.

Business Situation

Mr. Smith is president of the GBH Corporation, a manufacturer of chemicals and solvents. Mr. Smith founded the corporation 20 years ago, and it has grown steadily over the years.

The corporation has 900 shares of common stock outstanding, of which Mr. Smith owns 750 shares and Mrs. Smith owns the remaining 150 shares.

Personal Situation

Mr. Smith is 53 years old and his wife is 52. They have two children: a son, Bruce, aged 28, who is a dentist; and a daughter, Claire, aged 22, a music student at a conservatory in Rome. Bruce is married and has three children, aged 4, 3, and 1.

Neither Mr. Smith nor Mrs. Smith expects to receive a substantial inheritance from any family member in the future.

Wills and Other Information

Mr. Smith's will provides that, should Mrs. Smith survive him, his household and other tangible personal property are to go outright to her. The residue of his estate is to be divided as follows: one-half to Mrs. Smith outright; and the remaining one-half to be distributed outright in equal shares to Bruce and Claire or to their issue, per stirpes. All debts, administration expenses, and taxes are to be paid from the share of the estate going to Bruce and Claire. Mrs. Smith's will provides that her estate is to be divided equally and distributed outright to Bruce and Claire or to their issue, per stirpes.

Neither Mr. Smith nor Mrs. Smith has made any previous gifts.

Property Other Than Life Insurance

Mr. Smith owns the following property in his own name:

GBH Corporation stock	$5,250,000
Listed common stock	125,000

Marketable corporate bonds	90,000
Savings accounts	75,000
Household and other tangible personal property	70,000

Mrs. Smith owns the following property in her own name:

GBH Corporation stock	$500,000
Listed common stock	410,000
Checking account	12,000

Mr. Smith and Mrs. Smith own the following property as joint tenants with the right of survivorship:

Principal residence purchased in 1992. Entire purchase price contributed by Mr. Smith. No gift tax return was filed.	$450,000
Summer residence purchased in 1996. Entire purchase price contributed by Mrs. Smith from her separate funds. No gift tax return was filed.	320,000
Investment real estate purchased in 1997. Two-thirds of purchase price contributed by Mr. Smith, one-third by Mrs. Smith. No gift tax return was filed.	300,000

Life Insurance

Mr. Smith owns the following life insurance contracts on his own life:

Type	Age When Purchased	Beneficiary Designation	Settlement Arrangement	Face Amount
Life paid up at age 65	31	Mrs. Smith	Life income with no refund feature	$500,000
Ordinary life	35	Mrs. Smith	10-year fixed-period option with no right of withdrawal and with any remaining installments at Mrs. Smith's death to go to the Smith children in equal shares	250,000
Ordinary life	45	Mrs. Smith	Fixed-amount option with full right of withdrawal and with any remaining installments at Mrs. Smith's death to go to the Smith children in equal shares	150,000
Group life	38	Mr. Smith's estate	Lump-sum	100,000

Mrs. Smith owns the following life insurance contract on Mr. Smith's life:

Type	Age When Purchased	Beneficiary Designation	Settlement Arrangement	Face Amount
30-payment life	46	Bruce and Claire	Lump-sum equally	$200,000

ANSWERS TO MINI-CASE

The assets and their values that would be included in Mr. Smith's gross estate for federal estate tax purposes are as follows:

Property other than life insurance that Mr. Smith owns in his own name:

GBH Corporation stock	$5,250,000
Listed common stock	125,000
Marketable corporate bonds	90,000
Savings accounts	75,000
Household and other tangible personal property	70,000

These assets would be included in Mr. Smith's gross estate since they are owned solely by Mr. Smith. Property is included in a decedent's gross estate to the extent of his interest in the property at the time of his death (Sec. 2033).

Life insurance proceeds would be included in Mr. Smith's gross estate as follows:

Life paid up at age 65	$500,000
Ordinary life (purchased at age 35)	250,000
Ordinary life (purchased at age 45)	150,000
Group life	100,000

The proceeds of the foregoing would be included in Mr. Smith's gross estate since he was the owner of such policies at his death (that is, he possessed *incidents of ownership* in these policies at the time of death). In addition, the group life insurance is payable to Mr. Smith's estate. This would cause these proceeds to be included in his gross estate. In the absence of any problem concerning a gift within 3 years of death, the $200,000 proceeds payable under the 30-payment life policy that Mrs. Smith owns on

Mr. Smith's life would not be included in his gross estate for federal estate tax purposes since Mr. Smith possessed no incidents of ownership in this policy.

Properties that Mr. Smith and Mrs. Smith own as joint tenants with right of survivorship that would be included in Mr. Smith's gross estate are as follows:

Principal residence (50 percent)	$225,000
Summer residence (50 percent)	160,000
Investment real estate (50 percent)	150,000

The general principle applicable to joint property with right of survivorship held solely by spouses is that 50 percent of the date-of-death value is included in the estate of the first spouse to die. The percentage-of-contribution rule is irrelevant and does not apply to spousal joint tenancies with right of survivorship.

CHAPTER REVIEW

Key Terms and Concepts

annuity
joint and survivor annuity
reduction in value by mere lapse of
  time
lump-sum payments
percentage-of-contribution rule
basis
power of appointment
release

lapse
general power of appointment
special (limited) power of
  appointment
ascertainable standard
5-and-5 power
proceeds payable to or for the benefit
  of an estate

Chapter 12: Review Questions

1. When is the value of an annuity included in a decedent's gross estate? [LO 12.1]

2. Differentiate between annuities and amounts paid as life insurance proceeds. [LO 12.1]

3. What are the different types of annuities that are includible in a decedent's gross estate? [LO 12.1]

4. How will the following annuities be taxed under Sec. 2039 for federal estate tax purposes with respect to the decedent, Mr. Leonard?

   a.   Mr. Leonard purchases a life annuity for himself to end at his death.

   b.   Mr. Leonard purchases a life annuity for his wife 5 years before his death.

   c.   Mr. Leonard purchases a joint and survivor annuity for himself and his sister, Zelda, who furnished one-third of the purchase price. [LO 12.1]

5.   What is the general rule for determining the valuation of annuities in the gross estate? [LO 12.1]

6.   As of what date must annuities be valued for federal estate tax purposes? [LO 12.1]

7.   To what extent and under what conditions are benefits from a qualified retirement plan included in a decedent's gross estate? [LO 12.1]

8.   Explain the rule for estate taxation of jointly held property with right of survivorship when the only joint tenants are spouses. [LO 12.2]

9.   Ten years ago, Harry Hargrave and his son, Jimmy, acquired some real estate in Atlantic City for $50,000. Harry contributed 75 percent of the purchase price, and Jimmy contributed the remainder, using money that Harry gave him as a gift to pay for his share. They own the property as joint tenants with right of survivorship. The property was worth $200,000 at the beginning of this year when Harry died.

   a.   How much, if anything, is included in Harry's gross estate? Explain the reason for your answer.

   b.   Would your answer be different if Jimmy's contribution had been made with his own funds?

   c.   What would your answer be if the gift to Jimmy had been made 5 years earlier and Jimmy had used income generated by the gift to purchase his share of the jointly held property? [LO 12.2]

10. Tom and Mary Taylor acquired their personal residence 20 years ago for $150,000 and titled it jointly with right of survivorship. Tom furnished all the consideration for the property. Assume Mary dies this year when the house is worth $310,000.

   a.   How much of the value of the house, if any, is included in her gross estate for federal estate tax purposes?

   b.   Two years after Mary's death, Tom sold the property. Assuming that the house was worth $320,000 when he sold it, how much, if any, gain would he have? [LO 12.2]

11. What are three advantages for a married couple of owning property as joint tenants with right of survivorship? [LO 12.2]

12. What are two disadvantages for a married couple of owning property as joint tenants with right of survivorship? [LO 12.2]

13. How will property over which the decedent held a general power of appointment be treated for federal estate tax purposes? [LO 12.3]

14. Graham Green's wife gave him a general power of appointment in her will. Mrs. Green died 9 years ago. One year after Mrs. Green's death, Mr. Green exercised the power in favor of his two children. He died last year. The value of property subject to the power in the year he exercised it was $250,000. It had increased to $350,000 by the time of his death. How much, if anything, is includible in his gross estate? [LO 12.3]

15. If, at the time of his death, a person possesses a power of appointment that allows him to appoint property to himself, but that is limited by an ascertainable standard so that the property may be appointed to himself only for his health, education, support, or maintenance, how will the property subject to the power be treated for estate tax purposes? [LO 12.3]

16. a. What is the estate tax effect of a general power of appointment (created in 2018) that can be exercised only with the consent of another person who is not an adverse party?

   b. What if the power can be exercised only in conjunction with another person having a substantial adverse interest in the property?

   c. What is meant by an adverse interest in property?

   d. Describe the effects of the 5-and-5 power as a limitation on the general rule of estate tax inclusion for powers of appointment. [LO 12.3]

17. What is the effect of an individual's disclaiming a general power of appointment if she accepts the power and then tries to transfer it to another after 3 months? [LO 12.3]

18. Explain the general rule for estate taxation of life insurance proceeds. [LO 12.4]

19. In each of the following situations, indicate whether or not the life insurance proceeds on Edgar's life are includible in his estate at his death:

   a. a $25,000 policy owned by Edgar's wife and payable to Edgar's estate

   b. a $100,000 policy owned by Edgar and payable to Edgar's wife

   c. a $50,000 policy owned by Edgar's wife, Sue, and payable to herself as beneficiary. Sue possesses all ownership rights in the policy with the exception that Edgar may borrow the loan value of the policy without security

d. a $100,000 policy on Edgar's life transferred 12 years ago to an irrevocable trust for Edgar's children. The trustee is not authorized to use the proceeds to pay Edgar's estate tax. Edgar dies this year

e. a group term policy owned by Edgar and payable in equal shares to his wife and two daughters [LO 12.4]

20. Questions:

a. If the decedent owns life insurance on another party's life, will any part of the value of these policies be includible in the decedent's gross estate?

b. If so, how will it be valued? [LO 12.4]

21. How can life insurance proceeds payable on the death of the insured qualify for the marital deduction? [LO 12.4]

22. Garland Grant owned a life insurance policy on his life, with a face amount of $200,000. There were no policy loans outstanding. He made an absolute transfer of the policy to an irrevocable trust 2 years ago. He died this year. The named beneficiaries of the trust were his two nieces and two nephews in equal shares.

a. Are any or all of the proceeds includible in Mr. Grant's gross estate?

b. How will the proceeds be treated for estate tax purposes if he transfers the policy to the trust for the benefit of his nieces and nephews and dies 5 years afterward? [LO 12.4]

Chapter 12: Review Answers

1. The value of any annuity received by a beneficiary as a result of having survived the decedent is included in the decedent's gross estate. Payments that end at the decedent's death are not included in his or her estate.

2. Sec. 2039 of the Internal Revenue Code concerns the federal estate taxation of annuity products. With certain limited exceptions, a decedent's gross estate includes the present value of an annuity or other payment receivable by any beneficiary as a result of having survived the decedent. Included under this section are any agreements, commercial or private annuities, and employee retirement annuities (including all proceeds from qualified plans generally for decedents dying after December 31, 1984).

Specifically excluded from taxation under this Code section are all amounts paid "as insurance under policies on the life of the decedent." This is not to say that proceeds of life insurance will not be included in the decedent's gross estate. Proceeds of life insurance on the decedent's life are includible in the gross estate under another Code section (IRC Sec. 2042) if certain conditions exist. If a single contract contains or has contained both life insurance and annuity elements, the amount that is includible, if any, under this section is based on whether or not there was any insurance element in the contract at the moment of death.

3. Different types of annuities includible in a decedent's gross estate are

- an agreement under which the decedent was receiving or was entitled to receive payments before death and for the duration of his or her lifetime

- a joint and survivor annuity, under which the decedent was receiving payments before death with another person for their joint lives, with payments continuing to the survivor

- a contract between the decedent and his or her employer under which the decedent was receiving or entitled to receive an annuity after retirement for the duration of his or her life, with payments to designated beneficiaries upon the decedent's death

- a contract between the decedent and his or her employer that provided for an annuity to a designated surviving beneficiary if the decedent died before retirement

- an agreement under which the decedent was receiving or was entitled to receive annuity payments for a specified time period, with payments to continue to a named beneficiary if the decedent died before the time period expired

4. a. Since annuity payments cease with Mr. Leonard's death, the annuity will not be included in Mr. Leonard's gross estate, and there will be no estate tax.

   b. Mrs. Leonard's life annuity will not be included in Mr. Leonard's gross estate because he has no right to any of the annuity payments.

   c. To the extent that the survivor furnishes part of the purchase price of a joint and survivor annuity, that portion will not be included in the decedent's gross estate. Therefore, two-thirds of the value of Zelda's survivor annuity will be included in Mr. Leonard's gross estate.

5. Generally, an annuity is valued based on the cost of comparable contracts sold by the issuing company as of the date of the decedent's death.

6. The value of an annuity is determined on the primary annuitant's date of death.

7. Benefits under a qualified retirement plan are included in a decedent's gross estate unless one of the following exceptions applies:

    •   A non-employee-spouse's interest in plan proceeds arising solely because of the application of community-property laws is completely excluded from his or her estate if the non-employee-spouse predeceases the plan participant.

    •   If (1) plan proceeds were in pay status on December 31, 1984, and (2) prior to the enactment of the Deficit Reduction Act of 1984 (DRA 1984), the participant had irrevocably elected a beneficiary designation that would have qualified the plan proceeds for estate tax exclusion, the $100,000 exclusion amount is still available.

8. One-half of the value of jointly held property with right of survivorship held solely by husband and wife is included in the estate of the first spouse to die, regardless of which spouse furnished all or part of the consideration.

9. a. The entire value of the property ($200,000) will be includible in Harry's estate under the percentage-of-contribution (consideration-furnished) rule. Since the contribution furnished by Harry's son, Jimmy, was a gift from Harry, it is considered to have been furnished by Harry and not his son.

    b. Yes. In that case, only 75 percent of the value of the property ($150,000) would be included in Harry's estate.

    c. Only 75 percent of the value of the property ($150,000) would be included in Harry's estate in this event. Income generated by gifts of property made by the decedent can be applied as bona fide consideration by the recipient of the property to reduce the amount includible in the donor-decedent's estate.

10. a. One-half the value of the house ($155,000) will be included in Mary's gross estate for estate tax purposes. This results from the rule of 50 percent inclusion for the first tenant to die regardless of contribution for jointly held property with right of survivorship when only spouses are joint tenants.

    b. The amount of Tom's gain will vary according to the date the residence is sold. For home sales before May 7, 1997, Tom will have a capital gain of $90,000 determined as follows:

Original basis for half the property	$ 75,000
Plus stepped-up basis for half the property	155,000
Basis for property at time of sale	$230,000
Selling price	$320,000
Less basis	(230,000)
Capital gain	$ 90,000

For home sales after May 6, 1997 (the enactment date of the Taxpayer Relief Act of 1997), Tom will have no taxable gain. Up to $250,000 of gain is tax free for the sale of a personal residence by an individual. The exclusion is $500,000 for married couples who file joint income tax returns and if the sale occurs within two years of the death of a spouse.

11. Three advantages are as follows:

- Jointly held property with right of survivorship is generally nonprobate property, which means that it is not subject to estate administration.

- One-half of the property attributed to the decedent's interest and included in his or her estate is entitled to the full marital deduction. Thus, there is no estate tax liability because of the property's inclusion.

- Joint ownership often instills a feeling of comfort and harmony between spouses.

12. Two disadvantages are as follows:

- The surviving spouse gets full control of the disposition of the property, which may defeat a part of the estate plan of the first spouse to die.

- In a common-law state, only one-half of the property's value receives a step up in basis at the first joint tenant's death.

13. All property over which the decedent had a general power of appointment at the time of his or her death will be included in the decedent's gross estate for federal tax purposes.

14. Nothing will be includible in his gross estate. He exercised the power before his death and did not possess a general power of appointment or any rights over the property subject to it at his death. Property subject to a general power of appointment will be includible in a decedent's gross estate only if the decedent possessed the power at death. (Note that although none of the value of the property subject to the general power is included in Mr. Green's gross estate, Mr. Green's transfer of the property

during lifetime was gift taxable at the time of transfer because he held a general power of appointment.)

15. If the decedent's power to appoint property to himself or herself is limited to an ascertainable standard (such as for health, education, support, or maintenance), the power is generally considered to be a special power and not a general one, and the property is not included in his or her gross estate.

16. a. If a general power of appointment can be exercised only with the consent of another person who is not an adverse party, a fractional part of the property (determined by dividing the value of the property by the number of people in whose favor the power could be exercised) is included in the donee's estate.

    b. A power that can be exercised only with a person who has a substantial adverse interest in the property is not treated as a general power, and the property is not includible in the donee's estate.

    c. An adverse interest is one that, if the power is exercised, would not be in favor of the party holding the interest.

    d. If the decedent is given what is otherwise a general power of appointment, property is not included in his or her estate if the power is limited to the 5-and-5 rule. This rule restricts the decedent's noncumulative right to withdraw the greater of $5,000 or 5 percent of the aggregate value of the property each year. When the decedent dies, only the amount that the decedent could have appointed in his or her favor that year is includible in his or her estate.

17. For federal estate tax purposes, if an individual accepts a general power and disclaims it 3 months later, the disclaimer is ineffective. The value of the property subject to the power will be treated as a lifetime gift made by this individual to another. Once accepted, the property subject to the general power of appointment is within her control. This gives her ownership rights. Any subsequent transfer will be considered a gift potentially subject to gift tax.

18. In general, life insurance proceeds are included in the decedent's gross estate if one of the following occurs:

    - The decedent possessed incidents of ownership in the policy.

    - The proceeds are receivable by the estate.

    - The proceeds are receivable by another for the benefit of the estate.

19. a. Yes. The policy is payable to the decedent's estate.

    b. Yes. The decedent owned the policy.

    c. Yes. The right to borrow the loan value of the policy without security is an incident of ownership sufficient to require inclusion of the proceeds.

    d. No. The insurance was transferred to the trust more than 3 years before Edgar's death, and the trustee is not legally obligated to pay estate taxes from the proceeds.

e. Yes. The decedent owned the policy.

20. a. Yes. The value of life insurance policies the decedent owns on the life of another is included in the decedent's estate as property owned at death.

    b. If the policy is new, the gross premium paid is the value of the policy included in the decedent's estate. If the policy is paid up or a single-premium policy, the value is its replacement cost. If it is a premium-paying whole life policy, the value is determined by adding any unearned portion of the last premium to the interpolated terminal reserve. If it is a term life policy, the value is the unused premium.

21. Life insurance proceeds payable to the spouse or the spouse's estate in a lump sum qualify for the marital deduction only if the spouse survives the decedent by up to 6 months. If proceeds are left at the interest option for the life of the surviving spouse, they qualify for the marital deduction if they are payable to the spouse's estate or to persons to whom he or she appoints the proceeds at death. If the spouse does not exercise this power of appointment, proceeds may still qualify if they are received by named contingent beneficiaries as a result of the spouse's failure to appoint them.

    If proceeds are to be paid in installments or if there is a refund feature, they qualify for the marital deduction if payments following the surviving spouse's death are made to the beneficiaries the spouse designated to receive remaining payments. Proceeds also qualify if the spouse receives all the interest for life and the proceeds pass to a trust or named beneficiary at the spouse's death under the qualified terminable interest rules.

22. a. The full value of the proceeds will be includible in Mr. Grant's estate because the transfer was made within 3 years of his death.

    b. As long as Mr. Grant retained no incidents of ownership in the policy, the proceeds will not be included in his estate because the transfer was not made within 3 years of his death.

Chapter 13:

Deductions from the Gross Estate

Learning Objectives

An understanding of the material in this chapter should enable the student to do the following:

LO 13.1   Describe the deductions allowable from the gross estate.

LO 13.2   Explain any decisions that need to be made to minimize taxes.

THE TAXABLE ESTATE

adjusted gross estate

After the gross estate is determined, the next step in calculating the taxable estate is to determine the **adjusted gross estate**.

LO 13.1   Describe the deductions allowable from the gross estate.

Calculation of the Taxable Estate

1. Determine the gross estate

2. Determine the adjusted gross estate by deducting the following:[1]

    *   funeral expenses

    *   administration expenses attributable to property subject to claims against the estate

    *   claims against the estate

    *   unpaid mortgages

    *   other administration expenses

    *   losses

---

1.   Editor's Note: The adjusted gross estate calculation is not a required calculation on Form 706 (federal estate tax return). However, this calculation is required for a variety of other reasons: for example, to determine if a Sec. 303 redemption is permissible, where a formula marital deduction provision is used (for decedents who never amended the marital provisions since the enactment of the unlimited marital deduction), and where a closely held business is part of the gross estate; and to help ascertain whether installment payments of federal estate taxes are possible under Sec. 6166.

The deductions above are described in this chapter. It should be noted that, as an alternative, some of these items may be deducted from other tax returns that must be filed (for example, the decedent's last income tax return or the income tax return for the estate). However, if a certain deduction is taken on the income tax return, that same deduction cannot also be taken on the estate tax return (except as noted later under the heading "Taxes"). It is also important to remember that this chapter covers primarily the federal laws regarding deductions. While most of the time state estate deduction laws will be similar, they might vary a bit as to what can be deducted.

This chapter concludes with a discussion of the factors involved in determining where it might be best to take the deductions.

taxable estate

All the previous are allowable deductions from the gross estate to arrive at the *adjusted gross estate*. Three additional deductions are then permitted—the marital deduction, the charitable deduction, and the state death tax deduction (after 2004)—to arrive at the **taxable estate**. The marital and charitable deductions are treated in the next two chapters. The state death tax deduction is discussed in a later chapter.

Allowable Deductions from Gross Estate
- funeral expenses (reasonable amount)
- administration expenses (court costs, attorney/executor fees)
- claims against estate (decedent's debts; certain taxes, not including federal or state death taxes)
- unpaid mortgages
- other estate administration expenses
- theft/casualty losses

EXPENSES

Funeral Expenses

Certain expenditures, such as funeral expenses limited to a reasonable amount, are deductible for estate tax purposes only. Such expenses include costs associated with interment, a burial lot or vault, a grave marker or monument, the perpetual care of the grave site, and transportation of the body to the place of burial. The traveling costs of relatives are generally not an allowable deduction. Funeral expenses need to be reasonable and must be well-documented.

Expenses of Administering Certain Estate Property

estate administration expenses

The costs of administering property that is included in the decedent's gross estate are generally deductible from either the estate tax return (Form 706) or the estate's income tax return (Form 1041). Deductible items include expenses incurred in the collection and preservation of probate assets, the payment of estate debts, and the distribution of probate assets to estate beneficiaries. These **estate administration expenses** include court costs, executor's commissions, attorney fees, accounting fees, and miscellaneous costs, such as appraisers' fees, court costs, the expenses incurred on the sale of estate property if the sale is necessary to: pay the decedent's debts, expense of administration, estate taxes, or to preserve the estate, effect asset distribution, or was necessary to otherwise settle the estate. Selling expenses include brokerage fees among other expenses directly related to the sale of the property. Any expenses that were incurred for the benefit of the heirs individually are not deductible. The key question is whether the expenditure was essential to the proper settlement of the estate. For community-property states, the extent to which administration costs and claims are allowable deductions depends on the particular community state's law. Expenses and debts of community property are 50 percent deductible.

Medical Expenses

Medical expenses relating to the decedent's last illness may be deducted on either the estate tax return or the decedent's last income tax return (but in the latter case only if the estate files a statement waiving the right to an estate tax deduction).

Claims Against Estate

All claims against the estate, including any bona fide debts that the decedent was validly obligated to pay while alive plus interest accrued to the date of death, are deductible only from the gross estate. These obligations must be based on a promise or agreement. They are deductible only to the extent that they are based on adequate and full consideration in money or money's worth, and represent personal obligations of the decedent existing at the time of death, whether or not they have matured. Only claims enforceable against the decedent's estate may be deducted. The interest on the indebtedness is deductible, but is limited to the amount accrued to the date of death, although the executor may choose the alternate valuation date. Also, liabilities imposed by law or arising out of torts are deductible. If the decedent made a pledge or subscription that is evidenced by a promissory note or other proof, it may be deductible by the estate only to the extent that the liability contracted for was both bona fide and based on adequate consideration in cash or other property.

Taxes

Certain taxes are deductible on the estate tax return as claims against the estate and not as administration expenses. These include income taxes on income reported by the decedent (no deduction is allowed on income reported by the decedent's estate), unpaid gift taxes, and real property taxes accrued prior to the date of death as long as the property taxes are enforceable obligations at the time of the decedent's death. Federal income taxes owed to the date of death are deductible only on the federal estate tax return. After 2004, state death taxes are also a permissible deduction on the federal estate tax return, but death taxes paid to a city are not deductible. State, local, or foreign income taxes, as well as property taxes, may be deducted on either the federal estate tax return or the federal estate income tax return. Real estate taxes not accrued before death, as well as local and foreign income taxes on estate income, are deductible on the income tax return of the estate. Any federal income taxes on estate income are not deductible either on the estate tax return or for income tax purposes. There is, however, an exception to the general rule denying a double deduction: taxes, interest, and business expenses accrued at the date of the decedent's death that are attributable to income in respect of a decedent are deductible on both the decedent's final income tax return and also the estate tax return as administration expenses.

Mortgage Debt

A deduction is also allowed from the gross estate for the full unpaid balance of a mortgage or other indebtedness, including interest accrued to the date of death, if the following two conditions are met: (1) the full value of property that is not reduced by the mortgage amount or indebtedness must be included in the value of the gross estate; and (2) the decedent's estate must be liable for the amount of the mortgage or indebtedness.

OTHER ADMINISTRATION EXPENSES

Deductions allowed in this category refer to expenses in administering property not subject to claims. *Property that is not subject to claims* usually refers to the nonprobate estate. Jointly held property and life insurance are typical nonprobate assets. Expenses for administering nonprobate assets included in the gross estate are deductible, provided that the expense is paid before the time for filing the federal estate tax return.

Casualty and Theft Losses

casualty losses

theft losses

Casualty losses and **theft losses** are deductible expenses that are incurred during the estate settlement period but only to the extent that these losses are not compensated by insurance. Casualty and theft losses are deductible if the loss arose from fire, flood, storm, shipwreck, or other casualty or theft. The loss must have occurred during the estate settlement process and before the estate was closed. The loss is reduced to the extent that restitution was made through insurance or other compensation to offset the loss. Such a casualty loss to property permits a deduction from the gross estate for either estate tax or estate income tax purposes. However, the estate may not claim the same deduction on both returns.

LO 13.2   **Explain any decisions that need to be made to minimize taxes.**

DEDUCTION DECISIONS THAT MINIMIZE TAXES

Deductions from Either Estate Tax Return or Income Tax Return

As previously mentioned, the executor has discretion regarding the deduction of certain items on the federal estate tax return or on income tax returns. This choice does not apply to all debts and expenses. Some expenses are allowable on the federal estate tax return only. Some expenses may be allowed on either the estate tax return or the income tax return.

The primary reason for concern about where to take a deduction is the minimization of taxes. Before any administration expenses or casualty losses may be deducted for income tax purposes, the executor must file a timely statement waiving the right to claim these expenses on the decedent's federal estate tax return. Deductions for administration expenses and the decedent's medical expenses are not allowed from the income of either the estate or the beneficiary for income tax purposes. For most other expenses, the executor may file a waiver for a portion of the deductible items while the rest are allowed for estate tax purposes. Once the estate tax deduction waiver is filed, it cannot be revoked. The waiver should be filed with the income tax return in the year that the expenses are taken as deductions for income tax purposes. This statement does not apply to deductible expenses that relate to income in respect of a decedent (IRD).

Splitting Deductions Between Returns

Sometimes the best result is obtained by taking certain deductions on the estate tax return and other deductions on the income tax return. The regulations permit splitting deductions between the income and estate tax returns. This allows the executor to deduct some administrative expenses on the estate tax return and other allowable expenses on the estate income tax return. The Tax Cuts and Jobs Act of 2017 eliminated the deduction for many miscellaneous income tax deductions. Because of the change, the executor's only option may be to deduct these expenses on the estate tax return.

In situations where distributions are made to beneficiaries, the relative estate and income tax brackets of the beneficiaries must be examined. If the beneficiary is in a low-income tax bracket, tax savings may be achieved by splitting the deduction between the beneficiary's income and the estate's income. Also, proper timing of distributions may allow additional tax savings, particularly if the estate has chosen a fiscal year different from the taxable year of the beneficiary.

When the income tax rate is lower than the relevant estate tax rate (after the basic credit amount is applied), the "optional" deductions are generally more valuable on the estate tax return. However, many estates are not taxable due to the marital deduction and basic credit amount. In these cases, the deductions may be more useful on the estate's *income tax* return.

The executor often has to wait and see before making the appropriate choice. Quite often, the executor will deduct the expenses on both returns and later amend one return by removing the deduction after this choice is finalized.

Executor Fees as Either Bequest or Income

executor fees

Executors who are also named beneficiaries of the decedent may consider the desirability of waiving their **executor fees**, since they receive a bequest that is income tax free. All executors are entitled to reasonable compensation for their services. If an executor's commission is deductible on the federal estate tax return, it is then received as taxable income whether or not the executor is a beneficiary of the estate. However, if the commission or devise is considered a bequest, it is not deductible by the estate for either estate or income tax purposes. Executors must act promptly to waive any commissions if they find that more tax is saved by receiving the bequest income tax free than is saved by characterizing the executor's commission as a deductible expense of the estate. The critical factor to evaluate is whether greater tax savings results from a deduction on the federal estate tax return when the additional income tax incurred by the executor is taken into consideration. The executor need not turn down reasonable compensation because it will benefit the other heirs.

CHAPTER REVIEW

Key Terms and Concepts

adjusted gross estate

taxable estate

estate administration expenses

casualty losses

theft losses

executor fees

Chapter 13: Review Questions

1. What are the basic categories of deductions allowable from a decedent's gross estate to determine the adjusted gross estate? [LO 13.1]

2. What taxes are deductible on a decedent's federal estate tax return? [LO 13.1]

3. Melvin Marvel died leaving an $800,000 apartment complex as well as other items. He was not married and was the sole owner of the apartment complex. The apartment complex has a $300,000 mortgage on it, and the full value of $800,000 is included in his estate. Is the estate entitled to a deduction for the mortgage? Explain. [LO 13.1]

4. Simon Simple's estate included a yacht valued at $150,000 on the federal estate tax return. During the period of estate administration, it was severely damaged by fire. It cost $80,000 to repair the yacht. The estate received $55,000 under its insurance claim.

    a. State what amount, if any, the estate may deduct on the decedent's estate tax return.

    b. Would it be possible to deduct this or some other amount as a casualty loss on the decedent's final income tax return instead? [LO 13.1]

5. If an executor is also a beneficiary of the estate, when would it be wise for the executor to waive the fee? [LO 13.2]

Chapter 13: Review Answers

1. After the gross estate is determined, the next step in calculating the taxable estate is to determine the adjusted gross estate by deducting the following:

   - funeral expenses

   - administration expenses attributable to property subject to claims against the estate

   - claims against the estate

   - unpaid mortgages

   - other administration expenses

   - losses

2. Certain taxes are deductible on the estate tax return as claims against the estate. These include income taxes, unpaid gift taxes, and real property taxes accrued to the date of death. Federal income taxes owed to the date of death are deductible only on the federal estate tax return. However, state, local, or foreign income taxes, as well as property taxes, may be deducted on either the federal estate tax return or the federal estate income tax return. Real estate taxes not accrued before death, as well as local and foreign income taxes on estate income, are deductible on the income tax return of the estate. Any federal income taxes on estate income are not deductible either on the estate tax return or for income tax purposes.

3. A mortgage debt will be allowed as a deduction for federal estate tax purposes if the following two conditions are met: (1) the full value of the property unreduced by the mortgage amount or indebtedness must be included in the value of the gross estate; and (2) the decedent's estate must be liable for the amount of the indebtedness. Here the two foregoing conditions have been met. Therefore, a deduction of $300,000 is permitted for federal estate tax purposes.

4. a. The estate may deduct $25,000 as a casualty loss calculated as follows:

Cost of repair	$80,000
Less insurance	(55,000)
Loss	$25,000

   b. A casualty loss accruing during estate settlement may be deducted either from the federal estate tax return or the estate's income tax return, but not from the decedent's final income tax return.

5. Executors who are also named beneficiaries of the decedent may consider the desirability of waiving their executor fees, since they receive a bequest that is income tax free. If an executor's commission is deductible on the federal estate tax return, it is then received as taxable income whether or not the executor is a beneficiary of the estate. However, if the commission or devise is considered a bequest, it is not deductible by the estate for either estate or income tax purposes. Executors must act promptly to waive any commissions if they find that more tax is saved by receiving the bequest income tax free than is saved by characterizing the executor's commission as a deductible expense of the estate. The critical factor to evaluate is whether greater tax savings results from a deduction on the federal estate tax return when the additional income tax incurred by the executor is taken into consideration.

Chapter 14:
The Marital Deduction

Learning Objectives

An understanding of the material in this chapter should enable the student to do the following:

LO 14.1   **Describe the purpose behind the creation of an unlimited marital deduction, and explain what is meant by the net value of a qualifying interest passing to a surviving spouse.**

LO 14. 2   **Explain the requirements that must be met before property qualifies for the marital deduction.**

LO 14. 3   **Describe how either an overqualification or an underqualification may affect federal estate tax liability, and explain how formulas can be used to minimize the tax.**

LO 14. 4   **Describe the advantages and disadvantages of different forms of marital bequests, and explain the factors that should be considered in deciding to what extent the marital deduction should be used.**

LO 14.1   **Describe the purpose behind the creation of an unlimited marital deduction, and explain what is meant by the net value of a qualifying interest passing to a surviving spouse.**

In determining the taxable estate, property included in a decedent's gross estate for federal estate tax purposes that passes (or has passed) to a surviving spouse may qualify for a deduction from the adjusted gross estate. No deduction is more important to the typical married individual's estate than the estate tax marital deduction. It is often possible, through judicious use of this deduction, to reduce or eliminate the estate tax on the death of the first spouse. But if used improperly, the marital-deduction transfer can result in an overall combined estate tax on the total estates of both spouses that is far greater than if no transfer to a surviving spouse was made.

For these reasons, and because the rules in the Internal Revenue Code for qualifying for the marital deduction are strictly construed, a member of the estate planning team must have a thorough knowledge of the marital-deduction requirements.

BACKGROUND

Married residents of nine states (Arizona, California, Idaho, Louisiana, Nevada, New Mexico, Texas, Washington, and Wisconsin) operate under a community-property system. Therefore, all property acquired (other than by gift, devise, bequest, or inheritance) by a married couple during marriage while living in one of these states belongs to the *community*; that is, each spouse automatically and from the inception of ownership owns one-half of the property. Upon death, a decedent can dispose of only his or her share of the community property by will or trust. Because of this state property law concept, only one-half of the community property is includible in the estate of whichever spouse dies first.

EXAMPLE

Assume Herb and his wife, Roz, live in California. Herb's salary is large enough to allow him to save $50,000 a year. One-half of that, $25,000, is deemed to be Roz's property. Therefore, only one-half of the $50,000 is includible in Herb's estate if he dies first. Likewise, if Roz dies first, $25,000 is includible in her estate even though Herb earned the entire $50,000.

This tax advantage has been reflected in the income and gift taxation of community-property residents as well as in the estate taxation. As a result, residents of common-law states grew indignant, recognizing that their community-property neighbors were taxed more favorably under a state property law system that treated half of the earnings of either spouse as automatically belonging to the other.

Some traditionally common-law states (such as Pennsylvania, Michigan, Hawaii, and Nebraska) sought to achieve tax parity by converting to what was, in effect, a community-property system. Great interstate resentment and confusion about the disparities that developed prompted Congress to aim for tax parity by making a federal estate tax marital deduction available to married residents of common-law states.

Therefore, the Internal Revenue Code now allows a deduction for the value of any qualifying property interests includible in the decedent's gross estate that pass from the decedent to the surviving spouse.

Amount of Marital Deduction

Today, a federal estate-tax-free interspousal transfer is allowed either during lifetime or at death. In other words, the law now allows a deduction for unlimited assets passing from one spouse to another. Even residents of community-property states can take advantage of this unlimited marital deduction, because community property now qualifies for the marital deduction to the extent that it is includible in the decedent spouse's estate. Conceivably, this means that a decedent-spouse could leave his or her entire multimillion dollar estate to the surviving spouse and not pay any federal estate tax. However, the deduction cannot exceed the net value of the *qualifying interests* (defined below) passing to the surviving spouse.

LO 14. 2   **Explain the requirements that must be met before property qualifies for the marital deduction.**

Qualifications on Amount of Marital Deduction

The estate tax marital deduction is allowed on the net value of a qualifying interest passing to a decedent's surviving spouse. Therefore, it is necessary to define the term *net value.*

Net value refers to the gross estate tax value of a property interest—that is, its date-of-death value, or if applicable, its value as of the alternate valuation date, minus any charges against that interest.

Generally, this means that the gross value of a property interest passing to the surviving spouse must be reduced by (1) taxes payable out of the interest, (2) mortgages or liens against the interest, and (3) administration expenses payable out of the interest.

Taxes payable out of the interest include any federal estate tax or state death tax. The word payable is important because, in order to reduce the marital deduction, it is not necessary that the taxes actually be paid out of the marital share—only that they be *payable*.

> **EXAMPLE**
>
> Carlos left a taxable estate valued at $30 million when he died in 2019. His will directs that his two children are to receive $7.5 million each and the residue to his wife. Additionally the will provides for all estate taxes to be paid from the residuary estate. The tax on the transfer to his wife reduces her share of the estate. The reduced marital share in turn reduces the marital deduction, which then causes an increased estate tax. Assume for purposes of this problem that the tax on the estate is $2,000,000 (40% of $4 million), the wife's share constituting the marital deduction amount is only $13,400,000 ($15 million less $1,600,000 million).

If the surviving spouse takes an interest subject to a mortgage or a lien, the gross value of the interest is reduced by the amount of that obligation. For instance (ignore the annual exclusion), if Lara left her husband a $100,000 boat on which she owed $20,000, only $80,000 of qualifying property would pass. However, if Lara's will (or state law) required the debt to be discharged before the title to the boat was transferred to her husband, the gross value of the boat would be used in the marital-deduction computation; the amount of the lien would not reduce the marital deduction.

When administration expenses are chargeable (under a decedent's will or under state law) against the surviving spouse's share of the estate, the amount of those expenses reduces the allowable marital deduction.

These reductions are usually avoided by requiring in the decedent's will that expenses, debts, and taxes be paid out of the share of the estate passing to beneficiaries other than the spouse.

TRANSFERS QUALIFYING FOR MARITAL DEDUCTION

A number of very strictly construed technical requirements must be met before property qualifies for the marital deduction. There also are certain qualifications and limitations that must be considered:

- the citizenship requirement for the surviving spouse
- the requirement that property be included
- the requirement that property must pass or have passed
- the marital-status requirement
- the terminable interest rule

Citizenship Requirement for Surviving Spouse

The marital deduction is generally allowed only for transfers to a spouse who is, at the date of the decedent's death, a U.S. citizen. The marital deduction can be preserved if the surviving spouse becomes a citizen before the decedent's estate tax return is filed.

Transfers to a Surviving Resident-alien Spouse

resident alien

While the marital deduction provides an opportunity for a married couple to avoid federal estate taxes at the death of the first spouse, it is not available for property passing to a surviving resident-alien spouse. A **resident alien** is one who resides in the Unites States but is not a U.S. citizen.

This limitation on the use of the marital deduction reflects Congress's concern that if a surviving resident-alien spouse were to receive marital assets at the death of the citizen spouse, the survivor could return to his or her home country with such assets. Because the United States does not have jurisdiction to tax a nonresident alien for property located outside of the country, the assets transferred to the surviving resident-alien spouse could completely escape federal estate and gift taxation. This occurrence would be inconsistent with the underlying concept of the marital deduction—that is, that the wealth accumulated by a married couple will, to the extent it is unconsumed, be subject to transfer tax at the second spouse's death. The marital deduction is intended only to provide a deferral mechanism. If, however, the resident-alien spouse is the first spouse to die and property is transferred in a qualifying manner to the surviving citizen spouse, the marital deduction is allowed. In this case, transfer taxes can be imposed whenever the surviving U.S. citizen spouse transfers property.

Because the general rule is that transfers to a resident-alien spouse will not qualify for the unlimited federal estate or gift tax marital deduction, there is a special concern for marriages that include a resident-alien spouse. As previously mentioned, the transfer taxes facing such marriages often depend on which spouse survives. If the survivor is the resident alien, a substantial first-death estate tax may be payable. Fortunately, there are some exceptions to this harsh rule.

The Surviving Spouse Obtains Citizenship

Transfers to a surviving resident-alien spouse are eligible for the marital deduction if (1) the surviving spouse becomes a U.S. citizen before the decedent spouse's estate tax return is filed, and (2) the surviving spouse remains a U.S. resident after the death of the citizen spouse.

Qualified Domestic Trust (QDOT)

qualified domestic trust (QDOT)

If the surviving resident-alien spouse does not obtain U.S. citizenship, a **qualified domestic trust (QDOT)** can be used to transfer assets to a surviving resident-alien spouse while preserving the marital deduction for such transfer.

Congress created an exception for transfers to a qualified domestic trust to alleviate some of the harsh estate tax implications associated with the denial of the marital deduction for transfers to a resident-alien spouse. A QDOT is a unique transfer vehicle for marital-deduction transfers to surviving resident-alien spouses. Unfortunately, the QDOT rules also include a new type of transfer tax. Although the QDOT appears to provide all the usual tax benefits of the marital deduction, it has several disadvantages not applicable to transfers between citizen spouses. It is beyond the scope of this chapter to explore in depth the aspects of the marital deduction and marriages involving resident-alien spouses. The complex nature of this area requires the advice of an experienced estate planner.

Requirement That Property Be Included

A transfer does not qualify for the marital deduction unless the property interest is included in the decedent's gross estate for federal estate tax purposes. For example, no marital deduction is allowed when a wife purchases a life insurance policy on the life of her husband with her own funds and is the owner and beneficiary of such a policy. Because the proceeds of the policy are not includible in the husband's gross estate in the first place, they do not qualify for a marital deduction. However, if for any reason the life insurance proceeds are includible in the decedent's gross estate, they can qualify for the marital deduction if passing to the surviving spouse.

Requirement That Property Must Pass or Have Passed

The *pass-or-have-passed requirement* has two implications:

- An interest owned by the decedent must pass from the decedent to a surviving spouse; that is, the surviving spouse must receive the property by means of a transfer from the decedent, as opposed to a transfer from someone else.
- The surviving spouse must receive the interest as beneficial owner rather than as trustee or agent for someone else.

An interest can be transferred from the decedent to a surviving spouse in a number of ways that qualify for the marital deduction. These include transfers from the decedent:

- **by will, intestacy, or similar law.**
- **by election against the will.** In many states, a decedent cannot disinherit a surviving spouse because the survivor can elect to receive the amount that would have been received had the decedent died intestate—that is, without a will. The amount received as a result of the election is *property passing*.
- **by transfer to a spouse made by the decedent during lifetime and for some reason includible in the estate** (for example, a transfer the decedent made when a life estate was retained).
- **in the form of life insurance death proceeds.** This assumes the decedent retained incidents of ownership in the policy.
- **by survivorship** (for example, when the surviving spouse was a joint tenant with rights of survivorship). Note that, in this case, the marital deduction is allowed only to the extent the jointly held property is includible in the decedent's estate for federal estate tax purposes. Because only 50 percent of all spouse-owned jointly held property

(that is, spousal joint tenancies created after December 31, 1976) is includible, only the value of that portion is counted in computing the actual marital deduction even though the survivor receives title to the entire property.

- **by power of appointment.** For example, the surviving spouse could have been the appointee of a general power that the decedent, as donee, exercised, or a *taker in default* when the decedent failed to exercise a general power.

If the decedent leaves a bequest to a surviving spouse and the spouse *disclaims* (in other words, states in a timely disclaimer, "I renounce all my rights to the property"), the interest disclaimed is treated as if it never passed to the surviving spouse. Therefore, it does not qualify. But, if the bequest was first accepted by the surviving spouse and then transferred to a child, the property is considered to have passed from the decedent to the surviving spouse. (The spouse may be subject to gift tax on the value of the transfer to the child.)

EXAMPLE

Frank named his wife, Mary Jo, primary beneficiary of a $100,000 life insurance policy he owned on his life. He named his daughter, Julia, secondary beneficiary. At Frank's death, Mary Jo could have taken the proceeds in a lump sum. Instead she directed the insurance company to hold the proceeds at interest. In this case, an includible interest (the $100,000 in proceeds) is considered to have passed from the decedent to the surviving spouse. Her disposal of the property after that point does not affect the marital deduction. But if Mary Jo had made a timely disclaimer, she would have been treated as if she had never received the proceeds, and therefore no marital deduction would have been allowed.

There is another way a disclaimer can affect the marital deduction. Sometimes a decedent's will leaves the entire estate to a son or daughter. If the child makes a timely disclaimer, the result is the same as if no interest had ever passed to the child. If the child's refusal to accept the property causes all or a portion of it to pass to the surviving spouse, it qualifies as property passing from the decedent to a surviving spouse. In other words, if the effect of a disclaimer by a third party is to increase the amount of property passing from the decedent to the surviving spouse, the result may be to increase the marital deduction.

There is another implication to the pass-or-have-passed requirement. Regardless of whether the surviving spouse receives property outright or in trust for his or her benefit, the interest must be as an equitable owner in order to qualify; if the spouse is merely made a trustee for somebody else or is bound by agreement to transfer the property to another person, it is not considered to pass to the surviving spouse. So a bequest in a will providing that "my land in Wildwood is to go to my wife, Lynne, for the benefit of my invalid son, Marvin" does not qualify.

Types of Marital Deduction Transfers

Transferred by

- intestacy
  - will
  - election against the will
  - contract (Sec. 2042 life insurance inclusion)
  - survivorship (decedent's joint tenancy interest)
  - lifetime spousal transfers (Secs. 2036, 2037, and 2038 retained interests/inclusion)
  - successful will contest
  - qualified disclaimer

Marital Status Requirement

Appropriate marital status is an essential element. The decedent must have been (1) married at the date of death and (2) survived by the spouse receiving the property in question. The definition of the term *marital status* for purposes of the marital deduction has been expanded by a recent Supreme Court ruling. In June of 2013, the Supreme Court struck down Section 3 of the Defense of Marriage Act (DOMA) finding that this provision violates the Fifth Amendment's equal protection clause of the Constitution. This decision allows the marital deduction at the federal level for same-sex couples who were married in states recognizing same-sex marriage. Following a 2015 decision by the U.S. Supreme Court, same-sex marriage is both legal and recognized in all fifty states, and the tax issues at both the state and federal level that were distinct for same-sex couples are now moot.

Obviously, the words *surviving* and *spouse* present difficult questions in two situations: (1) when there has been a divorce or separation; and (2) when the decedent's and spouse's order of deaths cannot be established by proof.

The status of the surviving spouse is determined as of the date of a decedent's death. A legal separation or interlocutory (temporary and not yet final) decree of divorce that has not ended the marital relationship by the date of the decedent's death does not change the surviving spouse's status. So, a bequest to a spouse when the decedent is legally separated still qualifies for the federal estate tax marital deduction.

However, if, for example, a property interest passes from the decedent to a former wife who is not married to him at the date of his death, even though she may survive him, the interest does not pass to a surviving spouse.

If the decedent transferred property to someone who at the time of the transfer was not a spouse but who was a spouse on the date of death, the transfer is considered made to a surviving spouse. If for any reason that transfer must be included in the decedent's estate, it will qualify for the marital deduction. For instance, if Mary gives IBM stock to Pat but retains the right to the dividends that it produces, the stock is includible in her estate. If Mary has married Pat (either before or after the gift) and they are still married at the time of Mary's death, a marital deduction is allowed with respect to the stock.

The survivorship requirement is generally not difficult to meet in most cases. However, problems can occur when deaths result from a common accident, and the order of deaths cannot be determined.

At the time an estate is planned, a conflict of interest can develop. On the one hand, the marital deduction may be desirable only if it is likely that the surviving spouse will be able to use and enjoy the marital property for a relatively long period of time. If the surviving spouse dies immediately or shortly after receiving the marital share, that property (1) will be subject to a second probate and its consequent costs, (2) may be subject to federal estate taxation, and (3) will be subject to a second round of state inheritance tax in states that have neither a marital deduction nor a credit for previously paid taxes. Furthermore, the original decedent's property may pass to his or her spouse's heirs—a result the decedent may not have desired and would have taken steps to prevent had it been known that his or her spouse would live only a short period of time.

On the other hand, there are situations in which the use of the marital deduction makes good planning sense, even if the surviving spouse will probably not enjoy the property for long. One such case is when the original decedent has a large estate and the spouse has a small estate. The present value of the tax dollars saved through the use of the marital deduction at the first death, together with the availability of a second estate tax basic credit amount, can be a sizable advantage.

Will the marital deduction be allowed if there is no evidence as to the order of deaths? The regulations provide that when it is impossible to ascertain which spouse died first, any presumption—whether established by the decedent in a will, by state law, or otherwise—will be recognized. This means that, to the extent the presumption results in the inclusion of a bequest in the gross estate of the spouse deemed to have survived, a marital deduction is allowed.

This presumption is generally made in a will or life insurance settlement option in the form of a *presumption-of-survivorship* clause. A typical clause might read as follows:

> *In the event my wife and I die under such circumstances that there is no sufficient evidence to establish who survived the other, I hereby declare that my wife shall be deemed to have survived me, and this will and all its provisions shall be construed upon that assumption and basis.*

The importance of a presumption-of-survivorship clause in a decedent's will or life insurance settlement should not be underestimated. It can be an especially worthwhile tax-savings device when the spouse and/or nonmarital beneficiaries are less wealthy than the testator. This is because the clause makes optimal use of the marital deduction and multiple basic credit amounts possible. Assume that for 2019 a husband dies owning property in his own name worth $14,800,000 and the wife's assets are nominal. The husband leaves his entire estate to his wife. He has made no taxable lifetime gifts. If the wife either actually survives or, because of a presumption clause in a will or life insurance settlement option, is deemed to survive, the difference can be sizable, as the illustrations below show. (Assume funeral and administrative expenses of $40,000 as well as debts and taxes of $90,000.)

If the marital deduction is lost, the difference in cost in this hypothetical example (computed before credits) is $5,813,800, the difference between the tentative tax when no marital deduction is allowable ($5,813,800 [2019]) and the tentative tax if the marital deduction is obtained ($0).

<u>With the Marital Deduction</u>

Gross estate		$14,800,000
Funeral and administration costs	40,000	
Debts and taxes	<u>90,000</u>	
		<u>(130,000)</u>
Adjusted gross estate		14,670,000
Marital deduction		14,670,000
Taxable estate		$0
Adjusted taxable gifts		—
Tentative tax base		$0
Tentative tax		$0

<u>Without the Marital Deduction</u>

Gross estate		$14,800,000
Funeral and administration costs	40,000	
Debts and taxes	<u>90,000</u>	

	(130,000)
Adjusted gross estate	14,670,000
Marital deduction	<u>0</u>
Taxable estate	14,670,000
Adjusted taxable gifts	—
Tentative tax base	<u>14,670,000</u>
Tentative tax (2019)	<u>$5,813,800</u>

What happens if there is a common disaster in which both spouses die and no presumption-of-survivorship clause has been inserted in a will or life insurance settlement option? As mentioned above, state laws will govern.

Practically, all states have adopted the Uniform Simultaneous Death Act (USDA). This act provides that, if the order of the spouses' deaths cannot be determined and there is no presumption-of-survivorship clause in the will and/or life insurance contract, each decedent's estate will be distributed as though he or she was the survivor. In other words, in the probate of the husband's will, it will be assumed that he survived his wife. In the probate of the wife's will, it is presumed that she survived her husband. This results in a tax tragedy—the loss of the marital deduction, which, in the example above, would be quite costly to their heirs.

In 1991, a new Uniform Simultaneous Death Act (USDA '91) was enacted, with several technical amendments added in 1993. The original Uniform Simultaneous Death Act (USDA) was developed in 1940. Its application is limited to situations involving the simultaneous deaths of a testator and beneficiary. The original act is inapplicable to deaths that occur within short intervals of each other. The primary purpose of USDA '91 is to resolve survivorship dilemmas when the deaths occur within a close interval. One benefit of a survivorship clause is the avoidance of a double probate of the same property where the beneficiary does not survive long enough to truly use and enjoy the bequest. Additionally, the clause permits the parties involved in the common disaster to choose another beneficiary rather than having the bequest pass according to the primary beneficiary's will or intestate heirs.

Terminable Interest Rule

The term *qualifying interest* is used frequently in discussions of the marital deduction; the implication is that some transfers may not qualify for the marital deduction because of the nature of the property interest itself.

terminable interest rule

Why are some interests deductible and others nondeductible? Obviously, if the transfer does not meet the tests discussed, it is nondeductible. But there is a further roadblock to deductibility known as the terminable interest rule. To understand how the **terminable interest rule** operates—and when exceptions apply—it is necessary to review briefly tax history and philosophy.

The principal purpose of the marital deduction is to create tax parity after death between residents of common-law and community-property states—assuming, of course, equal estates. Given the same size estates and general dispository schemes, the federal tax consequences should be substantially equal, regardless of the decedent's domicile.

This thrust toward equalization grew out of the fact that in a community-property state, one-half of what one spouse acquired through earnings or as income from community property during the marriage was automatically considered the property of the other spouse. If the wife survived, she owned the property outright. She could give it away (and it would be subject to gift taxes), or she could keep it until death (and it would be subject to estate taxes). Regardless of whether she made a lifetime gift or a testamentary gift, the IRS had its proverbial bite of the tax apple.

The marital deduction was designed to give residents of common-law states the same federal estate tax treatment—but no more. In other words, because the share of a community-property decedent's surviving spouse has to be included in the surviving spouse's gross estate (the one-half portion not taxed at the decedent's death because community-property law deems it to be the surviving spouse's), it is only fair that when the surviving spouse of a decedent in a common-law state dies, the share of the decedent's estate that escapes estate taxation at the decedent's death by virtue of the marital deduction should be taxed at the surviving spouse's death. The marital deduction is, therefore, not a tax-avoidance device; it merely defers taxation until the death of the second spouse.

This is the terminable interest rule's general theory and goal: to allow the marital deduction only when the nature of the interest passing to the spouse is such that, if retained until death, it will be taxed in the surviving spouse's estate.

Emphasis should be placed on the words *general*, *theory*, and *goal*. Generally, the *intent* of the law is to deny a deduction for any interest acquired by a surviving spouse that would not be includible in the surviving spouse's estate for federal estate tax purposes if held until death. For example, if a wife in her will gives her husband the right to land in Wildwood for life, with the remainder going to their children at his death, no part of the land's value would be includible in the husband's estate. To allow a marital deduction for such a devise would favor common-law over community-property residents.

If an interest will be includible in a surviving spouse's estate if it is held until death, does the converse of the general rule make it deductible? The answer is no. There are situations in which an interest is nondeductible, even though it causes estate tax liability at the surviving spouse's death.

The *includible-in-the-surviving-spouse's-estate* rule should be remembered, therefore, only to review the basic intent of the law. But, to understand how the terminable interest rule is actually applied and when exceptions are operative, it is more helpful to examine the rule—and its exceptions—directly.

Actually, there are two terminable interest rules. The first provides that property is considered a nondeductible terminable interest if the following conditions exist:

- *It is a terminable interest*, that is, if it is an interest in property that will terminate or fail upon the lapse of time or upon the occurrence or nonoccurrence of some contingency. Life estates, annuities, and copyrights are good examples of this rule. Upon the death of a life beneficiary, a life estate or life annuity ends. Likewise, a patent will expire at the end of a given period of time. Other terminable interests include an estate for a term of years, such as "to my wife for 10 years," and a widow's support allowance that—under state law—ends when the widow dies or remarries. If Ed left Joyce property in Wildwood in the following manner, "to my wife, Joyce, during the time until she remarries," her interest would terminate at that event. If Ed had said, "to my wife, Joyce, absolutely but if she does not survive my father, then the property is to go to my sister," again Joyce's interest is terminable. Note that it is not necessary that the contingency or event actually occur—or fail to occur—in order that the interest be considered terminable; all that is required is that the surviving spouse's interest could terminate.

- *Another interest in the same property passed from the decedent to some person other than the surviving spouse or the spouse's estate.*

  For example, if the decedent gave her husband a life estate and provided that, at his death, their children would receive the remainder, such remainder interest would be *another interest in the same property*, and it would be passing from the decedent to someone other than the surviving spouse or his estate.

- *The interest passes or has passed to the "other person" for less than adequate and full consideration in money or money's worth.* In the example discussed above, the remainder interest would pass to the children without their payment in money or money's worth.

However, if the children had purchased the remainder interest for its fair market value and the proceeds were given to the decedent's estate, this provision would not be met (and therefore the interest would qualify for the marital deduction).

- *Because of its passing, the "other person(s)" or his or her heirs could possess or enjoy any part of the property when the surviving spouse's interest terminated.* Note that if a decedent left property "to my daughter, Pat, for life, then to my wife, Lynne, absolutely," the present value of the wife's interest (that is, the value after subtracting the daughter's life interest) is not disqualified for the marital deduction, since no one can possess or enjoy any part of the property when the wife dies. In fact, the wife's interest is not terminable.

Terminable Interests
- to spouse unless remarriage occurs
- to spouse for life, then to children
- to spouse on a condition/event
- to brother, then to spouse if spouse survives brother

So, generally a terminable interest such as a life estate is disqualified only if it falls within all of the last three categories. Therefore, a transfer "to my wife for life, then to her estate" qualifies for the marital deduction. This lifetime bequest to the surviving spouse qualifies, since the decedent designated his surviving spouse's estate (rather than their children) as the remainderperson; hence, no interest passes to someone other than the surviving spouse or her estate.

There is a second type of terminable interest that does not qualify for the marital deduction—even though no person other than the surviving spouse acquires an interest in the property. This is a situation in which the decedent in his or her will has directed the executor (or a trustee) to take assets ostensibly available to the surviving spouse and purchase a terminable interest with them. For example, if Al leaves $100,000 to his wife, Leslie, in a specific bequest in his will but directs his executor to use the $100,000 as the purchase price for a straight life annuity (no refund) for her, the $100,000 bequest will not qualify for the marital deduction. Likewise, if Al's executor is directed to use the $100,000 to purchase a patent, copyright, or other terminable interest for Leslie, such a bequest will not qualify.

Exceptions to Terminable Interest Rules That Qualify for the Marital Deduction

There are important exceptions to the terminable interest rules. Exceptions are listed directly below and are discussed in the paragraphs that follow.

- An interest will still qualify for the marital deduction (It will not be considered a nondeductible terminable interest solely because it will terminate or fail upon the surviving spouse's death.), if the bequest to the surviving spouse was conditional upon his or her surviving for up to 6 months after the decedent's death—as long as the surviving spouse does, in fact, survive for the specified period. (For example, an interest is not disqualified for the marital deduction merely because it states, "If my husband fails to survive me by 6 months, this will and all its provisions shall be construed as if he predeceased me.") However, if the specified termination does occur, the marital deduction is lost.

- A bequest of a life estate can qualify for the marital deduction if it is coupled with a general power of appointment. An interest passing to a surviving spouse for life with the remainder payable to his or her estate may also qualify for the marital deduction.

- A life insurance policy payable to the surviving spouse for life can qualify if the spouse has a general power of appointment over the proceeds.

- A qualified terminable-interest property election can also qualify.

Marital Deduction Requirements
- The surviving spouse must be a U.S. citizen.
- Marital status must exist.
- The property must be included in the decedent-spouse's gross estate.
- The property must pass to the surviving spouse.
- The transfer must not be a terminable interest.

Normally, these transfers of property would violate the terminable interest rules and, therefore, not qualify for the marital deduction. The exceptions to the terminable interest rules, however, specifically permit these kinds of transfers to a surviving spouse to qualify for the deduction if the requirements of the exceptions are met. All of the exceptions other than the 6-month survival contingency exception involve trust arrangements that qualify for the marital deduction.

Six-month Survival Contingency. The first exception to the terminable interest rule provides that an interest passing to a surviving spouse is not considered nondeductible merely because it will terminate or fail upon the surviving spouse's death within a period of not more than 6 months of the decedent's death. (This type of provision is sometimes used to prevent *double probate* and *double state death taxation* when the death of one spouse occurs within a short time of the other spouse's death.)

EXAMPLE

Ike leaves his land in Stone Harbor to his wife, Tina. But, Ike's will provides that Tina will receive no interest in the land if she does not survive Ike for 6 months. If Tina, in fact, survives the 6-month period, a marital deduction will be allowed in Ike's estate. If Tina does not survive Ike by the required period of time, no deduction will be allowed.

If Ike required Tina to survive him by some period in excess of 6 months (such as survival by one year or survival "until my estate is closed"), the transfer would not qualify because it exceeds or could exceed the 6-month permissible period. If Ike's will provided "my land is to go to Tina, my wife, for life, and the remainder, at her death, is to go to my son, Sophocles, but for my wife to receive her interest, she must survive me by 3 months," the interest would not qualify for the marital deduction even if Tina did survive the 3-month period. This is because the failure of a contingency to occur cannot convert what is otherwise a nonqualifying terminable interest (the life estate to the wife and remainder to the son) into a qualifying interest.

A second part of this exception deals with common-disaster provisions. Assume Ike's will stated, "I leave my entire estate to my wife, Tina, but if she and I die in a common disaster, my estate goes instead to my son, Sophocles." Assume also that state law defines a common disaster as an event in which both spouses die within 30 days from injuries attributable to a common accident. If Tina survived for 2 months and then died, she would have received Ike's estate. Since the terminating contingency—the deaths of both spouses in a common disaster as defined by state law—did not occur, the marital deduction would be allowed in Ike's estate. But if Tina died 3 weeks after the accident, no marital deduction would be allowed because the terminating contingency did, in fact, occur.

Power-of-appointment Trust. The second exception to the terminable interest rule is that the interest is not disqualified if it meets the following five conditions:

- The surviving spouse is entitled to all the income from the interest in question.

- The income is payable annually or more frequently. (The marital trust is the receptacle into which probate assets qualifying for the marital deduction are placed. If the marital trust has a specific provision either authorizing investment in non-income-producing assets or allowing the trustee to retain unproductive—that is, non-income-producing—assets, this requirement may not be satisfied. This militates against the purchase of life insurance by the marital trust or leaving closely held stock that has never paid a significant dividend or unproductive land in the trust, unless the surviving spouse has an unqualified right to demand that trust assets be sold and converted into income-producing property.)

- The surviving spouse has the power to appoint the interest to himself or herself or to his or her estate.

- The power must be exercisable by the surviving spouse alone and in all events. It can be a lifetime power or power exercisable by the surviving spouse only at death—that is, by will—or a power exercisable in either event.

- No person other than the surviving spouse has a power to appoint any part of the interest to anyone other than the surviving spouse.

power of appointment

This second exception makes the **power of appointment** trust the most widely used method of qualifying property in trust for the marital deduction. Essentially, the power-of-appointment trust is, as its name implies, a trust designed to hold assets for the surviving spouse and to qualify for the marital deduction by providing the surviving spouse with a general power of appointment over the corpus (see the following figure). The primary purpose of such a trust arrangement is to require the surviving spouse to take affirmative action to direct the corpus at death from the original estate owner's planned disposition.

Generally, the testator's will sets up two trusts: a marital (spouse's) trust (often referred to as the "A trust"), and a nonmarital (family) trust (or "B trust"). The marital trust is designed to hold assets that qualify for the marital deduction, while the nonmarital trust is intended to provide management for assets that are taxable at the testator's death.

Power-of-appointment Trust

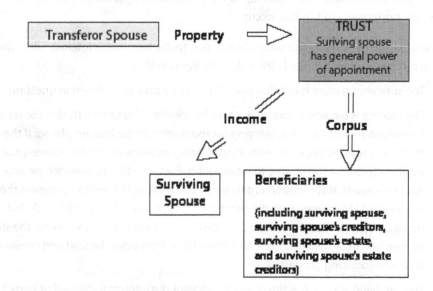

bypass trust

credit-exclusion/ equivalent bypass trust (CEBT)

If it is drafted properly, the nonmarital (family) trust provides the spouse with additional income and even limited amounts of principal without causing an inclusion of principal in the survivor's gross estate. In a sense, this trust is a **bypass trust**, because it provides security for the spouse but bypasses taxation in the surviving spouse's estate when the spouse dies. Quite often this trust is called a **credit-exclusion/equivalent bypass trust (CEBT)** because—ideally, at least—it should be funded with assets equivalent to the testator's exclusion amount (credit equivalent). However, in 2012 the American Taxpayer Relief Act allowed for the portability of the lifetime exclusion to the surviving spouse. As such, you no longer need to use all of your lifetime exclusion but can instead leave your $11.4 million (2019) to your surviving spouse. There are still some uses for CEBTs, mainly with regard to generation-skipping-transfer tax issues, because no portability is allowed with the GSTT. Additionally, CEBTs can still have other benefits like creditor protections, control of property, and removal of appreciating assets from both estates.

EXAMPLE

Assume Joan McFadden's adjusted gross estate was worth $17,400,000. The formula in her will for determining how assets are to be divided might provide that an amount equal to the basic exclusion amount (credit equivalent), that is, $11.18 million in 2019, goes to the CEBT and the balance of her estate to her surviving spouse. The federal estate tax on the $11.4 million that goes into the CEBT would be eliminated by the credit. The $6 million passing to her husband (either directly or in trust) would qualify for the unlimited marital deduction and, therefore, escape federal estate tax at Joan's death.

The advantage of *carving out* a CEBT before determining the marital deduction is that, when the first spouse dies, at least the basic exclusion amount in the CEBT escapes taxation on that particular spouse's estate. Through an effective use of the basic credit amount of the first spouse to die (and the avoidance of potential *stacking* assets into the second spouse's estate), significant estate tax savings can be realized. The results are even more dramatic if there is a substantial increase in asset values between the first and second deaths. For instance, in the previous example assume that the surviving spouse had no estate of his own. At his death, examine the following:

The same result is often obtained by establishing an inter vivos trust during the grantor's lifetime, and then *pouring over* probate assets by will into this trust and naming the trust as the direct beneficiary of death benefits from life insurance proceeds and employee benefit plans.

At the grantor's death, the trust is split into two (or more) trusts or two (or more) portions—marital and nonmarital—with the same functions as the testamentary trusts described above.

When the surviving spouse is given a general power of appointment over assets that are in the marital trust, the trust is known as a *power-of-appointment trust*.

The intended result can be accomplished by giving the surviving spouse a power to withdraw the property in the marital trust anytime during life, or to direct by will that the property is to become part of the survivor's estate or be used to satisfy creditors at death.

The surviving spouse can be restricted to a power exercisable only by will; the trust will qualify for the marital deduction even if the spouse has no power to withdraw the corpus during lifetime.

estate trust

Estate Trust. In addition to the power-of-appointment trust, the **estate trust** is also a viable method of obtaining a marital deduction. An estate trust is one in which the surviving spouse is given an interest for life, with the remainder payable to his or her estate. In effect, this gives the surviving spouse the equivalent of a general power of appointment by will, since that spouse can *transfer* (or, more correctly, shift) property subject to the power to anyone he or she chooses.

The estate trust does not run afoul of the nondeductible terminable interest rule for another reason: no interest passes to anyone other than the surviving spouse or to the surviving spouse's estate.

An estate trust is a useful alternative to the power-of-appointment trust for a number of reasons.

First, in contrast to the power-of-appointment trust, under which all income must be payable to the surviving spouse annually or more frequently, the trustee of an estate trust can accumulate income within the trust instead of paying it out. If the trust is in a lower income tax bracket than that of the surviving spouse, the power to accumulate can result in income tax savings. The income tax rates for trusts and estates enacted under the Revenue Reconciliation Act of 1993 (RRA '93), however, have generally eliminated this benefit.

Second, because the spouse does not have to receive all of the income annually, a trustee can either invest in nonproductive (non-income-producing) property or retain nonproductive assets, such as non-dividend-paying stock in a family-owned corporation.

These advantages must be weighed, however, against the certainty that any income accumulations (together with the original corpus) will be includible in the surviving spouse's estate. This in turn may result in increased administrative costs, be subject to the claims of creditors, and cause state inheritance taxes. (For example, compare this with the power-of-appointment trust, which, under the laws of a state such as Pennsylvania, is not part of the probate estate and the corpus that is not taxed for state inheritance tax purposes at the death of the donee of the power.)

Estate Trust

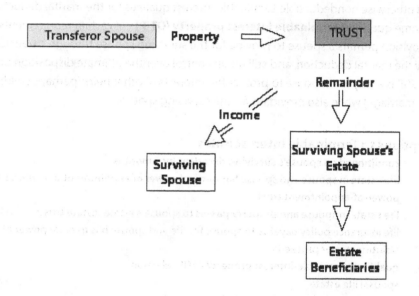

Interest in Life Insurance Proceeds. The third exception to the terminable interest rule parallels the second: an interest in life insurance proceeds (or an endowment or annuity contract) is treated as passing solely to the surviving spouse, if both of the following conditions exist:

- Under the settlement option, the surviving spouse is entitled to all of the interest for life (or the right to installment payments of the proceeds for life).

- The surviving spouse has the right to appoint to himself or herself, or to his or her estate, any proceeds or installment payments remaining.

This exception makes it possible to qualify life insurance proceeds under a settlement option if the surviving spouse is given the equivalent of a general power of appointment, even if there is a gift-over. For example, a settlement option could qualify for the marital deduction if it provided that: (1) the surviving spouse is to receive *interest only* for life; (2) there is an unlimited right of withdrawal or the right to a one-sum settlement; and (3) if no withdrawal is made, any proceeds remaining are to be paid to the children born of the marriage of the insured and said spouse.

qualified terminable interest property (QTIP)

Qualified Terminable-Interest Property. A fourth exception allows a qualifying terminable interest property to qualify for the marital deduction. A person can provide that his or her spouse will receive only the income from property and, at the death of the surviving spouse, the property must pass to the person or persons specified in the will of the original transferor spouse. This otherwise nondeductible terminable interest qualifies for the marital deduction—hence the name **qualified terminable interest property (QTIP)**—if certain requirements are met. This provision permits a spouse to provide for the surviving spouse through a transfer sheltered by the marital deduction, and still retain control over the ultimate disposition of the assets. The QTIP is a way for a spouse to protect the interests of other heirs (perhaps children from a prior marriage) while also providing for the surviving spouse.

Exceptions to Terminable Interest Rules

- conditioned on spouse's surviving decedent by 6 months
- life estate in spouse and spouse has general power of appointment over property
- power-of-appointment trust
- life estate in spouse and property passes to spouse's estate (estate trust)
- life insurance policy payable to spouse for life and spouse has general power of appointment over proceeds
- qualified terminable-interest property (QTIP) election
- spousal life estate
- first spouse to die controls remainder

There are four conditions that must be met before QTIP treatment is allowed. (Keep in mind that other property besides property that is placed in trusts can satisfy these requirements and achieve the same favorable results.)

- The decedent-spouse (or donor, in the case of a lifetime gift) must make a transfer of property. The transfer can be in trust or through insurance proceeds or in other forms, such as the death proceeds of a nonqualified deferred-compensation plan.

- The surviving spouse (donee, in the case of a lifetime transfer) must be given the right to all the income. The income must be payable at least annually, and the surviving spouse must be entitled to that income for life.

- No one can be given the right to direct that the property will go to anyone (other than the spouse) as long as the spouse is alive. (It is permissible to give someone other than the surviving spouse the power to appoint QTIP property, if that power can be exercised only after the surviving spouse dies.)

- The first decedent-spouse's executor must make an irrevocable election on the decedent's federal estate tax return. The election provides that, to the extent the QTIP property has not been consumed or given away during the lifetime of the surviving spouse, its date-of-death value (at the surviving spouse's death) will be included in the surviving spouse's estate. In the case of a lifetime gift of QTIP property, the donor spouse must file a similar election on the gift tax return so that the QTIP property will be in the estate of the donee spouse, unless disposed of during the donee spouse's lifetime.

In other words, under this elective provision even *terminable interests* passing to a spouse can qualify for a marital deduction. Property passing to a surviving spouse for life with the remainder going to some other person(s) is eligible for the marital deduction on the condition that the property will be subject to tax at the surviving spouse's death.

QTIP—The Problem of Unproductive Property

At first glance, it appears that the QTIP concept satisfies all needs for all people. However, this is not the case. If all or most of a client's estate consists of unproductive real estate (and/or stock in a closely held corporation that has not paid, and probably never will pay, any significant dividends), will the surviving spouse receive the statutorily required "all income at least annually"? Most authorities think the answer is no.

The surviving spouse must be given an interest that realistically is expected to produce income (or will be usable by the spouse in a manner consistent with its value). Most closely held stock will never pay dividends or realistically be expected to produce an income consistent with its value. Therefore, without planning, the marital deduction could be lost. What can be done to save the marital deduction? If there is no state law giving the surviving spouse the power to require that trust assets be sold and that trust property be made productive in a reasonable period of time, the attorney drafting the marital formula must insert a provision in the will or trust clearly giving the survivor that power. If the surviving spouse can demand that the trustee sell the stock (or other unproductive assets) and use the proceeds to purchase income-producing property, the marital deduction can be saved (even if the power is never actually exercised).

Unfortunately, even if the surviving spouse is given the power to demand that the trustee sell the stock, there are practical problems.

For example, suppose that a client's objective was to pass the stock to his daughter, an employee of the business, at his wife's death. If the wife can force a sale, what assurance does the daughter have that she will be the purchaser? Who would purchase the stock if it is a minority interest? If it is a majority interest, what would happen to the daughter's job if the stock is sold to a third party? Even if the wife is not given the power to require the trustee to sell the stock, can she obtain the corpus of the trust by electing against her husband's will? If the wife doesn't force a sale of trust assets, where will she obtain income sufficient to maintain her current standard of living?

Solutions include the creation of a life-insurance-funded irrevocable trust (ILIT) by the husband. At his death, the trust would provide income to the wife for life, and at the wife's death the corpus would pass to their daughter. This would relieve pressure on the wife to force the trustee to sell the stock in the QTIP trust. In fact, the irrevocable trust might provide income but make the surviving spouse's right to that income conditional on not demanding a sale of QTIP assets. If she demands that the trustee sell the QTIP assets, she loses her right to income from the irrevocable trust.

An alternative solution is a funded buy-sell agreement between the father and the daughter. If the daughter has the insurance proceeds at her father's death, she can purchase the stock from his estate. That way cash rather than stock goes into the QTIP trust. Another possibility is a recapitalization coupled with a Sec. 303 stock redemption and/or a cross-purchase agreement with the daughter.

LO 14. 3   **Describe how either an overqualification or an underqualification may affect federal estate tax liability, and explain how formulas can be used to minimize the tax.**

OVERQUALIFICATION AND UNDERQUALIFICATION

overqualification

Overqualification occurs when there is an underutilization of the estate owner's basic exclusion/credit amount. In 2019, overqualification and underqualification are generally not an issue due to the portability of the lifetime exclusion. However, if you are dealing with a GSTT issue - in which portability is not allowed, they could become issues. The result is that more property than necessary to reduce the estate owner's federal estate tax to zero goes to the surviving spouse. Thus, at the surviving spouse's death, more property than necessary is exposed to tax. This is where proper funding of a CEBT is important. It assures efficient use of both spouses' credit amounts and prevents unnecessary stacking of assets in the surviving spouse's estate.

underqualification

Underqualification means that less property passed to the surviving spouse in a qualifying manner than should have passed tax free. For instance, assume that in 2019 a wife had a $15,000,000 adjusted gross estate but left only $1,000,000 to her spouse in a qualifying manner. There is a $2,600,000 underqualification—$11.4 million (2019) goes to the CEBT and no tax is payable; that leaves $3,600,000 that could have qualified for the unlimited marital deduction outside of the lifetime exclusion amount of $11.4 million. In other words, the marital deduction is underutilized by $2,600,000. (However, keep in mind that for tax and other reasons planners sometimes deliberately utilize less than the maximum allowable marital deduction and thus deliberately underqualify). Underqualification can be a real issue even with portability if the surviving spouse dies with a small estate and does not use up all of his or her lifetime exclusion amount.

deceased spousal unused exclusion amount (DSUEA or DSUE)

The Tax Relief, Unemployment Insurance Reauthorization, and Job Creation Act of 2010 (TRA 2010) established a new and rather unique provision called the **deceased spousal unused exclusion amount (DSUEA or DSUE)**. Under the act, the DSUEA allows for the portability of any or all of a first-to-die spouse's unused exclusion amount to be carried over for use by the surviving spouse for the years 2011 and 2012. When Congress passed the American Taxpayer Relief Act of 2012 (ATRA 2012), the DSUEA was made permanent. Therefore, in 2019 when the basic exclusion amount is $11.4 million, a surviving spouse could possibly have an exclusion amount of $22.8 million if the decedent spouse did not use any of his or her basic exclusion amount. The DSUEA provision has the effect of minimizing concerns of some married couples about over and underqualification of the marital deduction.

Formulas for Minimizing Tax

formula bequests

Obviously, a clause is needed in the will that can provide, by formula, an amount or share of the estate that effectively utilizes the estate owner's basic credit/exclusion amount and is coordinated with the unlimited marital deduction. These are appropriately known as **formula bequests**.

Because of the basic credit amount, it is often desirable to provide that use of the marital deduction be limited to the amount required to reduce the estate owner's federal estate tax to the lowest possible figure after considering the basic credit amount for the year of death. For example, if in 2019 a decedent's adjusted gross estate is $12 million, and he leaves the full $12 million to his wife, there will be no federal estate tax at his death—but there may be a federal estate tax at the death of his wife that is equal to her tentative tax base less the basic credit amount, depending on the credit amount in the wife's year of death.

If instead of the unlimited marital share the decedent gave his wife an amount exactly sufficient (and no larger) to reduce the federal estate tax due at his death to the lowest possible figure, and gave the balance to his children (directly or through a CEBT), then (assuming the decedent dies in 2019) his children would receive $11.4 million (2019) and his wife would receive $600,000 (2019. Upon his wife's subsequent death, there could be less (depending on the credit amount in the wife's year of death) federal estate tax liability. In essence, the transfers result in "funding the residue" (the children's portion of the estate) to the extent of the basic exclusion amount before funding the marital gift.

There are two types of formula bequests:

- the pecuniary (dollar) amount
- the fractional share

pecuniary-amount bequest

The **pecuniary-amount bequest** provides that the survivor will receive a fixed-dollar amount and takes into consideration not only property passing under the will but all property qualifying for the marital deduction. The pecuniary-amount bequest might read as follows:

> If my wife, Allene, survives me, I give, devise, and bequeath to her a sum of money that shall be exactly sufficient to reduce the federal estate tax (after applicable credits) due as a result of my death to the lowest possible amount less the value of all interests in property, if any, that pass or have passed to her under other items of my will or outside my will, but only to the extent that such interests are included in determining my gross estate and allowed as a marital deduction.

fractional-share bequest

The **fractional-share bequest** is an attempt to accomplish the same goal by giving the surviving spouse a fractional share in the residue of the estate—that is, a fractional share of each asset after specific bequests have been made.

Marital Deduction Formula Bequests

- pecuniary amount
- fixed-dollar marital deduction amount
- fractional share
- fractional share of estate residue

How much should the surviving spouse be given under the marital bequest? Should the surviving spouse be given even less than the amount necessary to reduce taxes in the decedent's estate to zero? Should the surviving spouse be given only one-half of the estate? Will the time-use (or psychological) value of tax money saved on the death of the first spouse offset the cost, the (potential) increase in total taxes payable? Perhaps. Much depends on the size of the estates and the use to which tax savings are put at the first death. If the money is used to assure or enhance the lifestyle of the surviving spouse, then it will result in a long-run benefit.

However, if the excess of the amount necessary to *equalize the two estates* is invested by the surviving spouse and eventually taxed at a higher rate when he or she dies, the net result will be fewer assets passing to the next generation. Any planning and assumptions must take into consideration the increasing basic credit/exclusion amounts and portability of a deceased spousal unused exclusion (DSUE).

The actual solution varies according to the circumstances, needs, and desires of the parties involved. The time value of money, as well as the survivor's ability to consume or give away property, must be considered.

LO 14. 4   **Describe the advantages and disadvantages of different forms of marital bequests, and explain the factors that should be considered in deciding to what extent the marital deduction should be used.**

Forms of Marital Bequests: Advantages and Disadvantages

There are many means of obtaining the marital deduction. One method is the outright transfer of property to the surviving spouse by will or through life insurance death proceeds. There are advantages to an outright bequest:

- The surviving spouse has the right to use and manage marital assets as he or she desires.

- No trustee fees or court accountings are required.

- Giving the surviving spouse the marital share discourages him or her from electing against the testator's will.

- Assets the surviving spouse receives are available to his or her executor to meet estate liquidity needs.
- The surviving spouse can be given—and safely retain—non-income-producing assets, such as the non-dividend-paying stock in a family-owned corporation.

An outright bequest has a number of disadvantages:

- No protection is provided for a spendthrift spouse.
- There is no management with investment expertise.
- The surviving spouse's creditors can attach the bequest both during lifetime and at death.
- The surviving spouse can easily dispose of the bequest however he or she wishes during lifetime—even to the exclusion of his or her children and in favor of a second spouse and children.
- Assets the surviving spouse has not given away or consumed will be included in his or her probate estate.

A second method of providing a marital bequest is to leave property in a power-of-appointment trust. Typically, the power-of-appointment trust gives the spouse a lifetime interest in the trust property, coupled with the right to specify the identity of the remainderperson during lifetime or in his or her will. It usually also provides that if the surviving spouse fails to name the beneficiaries of trust assets, the trust corpus will go to a *taker in default*, a beneficiary named by the grantor of the trust. The trustee (as well as sometimes the surviving spouse) is often given additional powers over trust assets. These might include the right to use trust principal for emergencies or to make gifts to children and grandchildren.

The advantages of an irrevocable power-of-appointment trust include:

- As in the case of an outright gift, the surviving spouse may be discouraged from electing against the decedent's will.
- Protection is afforded to some degree against the surviving spouse's possible spendthrift habits.
- Protection is provided against the surviving spouse's creditors and the creditors of the spouse's estate.
- Principal distributions can be varied, depending on the surviving spouse's needs.
- The surviving spouse's right to dispose of the property during lifetime can be limited.
- Probate of the trust corpus can be avoided when the surviving spouse dies.
- Management and financial guidance are provided for the surviving spouse.

There are disadvantages of a power-of-appointment trust:

- Certain trustee fees and accounting costs are involved.
- Assets in a power-of-appointment trust may not be available to the surviving spouse's executor for the payments of costs and taxes (unless the surviving spouse appoints the assets to his or her estate).
- Non-income-producing property, such as life insurance, cannot safely be obtained or retained in the trust.

The third form of marital bequest under a will is known as an *estate trust*. This type of trust is not required to give the surviving spouse all the income during his or her lifetime, but pays all the accumulated income and the corpus to the surviving spouse's estate when he or she dies. (During lifetime, the surviving spouse can, of course, be given income or principal at the discretion of the trustee, but the surviving spouse personally has no lifetime right to demand either income or principal.)

Advantages of the estate trust include the following:

- Non-income-producing property can be purchased and safely retained by the trustee.
- Protection is provided against the surviving spouse's spendthrift habits, if any.
- Protection is afforded against the surviving spouse's creditors during lifetime.
- The surviving spouse is unable to make lifetime assignments of trust property.
- Assets are available to the surviving spouse's executor.

Disadvantages of the estate trust consist mainly of its inflexibility from the surviving spouse's viewpoint:

- The surviving spouse has no freedom to use and manage trust assets.
- The surviving spouse is restricted in disposing of any property in the trust during lifetime.
- Assets in the trust generate trustee fees and accounting costs.

The fourth form of marital bequest is through the QTIP trust. The QTIP trust gives the spouse a lifetime interest in the property but no general power either during lifetime or at death. At death, assets in the trust pass to the beneficiary or beneficiaries named by the testator.

The advantages of a QTIP trust include the following:

- The grantor can be more certain that the trust assets will eventually be received by the parties the grantor has designated.

- Protection is afforded against the surviving spouse's spendthrift habits, if any.
- Protection is provided against the surviving spouse's creditors and the creditors of the survivor's estate.
- The surviving spouse is given no power to dispose of the trust corpus.
- Probate of the trust corpus is avoided at the surviving spouse's death.

Note that in many states a surviving spouse may be able to *take against* the decedent-spouse's will and thereby defeat some of the objectives and advantages described above.

Disadvantages of the QTIP trust include the following:

- There may be a false sense of security that the first decedent-spouse's objectives will be accomplished.
- Non-income-producing property can be safely used to fund the trust only if the surviving spouse is given the power to demand that trust assets be made productive (income producing).
- The surviving spouse is restricted in the use of trust assets.
- Assets in the trust generate trustee fees and accounting costs.

Extent to Which Marital Deduction Should Be Used

There are a number of factors that should be carefully considered in deciding how much of a decedent's gross estate should be transferred to the surviving spouse. See Table 14-1 for a list of these considerations.

Table 14-1 Factors to Consider for Using the Marital Deduction	
Factor	**Consideration**
Tax savings desired at first death	Maximum utilization of marital deduction is indicated.
Tax savings—both estates	To the extent not consumed or given away through present-interest gifts, marital-deduction assets may compound estate tax problems at second death.
Lack of confidence in spouse's judgment	Marital assets are subject to spouse's dispository desires, either during lifetime or at death.
Fear of spouse's remarriage and aversion to the new spouse's obtaining marital property	Right of new spouse to elect against spouse's will indicates use of less than maximum marital transfer.
Size of surviving spouse's estate	Until size of surviving spouse's estate equals the exemption equivalent of the federal credit, assets should be transferred to him or her. But, if his or her estate is as large as or larger than the decedent-spouse's or a sizable inheritance from a third party is likely, the use of sizable marital transfers is contraindicated.
Time value of money	Tax money saved by maximum use of marital deduction can be invested and may offset any additional tax on second death. Investment opportunities available to the surviving spouse must be taken into account.
Availability of marital assets for spouse to give away and consume	Spouse's age, health, number of children and grandchildren, financial needs (including educational and health needs of children), living standard, and even inflation must be considered; generally, the younger the spouse, the greater the financial needs.
Income tax bracket of surviving spouse	If surviving spouse is already in a high-income tax bracket, additional income from marital assets may be counterproductive.
Liquidity needs of decedent's estate	If decedent's estate is relatively illiquid, maximum use of marital deduction is indicated.

Table 14-1	
Factors to Consider for Using the Marital Deduction	
Factor	**Consideration**
State death tax laws	Many states do not tax property subject to a power of appointment in donee's estate unless power is exercised by the donee. This makes it possible, in some cases, for property in a marital (spouse's) trust to escape state death taxation at the donee spouse's death.

Ethical Case

The ethical dilemmas presented in this text illustrate common scenarios that could present a financial or estate planner with an ethical predicament. The resolution of any dilemma, of course, depends on how one applies ethical codes, rules, and principles to the specific situation. The comments are meant to provide thought about these issues and not give a definitive resolution to them.

Peter Kim is an estate planner who moved to the small community of Ennetown about 18 months ago. His new practice has been steadily growing along with his increasing personal popularity. He enjoys socializing and makes the most of every opportunity that arises. He has often been called the life of the party.

Mr. Kim was recently invited to a party along with many prominent and wealthy Ennetown citizens. Mr. Kim considered the invitation an important opportunity and gladly accepted it. He arrived on time, introduced himself to everyone, and made everyone feel at ease. He clearly enjoyed entertaining the other guests. With so many prospects there, he was determined to make a strong impression.

At one point, Mr. Kim realized he had almost everyone's attention. He thought, "Everyone loves a good story." Only a few days earlier he had handled some very unusual situations involving humorous, though private, details concerning clients' marriages as well as their charitable intentions.

Mr. Kim paused. He would not want to breach the confidentiality of his clients regarding their personal affairs. But, he thought, "I could disguise the names so that it is not obvious who is involved. What harm could come of it?" As he turned back to his audience—eagerly waiting to hear more—he had to decide what to say.

Does Mr. Kim have an ethical dilemma?

A Possible Resolution

Mr. Kim does not have an ethical dilemma. He should not tell the story. He has a clear duty to respect confidentiality.

Mr. Kim is relatively new in town; he obviously wants to grow his estate planning practice; and he is eager to ingratiate himself with prospective clients. While humor can be an effective tool in increasing popularity, it is also important to guard against hurting the people who are the subjects of that humor.

Thus, Mr. Kim should not tell stories about clients to this group. It is a small community, and it is highly possible that no disguise would prevent the other guests from recognizing the subjects involved. Furthermore, Mr. Kim's behavior could be counterproductive since the possibility of gaining new clients dims considerably when prospective clients realize he cannot be trusted with confidences.

The responsibility for safeguarding confidentiality extends beyond mere direct disclosure. Clients have the right to have their affairs treated with respect, and the personal details of their circumstances should be kept private. Estate planners have the obligation to act responsibly and with discretion, being careful stewards of their clients' information.

CHAPTER REVIEW

Key Terms and Concepts

resident alien
qualified domestic trust (QDOT)
terminable interest rule
power of appointment
bypass trust
credit-exclusion/ equivalent bypass
   trust (CEBT)
estate trust

qualified terminable interest property
   (QTIP)
overqualification
underqualification
deceased spousal unused exclusion
   amount (DSUEA or DSUE)
formula bequests
pecuniary-amount bequest
fractional-share bequest

Chapter 14: Review Questions

1. Briefly explain the reason Congress enacted the marital deduction for married residents of common-law states. [LO 14.1]

2. What is meant by "net value of a qualifying interest passing to a surviving spouse"? [LO 14.1]

3. What are the requirements to qualify for the marital deduction? [LO 14.2]

4. Explain the circumstances under which a U.S. citizen decedent spouse's transfers to a resident-alien spouse are eligible for the unlimited marital deduction. [LO 14.2]

5. What is the effect of a valid disclaimer on the marital deduction if the disclaimed property passes to the surviving spouse? [LO 14.2]

6. a. What is meant by a presumption-of-survivorship clause?

    b. How does a survivorship clause affect the marital deduction? [LO 14.2]

7. What are the general theory and goal of the terminable interest rule? [LO 14.2]

8. a. Explain the terminable interest rule as it applies to a nondeductible terminable interest.

    b. What are the exceptions to the terminable interest rule? [LO 14.2]

9. Describe the requirements that must be met by a power-of-appointment trust before the property contained in such a trust will qualify for the federal estate-tax marital deduction. [LO 14.2]

10. In what way is an estate trust a useful alternative to the power-of-appointment trust? [LO 14.2]

11. Describe the four conditions that must be met before qualified terminable interest property (QTIP) can qualify for the marital deduction. [LO 14.2]

12. What is the role of the executor in qualifying property as QTIP? [LO 14.2]

13. a. Describe problems that may arise if unproductive property is transferred to a QTIP trust. [LO 14.2]

    b. How can these problems be resolved? [LO 14.2]

14. What important drawback generally is associated with overqualification of estate assets for the marital deduction? [LO 14.3]

15. Assume a decedent's estate consisted of $75,000 in cash or cash equivalents, $1,250,000 in life insurance payable in a lump sum to his wife, and a residence (purchased after 1976) valued at $520,000 that he owned as tenants by the entirety with his wife. There is no mortgage on the property. He also owned an automobile titled in his own name worth $10,000 and a sole proprietorship worth $10,600,000. His will states that his entire estate is to go to his wife. Assume debts and administrative expenses are $155,000. Assume also that the decedent had two adult children, one of whom was working with him in the business at the time of his death in 2019.

    a. Compute the gross estate.

    b. Compute the adjusted gross estate.

    c. Compute the marital deduction, listing all assets that qualify.

    d. Explain how estate taxes could have been minimized in the combined estates of the decedent and his wife by the use of trusts. [LO 14.3]

16. Describe the two types of formula bequests. [LO 14.3]

17. Under what circumstances might it be advantageous to qualify an estate for less than the maximum unlimited marital deduction? Explain. [LO 14.3]

18. What are the advantages and disadvantages of outright marital bequests? [LO 14.4]

19. Describe what constitutes a power-of-appointment trust: [LO 14.4]

    a. Compare power-of-appointment trusts with estate trusts. [LO 14.4]

    b. State the benefits and disadvantages of each. [LO 14.4]

Chapter 14: Review Answers

1. Because of the community-property-law concept, only one-half of the community property is includible in the estate of whichever spouse dies first. This tax advantage has been reflected in the income and gift taxation of community-property residents as well as in the estate taxation. As a result of this disparity between common-property and common-law states, Congress aimed for tax parity by making a federal estate tax marital deduction available to married residents of common-law states. Therefore, the Internal Revenue Code now allows a deduction for the value of any qualifying property interests includible in the decedent's gross estate that pass from the decedent to the surviving spouse.

2. Net value refers to the gross estate tax value of a property interest—that is, its date-of-death value or, if applicable, its value as of the alternate valuation date minus any charges against that interest. Generally speaking, this means that the gross value of a property interest passing to the surviving spouse must be reduced by (1) taxes payable out of the interest, (2) mortgages or liens against the interest, and (3) administration expenses payable out of the interest.

3. A number of very strictly construed technical requirements must be met before property qualifies for the marital deduction, and there are certain qualifications and limitations that must be considered:

    •   the citizenship requirement for the surviving spouse

    •   the requirement that property be included

    •   the requirement that property must pass or have passed

    •   the marital-status requirement

    •   the terminable interest rule

4. Transfers to a surviving resident-alien spouse are eligible for the marital deduction if (1) the surviving spouse becomes a U.S. citizen before the decedent spouse's estate tax return is filed, and (2) the surviving spouse remains a U.S. resident after the death of the citizen spouse.

If the surviving resident-alien spouse does not obtain U.S. citizenship, a qualified domestic trust (QDOT or QDT) can be used to transfer assets to a surviving resident-alien spouse while preserving the marital deduction for such a transfer.

5. If a third party makes a timely disclaimer, the result is the same as if no interest had ever passed to him or her. If the third party's refusal to accept the property causes all or a portion of it to pass to the surviving spouse, it qualifies as property passing from the decedent to a surviving spouse. In other words, if the effect of a disclaimer by a third party is to increase the amount of property passing from the decedent to the surviving spouse, the result may be to increase the marital deduction.

6. a. The regulations provide that when it is impossible to ascertain which spouse died first, any presumption—whether established by the decedent in a will, by state law, or otherwise—will be recognized. The importance of a presumption-of-survivorship clause in a decedent's will or life insurance settlement should not be underestimated. Having a presumption-of-survivorship clause can result in estate tax savings through utilization of the marital deduction and basic credit amount.

   b. To the extent the presumption results in the inclusion of a bequest in the gross estate of the spouse deemed to have survived, a marital deduction is allowed.

7. The marital deduction is not a tax-avoidance device; it merely defers taxation until the death of the second spouse. This is the general theory and goal of the terminable interest rule—to allow the marital deduction only when the nature of the interest passing to the spouse is such that, if retained until death, it will be taxed in the surviving spouse's estate. Emphasis should be placed on the words *general*, *theory*, and *goal*. Generally speaking, the *intent* of the law is to deny a deduction for any interest acquired by a surviving spouse that would not be includible in the surviving spouse's estate for federal estate tax purposes if held until death.

8. a. Actually there are two terminable interest rules. The first provides that property is considered a nondeductible terminable interest if the following conditions exist:

   - It is a terminable interest if it is an interest in property that will terminate or fail upon the lapse of time or upon the occurrence or nonoccurrence of some contingency.

   - Another interest in the same property passed from the decedent to some person other than the surviving spouse or the spouse's estate.

   - The interest passes or has passed to the "other person" for less than adequate and full consideration in money or money's worth.

- Because of its passing, the "other person(s)" or his, her, or their heirs could possess or enjoy any part of the property when the surviving spouse's interest terminated.

The second type of terminable interest that does not qualify for the marital deduction—even though no person other than the surviving spouse acquires an interest in the property—is a situation in which the decedent in his or her will has directed the executor (or a trustee) to take assets ostensibly available to the surviving spouse and purchase a terminable interest with them.

b. There are important exceptions to the terminable interest rules.

- An interest will still qualify for the marital deduction (it will not be considered a nondeductible terminable interest solely because it will terminate or fail upon the surviving spouse's death) if the bequest to the surviving spouse was conditional upon his or her surviving for up to 6 months after the decedent's death—as long as the surviving spouse does, in fact, survive for the specified period. (For example, an interest is not disqualified for the marital deduction merely because it states, "If my husband fails to survive me by 6 months, this will and all its provisions shall be construed as if he predeceased me.") However, if the specified termination does occur, the marital deduction is lost.

- A bequest of a life estate can qualify for the marital deduction if it is coupled with a general power of appointment. An interest passing to a surviving spouse for life with the remainder payable to his or her estate may also qualify for the marital deduction.

- A life insurance policy payable to the surviving spouse for life can qualify if the spouse has a general power of appointment over the proceeds.

- A qualified terminable-interest property election can also qualify.

Normally, these transfers of property would violate the terminable interest rules and therefore not qualify for the marital deduction. The exceptions to the terminable interest rules, however, specifically permit these kinds of transfers to a surviving spouse to qualify for the deduction if the requirements of the exceptions are met. All of the exceptions, other than the 6-month survival contingency exception, involve trust arrangements that qualify for the marital deduction.

9. The power-of-appointment trust exception to the terminable interest rule is that the interest is not disqualified if it meets all of the following five conditions:

- The surviving spouse is entitled to all the income from the interest in question.

- The income is payable annually or more frequently to the surviving spouse.
- The surviving spouse has the power to appoint the interest to himself or herself or to his or her estate.
- The power must be exercisable by the surviving spouse alone and in all events. It can be a lifetime power or a power exercisable by the surviving spouse only at death (that is, by will) or a power exercisable in either event.
- No person other than the surviving spouse has a power to appoint any part of the interest to anyone other than the surviving spouse.

10. An estate trust is a useful alternative to the power-of-appointment trust for a number of reasons. First, in contrast to the power-of-appointment trust, under which all income must be payable to the surviving spouse annually or more frequently, the trustee of an estate trust can accumulate income within the trust instead of paying it out. If the trust is in a lower income tax bracket than that of the surviving spouse, the power to accumulate can result in income tax savings. Second, because the spouse does not have to receive all the income annually, a trustee can either invest in non-productive (non-income-producing) property or retain nonproductive assets, such as non-dividend-paying stock in a family-owned corporation.

11. There are four conditions that must be met before QTIP treatment is allowed:
    - The decedent-spouse (or donor, in the case of a lifetime gift) must make a transfer of property.
    - The surviving spouse (donee, in the case of a lifetime transfer) must be given the right to all the income. The income must be payable at least annually, and the surviving spouse must be entitled to that income for life.
    - No one can be given the right to direct that the property will go to anyone (other than the spouse) as long as that spouse is alive.
    - The first decedent-spouse's executor must make an irrevocable election on the decedent's federal estate tax return.

12. The executor of the first decedent-spouse must irrevocably elect QTIP tax treatment on the decedent's federal estate tax return. The election provides that, to the extent the QTIP property has not been consumed or given away during the lifetime of the surviving spouse, its date-of-death value (at the surviving spouse's death) will be included in the surviving spouse's estate.

13. a. If all or most of a client's estate consists of unproductive real estate (and/or stock in a closely held corporation that has not paid, and probably never will pay, any significant dividends), the surviving spouse is unlikely to receive the statutorily required "all income at least annually."

    b. The surviving spouse must be given an interest that realistically is expected to produce income (or will be usable by the spouse in a manner consistent with its value). Most closely held stock will never pay dividends or realistically be expected to produce an income consistent with its value. Therefore, without planning, the marital deduction could be lost. If there is no state law giving the surviving spouse the power to require that trust assets be sold and that trust property be made productive in a reasonable period of time, the attorney drafting the marital formula must insert a provision in the will or trust clearly giving the survivor that power. If the surviving spouse can demand that the trustee sell the stock (or other unproductive assets) and use the proceeds to purchase income-producing property, the marital deduction can be saved (even if the power itself is never actually exercised).

14. Overqualification occurs when there is an underutilization of the estate owner's basic credit amount. The result is that more property than necessary to reduce the estate owner's federal estate tax to zero goes to the surviving spouse. Thus, at the surviving spouse's death, more property than necessary is exposed to tax. This is where the proper funding of a CEBT is important. It assures an efficient use of both spouses' basic credit amounts and prevents unnecessary stacking of assets in the surviving spouse's estate. Concerns about assets being stacked in a surviving spouse's estate have been lessened somewhat by the deceased spousal unused exclusion amount (DSUEA or DSUE) provision contained in The Tax Relief, Unemployment Insurance Reauthorization, and Job Creation Act of 2010 (TRA 2010) for 2 years—2011 and 2012. The DSUE provision was made permanent under the American Taxpayer Relief Act of 2012 (ATRA 2012). The DSUE allows for the portability of any or all of a first-to-die spouse's unused exclusion amount to be carried over for use by the surviving spouse. In 2019, when the exclusion amount is $11.4 million (2019 indexed for inflation), this means that a surviving spouse could possibly have a maximum exclusion of $22.8 million (or more with indexing if the decedent spouse did not use any of his or her basic exclusion amount. The DSUE provision has the effect of minimizing concerns about over and underqualification of the marital deduction.

15. a. The following property is included in the decedent's gross estate in whole or in part because he owned the property or had rights to the property at his death:

Gross Estate

Cash	$ 75,000
Life Insurance	1,250,000
Residence held as tenants by the entirety	260,000
(50 percent of property held as tenants by	
the entirety by spouses is included in the	
estate of the first spouse to die)	
Automobile	10,000
Sole proprietorship	10,600,000
Gross estate	$12,195,000

b. Debts and administrative expenses are $155,000. The adjusted gross estate before the marital deduction equals $12,040,000.

c. The marital deduction could potentially be $12,040,000 because the will provides that all property passes to the decedent's wife. Also, the life insurance that passes outside the will and is payable in a lump sum to his wife will qualify for the marital deduction as an interest in property that passes to the surviving spouse in a qualifying manner. The maximum marital deduction is an unlimited 100 percent marital deduction. Therefore, the deduction is the entire amount of the estate after reduction for debts and expenses, which leaves a taxable estate of zero.

d. Although there will be no federal estate taxes to pay when this decedent dies because all the property passing through his estate qualifies for the unlimited marital deduction, he has not taken advantage of the basic credit amount that exists for the estate of every decedent. Therefore, upon the death of the surviving spouse, if she has not remarried, there will be no marital deduction to shelter all property included in her estate in excess of the basic credit amount in the year of her death. A basic credit amount effectively exempts from estate tax an amount equal to $11.4 million in 2019 (as indexed). The decedent could have given his surviving spouse an amount exactly sufficient to reduce the federal estate tax due, at his death, to the lowest possible figure, and he could have bequested the balance equal to a *credit/exclusion (equivalent) bypass trust* (CEBT) to the children. In this way, he would have utilized the marital deduction as well as the basic credit amount existing at the time of his death to obtain the maximum federal estate tax savings both at his death and when his spouse dies. After 2010, the deceased spousal unused exemption (DSUE) provision in TRA 2010 and ATRA 2012 is also available for married couples. For some estates, using the DSUE will diminish or even negate the need for credit equivalent bypass trust (CEBT) planning.

16. There are two types of formula bequests:

   - the pecuniary (dollar) amount

   - the fractional share

The *pecuniary-amount bequest* provides that the survivor will receive a fixed-dollar amount, and it takes into consideration not only property passing under the will but also all property that qualifies for the marital deduction. The *fractional-share bequest* is an attempt to accomplish the same goal by giving the surviving spouse a fractional share in the residue of the estate—that is, a fractional share of each asset after specific bequests have been made.

17. It is advisable to determine how much the surviving spouse should be given under the marital bequest. It may be that the surviving spouse should be given less than the amount necessary to reduce taxes in the decedent's estate to zero. Perhaps the surviving spouse should be given only one-half of the estate. Although the time-use (or psychological) value of tax money saved on the death of the first spouse may offset the cost, the (potential) increase in total taxes payable should be considered. Such decisions may depend on the use to which tax savings are put at the first death. If the money is used to assure or enhance the lifestyle of the surviving spouse, then it is likely to result in a long-run benefit.

If the excess of the amount necessary to *equalize the two estates* is invested by the surviving spouse, greater estate taxation may result when he or she dies. The net result could be that fewer assets will pass to the next generation due to taxes. Equalization of spousal estates, however, is of decreasing importance while the basic credit amount is as high as $11.4 million in 2019 and the DSUE is available for spousal estate planning in 2019.

18. There are many means of obtaining the marital deduction. One method is outright transfer of property to the surviving spouse by will or through life insurance death proceeds. There are advantages to an outright bequest, as follows:

   - The spouse has the right to use and manage marital assets as he or she desires.

   - No trustee fees or court accountings are required.

- Giving the spouse the marital share discourages him or her from electing against the testator's will.

- Assets the surviving spouse receives are available to his or her executor to meet estate liquidity needs.

- The surviving spouse can be given (and can safely retain) non-income-producing assets, such as the non-dividend-paying stock in a family-owned corporation.

But an outright bequest has a number of disadvantages.

- No protection is provided for a spendthrift spouse.

- There is no management with investment expertise.

- The surviving spouse's creditors can attach the bequest both during lifetime and at death.

- The surviving spouse can easily dispose of the bequest however he or she wishes during lifetime—even to the exclusion of his or her children and in favor of a second spouse and children.

- Assets the surviving spouse has not given away or consumed will be included in his or her probate estate.

19. a. One method of providing a marital bequest is to leave property in a power-of-appointment trust. Typically, the power-of-appointment trust gives the spouse a lifetime interest in the trust property, coupled with the right to specify the identity of the remainderperson during lifetime or in his or her will. It usually also provides that if the surviving spouse fails to name the beneficiaries of trust assets, the trust corpus will go to a *taker in default*, a beneficiary named by the grantor of the trust. The trustee (and sometimes the surviving spouse) is often given additional powers over trust assets. These might include the right to use trust principal for emergencies or to make gifts to children and grandchildren.

   Another form of marital bequest under a will is known as an *estate trust*. This type of trust is not required to give the surviving spouse all the income during his or her lifetime, but pays all the accumulated income and the corpus to the surviving spouse's estate when he or she dies.

   b. The advantages of a power-of-appointment trust include the following:

   - As in the case of an outright gift, the surviving spouse may be discouraged from electing against the decedent's will.

- Protection is afforded to some degree against the surviving spouse's possible spendthrift habits.

- Protection is provided against the surviving spouse's creditors and against the creditors of the spouse's estate.

- Principal distributions can be varied, depending on the surviving spouse's needs.

- The surviving spouse's right to dispose of the property during lifetime can be limited.

- Probate of the trust corpus can be avoided when the surviving spouse dies.

- Management and financial guidance are provided for the surviving spouse.

But there are disadvantages of a power-of-appointment trust.

- Certain trustee fees and accounting costs are involved.

- Assets in a power-of-appointment trust may not be available to the surviving spouse's executor for the payments of costs and taxes (unless the surviving spouse appoints the assets to his or her estate).

- Non-income-producing property, such as life insurance, cannot safely be obtained or retained in the trust.

Advantages of the estate trust include the following:

- Non-income-producing property can be purchased and safely retained by the trustee.

- Income tax savings can be realized by the accumulation of the income in the trust in years when the trust's income tax bracket is lower than the surviving spouse's bracket.

- Protection is provided against the surviving spouse's spendthrift habits, if any.

- Protection is afforded against the surviving spouse's creditors during lifetime.

- The surviving spouse is unable to make lifetime assignments of trust property.

- Assets are available to the surviving spouse's executor.

Disadvantages of the estate trust consist mainly of its inflexibility from the surviving spouse's viewpoint.

- The surviving spouse has no freedom to use and manage trust assets.

- The surviving spouse is restricted in disposing of any property in the trust during lifetime.

- Assets in the trust generate trustee fees and accounting costs.

Chapter 15:

The Charitable Deduction

Learning Objectives

An understanding of the material in this chapter should enable the student to do the following:

LO 15.1   **Identify the general categories of organizations that entitle an estate to a charitable deduction as defined in the Internal Revenue Code.**

LO 15.2   **Identify the basic types of charitable bequests.**

LO 15.3   **Describe the various forms of charitable remainder and lead trusts and explain their differences.**

LO 15.4   **Describe the basic characteristics of charitable gift annuities.**

LO 15.5   **Describe the basic characteristics of community foundations.**

LO 15.6   **Describe the basic characteristics of donor-advised funds.**

LO 15.7   **Describe the basic characteristics of private foundations.**

LO 15.1   **Identify the general categories of organizations that entitle an estate to a charitable deduction as defined in the Internal Revenue Code.**

Types of Charitable Organizations

An estate tax charitable deduction is allowed for the full value of property transferred to a qualified charity, but only if the property is included in the donor's gross estate. Just as there are income tax rules about gifts to qualified charities, so are there specific rules governing charitable gifts of property included in an estate. Furthermore, it is possible for a charitable contribution made during the donor's lifetime to generate both an income tax deduction and an estate tax deduction if the value of the property is includible in the donor's gross estate. The value of a lifetime transfer may be included in the gross estate if the donor retains some interest in the property or powers over the property for life. A gift of a life insurance policy to a qualified charity, made within 3 years of the donor's death and includible in the gross estate, also qualifies for the deduction.

The charitable deduction is presently and has been an unlimited deduction for property passing to a qualified charity as defined in the Code. Qualified charitable organizations include

- corporations operated exclusively for religious, charitable, scientific, literary, or educational purposes, including the encouragement of art and the prevention of cruelty to children or animals

- the United States, any state or political subdivision, or the District of Columbia, provided that contributions are made exclusively for public purposes

- a fraternal society, order, or association, if the contributions are used exclusively for the charitable purposes listed above

- the use of any veterans' organization incorporated by an act of Congress or its departments, local chapters, or posts

DENIAL OF CHARITABLE DEDUCTION

A charitable deduction for any of the above bequests is denied if any part of the net earnings of these organizations inures to the benefit of a private stockholder or individual. The deduction is also denied if a substantial part of the charitable organization's activities involves preparation of propaganda or other methods that attempt to influence legislation. Likewise, a deduction is denied if the charity engages in any political campaign in behalf of a candidate for public office or other prohibited transactions. A deduction is also denied if, at the time of the donor-decedent's death, the gift is contingent upon the happening of an event or some act, unless the probability that this contingency will not occur is so remote that it is negligible. In addition, if the charitable beneficiary or a trustee has the power to use the property or funds contributed to the charity in whole or in part for noncharitable purposes or uses, the charitable deduction applies only to that part of the property or money not subject to this power.

Disclaimers

If property is transferred from a decedent's estate to a charitable organization because there has been a qualified disclaimer by a prior beneficiary, a charitable deduction is allowed for amounts that are actually transferred to the charity. For purposes of the charitable estate tax deduction, a complete termination of a power to consume, invade, or appropriate property for the benefit of an individual prior to the exercise of such power is considered to be a qualified disclaimer if the termination occurs before the due date for filing the estate tax return.

Payment of Death Taxes

If, under the terms of the will or provisions of local law, payment of death taxes or other deductible expenses is to be made from the charitable bequest, the charitable deduction is reduced by those amounts used to pay debts or taxes. In other words, the deduction is limited to the actual amount that passes free and clear to the charity for its charitable purposes. If the will provides that taxes and administration expenses are to be paid from the residue and the charitable bequest is also payable out of the residue, the residuary bequest is diminished by the amount of expenses and taxes paid. This creates a complex circular problem because a reduction of the charitable deduction has the effect of increasing the taxable estate as well as the estate tax. There is an estate tax regulation that addresses this situation where death taxes are paid from a deductible interest. It is called an *interrelated computation*; the text will not cover this calculation.

LO 15.2   Identify the basic types of charitable bequests.

TYPES OF CHARITABLE BEQUESTS

In addition to outright bequests of entire interests, charitable gifts can be in other forms including

- powers of appointment
- partial interests
- split gifts
- charitable remainder trusts
- charitable lead trusts
- charitable gift annuities
- community foundations
- donor-advised funds
- private foundations

Powers of Appointment

A charitable deduction is allowed for property that is included in the decedent's gross estate because the decedent possessed a general power of appointment over the property that passes to a charity by virtue of an exercise, release, or lapse of that power. It is considered to be a deductible bequest by the decedent to a charitable beneficiary.

Partial Interests

split-interest arrangement

There are many instances in which a donor, although wishing a charity to receive certain property eventually, wants a family member to enjoy the property first. This situation, called a **split-interest arrangement**, is governed by IRC Secs. 170, 2522, and 2055. Charitable income, gift, and estate tax deductions are allowed for the value of less than an entire interest passing to a charity if certain complex rules are met. The provisions in the tax law state that gifts of a remainder interest in trust are deductible for federal income, estate, or gift tax purposes only if the trust is a charitable remainder annuity trust, charitable remainder unitrust, or pooled-income fund. The valuation rules mandated by Secs. 664 and 7520 must be used to determine the specific amount of the deduction available. The tables of actuarial factors for calculating the deductions are found in *Actuarial Values Aleph Volume and Actuarial Values Beth Volume*, IRS Publications 1457 and 1458. The size of the deduction is based on the length of the noncharitable term or the measuring life of the noncharitable life interest(s), the size of annuity or unitrust payment paid to the noncharitable beneficiary, and the Sec. 7520 rate in effect at the time of the donation. The types of partial interests that may be bequeathed to a charity and qualify for the charitable deduction are:

- a testamentary gift of an undivided portion of the decedent's entire interest in property not held in trust. An undivided portion means a fraction or percentage of each interest or right owned by the decedent in the property. Furthermore, the decedent's interest in a fraction of every part of the whole must persist over the entire term that his or her interest in the property exists.

- a nontrust remainder interest in a personal residence. A charitable deduction is allowed for the transfer by the decedent at death of a remainder interest in his or her personal residence. The residence need not be the decedent's principal residence. It includes any residence used by the decedent for any part of the year (even as a vacation home). The charitable remainder interest pertains to the residence itself as opposed to any proceeds received on the sale of the residence.

- a nontrust remainder interest in a farm transferred by the decedent at death to a qualified charity, or a transfer of a partial interest in property to a charitable organization exclusively for conservation purposes. Special rules must be adhered to upon the transfer of these partial interests either in real estate or for conservation purposes.

- remainder interests in trust to charitable remainder trusts and pooled- income funds.

- a charitable lead trust.

LO 15.3   Describe the various forms of charitable remainder and lead trusts and explain their differences.

Charitable Remainder Trusts

charitable remainder trust (CRT)

A **charitable remainder trust (CRT)** occurs when a decedent transfers a remainder interest in property to a charity in trust. It must be made in the form of a charitable remainder annuity trust, unitrust, or pooled-income fund. Otherwise, no estate tax charitable deduction is allowed. These arrangements usually provide for an income interest to a noncharitable beneficiary with the remainder to the charitable organization. The trust instrument must provide that payments of the unitrust or annuity amounts begin as of the date of death if the charitable interest is to qualify for the estate tax charitable deduction. Gifts made in one of these forms are the only way to provide for income to individuals who are noncharitable beneficiaries while making a gift at the same time to a charitable organization that qualifies for an income, estate, or gift tax deduction. A donor transferring property to a CRT during his or her lifetime is entitled to a federal income tax deduction as well as a gift tax deduction. Both the federal income and gift tax deductions are limited to the actuarial value of the remainder interest. If the noncharitable beneficiary is someone other than the donor, the transfer may be subject to gift taxation. Both types of trusts may be created during lifetime or under a person's will.

The Taxpayer Relief Act of 1997 (TRA '97) imposed two limitations with respect to charitable remainder trusts (CRTs):

> For transfers in trust after June 18, 1997, the percentage of assets required to be distributed at least annually cannot exceed 50 percent of the initial fair market value of the trust assets for charitable annuity trusts, or 50 percent of the annual value of the trust assets for charitable unitrusts.

> For transfers in trust after July 28, 1997, the value of the remainder interest of a CRT must be at least 10 percent of the value of the property transferred to the trust. In other words, the value of the remainder interest must be at least 10 percent of the fair market value of all trust contributions. This limitation may affect the number of individuals who can qualify for CRT planning.

Although both the annuity trust and the unitrust are based on the same provisions in the tax law and exist for the same reasons, there are practical distinctions between the two types of trusts.

Annuity Trusts

charitable remainder annuity trust (CRAT)

A **charitable remainder annuity trust (CRAT)** is one that provides a noncharitable income beneficiary with a fixed sum annuity that is required to be worth at least 5 percent of the initial net fair market value of the property paid in trust. This amount must be paid at least annually to one or more noncharitable beneficiaries who are alive when the trust is created. Upon the death of the last income beneficiary or at the end of a term of years not greater than 20, the remainder interest must be held for or paid to a qualified charitable organization. (See the figure below.)

Charitable Remainder Trust

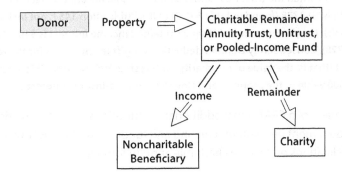

EXAMPLE

Dan Donor transfers property valued at $400,000 to a CRAT that provides for a 5 percent of the initial value of the principal payout for a 20-year term; consequently, $20,000 will be distributed annually to the noncharitable income beneficiary.

The payout amount and remainder amount vary inversely; that is, the greater the amount devoted to noncharitable payouts, the lesser the remainder passing to the charitable remainderman. Also, trust investment returns must be sufficient to maintain current distributions in order to avoid depleting the trust assets which eventually will pass to the charity. In other words, high-payout distributions to noncharitable beneficiaries may defeat the ability of assets to maintain their initial funding level. With a CRAT investment, risk is borne by the charitable remainderman. For the most part, the investment strategy of a CRAT is to allow for enough liquidity to pay the noncharitable distribution amounts, avoid decreases of initial trust funding, and at a minimum sustain long-term growth. Therefore, a lower payout rate such as 5 percent is more likely to maintain the original funding base over the term of the trust. Note, too, that charitable remainder annuity trusts are also subject to a 5-percent probability test as described in Revenue Ruling 77-374. This rule requires that, at the time of creation, all charitable remainder annuity trusts have a probability of 5 percent or less that the corpus will be exhausted and therefore pass minimal or no value to charity. An additional consideration is that when payouts to noncharitable beneficiaries are made with like-kind property, the recipient may be subject to gain recognition for income tax purposes. The appropriate Section 7520 (subtraction valuation method) rate is used for determining the present value of the remainder interest passing to charity for transfer-tax purposes.

EXAMPLE

Donna Donor, aged 65, creates a CRAT and funds the trust with $200,000. The trust terms provide for a payment of $10,000 from the CRAT annually. If the Sec. 7520 rate was 5.2 percent when the trust was funded and the single life annuity factor for someone aged 65 is 10.3728 (found in Table S (5.2) of IRS Publication 1457, not included in the materials), the present value of Donna's retained income interest is $103,728 ($10,000 x 10.3728). Consequently Donna's deduction for gift tax purposes for the remainder interest (that is, the value of the charity's interest) is $96,272 (the difference of the total $200,000 value of the property and Donna's retained-income interest).

One disadvantage of a CRAT is that additional contributions cannot be made to an existing trust. This requirement necessitates creating and funding another CRAT when a donor with charitable inclinations prefers the charitable annuity format.

Unitrusts

charitable remainder unitrust (CRUT)

A **charitable remainder unitrust (CRUT)** differs from an annuity trust in that a fixed percentage (not less than 5 percent of the net fair market value of the trust assets as annually revalued) is paid at least annually to one or more noncharitable income beneficiaries. Again, as with the annuity trust, the remainder interest will be paid to or held for the benefit of a qualified charitable organization, either at the death of the last income beneficiary or after a term of years not greater than 20.

In essence, the unitrust differs from the annuity trust in that the annual income is more in the form of a variable annuity. Another distinction between the two trusts concerns payment of income. Unlike the CRAT, CRUT trust assets are usually managed to produce at least moderate increases in short-term growth, but there is a greater emphasis on long-term, overall growth. In the annuity trust, if trust income is insufficient to meet the annual payment, the income beneficiary must be paid out of principal. In the case of the unitrust, however, the trust may provide that if income is insufficient, no payment will be made out of principal. Payments are made from income only. In any year when a trust has more than enough income to meet its present payments, the deficit of earlier years may be paid at that time. (See NIMCRUTs.) Since additional contributions may be made to unitrusts, donors have the ability to increase noncharitable distribution amounts and vary trust portfolios.

Planning Point: If a client is particularly concerned about the certainty of a fixed payout, the charitable remainder annuity trust is the better choice. The payout will not increase if the value of the trust assets increases during a period of inflation; likewise the payout will not decrease if the value of the trust corpus falls during an economic downturn.

On the other hand, if the client is more interested in an approach in which the payout depends on the annual value of the trust assets or the client wants increased payments over the trust term, the charitable remainder unitrust is more appropriate.

Net Income Unitrusts (NIMCRUTs)

NIMCRUT

One flexible payout pattern for charitable remainder trusts is called a net income unitrust or **NIMCRUT**. This type of arrangement is available only for CRUTs. In essence, NIMCRUTs are a regular unitrust except that the NIMCRUT's payout is limited to the lesser of the stated unitrust payout percentage or the net income earned by the CRUT during the year. What constitutes income is determined by a state's principal and income laws as modified by the CRUT document. NIMCRUTs are different from standard CRUTs in that if the NIMCRUT does not realize enough current income to make the stated unitrust payment, the annual payment is reduced to the amount of the actual income earned. Thus, the NIMCRUT protects the interests of the remainder beneficiary (that is, the charitable beneficiary) against invasion of principal, because the trustee is prohibited from invading principal for the benefit of noncharitable beneficiaries.

Beneficiaries of a standard CRUT receive their annual payments, regardless of the income the CRUT realizes, while beneficiaries of a NIMCRUT might receive smaller payments depending on trust income. There is one characteristic that makes NIMCRUTs especially unique. The NIMCRUT format provides for a make-up feature under which, in future years, noncharitable beneficiaries can receive payments in excess of the stated unitrust percentage to make up arrearages that might have occurred when the NIMCRUT did not have sufficient income to pay the full-stated-unitrust amount. NIMCRUTs, therefore, can offer good flexibility for CRTs that invest in property that produces little or fluctuating income and/or does not lend itself to be readily converted into cash to make a required payment on, for example, an undivided parcel of real estate. It is important for planners to be aware that NIMCRUT arrangements are scrutinized by the IRS.

Another CRUT variation is referred to as a FLIP-CRUT or FLIP UNITRUST. A FLIP-CRUT is essentially a NIMCRUT with a feature that allows the NIMCRUT, upon a qualifying-triggering event provided for in the trust instrument, to become a regular CRUT.

Planning Point: The flexibility of NIMCRUTs makes them popular charitable-planning devices. With a NIMCRUT, trustees and investment advisers are able to change asset allocations in order to plan and vary income distributions to noncharitable beneficiaries. For instance, assets within the trust could be selected to generate minimal income for a preretirement beneficiary and then reallocated to generate increased income for retirement years.

Pooled-income Funds

pooled-income fund (PIF)

A **pooled-income fund (PIF)** is much like a mutual fund maintained by a qualified charity. The fund contains commingled donations from many sources. In effect, a donor's donation purchases units in the fund consisting of diversified assets contributed by other donors. The income attributable to these units is paid at least annually to the noncharitable beneficiaries for life. An interest for a term of years is not permitted with a pooled-income fund. The fund does not distribute or invade corpus for the benefit of an income beneficiary. At the end of the life-income interest, the remainder goes to the charity maintaining the fund. A donor receives a transfer tax charitable deduction for the value of the charitable remainder interest. The value of the remainder interest is the amount by which the fair market value of the property exceeds the present value of the donor's retained income interest.

Pooled-income funds are popular with donors having relatively small amounts to contribute to charity. Donors are spared the expense and effort of having separate trusts drafted as would be the case with CRTs.

EXAMPLE

Derek Donor, aged 60, transfers $25,000 to a pooled-income fund. Assume that at the time the trust was funded, the Section 7520 rate was 4 percent and the single-life remainder interest factor (Single Life Table S (4.0) IRS Publication 1457, not included in the materials) for a 60-year-old is .47586.

$$\$25,000 \times .47586 = \$11,897$$

Therefore, the value of the remainder interest (and Derek's charitable deduction for gift tax purposes) is $11,897.

LO 15.4   Describe the basic characteristics of charitable gift annuities.

Charitable Lead Trusts

charitable lead trusts (CLT)

charitable lead annuity trust (CLAT)

These types of gifts work in reverse of the charitable remainder trusts; hence, they are commonly called **charitable lead trusts (CLT)**. (See the figure below.) The decedent transfers an income interest in property to a charity with the remainder to a noncharitable entity. The time period is not limited to 20 years as it is with a CRT. Unless this interest is in the form of a guaranteed-annuity interest or unitrust interest, the charitable deduction will be disallowed. These guaranteed interests refer to the right to receive a determinable amount at least annually for a specific term or for the life or lives of individuals living at the time of the decedent's death. With a **charitable lead annuity trust (CLAT),** a certain dollar amount is guaranteed to be paid to the charity at least annually as determined by the Sec. 7520 rates used to calculate the value of term interests, life estates, annuities, and remainder interests. The Sec. 7520 rate is 120 percent of the applicable federal midterm rate (AFMR). With a charitable lead unitrust (CLUT), a specified percentage amount (as revalued annually) is paid each year to the charity.

An insurance company or a similar organization regularly engaged in the business of issuing annuity contracts must pay the guaranteed annuity. A guaranteed unitrust interest refers to the right to receive payment of a fixed percentage of the net fair market value of the property that funds the unitrust revalued at least annually. The unitrust interest must be paid by an insurance company or any other similar organization, as mentioned above. The primary objective of a charitable lead trust is for the charity to benefit from the receipt of income for a term of years while also distributing the growth in trust value to the remaindermen at the end of the term at a significantly reduced transfer-tax cost. Like charitable remainder trusts, a CLT may be arranged during the donor's lifetime or at death. The annuity or unitrust interests of CLATs and CLUTs may vary as to the income, gift, and estate tax consequences. This device may be a useful income-tax-savings approach for lifetime transfers because the donor is allowed to take a current income tax deduction (subject to limitations) for the value of the income interest transferred to charity.

Charitable Lead Trust

Charitable Lead Trust
- income to charity
- remainder to noncharitable beneficiary

EXAMPLE

Linda, aged 60, established a charitable lead trust with $1 million of property. The trust is required to pay the charity $50,000 a year for a 20-year term. If the Sec. 7520 rate is 5 percent when the trust is funded and the term certain annuity factor for someone 60 years old is 12.4622, the present value of the charity's lead interest that Linda can take as a charitable gift tax deduction is $623,110 ($50,000 × 12.4622). Note that if the actual growth rate of the trust assets is greater than the Sec. 7520 5 percent rate, the distribution to the remaindermen will be greater than $1 million.

The manner in which CLT income is taxed depends on whether the CLT is characterized as a grantor or nongrantor trust. In essence, if the inter vivos trust is structured as a grantor trust for income tax purposes, the donor is responsible for paying income tax on the income generated by the trust property and is entitled to a charitable income tax deduction for the present value of the charity's income interest. The deduction is limited to certain income tax limitations. If the trust corpus (remainder interest) is to revert to the grantor, there is no gift liability upon creation of the trust. In this case, the donor may take an income tax deduction for the present value of the income stream passing to the charity and is liable for income tax on future income generated by the trust property. If the trust is a nongrantor trust for income tax purposes, the trust is responsible for income tax on income that exceeds what is paid to the charity. The trust receives a corresponding deduction annually for the amount of income paid to the charity. When, at the end of the trust term, the property is to pass to someone other than the donor or the donor's spouse, such as the donor's children, the donor has made a taxable future interest gift to the children. The value of the gift is reduced by the value of the lead interest passing to charity.

A testamentary CLT may also be used to reduce the estate tax burden on large estates because the estate may receive a charitable estate tax deduction for the value of the lead payments to charity. For example, suppose a wealthy decedent leaves his or her entire residuary estate to a CLT. The trust provides various charities, selected by the trustees, with a specified percentage of the initial value of the principal for 20 years. At the termination of the trust, the decedent's family will receive the remaining principal. Due to an assumed favorable Sec. 7520 interest rate in effect at the time of death, the estate tax charitable deduction could be a large percentage of the value of the decedent-transferor's residuary estate.

Planning Point: A charitable lead trust is a popular device when the donor wants to keep the property within the family unit but at the same time wishes to benefit one or more charities. This type of arrangement is beneficial in situations where the donor does not need the income for an established time period. Optimal results of CLTs occur when the assets appreciate significantly for the benefit of the remaindermen, and the trust earns sufficient income to make the required payouts to charity. With proper structuring, a CLT may cause the value of the remainder interest (which often passes to the grantor's children) to be zero, or approximately zero, for transfer tax purposes. This result occurs when the value of the payouts to charity over the charitable term closely approximates the value of the remainder interest at the creation of the trust. If the rate of return on trust property is greater than amounts necessary to sustain the charitable payments, the appreciated remainder interest may avoid all transfer taxation.

In addition to the more recognized charitable remainder trusts and charitable lead trusts, there are numerous charitable contribution devices that can be used in estate planning. General descriptions of the types of charitable arrangements frequently used in estate and gift planning are discussed below.

In summary: When an interest in property passes from a decedent to one or more charities, and an interest in the same property passes from a decedent to noncharitable beneficiaries for less than adequate and full consideration in money or money's worth, the value of the interest passing to charity is not allowed the estate tax charitable deduction unless it is in a specified form under Sec. 2055(e)(2).

Charitable Gift Annuities

charitable gift annuity (CGA)

A **charitable gift annuity (CGA)** is a contract entered into between a donor and a qualified charity. This type of charitable arrangement provides a deferred gift to a qualified charity and annual income payments to the donor for the rest of his or her life. The donor makes a transfer to the charity of cash or appreciated property. In return, the charity agrees to pay an annuity to an annuitant who may be the donor or one or more others chosen by the donor. In essence, the donor is purchasing an annuity from the charity and at the same time making a future-interest gift to the charity. The donation qualifies for a tax deduction because the fair market value of the contributed property is in excess of the present value of the life annuity. Because the charity's promise to pay must be unsecured, the donor bears the risk of the charity honoring the agreement. The precise income tax implications of charitable gift annuities vary according to the specific contract terms: whether there are one or more annuitants, when the annuity payments to the annuitant(s) commence, and so forth. The charitable gift annuity device is used when the donor wants to make a contribution to charity and at the same time receive or give to another an income stream—that is, make a charitable donation but get some value back from the gifted property. For income tax purposes, each annuity payment is composed of a return of principal, capital gain, and ordinary income. Although tax is avoided on any appreciation of capital gain at the time the property is transferred to the charity, a proportionate amount of the unrealized capital gain is allocated to each payment. If the annuitant lives beyond life expectancy, payments received are treated as ordinary income. If the annuitant dies prior to recovering his or her investment in the contract, a deduction on the decedent's final income tax return is allowed for the remaining balance.

Advantages of a charitable gift annuity include the following:

- The donor receives an immediate income tax deduction.
- If appreciated property is donated, the donor is able to defer gain over the donor's lifetime.
- It is simple in design and administration.
- No trust agreement or trustee's fees are required.
- The donor receives fixed annual payments for life that, among other possibilities, may be used to supplement retirement income.

As mentioned above, for gift tax purposes, the donation qualifies for a gift tax deduction because the fair market value of the contributed property will be in excess of the present value of the life annuity. The charity benefits because it will receive the excess value at the annuitant's death. The annual gift tax exclusion may apply if it is an immediate rather than deferred annuity. A 709 gift tax return should be filed for charitable gift annuities.

LO 15.5   Describe the basic characteristics of community foundations.

Community Foundations

community foundations

Community foundations have been a form of charitable organization for almost a century. They are grant-making entities that benefit the specified community. Generally speaking, a community foundation is a nonprofit grant-making organization that consists of an amalgamation of separate grant-making accounts. Donations to the organization are used to make grants for the benefit and needs of the general community. Community needs are determined through the efforts of foundation committee members, sometimes with the involvement of donors. Knowledgeable management and investment of donations by the foundation serve to maximize benefits provided to the local community. There may be separate funds or trusts within a community foundation. The separate funds may be either restricted or unrestricted. Committee members of the foundation determine how the unrestricted funds are used for community needs; donors are able to determine how restricted funds are spent.

Contributions of property to community foundations are popular when a donor wants to play a charitable and decision-making role in benefiting his or her local community. Donor contributions are used to establish a fund or account. The contributions made may be completely unfettered or may be bound by specific requirements. Although the focus of community foundations is usually to provide support for local charitable efforts, such as the ballet, art museum, and so forth, it is not uncommon for grants to be made on a nationally recognized basis such as to universities. Making gifts to community foundations is desirable because the organization is an already established charity and does not require the donor to bear the ongoing expenses that are associated with other charitable enterprises such as supporting organizations[1] and private foundations. There are no transfer tax consequences for donations to community foundations as a result of the charitable gift and estate tax deductions. Lifetime donations allow for income tax deductions.

---

1.   A supporting organization is created when a donor establishes a separate charitable trust or corporation affiliated with a community foundation. The resulting grant-making entity is classified as a supporting organization.

LO 15.6   Describe the basic characteristics of donor-advised funds.

Donor-advised Funds

donor-advised fund (DAF)

A **donor-advised fund (DAF)** is another type of charitable and estate planning technique. With this arrangement, a donor makes a donation to a public charity or community foundation, and the charity establishes a set-aside or subaccount fund named by the donor. Subject to the sponsoring charity's approval, the donor, or someone designated by the donor, makes recommendations for grants to be made from the fund for the benefit of certain permissible charitable beneficiaries. The donor may make the contributions to the charity anonymously or in his or her name or family name. Once the donor makes the contribution, the 501(c)(3) organization has legal control over the funds.

Again, there are no transfer tax ramifications due to the charitable gift and estate tax deductions. The donor is entitled to an income tax deduction that varies according to the donor's adjusted gross income and the type of property contributed to the donor-advised fund. Cash contributions are limited to 50 percent of a donor's adjusted gross income and 30 percent for gifts of appreciated property. Certain types of property, however, are allowed a deduction at full fair market value when contributed to a DAF. The 2006 Pension Protection Act put in new requirements and excise taxes to stop abuse of DAFs.

LO 15.7   Describe the basic characteristics of private foundations.

Private Foundations

private foundation

For federal tax purposes, there are two types of charities: public charities and private foundations. A **private foundation** is typically a charitable entity that is created, funded, and run by a donor or the donor's family. It is through the foundation organization that a donor makes contributions to one or more public charities. Private foundations are subject to strict and limiting tax rules and could, additionally, become subject to harsh excise taxes. Despite the rules and taxes associated with private foundations, they are an attractive charitable device because of the flexibility and control they offer to philanthropically inclined donors. Private foundations, also called family foundations, are created by donors who have substantial wealth. They provide an excellent means for combining family and philanthropic purposes because the organization provisions typically require family members to meet regularly to determine charitable expenditures. Original donors look to the family foundation as a way to instill social and philanthropic responsibility in their heirs in generations to come.

Private foundations are also advantageous because highly appreciated property contributed to the entity avoids capital gains taxes. If publicly traded securities are contributed, the full fair market value can be taken. Private foundations allow donors who desire visibility to receive public recognition of their philanthropic endeavors.

The disadvantages of private foundations include potentially costly administration expenses. The main administrative costs result from the creation of the organization and compliance with private foundation rules, maintenance of tax-exempt status, and annual reporting. Excise taxes are imposed on the foundation and its managers if the foundation fails to comply with the private foundation rules. For income tax purposes, lower annual charitable deduction percentages are allowed as compared to public charities: 20 percent instead of 30 percent of adjusted gross income for donations of capital gain assets, and 30 percent instead of 50 percent of adjusted gross income for cash donations. There are also restrictive rules pertaining to the donor-owners of closely held businesses.

Valuation

The gift of a partial interest (including a remainder interest to a charity) is valued at the fair market value of the interest on the appropriate valuation date. This may be the date of the gift or the date of death. The fair market value of an annuity, life estate, term of years, remainder, reversion, or unitrust interest is its present value. The present value of remainder interests in charitable remainder annuity trusts, unitrusts, or pooled-income funds is determined under the income tax regulations. The present value of a guaranteed annuity interest is determined under estate tax regulations. The present value of a unitrust interest is found by subtracting the present value of all interests in the transferred property other than the unitrust interest from the fair market value of the transferred property.

MINI-CASE: GEORGE JOHNSON

George Johnson, an executive employee of a Fortune 500 company, died in 2019, leaving property in his own name consisting of

Cash in the bank	$2,125,000
Real estate	$5,810,000
Municipal bonds	$500,000

In addition, George and his wife owned their home jointly with right of survivorship. The entire purchase price for this property, which was purchased 20 years ago, was $100,000, all paid by George. Its value at the date of his death was $1,370,000.

George made a gift of stock to his daughter early in the year of his death. The stock was worth $55,000 on the date of the gift. Assume the gift tax George paid after subtracting the annual gift tax exclusion was $8,200.

George owned three life insurance policies on his life: policy A for $500,000, payable in a lump sum to his wife; policy B for $1,500,000, payable to his wife with interest for life and full right to withdraw principal at any time, otherwise to her estate; and policy C for $130,000, payable to a qualified nonprofit educational institution.

In addition, his wife is the beneficiary of the death benefit under a qualified noncontributory retirement plan maintained by George's employer. The death benefit payable as an annuity is valued at $2,450,000 at the time of George's death.

When George died, his debts amounted to $2,000. Funeral expenses were $2,000, and the cost of the administration of his estate—including executor's and attorney's fees—is estimated at $50,000. Accrued taxes at the time of George's death were $7,000.

George's will leaves one-half of his probate estate outright to his wife and one-half outright to his daughter. All expenses, taxes, and debts are to be paid from the share given to his daughter.

1. List the items that will be included in George's gross estate, indicating whether they are probate or nonprobate assets (passing outside the will). Explain why each is included. Calculate his gross estate.

2. Determine George's adjusted gross estate before reduction by any marital or charitable deduction.

3. Compute the taxable estate, listing those items that qualify for the marital or charitable deduction and their values. Assume no death taxes are imposed by George's state of domicile.

CHAPTER REVIEW

Key Terms and Concepts

split-interest arrangement
charitable remainder trust (CRT)
charitable remainder annuity trust
   (CRAT)
charitable remainder unitrust (CRUT)
net income unitrust (NIMCRUT)
pooled-income fund (PIF)

charitable lead trusts (CLT)
charitable lead annuity trust (CLAT)
charitable gift annuity (CGA)
community foundations
donor-advised fund (DAF)
private foundation

Chapter 15: Review Questions

1. Describe the general rule for the charitable deduction and any limitations on the deduction. [LO 15.1]

2. How may a disclaimer be used to pass property to a charity? [LO 15.1]

3. Assuming that all debts, expenses, and taxes are to be paid from the residuary estate, how is the amount of a charitable bequest affected if the charitable gift is to be made from the residue? [LO 15.1]

4. Identify the basic types of charitable bequests that qualify for the charitable deduction. [LO 15.2]

5. Identify the four general types of partial interests passing to charity that can qualify for the charitable deduction. [LO 15.2]

6. Explain how transfers to charity may be split to take advantage of both the charitable and marital deductions. [LO 15.3]

7. What are the three ways that remainder interests in trusts may be given to charities so they will qualify for the charitable deduction? In all cases, assume that there is also a noncharitable beneficiary. [LO 15.3]

8. What is a charitable gift annuity and what are its advantages? [LO 15.4]

9. Explain how community foundations are grant-making entities. [LO 15.5]

10. Describe the basic characteristics of donor-advised funds. [LO 15.6]

11. Identify the advantages and disadvantages of private foundations. [LO 15.7]

Answers to Mini-Case

The calculation of the gross estate, adjusted gross estate, and taxable estate of George Johnson is as follows:

			Probate or Nonprobate	Value	
a. Gross estate					
	i. Property owned by decedent alone				
		Cash	P	$2,125,000	
		Real estate	P	5,810,000	
		Municipal bonds	P	500,000	
				8,435,000	8,435,000
plus	ii. One-half of jointly held spousal property		NP	685,000	685,000
plus	iii. Life insurance proceeds (included because decedent was owner)				
		Policy A—beneficiary W	NP	500,000	
		Policy B—beneficiary W	NP	1,500,000	
		Policy C— beneficiary — charity	NP	130,000	
				2,130,000	2,130,000
plus	iv. Qualified plan death benefit payable as annuity		NP		450,000
plus	v. Gift tax on taxable gift of $40,000 ($55,000 – $15,000 [annual gift tax exclusion] = $40,000			8,200	8,200
equals	*Gross estate*				$13,700,000
b. Adjusted gross estate					
minus	Debts and expenses			61,000	61,000
equals	*Adjusted gross estate*				$13,639,000
c. Taxable estate					
	Probate estate				
		Cash		2,125,000	
		Real estate		5,810,000	
		Municipal bonds		500,000	8,435,000
	Property qualifying for marital deduction				
		One-half of probate estate		$4,217,500	

		One-half of residence held as joint tenants with right of survivorship	685,000	
		Life insurance passing to surviving spouse	1,000,000	
		Qualified plan death benefit	450,000	
			8,352,500	8,352,500
		Adjusted gross estate		13,639,000
minus		i. Marital deduction	8,352,000	
minus		ii. Charitable deduction ($130,000 life insurance proceeds)	130,000	
		State death taxes	0	
		Total deductions	8,352,000	8,352,000
equals		*Taxable estate*		$5,156,500

Chapter 15: Review Answers

1. An estate tax charitable deduction is allowed for the full value of property transferred to a qualified charity, but only if the property is included in the donor's gross estate.

2. If property is transferred from a decedent's estate to a charitable organization because there has been a qualified disclaimer by a prior beneficiary, a charitable deduction is allowed for amounts actually transferred to the charity.

3. If, under the terms of the will or provisions of local law, payment of death taxes or other deductible expenses is to be made from the charitable bequest, the charitable deduction is reduced by those amounts used to pay debts or taxes. In other words, the deduction is limited to the actual amount that passes free and clear to the charity for its charitable purposes.

   If the will provides that taxes and administration expenses are payable from the residue and the charitable bequest is also payable out of the residue, the residuary bequest is diminished by the amount of expenses and taxes paid.

4. In addition to outright bequests of entire interests, charitable gifts can be in other forms, including

   - powers of appointment
   - partial interests
   - charitable remainder trusts
   - guaranteed annuity interests
   - split gifts

5. The four general types of partial interests passing to charity that can qualify for the charitable deduction are

    •   a testamentary gift of an undivided portion of the decedent's entire interest in property not held in trust

    •   a nontrust remainder interest in a person's residence

    •   a nontrust remainder interest in a farm transferred by the decedent at death

    •   remainder interests in trust to charitable remainder trusts and pooled-income funds

6. For transfers made after 1981, a donor-decedent may create a charitable remainder trust and obtain deductions for both the charitable and noncharitable bequests. If a spouse is the only noncharitable income beneficiary for life, the estate obtains a marital deduction for the income interest to the surviving spouse as well as a charitable deduction for the gift of the remainder interest to the charity. The result is that no transfer tax is imposed on the creation of a charitable remainder annuity or unitrust for either the remainder or income portion, provided that the income interest to a spouse qualifies under the new qualifying terminable interest rules. Thus, a split gift to a spouse and charity in the form of a charitable remainder annuity or unitrust may pass entirely estate tax free by using the combined marital and charitable deductions.

7. If the decedent transfers a remainder interest in property to a charity in trust, it must be made in the form of a charitable remainder unitrust, annuity trust, or pooled-income fund. Otherwise, no estate tax charitable deduction is allowed. These arrangements usually provide for an income interest to a noncharitable beneficiary with the remainder to the charitable organization.

8. A charitable gift annuity is a contract between a donor and a qualified charity. Under the agreement, the qualified charity receives a deferred gift. In addition the charity makes annual income payments to the donor or someone named by the donor for life. The advantages of a charitable gift annuity include the following:

    •   Donor receives an immediate income tax deduction.

    •   Donor may defer gain on contribution of appreciated property.

    •   Donor is able to receive fixed annual payments for life.

    •   It is simple in design and administration.

    •   There are no trust drafting or trustee expenses.

9. Community foundations are considered to be grantmaking entities because they are charitable organizations that consist of an amalgamation of separate accounts used to provide grants usually benefiting local communities.

10. In a donor-advised fund, a donor makes a donation to a public charity and the charity establishes a subaccount fund named by the donor. The donor can then make recommendations for grants to be made from the fund while receiving a transfer tax deduction.

11. Advantages of private foundations include that highly appreciated property can be contributed to the foundation while avoiding capital gains taxes. In addition, another advantage is that donors can receive public recognition for their charitable endeavors. Disadvantages of private foundations include costly administration expenses and a lower charitable deduction percentage.

Chapter 16:

State Death
Taxes and
Estate Planning

Learning Objectives

An understanding of the material in this chapter should enable the student to

LO 16.1   **Identify the types of state death taxes.**

LO 16.2   **Explain how states group beneficiaries who are entitled to receive estate assets into classes.**

LO 16.3   **Describe the three classifications of property subject to state death taxes.**

LO 16.4   **Explain how various types of property are affected by state death taxes.**

Frequently, the subject of state death taxes is overshadowed by the attention given to the federal estate tax. Although the emphasis on federal estate taxation is warranted for estates that have a value of more than the applicable exclusion amount, statistically this tax affects a relatively small percentage of all estates settled. On the other hand, most estates are within reach of the death taxes levied by states. Therefore, state death tax planning is an important component of the overall estate planning process, albeit to varying degrees.

LO 16.1   **Identify the types of state death taxes.**

TYPES OF STATE DEATH TAXES

State Inheritance Tax

state inheritance tax

The **state inheritance tax** is a tax imposed on an individual's right to inherit property from the estate of a decedent. The amount of inheritance tax is based on two factors: (1) the value of the property received by each beneficiary, and (2) the rate of the tax (and the amount of exemption, if any exists), which depends on the beneficiary's degree of blood relationship to the deceased. Generally, the closer the beneficiary's blood relationship is to the decedent, the lower the tax rate and the greater the exemption. During recent years, many states have opted for an estate tax, and less than one-half of the states currently impose an inheritance tax or any kind of death tax.

Estate Tax

state estate tax

A **state estate tax** is similar in nature to the federal estate tax. It differs from the inheritance tax in that the inheritance tax is imposed upon a beneficiary's right to inherit, while the estate tax is imposed on a decedent's right to *transfer* or pass property to beneficiaries.

Types of State Death Taxes

- inheritance tax—tax on right of beneficiary to receive estate property
- state estate tax—tax on right of decedent to leave property to beneficiaries

Economic Growth and Tax Relief Reconciliation Act of 2001

The Economic Growth and Tax Relief Reconciliation Act (EGTRRA) of 2001 made some significant changes to state death taxation. And, as previously stated, beginning in 2005, the state death tax credit was fully repealed and replaced with a deduction for any amount of state death taxes paid. The Tax Relief, Unemployment Insurance Reauthorization, and Job Creation Act of 2010 (TRA 2010) and the American Taxpayer Relief Act of 2012 (ATRA 2012) preserved the deduction for state death taxes paid.

EXAMPLE

In 2019 a decedent, Anne, a widow, has a gross estate of $18 million and an adjusted gross estate of $17.5 million. Because Anne was a widow, there is no marital deduction. Under her will, Anne directed her executor to leave $700,000 to her favorite charity, The Animal Humane Society. Her state has imposed $900,000 in state death taxes. Anne's taxable estate is $5,900,000:

$17,500,000	adjusted gross estate
– 700,000	charitable deduction
– 900,000	state death tax deduction
$15,900,000	taxable estate

The federal rules have encouraged the states, especially those states with only a federal state death tax credit, to legislate new state death tax laws.

Although many states have varying types of an inheritance tax and/or estate tax, in prior years *all* states used to take advantage of the tax credit pick-up tax—even those states that claimed to have no death tax. The states' rationale was, why turn down what the federal government will take out of its own pocket and allow the state to have? Clearly, under the EGTRRA 2001 rules, even states that claimed to have no death tax were left with *no* state death tax revenue. The loss of revenue had an understandably negative effect on the state treasuries.

decoupling

Consequently, many states have acted to prevent future death tax revenue losses by **decoupling** from the EGTRRA state credit repeal and federal exclusion amount increases. State decoupling in estate planning is the process of protecting the relevant parts of state tax law that ensure state death tax revenue is not reduced by federal law changes. Almost half of the states have decoupled from the current Federal system in order to protect revenue from their own state death tax system. In many cases, state death taxes can still be avoided by simply gifting property away while alive. Only a few states have state gift taxes. The states that have an estate tax now range from $0 exemption all the way up to the Federal lifetime exclusion.

Although the decoupling arrangements many states have made vary, the simplest form of decoupling is when a state references the full federal credit that was available prior to the 2001 changes. In other words, those states "froze" the amount of the state death tax credit allowed before EGTRRA was enacted for state death tax purposes. Complicating matters more, not only did the state death tax credit change under EGTRRA, but the *exclusion amounts* also changed with the phase-in of increasing exclusion amounts until 2010 when, for one year, the federal estate tax was completely repealed for those estates electing repeal (as allowed by TRA 2010). The final result of these EGTRRA 2001 rules is that some states have enacted legislation that froze the pre-EGTRRA state death tax credit; some states have enacted legislation that froze the basic exclusion amounts allowed under pre-EGTRRA law, and some states have enacted legislation that adopted both the prior state death tax credit amount and a specific prior federal basic exclusion amount.

As an example, under prior law, the federal exemption amount was $700,000 for deaths in 2003, rather than the $1 million allowed under EGTRRA in 2003. Prior law capped the $1 million amount after 2005 and beyond, while EGTRRA increased it through 2009. States that decoupled from EGTRRA have enacted legislation mandating certain previous exemption amounts to retain previous and relied-upon death tax revenue. For example, State X may retain the pre-2001 $600,000 federal exclusion amount before it imposes a state estate tax, while State Y may impose a state estate tax when a decedent-domiciliary's gross estate exceeds the 11.4 million under current law..

Although EGTRRA 2001 is a prior federal law, it had a significant impact on state death taxation. It is important for estate planners and advisers to keep current with the laws of states in which clients have a potential for transfer taxation.

LO 16.2   Explain how states group beneficiaries who are entitled to receive estate assets into classes.

BENEFICIARY CLASSES AND BENEFICIARY EXEMPTIONS

In the majority of states, state law sorts beneficiaries who are entitled to receive estate assets into classes. The closest blood relatives of the decedent have the lowest state death tax rate and the largest exemption. In a state that provides for two classes, class 1 (or class A) may include the deceased's surviving spouse, children, parents, and grandchildren. Class 2 (or class B) may include aunts, uncles, brothers, sisters, nephews, nieces, and all other beneficiaries. The class 2 individuals are subject to a higher tax rate than the members of class 1. If the particular state also provides exemptions, the beneficiaries in class 2 may have smaller exemptions than those in class 1. A state may also have different exemptions within a class according to how closely the beneficiary is related to the decedent.

Classes

Some states have numerous classes.

EXAMPLE

For inheritance tax purposes, state X has six possible classes:

Class	Class Member	Exemption
1	Spouse	Full
2	Lineal issues and adopted children	$25,000
3	Lineal ancestors	5,000
4	Siblings and their descendants; sons and daughters-in-law	500
5	Siblings of parents and their descendants	100
6	Others	None

Tax Rates

There are two types of tax rates used by states that have death taxes: (1) flat percentage rates, and (2) graduated percentage rates. In states with a flat rate, the value of the whole share passing to a beneficiary is taxed at the same percentage rate. The flat rate may vary, however, according to the beneficiary's degree of blood relationship to the decedent.

EXAMPLE

Tony, the decedent's son, inherited $100,000 from his father. The state provides for a flat tax rate of 6 percent for class 1 (direct lineal descendants of the deceased). There are no exemptions. Tony's state tax is $6,000. Martha, the decedent's niece, inherited $10,000. State law mandates that all beneficiaries other than direct lineal descendants and ancestors belong to class 2 and are taxed at a flat 15 percent rate. Martha's state tax is $1,500.

In states with graduated tax rates, a beneficiary's inheritance is broken down into sections. The first section is taxed at the lowest percentage rate. Each additional section is taxed at an increasing rate (similar to the federal gift, estate, and income tax rate schedules).

Two Types of State Death Tax Rates
- flat percentage rates—entire value of a beneficiary's share taxed at the same rate
- graduated percentage rates—progressive rates applied to a beneficiary's share

EXAMPLE

Assume the same facts as in the preceding example except that the state uses graduated tax rates. The inheritance tax rates are as follows:

Column (1) From	Column (2) To	Tax on (1)	Rate on Excess
Value of Property from Decedent to Class 1 Beneficiaries			
$ 0	$ 50,000	$ 0	0
50,000	150,000	0	3%
150,000	250,000	3,000	4%
250,000	300,000	7,000	5%
Value of Property from Decedent to Class 2 Beneficiaries			
$ 1,000	$ 6,000	$ 0	7%
6,000	25,000	350	8%
25,000	150,000	2,000	9%

Tony's state tax is $1,500 [.03 × $50,000, which is the amount Tony inherited in excess of $50,000 (in column 1)]. Martha's state tax is $670 [.07 × $5,000 ($6,000 – $1,000) = $350, + .08 × $4,000 ($10,000 – $6,000) = $320; or $350 + $320 = $670.]

Exemptions

If a state provides for exemptions within classes, the amount of the exemption usually depends on the closeness of the beneficiary's blood relationship to the deceased. (Some states reduce the exemption amounts for nonresident estates that have taxable property within the state.) The closest relatives receive the biggest exemptions and lowest tax rates. Where exemptions apply, it is important to determine when the exemption is taken. In some states, the exemption is taken from the entire share of property passing to the beneficiary prior to applying the tax rates. In other states, the exemption amount is deducted from the portion of the beneficiary's share in the bottom tax bracket. Because the lowest tax rate applies to the first or bottom section, only the amount in excess of the exemption gets the most favorable lowest percentage rate. This method is less beneficial to the beneficiary with regard to taxes.

> **EXAMPLE**
>
> Referring to the example and tax table for class 1, suppose that Tony, as a child of the decedent, is entitled to an exemption of $30,000. If the $30,000 exemption is taken from Tony's total inheritance of $100,000 before any tax rates come into play, for tax percentage rate and tax computation purposes, Tony would start with an inheritance of $70,000. According to the tax rate table in the example, the first $50,000 of property is taxed at a zero rate, so only the remaining $20,000 is subject to the 3 percent tax rate. In this case, Tony would owe $600 (.03 x $20,000) in state death taxes. Alternatively, if the state requires the exemption to apply to the first section or block of the tax table, only $20,000 of property is entitled to the zero percent rate and the remaining $50,000 is taxed at the 3 percent rate. In this situation, Tony's state death tax payable would be $1,500 (.03 x $50,000).

LO 16.3   **Describe the three classifications of property subject to state death taxes.**

Classifications of Property Subject to State Death Taxes

There are three main classifications of property: real property, tangible personal property, and intangible personal property.

- *Real property* is real estate and property that is permanently attached to the land. Generally, real property is taxable only by the state in which the property is located (situs).

- *Tangible personal property* is property such as cars, furniture, jewelry, and artwork. In general, tangible personal property is taxable by the state in which the property is usually kept, whether or not the state is the decedent's state of domicile.

- *Intangible personal property* includes stocks, bonds, insurance policies, mortgage liens, notes, debt instruments, and the like. These kinds of property may be taxable by more than one state if the states can establish a sufficient nexus or contact with the property. Therefore, intangible property may be subject to multiple state death taxation. Such taxation can occur in a number of different circumstances:

  - The decedent owned residences in more than one state.

  - It is unclear which of two or more states is the decedent's state of domicile.

  - Intangibles held in trust may be taxable by the deceased grantor's and the trustee's states of domicile.

  - Securities transferred due to the shareholder's death may be taxable by the shareholder's state of domicile and by the issuing company's state of incorporation.

Clearly, intangibles may present some unexpected tax results. Estates that have significant holdings of intangible assets may suffer disastrous consequences from the imposition of death taxes if several states have a nexus to the property. The right of more than one state to tax intangibles has been upheld in a number of Supreme Court decisions.[1] It is understandable that a decedent-owner's domiciliary state may levy a death tax. Other states' power to tax the property rests on whether the owner can seek state court protection of his or her rights in the property. In other words, if the intangibles had sufficient nexus with another state so as to provide the decedent's rights in the property some protection under the law of that state, the state has the power to tax the property.

State Death Taxation of Types of Property
- real property (land, buildings)
  - taxed by state of location
- tangible personal property (cars, furniture, artwork)
  - taxed by state of location
- intangible personal property (stocks, bonds, notes)
  - multiple state taxation possible
    ◊ decedent's state of domicile
    ◊ states having significant contacts with property
      ○ state of trust situs
      ○ state of incorporation

---

1. *Curry et al. v. McCanless*, 307 U.S. 357 (1939); *Utah v. Aldrich*, 316 U.S. 174 (1942); *Graves v. Elliott*, 307 U.S. 383 (1939).

LO 16.4 **Explain how various types of property are affected by state death taxes.**

PROPERTY SUBJECT TO STATE DEATH TAXES— GENERAL PRINCIPLES

The laws of each state determine the specific types of property that are taxable by the state as transfers taking effect at death. Death tax statutes of many states have some similarities to federal estate tax provisions. Generally speaking, property is taxable if the decedent directly owned the property at death, retained certain rights or powers over the property during lifetime, made lifetime transfers of property in contemplation of death and within a certain period (one to 3 years) of death, held the property in a revocable trust, or made vesting of the property in another dependent upon surviving the decedent.

Property Jointly Held With Right of Survivorship

As might be expected, the rules regarding property held jointly with right of survivorship vary widely among the states. Some states do not tax jointly held property that passes from a decedent to a surviving spouse. Other states completely exempt all survivorship joint property from state transfer taxation. Still other states tax the full fair market value of the property in the estate if the joint tenant dies absent proof of contribution by the surviving tenant(s). A few states divide the property's value by the number of joint tenants and tax the decedent's fractional share.

Life Insurance

Again, there is a wide variation among the states. If the proceeds are payable to or for the benefit of the decedent-insured's estate or to a personal representative, the proceeds are taxable in most states. A few states, however, exempt a portion or all of such proceeds. In many states, if the proceeds are payable to named beneficiaries other than the estate or personal representative, they are not taxed. Exemptions from tax may vary according to the beneficiary designation. For instance, if a surviving spouse or children are the named beneficiaries, the proceeds may pass tax free; whereas if the proceeds are payable to any other beneficiary, they are taxable. Some states tax the proceeds if the decedent held certain incidents of ownership. If the decedent did not possess any incidents of ownership and did not name the estate as beneficiary, the proceeds usually are not taxed.

Annuities

As a general rule, if a decedent-annuitant held a period-certain or refund annuity and payments are made to a beneficiary, the payments are taxable. State death taxes often apply to survivor interests in joint-and-survivor annuities.

Business Situs of Intangible Property

Owners of intangible property should think carefully before using that property for business-related purposes in a state other than the business's state of domicile (that is, the state of incorporation or main headquarters). If intangibles are given business applications in another state, that state may be able to claim the intangibles are taxable because they have a business situs in the state. For instance, if business property is used to secure a loan in another state, the state may claim the intangible has a business situs within the state and, therefore, is subject to tax.

Powers of Appointment

There is wide variation in the states' death tax treatment of powers of appointment. If a state does not have statutory law concerning death taxation of powers of appointment, common law may prevail, resulting in taxation at the decedent-donor's death. In other states, the value of the property subject to a power is taxed in the estate of the donee (the individual with the power to appoint the property). In some instances, it is the distinction between the exercise and nonexercise of the power or general power versus limited or special power that determines tax liability. In Pennsylvania, assets under a general power of appointment are exempt from taxation in the power holder's estate.

Retirement Benefits

The majority of states have statutes that closely track federal law regarding death taxation of retirement benefits. Benefits payable to the decedent-employee's estate are generally taxable. Benefits paid to other beneficiaries are exempt from state death tax to the extent of the decedent's contributions. Although the death benefits and survivor benefits of qualified plans and governmental retirement arrangements are usually taxable in states that have inheritance taxes, most states have exemption provisions.

Community Property

A decedent-spouse's one-half interest in community property is subject to death taxation in most of the community-property states.

Nonresident Exemptions

Fortunately, the likelihood of multiple taxation is decreased by the fact that many states either exempt the intangible property of nonresidents or grant a reciprocal exemption for nonresident-decedents. Reciprocity laws typically serve to exempt a nonresident's intangibles from tax if the nonresident's domiciliary state also exempts the intangibles of nonresidents. To avoid duplicate taxation, some states have adopted the Uniform Interstate Compromise of Death Taxes Act,[2] under which state tax authorities and executors agree on a compromise of state taxes owed. Some states provide for arbitration concerning death tax disputes. Most multiple tax dilemmas arise when the decedent's state of domicile is not definitively established, when intangibles were used for business purposes in other states, or when trusts are located in other states.

Time of Payment

The point at which state death taxes become due varies among the states. Many states have adopted the same time frame for filing and paying as the federal government's 9 months from the date of the decedent's death.

It is a common policy for many states to allow a discount for early payment. For instance, in a manner similar to the federal estate tax return, Pennsylvania requires inheritance tax returns to be filed and payment made within 9 months of the decedent's death (assuming no extensions have been granted). However, Pennsylvania allows a 5 percent discount from the inheritance tax due for payments made within 3 months of the decedent's death. In turn, interest and penalties are charged for late payment. Extensions for filing are granted if there is proof of sufficient cause for the delay.

Responsibility for Payment

Generally, the decedent's personal representative is responsible for paying state death taxes. Unless the decedent directed otherwise through a tax apportionment clause in his or her will, the personal representative deducts the tax proportionately from each beneficiary's interest in the estate prior to distribution.

---

2.   *Uniform Laws Annotated*, vol. 8A (St. Paul: West Publishing Co.).

CHAPTER REVIEW

Key Terms and Concepts

inheritance tax   decoupling
state estate tax

Chapter 16: Review Questions

1. Briefly describe the two current types of state death taxes. [LO 16.1]

2. What effect do beneficiary classes and exemptions have on state death taxation? [LO 16.2]

3. Describe the general rules used to determine which state has the right to tax the following types of property:

    a. real estate,

    b. tangible personal property,

    c. intangible personal property. [LO 16.3]

4. Describe the most common circumstances in which intangible property is subject to double or multiple state death taxation. [LO 16.3]

Chapter 16: Review Answers

1.   *Inheritance Tax*

The inheritance tax is a tax imposed on an individual's right to inherit property from the estate of a decedent. The amount of inheritance tax is based on two factors: (1) the value of the property received by each beneficiary, and (2) the rate of the tax (and the amount of exemption, if any exists), which depends on the beneficiary's degree of blood relationship to the deceased.

Estate Tax

A state estate tax is similar in nature to the federal estate tax. It differs from the inheritance tax in that the inheritance tax is imposed on a beneficiary's right to inherit, while the estate tax is imposed on a decedent's right to transfer or pass property to beneficiaries.

2.   In the majority of states, state law sorts beneficiaries who are entitled to receive estate assets into classes. The closest blood relatives of the decedent have the lowest state death tax rate and the largest exemption. In a state that provides for two classes, class 1 (or class A) may include the deceased's surviving spouse, children, parents, and grandchildren. Class 2 (or class B) may include aunts, uncles, brothers, sisters, nephews, nieces, and all other beneficiaries. The class 2 individuals are subject to a higher tax rate than the members of class 1. If the particular state also provides exemptions, the beneficiaries in class 2 may have smaller exemptions than those in class 1. A state may also have different exemptions within a class according to how closely the beneficiary is related to the decedent.

3.   a.   Real property is real estate and property that is permanently attached to the land. Generally, real property is taxable only by the state in which the property is located (situs).

   b.   Tangible personal property is property such as cars, furniture, jewelry, and artwork. Tangible personal property, generally, is taxable by the state in which the property is usually kept, whether or not the state is the decedent's state of domicile.

   c.   Intangible personal property includes stocks, bonds, insurance policies, mortgage liens, notes, debt instruments, and the like. These kinds of property may be taxable by more than one state if the states can establish a sufficient nexus or contact with the property.

4. Intangible property may be subject to multiple state death taxation under the following circumstances:

   - The decedent owned residences in more than one state, and it is unclear which of the states was the decedent's state of domicile.

   - Intangibles held in trust may be taxable by the deceased grantor's state of domicile and the trustee's state of domicile.

   - Securities transferred due to the shareholder's death may be taxable by the shareholder's state of domicile and by the issuing company's state of incorporation.

Chapter 17:

Computation and Payment of Federal Estate Tax

Learning Objectives

An understanding of the material in this chapter should enable the student to do the following:

LO 17.1   **Explain how the tentative tax base is determined.**

LO 17.2   **Describe how the estate tax payable before credits is computed.**

LO 17.3   **Describe the credits that may be applied in determining the net federal estate tax payable.**

LO 17.4   **Explain when a federal estate tax return must be filed, when the tax due must be paid, and when payment of a tax may be delayed.**

As stated in prior chapters, the taxable estate is found by deducting from the gross estate all allowable estate debts, taxes, and administration expenses. Further reductions that may be applicable are the marital deduction and the charitable deduction. As previously stated, beginning January 1, 2005, a state death tax deduction replaced a state death tax credit. After the above mentioned deductions, the result is the *taxable estate*.

In this chapter the remaining steps necessary to compute the federal estate tax are discussed. These include

- the determination of the tentative tax base
- the determination of the estate tax before credits
- the determination of the net federal estate tax payable

A convenient chart for computing the federal estate tax is located near the end of this chapter.

In addition, the chapter discusses who must file an estate tax return, the procedures for filing the estate tax return, and payment of the estate tax.

LO 17.1   **Explain how the tentative tax base is determined.**

DETERMINATION OF TENTATIVE TAX BASE

Recall from earlier discussions that the federal estate and gift tax are unified. This means that for tax calculation purposes, taxable gifts are added to the taxable estate in order to calculate the total amount of federal gift and estate tax liability. Once the taxable estate is determined, the amount of adjusted taxable gifts made after 1976 is added to the taxable estate. The result is the *tentative tax base*.

adjusted taxable gifts

Adjusted taxable gifts are taxable gifts made after 1976 that are not includible in the decedent's gross estate. (The term taxable in this context means either that gift tax liability occurred or that the basic exclusion amount [credit equivalent] applied to the gift.) Consequently, the following are excluded from treatment as adjusted taxable gifts:

- post-1976 gifts within the amount of the annual exclusion ($3,000 after 1976; $10,000 after 1981; $11,000 after 2001; $13,000 after 2008; $14,000 in 2016; and $15,000 in 2019)
- gifts made to a spouse that qualified for the gift tax marital deduction
- gifts that qualified for the gift tax charitable deduction
- gifts that have already been included in the decedent's gross estate for whatever reason. In this latter category is the value of certain transfers that were included in the decedent's gross estate because the decedent retained certain interests, rights, or powers in the property for life, or because such interests were retained initially and were given away less than 3 years before death.
- educational and medical expense exclusion amounts

Tentative Tax Base

taxable estate

+

adjusted <u>taxable</u> gifts
(all post-1976 <u>taxable</u> gifts decedent made during lifetime
that are <u>not</u> included in the gross estate)

=

tentative tax base

Estate Tax Treatment of Split Gifts

Inclusion or Exclusion of the Gift Value

If the split gift does not exceed the annual exclusion amount per donee, nothing is included in the gross estate or adjusted taxable gifts of the donor-decedent.

If the split gift does exceed the annual exclusion (and is not includible in the gross estate because of retained interests or powers), the excess over the annual exclusion amount becomes an adjusted taxable gift in the estate tax computation of the donor-decedent.

If a donor-decedent made a split gift within 3 years of death and retained certain interests or powers (for example, retained income for life) or transferred certain types of property (such as insurance policies on his or her life), the entire value of the gifted property is brought back into the gross estate of the donor-decedent. If, subsequent to the death of the donor spouse, the consenting spouse died (within 3 years of a gift with retained interests or powers), the consenting spouse's portion of the gift is not includible in his or her gross estate, since the entire value of the gift had already been included in the donor spouse's gross estate.

Includibility of Gift Tax Paid within 3 Years of Death

With respect to the gift taxes paid on the split gift made within 3 years, only the gift tax paid by the donor spouse is includible in the donor spouse's gross estate. Indeed, the gift tax paid by the consenting spouse will be includible in his or her own gross estate. (On the other hand, if the donor spouse pays the entire gift tax, then the total amount of the gift tax is included in the donor spouse's gross estate and no gift tax is included in the consenting spouse's gross estate.)

Credit for Gift Taxes Paid

When the entire gift is includible in the donor spouse's gross estate, any tax that was actually paid by the consenting spouse is allowed as a credit in computing the donor spouse's estate tax. Therefore, any credit allowed in the donor spouse's estate is not allowed as a credit for gift tax paid by the consenting spouse.

The foregoing concept involves computations beyond the scope of this chapter and is presented for informational purposes only.

LO 17.2   Describe how the estate tax payable before credits is computed.

Determination of Estate Tax Before Credits

Under the Tax Reform Act of 1976 (TRA 1976), a unified estate and gift tax system was created. This means that the same rate schedule was applied to transfers both during a decedent's lifetime and at death. The system used a cumulative approach to all transfers made during lifetime, culminating in the final gratuitous transfer of property at death. Cumulating taxable lifetime gifts with dispositions at death had the net effect of increasing the tax rates applied to the taxable estate by adding adjusted taxable gifts to the value of transfers taking effect at death. Because the estate and gift tax rate schedule is progressive, any individual who made lifetime taxable gifts after 1976 was subject to a higher combined estate tax rate than if the computation did not include lifetime gifts. That was the rationale for adding adjusted taxable gifts to the taxable estate to arrive at the tentative tax base—the amount to which tax rates are applied. In other words, the transfer tax rate schedules (near the end of this chapter) apply to cumulated transfers, and the result is the tentative tax.

Once the tentative tax is determined, gift taxes generated by taxable gifts made after 1976 in excess of the basic credit amount are subtracted from this figure. The determination of the amount of reduction allowable because of taxes attributable to post-1976 taxable gifts is made through the following steps:

1. Total all post-1976 taxable gifts.

2. Compute the gift tax payable by applying the rate schedule in effect at the decedent's death (see "Chart for Computing Federal Estate Tax and Estate Tax Credit Schedule" which is located near the end of this chapter) to the total taxable gifts. In other words, all the post-1976 taxable gifts are treated as if they were made at one time—the date of the decedent's death.

3. Reduce the gift tax payable by the basic credit amount for the year of the decedent's death (for gift tax purposes, the credit amount is $4,505,800 for 2019 as indexed for inflation).

4. If the gift tax payable exceeds the basic credit amount, subtract the excess from the tentative tax.

The result is the *estate tax payable before credits*.

LO 17.3 **Describe the credits that may be applied in determining the net federal estate tax payable.**

DETERMINATION OF NET FEDERAL ESTATE TAX PAYABLE

Once the estate tax is computed, there are currently four possible credits that may be applied against the tax to arrive at the *net federal estate tax payable*. As with income tax credits, these credits are allowed as a dollar-for-dollar reduction of the estate tax. They are the

- basic credit amount
- credit for foreign death taxes
- credit for gift tax paid on pre-1977 gifts (irrelevant for this course)

- credit for taxes paid on prior transfers

No refund is allowed if the sum of the credits exceeds the estate tax otherwise payable.

Basic Credit Amount

basic credit amount

Under TRA 1976, the unified estate and gift tax credit came into existence for estates of decedents dying after December 31, 1976. The term *unified credit* was adopted because the credit may be used as an offset against gift taxes as well as estate taxes. Actually, the credit must first be used to offset gift taxes on lifetime transfers. Any remaining credit is applied as a credit against the federal estate tax. The unified credit was gradually increased each year until it reached $192,800 in 1987. At that time, a unified credit of $192,800 was equivalent to $600,000 of taxable transfers. Thus, the unified credit was commonly, albeit mistakenly, referred to as a $600,000 credit; stated correctly, the $600,000 amount was a credit *equivalent*.

After 1997 and until 2011, the unified credit became known as the *applicable credit amount*. The credit increased incrementally until the Economic Growth and Tax Relief Reconciliation Act of 2001 (EGTRRA). The Tax Relief, Unemployment Insurance Reauthorization, and Job Creation Act of 2010 (TRA 2010), the American Taxpayer Relief Act of 2012 (ATRA 2012), and the Tax Cuts and Jobs Act of 2017 (TCJA 2017) refer to the credit as the **basic credit amount** (rather than the prior applicable credit amount terminology).

Basic Credit Amount

In 2019, an estate tax credit of $4,505,800 is allowed to offset estate taxes on the equivalent of $11.4 million of taxable transfers at death.

The federal exemption is not directly applied in the calculation of the gift and estate tax. Instead, the basic credit amount, which offsets the tax that would have been owed on assets totaling the federal exemption amount, is applied instead. This also means that if there is any tax liability still owed after all credits have been applied, the taxpayer is already in the top marginal tax bracket.

The basic credit amount, therefore, has the effect of eliminating the lower brackets allocated to taxable transfers below the basic exclusion amount. As the gift and estate tax rate schedule for 2018 and beyond near the end of this chapter indicates, the first dollar of transfer tax imposed above the credit exclusion amount is paid at a marginal rate of 40 percent for gift, estate and generation-skipping tax purposes.

Prior Law: State Death Tax Credit (Repealed)

state death tax credit

adjusted taxable estate

After repeal of the **state death tax credit**, beginning in 2005 through 2016, an estate may take a deduction on the federal estate tax return for any estate, inheritance legacy, or succession taxes actually paid to a state, if the state death tax was attributable to property included in the decedent's gross estate. TRA 2010 and ATRA 2012 retain the state death tax deduction from a decedent's adjusted gross estate (**adjusted taxable estate**).

Credit for Foreign Death Taxes

credit for foreign death taxes

There is a credit allowed against the federal estate tax for taxes actually paid by the decedent's estate to any foreign country for any estate, inheritance, legacy, or succession taxes. The purpose of the **credit for foreign death taxes** is to prevent double taxation. It is allowable only to the estate of a decedent who was either: (1) a citizen of the United States or (2) a resident of the United States who was not a citizen at the time of death. Nonresident aliens are denied the foreign death tax credit. The credit exists for taxes actually paid by the decedent's estate to any foreign country, U.S. possession, or political subdivision of a foreign state.

Credit is given for death taxes paid on property that is located within the foreign country to which the tax is paid and that is also included in the decedent's gross estate for U.S. federal estate tax purposes. In other words, the property taxed by a foreign jurisdiction must also be taxed by the United States under our estate tax system. The United States recognizes that the same property is taxed doubly and allows a credit for taxes paid to the foreign jurisdiction. This credit is limited to the proportionate share of federal estate tax attributable to the property located in and taxed by the foreign country.

The maximum credit allowed is the *lesser* of: (1) the amount of foreign death tax imposed on the property situated in the foreign country that was also included in the decedent's gross estate for federal estate tax purposes, and (2) the amount of federal estate tax attributable to that same property located and taxed in the foreign country that also is included in the decedent's gross estate for federal estate tax purposes. In comparing the two taxes to determine which is the lesser, the exchange rate used is the one that converts foreign currency into U.S. dollars in effect when each foreign tax payment is made. No credit is given for interest owed or penalties connected with the payment of foreign death taxes.

If the federal estate tax is attributable to a remainder or reversionary interest in the foreign property and an election is made to postpone payment of that part of the tax, the credit applies to the portion of foreign death taxes that are paid and claimed as a credit before the time for payment expires. The credit must be claimed by the *latest* of the following: (1) 4 years from the time the estate tax return is filed, (2) the expiration of any extension for paying the tax, and (3) 60 days after the Tax Court has reached a decision on a petition for redetermination of a deficiency.

Credit for Gift Tax Paid on Pre-1977 Gifts

Gift tax payable on post-1976 gifts becomes part of the computation for determining estate tax liability under the gift and estate tax system, as explained earlier. Therefore, no separate credit is allowed for taxes attributable to these gifts. However, a credit still exists for federal gift tax paid by a decedent on taxable gifts made before 1977 if the property is included in the gross estate. This concept is illustrated by the following example.

EXAMPLE

A grantor, Michael, established a trust for the benefit of his son before 1977. The grantor reserved the right to all income from the trust during his life. The gift of the remainder interest was a taxable gift on which gift tax was paid. The grantor died last year and the trust property was includible in his gross estate because of the retained life interest. A credit was allowed (within certain technical limitations) for the gift tax paid on the pre-1977 gift.

Additional complications arise if there are several pre-1977 gifts to which this credit could be applicable. A discussion of the rules regarding these complications and technical limitations of this credit is beyond the scope of this chapter.

Credit for Tax on Prior Transfers

credit for tax on prior transfers

Circumstances may arise in which a decedent has inherited property from someone who died less than 10 years before the decedent's death or within 2 years following the decedent's death, and the property transferred to the decedent was already taxable in the estate of the transferor-decedent. To avoid double taxation on double transfers of property occurring within a reasonably short time period (that is, 10 years before or 2 years after the decedent's death), a credit (a **credit for tax on prior transfers**) is allowed against the federal estate tax paid by the present decedent as a result of this inherited-property inclusion in the decedent's gross estate. (See the table below.)

Credit for Tax on Prior Transfers	
Percent Allowable	**Period of Time Between Transferor's Death and Death of Present Decedent**
100 percent	up to 2 years after
100 percent	up to 2 years before
80 percent	2 to 4 years before
60 percent	4 to 6 years before
40 percent	6 to 8 years before
20 percent	8 to 10 years before
0 percent	more than 10 years before

Amount of Credit

If the decedent's death occurs within 2 years before or after the transferor's death, the credit is limited to the lesser of: (1) the amount of the federal estate tax attributable to the transferred property in the transferor's estate, or (2) the amount of the federal estate tax attributable to the transferred property in the present decedent's estate. If the transferor died within 2 years before or 2 years after the death of the present decedent, the allowable credit for the tax on the prior transfer is determined by the lesser of (1) or (2) above. In other words, the full credit is allowed if both deaths occur within 2 years of each other. However, if the transferor died more than 2 years before the present decedent, the credit is reduced by 20 percent for each 2-year period in excess of 2 years.

EXAMPLE

If the transferor died 3 years before the present decedent, 80 percent of the credit will be allowable. The allowable percentages are provided in the table above.

A formula for determining the credit is contained in the Treasury regulations. The Code further defines how the property transferred to the present decedent from the transferor's estate shall be valued.

Allowance of Credit

Property included in the transferor's gross estate that is eligible for the credit includes any beneficial interest in property received by the present decedent from the transferor. The credit may also be allowed with respect to property received by the present decedent as the result of the exercise or nonexercise of a general power of appointment by the transferor-decedent.

Of course, if the present decedent was the surviving spouse of the transferor, the credit will be disallowed to the extent that property included in the transferor's gross estate qualified for the marital deduction. The credit pertains to many types of property interests that the present decedent may have received from the transferor, including annuities, life estates, terms for years, remainders, and other interests. The necessary ingredient is that the present decedent inherited these interests from the transferor and became the beneficial owner of the interest. Determining the credit may be further complicated if property for which the credit on prior transfers was sought is also subject to a generation-skipping tax. (The interaction of the credit and the generation-skipping tax is complex and beyond the scope of this chapter.)

LO 17.4   **Explain when a federal estate tax return must be filed, when the tax due must be paid, and when payment of a tax may be delayed.**

Filing an Estate Tax Return

The personal representative of the estate of every U.S. citizen or resident must file Form 706—The United States Estate Tax Return—if the value of the taxable estate plus adjusted taxable gifts on the date of death exceeds the statutory filing requirement. The taxable estate and adjusted taxable gifts must exceed the basic exclusion amount for filing to be required. In other words, these statutory filing limitations are applied to the value of all property included in the gross estate plus the total amount of taxable gifts made after 1976 that were not included in the decedent's estate. (Note that the value of adjusted taxable gifts is included for this purpose at the date-of-gift value, not the value at the date of death.) The value of these lifetime gifts also plays a part in establishing the rate of estate tax to be applied.

PAYMENT OF ESTATE TAX BY PERSONAL REPRESENTATIVE

A primary duty of the personal representative is to file the federal estate tax return when due and to see that estate taxes are timely paid. The personal representative must also timely file any estate income tax returns when they are due. If the estate is sizable enough to warrant filing a federal estate tax return, the return is due no later than 9 months after the decedent's death unless an extension is granted (IRC Sec. 6075(a)).

The personal representative is required to gather and retain records as well as supplemental data supporting the amounts stated or claimed on the federal estate tax return. If the estate assets are insufficient to pay all the decedent's taxes, the decedent's federal tax liabilities must be paid first. This includes the decedent's income tax liabilities up to the time of death, the income tax liability of the estate, and the estate tax liability. An executor (or administrator) will be held personally liable for the tax if he or she was aware of a potential tax liability or failed in the responsibility to determine if any such tax obligations existed prior to distribution of the estate's assets and the executor's discharge from responsibility (IRC Sec. 2202). In other words, an executor will be liable if he or she was either aware of or should have been aware of the existence of tax obligations. In addition, if the estate is insolvent, the individual beneficiaries will be responsible for paying any federal estate tax accruing from the inclusion of their inheritances in the decedent's gross estate.

Extension for Filing

Generally, a personal representative may obtain an extension for filing a return if it is either impossible or impractical to complete the return within the 9-month period after the decedent dies. This extension is limited to 6 months, unless the personal representative is abroad (IRC Sec. 6081(a)). The estate tax payable, if any, is due nine months after the decedent's death (even if an extension to file the return is granted).

Although a 6-month extension is automatically granted, the personal representative of an estate must file Form 4768 with the Internal Revenue Service for the 6-month extension on or before the original due date of Form 706, along with an estimate of the full amount of tax due. An extension of the time for filing an estate tax return does not prevent interest from accruing on any unpaid taxes beginning on the date the return was originally due (IRC Sec. 6601(b)(1)). Also, an extension of time to file does not automatically extend the time for payment. In addition to providing information concerning requests for an extension to file, Form 4768 also contains sections pertaining to requests for an extension to pay tax. Penalties of 5 percent per month up to 25 percent will be added to the final tax liability unless reasonable cause is shown (Treas. Reg. Sec. 20.6081–1(a)). Thus, if it is impossible or impractical to file a return by the due date, consideration should be given either to paying the estimated amount of estate tax by the due date for filing or to obtaining an extension for payment of the tax.

Extension for Tax Payment

There are mitigating circumstances that the IRS will accept for granting an extension of time to pay the estate tax. An extension for up to 12 months to pay the estate tax will be granted if the Internal Revenue Service determines there is reasonable cause (IRC Sec. 6161(a)). While no definition of reasonable cause is given in the Code or regulations, the following situations are provided in the regulations as a basis for granting an extension of time to pay the tax:

- Although an estate includes sufficient liquid assets, assets are located in several jurisdictions and cannot be marshaled readily by the executor, despite a diligent effort to do so by the time for filing the return.

- A great part of the estate consists of assets that will provide future payments, such as annuities, copyright royalties, contingent fees, or accounts receivable. Because these assets constitute the major part of the estate, the estate does not contain sufficient cash to pay the estate tax within the due period. Borrowing against these assets would inflict considerable losses upon the estate.

- The estate includes a major asset that cannot be collected without litigation. It is unknown whether this asset will ever be collectible, and the size of the gross estate is not determinable at the time for filing the return.

- Unless the estate borrows at a higher-than-normal rate of interest, it does not have sufficient funds to pay the entire estate tax when due as well as to provide reasonable subsistence for the decedent's spouse and dependent children during the remaining period of estate administration. Also, funds are insufficient to satisfy claims currently due against the estate despite reasonable efforts by the personal representative to convert assets into cash (other than an interest in a closely held business to which Sec. 6166 applies).

While the initial extension for *reasonable cause* pertains to a 12-month period from the time the estate tax return is due, a finding of reasonable cause may allow a deferral of payment of estate taxes for reasonable periods up to 10 years for decedents dying after December 31, 1976 (IRC Sec. 6161(a)(2)).

Extension for Paying Tax on Closely Held Business Interests

There is a special provision that allows the personal representative to elect a deferral for payment of estate tax attributable to the inclusion of a closely held business or farm in the decedent's gross estate if certain conditions are met (IRC Sec. 6166). The law provides that an executor may elect to defer payment of estate tax attributable to inclusion in the estate of a farm or other closely held business if that business consists of more than 35 percent of the adjusted gross estate. If the estate qualifies, such an election is made at the sole discretion of the estate's personal representative. Payments of tax attributable to the business interest may be deferred for 5 years from the due date. Interest only on the unpaid balance is due annually for the initial 4 years (four annual installments of interest only). In the fifth year and thereafter, the tax plus installments of interest on the unpaid balance is payable in equal annual installments over a maximum of 10 more years. Note that the total payment period actually extends over 14 years and 9 months (9 months is the time period allowed for filing the federal estate tax return) rather than 15 years because the first installment of tax becomes due simultaneously with the last payment of interest. To determine whether more than 35 percent of the adjusted gross estate is made up of a closely held business or farm, the adjusted gross estate is defined as the gross estate reduced by deductible debts, expenses, claims, and losses, but before reduction by the marital or charitable deductions (IRC Sec. 6166(b)(6)).

Filing and Tax Payment Extensions

- 6-month extension
  - easily granted
  - extension Form 4768 filed on or before 9 months of death
  - interest on estate tax due commences to run 9 months after death
- 12-month extension [Sec. 6161(a)]
  - granted for "reasonable cause"
    - pending estate litigation
- 10-year extension [Sec. 6161(a)(2)]
  - difficult to marshal assets
  - assets providing future payments
  - only higher than normal rate of interest for loan available
- 14-year extension for closely held business or farm interest [Sec. 6166]

For purposes of the 35 percent rule, an interest in a closely held business is defined as: (1) an interest in a proprietorship, (2) an interest in a partnership carrying on a trade or business with no more than 45 partners or where 20 percent or more of its assets helped determine the decedent's gross estate, or (3) stock in a corporation with no more than 45 shareholders or where 20 percent of its voting stock is included in the decedent's gross estate (IRC Sec. 6166(b)(6)(1)). Property owned by a corporation, partnership, estate, or trust is regarded as owned proportionately by its shareholders, partners, or beneficiaries. In addition, for purposes of this election, interests in two or more closely held businesses are treated as a single closely held business if 20 percent or more of the total value of each business is included in the decedent's gross estate (IRC Sec. 6166(c)). Also, all stock and partnership interests belonging to a decedent and any family members will be aggregated in order to meet the requirements of stock ownership. The family members whose interests are considered as held by the decedent are the decedent's brothers, sisters, spouse, parents, grandparents, children, and grandchildren. For purposes of this election, stock in a closely held business must be stock that is not readily tradable. At the time of the decedent's death, this means stock that is not listed on a stock exchange and for which there is no market in over-the-counter trading. When a farm or other business is included in the estate and the executor has elected special-use valuation, the special-use value is treated as the property value to which Sec. 6166 applies.

In some cases, an executor may be uncertain whether the estate will need to defer payment of tax or will qualify for deferred payment of tax. In that event, the executor may file a protective election with the estate tax return. Filing such an election preserves the executor's right to elect estate tax deferral.

Special 2 Percent Interest Rate

The present law contains a special 2 percent rate of interest (compounded daily) attributable to the deferred estate tax on the first $1 million of closely held business or farm property included in the gross estate. The $1 million figure for purposes of calculating the 2 percent portion of deferred estate taxes is indexed for inflation under TRA 1997 ($1,550,000 in 2019). The special interest rate applies to installment payments. For decedents dying in 2019, the interest rate is 2 percent on the lesser of $620,000 (the product of multiplying the top tax rate of 40% times the $1,550,000 for 2019) or the amount of the estate tax that is attributable to the closely held business and that is payable in installment. This number is found on the IRS Form 706 for the year of death.

It should be noted, however, that the tax for which the 2 percent rate is available is in addition to the basic credit/exclusion amount. The remaining amount accrues interest at 45 percent of the applicable federal rate on underpayments of tax (compounded daily) determined on a calendar-quarter basis.

Note: Students will not be expected to know how to make this Sec. 6166 calculation.

It is also interesting to note that interest begins to accrue on the date the tax was required to be paid without regard to any allowable extensions. However, the adjusted gross estate is determined on the date the estate tax return is filed, including any extensions of time for filing (IRC Sec. 6166(b)(6)). This differential allows the estate to deduct the interest payments that accrue up to the date the return is actually filed. Thus, an estate that barely misses qualifying under the 35 percent rule may qualify for tax deferral by delaying filing and accruing interest. The interest deduction accrued from 9 months after the date of death to the date of filing will increase the amount of deductible expenses from the gross estate in arriving at the adjusted gross estate. This will decrease the value of the adjusted gross estate and increase the percentage of the closely held business or farm relative to the adjusted gross estate. Thus, an estate that came close to qualifying but failed to do so under the 35 percent eligibility rule may then qualify for installment payment of tax.

Acceleration

Under certain circumstances, the estate forfeits its right to installment payments of tax. If any of the following actions occurs, all remaining unpaid estate tax becomes due and payable immediately upon notice and demand by the Internal Revenue Service. The events that cause acceleration are

- late payment or failure to pay any individual installment
- withdrawal of 50 percent or more of the assets (including cash and property) from the business
- distribution, sale, exchange, or disposition of 50 percent or more of the value of the business interest to anyone other than a beneficiary who is entitled to receive the interest under the decedent's will or trust or under state intestacy laws

These withdrawals are cumulative. If the decedent's interest in a closely held business is transferred because of either the death of the original heir or the death of any subsequent transferee receiving the interest as a result of the prior transferor's death, acceleration of taxes will not be triggered if each subsequent transferee is a family member of the transferor. The term *family member* for the purposes of Sec. 6166 acceleration is determined under Sec. 267(c)(4), which includes brothers, sisters, spouse, ancestors, and lineal descendants as family members of the transferor.

Furthermore, acceleration will not be triggered by late installment payments of tax by the executor in the first 6 months. An executor is now given a grace period of 6 months after each installment is due within which to pay the tax without causing acceleration of the unpaid tax. However, late payment causes the estate to lose the benefit of the 2 percent interest rate with respect to that payment. In addition to the higher interest rate, the estate will be required to pay a penalty of 5 percent for each month or part of a month that the payment is overdue.

Because an executor may be held personally liable if other distributions are made from the estate prior to payment of the estate tax, installment payment of the estate tax could leave executors vulnerable over a long period of time. To alleviate this problem, there is a special lien procedure available that relieves the executor from personal liability for the entire installment period. It may be elected if the executor, as well as all parties having any interest in the property to which the lien will attach, files a written agreement consenting to creation of the lien in favor of the federal government instead of a bond. This agreement must name a responsible individual to deal with the Internal Revenue Service on behalf of the beneficiaries and all other parties who consented to the lien. A bond may not be required by the IRS except to the extent that no adequate security exists for the unpaid principal plus interest.

Additional Sec. 6166 Considerations

Other considerations concerning Sec. 6166 include recognizing some of the downsides of being successful in meeting the requirements of the 6166 election. For example, Sec. 6166 does not in itself actually provide the cash to pay the tax. It simply allows for the deferral of paying a portion of the tax through installments. There is also the expense of the interest, albeit low, which increases total costs. Personal representatives and estate advisors also need to be aware that in addition to federal estate taxes, the estate has to have cash to pay state death and income taxes, administrative expenses, estate debts, and so forth. Sec. 6166 addresses only the postponement of a portion of federal taxes. Last, as previously stated, personal representatives are loath to remain personally liable for the unpaid taxes, possibly for as long as 14 years. And, as part of the ripple effect, Sec. 6166 has the result of delaying distribution to beneficiaries. Few beneficiaries and heirs want to wait for such a long period for their interests.

> **Sec. 6166 Installment Payment of Estate Tax**
> - inclusion in decedent's estate of closely held business interest or farm valued at more than *35 percent of adjusted gross estate*
> - deferral of tax payments for 5 years from return due date
> - interest payments only on unpaid balance for first 4 years
> - overlapping tax and interest payments in fifth year
> - acceleration of full estate tax balance if Sec. 6166 requirements not met

MINI-CASE: MR. X

Mr. X is a successful businessman who owns a one-half interest in a profitable partnership that he and his brother, Y, organized to develop real estate. He has also engaged from time to time in other real estate ventures with his brother independently of the partnership. X and his wife are both 59 years old.

X holds personal assets in his own name as follows:

One-half of the partnership interest in the XY Company	$7,000,000
Common stock	3,040,000
Cash in bank	180,000
Household furnishings and personal effects	200,000
Municipal bonds—face amount	1,440,000

X holds the following property in joint tenancy with Mrs. X (who has made no contribution to the cost of these assets):

Bank checking account	$ 80,000
Corporate bonds (purchased in 1995)	460,000
Cash in bank	60,000

X and Mrs. X hold their residence, purchased in 1996 and valued at $900,000, as tenants by the entirety. Mrs. X paid 20 percent of the original purchase price from an inheritance that she received from her father. In addition, X and his brother own, as tenants in common, equal shares of undeveloped commercial real estate with a total value of $4,000,000. Assume a hypothetical basic credit amount of $4,000,000.

X owns life insurance on his own life as follows:

Policy	Age at Issue	Face Amount	Beneficiary	How Payable
30-payment life	28	$200,000	X's estate	Lump sum
Ordinary life	34	200,000	Mrs. X	Lump sum
Ordinary life	38	400,000	Mrs. X and then her estate	Installments certain for 10 years
20-year term	48	100,000	Mrs. X	Lump sum

1. Assume that no change has been made in the manner in which X and Mrs. X hold title to their property, and that the values of their assets at X's death in 2019 are those shown above. Prepare a list of assets, with their values, that would be included in X's gross estate for federal estate tax purposes if he predeceases Mrs. X.

2. X's will leaves the entire residue to his wife except his partnership interest, which he leaves to his two sons in equal shares. Assume X dies in 2019. Compute the federal estate tax payable. Assume that funeral and administration expenses are $130,000, that the state death tax is $65,000, and that X's executor will utilize X's basic credit/exclusion amount.

MINI-CASE: EMILY SMITH

Emily Smith, a widow, died in 2019 at age 75. Prior to her retirement 10 years ago, Emily had been a corporate secretary. Emily is survived by a daughter, Eva, a son-in-law, and three grandchildren. Most of Emily's assets were left to her by her late husband, Henry Smith, who was an airline executive when he died 12 years ago.

After Henry's death, Emily became the sole owner of their personal residence. Eight months before her death, Emily deeded the property to her daughter Eva in exchange for a written agreement stating that she would be allowed to live in the house for as long as she wanted. Emily retained title to the furnishings.

Under Emily's will, she left $500,000 to State University. Her deductible funeral and administration expenses are $125,000, and her deductible debts are $75,000. The full amount of the basic credit amount is available for her estate, and state death taxes are $60,000. Emily's date of death is the applicable date for federal estate tax valuation.

Emily's Situation on the Date of Her Death

Type of Asset	Fair Market Value	Owner(s)
Checking account	$20,000	Emily
Money market funds	$1,540,000	Emily
Common stock	$7,200,000	Emily and Eva, as joint tenants with right of survivorship. Emily and Eva equally contributed to the purchase of the stock.
Personal residence	$1,550,000	Eva
401(k) plan benefit	$1,900,000	Emily. At Emily's death the plan trustees are to pay the plan benefit to her husband, Henry, if living, otherwise to her estate in a lump sum.
Household furnishings	$130,000	Emily
Automobile	$15,000	Emily
QTIP trust	$1,750,000	Trustee, under the provisions of Henry Smith's testamentary trust. Emily receives the annual income, and at her death the trust corpus passes to Eva.

1. Prepare a list of assets, with their values, that would be included in Emily's gross estate for federal estate tax purposes.

2. Compute the federal estate tax payable for Emily's estate if the basic credit in the year of death is $4,000,000.

Chart for Computing Federal Estate Tax

CHART FOR COMPUTING FEDERAL ESTATE TAX

	STEP 1	(1)	Gross Estate		$_____
minus		(2)	Funeral and administration expenses (estimated as_____ % of_____	$_____	
		(3)	Debts and taxes	_____	
		(4)	Losses	_____	(–)_____
equals	STEP 2	(5)	Adjusted gross estate		$_____
minus		(6)	Marital deduction	$_____	
		(7)	Charitable deduction	_____	
		(8)	State death tax deduction	_____	(–)_____
equals	STEP 3	(9)	Taxable estate		$_____
plus		(10)	Adjusted taxable gifts (taxable portion of post-1976 lifetime taxable transfers not included in gross estate)		+_____
equals		(11)	Tentative tax base (total of taxable estate and adjusted taxable gifts)		$_____
compute		(12)	Tentative tax		$_____
minus		(13)	Gift taxes payable on post-1976 gifts[1]		(–)_____
equals	STEP 4	(14)	Estate tax payable before credits		$_____
minus		(15)	Tax credits		
		(a)	Basic credit amount	$_____	
		(b)	Credit for foreign death taxes[2]	_____	
		(c)	Credit for gift tax for pre-1977 gifts[3]	_____	
		(d)	Credit for tax on prior transfers	_____	(–)_____
equals	STEP 5	(16)	Net federal estate tax payable	_____	$_____

1. Once the tentative tax is determined, gift taxes generated by taxable gifts made after 1976 in excess of the basic credit amount are subtracted from it.

2. Irrelevant credit for calculation purposes in this course.

3. Credit still exists for gift taxes paid by a deceased on taxable gifts made before 1977 if the property is included in the gross estate. Irrelevant credit for calculation purposes in this course.

Estate Tax Credit Schedule

ESTATE TAX CREDIT SCHEDULE

The basic credit amount applies to both lifetime and at death transfers. The credit is first used to offset taxable gifts made during lifetime, with any remaining credit to be applied as a credit against federal estate taxes. The following chart shows the relevant credit amount per year as it is phased in for different time periods and the equivalent value of the gross estate exempted from taxation.

Year	Credit Amount	Exclusion Amount
1982	$62,800	$225,000
1983	79,300	275,000
1984	96,300	325,000
1985	121,800	400,000
1986	155,800	500,000
1987 to 1998	192,800	600,000
1998	202,050	625,000
1999	211,300	650,000
2000 and 2001	220,550	675,000
2002 and 2003	345,800	1,000,000
2004 and 2005	555,800	1,500,000
2006, 2007, and 2008	780,800	2,000,000
2009	1,455,800	3,500,000
2010	Repeal (if elected) or 1,730,800	Repeal (if elected) or 5,000,000
2011	1,730,800	5,000,000
2012	1,772,800	5,120,000
2016	2,125,800	5,450,000
2017	2,141,800	5,490,000
2018	4,417,800	11,180,000
2019	4,505,800	11,400,00

The requirement to file an estate tax return has been adjusted upward to reflect increases in the basic credit amount. Executors of estates (including lifetime adjusted taxable gifts) having a gross value of less than the basic exclusion amount shown in the right column above are not required to file federal estate tax returns.

Only estates having values exceeding the exclusion amount are potentially subject to the federal estate tax.

CHAPTER REVIEW

Key Terms and Concepts

adjusted taxable gifts   credit for foreign death taxes
basic credit amount   credit for tax on prior transfers
state death tax credit   Sec. 303 redemption
adjusted taxable estate

Chapter 17: Review Questions

1. Given the taxable estate, explain how the tentative tax base is obtained. [LO 17.1]

2. Mr. Bowden died in 2019 with a gross estate valued at $7,800,000. His funeral and administration expenses are $100,000. At his death, Mr. Bowden owed $25,000 in accrued personal property and realty taxes. Mr. Bowden's estate left $2,375,000 to his wife outright and the remainder in trust for his two sons. At no time during his life did Mr. Bowden make any taxable gifts. His state of domicile has imposed $50,000 of state death taxes. Calculate the tentative tax (before credits) due on the transfer of Mr. Bowden's estate. [LO 17.1]

3. What amount may be deducted from the tentative tax before credits are determined? [LO 17.2]

4. What are the credits that may be deducted from the tentative tax, and what is the effect of a tax credit? [LO 17.2]

5. Sam, a widower, died in 2019 with a gross estate of $16,320,000; deductible administration expenses and debts totaled $140,000. Sam's three children, who are his sole beneficiaries, will receive equal shares of his estate. Their ages are 26, 23, and 21. Under his will, Sam donated $250,000 to his university. He also made post-1976 adjusted taxable gifts of $60,000, for which there was no gift tax liability. Assuming the state death taxes are $70,000, calculate the net federal estate tax by using a hypothetical $4,000,000 basic credit amount in the year of death. [LO 17.3]

6. What is the purpose of the basic credit amount, and how does its use during lifetime affect its availability at death? [LO 17.3]

7. What is the purpose of the credit for foreign death taxes paid, and to whom does it apply? [LO 17.3]

8. Tom Grigson died in 2019 with a taxable estate valued at $4,825,000. Will the following amounts paid be allowed as credits against his estate tax liability?

    a. His estate paid $250,000 in state inheritance taxes.

    b. Tom's sister, who died 3 years before Tom, had an estate valued at $500,000 after payment of debts and taxes. He was the sole heir of his sister's estate, which was settled shortly before Tom died. His gross estate included the $500,000 received from his sister. Assume federal estate taxes paid on her estate were $155,800. [LO 17.3]

9. Explain the credit for tax on prior transfers and its purpose. [LO 17.3]

10. In which of the following situations is the executor required to file a federal estate tax return?

    a. George Jessup died in 2019 with a gross estate valued at $4,875,000.

    b. Jim's gross estate is valued at $11,600,000, and the estate had $100,000 of deductions in debts and unpaid federal income taxes as well as funeral and administration expenses.

    c. Sarah does not have a taxable estate because she left all of her property to her husband. [LO 17.4]

11. Describe the duties of the personal representative of an estate with respect to the filing of federal tax returns. [LO 17.4]

12. For what reasons might an extension of time to pay the federal estate tax usually be allowed? [LO 17.4]

13. Describe the circumstances that must exist before the estate tax may be paid in installments. [LO 17.4]

14. The following situations describe two sets of circumstances under which an extension of time for paying all or part of the estate tax liability may be obtained. Explain whether the extension in each case is granted at the discretion of the Internal Revenue Service or whether it may be elected by the executor as a matter of right.

a. Albert, a widower, died in 2019 leaving a gross estate of $16,850,000 and an adjusted gross estate of $16,700,000. Albert's taxable estate is also $16,700,000. The executor has determined that a portion of the estate must be sold in order to pay the estate tax within the 9-month time limit. The only portion of the estate that can be sold is Albert's interest in a partnership in which he and his brother, Sam, were equal partners. Albert's partnership interest has an estate tax value of $2,200,000, and the executor has found a buyer at that price. However, the buyer will need several months to raise that amount of money.

b. Benjamin died recently leaving a gross estate of $17,800,000, an adjusted gross estate of $17,725,000, and a taxable estate of $17,650,000. Benjamin's executor has determined that the estate does not contain sufficient liquid assets with which to pay the estate tax. The only portion of the estate that could be converted to cash in time to pay the taxes is his interest in a closely held corporation engaged in the heating oil business. The estate owns 30 percent of the stock, which had a fair market value of $13 million at the time Benjamin died. The two surviving stockholders are Benjamin's sons who inherited the stock; they are attempting to raise the money to pay the tax themselves so it will not be necessary to sell the stock to an outsider. [LO 17.4]

15. Describe what circumstances will trigger an acceleration of the estate tax payable when installment payments are being made. [LO 17.4]

Answers to Mini-Cases

1. Mini-case: Mr. X

    a. The assets includible in X's gross estate for federal estate tax purposes if he predeceases Mrs. X are as follows:

Property in his own name

One-half of partnership interest in the XY Company	$7,000,000
Common stock	3,040,000
Cash in bank	180,000
Household furnishings and personal effects	200,000
Municipal bonds—face amount	1,440,000
One-half of real estate held as tenants in common with brother, Y	2,000,000
	$13,860,000

Life insurance owned by X

Policy	Face Amount
30-payment life	$ 200,000
Ordinary life	200,000
Ordinary life	400,000
10-year term	100,000
	$ 900,000

One-half of all property held jointly or by the entirety with Mrs. X

Personal residence	$ 450,000
Bank checking account	40,000
Corporate bonds	230,000
Automobile	30,000
	$ 750,000
Total value of assets included in X's gross estate	$15,510,000

b. CHART FOR COMPUTING X's FEDERAL ESTATE TAX

	STEP 1	(1)	Gross estate	$15,510,000
minus		(2)	Funeral and administration expenses (estimated as _____ % of _____	($130,000)
		(3)	Debts and taxes	—
		(4)	Losses	—
			Total deductions	($130,000)
equals	STEP 2	(5)	Adjusted gross estate	$15,380,000
minus		(6)	Marital deduction*	($8,510,000)
		(7)	Charitable deduction	—
		(8)	State death tax deduction	(65,000)
			Total deductions	(8,575,000)
equals	STEP 3	(9)	Taxable estate	$6,805,000
plus		(10)	Adjusted taxable gifts (post-1976 lifetime taxable transfers not included in gross estate)	—
equals		(11)	Tentative tax base (total of taxable estate and adjusted taxable gifts)	$6,805,000
compute		(12)	Tentative tax ($345,800 + .4*(tentative tax base less $1m))	$2,667,800
minus		(13)	Gift taxes payable on post-1976 gifts	—
equals	STEP 4	(14)	Estate tax payable before credits	$2,667,800
minus		(15)	Tax credits	
			(a) Basic credit amount (hypothetical year)	$4,000,000
			(b) Credit for foreign death taxes	—
			(c) Credit for gift tax for pre-1977 gifts	—
			(d) Credit for tax on prior transfers	—
			Total credits	$4,000,000
equals	STEP 5	(16)	Net federal estate tax payable	$0

*This amount is determined after other deductions from the adjusted gross estate. (The marital deduction is equal to the amount of all assets passing to Mrs. X, which include the entire estate less the $7 million partnership interest passing to the sons. All the life insurance qualifies for the marital deduction as it is payable directly to Mrs. X or X's estate and passes to her under his will or paid to her in such a way that any payments left at her death will pass to her estate.

2. Mini-Case: Emily Smith

    a. The assets includible in Emily's gross estate for federal estate tax purposes are the following:

Checking account	$ 20,000
Money market funds	1,540,000
Common stock (one-half)	3,600,000
Personal residence	1,550,000
401(k) plan benefit	1,900,000
Household furnishings	130,000
Automobile	15,000
QTIP trust	1,750,000
Total value of assets included in Emily's gross estate	$10,505,000

    The personal residence is included in Emily's gross estate under Sec. 2036 since Emily retained a life interest in the property at death.

b. CHART FOR COMPUTING EMILY SMITH'S FEDERAL ESTATE TAX

	STEP 1	(1)	Gross estate		$10,505,000
minus		(2)	Funeral and administration expenses (estimated as ____% of _____)	($125,000)	
		(3)	Debts and taxes	(75,000)	
		(4)	Losses	—	
				Total deductions ($200,000)	
equals	STEP 2	(5)	Adjusted gross estate		$10,305,000
minus		(6)	Marital deduction	—	
		(7)	Charitable deduction	($500,000)	
		(8)	State death tax deduction (2019)	(60,000)	
				Total deductions ($560,000)	
equals	STEP 3	(9)	Taxable estate		$9,745,000
plus		(10)	Adjusted taxable gifts (post-1976 lifetime taxable transfers not included in gross estate)	—	
equals		(11)	Tentative tax base (total of taxable estate and adjusted taxable gifts)		$9,745,000
compute		(12)	Tentative tax	$3,843,800	
minus		(13)	Gift taxes payable on post-1976 gifts	—	
equals	STEP 4	(14)	Estate tax payable before credits		$3,843,800
minus		(15)	Tax credits ($345,800 + .4*(tentative tax base less $1m))		
			(a) Basic credit amount (hypothetical year)	$4,000,000	
			(b) Credit for foreign death taxes	—	
			(c) Credit for gift tax for pre-1977 gifts	—	
			(d) Credit for tax on prior transfers	—	

			Total credits	($4,000,000)
equals	STEP 5	(16)	Net federal estate tax payable	$0

Chapter 17: Review Answers

1. Once the taxable estate is determined, the amount of adjusted taxable gifts made after 1976 is added to the taxable estate. The result is the tentative tax base.

2. Federal estate tax is computed by subtracting certain allowable deductions from the gross estate to arrive at the adjusted gross estate; other deductions may then be taken to find the taxable estate. Any adjusted taxable gifts (post-1976 taxable gifts that are not included in the gross estate) are added to the taxable estate to form the tentative tax base. A tentative tax is derived by multiplying the tentative tax base rate by an applicable rate found in the gift and estate tax rate schedule. Any gift taxes payable (in excess of the basic credit amount in the year of the decedent's death) after 1976 may then be subtracted from the tentative tax. The tentative tax may also be reduced by certain credits. The most notable credit is the federal estate tax basic credit amount, which is $4,505,800 in 2019 (as indexed).

   In Mr. Bowden's case $100,000 of funeral and administration costs and $25,000 in accrued taxes may be subtracted from the gross estate of $7,800,000. The adjusted gross estate is $7,675,000, from which the estate of Mr. Bowden is entitled to subtract a marital deduction for property passing to a surviving spouse in a qualifying manner. In this case, the marital deduction is $2,375,000—the amount left outright to his surviving spouse. Mr. Bowden's estate may also deduct $50,000 of state death taxes (2019). The taxable estate is $5.25 million. Since Mr. Bowden made no taxable life-time gifts, the tentative tax base consists solely of the taxable estate of $5.25 million. Applying the appropriate tax rate, the tentative tax is $2,045,800 (2019). The tentative tax may be reduced by any gift taxes payable after December 31, 1976 (there are none here), and, thus, the estate tax payable before credits is also $2,045,800.

3. After the tentative tax is determined, gift taxes generated by taxable gifts made after 1976 in excess of the basic credit amount are subtracted from this figure. The determination of the amount of reduction allowable because of taxes attributable to post-1976 taxable gifts is made through the following steps:

   a. Total all post-1976 taxable gifts.

   b. Compute the gift tax payable by applying the tax rate schedule in effect at the decedent's death to the total taxable gifts. In other words, all the post-1976 taxable gifts are treated as if they were made at one time—the date of the decedent's death.

   c. Reduce the gift tax payable by the relevant credit amount for the year of the decedent's death (for example, $4,505,800 for 2019 (as indexed)).

   d. If the gift tax payable exceeds the basic credit amount, subtract the excess from the tentative tax.

The result is the estate tax payable before credits.

4.   Once the estate tax is computed, there are four possible credits in 2019 that may be applied against the tax to arrive at the net federal estate tax payable. As with income tax credits, these credits are allowed as a dollar-for-dollar reduction of the estate tax. They are the

- basic credit amount
- credit for foreign death taxes
- credit for gift tax paid on pre-1977 gifts (irrelevant for this course)
- credit for taxes paid on prior transfers

5.   The net federal estate tax payable on Sam's estate is calculated as follows:

Gross estate		$16,320,000
	Less administration expenses and debts	(140,000)
Adjusted gross estate		16,180,000
	Less charitable deduction	(250,000)
	Less state death taxes	(70,000)
Taxable estate		15,860,000
	Plus adjusted taxable gifts	60,000
Tentative tax base		15,920,000
Tentative tax ($345,800 +40% x $14,920,000)		6,313,800
	Less gift taxes payable on post-1976 gifts	0
Estate tax payable before credits		6,313,800
Less basic credit amount (hypothetical year)		(4,000,000)
Net federal estate tax payable		$ 2,313,800

6.   The estate and gift tax credit came into existence for estates of decedents dying after December 31, 1976. The term *unified credit* was adopted under the 1976 act because the credit may be used as an offset against gift taxes as well as estate taxes. Actually,

the credit must first be used to offset gift taxes on lifetime transfers. Any remaining credit is applied as a credit against the federal estate tax.

The basic credit amount is $$4,505,800 and the basic exclusion amount is $11.4 million for 2019, as indexed for inflation. TRA 2010 and ATRA 2012 refer to these numbers as the *basic credit amount* and *basic exclusion amount*. The credits and exclusion amounts for gift, estate, and generation-skipping tax are currently "unified" and are, therefore, the same.

7. There is a credit allowed against the federal estate tax for taxes actually paid by the decedent's estate to any foreign country for any estate, inheritance, legacy, or succession taxes. The purpose of the *credit for foreign death taxes* is to prevent double taxation. It is allowable only to the estate of a decedent who was either (1) a citizen of the United States, or (2) a resident of the United States who was not a citizen at the time of death. Nonresident aliens are denied the foreign death tax credit. The credit exists for taxes actually paid by the decedent's estate to any foreign country, U.S. possession, or political subdivision of a foreign state.

8. a. State death taxes are a deduction and are not a credit. However, Tom Grigson's estate will be able to deduct the entire amount of $250,000 in state inheritance taxes from the adjusted gross estate.

    b. A credit for tax in prior transfers is permitted when the first decedent dies less than 10 years before the second decedent. In this case, the property was inherited 3 years before the death of the second decedent. Under these circumstances, the credit is limited to 80 percent of the taxes paid in the first decedent's estate.

9. Circumstances may arise in which a decedent has inherited property from someone who died less than 10 years before the decedent's death or within 2 years following the decedent's death and the property transferred to the decedent was already taxable in the estate of the transferor-decedent. To avoid double taxation on double transfers of property occurring within a reasonably short time period (that is, 10 years before or 2 years after the decedent's death), a credit is allowed against the federal estate tax paid by the present decedent as a result of this inherited-property inclusion in the decedent's gross estate.

10. a. The basic credit amount for estate tax purposes currently available (2019) is $4,505,800. However, the equivalent value of the estate credit amount in 2019 is $11.4 million. George Jessup's gross estate is less than the equivalent value required to file an estate tax return, assuming there are no adjusted taxable gifts. Therefore, the executor of the estate is not required to file an estate tax return.

b.   Jim's gross estate is valued at $11,500,000, which is $100,000 more than the basic exclusion amount in 2019. It means that Jim's executor must file a federal estate tax return. The $100,000 of deductions is, of course, important in that the $100,000 will be deducted from the gross estate of $11,600,000, which will reduce the estate value to $11,500,000. Even when no federal estate tax is payable, an estate tax return must still be filed as required under certain circumstances. In this case, it is likely that he will owe taxes on a portion of the estate.

c.   A Form 706 must be filed by the executor of the estate of every U.S. citizen or resident when the executor elects to transfer the DSUE amount to the surviving spouse, regardless of the size of the decedent's gross estate. Since she is married, her executor should transfer the DSUE to the surviving spouse.

11. A primary duty of the personal representative is to file the federal estate tax return when due and to see that estate taxes are timely paid. The personal representative must also timely file any estate income tax returns when they are due. If the estate is sizable enough to warrant filing a federal estate tax return, the return is due and the tax is payable no later than 9 months after the decedent's death unless an extension is granted.

12. There are mitigating circumstances that the IRS will accept for granting an extension of time to pay the estate tax. An extension for up to 12 months to pay the estate tax will be granted if the Internal Revenue Service determines there is reasonable cause.

13. There is a special provision that allows the personal representative to elect a deferral for payment of estate tax attributable to the inclusion of a closely held business or farm business in the decedent's gross estate if certain conditions are met (IRC Sec. 6166). The law provides that an executor may be able to elect to defer payment of estate tax attributable to inclusion in the estate of a farm or other closely held business if that business consists of more than 35 percent of the adjusted gross estate. If the estate qualifies, such an election is made at the sole discretion of the estate's personal representative.

To determine whether more than 35 percent of the *adjusted gross estate* is made up of a closely held business or farm, the adjusted gross estate is defined as the gross estate reduced by deductible debts, expenses, claims, and losses, but before reduction by the marital or charitable deductions (IRC Sec. 6166(b)(6)).

For purposes of the 35 percent rule, an *interest in a closely held business* is defined as (1) an interest in a proprietorship, (2) an interest in a partnership carrying on a trade or business with no more than 45 partners or where 20 percent or more of its assets helped determine the decedent's gross estate, or (3) stock in a corporation with no more than 45 shareholders or where 20 percent of its voting stock is included in the decedent's gross estate. Property owned by a corporation, partnership, estate, or trust is regarded as owned proportionately by its shareholders, partners, or beneficiaries. In addition, for purposes of this election, interests in two or more closely held businesses are treated as a single closely held business if 20 percent or more of the total value of each business is included in the decedent's gross estate. Also, all stock and partnership interests belonging to a decedent and any family members will be aggregated in order to meet the requirements of stock ownership.

14. a.   If requirements are met to qualify for installment payment of tax, the executor may elect to defer payment of tax as a matter of right. The estate tax value of the closely held business must comprise more than 35 percent of the adjusted gross estate. Albert's adjusted gross estate is $16,700,000 and the partnership interest is $2,200,000, which is less than 35 percent of the adjusted gross estate. Therefore, the executor cannot elect deferred payment of estate tax. However, there is a discretionary extension allowed by the IRS for one year and up to 10 years if the executor can show reasonable cause to extend time for the payment. Because of the liquidity problem, the estate could probably qualify for a delayed payment of tax under the Code if reasonable cause exists. Granting an extension for reasonable cause is at the discretion of the IRS.

   b.   Benjamin's adjusted gross estate was $17,725,000 and the stock in the closely held corporation was valued at $13 million, which is more than 35 percent of the adjusted gross estate. Therefore, the executor has a right to elect to extend tax payment attributable to the closely held stock over a 14-year deferral period. Interest at the rate of only 2 percent (subject to certain qualifying limitations) will be due for the first 4 years, with equal annual installments of interest and principal payable beginning in the fifth year and continuing over the following 10-year period, unless certain changes occur that would cause acceleration of the tax.

15. The events that cause acceleration are

   •   late payment or failure to pay any individual installment

   •   withdrawal of 50 percent or more of the assets (including cash and property) from the business

   •   distribution, sale, exchange, or disposition of 50 percent or more of the value of the business interest to anyone other than a beneficiary who is entitled to receive the interest under the decedent's will or trust or under state intestacy laws

16. Sec. 303 of the Code allows a redemption of stock for the purpose of paying funeral and administrative expenses and death taxes without the redemption being treated as a dividend. If the redemption qualifies, it is treated as a sale, and the gain is treated as

capital gain if the stock was held as a capital asset in the hands of the decedent at the time of the exchange. In order to qualify for capital-gain treatment under this section, the decedent's stock must represent more than 35 percent of the adjusted gross estate. Ownership of 20 percent or more of the stock of each of two or more corporations may be aggregated to satisfy this 35 percent test.

Chapter 18:

The Basis Rules for Property Transferred during Lifetime or at Death

Learning Objectives

An understanding of the material in this chapter should enable the student to do the following:

> **LO 18.1**   **Explain how basis is used to determine gain or loss when property changes hands in a taxable transaction.**
>
> **LO 18. 2**   **Explain the rules for determining the basis of property transferred at death.**
>
> **LO 18. 3**   **Explain the rules for determining the basis of property transferred during lifetime by gift or bargain sale.**

LO 18.1   **Explain how basis is used to determine gain or loss when property changes hands in a taxable transaction.**

COMPUTING GAIN OR LOSS

One cannot compute the amount of gain or loss on the sale of an asset without knowing its cost. In most cases, the basis of an asset is the original price paid to acquire the property increased by certain adjustments (such as expenditures for improvements) and decreased by certain tax benefits (such as depreciation taken during the term of ownership).

Before an asset is transferred, four factors must be established. The first is the basis in the hands of the transferor; second, whether the asset is characterized as a capital or noncapital asset; third, the holding period in the hands of the transferor; and fourth, the fair market value of the asset at a relevant point in time.

Function of Basis

The main function of basis is to measure gain or loss when property is sold, exchanged, or transferred in a taxable transaction. (A second function of basis—to serve as a departure point for depreciation—is not discussed here.) Basis becomes important when property changes hands. If the transaction is taxable, the transferor must establish the basis in order to calculate gain or loss on the transaction. The transferee's basis determines gain or loss on a later transfer. The basis assumed by the transferee varies depending on the character of the transfer—that is, whether the transfer is a taxable sale or exchange, a nontaxable transfer by gift or inheritance, or a tax-free exchange. The transferee's basis is used to determine gain or loss when the asset is sold.

Capital Assets

capital asset

The Internal Revenue Code defines a **capital asset** as "property held by the taxpayer with specified exceptions." A major exception under this definition is inventory or property held primarily for sale to customers in the ordinary course of business. A second exception is certain depreciable real property used in a trade or business (which receives special tax treatment); this property is also considered ordinary income property. All gain or loss on the sale of property other than capital assets is taxable as ordinary income. If the asset is treated as a capital asset, however, it receives capital-gains tax treatment and the seller is taxed only to the extent of gain.

Holding Period

holding period

The **holding period** is determined with regard to whether the taxpayer has long-term or short-term capital-gain or capital-loss treatment. Long-term capital gains or losses result in most cases from the sale of a capital asset held for more than 12 months. Property held at death and included in a decedent's estate is treated for income tax purposes as long-term capital-gains property to the beneficiary, no matter what the decedent's holding period was.

Fair Market Value

The fourth element, the fair market value of an asset, may become important in determining basis for special situations involving gratuitous transfers at death. As previously discussed, fair market value can be defined as the price agreed upon by a willing buyer and a willing seller, neither being under compulsion either to buy or to sell.

LO 18. 2   **Explain the rules for determining the basis of property transferred at death.**

BASIS OF PROPERTY TRANSFERRED AT DEATH

General Rule

The way property was acquired will influence its basis on future disposition. There are special rules pertaining to the basis of property transferred at death. When property is acquired from a decedent, it acquires a new basis equal to the value of the property either on the date of death or on the alternate valuation date (6 months after death) if the estate is eligible to use the alternate valuation date and an election is made by the executor to use it. When an individual dies, the original basis becomes irrelevant. Property included in the decedent's gross estate acquires a new basis, which is either increased or decreased to the fair market value of the asset on the date of death. Basis changes occur even when no estate tax return is filed or there is no tax liability. The stepped-up or stepped-down basis rules apply to property included in the estate irrespective of its size. The value depicted on the estate tax return establishes the basis. Therefore, in cases where the alternate valuation date under Sec. 2032 or special-use valuation under Sec. 2032A is elected, the value of assets shown on the return determines basis.

stepped-up basis

In the past two or three decades, the fair market value of property has steadily increased as a result of our inflationary economy. These upward trends have caused the basis of property inherited from a decedent to be adjusted in an upward direction more often than not. This increased basis is known as a **stepped-up basis**. The stepped-up basis can result in a windfall to the transferee of the property. Property transferred by reason of death and included in a decedent's gross estate receives a step up in basis, regardless of whether or not a federal estate tax return is filed. The stepped-up-basis-at-death rule effectively eliminates the income tax on all potential gain accrued to the date of death. In those cases where property has greatly appreciated in value, there is a substantial income tax advantage to the estate or beneficiaries. Actually, the stepped-up-basis rule is a form of tax relief afforded to those people receiving property transferred at death.

Because the rule provides that basis becomes the fair market value on the date of death, it may also be *stepped down* if the asset has declined in value from the time it was acquired by the decedent. If the decedent possessed an asset that declined in value, he or she would have been wise to sell the asset or give the asset away while alive, thereby taking advantage of the loss on the sale. If a property that declined in value was not sold during the decedent's lifetime, the cost basis to the beneficiary becomes the fair market value at death. Any tax benefit from the unrealized loss is gone forever.

During periods when inflation slows down, this factor, if coupled with a recessionary economy, may reduce the benefit of this special-basis rule in the future. More properties may be *stepped down* to their fair market value on the date of death than have been in recent decades. Lifetime estate planning judgments regarding the holding or disposition of assets should be made. Unquestionably, the basis rules should be factored into such decisions. The financial services professional has a responsibility to advise clients to take losses during lifetime if the property is not being held for sentimental value. Basis is stepped up or down to fair market value at the date of death or the alternate valuation date.

Property Subject to Power of Appointment

If property passes to another because the decedent exercised a general power of appointment over the property under his or her will, that property is treated as property transferred by a decedent at death. Therefore, the value of the property is included in the decedent's gross estate. The property subject to the power receives a new basis stepped up to its fair market value on the date of the decedent's death. Conversely, if property is transferred to another because the donee-powerholder exercised a general power over the property during lifetime, the property is treated as having a carryover basis.

Retained Powers

There are adjustments to basis for property included in the decedent's gross estate either as a retained lifetime interest or because the decedent possessed certain powers over the transferred property that were not released during the 3-year period prior to death. These powers include the right to revoke the transfer as well as the right to alter or control the beneficial enjoyment or the income from the property. The stepped-up-basis rules apply to these properties transferred during lifetime that were brought back into the gross estate for valuation purposes because of the retained powers.

EXAMPLE

If the decedent transferred real estate to a son but retained the right to use the property for life or the right to income from the property for life, the property is included as a retained life income interest in the decedent's estate at its value on the day the decedent died. In that case, the property then receives a new basis equal to the fair market value for federal estate tax purposes. Thus, if highly appreciated property is given away, the donee may benefit from the inclusion of that property in the decedent's gross estate since the donee receives new stepped-up basis. When the property is subsequently sold, the new owner will have a smaller capital gains tax to pay.

Effect of Step Up in Basis on Jointly Held Property

The general rule that all property included in the gross estate receives a stepped-up basis at death also applies to property held jointly with right of survivorship. In the case of nonspousal joint tenancies or spousal joint tenancies created prior to January 1, 1977 (under the consideration-furnished rule), whatever value is attributed to the property that represents the decedent's joint interest receives a stepped-up basis to the date-of-death value in the hands of the surviving joint tenant or tenants. Should the entire value of jointly held property be included in the decedent's gross estate, the property will receive a fully stepped-up basis equal to the value on the date of death or alternate valuation date, if applicable. This value then becomes the new basis in the hands of the surviving joint tenant for later sale purposes.

This rule has a strange effect on joint tenancies between spouses. Because only one-half of the property can now be included in the gross estate of the decedent-spouse, the property receives a stepped-up basis for the value of one-half of the property only. The original basis of the other half of the property is retained by the surviving spouse. This affects the amount of gain realized should the property be sold during the surviving spouse's lifetime. If, however, the surviving spouse holds the property until death, the entire property will be included in the survivor's estate. The entire property will then acquire a fully stepped-up basis in the hands of the beneficiaries.

EXAMPLE

Mary Beth and her husband, a decedent, acquired a principal residence 15 years ago for $250,000 and titled it in joint names with right of survivorship. At the decedent's death last year, the fair market value of the property was appraised at $800,000. Under current law, only one-half of the value of the property (the one-half that is included in the decedent's gross estate) receives a stepped-up basis. The new basis is computed as follows: the one-half included in the decedent's estate receives a new basis of $400,000 and the one-half of the property owned by Mary Beth retains its original basis, $125,000. The total basis of the property is now $525,000. If Mary Beth later sells the property for fair market value, the combined basis will be $525,000 ($400,000 plus $125,000), and a taxable gain will occur. Note that under current law, Mary Beth, as a single individual, is able to exclude $250,000 of taxable gain on the sale of a principal residence (if she sells within two years of death, she can claim $500,000). If Mary Beth sells the house for $800,000, she may have taxable gain on $25,000 ($800,000 less basis of $525,000 = $275,000, less $250,000 of capital gains exclusion). One way to avoid this additional gain is for the surviving spouse to hold the property until death.

To summarize, the current rule for estate tax inclusion with respect to jointly held property with right of survivorship is actually two separate rules depending on whether the property is held by the spouses alone or by the decedent and one or more persons. For all joint tenancies other than spousal joint tenancies, the consideration-furnished rule applies. The rule pertaining to spousal joint tenancies has been amended in the Code to define a qualified joint interest as any interest held by the decedent and the decedent's spouse as joint tenants with right of survivorship or as tenants by the entirety, if they are the only joint tenants. All former requirements pertaining to qualified joint interests have been eliminated, including filing a gift tax return on the creation of the joint tenancy as well as making elections under the gift tax provisions to treat the creation as a gift.

Exceptions to the General Stepped-Up-Basis Rule

Basis of Income in Respect of a Decedent (IRD)

The stepped-up-basis rules do not apply to income that is included in the decedent's gross estate as *income in respect of a decedent (IRD)*. Income in respect of a decedent is any income that the decedent was entitled to (but did not receive) while alive. The income is includible at full value for estate tax purposes. It is then also taxed to the beneficiary of the income as ordinary income for income tax purposes. However, the beneficiary is allowed an income tax deduction for the additional estate tax paid due to the IRD being included in the gross estate.

Receipt of Property in Kind

Also, if the beneficiary receives property in substitution for a cash bequest, the basis of the property in the beneficiary's hands equals the amount of cash bequest that the property transferred satisfies.

EXAMPLE

Suppose the decedent leaves $20,000 to a cousin. Instead of paying the cousin $20,000, the executor transfers property worth $20,000 to the cousin. The cousin acquires a basis of $20,000 for the property. If the fair market value of the property on the date of death was $17,000, the basis to the estate is the date-of-death value, or $17,000. Because this property appreciated in value after the date of death and was distributed in lieu of $20,000 cash, the estate (being a separate tax paying entity) realizes a gain of $3,000.

Basis of Community Property

A special rule pertains to community property held by the decedent and the surviving spouse when the decedent spouse leaves his or her share of community property to the surviving spouse. If at least one-half of the community property vesting in the surviving spouse was includible in the decedent's gross estate and received a basis equal to the value of that share on the date of death, the property that represents the surviving spouse's one-half share of community property receives a new basis in the property adjusted to the full fair market value of the property at the decedent's death. In other words, if a decedent's share of community property passes to the surviving community spouse, the surviving spouse receives a step up in basis equal to the full value of the property. This full step-up rule is different from the basis rules that apply in common-law states. In those states, a surviving spouse receives a step up only for the value of property included in the decedent's gross estate.

Certain Property Acquired by Gift within One Year of Death

The stepped-up-basis-at-death rule is ignored under certain circumstances. The rule does not apply when appreciated property is acquired by the decedent by gift within one year before death if, upon death, the property then passes directly or indirectly back to the original donor or the original donor's spouse. This exception was carved out to eliminate schemes to obtain the stepped-up basis for certain property that, in actuality, did not belong to the decedent and was intended to return to the original owner at the decedent's death. This scheme involves a sham transfer made for the purpose of increasing the basis of the asset to the original owner. The nature of the bequest does not change the application of this exception to the basis rules.

The following situation illustrates the type of scheme this provision is designed to thwart.

EXAMPLE

Sam Summers owns 500 shares of IBM stock that he acquired 20 years ago for one-tenth of its present value. Martin Summers, his brother, is terminally ill and expected to die shortly. Sam transfers stock that cost him $100,000 to Martin when the shares are worth $1,000,000. Martin subsequently dies and, under the terms of his will, there is a specific bequest of the IBM stock to his brother, Sam. At the time of Martin's death, the stock has a fair market value of $1,000,000. Sam sells the stock 2 months later for $1,100,000. If he had never transferred the stock to his dying brother, Sam would have had a long-term capital gain of $1,000,000. If Sam were allowed to obtain a stepped-up basis as a result of this sham transfer, he would avoid $900,000 of gain and would receive a stepped-up basis of $1,000,000 that would provide him with a long-term gain of only $100,000.

To prevent this type of windfall, Congress enacted a rule that any property transferred by gift to the decedent within one year of death that reverts to the original donor or the donor's spouse as a bequest from the decedent (either directly or indirectly) will not receive a stepped-up basis when the property is sold or exchanged. The property retains the same basis in the hands of the donor-heir that it had in the hands of the decedent immediately before death. This rule applies to property acquired after August 13, 1981 (the date the law was signed), by decedents dying after December 31, 1981. It also applies to gift transfers between spouses.

The stepped-up basis is denied only to the extent that the donor-heir is entitled to receive the appreciated value. Thus, if the heir inherits only a portion of the property that was transferred because it was used to satisfy debts or administrative expenses, the rule applies on a pro rata basis. It should be noted that if the decedent lives more than one year after the original transfer, the general stepped-up-basis rule is applicable. The general rule also applies to transfers made by the decedent to someone other than the original donor or the donor's spouse, although the property was transferred to the decedent within one year of death. If, in the preceding illustration, the decedent, Martin Summers, left the IBM stock to his brother's grandchildren rather than to his brother or his brother's wife, the stepped-up-basis rule would apply. This one-year rule was enacted to prevent a windfall to an heir who transfers appreciated property to a terminally ill relative shortly before the relative's death with the knowledge that the heir will get the property back through inheritance after the relative's death occurs, thus receiving a new basis equal to the fair market value of the property on the date of death.

The stepped-up-basis provision offers excellent estate planning opportunities. Because there are relatively few ways to successfully avoid taxation of gain, the stepped-up-basis rules create an opportunity for elimination of potential gain when property has greatly appreciated in value. Any substantially appreciated property owned by the decedent at death is passed on to the heirs with a higher basis. That increment of gain (from the time the property was obtained until the decedent's death) is wiped out or eliminated when the property is subsequently sold. In effect, what exists is a loophole in the tax law because some gain escapes taxation entirely.

The estate owner can avoid potential tax by determining whether it would be more advantageous to hold the property for life or if a greater tax benefit would be derived if the property was disposed of during lifetime. Certainly the stepped-up-basis rule should be taken into consideration when a decision to hold or sell property is made by a mature estate owner. Again, the decision will vary depending on many factors, including the following: (1) whether property has substantially increased in value, (2) whether the basis is close to or greater than the fair market value when a transfer is contemplated, (3) whether there is the potential for future increase in value, and (4) the relative impact of the estate and gift taxes compared with the income tax if the property is sold.

There is yet another tax consideration when property is transferred at death, which pertains to the holding-period rules for long-term capital-gains treatment. The length of time property was held by the decedent prior to death and the holding period by the estate or beneficiary afterward are not determinative for long-term capital-gains treatment on a later sale. The general rule is that any person acquiring property from a decedent that was included in the gross estate and to which the stepped-up-basis rules apply is considered to have held the property for more than 12 months. In other words, when an asset is transferred as a result of death, the transferee receives long-term capital-gains treatment, regardless of the holding periods before and after death.

LO 18. 3 **Explain the rules for determining the basis of property transferred during lifetime by gift or bargain sale.**

PROPERTY TRANSFERRED DURING LIFETIME BY GIFT (SEC. 1015)

The stepped-up basis rule for property passing at death does not apply to property transferred during lifetime by gift. A carryover or substituted basis rule applies to property transferred gratuitously during lifetime. For a gift made after December 31, 1976, the donee acquires the donor's basis increased by any gift tax paid on the net appreciation at the time of the gift. The net appreciation is the amount by which the fair market value at the time of the gift exceeds the donor's adjusted basis. The amount of gift tax paid that can be added to the donee's basis is computed by taking the ratio that the net appreciation bears to the fair market value of the gift and applying that ratio to the total gift tax paid (IRC Sec. 1015(d)(6)).

carryover basis rule

Any appreciation in the property that might result in capital gains if the property is sold is deferred until such later time as the donee disposes of the property. The increment of gain or appreciation in the value of the property between the date of the gift and the time it is transferred in a taxable exchange does not avoid taxation because the property was given away. It is merely deferred until the time of sale. This is called the **carryover basis rule**, or substituted basis rule. When a gift is made, the basis of the property in the hands of the donor is carried over and becomes the basis in the hands of the donee.

The following situation illustrates the basis rule for property that is transferred by gift.

EXAMPLE

Early in the year, a father made a gift equal to the annual exclusion amount to his daughter. This gift was gift tax free because of the annual gift tax exclusion. Later that same year, the father made a gift to the daughter of property having a fair market value of $60,000. He originally acquired the property for $20,000. Because this transfer is a taxable gift, it is valued for gift tax purposes at $60,000. Assuming he did not make any other taxable gifts, his gift tax liability is $24,000 (60,000 × 40%). The gift tax attributable to the net appreciation in the property from the time he acquired it to the time of the gift is $16,000. Therefore, the daughter's basis is her father's basis of $30,000, plus that portion of the gift tax paid attributable to the net appreciation in the value of the gift (or $16,000). Thus, the daughter's basis is $36,000 (20,000 + 16,000).

General Rule for Basis of Gifted Property

When property is acquired by gift, the basis to the donee remains the same basis that the donor had in the property increased (but not above fair market value) by the portion of the gift tax paid attributable to the net appreciation in the value of the gift. To determine the net appreciation, the fair market value of the property at the time of the gift is reduced by the donor's adjusted basis.

The rule is different when the donor gives away property whose fair market value is less than the adjusted basis. For purposes of loss, the donee's basis is the lesser of: the donor's basis, or the fair market value at the time of the gift. For purposes of gain, the donee's basis is the greater of: the donor's basis, or the fair market value at the time of the gift. If the property is sold between the donor's basis and the fair market value on the date of the gift, there is no gain or loss.

EXAMPLE

Suppose James gives away property worth $30,000, which had cost him $50,000, to Sally. If Sally then sells the property for any price between $50,000 and $30,000, she does not realize either a gain or a loss on the sale.

Bargain Sales to Individuals

A gift between individuals is not always entirely gratuitous. A bargain sale, rather than an arm's-length transaction, occurs when the purchaser (donee) pays less than fair market value for the property to the seller (donor). The transaction can be viewed as consisting of two components—part sale and part gift. In this circumstance, the seller cannot realize a loss on the sale if the proceeds received are less than the basis. However, a gain is realized if the proceeds received exceed the basis. The seller (donor) is deemed to make a gift of the excess of the fair market value over the amount received for the property.

EXAMPLE

Sam sells property with a current fair market value of $100,000 to his son for $60,000. Sam had a basis in the property of $75,000. Sam has made a gift to his son of $40,000 ($100,000 − $60,000). Sam realizes no loss on the sale despite receiving proceeds less than his basis.

The basis rules for the purchaser (donee) in the bargain sale situation require careful study. The purchaser (donee) acquires a basis equal to the greater of: (1) the amount paid for the property increased by the gift tax paid by the seller (donor) attributed to the appreciated portion of the property while held by the seller, and (2) the seller's (donor's) basis at the time of the transfer increased by the gift tax paid by the seller (donor) attributed to the appreciated portion of the property while held by the seller. However, the basis of the purchaser cannot exceed the fair market value of the property at the time of the original transfer for the purpose of determining loss on the part of the purchaser.

EXAMPLE 1

Sam transfers property with a fair market value of $100,000 to his son for $60,000. Sam had a basis of $75,000 in the property and paid gift tax on the transaction. The son gets a basis in the property of $75,000 plus the amount of gift tax paid that is attributable to the appreciation in the property.

EXAMPLE 2

Same facts as above, except the son pays $80,000 for the property. The son now has a basis in the property of $80,000 plus the amount of the gift tax paid that is attributable to the appreciation in the property.

EXAMPLE 3

Sam transfers property with a fair market value of $75,000 to his son for $60,000. Sam had a basis of $100,000 in the property at the time of the transfer but paid no gift tax on the transfer. If the son later sells the property at a gain, the basis of the property in the hands of the son is $100,000 for the purpose of determining gain. However, if the son subsequently sells the property at a loss, the son's basis is limited to $75,000 (fair market value at the time of the original transfer) for the purpose of determining the amount of the loss.

Bargain Sales to Charity

The transfer of property to a charity for less than fair market value has some advantages for planning purposes. However, the transaction creates some unique tax effects. For the purpose of determining the gain realized by the transferor, the transaction is fictionally divided into two components—part sale and part gift. The basis of the property sold must be allocated to the portion of the property deemed sold and to the portion deemed a gift to charity. The ratio of the basis of the property allocated to the sale portion of the transaction to the total basis is the same as the ratio of the amount realized on the sale to the fair market value of the property. The formula for determining the basis for the sale is as follows:

$$(\text{Amount realized} \div \text{Fair market value}) \times \text{basis for property} = \text{basis for sale}$$

The portion of the basis deemed gifted to the charity is determined by subtracting the basis allocated to the sale from the total basis held by the transferor.

EXAMPLE

Bert makes a part sale/part gift of some of his valuable collection of watercolors by recognized artists to The American College for its lobby. Ignoring the annual gift tax exclusion, the collection sold and donated is valued at $1 million. Bert's basis in the watercolors is $200,000. The American College paid Bert $400,000. Bert's basis for the sale is $80,000:

$$(\$400,000 \div \$1,000,000) \times \$200,000 = \$80,000$$

CHAPTER REVIEW

Key Terms and Concepts

capital asset
holding period

stepped-up basis
carryover basis rule

Chapter Eighteen Review Questions

1. What is the function of *basis* with respect to an asset? [LO 18.1]

2. On the day he died, Mr. Jones owned 1,000 shares of IBM stock valued at $80 per share. When he had bought the stock 2 years earlier, he paid $65 per share. He also owned real estate at the time of his death in Atlantic City, New Jersey, valued at $200,000. He had purchased the property 4 years earlier for $60,000. His sole heir is his son, Richard. Assuming no alternate valuation date has been elected, what will be Richard's basis in each of these assets if he decides to sell them? [LO 18.2]

3. Nine months before his death, Mr. Jones purchased gold coins for which he paid $120,000. At the time of his death, the price of gold had dropped, and the coins were worth $75,000. His executor sold the coins at auction for $90,000. [LO 18.2]

    a. What was the basis to the estate?

    b. How much, if any, capital gain was realized?

4. Define income in respect of a decedent, and explain the tax treatment for a beneficiary in receipt of such income. [LO 18.2]

5. a. After it had appreciated to $50 a share, Tom Taylor gave his Uncle Ed 1,000 shares of XYZ Corporation stock that he had purchased for $10 a share. He knew that Uncle Ed was dying of cancer. Uncle Ed died 6 months after the transfer and left the XYZ Corporation shares to Tom. What will be Tom's basis in the shares?

    b. Assume instead that when Uncle Ed died, he left the shares to Tom's son instead of Tom. What basis will Tom's son have in the shares of XYZ Corporation? [LO 18.2]

6. Suppose Joe gifts property to Sam that cost $80,000, but is now worth only $40,000. If Sam then sells the property for $60,000, how much capital gain does he realize on the transaction? [LO 18.3]

7. Adam made a part sale/part gift to The American Cancer Society. The fair market value of the property is $1.6 million and the basis to Adam is $600,000. The American Cancer Society paid Adam $700,000. Ignoring the annual exclusion for gift tax purposes, what is the basis for the sale? [LO 18.3]

Chapter Eighteen Review Answers

1. The main function of basis is to measure gain or loss when property is sold, exchanged, or transferred in a taxable transaction.

2. The basis of property transferred at death in this case would be stepped up to the date-of-death basis as follows:

IBM shares	$80,000 ($80 x 1,000)
Real estate	$200,000

3. a. Property transferred at death acquires a new basis increased or decreased to the fair market value of the asset on the date of death. Here the property's basis in the estate would be stepped down to $75,000, since the value declined from the time the asset was acquired from the decedent.

   b.

Auction price	$90,000
Less basis	(75,000)
Long-term capital gain	$15,000

4. *Income in respect of a decedent* (IRD) is any income that the decedent was entitled to (but did not receive) while alive. The income is includible at full value for estate tax purposes. It is then also taxed to the beneficiary of the income as ordinary income for income tax purposes. However, the beneficiary is allowed an income tax deduction for the additional estate tax paid due to the IRD being included in the gross estate. The stepped-up-basis rules do not apply to income that is included in the decedent's gross estate as IRD.

5. a. Tom's basis in the shares is $10 a share because of the one-year rule.

   The stepped-up-basis-at-death rule is ignored under certain circumstances.

   The rule does not apply when appreciated property is acquired by the decedent by gift within one year before death if, upon death, the property then passes directly or indirectly back to the original donor or the original donor's spouse.

b. Tom's son's basis in the shares is $50 a share because the transfer was not to the original donor of the shares and, therefore, is outside of the one-year rule.

6. Sam does not realize either a gain or a loss on the sale. The property could have been sold for any price between $40,000 and $80,000 without Sam realizing a gain or a loss.

7. The basis for the sale is $262,500, computed as follows:

$$\$700,000 \text{ (amount realized)} \div \$1,600,000 \text{ (fair market value)} =$$
$$.4375 \times \$600,000 \text{ (basis)} = \$262,500$$

Chapter 19:

Income Taxation of Estates and Trusts

Learning Objectives

An understanding of the material in this chapter should enable the student to do the following:

LO 19.1   Describe in general the income of estates and trusts.

LO 19.2   Explain how the income of estates is taxed.

LO 19.3   Explain how the income of trusts is taxed.

Trusts and estates are separate taxpaying entities. As such, both trusts and estates may provide opportunities for tax savings through income allocation among taxpayers so that the most favorable tax treatment is achieved. While income tax saving is not the primary purpose of either trusts or estates, the financial services professional should not overlook potential tax savings. Knowledge of this area enables him or her to make recommendations regarding the creation of trusts, which may be structured so that the trustee is given discretionary powers to either accumulate or distribute income earned by the trust.

A critical question is: To which taxpaying entity should the income be taxed and in what proportion? Should it be taxed to the taxpayers to whom income may be allocated, or to the trust or estate, the beneficiaries, or the grantor? Sometimes, because of poor planning, the grantor is inadvertently the taxpayer. In addition, the rules pertaining to the unearned income of children under 19 (or 24 if a full-time student) years of age (kiddie tax) may have an impact on planning.

In order to both maximize tax savings and to avoid taxing the wrong taxpayer, an estate planner must understand the rules pertaining to income taxation of estates and trusts.

ESTATES

Status of Estates

A decedent's estate exists for a limited time—the estate appears when the decedent dies, and then it ceases to exist when all its functions are ended. It exists for a finite time because its purposes are limited. One primary purpose is to effectuate the orderly, legal transfer of property. Until this task is accomplished, the personal representative must manage and safeguard the property within his or her control. The personal representative has a duty to keep the property both invested and income producing. Income earned from estate assets is taxable to the estate. As a separate taxpayer, the estate must file timely income tax returns. One of the first tasks of the personal representative is to obtain a special tax identification number for the estate.

The estate maintains its separate tax status until it is closed, which may take several months or years. An estate's duration varies with the complexity of estate assets. The estate may contain a business interest or assets in a foreign country as well as other complicated ownership interests or rights that require it to be held open for an extended period. Technically, estates should not be closed before the federal estate tax return (if one is required), is filed and cleared. The typical length of time that an estate remains open is one to 3 years. The state has an interest in the settlement and distribution of a decedent's estate to its beneficiaries. Furthermore, the personal representative may become liable to beneficiaries and creditors of the estate for negligence or fraud in the management of estate assets and, therefore, the personal representative also has an interest in settling the estate. An estate should not be kept open without reason. Any tax benefits derived from the use of an additional taxpayer are not sufficient reasons by themselves to keep the estate open, and an estate that unreasonably prolongs administration will lose its status as an estate for tax purposes. However, there may be income tax benefits to be derived from properly using the estate as a separate taxpaying entity. Income tax considerations should not be overlooked by the personal representative.

LO 19.1   **Describe in general the income of estates and trusts.**

SIMILARITIES AND DIFFERENCES BETWEEN ESTATES AND TRUSTS

Similarities Between Estates and Trusts

Estates and trusts have many similarities. The personal representative has duties and responsibilities similar to those of the trustee of a trust.

- Both administer property in a fiduciary capacity.
- Property is transferred from the decedent to the estate in a manner similar to the transfer of property by a grantor to a trust.
- Both decedents and grantors are responsible for the creation of the estate or trust.
- Beneficiaries of an estate have a relationship to the estate that is similar to that of the beneficiaries of a trust.

Estate and Trust Similarities
- fiduciary duties and responsibilities
- property transfers
- beneficiary relationships
- income taxation rate
  - different computational system from
    - individuals
    - corporations
    - partnerships

Differences between Estates and Trusts

There are, however, important differences. An estate comes into existence involuntarily by operation of law upon the decedent's death. A living trust is created intentionally and voluntarily by a specific action of the grantor. Estates exist for a limited time period. Trusts generally exist for many years and possibly span more than one generation.

The primary function of many trusts is to provide sound, professional asset management. Use of a trust can give the grantor a sense of security, peace of mind, and possibly some control over the management of one's property. The trustee's primary duty is to be a good manager. Whether an individual or institution, the trustee will be in charge of the management of the trust property for the duration of the trust. This period may extend over a long time.

On the other hand, an estate serves as a temporary receptacle for assets pending distribution to the new owners. The personal representative functions primarily as a liquidator who must marshal the decedent's assets, advertise the estate for the benefit of creditors, and pay its debts, expenses, and taxes. The personal representative must settle any claims against the estate and has a duty to keep the property income producing until its distribution.

Another significant difference between the two entities is their relationship to the court. An estate is created by operation of law and is supervised by the court until it is terminated. A trust, on the other hand, is generally a private arrangement. Unless a court accounting is requested by the beneficiaries or a court interpretation of trust terms is requested by the trustees or beneficiaries, in most cases the trust neither has direct contact with the court nor is guided by the court in its actions or investments.

Estate and Trust Differences

Estates created involuntarily by operation of law	Trusts created by grantor's voluntary action
• limited duration	• extended duration possible
• primary purpose: predistribution asset receptacle	• primary purpose: asset management
• court supervision	• private arrangement

General Income Taxation of Estates and Trusts

Trusts and estates are subject to the same rate of income taxation. However, they are subject to a slightly different computational system of taxation than are individuals, corporations, or partnerships, because they exist for the benefit of others. Not operating as mere conduits, they are taxable on income withheld but receive deductions for income distributed. If Congress had chosen to tax estates and trusts in a manner similar to corporations, double taxation would have resulted. If taxed like a corporation, the trust or estate would be taxed on income earned during its taxable year. Beneficiaries would then be treated as shareholders who would be taxed on the distribution when received, just as dividends are taxable to shareholders in the year received. The result would be double taxation. This tax burden undoubtedly would have detracted from the desirability of maintaining trusts.

Alternatively, if a trust or estate was taxed as a partnership, all income would be passed through to the individual beneficiaries in a manner similar to the way it is passed to partners. Using this method would be detrimental in cases where the grantor did not intend beneficiaries to be entitled to the income automatically. First of all, there would be a potential conflict with the law of trusts. Trustees normally derive their powers from the trust instrument. Taxation as a partnership would defeat the right of the grantor to give the trustee discretion to accumulate or distribute income. Also a personal representative of an estate does not have a duty to distribute income before the estate makes final distribution to the beneficiaries. Under the theory of partnership taxation, a beneficiary would pay tax on amounts not yet received.

Having considered these various possibilities, Congress wisely adopted a hybrid method for income taxation of estates and trusts, which is known as the *sharing concept*. The general rule is that the trust or estate pays income tax on amounts of income retained, while the beneficiaries pay tax on trust or estate income distributed, or deemed distributed, to them. The result is that trust or estate income is generally taxed only once. To the extent it remains in the estate or trust, income is taxed to that entity. To the extent distributed, income is taxed to the beneficiaries (with certain limitations that are discussed later). With estates, the personal representative has discretion regarding retention or distribution of income. As for trusts, the trust instrument provides the standards and directions for taxation of trust income. Much depends on the type of trust and the trustee's exercise of any discretionary powers regarding distribution or accumulation of trust income.

LO 19.2   **Explain how the income of estates is taxed.**

INCOME TAXATION OF ESTATES

Decedent's Final Return

An executor or administrator has the duty to file two different types of income tax returns for a decedent—a decedent's last life return and an estate's income tax return.

A deceased taxpayer's tax year ends with the date of death. For example, if Greg dies on March 30, an income tax return must be filed for the short year of January 1 to March 30. The return must be filed by the regular due date, April 15, of the following year. The amounts of income and deductible expenses that must be reported depend on the deceased taxpayer's regular method of accounting.

For cash-basis taxpayers, only income actually or constructively received must be reported. Deductions can be taken only for expenses that were actually paid during the decedent's lifetime. If the decedent was on the accrual method, the return will show all income and deductions accrued through the date of death.

Even a decedent who did not live the entire year is still entitled to use the full standard deduction and personal exemption. If the taxpayer has a surviving spouse, the spouse can still file a joint return with the decedent for the year of the decedent's death.

Tax Return Filings
- decedent's final federal income tax return
- decedent's final state income tax return
- decedent's final local income tax return
- federal estate tax return
- state death tax return
- federal estate income tax return
- state estate income tax return
- local estate income tax return

Income in Respect of a Decedent (IRD)

income in respect of a decedent (IRD)

Because this is the final income tax return for the individual, if he or she was a cash-basis tax-payer, income that was earned but had not been received by the date of death would not be included in the decedent's final return (**income in respect of a decedent (IRD)**), because the individual did not actually or constructively receive the item by the date of death. For example, an insurance agent's renewal commissions paid after death cannot be included in a last life return, assuming the deceased agent was a cash-basis taxpayer.

Income that the decedent would have included in gross income had he or she lived does not escape taxation. Instead, it is taxed to the recipient of that income. In other words, the estate or the beneficiary who receives the income is taxed on it in the same manner in which the income would have been taxed to the decedent. If it would have been ordinary income to the decedent during lifetime, it will be ordinary income to the estate or beneficiary.

As mentioned previously, income in respect of a decedent is also subject to estate taxes. The estate or beneficiary that includes in income an item of income in respect of a decedent is entitled to a deduction on the same income tax return. This deduction is for the amount of additional federal estate tax attributable to inclusion of that item in the decedent's gross estate.

Income in Respect of a Decedent (IRD)

- **earned by decedent but not received by death (would be included on decedent's final income tax return if received prior to death)**
- **taxable to beneficiary or entity (estate) receiving it**
- **subject to estate tax (with corresponding deduction to income recipient)**
  possible for IRD to be included on both the estate's income tax and estate tax returns

Additional Considerations

As a taxable entity, an estate must pay tax on its income. If the income of the estate consists of dividends from stock and interest from bonds, these items constitute the gross income of the estate. Likewise, if there is rental income, royalty income, income from the sale or exchange of property, or income from a business carried on by the executor or administrator, then the income of the estate includes those items as well.

Because an estate is considered a separate tax entity, it has not only income but also deductions. Since an estate calculates income tax like other taxpayers, miscellaneous itemized deductions subject to the 2 percent of adjusted gross income floor are suspended from 2018 through 2025.

However, expenses that are incurred solely by reason of estate or trust administration are deductible in full. An estate may deduct reasonable amounts paid for administration costs, including executor fees and legal fees in connection with the administration of the estate. Some of these expenses may be taken on either the income tax return of the estate or as deductions from the gross estate to obtain the adjusted gross estate for federal estate tax purposes.

An estate is also entitled to a deduction for amounts of income distributed. It is not entitled to the standard deduction. An estate may take a $600 personal exemption. As previously mentioned, to the extent that the estate retains income, it is taxed; to the extent that the beneficiaries receive income, they are taxed. Furthermore, estates that are open for tax years ending 2 or more years after the decedent's death are subject to the estimated tax rules.

The only beneficiaries who do not pay income tax on distributions of income from estates are those who receive specific bequests under the will in three installments or less.

EXAMPLE

Assume that the will of the decedent, Leslie Little, states: "I give $5,000 to my favorite nephew, Al, and all the rest, residue, and remainder to my cousin, Jeffrey Little." During the first year of the estate, assets held by the executor generate $16,000 of income. The executor distributes $5,000 to Al and $11,000 to Jeffrey. Because Al's $5,000 was a specific bequest, he is not taxed. This amount is considered a distribution of estate corpus for tax purposes. In this case, Jeffrey would be taxed on the $11,000 he received, and the estate would be taxed on the remaining $5,000 of income.

On the other hand, if Leslie's will stated that the $5,000 bequest to Al was to be paid in five equal annual installments and in the first year he received $1,000, he would be taxed on the $1,000 only if the payment is made out of income. Beneficiaries are taxed on any specific bequests that are required to be paid out of income.

income-first rule

Aside from the foregoing rule regarding specific bequests, there is an **income-first rule** requiring that all distributions are deemed to be paid out of income first, even if the executor, administrator, or trustee in fact distributes corpus in the form of cash or property. For example, assume in the previous example that the distribution to Jeffrey consisted solely of stock. Jeffrey would still be deemed to have received income.

Estate Income Taxation

- Estate income is taxed to either the beneficiaries or the estate.
- An income tax return must be filed.
- Estate administration expenses are deductible.
- Deductions are allowed for income distributed.
- The estate may take a $600 exemption (no standard deduction allowed).

Fiscal Year for Estate Income Taxation

Unlike trusts, the personal representative of a decedent's estate is able to select the estate's income tax year. This means the representative can select the last day of any month for the estate's income tax year to end. All income tax years, however, must be 12 months in length except for the first and last years. If the personal representative chooses the end of any month other than December 31, the estate is reporting income tax for a *fiscal year*. If December 31 is selected as the end of the estate's income tax year, the estate is reporting its income as a calendar-year taxpayer. The decedent's personal final tax year ends on the date of death, no matter how soon death occurs after January 1 of his or her calendar tax year. For example, if Marge dies on January 4 this year, the decedent's final tax year is January 1 through January 4.

Income tax savings can result for the estate if the fiscal year is carefully chosen. Savings are possible because for tax purposes income is treated as if it was distributed to beneficiaries on the last day of the estate's fiscal tax year even though the income may have been distributed much earlier in the tax year.

EXAMPLE

Derek's executor wants to make distributions of estate income to the beneficiary, Derek's son Darrell. The executor distributes the income to Darrell in early December of year 1 even though the estate taxed the income in April of year 1. Because the estate's fiscal year ends on January 31, the income is treated as received on January 31 of year 2. Therefore, Darrell will not have to report the income on his income tax return until April 15 of year 3. The income avoids income taxation for 2 years from the time the estate actually received it.

LO 19.3   Explain how the income of trusts is taxed.

INCOME TAXATION OF TRUSTS

nongrantor trust

A trust that is deemed irrevocable (a nongrantor trust) is considered a separate taxpayer. These trusts may be testamentary (made irrevocable on the death of the testator) or inter vivos (living) trusts. On the other hand, income from property in revocable trusts (grantor trusts) is taxed to the grantor rather than to the trust, because the power to revoke the instrument gives the grantor control over the trust assets. Trustees of irrevocable trusts may be given discretionary powers to distribute or accumulate income. To the extent a trustee exercises the right to distribute that income and sprinkle it among more than one taxpayer within the family group, the income may be shifted to a lower tax bracket and can be sheltered by multiple personal exemptions.

Trust Income—General Taxation

The essential concept of trust taxation is that trust income is taxed once, either (1) to the beneficiary(ies) or (2) to the trustee. If a trustee is required to distribute the entire income of the trust annually, that income is taxed to the recipient(s). However, some trusts authorize the accumulation of all or part of the income at the trustee's discretion. The tax law does not tax prospective beneficiaries on amounts they may never receive.

A system has been devised that taxes the trustee on income accumulated by the trust and the beneficiary on income receivable. To thwart tax avoidance, the beneficiary is taxed on the amount *distributable* to him or her rather than on the amount actually paid to him or her. This prevents the trustee from arbitrarily deferring payments in an attempt to keep trust income in lower brackets.

Trust Income Taxation
- irrevocable trusts—separate taxpaying entities
- revocable trusts—the grantor pays tax under grantor trust rules

Although the details of trust taxation are quite complex, they can be summarized: Income that is accumulated by the trust is taxable to the trust; income that is payable to the beneficiary is taxable to the beneficiary; and income either accumulated or distributed by a grantor trust is taxable to the grantor.

Irrevocable Trust Income Taxation
- trust income taxed to either the beneficiary or the trust
  beneficiary taxed on distributable net income (DNI) (whether or not distributed)
- trust taxed on accumulated/retained income
- two types of trusts for income tax law
  simple trusts
  complex trusts—may change from year to year

Simple Trusts

The income tax law classifies trusts into two types—simple and complex. A trust's designation as simple or complex may change from year to year; however, a trust will always be complex in its final year.

simple trust

A **simple trust** is one in which the trust agreement requires that all trust income be distributed currently to the beneficiaries. As long as the trust instrument provides for the trustee to distribute all of the trust's current year's income, the beneficiaries are treated as having received the income for taxation purposes, whether the income is distributed or not. If, on the other hand, the trust terms do not require that all trust income be distributed each year, the trust is treated as a complex trust despite the fact that the trust actually did distribute all trust income for the year. In any year, a simple trust may not make distributions from amounts other than current income. Principal may not be distributed, and no charitable gifts can be made by this type of trust; otherwise, it will be deemed to be a complex trust for that taxable year. Although the trust terms may grant the trustee a power to distribute corpus, as long as no distribution is actually made during the tax year, the trust is considered simple for that year. On the other hand, if the trust terms allow the trustee to make a charitable contribution that would qualify for a charitable deduction, the trust will not be treated as a simple trust whether or not a charitable distribution is made.

Simple Trusts
- treated as conduits to pass trust income directly to beneficiaries
- require current distribution of all net income
- deduction for distributable income
- no distributions of corpus
- $300 exemption (no standard deduction)
- no charitable contributions/distributions
- beneficiaries taxed on distributable net income

A simple trust is treated as a separate tax entity subject to a $300 personal exemption. As such, it has—subject to certain exceptions—the same deductions as an individual. It also has a special deduction for income that is distributable to its beneficiaries. The net result is that a simple trust does not pay tax on income it pays out. The beneficiary of a simple trust in turn reports the income received—or receivable. In other words, a simple trust acts like a funnel—a conduit for passing the trust income from the grantor to the beneficiaries.

Most trusts operate as simple trusts. For example, a trust that provides income "to my wife for life with remainder to my children" or "income to be distributed to and among my spouse and children in such amounts and such proportions as my trustee may determine" is a simple trust until and unless a distribution of corpus is made. All trusts are complex trusts in the final year because in the year of termination, trusts must distribute all trust corpus.

Complex Trusts

complex trust

The second type of trust is known as a complex trust. A **complex trust** is any trust that is not a simple trust; that is, a complex trust is one in which the trustee either must or may accumulate income. The trustee of a complex trust—unlike the trustee of a simple trust—can distribute corpus (principal). The trustee can also make gifts to charities. A complex trust—like a simple trust—is a separate taxpaying entity. It is allowed a special deduction for actual distributions of income but pays tax on any income it does not distribute. Generally, the same rules that govern complex trusts apply also to the income taxation of a decedent's estate.

It is impossible to understand the taxation of trusts unless the term *income* is defined. There is income in the trust sense and income in the tax sense.

Most states have a *Principal and Income Act* that allocates receipts and payments between estate or trust income and principal. For example, if the trustee is required to pay out "all the income," then, under the trust law definition of income, the trustee would not be required to pay out capital gains or other items classified as corpus (as opposed to income). Capital gains are excluded from the trust law definition of income and treated as additions to corpus rather than income. But, generally, the grantor or decedent may override these rules. For example, gains from property can be designated by the grantor as trust income.

Complex Trusts
* accumulation of income allowed
* distributions of corpus allowed
* charitable contributions allowed
* taxed on income retained
* deduction for actual distributions
* $100 exemption (no standard deduction)
* beneficiaries taxed on distributable net income
* all trusts are complex trusts in their last year because corpus is distributed

(The income taxation of complex trusts is similar to the income taxation of estates.)

Note that a capital gain is every bit as much income in the tax sense as dividend income, rental income, or interest on a loan. Therefore, it is possible that, even though a trustee of a simple trust is required to distribute all the income (and, thus, that amount is taxable to the beneficiaries rather than the trust), the difference between the total income in the tax sense and the total income in the trust sense is taxable to the trust.

EXAMPLE

Suppose a trust received $3,000 in capital gains from the sale of trust assets and $5,000 from dividends on stock it held. A trust that was required to pay out "all the income" to the beneficiaries would make a distribution of only $5,000 (the amount of dividends). The beneficiaries, rather than the trust, would be taxed on that $5,000. However, the remaining income in the tax sense, $3,000, would not be distributable by the trust because it is treated as an addition to corpus instead of income and, therefore, would be taxed to the trust. For this reason, a simple trust may be taxed even though it is required to distribute all of its income in the trust-law sense.

A complex trust that is required to distribute all of its income currently has an exemption of $300. For a complex trust (sometimes called an *accumulation trust*) that is not required to distribute income, the regular exemption is $100. No type of trust (or estate, for that matter) may deduct the standard deduction allowed to individual taxpayers.

Distributable Net Income

distributable net income (DNI)

The mechanical approach to the sharing concept (the trust pays income tax on the amount it retains, while the beneficiaries pay tax on the income of the trust distributable to them) occurs through the utilization of a concept known as **distributable net income (DNI)**. In general, distributable net income means taxable income before the deduction for distributions and before the $300 personal exemption for simple trusts ($100 for complex trusts and $600 for estates) but after the exclusion of capital gains and losses. The concept of DNI is used to achieve three main results:

- First, it provides a limit on the deduction that a trust or estate may receive for amounts distributed to beneficiaries.

- Second, it limits the amount of distributions that may be taxable to the beneficiaries.

- Third, it establishes the character of the amounts taxable to the beneficiaries.

As a general rule, income retains the same character in the hands of the beneficiaries as it had in the hands of the trust. Therefore, tax-exempt income to the trust retains its tax-exempt status when distributed to the beneficiary.

The first purpose of DNI ensures that the trust or estate receives a deduction for amounts that it distributes and then provides a limit for that deduction. For example, assume that a trust earns $10,000 in taxable income and distributes $6,000 of that income to its sole beneficiary. The DNI is $10,000. Accordingly, the estate or trust deducts $6,000. The trust will be taxed on the amount that it retains, $4,000.

The second purpose of DNI is to limit the portion of distributions that are taxable to beneficiaries. If the trust in the above example distributed $12,000 to the beneficiary, the trust would be allowed to deduct $10,000, the DNI. The trust, therefore, would have no tax liability. The beneficiary would be taxed on $10,000 of the $12,000 received. The first $10,000 would be considered to have come from income, while the remaining $2,000 would be considered an income-tax-free distribution of trust corpus. The DNI rule does not allow a trustee to determine whether income or corpus has been distributed. Instead, arbitrarily and automatically, all amounts distributed are first deemed to be income—to the extent of DNI.

The following examples illustrate trust income taxation with respect to DNI.

EXAMPLE 1

A simple trust has long-term capital gain allocable to corpus of $12,000, taxable income of $3,000, and dividends from a taxable U.S. corporation of $4,000. The trust's distributable net income is the $3,000 of income plus the $4,000 of dividends.

EXAMPLE 2

For this year, the estate's DNI is $48,000. Under the terms of his will, Sam Snead left $24,000 a year to be paid to his surviving spouse and $18,000 to each of his two daughters out of the income his estate earned during its administration. Because the amount taxable to the beneficiaries is limited to the estate's DNI, if distributions are greater than DNI, a proportional amount of DNI must be allocated to each beneficiary based on the total distributed to all beneficiaries. Mrs. Snead's proportional share is determined by dividing her portion by the total amount distributed to all beneficiaries: $24,000 ÷ $60,000 (the total amount of distributions is $24,000 + $18,000 + $18,000) = 2/5. Two-fifths of the estate's total DNI of $48,000 is $19,200. This is the amount that the surviving spouse must include in gross income. The balance of the estate's distribution to Mrs. Snead is treated as a distribution of corpus and is not included in income.

According to this arbitrary DNI rule, a beneficiary can be taxed even if the distribution received is actually from corpus. For example, assume a trust has interest income of $10,000 that the trustee decides to accumulate. If the trustee then decides in the same tax year to distribute $10,000 of corpus to one of its beneficiaries, the beneficiary will be deemed to have received $10,000 of income, even though the trustee is actually making a distribution from corpus.

The third function of DNI is to ensure that the character of the amounts in the hands of a beneficiary is the same as that in the hands of a trust or estate. Therefore, if dividends are received by a trust and distributed to a beneficiary, the dividends retain their character as dividends.

Likewise, if the trust receives tax-free income (such as from a municipal bond), the income remains tax free in the hands of the beneficiary. This result is achieved mechanically by limiting the trust's deduction to DNI determined without regard to tax-free income.

DNI
- limits trust/estate deductions for distributions
- limits taxable distributions to beneficiaries
- establishes the tax character of distributions
- is income in a trust sense
- is income in a tax sense

EXAMPLE

Assume a trust has $4,000 of tax-exempt interest and $6,000 of dividend income. Its distributable net income is $10,000, but the DNI for deduction purposes is $6,000. The $10,000 distributed would be the same in the hands of the beneficiary as it would be in the hands of the trustee—$4,000 of the interest would be tax-exempt and $6,000 of the dividend income would be taxable because the DNI received by the beneficiary will be $6,000.

Effect of Multiple Beneficiaries

When there is more than one beneficiary, each is taxed on his or her share of DNI. When special items are distributed (such as tax-exempt interest, dividends, and so forth), a beneficiary is considered to have received a proportionate share unless the trust agreement earmarks a particular type of income for a specified beneficiary. This makes it possible to pay out tax-exempt income to high-income-tax-bracket beneficiaries and to pay other income to lower-bracket beneficiaries and also to lower-bracket family members. (The distribution provisions cannot be arbitrary and must have some significance apart from their tax sense.) For example, it would be permissible to require that 40 percent of the trust corpus be invested in tax-exempt securities and that the grantor's spouse receive all such income.

Taxation of Grantor Trusts

A trust is typically created by a grantor with substantial assets, who sets aside the trust property for the benefit of less wealthy family members. Quite often, one purpose for this transfer is to shift income, and the taxation thereof, from a higher-bracket grantor to lower-bracket beneficiaries, resulting in the availability of a greater amount of funds to the beneficiaries than if the grantor had received the income and paid the after-tax proceeds to the beneficiaries directly.

grantor-trust

Trusts would be very popular indeed if the grantor could shift the taxation of trust income to lower-bracket beneficiaries while maintaining substantial control over the trust property and income. Congress recognized this possibility for abuse and devised the **grantor-trust** rules, which provide that the income from a trust is taxed to the grantor if the grantor retains certain proscribed powers and controls over the trust.

The grantor-trust rules also apply if the spouse of the grantor, living with the grantor at the time of creation of the interest, is given any of the proscribed powers that invoke the grantor-trust rules. In the case of a grantor trust, the trust is disregarded for income tax purposes; all income, deductions, and credits attributable to any portion of a trust declared a grantor trust are taken into account directly on the grantor's individual income tax return. The financial services professional should be aware of these rules to alert a client-grantor whose trust could be inadvertently designed as a grantor trust.

Trust Income Available for the Benefit of the Grantor

Grantor-trust taxation is applied to all or part of the trust income that is provided for the grantor or the grantor's spouse without the consent of an adverse party. Furthermore, the income will be taxed to the grantor for any portion of the trust if the income may be provided for the grantor or the grantor's spouse at the discretion of the grantor or a nonadverse party. In the same manner, a trust is considered a grantor trust if it accumulates taxable or tax-exempt income for future distribution to the grantor or the grantor's spouse. The grantor will also be taxed on any portion of a trust in which the income may be applied to pay premiums for life insurance on the life of the grantor or the grantor's spouse.

The income from a trust that is applied to satisfy the legal support obligations of the grantor is paid to the benefit of the grantor and also causes grantor-trust tax treatment. However, the grantor is not taxed on this income if it is merely payable for a support obligation of the grantor at the discretion of the trustee unless the income is actually so applied.

Revocable Trusts

The revocable trust is an example of a trust in which the grantor has strings attached to the trust property and income. In this case, the grantor has not completed a transfer for tax purposes if the power is retained, at any time, to return the trust property to the grantor's possession. For this reason, the revocable trust is taxable as a grantor trust, and its creation does not alter the federal income tax picture of the grantor or the beneficiaries.

The grantor will also be treated as the owner of the trust if the power to revoke the trust is similarly held by either the grantor's spouse or a nonadverse party. For the purposes of the grantor-trust rules, a nonadverse party is any individual who does not possess a substantial beneficial interest in the trust that would be adversely affected by the exercise or nonexercise of any power held by the individual with respect to the trust. For example, a trust beneficiary who loses the benefit of the trust if the grantor revokes would be an adverse party.

Reversionary Interest

Grantor-trust tax treatment will occur for any portion of the trust in which the grantor retains a reversionary interest in either the trust corpus or the trust income if, at the creation of the portion of the trust in which the grantor holds the reversionary interest, the value of this reversionary interest exceeds 5 percent of the value of this portion of the trust. The IRS valuation rules are to be used to determine the value of any reversionary interest. Generally, the trust income interest would have to be gifted for a significant period of time (over 30 to 40 years, depending on the current AFMR) before the grantor-trust rules can be avoided. Thus, a temporary gift of an income interest followed by a reversionary interest in the grantor will rarely cause a shifting of income for tax purposes.

As an exception to the reversionary-interest rule, the grantor will not be treated as the owner of the income portion of a trust if the reversionary interest will take effect at the death of the beneficiary who: (1) is a lineal descendant of the grantor, and (2) has not attained age 21. These reversionary-interest provisions apply to transfers and trusts made after March 1, 1986.

Controls Retained by the Grantor

The grantor-trust rules contain a series of proscribed controls and powers that the grantor might desire to retain over a trust. These are included in the grantor-trust category to prevent the grantor from shifting taxation of the trust income while retaining enough control over the trust to possess substantial beneficial enjoyment of the trust income and property.

Power to Control Beneficial Enjoyment

Grantor-trust tax treatment occurs if the grantor retains (1) the beneficial enjoyment of the trust corpus and/or (2) the power to dispose of trust income without the approval or consent of an adverse party. The general rule provides that the grantor is taxed on the income when the grantor or nonadverse party holds the right to add or delete beneficiaries, to alter the shares of the beneficiaries in the income or principal, or to determine the timing of distributions. Fortunately, this general rule is subject to several exceptions which allow the grantor some flexibility in the design of the trust. Powers that may be held by the trustee, regardless of who the trustee is, that do not cause grantor-trust taxation include the following:

- the power to apply income toward the support of the grantor's dependents except to the extent that the income is actually applied to satisfy the grantor's legal support obligation

- the power to appoint the income or principal of the trust by will, other than income accumulated in the trust at the discretion of the grantor or nonadverse party

- the power to allocate income among charitable beneficiaries

- the power of the trustee to sprinkle or accumulate income, including

    - the power to invade corpus for the benefit of a beneficiary or beneficiaries provided that the trustee's power is limited by some definite standard (for example, the power to distribute corpus for the education, support, maintenance, or health of a beneficiary)

    - the power to withhold income temporarily from a current-income beneficiary

    - the power to withhold income during the legal incompetency or minority of a current-income beneficiary (this provision allows accumulation for the minor-beneficiary of a Sec. 2503(c) trust)

- the power, exercisable only by an independent trustee (an individual not subordinate to the grantor), to sprinkle income and principal among a class of beneficiaries
- the power to apportion income by a trustee (not the grantor or the grantor's spouse) among a class of beneficiaries guided by some reasonably definite standard in the trust instrument

Administrative Powers

Certain powers of administration over a trust held by the grantor or a nonadverse party create grantor-trust taxation. Basically, the powers included in the grantor-trust rules are ones that allow the trust to be operated substantially for the benefit of the grantor. These powers include disposing of trust property or income for less than adequate consideration or obtaining a loan from the trust without adequate interest or security.

Grantor Trust Taxation (without Consent of Adverse Party)
- power to revoke trust
- income for grantor's/spouse's benefit
- income used for life insurance premiums on grantor's/spouse's life
- reversionary interest
- power to control beneficial enjoyment
- retention of controls over trust

Intentionally Defective Grantor Trust

An intentionally defective grantor trust (IDGT), sometimes referred to as an intentionally defective irrevocable trust (IDIT), is a trust that is designed (among other reasons) to purposefully attribute the income to the grantor for income tax purposes under one of the grantor trust Code Secs. 671–677, but exclude the trust corpus from the grantor's estate for estate tax purposes under Code Secs. 2036–2038. In other words, transfers to an IDGT are intended to be completed gifts for federal gift and estate tax law but incomplete gifts for income tax law. This type of trust is a beneficial tax savings technique because it allows the grantor to transfer property out of his or her estate. Simultaneously, the grantor can further reduce his or her estate by paying income tax on trust income that the trust or the trust beneficiaries would otherwise pay. Note that trust provisions *requiring* the grantor to bear the trust's income tax liability may result in the IRS treating the grantor's income tax payments as additional gifts to the trust beneficiaries.

EXAMPLE

To avoid paying any gift tax on the transfer, Linda transfers the cash equivalent of the gift tax basic exclusion amount and the annual exclusion amount to an IDGT for the benefit of her adult son. (Assume Linda has retained a prohibited power under one of the Secs. 671–677 grantor trust rules, but one that does not violate any of the prohibited transfer tax rules.) If the trust earns $45,000 its first year and Linda is in a 33 percent income tax bracket, Linda will transfer an additional $14,850 ($45,000 × .33) out of her estate. By paying the trust income tax each year, Linda will be able to further reduce her estate.

Kiddie-tax Rules

Taxation of Unearned Income of Children under the "Kiddie-tax" Rules

A popular income tax planning technique—shifting income from a high-bracket individual to the person's lower-bracket children—was curtailed severely by several acts: the Tax Reform Act of 1986 (TRA '86), the Tax Increase Prevention and Reconciliation Act of 2006 (TIPRA 2006), the Small Business and Work Opportunity Tax Act of 2007 (the Small Business Act 2007); and the Tax Cuts and Jobs Act of 2017. The current rules provide that a portion of the unearned income of a child under 19 years of age (age 19 to 24 if a full-time student) is taxed at the top rate of the the compressed income-tax rates for trust. The requirement does not apply if the earned income of a child under age 19 (or age 19 to 24 if a full-time student) exceeds one-half of his or her support for the tax year.

The provisions apply to all net unearned income of a child under age 19 and under age 24 for a full-time student, including income from a trust. The rules apply regardless of when and from whom the child receives the income-producing property. Therefore, as seen below, there are limited income tax savings if a parent transfers property to a trust that pays out income to a child-beneficiary under age 19 (under age 24 for a full-time student). Moreover, trusts in existence before these rules were established are also subject to the current rules.

Calculating the Kiddie Tax

kiddie tax

The procedure for calculating the **kiddie tax** is complex and is not described fully here. However, the law provides that the child pays tax on net unearned income according to the trust income tax rates. Prior to the TCJA (Tax Cuts and Jobs Act) of 2017, individual income tax rates were used to assess this tax.. The net unearned income of the child is the child's unearned income less the sum of the $1,100 standard deduction for dependents (2019) as indexed for inflation, and an additional amount, which is the greater of (1) $1,100 (2019), as indexed for inflation) and (2) allowable deductions directly related to the production of the child's unearned income. The intent of this procedure is to apply no tax to the first $1,100 (2019) of unearned income due to the standard deduction. The next $1,050 of unearned income is taxed at the child's bracket, and income in excess of $2,200 (2019) is taxed at trust tax rates.

Under *The Small Business Act of 2007*, extending the kiddie tax rules to age 19 and up to age 24 for full-time students affects tax planning for minors and young adult children in general. It also affects existing tax plans created under prior law when the expectation was that investment income would be taxed at the child's low rates upon their attaining the lower age of 14. Now the investment income exceeding $2,200 (2019) of a minor under age 19 and a full-time student under age 24 is taxed at trust tax and estate rates. In other words, a child's interest income may be taxed at the maximum income tax rate instead of at the child's potentially lower 10 percent or 15 percent rates. In addition, a child's qualified dividends and adjusted net capital gain may possibly be taxed at a higher percentage than at 15 percent or 0 percent.

EXAMPLE 1

Sara Jones, aged 18, receives $1,100 of unearned trust income and no earned income in 2019. Sara's $1,100 (2019) standard deduction is allocated against this, leaving a net unearned income of $50, which will be taxed at Sara's tax rate.

EXAMPLE 2

Suppose instead that Sara had $3,000 of unearned trust income and no earned income. After applying Sara's $1,100 (2019) standard deduction, a net unearned income of $1,900 remains. The next $1,100 is to be taxed at Sara's rate, while the remaining $800 will be taxed at the federal income tax rate for trusts for the year.

Minimizing the Kiddie-tax Impact

It is obvious that the kiddie tax provides little or no income tax benefit to shifting income to children under 19 years of age (or 24, if a full-time student). However, there are still some estate planning benefits to transferring income to children along with many personal nontax benefits for the creation of trusts for minor children. To minimize the impact of the kiddie tax when planning a transfer in trust for minor children, the client might consider the following:

- The trust can be designed to accumulate income until the child reaches age 19 or later. Under the grantor-trust rules that while the child is a minor, a Sec. 2503(c) trust can be used to allow the trust to accumulate income that is taxable to the trust. Income paid out to the child from the Sec. 2503(c) trust after the child attains age 19, or 24 if relevant, is taxed at the child's—not the trust's—marginal tax rate. In general, the trust document may provide discretion for the trustee to temporarily withhold income from a trust beneficiary without the application of the grantor-trust rules.

- The trust property can be invested in assets in which income will be deferred—presumably until the child-beneficiary reaches the relevant kiddie tax age. Examples of investments that are suitable for this purpose include the following:

  - Series EE U.S. government bonds defer income until the bond is redeemed. For this purpose, the child must not already own Series EE bonds on which each year's income is being declared.

  - Growth stocks could be purchased with trust assets that pay little or no current dividends. The stock can be held until the child reaches the appropriate kiddie tax age, at which time any gain would be taxed at the child's bracket.

  - Deep-discount tax-free municipal bonds can be purchased that mature after the child reaches the appropriate age. The current interest will be tax free and any later gain will be taxed at the child's tax rate when the bond is redeemed.

  - Life insurance or annuity policies can be purchased on the life of the child-beneficiary without incurring either a grantor-trust or kiddie-tax problem. Any gain on a policy held until after the child reaches age 19, or 24 when relevant, will be taxed at the child's rate. These policies are highly liquid since they may be surrendered at any time for the cash surrender value and, unlike stocks or bonds, are not subject to market risk. However, it is important to remember that tax on the policy earnings is deferred only if the policy meets the statutory guidelines for the definition of life insurance.

- Investments in mutual funds, growth stocks, or preferred stocks will generate gain or qualified dividends taxed at a trust's capital gain rate rather than trust's higher ordinary income tax rate and, when the child is no longer subject to the kiddie tax, will be taxed at the child's lower capital gain rate.

- A family business may be able to employ a child. A child's earned income from employment is not subject to the kiddie tax. The child's compensation provides a deduction for the business. A child's earned income not sheltered by his or her standard deduction will be taxed at the child's income tax rate.

- Instead of parents (and grandparents) putting funds in a child's name as a way of saving for college, parents should consider other tax-favored means of college saving, such as establishing a tax-free Code Sec. 529 qualified tuition program and/or a tax-free Code Sec. 530 Coverdell Education Savings account (ESA).

Kiddie Tax Considerations

- Design the trust to accumulate income until the child attains age 19 (or 24 if a full-time student).
  - Sec. 2503(c) trust
- Invest in income-deferred assets:
  - Series EE U.S. government bonds
  - growth stocks
  - deep-discount tax-free municipal bonds
  - life insurance or annuity policies on child-beneficiary's life
- Invest in capital gain/qualified dividend-producing assets.
- Employ the child in the family business.
- Establish Sec. 529 and/or 530 college savings plans.

Multiple Trusts

Prior to the enactment of the *Revenue Reconciliation Act of 1993 (RRA 1993)*, a popular technique for saving income taxes was to use separate or multiple trusts. Rather than create a single trust in which each beneficiary was given a fractional interest, a grantor could create one trust for each beneficiary. In other words, instead of the grantor providing that the residue of the decedent-grantor's estate was to be held in trust and that each of the decedent's four children was to receive one-fourth of the income each year and a one-fourth share of the principal on termination of the trust, the grantor could provide for separate trusts for each beneficiary. Therefore, if the same assets were divided into four equal shares and held in separate and distinct trusts (one trust for each child), each trust would have its own exemption, and each would have been subject to the lower trust income tax rates that prevailed before the 1993 Act. Because RRA '93 imposes higher income-tax rate brackets on trusts and estates at lower income thresholds, the use of separate or multiple trusts for the purpose of saving income taxes often results in only nominal savings.

It is possible to create several trusts for the same or different beneficiaries. If the tax law recognizes the existence of multiple trusts, then the income is taxed separately to each trust, which means that each trust receives a separate exemption, and each trust is treated as a separate tax entity for all income tax purposes. Conversely, if multiple trusts are considered by the IRS to be one trust, only one exemption is allowed. All of the trusts are treated as one entity for income tax purposes.

The grantor's intention is examined by studying the various trust instruments to determine whether or not more than one trust was established. The IRS will not question the separate tax status of multiple trusts if the following criteria are met:

- The trusts have substantially different grantors and/or substantially different beneficiaries.

- The trusts have substantially independent purposes or objectives, such as different dispositive goals for each beneficiary.

- The principal purpose for creating multiple trusts was not avoidance, deferral, or mitigation of the progressive income tax rates.

The trusts should also be separately maintained (that is, separate books and records should be kept for each trust, each trust should have its own bank account, and separate returns should be filed).

Accumulation of Income in Trusts

One frequently used technique of estate planning is to give a trustee the discretionary power either to pay income to beneficiaries or to accumulate it. If a beneficiary has sufficient other income, a trustee may decide to retain income from the trust and pay it out in some year when the beneficiary is in a lower tax bracket or more in need of the money. If the beneficiary has more than sufficient income, it is improper tax planning for the terms of the trust to require a distribution of income since the income, if distributable, is taxable to the beneficiary whether or not it is actually received.

RRA '93, however, has diminished the advantages of income accumulation trusts. Because trusts and estates are taxed at higher rates on taxable income at the lower thresholds of income than individuals are taxed, it is likely that many beneficiaries will be in a lower tax bracket than the trusts benefiting them. Thus, there is pressure on trustees with the discretion to accumulate or distribute income to make income distributions before trust income reaches the higher tax brackets. In many instances, current distributions of income to beneficiaries (such as minors) defeat the very purpose for which the trust was originally established. A discretionary trustee is caught in a bind because if, in keeping with the trust purpose, the trustee does not distribute income currently and trust income is then taxed at tax rates higher than the beneficiary's rate, the trustee will overpay taxes.

Investing trust principal in securities having growth potential rather than current income may be one solution to the dilemma. Another is to make periodic income distributions to children over age 19 (24 if still in school) so that income is taxed at the children's lower individual rates.

The practical consequence of the new income tax rates is that planners and fiduciaries may have to weigh numerous factors concerning income distributions to beneficiaries who are subject to lower tax rates, especially where there are conflicting nontax considerations.

Purchase of Life Insurance by a Trustee

A trust instrument may authorize a trustee of a testamentary trust to purchase life insurance on the lives of the beneficiaries. State law must be examined to see if there is a prohibition against the use of income for this purpose. From a tax viewpoint, income used to purchase life insurance on the lives of beneficiaries is considered accumulated income; therefore, income used to purchase life insurance by the trustee of the testamentary trust is taxed to the trust. However, trust income used for premium payments for insurance on the life of the grantor of the trust (and/or on the life of the grantor's spouse) is taxed to the grantor.

Authorizing a trustee to purchase life insurance on the lives of the beneficiaries can yield some limited benefits under current income tax law. For example, suppose one of the trust beneficiaries has a significant amount of taxable income this year and is already in a high-marginal tax bracket. Suppose also that the trust has taxable income that will be taxed in one of the lower-marginal-tax brackets. If the trustee distributes the trust income to the beneficiary, it will be taxed at the beneficiary's higher rate, leaving less income for the beneficiary to purchase life insurance and pay premiums. If, however, the trust itself purchases the life insurance and pays the premiums with the income, more income is available for the purchase and premium payments because of the trust's exemption and lower income-tax bracket.

Sprinkle Provisions

One of the principles of proper tax planning is that income should be divided among family members whenever possible in order to lower the rate at which the income will be taxed as well as to take advantage of the multiple individual personal exemptions.

EXAMPLE

Assume a grantor's son, Jerry, is in the 37 percent income tax bracket. If the grantor left income-producing property in trust with the provision that the income was payable to Jerry, $10,000 of additional income would net Jerry approximately $6,300. But if for tax purposes the same $10,000 was spread among Jerry and his three children, the total intrafamily *net dollars* might be more than if all the income was paid to Jerry.

However, referring to the preceding example, because the kiddie tax is applicable to the unearned income of children under the relevant kiddie-tax age, the trust income distributed to children under the appropriate kiddie-tax age may be subject to the same maximum tax rate. This results in no tax savings if the income is shifted to Jerry's children under age 19 or 24. Any income shifted to Jerry's children over the appropriate kiddie tax age may result in tax savings if the children are in a lower income tax bracket.

Assuming Jerry's children are all past the relevant kiddie-tax age, one way to accomplish the objective of shifting income to lower brackets is to require the trustee to pay the income to Jerry and his children in four equal shares. Yet, the same tax savings may be accomplished with more flexibility if the trustee is authorized, rather than mandated, to pay income to Jerry or any one or more of his children at the trustee's discretion. The trustee can then allocate income among the family members in any manner that seems desirable from tax year to tax year. In exercising that discretion, the trustee would consider the individual needs of the various beneficiaries, the ultimate use to which the income would be put, and the collective as well as individual tax burdens.

sprinkle provision

There are also nontax advantages to clauses that *sprinkle* income according to needs. An example is a testator who wants to provide for the family of a deceased child but does not want to pay income for the lifetime of a deceased child's spouse. The testator may fear that if the surviving spouse remarries, income will go to the new spouse or the new spouse's children rather than to the testator's grandchildren. The **sprinkle provision** in a trust enables a trustee to pay income to the spouse only as long as the children are young or have varying needs and as long as the spouse does not remarry.

It should be noted that a possible tax consequence of using a sprinkle provision to provide financial protection to the family of a deceased child of the grantor is that, if trust income is used to support a dependent, the income will be taxed to the person who is obligated to provide the support. In a trust with a sprinkle provision, to the extent that the trustee applies income for the support of a minor, the IRS may attempt to tax this income to the parent. *Obligation to support* means the duty imposed by law to support another person. In most cases, an obligation to support pertains to a taxpayer's minor child or children.

Trust income, though, is not generally considered to be used for the support of a dependent. There are a number of reasons that income will not be considered to be used for the discharge of the parent's obligation. First, if the beneficiary is over the age of majority, the obligation to support that child may be limited. However, some states hold that support obligations include college costs. A family court decree may create an obligation to support post-majority child costs. Second, a trustee would generally accumulate income when a minor is involved. Third, if the finances of a parent are limited, income used by the trustee for support may be over and above the parent's obligation.

Conservative planning suggests that a trust provision be included stating that income may be used only if the parent's funds are inadequate for the desired purpose. Alternatively, such funds can be used to provide nonsupport items such as toys, music lessons, travel, entertainment, cars, or other items that will not fall into the category of "legal obligation to support."

CONCLUSION

Trusts and estates, creatively structured, can provide some income tax advantages for the beneficiaries. Full utilization of tax planning opportunities for estates, trusts, and beneficiaries is generally overlooked by all but the most sophisticated tax planners. While the income taxation of estates and trusts is complicated to master, it may be worth the effort when considering potential tax savings.

CHAPTER REVIEW

Key Terms and Concepts

income in respect of a decedent (IRD)	distributable net income (DNI)
income-first rule	grantor trust
nongrantor trust	kiddie tax
simple trust	sprinkle provision
complex trust	

Chapter 19: Review Questions

1. When and for what purposes does an estate come into existence? [LO 19.1]

2. Over what period of time is the estate held open? [LO 19.1]

3. What are the similarities between estates and trusts? [LO 19.1]

4. Explain the differences between estates and trusts with regard to purpose, mode of creation, and duration. [LO 19.1]

5. How does the taxation of estates and trusts differ from the taxation of corporations or partnerships? [LO 19.1]

6. Describe the income tax returns required to be filed by the personal representative of the estate with respect to filing dates, income, expenses, and accounting methods. [LO 19.2]

7. Why may a deduction that involves income in respect of a decedent be allowable on the income tax return? [LO 19.2]

8. What are the exemptions available to

   a. an estate

   b. a simple trust

   c. a complex trust [LO 19.2]

9. How are specific bequests distributed by an estate in more than three installments treated for income tax purposes? [LO 19.2]

10. An estate receives dividends of $15,000 during its second year of operation. The executor determines that $25,000 of corpus should be paid to a beneficiary and that the dividends should be retained and added to corpus. Explain how the $25,000 distribution will be treated for income tax purposes under the *income-first rule*. [LO 19.2]

11. Briefly describe why an estate's personal representative would select a fiscal year for reporting the estate's income taxation. [LO 19.2]

12. How is trust income taxed to

   a. a beneficiary

   b. a trust [LO 19.3]

13. Larry Ladnor created a trust for the benefit of his mother, Laura. The trust provides that all income may be distributed annually to Laura for life. Any income not distributed is to be accumulated. The trust corpus generates $25,000 of taxable income annually, unless otherwise stated. Explain whether the trust is a simple trust or a complex trust in each of the following years:

   a. Five years ago, the trust distributed $25,000 to Laura.

   b. Four years ago, the trust distributed $22,000 to Laura and made a gift of $3,000 to Duke University, her alma mater.

   c. Three years ago, the trust distributed $20,000 to Laura and credited her trust account with $5,000 of income that was retained in the trust.

   d. Two years ago, the trust distributed $27,000 to Laura. The trust earned only $21,000 of income that year and $6,000 was a distribution from corpus.

   e. Last year, the trust earned $20,000 and distributed all of it to Laura. [LO 19.3]

14. a. Identify the three main results of distributable net income (DNI). [LO 19.3]

    b. How is DNI affected by multiple beneficiaries? [LO 19.3]

15. What is meant by the statement that items of income retain their character? [LO 19.3]

16. Assume that the sole income of the Madison family trust is $18,000 of tax-exempt interest from municipal bonds. Fifteen thousand dollars is distributed to the sole beneficiary. How much of this income will be taxable to the trust, and how much will be taxable to the beneficiary? [LO 19.3]

17. Explain who is liable for the tax resulting from income earned by a grantor trust. [LO 19.3]

18. Mr. X creates a trust for the benefit of his children. How will the taxation of the trust income be affected if Mrs. X holds the power to revoke the trust? [LO 19.3]

19. In 2019 Paul creates an irrevocable trust providing that all income be distributed to Sheila, his 12-year-old daughter. If the trust distributes $2,000 of income to Sheila and she has no other income for the year, explain the tax consequences. [LO 19.3]
    Note: For 2019, the standard deduction for a person who may be claimed as the dependent of another (whether actually claimed or not) is $1,100 or the amount of the child's earned income. (For kiddie tax purposes in 2019, the net unearned income is generally equal to a child's unearned income less the greater of (1) $2,200 or (2) $1,100 (plus certain itemized deductions).

20. Explain the use of multiple trusts. [LO 19.3]

21. Describe the income tax consequences of the accumulation of income in trusts. [LO 19.3]

22. What benefits may be derived from having the trustee purchase life insurance on a beneficiary's life rather than having the trustee distribute income to the beneficiary who then uses such income to make life insurance premium payments? [LO 19.3]

23. a. Explain how the existence of a sprinkle provision in a trust may enable the trust to save income taxes. [LO 19.3]

    b. For what purposes, other than tax reasons, would a grantor use a sprinkle provision in a trust? [LO 19.3]

24. What is the tax effect when trust income is used to support a grantor's dependent? [LO 19.3]

25. Mr. Smith has a son, Harris, who has a sizable estate in his own right. Mr. Smith would like to give his son income from his property for life under a testamentary trust with the principal payable to Harris's children upon Harris's death. If the trustee of this trust is authorized in his sole discretion to use a portion of the trust income to purchase life insurance on Harris's life, how will the trust income used to pay such life insurance premiums be taxed for federal income tax purposes? Explain. [LO 19.3]

Chapter 19: Review Answers

1. An estate is a taxpaying entity that comes into being when a taxpayer dies for the purpose of effectuating the orderly, legal transfer of the decedent's property.

2. A decedent's estate exists for a limited period of time—typically 1 to 3 years.

3. Estates and trusts have many similarities.

   - Both administer property in a fiduciary capacity.
   - Property is transferred from the decedent to the estate in a manner similar to the transfer of property by a grantor to a trust.
   - Both decedents and grantors are responsible for the creation of the estate or trust.
   - Beneficiaries of an estate have a relationship to the estate similar to that of the beneficiaries of a trust.

4. Estates and trusts have some important differences. An estate comes into existence involuntarily by operation of law upon the decedent's death. A living trust is created intentionally and voluntarily by a specific action of the grantor. Estates exist for a limited time period. Trusts generally exist for many years and possibly span more than one generation.

   The primary function of many trusts is to provide sound, professional asset management. The trustee's primary duty is to be a good manager. Whether an individual or institution, the trustee will be in charge of the management of the trust property for the duration of the trust.

   On the other hand, an estate serves as a temporary receptacle for assets pending distribution to the new owners. The personal representative functions primarily as a liquidator who must marshal the decedent's assets, advertise the estate for the benefit of creditors, and pay its debts, expenses, and taxes. The personal representative must settle any claims against the estate and has a duty to keep the property income producing until its distribution.

   Another significant difference between the two entities is their relationship to the court. An estate is created by operation of law and is supervised by the court until it is terminated. A trust, on the other hand, is generally a private arrangement.

5. Trusts and estates are subject to income tax. However, they are subject to a slightly different computational system of taxation than are individuals, corporations, or

partnerships, because they exist for the benefit of others. If Congress had chosen to tax estates and trusts in a manner similar to corporations, double taxation would have resulted. If taxed like a corporation, the trust or estate would be taxed on income earned during its taxable year. Beneficiaries would then be treated as shareholders who would be taxed on the distribution when received, just as dividends are taxable to shareholders in the year received.

Alternatively, if a trust or estate was taxed as a partnership, all income would be passed through to the individual beneficiaries in a manner similar to the way it is passed to partners. Using this method would be detrimental in cases where the grantor did not intend beneficiaries to be entitled to the income automatically. Taxation of a partnership would defeat the right of the grantor to give the trustee discretion to accumulate or distribute income. Also, a personal representative of an estate does not have a duty to distribute income before the estate makes final distribution to the beneficiaries. Under the theory of partnership taxation, a beneficiary would pay tax on amounts not yet received.

6. An executor or administrator has the duty to file two different types of income tax returns for a decedent—a decedent's last life return (Form 1040) and an estate's income tax return (Form 1041).

    A deceased taxpayer's tax year ends with the date of death. The return must be filed by the regular due date, April 15, of the following year. The amounts of income and deductible expenses that must be reported depend on the deceased taxpayer's regular method of accounting.

    For cash-basis taxpayers, only income actually or constructively received must be reported. Deductions can be taken only for expenses that were actually paid during the decedent's lifetime. If the decedent was on the accrual method, the return will show all income and deductions accrued through the date of death.

7. If income in respect of a decedent is included in the decedent's gross estate for estate tax purposes, the estate tax attributable to the inclusion of those income items in the estate will be deductible by the recipient of the income as and when it is received.

8. Exemptions available to a trust are

    a. an estate—$600

    b. a simple trust—$300

    c. a complex trust—$100

9. The only beneficiaries who do not pay income tax on distributions of income from estates are those who receive specific bequests under the will in three installments or less. Therefore, beneficiaries are taxed on payments from income in four or more installments.

10. The income-first rule requires that all distributions be made first out of income. Since the estate received $15,000 of income and made a distribution of $25,000 to its beneficiary, the beneficiary would be taxed upon receipt of $15,000 of income and receive a nontaxable distribution of corpus in the amount of $10,000. The estate will receive a deduction for the $15,000 of income distribution. The distribution of corpus is neither deductible to the estate nor taxable to the beneficiary.

11. Estates are permitted to have a fiscal income tax year rather than being restricted to a calendar year. By carefully selecting the estate's fiscal year for reporting the estate's income and giving consideration to the timing of distributions of estate income to estate beneficiaries, the beneficiary's payment of the tax on the income earned by the estate can be delayed for years.

12. a. The essential concept of trust taxation is that trust income is taxed once, either: (1) to the beneficiary(ies), or (2) to the trustee. If a trustee is required to distribute the entire income of the trust annually, that income is taxed to the recipient(s). However, some trusts authorize the accumulation of all or part of the income at the trustee's discretion. The tax law does not tax prospective beneficiaries on amounts they may never receive.

     b. The trustee is taxed on income accumulated by the trust. In essence, the taxation of trust income can be capsulized thus: income that is accumulated by the trust is taxable to the trust; income that is payable to the beneficiary is taxable to the beneficiary; and income either accumulated or distributed by a grantor trust is taxable to the grantor.

13. a. Five years ago, the trust was a simple trust.

     b. Four years ago, the trust was a complex trust since it made a gift to a qualified charity that year.

     c. Three years ago, the trust was a complex trust since it accumulated $5,000 of income.

     d. Two years ago, the trust was a complex trust because it made a distribution from corpus in addition to distributing all the income earned that year.

     e. Last year, the trust was a simple trust because all the income earned was distributable to the beneficiary.

14. a. The concept of DNI is used to achieve three main results:

    - First, it provides a limit on the deduction that a trust or estate may receive for amounts distributed to beneficiaries.

    - Second, it limits the amount of distribution that may be taxable to the beneficiaries.

    - Third, it establishes the character of the amounts taxable to the beneficiaries.

    b. When there is more than one beneficiary, each is taxed on his or her share of DNI. When special items are distributed (such as tax-exempt interest, dividends, and so forth), a beneficiary is considered to have received a proportionate share unless the trust agreement earmarks a particular type of income for a specified beneficiary.

15. One function of DNI is to ensure that the character of the amounts in the hands of a beneficiary is the same as that in the hands of a trust or estate. Therefore, if dividends are received by a trust and distributed to a beneficiary, the dividends retain their character as dividends.

    Likewise, if the trust receives tax-free income (such as from a municipal bond), the income remains tax free in the hands of the beneficiary.

16. Although the total tax-exempt interest is $18,000, with $15,000 distributable to the beneficiary and $3,000 left in the trust, neither the beneficiary nor the trust will be subject to tax on their respective sums since the interest is tax exempt.

17. In the case of a grantor trust, the trust is disregarded for income tax purposes and all income, deductions, and credits attributable to any portion of a trust declared a grantor trust are taken into account directly on the grantor's individual income tax return.

18. The grantor-trust rules also apply if the spouse of the grantor, living with the grantor at the time of creation of the interest, is given any of the proscribed powers that invoke the grantor-trust rules.

19. The trust income is treated as unearned income of minors under age 19 or 24, if a full-time student. The net unearned income of the trust is determined as follows:

Sheila's unearned income	
Less the sum of (2019)	$2,000
a. the standard deduction, as indexed for inflation	(1,100)
b. $1,100, as indexed for inflation (taxed at child's rate)	(1,100)
Net unearned income to be taxed at the trust marginal bracket	$0

20. Because the *Revenue Reconciliation Act of 1993 (RRA '93)* imposes the higher tax rates on trusts and estates having taxable income at lower thresholds than individuals are subject to, the use of separate or multiple trusts for the purpose of saving income taxes often results in only nominal savings.

    It is possible to create several trusts for the same or different beneficiaries. If the tax law recognizes the existence of multiple trusts, then the income is taxed separately to each trust, which means that each trust receives a separate exemption, and each trust is treated as a separate tax entity for all income tax purposes. Conversely, if multiple trusts are considered by the IRS to be one trust, only one exemption is allowed. All the trusts are treated as one entity for income tax purposes.

21. As stated above, the RRA '93 has clearly diminished the advantages of income accumulation trusts. Since trusts and estates are taxed at higher rate brackets for taxable income at lower threshold amounts than individuals are taxed, it is likely that many beneficiaries will be in a lower tax bracket than the trusts benefiting them.

22. Authorizing a trustee to purchase life insurance on the lives of the beneficiaries can yield some limited benefits under current income tax law. Suppose one of the trust beneficiaries has a significant amount of taxable income this year and is already in a high marginal tax bracket. Suppose also that the trust has taxable income that will be taxed in one of the lower marginal tax brackets. If the trustee distributes the trust income to the beneficiary, it will be taxed at the beneficiary's higher rate, leaving less for the beneficiary to purchase life insurance and pay premiums. If, however, the trust itself purchases the life insurance and pays the premiums with the income, more income is available for the purchase and premium payments because of the trust's exemption and lower income tax bracket.

23. a. One of the principles of proper tax planning is that income should be divided among family members whenever possible in order to lower the rate at which the income will be taxed as well as to take advantage of the multiple individual personal exemptions. Tax savings may be accomplished with more flexibility if the trustee is authorized, rather than mandated, to pay income to trust beneficiaries at the trustee's discretion. The trustee can then allocate income among the

family members in any manner that seems desirable from tax year to tax year. In exercising that discretion, the trustee would consider the individual needs of the various beneficiaries, the ultimate use to which the income would be put, and the collective as well as individual tax burdens.

b.   There are also nontax advantages to clauses that sprinkle income according to needs. An example is a testator who wants to provide for the family of a deceased child but does not want to pay income for the lifetime of a deceased child's spouse. The testator may fear that if the surviving spouse remarries, income will go to the new spouse or the new spouse's children rather than to the testator's grandchildren. The sprinkle clause in a trust enables a trustee to pay income to the spouse only as long as the children are young or have varying needs and as long as the spouse does not remarry.

24. If trust income is used to support a dependent, that income will be taxed to the person who is obligated to provide the support. In a trust with a sprinkle clause, to the extent that the trustee applies income for the support of a minor, the IRS may attempt to tax this income to the parent. Obligation to support means the duty imposed by law to support another person.

25. If the trustee is authorized in his sole discretion to use a portion of the trust income to purchase life insurance on Harris's life, the trust income used to pay premiums will be taxed to the trust. It should be noted that Harris is a life income beneficiary of a trust created by his father and not the grantor of the trust. To the extent the income is used to pay premiums, it will not be distributed to Harris and, therefore, will not be included in Harris's gross income for income tax purposes. This result may be an advantage if Harris is already in a relatively high income tax bracket and has a sizable estate of his own.

Chapter 20:

The Generation-Skipping Transfer Tax

Learning Objectives

An understanding of the material in this chapter should enable the student to do the following:

LO 20.1 Describe the types of transfers that are subject to the generation-skipping transfer tax (GSTT).

LO 20.2 Explain the importance of exemptions and exclusions from the GSTT and how a client should plan for allocation of the GSTT exemption.

LO 20.3 Describe in general the calculation of the GSTT.

LO 20.4 Determine who has liability for the GSTT.

LO 20.5 Identify the different aspects of planning for the GSTT.

LO 20.1 Describe the types of transfers that are subject to the generation-skipping transfer tax (GSTT).

Introduction to the Generation-Skipping Transfer Tax

generation-skipping transfer tax

The first **generation-skipping transfer tax (GSTT)** was enacted in 1976. However, when Congress made sweeping revisions to the federal tax code in 1986, it totally revamped the GSTT.

The Tax Reform Act of 1986 (TRA '86) repealed the prior system of taxing generation-skipping transfers and replaced it with a completely different framework for the imposition of the GST tax. The present approach imposes a flat rate on taxable transfers that is equal to the highest current federal estate and gift tax rate—40 percent after 2012. The objectives of the GSTT are to obtain at least one transfer tax per generation and to discourage the transfer of substantial assets to more distant family members in order to reduce transfer taxes.

GSTT
- 40 percent FLAT rate after 2012
- imposed on
  - gifts
  - bequests
  - transfers
  - distributions to skip beneficiaries
- *in addition* to gift and estate taxes on same property

The American Taxpayer Relief Act of 2012 (ATRA 2012) increases the top estate tax rate to 40 percent after 2012. The GSTT rate has historically been equivalent to the top marginal income tax rate. However, the GST rate remains at 40% (2019) even though the TCJA 2017 lowered the top income tax rate from 40% to 37%.

Generation-Skipping Transfer Tax Rate Schedule	
Year	**Rate**
2001	55%
2002	50%
2003	49%
2004	48%
2005	47%
2006	46%
2007–2009	45%
2010	GSTT (elective repeal) or 35%
2011 and 2012	35%
2013 and beyond	40%
Beginning in 2004, the GSTT exemption amount equals the federal estate tax exclusion amount.	

The table below shows the increase in the GSTT exemption amount under EGTRRA 2001, TRA 2010, and ATRA 2012.

Increase in GSTT Exemption	
Year	**GSTT Exemption**
2001–2003	$1,000,000
2004–2005	$1,500,000
2006–2008	$2,000,000
2009	$3,500,000
2010	$5,000,000 (unless repeal is elected)
2011	$5,000,000
2012	$5,120,000
2013	$5,250,000
2014	$5,340,000
2015	$5,430,000
2016	$5,450,000
2017	$5,490,000
2018	$11,180,000
2019	$11,400,000

TAXABLE TRANSFERS

The GSTT applies when a taxable transfer is made to a transferee more than one generation level below the transferor. For example, a generation-skipping transfer occurs when a grandparent transfers property to a grandchild. However, the GSTT applies only if the transfer avoids estate or gift tax one generation level above the transferee. That is, the GSTT applies only if a generation is "skipped" by the estate and gift tax system. Thus, a gift from a grandparent to a grandchild that causes estate and gift tax on such transfer at the parent's level will not invoke the generation-skipping tax. It is important to remember, however, that estate or gift tax in addition to the GSTT may be applicable on such generation-skipping transfers because a *grandparent* will probably be subject to the federal estate and gift tax system as well as the GSTT system when making gifts to a grandchild.

The GSTT is imposed on gifts, bequests, or other distributions to skip beneficiaries. A *skip beneficiary* is either: (1) a person who is at least two generations below the level of the transferor, or (2) a trust in which the beneficiaries are skip persons and from which no nonskip person (a person only one generation below the transferor) will benefit. In most instances, a skip person is a grandchild of the transferor and a nonskip person is a child of the transferor.

EXAMPLE

Grandfather Joe is survived by his wife, Jennie. Joe and Jennie had two children—Jack and Jake. Jack is married and has three children—James, Jason, and Julia. Jennie (the grandmother) and Jack and Jake (the children) are nonskip persons. James, Jason, and Julia are skip persons.

Although most generation-skipping transfers are to family members, usually grandchildren, transfers may be made to nonrelatives and be subject to GST taxation. For purposes of nonrelated donees, a person born not more than 12½ years after the transferor's date of birth is treated as being in the transferor's generation. Persons born more than 12½ years but not more than 37½ years after the transferor's date of birth are considered to be within the first generation below the transferor. Therefore, an unrelated individual born more than 37½ years after the transferor is considered a skip person for GSTT purposes. Spouses are treated as being of the same generation despite any age differences.

The taxes are imposed on three possible taxable events:

- direct skips
- taxable distributions
- taxable terminations

Direct Skips

direct-skip transfer

As defined in the generation-skipping transfer tax system, a **direct-skip transfer** is a taxable transfer to a skip person. A direct skip can be either an outright transfer or a transfer in trust for the benefit of a skip person. A transfer in trust will be treated as a direct skip if

- the trust benefits only one individual
- no portion of the income or corpus may be distributed to anyone else during the beneficiary's lifetime
- the corpus will be included in the beneficiary's estate if the beneficiary dies before the termination of the trust

Thus a transfer to a life insurance trust will qualify as a direct skip if the trust meets the above requirements and provides current withdrawal powers, such as Crummey withdrawal powers. Under the predeceased ancestor rules, in most cases, direct skips, taxable distributions, and taxable terminations are not treated as taxable generation-skipping transfers if, at the time of the transfer, the parent of the skip person is already deceased. In this instance, the GSTT is eliminated because the grandchild is the natural recipient of the grandparent's wealth if the grandchild's parent is deceased.

EXAMPLE

James Dallop left a fully furnished condominium that he had owned for 14 years to his grandson, Scott, under the terms of his will. This transfer is *not* considered a direct skip triggering the GSTT if Scott's parent, who is the son or daughter of James, has predeceased James. If Scott's parent who is the son or daughter of James is alive at the time of James's death, the generation-skipping tax does apply to this direct–skip bequest. In either event, the regular federal estate tax applies to this transfer.

skip beneficiary

Skip Beneficiary
- A **skip beneficiary** is a person two or more generations below the transferor (exception: grandchild [skip person] of deceased parent) OR
- a trust with skip beneficiaries and no nonskip beneficiaries benefiting

Taxable Distributions

In addition to direct-skip situations, the GSTT may apply to what is known as a taxable distribution.

taxable distribution

A **taxable distribution** is any distribution of either income or principal from a trust to a person two or more generations junior to the trust settlor's generation. The recipients of a taxable distribution are called skip beneficiaries. To be taxable as a generation-skipping transfer, the distribution must otherwise escape federal estate and gift taxation at the first generation level below the original transferor.

The taxable amount in this scenario is the net value of the property received by the skip beneficiary reduced by any amount the beneficiary may have paid in order to receive the property. In addition, the taxable amount includes any GSTT paid by the *trustee* on such taxable distribution. The reason for this "gross-up" rule is that the GSTT liability falls on the skip beneficiary, not the trustee.

> **EXAMPLE**
>
> Ethel Bally created an irrevocable trust eleven years ago for the benefit of her son, Carlos, and her grandson, Julio. In December of this year, the trustee made a distribution of $20,000 of trust income to Carlos and $18,800 of trust income to Julio. The distribution to Julio is characterized as a taxable distribution that triggers GSTT. Note that the original transfer to the trust could have been subject to taxation through the gift tax rules at that time.

Taxable Terminations

taxable termination

A **taxable termination** is defined as a situation in which there is a termination of a property interest held in trust, the termination occurring by death, lapse of time, release of a power, or otherwise, that results in skip beneficiaries holding the property interests in the trust. Four miscellaneous points must be noted:

- A taxable termination cannot take place if a skip beneficiary could not receive a distribution after the termination.

- A taxable termination cannot occur as long as at least one nonskip beneficiary has an interest in the property.

- There will be no taxable termination if an estate or gift tax is imposed on the trust property one generation level below the transferor at the time of the termination.

- A partial termination subject to GSTT is possible if a specified, separate portion of the trust is available only to skip persons after the termination.

GSTT Events
- **direct skips**
  - outright transfer or
  - trust with only one lifetime and at death beneficiary
- **taxable distributions**
  - trust distributions (income/principal) to skip beneficiaries (two or more generations below)
- **taxable terminations**
  - trust termination with property passing to skip beneficiaries

The taxable amount in the case of a taxable termination is the value of all property involved reduced by any amounts the recipient paid for it and any expenses, debts, and income or property taxes triggered by that property.

EXAMPLE

Rosemary's will directed that the income from her marketable securities was to pass to her daughter, Kim, for life, with the remainder interest to pass at Kim's death to Rosemary's granddaughter, Heather. When Kim died, her life interest in the trust property terminated, and Heather received the underlying property. Heather is the skip beneficiary. A taxable termination occurred at Kim's death.

LO 20.2   **Explain the importance of exemptions and exclusions from the GSTT and how a client should plan for allocation of the GSTT exemption.**

EXEMPTIONS AND EXCLUSIONS

Although the scope of the GSTT is broad and could have a dramatic effect on a client's tax planning, it must be emphasized that there are several exemptions to, and exclusions from, this tax.

The GSTT Exemption

The most basic GSTT exemption is that every taxpayer is permitted to make aggregate transfers (which, in the past, increased over time) either during lifetime or at death that will not attract the GSTT. In 2019, a transferor has a $11.4 million exemption and the transferor's spouse also has a $11.4 million exemption against generation-skipping transfers. Therefore, a total family basic exemption amount of $22.8 million is available for 2019.

GSTT Exemptions

$11.4 million exemption in 2019 (indexed amount)
- per donor, not per donee
- lifetime/death
- $22.8 million for both spouses (double the amount of an individual single transferor)

The Annual Exclusion Transfer

As with the annual per-donee exclusion from gift tax, a similar exclusion from the GSTT is available for direct skips. A direct skip is either: (1) an outright gift providing the donee with immediate possession, or (2) certain gifts in trust providing a present interest to a skip person.

For GSTT purposes, the annual exclusion is more restrictive than the gift tax annual exclusion for gifts in trust. The gift in trust qualifies for the GSTT exclusion if it provides a present interest such as a current income interest or Crummey withdrawal power. In addition, the trust must limit distributions of income and corpus to a single beneficiary and must provide that the corpus will be included in the estate of the beneficiary if he or she dies prior to the termination of the trust. Thus, because only one beneficiary is permitted, the GSTT annual exclusion cannot be used on the typical inter vivos trust with sprinkle provisions. It is possible, however, to create a separate trust for each grandchild, such as a Sec. 2503(c) trust, that will qualify for both the gift tax and GSTT annual exclusions.

GSTT Exclusions

$15,000 annual exclusion (2019)
- outright gifts
- in trust
    - requires present interest (current income interest or Crummey power)
    - only one beneficiary with lifetime/death receipt of property

Exclusion for Transfers for Educational or Medical Expenses

Tuition or medical expense payments on behalf of a donee are also excluded from both gift tax and GSTT. Such gifts must be provided directly to the educational institution or medical provider for expenses incurred by the donee. The transfers excludible under this provision are not limited in amount, but the tuition payment exclusion is limited to transfers to educational institutions eligible for income-tax-deductible charitable contributions covering the direct tuition costs for the education or training of the donee. Direct tuition payments are an excellent gift for wealthy grandparents to consider because they (1) are not subject to gift or GSTT taxes, (2) do not reduce the annual exclusion gifts, and (3) do not reduce the GSTT exemption.

Medical expenses eligible for the exclusion are those expenses normally deductible by the donee under the income tax rules.

GSTT Exemptions and Exclusions
- unlimited educational/medical expenses
- direct payments to provider
- $11.4 million GSTT exemption (2019) unaffected

LO 20.3 Describe in general the calculation of the GSTT.

Calculation of the GSTT

The GSTT is calculated by a somewhat unusual process, which is discussed herein primarily to demonstrate the effect of the GSTT exemption. The GSTT is determined by multiplying the taxable amount by the GSTT rate. The taxable amount is the value (less certain expenses) of any direct skip, taxable termination, or taxable distribution.

inclusion ratio

The applicable GSTT rate is the highest federal estate and gift tax rate (40 percent in 2019) multiplied by an inclusion ratio. The **inclusion ratio** is determined by the following formula:

$$\text{Inclusion ratio} = 1 - (TE \div (VT - (ET + CD)))$$

TE	=	transferor's exemption allocated to the transfer
VT	=	value of the transferred property
ET	=	amount of federal estate tax or state death tax recovered from the trust attributable to the transferred property
CD	=	charitable deduction attributable to the transferred property

Assuming no estate tax or charitable deduction, the inclusion ratio is one (and the current applicable rate is 40) if no exemption is allocated to the transfer. If the amount of the exemption is allocated equivalently to the value of the transferred property, the applicable rate is zero and the transfer is exempt from GSTT. It is possible, of course, to have an applicable rate somewhere between zero percent and 40 percent if the transfer is only partially exempt. However, a partially exempt trust should generally be avoided unless the transferor has insufficient remaining exemption to fully shelter the trust from GSTT. Partially exempt trusts will generally increase the complexity and fiduciary costs associated with the administration of the trust.

EXAMPLE

Using the 2019 GSTT exemption amount and tax rate of 40 percent:

In 2019, a widower grandfather transfers outright (direct skip) $15,000,000 to his grandson. Ignore the annual exclusion for this example. His entire 2019 exemption of $11.4 million is allocated to the transfer. The fraction is

$$\$11,400,000 \div \$15,000,000 = 0.76$$

0.24 (1 - 0.76) is the inclusion ratio

0.24 of 40% yields a tax rate of 0.096

0.096 of $15,000,000 equals a GSTT of $1,440,000 (for direct skip where GSTT is paid from other property)

Keep in mind that, although not addressed in this example, gift tax will also apply to this transfer from grandfather to grandson.

LO 20.4   Determine who has liability for the GSTT.

Liability for the Tax

The liability for tax payment depends on the type of generation-skipping transfer. Therefore, in choosing the transfer mechanism, the transferor must consider the net amount the skip beneficiary will receive.

- For direct skips, the tax is imposed on the transferor or the transferor's estate. Therefore the direct-skip beneficiary receives the full amount of the transfer while the remainder of the transferor's estate is diminished by the transfer.

- In the case of a taxable distribution, the liability for the tax falls on the transferee. That is, the tax that is imposed reduces the amount of the transfer available to the beneficiary. Because the rate of tax is 40 percent (2019), the amount of the taxable distribution available to the skip beneficiary is substantially reduced after the GSTT liability.

- The tax is paid by the trustee in the event of a taxable termination. Thus, at the time of the termination, the skip person receives the proceeds reduced by the tax.

The GSTT is imposed by statute on the property transferred unless the transferor specifically allocates the tax elsewhere by the terms of a will or trust document. As with the federal estate and gift taxes, a lien is applicable against the transferred property for collection of the tax.

Liability for GSTT

Taxable GSTT Event	Liability
– direct skip	– transferor/ transferor's estate
– taxable distribution	– transferee (beneficiary)
– taxable termination	– trustee

LO 20.5   **Identify the different aspects of planning for the GSTT.**

PLANNING FOR THE GSTT

Because the GSTT is imposed at the highest marginal federal estate tax bracket, the tax will represent the highest percentage burden of any federal tax in the future. Because generation-skipping transfers are also potentially subject to estate or gift taxes, the combination of estate or gift tax and GSTT rates can be considerable. Obviously, this tax creates a substantial incentive to transfer property in a manner exempt from the tax.

Allocating the GSTT Exemption

Lifetime Transfers

indirect skip

One choice available to the taxpayer for allocating the GSTT exemption is to apply such exemption affirmatively to lifetime gifts. The allocation of such exemption to lifetime gifts is particularly appropriate because the exemption is leveraged. That is, the exemption need shelter only the value of the contribution at the time of the gift on a dollar–for–dollar basis. It is important to note, that under Sec. 2632(b), the GSTT exemption is automatically allocated to lifetime direct skips unless the donor elects otherwise on a gift tax return (709) that is timely filed. EGTRRA 2001 added Sec. 2632(c) that provides that any unused GSTT exemption is automatically allocated to indirect skips made to a GST trust for the years 2001 to 2009. An **indirect skip** is any transfer of property, other than a direct skip, that is subject to the GSTT made to a GST trust. A transferor has the option to elect out of the automatic allocation rules by making the election on the appropriate return.

Gifts of appreciating property are good targets for lifetime gifts to take advantage of the GSTT exemption. The exemption will be applied to the value of the property at the time of the transfer, and any posttransfer appreciation will not be subject to the tax and need not be sheltered by part of the exemption. In addition, the exemption can be used to provide for skip persons through transfers in trust. The exemption must be allocated against current additions to the trust on a timely filed gift tax return. However, the appreciation on the corpus will avoid GSTT if all *additions* to the trust are sheltered by the exemption. Therefore, because the GSTT exemption is leveraged, wealthy clients can transfer appreciating property that will eventually expand into substantial wealth at a huge total transfer tax savings.

The irrevocable life insurance trust discussed earlier is an excellent device for using the GSTT exemption. Unless the trust has one beneficiary, the premium additions to a Crummey life insurance trust will not be eligible for a GSTT annual exclusion. However, the gift tax annual exclusion will be available, and the GSTT exemption will shelter the trust from GSTT unless aggregate premiums exceed the GSTT exemption amount. In this manner, substantial wealth may be transferred to the trust and avoid the gift tax or GSTT. The cash contributed to the trust can be used to purchase a life insurance policy on the life of the grantor. Therefore, the appreciation in the life insurance policy and subsequent proceeds at the death of the grantor are beyond the reach of the estate tax or GSTT. The life insurance received by the beneficiaries will prevent the diminution of the grantor's estate caused by the total transfer taxes imposed on any wealth *retained* by the grantor until death.

For example, suppose a $3.5 million policy is placed in the trust and will be paid up with 20 annual premium contributions of $100,000. The grandparent could shelter such a transfer with $2 million of his or her exemption and apply the remaining exemption amount to a different type of gift.

Testamentary Transfers

Any exemption not used at the time of the taxpayer's death and not made by the taxpayer's executor is allocated according to the default rules. The unused portion of the decedent's GSTT exemption at the time of death is allocated under the following priorities:

- First, the GSTT exemption is applied to a direct skip of property (a specific outright bequest or devise of property) occurring at the individual's death.

- Second, the exemption is allocated to trusts in which the decedent is treated as the transferor and from which a taxable GSTT event might occur after the individual's death.

These rules provide that the exemption is allocated ratably to the priority list above based on the nonexempt portion of the properties included in such bequests or trusts. The nonexempt portion of such bequests is the amount of the property to which the GSTT exemption has not been previously allocated.

EXAMPLE

Grandparent (GP) died in 2019. GP left separate $11.4 million parcels of real estate to each of his grandchildren, GC1 and GC2.

GP had not used any of his $11.4 million (2019) GSTT exemption while he was alive and had not allocated any of the exemption affirmatively through the provisions of his will. The IRS allocation rules would apply the GSTT exemption ratably to the two pieces of property. Thus, $5,700,000 of each parcel of real estate left to the grandchildren will be exempt, and the remaining $5,700,000 of each parcel will become subject to the GSTT.

These exemption allocation rules do not add complexity to a grandparent's estate if substantial direct-skip bequests are made to grandchildren. The exemption is simply allocated ratably among the bequests. If the grandparent leaves no such direct-skip bequest, however, the allocation rules add to the cost and complexity of administering testamentary trusts. The allocation of the exemption to such trusts is applied ratably against any trust that might result in a taxable distribution or termination subject to GSTT. In the usual marital-deduction will, the will divides the property between a marital trust and a credit-equivalent bypass trust. In either trust the property might later be subject to a GSTT, because grandchildren are almost certainly contingent or remainder beneficiaries. The allocation rules cause the exemption to be allocated ratably between the marital and the (bypass) trust. The result is that each trust would likely become partially exempt and partially nonexempt from GSTT. This adds to the administrative complexity for the trustee and, most likely, to the costs of administering the trust.

The mechanics of the GSTT calculation make it preferable to leave trusts either wholly exempt or wholly nonexempt. Of course, the taxpayer would prefer that the trust more likely to result in a GSTT liability receive the exemption and become wholly exempt. The taxpayer is incapable of controlling the allocation of such exemption unless he or she allocates the exemption affirmatively to lifetime gifts or directs the executor in the allocation of such gifts after the individual's death. The directions to the executor should be included in the decedent's will along with the normal directions with respect to estate tax elections. By giving the executor the appropriate discretion, the taxpayer is able to take a wait-and-see approach, and the executor will be able to make appropriate allocation of the exemption after the decedent's death.

Both spouses should make full use of their GSTT exemptions. The allocation of the exemption in the wills of both spouses should be carefully planned. The spouses should avoid wasting the exemption by allocating both exemptions to the same assets. A popular method is to provide the executors of the will with discretionary power in allocating the exemptions. After viewing the facts at the time of estate administration, the executor then allocates the exemption where it is most appropriate. The exemption should be allocated to a transfer, perhaps a credit-equivalent bypass trust, that is most likely to benefit skip persons. In addition, the executor should avoid allocating the exemption to a transfer if the surviving spouse's exemption will be available.

If one spouse does not have sufficient assets to use the exemption, an interspousal transfer may be indicated. By using the unlimited marital estate or gift tax deduction, the wealthy spouse can transfer assets to the other spouse without incurring transfer tax. These assets may enable the less-wealthy spouse to use the GSTT exemption.

CHAPTER REVIEW

Key Terms and Concepts

generation-skipping transfer tax
direct-skip transfer
skip beneficiary
taxable distribution

taxable termination
inclusion ratio
indirect skip

Chapter 20: Review Questions

1. What types of transfers will result in taxation under the GSTT rules? [LO 20.1]

2. What is the current exemption amount against the GSTT, and how should the taxpayer allocate the exemption? [LO 20.2]

3. How must a trust be designed for transfers to the trust to qualify for the annual gift tax exclusion from the GSTT? [LO 20.2]

4. How might a grandparent make gifts to a grandchild free of the GSTT without using either the annual exclusion or GSTT exemption amount? [LO 20.2]

5. How might an irrevocable life insurance trust be used in conjunction with the GSTT exemption amount? [LO 20.2]

6. Who is responsible for paying the GSTT? [LO 20.4]

7. Describe the manner in which the IRS will allocate the GSTT exemption amount at a transferor's death if the exemption is not allocated by the decedent. [LO 20.5]

8. Describe the calculation of the GSTT [LO 20.3]

Chapter 20: Review Answers

1. Imposition of the GSTT results when a taxable transfer is made to a transferee who is more than one generation level below the generation level of the transferor. The GSTT applies only if a generation is "skipped" by the estate and gift tax system.

2. The GSTT exemption amount ($11.4 million in 2019 (indexed for inflation)) is the most basic exemption that every taxpayer is entitled to make in the aggregate for transfers up to and including the exemption amount without having to pay the GSTT. Although the Code provides allocation rules of the GSTT exemption, by electing not to have the automatic rules apply, the allocation of the exemption is according to the transferor's wishes as it may be utilized partially or fully during lifetime and/or at death.

3. A gift in trust qualifies for the GSTT annual exclusion if it provides a present interest or Crummey withdrawal power. Also, the trust must limit distributions of income and corpus to a single beneficiary and must provide that the corpus be included in the beneficiary's estate should he or she die prior to the trust's termination.

4. Direct education tuition payments are an excellent gift for grandparents to make to a grandchild since they are not subject to gift tax or the GSTT, and they do not reduce either annual exclusion gifts or the GSTT exemption amount. The same rules apply for direct medical payments.

5. The irrevocable life insurance trust provides an opportunity for a grantor to affirmatively allocate the GSTT exemption amount to premium gifts to the trust. It should be used when beneficiaries are (or are likely to include) grandchildren. The exemption allocated in this way gives the grantor the opportunity to leverage the exemption. This is because all proceeds will be exempt from GSTT if the premiums are sheltered by allocating the exemption to them on a timely filed gift tax return. Annual Crummey powers should shelter the premiums from gift tax if the annual gift tax exclusion is not exceeded.

6. For direct skips, the transferor or the transferor's estate has liability for the tax. For taxable distributions, the liability for the tax belongs to the transferee. For taxable terminations, the tax is paid by the trustee.

7. Any exemption not used at the time of the taxpayer's death and not made by the taxpayer's executor is allocated according to the default rules. The unused portion of the decedent's GSTT exemption at the time of death is allocated under the following priorities:

- First, the exemption is applied to a direct skip of property (a specific outright bequest or devise of property) occurring at the individual's death.

- Second, the exemption is allocated to trusts in which the decedent is treated as the transferor and from which a taxable GSTT event might occur after the individual's death.

These rules provide that the exemption amount is allocated ratably to the priority list above based on the nonexempt portion of the properties included in such bequests or trusts. The nonexempt portion of such bequests is the amount of the property to which the GSTT exemption has not been previously allocated.

8. The applicable GSTT rate is the highest federal estate and gift tax rate (40 percent in 2019) multiplied by an inclusion ratio, which is determined by the following formula:

Inclusion ratio = 1 - (TE divided by (VT-(ET + CD)))
TE = transferor's exemption allocated to the transfer
VT = value of transferred property
ET = amount of federal estate tax or state death tax recovered from the trust attributable to the transferred property
CD = charitable deduction attributable to the transferred property

Example: In 2019 a widower grandfather transfers outright (direct skip) $15,000,000 to his grandson. Ignoring the annual exclusion, his entire 2019 exemption of $11.4 million is allocated to the transfer. The fraction is: $11.4 million divided by $15 million = 0.76

0.24 (1-0.76) is the inclusion ratio
0.24 of 40% yields a tax rate of .096.
.096 of $15 million = GSTT of $1,440,000

Chapter 21:

Other Estate Planning Techniques

Learning Objectives

An understanding of the material in this chapter should enable the student to do the following:

LO 21.1   **Describe the advantages, disadvantages, and tax treatment of installment sales.**

LO 21.2   **Define private annuities and explain their tax treatment.**

LO 21.3   **Describe the gift and estate tax treatment of grantor-retained annuity trusts and grantor-retained unitrusts.**

LO 21.4   **Describe the design considerations and transfer tax treatment of a qualified personal residence trust.**

LO 21.5   **Describe the basic concept of family limited partnerships and limited liability companies.**

LO 21.6   **Explain what is meant by a Sec. 303 redemption.**

LO 21.7   **Describe other issues that arise during modern estate planning, such as providing equity, pet trust, and ethical issues.**

Recent tax reforms have increased the significance of planning for federal transfer tax reduction. In many ways, the planning for estate and gift tax reduction can result in far greater gains to the taxpayer than planning for other taxes. This is particularly true for wealthy individuals with substantial estates. Reasons for the increased importance of estate planning include:

- The federal transfer tax rates have increased in relation to the marginal income tax rates. (Currently, marginal income tax rates peak at 37 percent in 2019. For 2019, the federal estate and gift tax rates have a 40 percent maximum).

- The generation-skipping transfer tax is applicable to many transfers to skip beneficiaries at a flat rate equal to the highest current federal estate and gift tax rate.

- The combination of federal estate or gift taxes with generation-skipping transfer taxes can result in doubling high marginal rates for certain transfers to skip beneficiaries.

- The anti-freeze rules under Chapter 14 of the Internal Revenue Code present a new estate tax trap for the unwary, since they may cause additional unforeseen estate or gift taxes if property gifted during a donor's lifetime is returned to his or her gross estate.

- The population of the elderly in the United States has been increasing faster than the overall population.

- The unlimited marital deduction has delayed payment of estate taxes until the death of the surviving spouse, which occurs on average about 10 years after the first spouse's death.

To prevent the government from confiscating the wealth of those individuals who accumulate substantial assets, estate planning is particularly important. There are also several other estate planning considerations that a client and estate planner should discuss.

In conjunction with planning for transfer tax reduction, estate planners must also be cognizant of health care considerations. Health care and incapacity issues are not necessarily reserved until old age. To at least some extent, depending on the particular circumstances, these matters should be addressed in a comprehensive estate plan.

Last, the planner should be aware of the special circumstances that are often involved in estate planning for the elderly, the incapacitated, married couples, and nonmarital partners.

LO 21.1   **Describe the advantages, disadvantages, and tax treatment of installment sales.**

INSTALLMENT SALES

installment sale

An installment can be a useful technique for financial and estate planning purposes. It is a taxable sale of a property with the income tax reporting of gain accounted for under the installment accounting provisions of the Internal Revenue Code. An **installment sale** is any sale in which at least one principal payment is received in a year other than the year of the sale (See 26 U.S.C. Sec. 453). The installment reporting provisions are the general rule when this definition for an installment sale is satisfied. However, the seller can elect to use normal accounting for an installment sale and recognize all gain in the year of sale.

Advantages of Installment Sales

From the seller's standpoint, an installment sale of property can provide both income tax and estate tax benefits. If installment reporting is available, the gain of the sale of property in exchange for an installment note will be delayed and recognized gradually over the installment period. Thus, it is possible to sell highly appreciated property without immediate recognition of the full taxable gain. On the other hand, the ability to elect out of installment reporting provides the taxpayer with the possibility of recognizing all taxable gain immediately. For example, a taxpayer may elect to recognize all gain at the time of an installment sale in a year when the taxpayer either has little other income or shows a loss for income tax purposes. Under these circumstances, reporting the gain immediately on an installment sale could prevent the taxpayer from wasting other deductions and tax benefits. The flexibility of an installment sale's reporting rules permits a taxpayer to defer gain recognition and, to some degree, plan the timing of gain recognition on the sale of property.

The installment sale also provides estate tax saving possibilities for the seller. The installment sale, a particularly useful device for family estate planning, may be used when a senior family member wishes to pass property on to a successor in the family. Be aware that special related-party rules apply to installment sales between family members. For estate planning purposes, an installment sale is one method of "freezing" the seller's estate and shifting the appreciation potential to a junior family member. If performed properly, and if the installment note is equal to the fair market value of the property at the time of the sale, the installment sale shifts the postsale appreciation to the junior family member without any transfer taxes being payable on the transferred property.

From the buyer's standpoint, the installment sale permits the buyer to defer some or all of the principal payments on the sale. This is particularly important for buyers without the funds for the entire purchase price. Quite often, the purchase and sale would be impossible without the payment deferral available in an installment sale. Installment sale treatment is not permitted where sales result in a loss.

Income Tax Treatment of Installment Sales

The sale of appreciated property in exchange for an installment note provides that some or all of the purchase price will be payable at some date in the future. From the seller's standpoint, the future payments can be broken down into three components for income tax purposes.

- One component of each annual payment on the installment note is treated as a return of the seller's original basis of the property. This return of basis is not taxable, because the seller is merely recovering his or her cost of the property.

- A second component of each payment received is treated as taxable gain.

- The third and final component of each payment is deemed interest. This interest is taxable to the seller as ordinary income.

Under the installment sales rules, the taxable gain component is recognized proportionally over the period in which the installment payments are made. The formula for recognizing gain from any particular installment payment is as follows:[1]

Capital gain = payment received during the year × (gross profit ÷ total contract price)

EXAMPLE 1

Ignoring the interest component in this case, assume that Tom Taxplanner, aged 52, would like to sell his vacation home to his daughter, Julia. The vacation home is valued at $200,000 and Tom's basis in the property is $50,000. Julia proposes an installment sale with a $50,000 down payment and the remaining principal payable in 10 annual installments of $15,000 beginning one year from settlement. Tom's gross profit is $150,000 and the contract price is $200,000. Thus, Tom will recognize 75 percent ($150,000 divided by $200,000) of each payment, or $11,250 (75% × $15,000) as gain.

EXAMPLE 2

Recently, Martin sold his collection of watercolors by recognized artists to his son, Roger, for $100,000. Roger made a down payment of $10,000 and will make principal payments in eight equal installments of $11,250 each year. Roger will also make monthly payments of interest. Because Martin's adjusted basis in the artwork is $40,000, Martin has a gross profit of $60,000. Each year he will recognize a capital gain of 60 percent ($60,000 ÷ $100,000) of the principal amount received. Therefore, in the year of the installment sale, Martin must report $6,000 of gain from the $10,000 received from Roger. For the next 8 years, he will have a gain of $6,750 (60% × $11,250).

Income Taxation of Installment Sales
- seller
  - three components of each installment payment
    - return of seller's basis: not taxable
    - taxable gain
    - interest: taxable as ordinary income
- buyer
  - interest paid may be deductible
  - principal payments constitute basis

---

1. This formula is simplified to demonstrate the gain recognition process without adding federal income tax complexity that is beyond the scope of this chapter.

Interest on Installment Sales

Interest paid by a buyer on an installment sale is potentially deductible for income tax purposes. Thus it might be to the benefit of the buyer to recharacterize some of the purchase payment as interest if the interest on the transaction is deductible.

On the other hand, the buyer may wish to minimize the interest element of the installment sale if the interest is nondeductible. Under these circumstances, it may be more advantageous for the buyer to characterize the payments as principal. The additional amount of principal will provide the buyer with a higher basis, which may be available for depreciation deductions at a later date. Certainly the interest rate might be a consideration in the negotiation process for the installment sale.

Unfortunately, the tax rules provide for target rates of interest on installment obligations under either the imputed interest rules (Code Sec. 483) or original-issue-discount (OID) rules (Code Secs. 1271–1274). These rules minimize the flexibility by specifying a rate of interest that is deemed to apply for installment obligations falling within these rules. As such, you must use the applicable federal rate (AFR) to figure out the amount of stated principal recharacterized as unstated interest or original issue discount if the original sales contract does not provide for adequately stated interest. Currently, these rates are near historical lows (about 3%), creating the opportunity to engage in intrafamily sales at favorable rates. You generally need to report installment sale interest as ordinary income. Although these rules are beyond the scope of this book, the estate planner should be aware that the appropriate tax advice should be sought for determining the rate of interest on an installment obligation.

Gift Tax Treatment of Installment Sales

There will be no gift tax ramifications for an installment sale if the transaction is a fair, arm's-length arrangement made for full and adequate consideration. When the parties to an installment sale are family members, the seller (usually the senior family member) may forgive an occasional future payment by the buyer (junior family member). Generally, the forgiven amount qualifies for the annual exclusion. Any amount forgiven in excess of the annual gift tax exclusion constitutes a taxable gift. Care, however, must be taken that the forgiveness of payments is not the result of a presale understanding between the parties to the sale. The appearance of a preunderstanding could result in an IRS challenge that the entire sale is a taxable gift to the purchaser.

Estate Tax Treatment of Installment Sales

An installment sale is a useful device in a family's financial and estate planning. The income tax advantages of installment reporting have been discussed above. In addition, the seller receives estate tax advantages. The transaction is particularly useful when a senior family member sells property to a junior family member. An installment sale for estate planning purposes is one of the methods of "freezing" the seller's estate and shifting the growth in family property to the next generation without the payment of transfer taxes on the growth element.

In our previous example, Tom Taxplanner sold a family vacation home to his daughter. To avoid any transfer tax consequences, the home was sold for an installment note equivalent to the fair market value of the home—$200,000. This transaction is one type of estate freeze. The maximum total value of the vacation home in Tom's estate will be $200,000. If Tom survives the 10-year installment period, no value of the home or the installment note will be included in his gross estate. Only the unconsumed amounts of the principal and interest payments received in the installment sale will remain in his estate. If Tom dies during the period of the installment term, the present value of the remaining installment payments will be included in his estate. In either event, none of the growth on the property following the sale to his daughter will be included in Tom's estate. The growth element has been transferred to his daughter free of transfer taxes. The transfer tax savings are substantial if rapidly appreciating property is transferred to the next generation in exchange for an installment note.

Installment Sales

- sale with one or more principal payments in year other than year of sale
- income tax treatment under installment accounting method
- seller's income tax gain recognized over each installment
- used to freeze gift/estate value and remove appreciation potential
- payments deferred for buyer
- estate inclusion of present value of remaining payments at seller's death

Self-Canceling Installment Notes (SCINs)

self-canceling installment note (SCIN)

One variation of an installment note is an intrafamily installment note that includes a self-cancellation provision at the seller's death. The **self-canceling installment note (SCIN)** is designed like an installment note and is subject to normal installment-sale reporting rules but is automatically canceled by the terms of the sale contract if the seller dies before all the remaining principal payments are made. Because the mortality risk is borne by the seller, the buyer has to pay a higher than fair market price for the business, usually with a higher principal amount, or greater interest rate in order to compensate the seller. The seller's age and health are also factors in the sale price. The older the seller is, the more the consideration is increased. The typical seller of a SCIN has a relatively large estate, is at least 70 years old, and has somewhat less than the best of health. The price is increased by the actuarial value of the contingency that not all installment payments will be made if the seller dies during the term period.

It is particularly important in a family transaction that the IRC valuation rules under Sec. 7520 be followed carefully. The SCIN should be equal in value to the property transferred or a gift is made to the buyer to the extent that full and adequate consideration is not received in the transaction. To rebut a presumption by the IRS that an intrafamily SCIN is a gift rather than a bona fide sale transaction, at the seller's death the buyer may need to show that when the transaction was created, there was an expectation of and intention to enforce repayments.

As previously stated, because the note cancels automatically at the death of the seller, there is nothing left to be included in the seller's estate for estate tax purposes if he or she dies during the term. When, however, the seller dies prior to the installment sale period and remaining payments are canceled, the entire amount of the remaining gain on the deceased seller's note must be included on the decedent's fiduciary (estate) income tax return (Form 1041). Although the gain constitutes income in respect of a decedent (IRD), no corresponding income tax deduction is available for the proportionate amount of estate tax because the note is canceled at death and therefore is not included in the decedent's gross estate. If the seller lives for his expected life span, there are drawbacks for both the seller and buyer. The seller not only does not reduce the size of his estate but also may end up having a larger estate because of the risk premium the buyer paid. The buyer, on the other hand, paid more (the premium) for the potential premature release from his or her payment obligation. Aside from the drawbacks, however, through the use of the SCIN, there is the potential to pass property to the next generation, producing a windfall to the junior family member buyer and a substantial reduction in the net proceeds received from the sale by the senior family member.

Both SCINs and installment sales are freezing techniques, which allow the grantor to engage in a transaction that freezes the value of an asset for purposes of determining the transfer tax base. Estate planning freezes have been a popular technique for high-net-worth clients. Another strategy is to engage in an installment sale to an intentionally defective grantor trust.

Self-Canceling Installment Note (SCIN)
- The buyer's remaining principal payments are canceled at the seller's death prior to the installment term period.
- The buyer pays an increased price for the seller's bearing the mortality risk.
- The seller has no estate inclusion of (canceled) remaining payments.

LO 21.2   Define private annuities and explain their tax treatment.

Private Annuities

private annuity

The private annuity is a variation of the installment sale with particular estate planning benefits. However, the rules and tax advantages are somewhat different. A **private annuity** is a sale
of property, such as a family business, in exchange for the buyer's agreement to make periodic
payments of a specified sum for the remainder of the seller's life. The amount of the payments
is based on the actuarial factors determined under the rules of Sec. 7520.

> ### EXAMPLE
>
> On her 65th birthday, Melanie transferred property valued at $800,000 to her daughter
> according to a private annuity agreement. Suppose the federal rate for valuing annuities
> is 1.4 percent. Based on a Single Life expectancy under government Table S, Melanie
> will receive $52,575.20 a year for life. (The term of the annuity based on Melanie's life
> expectancy is 20 years. For purposes of this example a zero growth rate of the property
> value was used.)

Because the value of the property being transferred equals the present value of the expected
and properly valued annuity, there are no gift tax consequences for the transaction. If the
private annuity is not properly valued and a gift element exists, the annuitant will be treated
as having a retained life interest at death under Sec. 2036, causing inclusion of the value of the
transferred asset in the decedent-annuitant's gross estate. The U.S. Treasury's actuarial tables,
the Alpha Tables, are used for the valuation of private annuities unless, at the time the private
annuity is executed, the annuitant had a 50 percent or less probability of living one year.

A major advantage of the private annuity is its estate tax treatment. In a regular installment
sale, some amount is included in the seller's estate if the seller dies holding the installment
note. In this case, the remaining payments are an enforceable obligation held by the estate and,
therefore, are a valuable asset to the estate. However, in a private annuity no further payments
are due when the seller dies. Thus, there is nothing to include in the estate of a seller who dies
holding a private annuity. For estate tax purposes the private annuity terminates at the seller-annuitant's death, and no amount of the annuity is included in the seller's estate. (Of course,
any annuity payments the seller received that are not consumed before the seller's death are
included in the seller's estate.)

EXAMPLE

If, in the prior example, Melanie dies 3 years after creating the private annuity, her daughter will have paid only $157,725.60 (3 x $52,575.20) for the property.

Any appreciation in the property after the exchange escapes gift or estate taxation. In other words, if the seller dies after one year, the property passes to the buyer (usually a family member) for only one annual payment. Keep in mind, however, that the buyer bears the risk of the seller's living beyond his or her life expectancy and the annual payments continuing until the seller's death.

Unlike the installment sale, no part of the purchase payments is deductible as interest by the buyer. Another distinguishing characteristic of the private annuity is the fact that the seller cannot take a security interest as collateral when receiving the private annuity. This lack of security can be disturbing to an annuitant who depends on the annuity payments for support. In other words the structure of a private annuity is based on an unsecured promise that the buyer of the property makes to the seller. If private annuities are secured, the seller annuitant could be deemed to have a Sec. 2036 retained life interest causing inclusion of the value of the entire property in the seller's estate. Another concern for the seller may be the buyer's premature death. This concern, however, could be resolved if the seller purchases life insurance on the buyer's life. Private annuity payments are generally limited to family situations where a senior family member is transferring property to the next generation.

In an effort to stymie perceived abusive tax strategies, proposed regulations issued by the IRS and Treasury Department drastically change the tax treatment for private-annuity transactions that take place after October 18, 2006 (Proposed Red-141901-05). In essence, the proposed regulations under Secs. 72 and 1001 of the Internal Revenue Code end the capital-gain-tax deferral previously permitted for private-annuity trusts. Under prior law concerning private-annuity arrangements, sellers exchanged appreciated assets for fixed annuity payments. The transaction allowed the seller's capital gain to be spread out over numerous years because capital gain was taxed on the annuity payments as they came out of the trust. This treatment avoided paying capital gain up front as is required when a seller sells an asset outright instead of exchanging it for a private annuity. After October 18, 2006, a seller's capital gain is taxable at the time of the transaction, rather than over the seller's lifetime. The effect of the new rules is that for income tax purposes, the transferor is treated as having sold the property for cash and then using the cash to purchase an annuity contract. Therefore, the annuitant-seller is treated as having realized an amount equal to the contract's fair market value according to the Sec. 7520 actuarial tables used to compute the present value of annuities. In other words, the entire amount of the annuitant-seller's gain or loss, regardless of the annuitant-seller's accounting method, is recognized on the date of the exchange because sellers are no longer permitted to defer recognition of gain with private-annuity arrangements. There are some limited exceptions and the proposed regulations do not apply to private-annuity arrangements created prior to October 19, 2006. Unfortunately, in addition to tax-driven private annuities, the new rules also affect transactions that were created purely for nontax reasons.

Private Annuity Summary

- seller's (senior family member) sale of property (family business) to buyer (junior family member)
  - appreciation out of estate
  - cash flow to annuitant-seller
  - seller's premature death: estate inclusion of only unconsumed payments
- buyer's unsecured agreement to pay seller periodic specified amounts for seller's life
  - no portion of payments deductible to buyer
  - termination of payments at seller's death
- risks
  - seller's longevity: buyer pays more than property value
  - buyer unable to make payments
  - buyer's premature death
  - inaccurate valuation at time of creation results in inclusion in annuitant-seller's estate

As a result of the proposed regulations, many practitioners believe private annuities will decline in popularity or, worse, will no longer be a useful planning device because few individuals will want to pay the full capital gain at the onset of the transaction. Some advisors, however, have determined that private annuities may still be useful in estate plans after calculations and comparisons of potential estate tax savings and capital gain costs are made. In addition, the proposed regulations are relevant primarily in situations where significantly appreciated assets are exchanged for an annuity. Private annuities could still be useful in cases involving exchanges of assets having minimal or no appreciation as the amount of taxable gain will also be insignificant or nil. These proposals have not yet been finalized.

Planning Point: Private annuities can be especially useful when a client: for health reasons, does not expect to survive his or her life expectancy term; needs a steady flow of cash; can depend on the purchaser to make timely payments; wishes to save estate taxes; and has a desire to pass specific assets to certain individuals or retain those assets within the family unit.

LO 21.3   Describe the gift and estate tax treatment of grantor-retained annuity trusts and grantor-retained unitrusts.

ESTATE FREEZES THROUGH USE OF FAMILY TRUSTS

Irrevocable trusts provide an excellent opportunity for a wealthy individual to reduce total transfer tax. Property transferred to an irrevocable trust will be treated as a current gift for gift tax purposes. However, the gift tax annual exclusion, the GSTT annual exclusion, the basic credit amount against estate or gift taxes, and the GSTT exemption may be used to reduce the actual current gift or GSTT liability to zero.

The estate tax treatment of the transfer to the irrevocable trust depends on the circumstances with respect to the terms and administration of the trust. Recalling the Sec. 2702 rules discussed previously, note that transfers with retained rights for the donor may cause serious estate or gift tax consequences for the donor. For example, the wrong retained rights could cause the entire property to be treated as a taxable gift. A retained right that does not end before the grantor's death will cause all, or a portion of, the trust property to be included in the donor's gross estate even if the transfers are treated as current gifts for gift tax purposes.

These estate tax rules are very important for designing a successful trust freeze. The grantor quite often would like to retain some use of the donated property. First, this gives the grantor the opportunity to draw on the trust income or principal to receive income payments during retirement, for instance. In addition, the retained rights held by the grantor may have value for gift tax purposes that can be used to offset the gift tax cost of transferring the property to the trust. The subtraction method of valuation permits retained rights with "value" to reduce the gift tax cost of transfers subject to grantor-held retained rights.

Grantor-Retained Annuity Trust or Unitrust Freezes

grantor-retained annuity (GRAT)

Two examples of retained rights (qualified interests) that are treated as having value for gift tax purposes are the **grantor-retained annuity trust (GRAT)** and *grantor-retained unitrust (GRUT)*. A GRAT is an irrevocable trust in which the grantor retains the right to receive fixed amounts payable at least annually for life (or the joint lives of the grantor and others) or for a term of years. A GRAT is actuarially similar to a charitable remainder annuity trust (CRAT). The GRAT payments to the grantor are subject to income taxation. Thus, the grantor can gift property to a trust and retain a fixed annuity for life or for a period of years. A fixed annuity is a stated annual dollar amount or a stated percentage of the initial value of the trust property. At the end of the life interest or term, the remaining trust corpus is paid to the remainderperson(s). After the initial gift to the trust, no additions are permitted.

Grantor-Retained Annuity Trust (GRAT)

The grantor has the right for life or a term of years to receive at least annually a stated dollar amount or stated percentage of the initial value of property transferred to an irrevocable trust.

EXAMPLE

Maxwell contributes $1.3 million in securities to an irrevocable trust. He retains the right to receive $80,000 per year from the trust for the next 10 years. At the end of 10 years, the trust will terminate and the remainder will be paid in equal shares to his grandchildren. The retained interest is a qualified annuity interest and will be given full actuarial value under the Sec. 7520 valuation rules. Thus the value of the gift is equal to $1.3 million minus the value of a 10-year $80,000 annual annuity.

grantor-retained unitrust (GRUT)

A **grantor-retained unitrust (GRUT)** is an irrevocable trust in which the grantor retains the right to receive amounts payable, which are a fixed percentage of the trust's assets (as valued each year), at least annually for life (or the joint lives of the grantor and others) or for a term of years. A GRUT is actuarially similar to a charitable remainder unitrust (CRUT). Thus, the grantor retains a variable annuity and the annual payout is based on the value that the trust grows (or contracts) to each year. The trust payments to the grantor are subject to income taxation. The term of the trust may be based on the life of the annuitant or a specified term of years. At the end of the term of the trust, all remaining trust assets pass to the designated remainderpersons. The gift tax value of the GRUT may be subtracted from the value of the property transferred to the trust to determine the gift tax value of the remainder interest. In contrast to the rules for a GRAT, the grantor may make additional gifts to a GRUT.

EXAMPLE

Assume the same facts as the previous example. However, Maxwell instead retains the right to receive payments equal to 7 percent of the trust based on its current value each year. The retained interest is a qualified unitrust interest and will be given full actuarial value under the Sec. 7520 valuation rules. Thus the value of the gift is equal to $1.3 million minus the value of a 10-year unitrust interest.

Grantor-Retained Unitrust (GRUT)

The grantor has the right for life or a term of years to receive at least annually amounts that are a fixed percentage of an irrevocable trust's assets (as valued annually).

Gift Tax Treatment of the GRAT or GRUT

The irrevocable transfer of the remainder interest in the GRAT or GRUT is a current gift for gift tax purposes. Because the gift provides a future interest to the donees, the gift does not qualify for the annual exclusion. However, the gift is discounted from the full fair market value of the corpus by subtracting the value of the grantor's retained interest valued under the Sec. 7520 rules. This discounted gift can be sheltered by the grantor's basic credit amount. Any retained trust interest other than a GRAT or a GRUT is generally valued at zero for gift tax purposes and the grantor will be treated as having gifted the entire remainder with no discounting for other retained rights.

EXAMPLE

Suppose Tom Taxplanner rents out his vacation home, valued at $200,000. If he transfers the home to a GRAT and retains a $12,000 (assume this is the actual net rental amount) annuity for 10 years, while gifting the remainder to Julia, he will be able to value the gift by subtracting the value of the annuity from the full value of the property. Assuming the Sec. 7520 monthly rate is 1.4 percent, the value of the retained annuity is $111,254.40. Thus the taxable value of the gift is $88,745.60 ($200,000 less $111,254.40).

Estate Tax Treatment of the GRAT or GRUT

If the grantor survives the retained interest term in a qualified GRAT or GRUT, Sec. 2036 does not apply and the corpus, including any posttransfer appreciation, is excluded from the gross estate of the grantor. In other words, a growing property interest can be transferred to family heirs for a significantly discounted transfer tax cost.

The estate tax benefits are reduced, however, if the grantor fails to survive the term. The amount included is the amount of principal of the trust that would be required under actuarial valuation principles to produce the annuity or unitrust payout. The upper limit on the inclusion is the actual amount of principal at the time of death. In many circumstances, the includible amount may be less than the entire trust principal. The amount includible is based on the annuity or unitrust amount and the Sec. 7520 discount rate at the time of the grantor's premature death. Presumably, the Sec. 7520 rate 6 months after the grantor's death can be used if the alternative valuation date is selected. In other words, the GRAT and GRUT could result in transfer tax savings even if the grantor does not survive the retained-interest term. Be aware, however, that the IRS has ruled privately that the full GRAT principal is includible in the gross estate of an annuitant who dies prior to the termination of a GRAT.

Planning Point: Because a major objective of a GRAT or GRUT is an estate freeze and the reduction of the grantor's estate, the more an asset is expected to appreciate after the transfer, the better it is as a trust investment. Securities and real estate are typically excellent assets to consider. Closely held corporate stock may be a less advisable investment because the GRAT or GRUT trustee would need to receive taxable dividends to make payments to the annuitant.

LO 21.4   **Describe the design considerations and transfer tax treatment of a qualified personal residence trust.**

QUALIFIED PERSONAL RESIDENCE TRUSTS

qualified personal residence trust (QPRT)

A **qualified personal residence trust (QPRT)** is specifically excepted from the treatment of the anti-estate-freeze rules. By excepting the personal residence, Congress intended that a transfer of a personal residence to a trust can provide a retained interest to the grantor that is not limited to the GRAT or GRUT. The regulations on QPRTs make it clear that the Treasury Department intended to limit the corpus of these trusts to personal residences and other *de minimis* property.

In the typical QPRT, the grantor (usually a senior family member) retains the use of the home for a specified number of years. One or more remainder beneficiaries receive the personal residence at the termination of the trust. The longer the term of the grantor's retained interest in the QPRT, the lower the value of the gift to the remainderperson. To determine the value of the gift to the remainderperson, the value of the grantor's retained interest (as measured according to the Sec. 7520 valuation rules) is subtracted from the value of the residence placed in the trust. Thus, the gift tax value of the transfer is frozen at the present value of the remainder interest at the time of the transfer to the QPRT, since Sec. 2702 does not apply.

The personal residence is defined as the grantor's principal residence and a second home. The second home must be used for personal use by the grantor the greater of 14 days or 10 percent of the time the property is rented. Consequently, a vacation home that is both rented and used by the grantor can be used in the personal residence trust.

The QPRT may include a dwelling used as (1) the principal place of the taxpayer's business or (2) a place where the taxpayer sees customers, clients, and patients in the ordinary course of business. Thus, a personal residence trust could include a home with a qualified home office for income tax purposes as well as a vacation home rented part of the year.

A QPRT may also include appurtenant structures used for residential purposes and adjacent land not in excess of that which is reasonably appropriate for residential purposes (taking into account the residence's size and location). The personal residence subject to a mortgage can be contributed to a QPRT. However, the regulations will not permit corpus to include any personal property (for example, household furnishings). Therefore, the grantor continues to own household furnishings individually. To pay the essential expenses of the personal residence trust, the trustee may hold cash that is limited in the amounts and purposes for which it may be used. A taxpayer is limited to being a term holder in only two QPRTs at any point in time.

The regulations add some flexibility and permit the trustee to sell the residence held by the personal residence trust, but require that the trustee do one of the following or the gift tax advantages will be lost:

- Replace the residence with another qualifying residence within 2 years.

- Distribute the cash to the term holder.

- Convert the QPRT to a qualified grantor-retained annuity trust (GRAT).

The personal residence trust is a valuable transfer tax saving tool, but the trust must be drafted and administered with extreme care. The penalty for a drafting error is severe, because the full Sec. 7520 value of the grantor's retained interest will be treated as an additional gift at the time the IRS discovers the fact that the trust fails to qualify.

QPRT Gift Tax Consequences

The QPRT is irrevocable, and a completed gift of the remainder interest is made for tax purposes when the grantor establishes the trust. The value of the property for gift tax purposes is reduced by the present value of the retained-income interest. This is appropriate enough, although the grantor retains only the *use* of the corpus and not a right to cash payments. The taxable gift at the time of the establishment of the QPRT is merely the present value of the remainder interest. This taxable gift constitutes a future-interest gift that does not qualify for the gift tax annual exclusion. Frequently, the grantor will have his or her basic credit amount available to shelter some or all of the transfer from gift tax.

The purpose of the QPRT is to reduce the overall transfer tax costs of passing the grantor's assets to his or her beneficiaries. Therefore, the key to the technique is establishing the highest value possible for the grantor's retained-income interest. This will result in a low present value for the remainder interest, and therefore the total amount subject to gift tax can be minimized.

Estate Tax Consequences

If the Grantor Survives the Retained-Interest Term

If the QPRT is properly designed, none of the property will be in the grantor's estate if the grantor survives the term period. If, however, the grantor survives the term of the retained interest and no trust property is included in the gross estate, the basis step up for the personal residence at the grantor's death is not available.

If the Grantor Dies During the Retained-Interest Term

The transfer tax savings available through the use of a QPRT are realized only if the grantor survives the term of the retained-income interest. You will recall that a transfer with a retained interest that does not end before the transferor's death is included in the gross estate under Sec. 2036(a). Therefore, the full value of the trust property, not just the value of the remaining term, will return to the grantor's estate if the grantor fails to survive the term. However, the basic credit amount used on the original transfer, plus any gift tax actually paid, is allowed as a credit against the estate tax due. Furthermore, the benefit of the income tax basis step up is available because the assets are included in the gross estate.

Because the planning value of the QPRT is eliminated if the grantor does not survive the retained-interest term, it is advisable to select a term that the grantor is likely to survive. If the term of the QPRT must be kept short due to the health or age of the grantor, the value of the remainder interest increases, which in turn reduces the potential transfer tax savings of the technique. However, from a federal tax viewpoint, the downside risk of attempting a QPRT is small, since it leaves the grantor's estate with no greater tax liability than it would have had if nothing had been done.

Income Tax Consequences

A QPRT is a grantor trust for income tax purposes during the retained-interest term. Therefore, the grantor bears all of the income tax consequences during the term of the trust. If there is income from the property (for example, if the home is rented during part of the year), the grantor is taxed on the income. If deductible expenses are incurred, the expenses are also passed through to the grantor.

Effect of a Mortgage

A mortgage on the property may create some complicated income and gift tax issues. For instance, the transfer of property with a mortgage greater than the transferor's adjusted basis usually triggers gain for income tax purposes. However, because the QPRT is a grantor trust, the gain is not recognized by the grantor until the retained-interest term ends. Furthermore, depending on who is responsible for the mortgage expenses under state law, if the grantor makes additions of cash to pay mortgage principal and interest, such additions could be treated as further gifts to the remainderpersons. This occurs when the remainderpersons-beneficiaries are responsible for the expenses but the grantor pays them. Tax counsel should be sought prior to gifting mortgaged property to a QPRT.

LO 21.5   Describe the basic concept of family limited partnerships and limited liability companies.

Family Limited Partnerships and Limited Liability Companies

family limited partnerships

Family limited partnerships, usually referred to as FLPs, are another popular estate planning technique used to transfer wealth from senior to junior generations. With an FLP, generally one or more members of the older generation, usually one or both parents, transfer cash or property to a newly created limited partnership according to a state's limited partnership act in exchange for general and limited partnership ownership interests. Following this original exchange, a portion or all of the limited partnership interests are then transferred by gifts or sales to members of the younger generation(s). In most situations, the basic credit amounts must be used; gift tax liability may be generated by the transfers since annual exclusions alone are usually insufficient to accomplish the transfers tax free. Values of the partnership and partnership interests, of course, should be established by appropriate appraisals. Partnership agreements generally provide for a partnership term of 50 years. However, provisions in the agreement usually state that after one or both of the general partners die, the limited partners may liquidate the partnership.

By doing so, the senior generation transferor removes the value of the limited partnership interests and future appreciation with respect to those interests from his or her taxable estate while still retaining all managerial control over the FLP and its assets via continued ownership of the general partnership interest. For instance, the parent general partner would be able to determine if and when income distributions are made to the partners and whether or not to reinvest income in the entity. The limited partners are not involved in actual business management.

Additional leverage for the transfer of wealth between generations is provided by significant discounts pertaining to the value of the limited partnership interests. In some cases, the discounts can range between 20–50 percent. However, make sure that any discount or appraisal is legitimate as the IRS closely watches these transactions of late. These discounts are based on the following:

- a lack of marketability of a privately owned partnership interest
- a lack of control by the limited partner(s) over partnership property and distributions
- limitations on the limited partner's ability to sell his or her partnership interests, manage partnership matters, force liquidation, and/or receive repayment of his or her capital account

When the senior transferor/family member dies, only the value, often discounted, of the retained partnership interest(s) is typically included in his or her estate. Clearly, transfer tax benefits can be achieved through the use of FLPs. With respect to income taxation, family partnerships generally are taxable under normal partnership tax rules if the family partnership rules of Sec. 2704 are followed. Partnership income is passed to partners as distributive shares of income as determined by the partnership agreement. There may also be opportunities, subject to limitations, to shift income to junior generations. Therefore, significant income tax savings may be achieved if the senior family member is in a top income tax bracket and the junior limited partner is in a low one. One of the best benefits of a family limited partnership is the ability to transfer wealth to family members without giving up control of the family business. This allows the older generation to watch the younger generation in action before giving up full control.

Another advantage of FLPs is the potential for asset protection. It is very difficult for the creditors of limited partners to reach assets inside the FLP. Although property cannot avoid the reach of creditors when transfers occur during impending insolvency of a transferor, the assets can no longer be attached by the transferor's personal creditors without more complex legal efforts, if at all, after a sufficient time period determined by state law has elapsed. FLPs also may afford protection against a younger family member's divorce because the partnership interest is established as the limited partner's separate property. Additionally, gifts to one community spouse are not subject to division under the community-property laws in community states.

A disadvantage of transferring limited partnership interests with FLPs is the carryover basis rules. If the assets have a low tax basis, capital gain will be increased if and when the business is sold. Even if capital gain does result, however, it may still be less than transfer taxation without formation of the FLP.

Over the last few years there has been an increase in litigation in this area by the IRS. Previously, most IRS litigation focused on disallowance of discounts for intrafamily transfers. Currently, however, the IRS is concentrating on Sec. 2036 arguments, specifically the degree to which a transferor retained lifetime control and enjoyment of partnership assets. In spite of greater IRS scrutiny, however, with careful planning and properly drafted governing instruments, FLPs are and should continue to be a valuable device for the tax-efficient transfer of wealth to younger family members.

Family limited liability companies (FLLCs) are similar to FLPs for estate planning purposes and are often used for discounted gifts in lieu of an FLP. A primary difference between FLLCs and FLPs is that FLLCs are created with some corporate characteristics. FLLCs allow business owners, called members, to have the limited liability that corporations enjoy and the pass-through tax benefits associated with partnerships. With limited liability, a member is liable only for negligence in which he or she participated. Other members avoid liability with respect to the particular matter. Consequently, if one member is responsible for an incident in which others suffer injuries, only that member and the business are liable. With FLPs a general partner is exposed to unlimited personal liability.

LO 21.6   Explain what is meant by a Sec. 303 redemption.

IRC SEC. 303 REDEMPTION

Sec. 303 redemption

The purpose of Sec. 303 is to reduce the tax impact on the estates of decedents who owned incorporated businesses. This Code section is an income tax provision rather than an estate tax Code section. An IRC **Sec. 303 redemption** allows a redemption of closely held stock for the purpose of paying funeral and administrative expenses and death taxes without the redemption being treated as a dividend. If the redemption qualifies, it is treated as a sale, and the gain is treated as capital gain if the decedent held the stock as a capital asset at the time of the sale.

Sec. 303 provides a means to have sufficient liquidity to pay death taxes and funeral and administrative costs of an estate without the stock or business interest being sold to persons who are not within the partnership or closely held business group. This is especially important when the stock or partnership interest is not readily marketable but liquidity is needed.

EXAMPLE

(Ignore basic exclusion amounts relevant to a particular year for this example.) At his death, Marvin owned 10,000 shares of Marvalus, his closely held business, which were included in his estate. Each share had an estate tax value of $90 at his death and an adjusted basis of $0. Marvin's estate is responsible for $400,000 in funeral costs, federal and state death taxes, and administration expenses. Several months after Marvin's death, when the value of the stock was $100 per share, the corporation redeemed 4,000 shares of Marvalus, Inc., for $100 per share. If this redemption qualifies for Sec. 303 treatment, the estate will have long-term gain of $40,000 due to the per-share gain of $10 from the date-of-death value. If the redemption does not qualify for Sec. 303 treatment (that is, capital-gain treatment), the estate will be treated as having received a dividend of $400,000 (4,000 shares x $100 a share). The $400,000 dividend will be taxed as ordinary income.

In order to qualify for capital-gain treatment under this section, the decedent's stock must represent more than 35 percent of the adjusted gross estate. Ownership of 20 percent or more of the stock of each of two or more corporations may be aggregated to satisfy this 35 percent test.

If any redemption is made more than 4 years after the decedent's death, capital-gains treatment is available only for the distribution that represents the lesser of: (1) the amount of the qualifying death taxes and funeral and administration expenses unpaid immediately before the distribution, or (2) the aggregate of these amounts paid within one year after the distribution.

This favorable tax treatment applies to the distribution by a corporation only to the extent that the interest of a shareholder is reduced directly or through a binding obligation to contribute to the payment of the estate's expenses or taxes. In other words, the party whose shares are redeemed must be the one who actually bears the burden of the estate and other death taxes, or funeral and administration expenses in an amount equal to the redeemed value of the stock. This rule can be illustrated by the following example. Assume a block of otherwise qualifying stock is left to a surviving spouse in a manner that qualifies for the marital deduction, and that the decedent's will provides that the marital bequest will bear no portion of taxes or administrative costs (a common provision). In this case, the stock left to the surviving spouse could not be redeemed under Sec. 303 even though in all other respects it qualified, because there is no liability on the marital bequest to pay death taxes or administrative costs.

It should be noted that if a redemption qualifies for capital-gains treatment under Sec. 303 or under other Code sections, an estate recognizes less or no taxable gain because the stock receives a new stepped-up basis. However, should a redemption not qualify for capital-gains treatment, it is treated as a dividend distribution, and the estate will recognize ordinary income on the full value of the stock on the applicable valuation date.

Sec. 303 Stock Redemption

- *Without* its being treated as a dividend with capital gain, it allows the redemption of stock up to the amount of
  - funeral costs
  - estate administration expenses
  - death taxes
- Redemption of stock is treated as an exchange.
- Decedent's stock has to represent more than 35% of the adjusted gross estate.

Planning Point: With proper advance planning, a closely held business that otherwise does not meet the greater than 35 percent test can be made to qualify for Sec. 303. For instance, by making lifetime gifts of nonbusiness property, the business owner can reduce his or her adjusted gross estate and thereby increase the percentage of the business included in the estate. When a gifting program, however, is implemented to increase the percentage of a business included in an estate, planners must be aware that the 3-year rule under Sec. 2035 pulls the value of gifts made within 3 years of the donor's death solely for the purpose of calculating qualification for certain favorable tax treatment Code sections such as Secs. 303 and 6166.

EXAMPLE

Mae died with an adjusted gross estate of $10 million and a business valued at $3.6 million that was included in her estate.

Based on these simple facts, Mae's estate meets the 35 percent test and qualifies for Sec. 303 (or Sec. 6166) treatment. Suppose, however, that a year and a half before her death Mae gave $500,000 to each of her two sons. Because the 3-year rule of Sec. 2035 requires the $1 million in gifts to be included in Mae's gross estate for purposes of determining Sec. 303 qualification, the business does not meet the 35 percent test (35 percent of $11 million [the amount of the adjusted gross estate when the two $500,000 gifts are added back in] adjusted gross estate requires that the business be valued in excess of $3.85 million).

LO 21.7   Describe other issues that arise during modern estate planning, such as providing equity, pet trust, and ethical issues.

Equity of Inheritance

There are many estate planning situations in which it is the estate owner's wish to equalize inheritances among children. A prime example is when an estate owner has brought some of his or her children into a family business and intends to give these children an ownership interest in the enterprise. The plan may be to pass the interest to these children either during his or her lifetime or after death. If there are other children in the family who have no contact with the business, however, the estate owner may wish to provide for them in some other way so that there is equality among the children. Life insurance in this context is appropriate.

EXAMPLE

Marcus is president and sole shareholder of Zipper-Do, Inc., a highly successful manu-facturer of snag-proof zippers. He has three adult children—two sons and one daughter. The daughter and one of the sons work for Marcus and would like to take over the busi-ness when Marcus retires. The other son, a musician, has no interest in this business.

Marcus arranges for the two employee-children to receive the business at his retirement or death. He also acquires life insurance on his life in an amount equal to the anticipated fair market value of Zipper-Do, Inc. that each employee-child will receive. Marcus pays the premiums, and the musician son is the designated beneficiary of the policy. Equity of inheritance has been achieved.

Pet Trusts

Under common law, a pet cannot be a beneficiary of a trust and the duration of a trust cannot be linked to a pet's life. In recent years, however, pet trust legislation has been promulgated in a majority of the states and Washington, D.C. Pet trust statutes enacted in these states recognize and enforce pet owners' wishes to provide for their pets upon the owner's death or inability to give care. In addition, a traditional legal trust, rather than a pet trust arrangement, may also be established for the care of pets. An advantage of traditional trusts is that they are enforceable in all states. They may be established during lifetime as a revocable living trust or under a will. If the trust is created in a will, the pet owner should be made aware that wills are subject to the delay of probate and are not useful when an owner becomes disabled or is otherwise unable to care for the pet. A trust or power of attorney can provide for pets immediately and therefore may prove to be an appropriate solution when there are concerns about the delay of having a will probated, illness, or incapacity.

A revocable living trust must be funded. The person who will provide future care for the animal is the trust beneficiary for the pet's life conditioned on the trustee's taking care of the pet. Clearly, the selection of a caretaker and successor caretaker is crucial to the premise of the arrangement. Once the pet dies, remaining trust corpus passes to the remainder beneficiaries. In establishing a trust for the benefit of pets, a planner needs to make certain that the docu-ment is valid and enforceable under relevant state law. Life insurance on the owner's life may be used to fund the costs of caring for the animal.

Ethical Dilemma

The ethical dilemmas presented in this text illustrate common scenarios that could present a financial or estate planner with an ethical predicament. The resolution of any dilemma, of course, depends on how one applies ethical codes, rules, and principles to the specific situation. The comments are meant to provide thought about these issues and not give a definitive resolution to them.

Beatrice Porter is an estate planning attorney who recently drafted an irrevocable life insurance trust for one of her clients. Beatrice has just become aware that when applying for a large life insurance policy, her client stated he was a non-smoker and avoided alcohol except for a minimal amount at social events. Beatrice knows that both of her client's statements could not be further from the truth.

- **What should Beatrice do?**

A Possible Resolution

The dilemma for Beatrice involves a conflict between her responsibility to represent her client's interests and her responsibility to the truth. As an attorney, she is obligated to refrain from knowingly perpetuating a fraud. Although Beatrice lacks actual knowledge of a misrepresentation, in this instance it could be argued that she has constructive knowledge. Beatrice could ask her client about his smoking and drinking, but if she challenges him, she could risk losing him as a client.

To resolve this dilemma, it is perhaps helpful for Beatrice to consider her responsibility to provide proper representation to her client. Aside from personal ramifications for her, if it is subsequently determined that her client submitted false information, it could invalidate the ILIT. Regardless of possible negative consequences to her, Beatrice cannot responsibly submit this paperwork or knowingly allow her client to submit it on his own. False representations, if found out, could jeopardize the very ILIT for which he is applying.

CHAPTER REVIEW

Key Terms and Concepts

installment sale
self-canceling installment note (SCIN)
private annuity
grantor-retained annuity (GRAT)

grantor-retained unitrust (GRUT)
qualified personal residence trust (QPRT)

Chapter 21: Review Questions

1. Identify the advantages of an installment sale from the standpoint of

    a. the seller

    b. the buyer [LO 21.1]

2. Suppose a parent (P) would like to sell a rental property to a child (C) for $100,000 payable in five annual installments beginning one year after settlement. If P's basis in the property is $25,000, calculate how each installment will be treated for income tax purposes by P when paid. [LO 21.1]

3. How can an installment sale be used as an estate-freezing technique? [LO 21.1]

4. What is the gift tax treatment of an installment sale? [LO 21.1]

5. Under what circumstances might a self-canceling installment note (SCIN) be useful for estate planning purposes? [LO 21.1]

6. Explain why with a SCIN the buyer pays more than the fair market value for the property subject to the sale. [LO 21.1]

7. What is a private annuity? [LO 21.2]

8. What are the transfer tax implications if a private annuity is not properly valued? [LO 21.2]

9. GRATs and GRUTs are retained trust interests having value that, in turn, reduces the gift tax cost of transferring a remainder interest in trust. What are the permissible payment forms for GRATs and GRUTs? [LO 21.3]

10. In general, how are GRATs and GRUTs treated for gift and estate tax purposes? [LO 21.3]

11. Explain the design and transfer tax considerations of a qualified personal residence trust (QPRT). [LO 21.4]

12. What type of property can be placed in a QPRT if a retained interest in such trust by the grantor will be valued at greater than zero for gift tax purposes? [LO 21.4]

13. Explain the gift tax consequences when a grantor transfers a personal residence to an irrevocable trust and retains a term interest with the remainder to his or her children. [LO 21.4]

14. Explain the type of person that would be interested in a family limited partnership. [LO 21.5]

15. Explain a Sec. 303 stock redemption and when it can be used. [LO 21.6]

16. How does the planner establish a trust for the benefit of pets? [LO 21.7]

Chapter 21: Review Answers

1. a. For a seller, an installment sale of property can provide both income tax and estate tax benefits. If installment reporting is available, the gain on the sale of property in exchange for an installment note will be delayed and recognized gradually over the installment period. Thus it is possible to sell highly appreciated property without immediate recognition of the full taxable gain. On the other hand, the ability to elect out of installment reporting provides the taxpayer with the possibility of recognizing all taxable gain immediately. For example, a seller may elect to recognize all gain at the time of an installment sale in a year when the taxpayer either has little other income or shows a loss for income tax purposes. Reporting the gain immediately on an installment sale could prevent the seller from wasting other deductions and tax benefits. The flexibility of an installment sale's reporting rules permits a seller to defer gain recognition and, to some degree, plan the timing of gain recognition on the sale of property.

The installment sale also provides estate tax saving possibilities for the seller. The installment sale, a particularly useful device for family estate planning, may be used when a senior family member wishes to pass property on to a successor in the family.

　　b. From the buyer's standpoint, the installment sale permits the buyer to defer some or all of the principal payments on the sale. This is particularly important for buyers without the funds for the entire purchase price.

Interest paid by a buyer on an installment sale is potentially deductible for income tax purposes. Thus it might be to the benefit of the buyer to recharacterize some of the purchase payment as interest if the interest on the transaction is deductible.

On the other hand, the buyer may wish to minimize the interest element of the installment sale if the interest is nondeductible. Under these circumstances, it may be more advantageous for the buyer to characterize the payments as principal. The additional amount of principal will provide the buyer with a higher basis, which may be available for depreciation deductions at a later date. Certainly, the interest rate might be a consideration in the negotiation process for the installment sale.

2. The taxable amount of each installment is calculated as follows:

$$\text{amount of payment} \times (\text{gross profit} \div \text{total contract price})$$

Thus, 3/4 (75,000 ÷ 100,000) of each payment will be reported as gain in the year received.

year 1	¾	×	20,000	=	15,000 gain reported
year 2	¾	×	20,000	=	15,000 gain reported
year 3	¾	×	20,000	=	15,000 gain reported
year 4	¾	×	20,000	=	15,000 gain reported
year 5	¾	×	20,000	=	15,000 gain reported

There will also be an interest component attributed to the deferred installments, but these facts and the material in the text do not provide enough information to calculate the interest required.

3. For estate planning purposes, an installment sale is one method of "freezing" the seller's estate and shifting the appreciation potential to a junior family member. If performed properly, and if the installment note is equal to the fair market value of the property at the time of the sale, the installment sale shifts the postsale appreciation to the junior family member without any transfer taxes being payable on the transferred property.

4. If the arrangement is a fair, bona fide, arm's-length sale made for fair market value, there will be no gift tax consequences.

5. Because a SCIN cancels automatically at the seller's death, there is nothing left to be included in the seller's estate if he or she dies during the term. Through the use of the SCIN, a senior family member can transfer property to the next generation, which may result in a substantially discounted purchase price for the junior family-member purchaser and the receipt of significantly less in net proceeds for the senior family member-seller. This arrangement may remove appreciated property from the seller's estate and reduce the seller's transfer taxes.

6. The buyer of a SCIN has to pay a price in excess of the fair market value for the sale property because the risk of a premature death and loss of remaining installment payments is borne by the seller.

7. A private annuity is a sale of property, such as a family business, in exchange for the buyer's agreement to make periodic payments of a specified sum for the remainder of the seller's life. In a private annuity, no further payments are due when the seller dies. Thus, there is nothing to include in the estate of a seller who dies holding a private annuity. For estate tax purposes, the private annuity terminates at the seller-annuitant's death and no amount of the annuity is included in the seller's estate. (Of course, any annuity payments received by the seller that are not consumed before the seller's death are included in the seller's estate.) Any appreciation in the property after the exchange escapes gift or estate taxation.

8. If a private annuity is not properly valued and a gift is present, the seller-annuitant will have inclusion of the property in his or her gross estate under the retained life interest rules of Sec. 2036.

9. A GRAT is an irrevocable trust in which the grantor retains the right to receive fixed amounts payable at least annually from the trust. Thus, the grantor can gift property to a trust and retain a fixed annuity for life or for a period of years. A fixed annuity is a stated annual dollar amount or a stated percentage of the initial value of the trust property.

   A GRUT is an irrevocable trust in which the grantor retains the right to receive amounts payable at least annually that are a fixed percentage of the trust's assets as valued annually. Thus, the grantor retains a variable annuity and the annual payout is based on the value that the trust grows (or contracts) to each year.

10. The irrevocable transfer of the remainder interest in the GRAT or GRUT is a current gift for gift tax purposes. Since the gift provides a future interest to the donees, the gift does not qualify for the annual exclusion. However, the gift is discounted from the

full fair market value of the corpus by subtracting the value of the grantor's retained interest valued under the Sec. 7520 rules.

If the grantor survives the retained-interest term in a qualified GRAT or GRUT, Sec. 2036 does not apply and the corpus, including any posttransfer appreciation, is excluded from the gross estate of the grantor.

The estate tax benefits are reduced, however, if the grantor fails to survive the term. The amount included is the amount of principal of the trust that would be required under actuarial valuation principles to produce the annuity or unitrust payout. The upper limit on the inclusion is the actual amount of principal at the time of death. In many circumstances, the includible amount may be less than the entire trust principal. The amount includible is based on the annuity or unitrust amount and the Sec. 7520 discount rate at the time of the grantor's premature death.

11. Congress intended that a transfer of a personal residence to a trust can provide a retained interest to the grantor that is not limited to the GRAT or GRUT. The regulations on QPRTs make it clear that the Treasury Department intended to limit the corpus of these trusts to personal residences and other *de minimis* property.

    In the typical QPRT, the grantor (usually a senior family member) retains the use of the home for a specified number of years. One or more remainder beneficiaries receive the personal residence at the termination of the trust. The longer the term of the grantor's retained interest in the QPRT, the lower the value of the gift to the remainderperson. To determine the value of the gift to the remainderperson, the value of the grantor's retained interest (as measured according to the Sec. 7520 valuation rules) is subtracted from the value of the residence placed in the trust. Thus, the gift tax value of the transfer is frozen at the present value of the remainder interest at the time of the transfer to the QPRT since Sec. 2702 does not apply.

12. The QPRT may include a dwelling used as (1) the principal place of the taxpayer's business or (2) a place where the taxpayer sees customers, clients, and patients in the ordinary course of business. Thus, a personal residence trust could include a home with a qualified home office for income tax purposes as well as a vacation home that is rented part of the year.

    A QPRT may also include appurtenant structures used for residential purposes and adjacent land not in excess of that which is reasonably appropriate for residential purposes. The personal residence subject to a mortgage can be contributed to a QPRT. However, the regulations will not permit corpus to include any personal property (for example, household furnishings). Therefore, the grantor continues to own household furnishings individually. To pay the essential expenses of the personal residence trust, the trustee may hold cash that is limited in the amounts and purposes for which it may be used.

13. The QPRT is irrevocable, and a completed gift of the remainder is made for tax purposes when the grantor establishes the trust. The value of the property for gift tax purposes is reduced by the present value of the retained-income interest. This is true even though the grantor retains only the use of the corpus. The taxable gift at the time of the establishment of the QPRT is merely the present value of the remainder interest. This taxable gift constitutes a future-interest gift that does not qualify for the federal gift tax annual exclusion.

14. The person that would be interested in a family limited partnership would be facing some type of estate or gift tax. Additionally, he would have a valuable small business or investment property that he wants to transfer to his heirs. However, the person would also have some reservations about outright transferring the property as he still wants to control the business for the near future. Additionally, the person might be concerned about protecting assets from his children's creditors but at the same time not overly concerned about his own personal liability. If he was concerned about his own personal liability, a FLLC would be more beneficial than remaining a general partner of a FLP.

15. The purpose of Sec. 303 is to reduce the tax impact and increase liquidity for the estates of decedents who owned incorporated businesses. This Code section is an income tax provision rather than an estate tax Code section. A Sec. 303 redemption allows a redemption of closely held stock for the purpose of paying the funeral and administrative expenses and death taxes without the redemption being treated as a dividend (and therefore taxed as ordinary income). If the redemption qualifies, it is treated as a sale, and the gain is treated as a capital gain (and therefore, taxed at capital gains rates). Because capital gains tax rates are generally lower than the related income tax rates, the estate realizes tax savings. In addition, because the stock receives step-up basis treatment at the decedent's death, most or all capital gains will be eliminated and the estate may pay little to no capital gains tax on the redemption.

In addition to tax savings, Sec. 303 redemptions help estates by providing a means to generate liquidity to pay the death taxes and administrative costs of an estate, and helps avoid the risk that stock may pass to beneficiaries or third party purchasers who may upset the existing harmony of the corporation.

16. In establishing a trust for the benefit of pets, a planner needs to make certain that the document is valid and enforceable under relevant state law. Life insurance on the owner's life may be used to fund the costs of caring for the animal.

Chapter 22:

The Role of Life Insurance in Estate Planning

Learning Objectives

An understanding of the material in this chapter should enable the student to do the following:

LO 22.1   **Explain why life insurance can be an important asset in estate planning.**

LO 22.2   **Identify basic types of life insurance products.**

LO 22.3   **Explain in general the estate taxation of life insurance and how an irrevocable life insurance trust can be designed to provide estate liquidity without adding to the estate tax burden.**

LO 22.4   **Describe the structure, tax implications, and strategies for using Irrevocable Life Insurance trusts (ILITs).**

LO 22.5   **Explain the gift tax treatment of life insurance polices.**

LO 22.6   **Describe the practical uses for life insurance in estate planning.**

Planning with Life Insurance

LO 22.1   **Explain why life insurance can be an important asset in estate planning.**

Life insurance planning is an essential component of the estate planning process for wealthy individuals. For individuals of modest wealth, life insurance coverage may be the most significant asset they leave to their heirs. Remember that life insurance is an intangible property item, as stated earlier in the text. This means that the life insurance contract, while representative of the right, is really just a representation of your property rights. When developing wills or trusts you must be sure to address the intangible property, including life insurance.

Several unique aspects of life insurance make the product a vital asset in the estate planning process. For instance, some favorable tax rules apply only to life insurance; life insurance enjoys a significant appreciation in value upon the death of the insured; life insurance provides benefits when estate taxes and other settlement costs have to be paid and the income or other services of the insured must be replaced. Furthermore, life insurance products offer a substantial degree of flexibility in the estate planning process.

The goal of life insurance in the estate plan depends on many factors specific to the estate owner. Life insurance goals in general can be divided into two categories: estate enhancement, and estate liquidity.

Clients generally have estate enhancement as the primary goal for their life insurance coverage because they are either too young or have otherwise failed to accumulate sufficient wealth to provide for their heirs in the event of their passing. Life insurance is an excellent device to replace the financial loss created by premature death. Life insurance should be coordinated with your client's overall estate, retirement, and financial plan. The value of the life insurance policy should account for lost wages and other lost income sources like Social Security or a pension. Life insurance for non-working individuals should account for the value of lost services and income sources that would need to be replaced, such as household services and lost Social Security benefits. Life insurance can also be a way to generate increased wealth due to the potentially large death benefit and the tax-free and tax-deferred internal growth of most policies. In some cases, life insurance can also be used as an effective investment option inside of a retirement plan. However, life insurance as an investment asset inside of a 401(k) plan or other ERISA plan is subject to a certain amount of current taxation for the purse cost of insurance coverage. However, most people get to recover the taxes paid as cost basis later on when the policy is distributed.

For older clients or clients with large estates, estate liquidity planning is the primary goal of life insurance coverage. Even for estates that may not be subject to federal estate/gift taxes or generation skipping transfer tax, liquidity is needed for administrative costs, executor fees, fees for specialized services such as attorney and CPA services, and probate costs. If older estate owners have accumulated enough wealth and/or have an adequate retirement plan, the need for estate enhancement from life insurance is diminished in importance relative to their estate liquidity needs. For example, life insurance is appropriate for liquidity concerns when federal, state, and generation-skipping transfer taxes are significant and also when estates contain illiquid assets such as closely held businesses.

Life insurance can be used to pay for a variety of estate costs, such as:

1. federal estate taxes

2. state estate taxes

3. home mortgages

4. college expenses

5. long-term care premiums or expenses

6. end of life medical expenditures

7. attorney or other administrative estate costs

8. funeral costs

9. other estate expenses

Life insurance is a particularly important tool to generate liquidity in estates which contain small businesses or substantial real estate, which are considered illiquid assets. These assets typically make up a large percentage of the estate value, but cannot be easily converted to cash, which causes financial strain on the estate.

LIFE INSURANCE PRODUCTS

LO 22.2   Identify basic types of life insurance products.

Today, there are many types of life insurance products. A general knowledge of the types of products is necessary to understand the uses of the products in the estate plan. Clearly, the services of a competent life underwriter are essential to the estate planning process because the selection of the most appropriate product in a particular estate planning case will maximize the efficiency of an entire financial plan. For the purposes of this course, the types of life insurance products are separated into single life policies and multiple life policies.

Single Life Coverage

Term Life

Term life insurance provides coverage for a finite period of time expressed as a number of years such as one, 5, or 10. The specified face amount of the policy will be paid to a designated beneficiary if the insured dies during that time period. If the insured survives the time period, the policy expires and the coverage terminates. If the coverage needs are longer than the specific term, a renewability provision may be considered. This provision allows the insured to renew without providing new evidence of insurability.

Conversion privileges that permit the insured to change a term policy for a permanent life policy without giving evidence of insurability are often included with term insurance policies. Term insurance is generally appropriate for estate planning uses only if the coverage need is temporary.

Permanent Life Insurance

Permanent insurance is coverage that is designed to exist for the entire life of an insured. A distinguishing characteristic of permanent insurance is the existence of a cash value or accumulation buildup within the policy. Permanent coverage can be designed either on a fixed-price premium or flexible-premium basis.

Simply stated, fixed-price premium life insurance, traditionally called whole life insurance, is life insurance coverage in which a constant guaranteed premium is paid for a specific face amount of coverage.

In flexible-premium life insurance policies (generally referred to as universal life policies), the insured pays a stipulated premium in the first year of coverage. Afterward, the policyowner may choose to pay whatever amount of annual premium he or she desires. Because flexible premiums provide for a cash-value accumulation similar to fixed-premium policies, the cash value will either grow or be expended to pay required annual policy charges after the first year. The policy's performance and the size of premiums the policyowner actually contributed after the first policy year will determine the growth (or shrinkage) of the cash value. The actual death benefit of a universal life policy is similarly flexible. The amount of the death benefit paid will depend on the actual premiums contributed by the insured and the policy options selected.

With variable life insurance, the policyowner has the ability to select the investment vehicle for the cash value of the policy. The investment risk for the cash value falls entirely on the policyowner. Both fixed-premium and flexible-premium variable life insurance products are available.

Multiple Life Policies

Survivorship Life Insurance

Survivorship life insurance (also called second-to-die or last-to-die insurance) is a permanent life insurance policy that provides coverage on the lives of two individuals. The death benefit under the survivorship policy is payable upon the death of the survivor of the two insureds. Survivorship life insurance is generally used to provide coverage for a married couple. It is popular because the estate tax rules allow an unlimited federal estate tax marital deduction at the first death of a married couple.

Survivorship life insurance coverage can be designed as fixed-premium or flexible-premium survivorship coverage.

Joint Life Insurance

Joint life insurance (also called first-to-die insurance) covers the joint lives of multiple insureds and provides its death benefit at the first death of the joint insureds. Joint life insurance is often used in buy-sell agreements in which the first death of two or more co-owners of the business will create the need to fund the purchase price required under the buy-sell agreement. The premium required for joint life coverage is attractive compared with the premiums for individual policies on each of the co-owners.

FEDERAL ESTATE TAXATION OF LIFE INSURANCE

LO 22.3   **Explain in general the estate taxation of life insurance and how an irrevocable life insurance trust can be designed to provide estate liquidity without adding to the estate tax burden.**

Life insurance is often the single largest asset or group of assets in an individual's gross estate. The inclusion of life insurance can often mean the difference between a federal estate tax liability and no tax liability. There are four basic instances when life insurance is included in a decedent's gross estate:

- when it is payable to the insured's estate
- when the insured possessed incidents of ownership in the policy at the time of death
- when the insured transferred incidents of ownership by gift within 3 years of death
- when life insurance is placed in a trust that is required to pay for the estate's costs

Proceeds Payable to Estate

Life insurance proceeds payable to the executor (that is, to or for the benefit of an insured's estate) are includible in the estate, regardless of who owned the contract or who paid the premiums. There are many reasons in addition to avoiding federal estate taxation why estate planners seldom recommend that life insurance be payable to a decedent's estate:

- Insurance payable to a decedent's estate subjects the proceeds to the claims of creditors.

- Insurance payable to a decedent's estate subjects the proceeds to costs of probate administration.

- Life insurance proceeds in many states, otherwise exempt from state death taxes (either fully or partially) if payable to a named beneficiary, become subject to such taxes if they are payable to the decedent-insured's estate.

In some instances, death benefits payable to named beneficiaries are included in an insured's gross estate if the proceeds can or must be used to pay settlement costs. The regulations under Sec. 2042 make it clear that proceeds payable to a named beneficiary (such as a trustee) are includible in the insured's gross estate if the beneficiary has a legal obligation to use the proceeds to pay the settlement costs for the estate. Failure to make an effective beneficiary designation could also cause the proceeds to be payable to the estate.

In addition to problems created by making life insurance payable to a decedent's estate, there are complications if life insurance is owned by a third party and made payable to a decedent's testamentary trust. Because a testamentary trust is created in a decedent's will and takes effect only at death, life insurance payable to a decedent's testamentary trust might be considered payable to his or her estate, depending on the trust law of the particular state. This could cause inclusion of the proceeds in the gross estate and might subject the proceeds to the expenses of probate and the claims of creditors. The result will vary from state to state.

Possession of Incidents of Ownership

A policy is also included in an insured's estate if he or she possessed an "incident of ownership" in the policy at the time of his or her death. When insurance proceeds are paid to a named beneficiary other than the insured's estate, incidents of ownership in the policy at the time of death are the key criteria for inclusion. An incident of ownership is broadly defined as any right to the economic benefits of the policy. The regulations provide that incidents of ownership include (but are not limited to) the power to

- change the beneficiary
- assign the policy
- borrow on the policy
- surrender the policy
- exercise any of the other essential contract rights or privileges

To remove life insurance proceeds from the reach of the federal estate tax, the insured must divest himself or herself of all significant rights and privileges under the contract.

EXAMPLE

Brenda, a widow, transferred ownership of three whole life insurance policies to her daughter, Sara, 6 years ago. However, it was clear at the time of the transfer that Brenda still had the right to borrow against the policies' cash values and the right to change the beneficiary by written notification to the insurance company. Although Brenda effectively transferred title in the policies to her daughter, the policies' proceeds will still be included in her gross estate for federal estate tax purposes because she retained the right to borrow against these policies and to change the beneficiary. To have successfully removed the proceeds from the gross estate, Brenda must not have reserved these rights.

It is clear that a directly held incident of ownership will cause inclusion, even if the incident is exercisable only with another's consent. However, planners must also be aware that inclusion may occur even if the insured is unaware that such incidents are held or is incapable of exercising the incidents. In other words, there have been instances when there are some hidden incidents of ownership that exist after it appears that the owner has effectively transferred all *traditional* ownership rights to a life insurance policy. For example, the Treasury regulations provide that incidents of ownership held by a corporation will, in some circumstances, be attributed to a majority shareholder.

Transfers within 3 Years of Death

In addition, under the unique rules of Sec. 2035, life insurance is included in the gross estate of an insured who transferred incidents of ownership in the policy by *gift* within 3 years of his or her death. Transfers made more than 3 years before the insured's death should not normally be includible in the insured's estate, assuming the insured has retained no incidents of ownership.

Life Insurance and the Marital Deduction

Life insurance proceeds that are payable at the insured's death to the insured's surviving spouse can qualify for the federal estate tax marital deduction if the requirements for the deduction are met. Because the marital deduction is unlimited, the full value of life insurance proceeds payable in a qualifying manner to the surviving spouse is deductible from the insured's gross estate.

Qualification for the marital deduction, however, is more complicated if the surviving spouse does not receive the proceeds outright. For example, life insurance proceeds payable to a surviving spouse under available settlement options may or may not qualify for the marital deduction. Some settlement options terminate payment at the surviving spouse's death. If the remaining payments are not payable to the surviving spouse's estate or subject to the surviving spouse's control, the marital deduction will not be available unless the estate is eligible to make the QTIP election.

If the proceeds of a life insurance policy are payable to a trust that benefits the surviving spouse, the trust's remainder interest must be payable to the surviving spouse's estate or be subject to the surviving spouse's general power of appointment to qualify for the marital deduction. Without these provisions, the trust can qualify only if the decedent-spouse's executor makes the QTIP election.

Gross Estate Inclusion of Life Insurance

Policies on Life of Decedent

If a life insurance policy must be included in the decedent-insured's gross estate for federal estate tax purposes, the amount included is the death benefit of the policy. The *death benefit* of the face amount is adjusted by: (1) deducting any policy loan, or other encumbrance and (2) adding any accrued or terminal dividends. Such concepts as cash value, total premiums paid, or reserves in the policy are irrelevant in this context and have nothing to do with determining the amount included in the decedent-insured's gross estate.

Policies Owned by Decedent on Lives of Others

Under third-party ownership of life insurance, it is possible that a policyowner will die before the insured. In this case, the policy is included in the decedent's gross estate at its fair market value at the time of the decedent's death.

The fair market value of the unmatured life insurance policy at a given point in time depends on the type of coverage. If the policy is currently paid up, its value is equal to the sale price of the insurance company's comparable contracts, which is typically the single-premium cost of a similar policy on the life of a person at the insured's attained age. Sometimes, a policy does not have a readily ascertainable value through the sale of a comparable contract. Generally, no ascertainable value is available when a contract has been in force for some time and still has future premium payments to be made. In this case, the value is equal to the policy's *interpolated terminal reserve* at the date of the decedent's death *plus* the proportionate part of the *unearned premium* (the amount of premium already paid covering the period after the policyowner's death).

Be aware, however, that if the alternate valuation date is used for purposes of valuing the policy in the decedent-policyowner's gross estate and if the insured dies within the 6-month alternate valuation period, there is inclusion of the full amount of the death proceeds in the decedent-policyowner's estate instead of just the fair market value of an unmatured life insurance policy.

Code Sec. 2206 stipulates that federal estate taxes attributable to life insurance proceeds included in the decedent's gross estate may be recovered by an executor from the beneficiary of the life insurance policy unless the decedent's will provides a contrary provision for tax apportionment.

Removal of Life Insurance from Insured's Gross Estate

There are two possible ways to remove life insurance from the insured's gross estate:

- *cross-ownership between spouses*—a criss-cross method wherein one spouse owns the life insurance on the other spouse's life and that spouse owns the life insurance on the opposite spouse's life

- *irrevocable life insurance trust*—a trust created for the express purpose of holding the life insurance policies involved

Cross-Ownership

Because of the incidents-of-ownership test, cross-ownership is a useful technique. If new life insurance is being acquired on one spouse's life, the other spouse should act as owner and applicant of the policy. If the spouse other than the insured spouse owns the policy from the outset, there is no transfer of life insurance and therefore no Sec. 2035 3-year-rule problem. If the insured already owns the policy, the ownership should be assigned to the spouse. This method also removes the death proceeds from the insured's gross estate, except that the transferor must live for more than 3 years after the assignment to avoid inclusion of the proceeds in his or her gross estate under Sec. 2035.

Although cross-ownership of life insurance is an effective way to defeat the incidents-of-ownership test, the arrangement is not without problems. First, if the spouses divorce, the life insurance arrangement will have to be restructured according to the specifics of the property settlement. If cross-ownership is not involved, the divorce settlement has one less element of complexity.

Another problem with cross-ownership is the unpredictability of the order of spouses' deaths. In the event that the spouse other than the insured predeceases the insured, the insurance will likely end up back in the insured's gross estate. Cross-ownership will have accomplished nothing.

In essence, even though cross-ownership defeats the incidents-of-ownership situation, there are many potential problems with its use.

Irrevocable Life Insurance Trust

irrevocable life insurance trust (ILIT)

LO 22.4 **Describe the structure, tax implications, and strategies for using Irrevocable Life Insurance trusts (ILITs).**

The **irrevocable life insurance trust (ILIT)** can be of particular benefit for estate planning purposes. Placing ownership of a policy with an ILIT aims to make the trustee the effective owner of a policy that will fund the trust upon the death of the insured. This arrangement allows the individual who set up the trust to avoid the proceeds of the policy being included in his gross estate, thus diminishing or eliminating the federal estate tax burden. All the while, practical control remains in that individual's hands. It is then up to the trustee to manage or distribute the funds in accordance with the terms of the trust agreement. Therefore, ensuring that the ILIT instrument is effectively drafted is an essential part of the success of this strategy. A poorly worded trust agreement can cause undesirable results that run counter to the intentions of the original policy purchaser or subject the proceeds to unnecessary taxation. An ILIT should be used when the goal is exclusion of the life insurance proceeds from the estate of both spouses. The drawback to this arrangement is that the insured relinquishes any control over the policy. Further, the irrevocable nature of the trust means that the trust cannot be revoked. The irrevocable life insurance trust can provide the following benefits:

- Gift taxes can be avoided for premiums contributed to the trust.

- Estate taxes can be avoided when the proceeds are received.

- Generation-skipping transfer taxes can be avoided if the insured's exemption is allocated to the trust.

- The insured's transferable wealth can be enhanced through leveraging.

- The expenses and publicity of probate can be avoided for transfers to the trust.

- Estate liquidity can be enhanced by the trust.

- The grantor-insured can control the disposition of the proceeds before the fact through the trust provisions.

- Income taxes can be avoided on the corpus buildup and receipt of proceeds.

Essentially, there are two rules that create problems for purposes of the irrevocable life insurance trust. If these two problems are avoided, the life insurance trust will be able to provide for heirs or for the liquidity of the insured's estate without increasing the estate tax liability.

First, life insurance proceeds are included in the insured's gross estate if they are payable to the executor. Therefore the grantor generally avoids directly naming his or her estate as beneficiary of the trust. The hidden trap is indirectly causing the trust to be deemed payable to the executor, which could occur if the trustee is directed to pay the expenses of the estate or merely given the discretion to pay the expenses of the estate. Because these trust provisions cause some, or all, of the proceeds to be included in the insured's gross estate, they should be avoided.

Trust provisions that can be used in the insurance trust to provide liquidity to the estate are discretionary powers to the trustee to lend trust funds to the insured's estate or to purchase assets from the estate. The loan or sale should follow normally acceptable commercial standards and be within the explicit powers of the fiduciaries involved. The purchase of assets should be for fair market value, and the loan should be secured and bear adequate interest. These provisions allow the cash proceeds held by the trustee to be transferred to the estate to increase estate liquidity without causing unnecessary additional estate taxes.

The second possibility for estate inclusion is the retention of any incidents of ownership by the insured with 3 years of death. Although this test sounds simple enough, it can be an additional trap for the unwary. First, the insured should possess no rights to the trust that would provide him or her with incidents of ownership in the corpus. The trust must be a truly irrevocable, no-strings-attached gift. Therefore, the insured is not able to change beneficiary designations on the policy or within the trust once the trust is executed, and he or she is not able to receive policy loan proceeds or use the trust as collateral for a loan.

Assuming a trust is drafted to avoid attributed incidents of ownership to the insured, there are further concerns. First, the insured should avoid obtaining incidents of ownership in the policy prior to the gift to the trust. This may be unavoidable if an existing policy is used to fund the trust. In this case, the insured must live 3 years after the transfer of the policy to the trust, or Sec. 2035 brings the proceeds back into the estate. This transfer is often recommended regardless of the Sec. 2035 risk. Quite often, an older insured may use an existing policy to fund an irrevocable trust as estate tax concerns increase. The insured should do this when he or she is prepared to irrevocably name the beneficiaries of the trust and when it is economically impractical to purchase a new policy within the trust.

If a new policy is used to fund the trust, it would be a serious estate tax mistake for the insured to acquire incidents of ownership. In this case, the 3-year rule is a trap even if the intent is for the policy to be held in all events by an irrevocable trust. The insured should participate in the process only as trust grantor and insured. The insured should not sign as applicant or owner on the policy application. The trustee is the applicant and owner of the policy, and the trust should exist at the time of application.

Irrevocable Life Insurance Trust

- The trust must not have direct or indirect responsibility to pay the insured's estate expenses.
- The grantor must not have incidents of ownership within 3 years of death.

If the trust is not in place and the application and underwriting process must be started, the child of the insured could be the applicant and owner. Then a transfer to an irrevocable trust can be made when the trust is drafted. If these steps are followed, current case law indicates that the insured does not hold incidents in the policy even if the insured actually makes all premium payments to the trust.

The ILIT can be designed to bypass both spouses' estates. The dispositive provisions should not give the surviving spouse any powers that will cause inclusion in his or her estate. For example, the surviving spouse should not have a general power over the corpus or have unlimited invasion powers. However, the surviving spouse could be given a life estate with limited invasion powers (that is, the 5-and-5 powers). In addition, a discretionary invasion power in favor of the surviving spouse can be given to the trustee if the invasion is subject to ascertainable standards. A properly designed trust can also be the owner of a second-to-die policy that covers the spouses, and the second-death benefits avoid inclusion in either spouse's estate.

As this discussion demonstrates, the ILIT might be the most advantageous estate preservation technique available under current tax law. However, the potential hazards discussed above indicate that the trust should be drafted and administered only with the advice of an attorney experienced in estate planning matters.

Gift Tax

gift tax

A third consideration is the **gift tax**. A lifetime transfer of a life insurance policy will likely be considered a taxable transfer if the value of the policy exceeds the annual exclusion amount (currently $15,000, as of 2019). In order to be considered gifts, the transfer could be direct or indirect. A direct transfer occurs when the policy owner is also the insured and transfers or assigns the policy to another person. Any time someone is named as the beneficiary for a policy that the owner purchased on his own life, the beneficiary is receiving a direct gift transfer. An indirect transfer would include payment of another person's premium or transferring employer-provided coverage to another person. In order to determine whether the amount of the policy exceeds the gift tax exclusion, and by how much, the government will look to the fair market value, which could be either the actual cost or replacement cost of the policy. This can be determined by comparing the policy transferred to the cost of a similar policy sold by another company around the time of purchase. The recipient of the gift must also have a present interest in the policy he or she received in order for the annual exclusion to apply. If the recipient had unrestricted ability to use the policy, he or she had a present interest.

Gifts of Life Insurance. An outright, no-strings-attached gift of life insurance qualifies for the annual exclusion. Life insurance (and annuity policies) are subject to the same basic test as any other type of property in ascertaining whether the interest created is a present or future interest, even though the ultimate obligation under a life insurance policy—payment of the death benefit—is discharged in the future. It is not necessary that a policy have cash value at the time of the gift for the transfer to be a present interest. However, the annual exclusion is lost if the donor prevents the donee from surrendering the policy or borrowing its cash value, or limits the donee's right to policy cash values in any way.

Gifts of Life Insurance to Trusts. If the grantor transfers a life insurance policy to a trust, the present-interest rules apply—not the future-interest rules discussed above. That is, the annual exclusion is available only if the donee beneficiaries receive a present interest. Simply transferring life insurance to a trust does not typically create a present-interest gift. The life insurance trust usually pays no income, or the income is used to provide premium payments and is not currently available to donees. Qualifying as a present interest would be a significant hurdle for the life insurance trust if there were no exceptions to the general rule. Remember that, typically, the initial cost of the life insurance policy transferred to the trust and the annual premiums that must be contributed to the trust by the grantor each year are under the current annual gift tax exclusion amount. Therefore, if the annual exclusion applies, most irrevocable life insurance trusts will not incur gift tax liability. Fortunately, it is possible to design an irrevocable life insurance trust that qualifies as a present-interest gift for annual-exclusion purposes.

Advantages of ILITs

The ILIT is a particularly advantageous vehicle for making a lifetime gift and discussion of the gift tax provides a good opportunity to begin an expanded discussion of the advantages of the irrevocable life Insurance trust.

LO 22.5   Explain the gift tax treatment of life insurance policies

Gift Tax Advantages

The gift tax annual exclusion is limited to gifts of a present interest up to $15,000 per donee (as indexed for 2019). If the grantor is married and his or her spouse elects to split gifts, the annual exclusion can be increased to $30,000 per donee. Thus, the grantor is able to contribute up to $30,000 (2019) for each beneficiary of the ILIT without any gift tax consequences. The annual-exclusion gift is the single most beneficial estate planning technique because the cash or other property that is transferred through annual exclusions is forever removed from the donor's transfer-tax base.

The donor's applicable credit amount (gift tax exemption) will shelter up to $11,400,000 (2019 indexed amount) cumulative taxable transfers for amounts contributed to an ILIT in excess of the grantor's annual exclusions. If it is feasible for the donor's spouse to contribute to the ILIT (for example, the ILIT will invest in a survivorship life insurance policy on the donor and his or her spouse), a second applicable credit amount is available. Thus a married couple can contribute to an ILIT as much as $22.8 million in premiums in excess of the donor's annual gift tax exclusions without incurring gift taxes.

In the largest estate planning cases, the annual exclusions and applicable credit amount(s) will not entirely shelter the required premium gifts to the ILIT. Nevertheless, the ILIT continues to be a useful planning technique in these cases. Gift taxes paid on taxable gifts made more than 3 years prior to the grantor's death will be removed from the donor's gross estate—that is, the gift tax system is tax-exclusive. This means that the donor will not have to pay transfer taxes on gift taxes paid on gifts made more than 3 years before his or her death. The payment of gift taxes on lifetime gifts in excess of the annual exclusions and applicable credit amount might be beneficial.

Compare this either to transfers made within 3 years of death or that are transfers made at death. For these transfers, the transferor will pay tax not only on the property transferred but also on the tax payable on the transfer. Thus, the transfer-tax system is tax-inclusive for gifts that are made within 3 years of death and for transfers that are made at death. Since lifetime gifts decrease the ultimate size of the taxable estate, even if they are taxable, lifetime gifts will be an effective transfer-leveraging technique.

Generation-Skipping Transfer Tax (GST) Advantages

Sometimes, the ILIT will be used to bypass the next generation and provide benefits for the insured's grandchildren and great grandchildren. In such cases, the ILIT will be immediately subject to the GST rules. In other instances, the insured's grandchildren will benefit after, or in conjunction with, the insured's children. In these cases, the GST will be applicable when the grandchildren benefit from the ILIT. Its application to ILITs is more confusing than with the estate and gift tax systems. Only in the rarest instance would a transfer to an ILIT be a direct skip. Thus, the GST taxable event for an ILIT is delayed until a later taxable termination or distribution. If the GST is in place at the time such event occurs, it may be imposed even if the ILIT was funded when the GST was subject to repeal unless GST exemption was allocated to the transfer when the ILIT was funded.

Generally, the insured can avoid any GST consequences by allocating his or her GST exemption against premium gifts to the ILIT. In some instances, the allocation is automatic for lifetime gifts to a trust. This represents a tremendous opportunity to use an ILIT for transfer-tax leveraging against the GST.

Probate Expenses and Publicity Are Avoided

Much has been made recently of the use of living trusts as a probate-avoidance technique. Living trusts are designed to reduce the probate estate held by the grantor of the trust at the time of death. Probate expenses are substantial if professional help is required.

The ILIT is a type of living trust with these probate-avoidance advantages: The death benefits paid to the ILIT avoid the expenses of probate when the grantor-insured dies. In addition, the ILIT is a private, nonprobate document, and the beneficial provisions of the ILIT are known only by the grantor, trustee, and trust beneficiaries. Thus, the grantor of the irrevocable life insurance trust has the ability to create a completely private estate that avoids the scrutiny of the grantor's other heirs.

Trust Terms Give Grantor Dispositive Flexibility

The ILIT is a private document that directs a trustee to manage the trust according to its specified terms. To succeed in meeting the transfer-tax planning goals for the ILIT, the grantor can retain no control over the disposition of the trust after the trust is created. However, the trust terms can be designed to give an independent trustee significant flexibility in managing the trust. The ILIT permits the grantor to defer distributions to beneficiaries and empower a mature, competent trustee to make dispositive decisions for the grantor after the grantor's death.

For example, the trustee can be given discretionary powers to sprinkle trust income or principal among the various beneficiaries after the death benefits are paid to the trust. The grantor can specify that his or her children have merely an income interest in the trust during their lives. The remainder of the trust corpus can be distributed according to the dispositive terms specified by the grantor at the time the ILIT is created, or it can be distributed under powers of appointment granted to the trustee or beneficiaries of the trust.

Compare an ILIT's dispositive flexibility with the outright payment of death benefits to the insured's beneficiaries. With an outright payment nobody but the beneficiary is responsible for managing the death proceeds. The proceeds could be consumed or given away quickly by the beneficiary or assigned to the beneficiary's creditors. A large death benefit designed to last a lifetime or into the next generation, therefore, could be wasted in a short period of time.

If the life insurance is instead acquired by an ILIT, the grantor's specified terms will provide for the disposition of the asset. Thus, the death proceeds from the life insurance policy will be invested and managed by a selected individual or institution. The payment of any income or principal could be limited by the predetermined terms of an ILIT or placed in the hands of a responsible and reliable trustee.

Irrevocability Concerns Can Be Addressed

The irrevocability of the ILIT is, of course, a disadvantage from the grantor's standpoint. Fortunately, the grantor can, through careful trust drafting, give the independent trustee a great deal of flexibility in managing the trust. If it is desirable, the independent trustee can transfer the policy from the ILIT. For example, the policy can be distributed to beneficiaries or it can be sold to anyone, including the grantor, provided the trustee exercises independent judgment. The grantor can provide a limited power of appointment for another individual to invade the ILIT. This power of appointment can give access to the policy's cash surrender value or provide for the distribution of the life insurance policy.

Gift Tax Planning for ILITs

The gift tax planning involved in creating and funding an ILIT is the most complex aspect of such trusts. It is essential that the trust be created and managed properly to benefit from the available gift-tax-avoidance provisions of the tax rules. For example, the donor should take advantage of every available annual exclusion. The applicable credit amount should be used only as necessary; if the credit is used to avoid gift taxes, it must be used as efficiently as possible.

Most individuals considering an ILIT have substantial estates. They also are generally older on the average than people who purchase life insurance outright. They usually have significant unearned income, their estates are growing larger all the time, and they are using the ILIT to save estate taxes. In many cases, they own closely held businesses or professional practices. These individuals should be considering the use of every gift-tax-saving avenue for the remainder of their lives. If the premium gifts to an ILIT are not designed in the most gift-tax-efficient manner, the grantor will be wasting estate planning opportunities. Any inefficient use of the gift tax shelters will ultimately result in increased estate tax costs and decreased family wealth for the next generation.

QUALIFYING GIFTS TO ILIT FOR ANNUAL GIFT TAX EXCLUSION

Advantages of Annual Exclusion

The annual exclusion was created to prevent taxation of de minimis gifts to family members through the gift tax system. Think of the compliance difficulty that would occur if every birthday or holiday present to a child or grandchild were subject to gift tax reporting. However, the annual exclusion creates an estate planning opportunity that goes far beyond de minimis gifts. A wealthy donor can transfer up to $15,000 (2019 indexed amount) to any number of individuals without gift tax consequences. Annual-exclusion gifts are not defined as taxable gifts under the unified estate and gift tax system. Thus such gifts never become part of the donor's transfer-tax base.

Taxable gifts (gifts in excess of the annual exclusions and marital deduction) are, on the other hand, returned to the donor's estate tax base as adjusted taxable gifts, even if the taxable gifts were fully sheltered by the applicable credit amount. Therefore, annual-exclusion gifts represent a rare opportunity to avoid the federal tax system entirely. If the grantor makes systematic annual-exclusion gifts to his children and/or grandchildren over a number of years, a significant estate tax savings will result. If the donor is married and his or her spouse elects to split gifts each year, the transfer tax savings can be doubled by increasing the annual exclusion to $30,000 per donee.

EXAMPLE

Tom Taxplanner, a widower aged 65, has two children and four grandchildren. In 2019, Tom can make up to $90,000 of total qualifying gifts annually to his children and grandchildren without ever subjecting this property to the transfer tax base. If Tom lives another 20 years, he can give away a total of $1,800,000 at a minimum (ignoring further inflation adjustments to the annual exclusion) to these donees. If there is a federal estate and/or state death tax imposed on his estate, the tax savings could be significant. The savings are further enhanced because the appreciation of the property transferred through annual-exclusion gifts is also removed from Tom's estate tax base.

The example above demonstrates tremendous potential estate-tax savings if the annual exclusion is used effectively. The savings demonstrated above could be even greater if the annual exclusion gifts are made to an ILIT and invested in a life insurance policy covering the donor's life (or perhaps the lives of the donor and his or her spouse).

Present-Interest Dilemma

Unfortunately, annual exclusion from gift taxes is not available for all gifts. The rules of Sec. 2503 state that the annual exclusion is available only for gifts of a present interest. That is, an annual-exclusion gift must give the donee a present right of enjoyment. Certainly, all outright transfers of cash or property to a donee qualify for an annual exclusion. Even property such as life insurance, which provides for death benefits at a later date, will qualify as a present interest if it is transferred directly to the donee.

A problem arises in creating a present interest when a gift is made to a trust for the benefit of the donee-beneficiaries. If the trust does not provide for immediate benefits and delays income and principal distribution to a future date, the trust provides a future interest to the beneficiaries. An ILIT is a future-interest trust. The grantor-insured of an ILIT has no intention of providing any current benefits to the ILIT's beneficiaries. The beneficiaries are not expected to benefit until the grantor-insured's death when the death proceeds are received by the trustee. Can irrevocable trusts that defer beneficiaries' receipt of benefits be designed to qualify as present-interest gifts sheltered by the annual exclusion? The answer is yes, through the granting of Crummey withdrawal powers.

"Crummey" Withdrawal Powers

Fortunately, gifts to trusts can qualify for the annual exclusion if they are appropriately designed. However, the trust must provide current enjoyment rights to the donee-beneficiaries. With an ILIT this is accomplished by giving each donee who will receive annual-exclusion gifts the right to receive the gift outright immediately. These withdrawal powers (referred to as Crummey powers) are a powerful-planning technique. Remember that the Crummey demand must be for a certain time period that is no less than 30 days. The goal is to give the beneficiary access to the money but to inform the beneficiary when you set up the trust to not take the premiums so it can fund the policy or trust.

The Crummey Case

The Crummey doctrine is derived from the case of _Crummey v. Comm'r_, 397 F.2d 82 (9th Cir. 1968). In this case, the taxpayer, Clifford Crummey, created four irrevocable living trusts for the benefit of his four children, aged 22, 20, 15, and 11. Because the transfer of property into the trusts qualified as a taxable gift, the taxpayer took the annual exclusion (at that time, $3,000 per donee) for each child.

The IRS, however, stepped in and disallowed the annual exclusion for those beneficiaries under the age of 21.

IRS Position in the Crummey Case

Because three of the beneficiaries of the trusts that Crummey had created were minors, the IRS asserted that a present-interest gift was not possible. The IRS was applying the doctrine of property law that states that a minor cannot own property in a highly literal and restrictive manner. Because the minors in the Crummey case could not own the gifted property or even "own" the benefits created under the terms of the trust, according to the IRS, present-interest gifts were impossible. Therefore, the annual exclusion was disallowed.

Holding of the Court in the Crummey Case

The court in Crummey rejected the IRS's position and held that a present-interest gift had been made because the guardian named by the taxpayer in the trust had been given the power to demand distribution on behalf of the minors. In essence, although the actual Crummey case had nothing to do with transfers of life insurance policies into trust, the case has come to stand for the principle that the annual exclusion is available if a power to demand the addition to trust property is given to the beneficiaries.

Thus annual exclusions are available for premiums given to an ILIT as long as the ILIT contains language that requires the trustee to notify the trust beneficiaries that payments to cover premiums have been transferred to the trust and that the trust's beneficiaries have the right to demand distribution of these payments.

Application of Crummey Power to ILITs

The Crummey case has taught us that as long as a trust contains a power allowing beneficiaries to demand distribution, a present-interest gift will be considered to have been made. This guarantees the availability of the annual exclusion. Therefore, since there will be a possible federal gift tax created: (1) by transferring existing life insurance policies into a trust, and/or (2) by gifting premiums to the trustee, the availability of the annual exclusion becomes very important because it is a method to reduce or even eliminate federal gift tax liability. Thus, qualifying gifts to an ILIT for the annual-gift-tax exclusion is essential if the grantor hopes to maximize his or her potential gift and estate tax savings.

According to the principles set forth in the Crummey case, a clause that allows the beneficiary to demand distribution must be included in the ILIT. This is true regardless of whether or not minors and a guardian are involved. As long as the named beneficiaries of the trust have been given ample notice of their right to demand distribution, a present-interest gift is deemed to exist. Therefore, the annual exclusion will be available.

EXAMPLE 1

Marvin has created an ILIT and has transferred a life insurance policy into the trust. The face amount of the policy is $300,000, and its gift tax value is $4,700 on the day of the transfer. Premiums of $903 are payable annually on March 1. The beneficiary of the policy is the ILIT, and the beneficiary of the ILIT is Marvin's daughter, Ellen, age 28. Because Ellen is not a minor, there is no guardian involved. There is a provision in the ILIT that Ellen, as beneficiary, will be notified within 60 days of receipt if Marvin makes any gifts to the ILIT. Furthermore, Ellen has been given the "power to demand distribution" of this gifted property.

When Marvin's next annual premium is due, he makes a gift of an amount roughly equal to the premium amount to the trustee. The trustee notifies Ellen in writing that she has the right to demand this gift. She, of course, does not demand it. The federal gift tax annual exclusion is available for both the policy's value of $4,700 when it was originally transferred and for the premium payment of $903. Therefore, no federal gift tax liability is triggered.

EXAMPLE 2

John has created an ILIT and has transferred a life insurance policy into the trust. The face amount of the policy is $100,000, and the policy's fair market value is $3,100 on the day of the transfer. Premiums of $811 are payable annually on January 14. The beneficiary of the policy is the ILIT, and the beneficiary of the ILIT is John's daughter, Jennifer, age 3. John's brother, Ed, is named guardian on behalf of Jennifer, and under the terms of the ILIT, Ed is given the power to demand distribution on Jennifer's behalf when John transfers funds to the ILIT.

When John's next annual premium is due, he makes a gift of an amount equal to the premium amount plus anticipated expenses of the trust to the trustee. The trustee notifies Ed that he has the right to demand this gift as guardian for Jennifer. Ed does not demand it. The federal gift tax annual exclusion is available for both the policy's value of $3,100 when the policy was originally transferred and for the premium payment. Therefore, no federal gift tax liability exists.

Avoid Crummey Powers for Special-Needs Beneficiaries

Although it is generally considered important to shelter gifts to an irrevocable trust by the use of the federal gift tax annual exclusion, the provision of a Crummey power for a special-needs beneficiary should be avoided. A Crummey power is a general power of appointment and the beneficiary provided with this right must have no legal impediments that would prevent the withdrawal of any funds subject to the power.

A special-needs beneficiary of a third-party supplemental needs trust should not be provided with any type of power of invasion. The ability to take any principal or income from the trust would be treated as an available asset to the holder of a Crummey power. In applying the test for SSI (Supplemental Security Income) and Medicaid, the state would consider any assets subject to a Crummey power to be an available asset for the beneficiary. This would be true even though the Crummey power is temporary and subject to lapse in a short period of time. A lapsing Crummey power would be treated as income to the extent of the withdrawal power in any month that the special-needs beneficiary held the power. This would cause the beneficiary to exceed the SSI income limitations for the respective months and cause disqualification from

Medicaid. The failure to exercise the power and make the asset available would be subject to challenge by the Department of Welfare whether the powers held directly by the special-needs beneficiary or by a guardian or other representative.

A third-party supplemental needs trust will certainly have other family members as vested remainder beneficiaries. It probably is appropriate to provide Crummey powers for other beneficiaries of the supplemental needs ILIT who do not have SSI and Medicaid concerns or other creditor problems. The trust provisions granting the Crummey powers should be drafted carefully to explicitly avoid providing a Crummey power to a special-needs beneficiary. If the beneficiaries forced by the state to withdraw under the Crummey provision, the life insurance policy funding the supplemental-needs ILIT could be jeopardized by the reduced funds available to pay the annual premium.

LO 22.6   **Describe the practical uses for life insurance in estate planning**

Keeping ILIT Proceeds Out of Grantor's Estate

Life insurance is included in the gross estate under the rules of Sec. 2042 in conjunction with the special rules of Sec. 2035. Under Sec. 2042, life insurance proceeds are included in the gross estate of a decedent-insured if: (1) the policy proceeds are payable to the decedent's executor (that is, for the benefit of the decedent's estate), or (2) the decedent-insured owned incidents of ownership in the policy at the time of his or her death. The special rules of Sec. 2035 also cause inclusion in the decedent-insured's estate if he or she made a gratuitous transfer of the policy within 3 years of his or her death.

ILIT Terms Should Avoid Directly Benefiting Insured's Estate

In the typical ILIT, the trustee is the owner and named beneficiary of the policy held by the ILIT. The ILIT terminology instructs the trustee on how investments should be managed and how the death proceeds will ultimately be provided to the beneficiaries. The proceeds could be payable to the ILIT beneficiaries outright at the decedent's death. In most circumstances, however, the ILIT will continue beyond the life of the insured and provide income and/or principal gradually to the beneficiaries. In many instances, the trustee is given a discretionary power to choose the size and timing of distributions to the beneficiaries.

Caution should always be exercised in drafting the terminology of an ILIT. Sample ILIT documents received from insurance companies, banks, or law libraries should be examined carefully to ensure that the terminology will not cause tax problems for the insured. In particular, the ILIT terminology should not direct the trustee to use policy proceeds to pay the expenses of the insured's estate. If the trustee is directed to pay the expenses of the estate, the IRS will deem the policy payable to the executor, and the proceeds will be included in the insured's estate. If the trustee is given the mere discretionary power to pay estate expenses with the proceeds, this should not cause the proceeds to be treated as "payable to the executor" under Sec. 2042(1). However, any amounts so used will be included in the insured's gross estate. Since the typical ILIT is designed to remove the death proceeds from the insured's gross estate, terminology that directs the trustee to use the death proceeds to pay estate expenses would be a costly mistake, while terminology that permits the trustee to use the death proceeds for estate expense purposes should be used only after careful consideration of all the tax consequences.

ILITs and Sec. 2035 3-Year Rule for Existing Policies Owned by Insured

Policies owned by the insured are subject to the 3-year rule regarding gratuitous transfers. That is, the proceeds will be included in the insured's gross estate if the insured's death occurs within 3 years of the policy's gratuitous transfer to a third party. This 3-year rule, of course, applies to transfers of existing policies to ILITs. Regardless of this rule, transferring an existing life insurance policy to an ILIT is an appropriate planning technique under certain circumstances.

Transferring an existing life insurance policy to an ILIT created by the insured is recommended when the estate-planning objectives for the transfer are more important than other goals. The transfer of a policy to an ILIT should not be made until after the insured feels comfortable that he or she will not require further access to the policy's cash value. The grantor-insured should be relatively older and financially more secure. Furthermore, he or she should be certain of his or her ILIT beneficiary selections before implementing the transfer. After the transfer, the trustee will become the owner and named beneficiary of the policy, and the proceeds will be distributed according to the ILIT's terms. Since the trust is irrevocable, the grantor-insured will not be able to retrieve the policy or change the trust's terms.

To achieve estate tax advantages, a grantor-insured will have to survive more than 3 years following the transfer of his or her life insurance policy to an ILIT. However, this transfer is still a useful planning technique since the full amount of policy proceeds will avoid estate taxation if the grantor-insured survives the 3-year period. Even if the grantor-insured does not survive the 3-year period, his or her estate will be no worse off than if the transfer had not been made. That is, absent the gift of a policy to an ILIT, the insured's estate would already have included the full proceeds because the insured would have continued to hold incidents of ownership in the policy until the time of his or her death.

Avoiding Estate Inclusion with Newly Acquired Policies

Following the decision in the Headrick case (ESTATE OF Eddie L. HEADRICK, Cleveland Bank and Trust, Company and Charles L. Almond, Petitioners-Appellees, v. COMMISSIONER OF INTERNAL REVENUE, Respondent-Appellant.), the IRS indicated that it will no longer litigate the Sec. 2035 3-year-rule implications of life insurance policies newly acquired by an ILIT. Thus a client will be within a safe harbor if an ILIT is created and administered according to the facts of the Headrick case. If the ILIT is created and administered in a more aggressive manner, there is a risk that the IRS will deem that the policy newly acquired by the ILIT was, in fact, transferred to the ILIT by the grantor-insured and thus subject to the Sec. 2035 3-year rule. If the IRS is successful in this endeavor, the grantor-insured of the ILIT could have the full amount of proceeds included in his or her gross estate if the grantor dies within 3 years of the acquisition of the policy. Since the facts of Headrick give us careful guidance, it is important to review the events of the Headrick case in detail here.

EXAMPLE

Eddie Headrick, an attorney, approached a local bank and trust company and explained his plan to create an irrevocable trust. The trust was executed the same day and funded by a check Eddie wrote to the bank as trustee. The terminology of the trust permitted many types of investments, including the purchase of life insurance on the grantor's life. The trust terminology did not, however, direct the trustee to purchase such insurance.

The following day, the bank, as trustee, applied for a life insurance policy on the life of the grantor— Eddie Headrick. Within 10 days, Eddie submitted to a physical examination for the purpose of securing the insurance. Eddie was found to be insurable, and the trust paid the first premium. Within one month after the trust was created, a policy was issued.

Mr. Headrick died approximately 2 years later, and the IRS attempted to treat the transaction as if Eddie controlled the trustee and, in effect, caused a transfer of a policy on his life in which he had incidents of ownership to the trust. Thus, Sec. 2035 would require that the proceeds be included in Eddie's gross estate since he died within 3 years of this "deemed transfer." The court held for the estate of Mr. Headrick, based on the grounds that no transfer had actually taken place. The trustee was merely investing trust funds irrevocably transferred to the trust by the grantor. Therefore, the policyowner of the life insurance at the time of its purchase was established unequivocally to be the ILIT and not Mr. Headrick.

The facts of the *Headrick case* can be listed in the following steps that are recommended to anyone establishing an ILIT:

Step 1: The ILIT is executed before the final policy application is made and any premium is paid.

Step 2: The grantor transfers funds to the ILIT (and makes further gifts, as necessary, when premium payments are due).

Step 3: The trustee sends notice to the beneficiaries of their Crummey withdrawal rights. (This step is repeated each time additional gifts are transferred to the ILIT.)

Step 4: The trustee applies for the policy on the grantor's life and is named as owner and beneficiary of the policy. (The insured participates in the transaction only for the purpose of establishing his or her insurability and signs only the "insured" signature block on the policy application.)

Step 5: The trustee pays the policy's annual premium to the insurance company when the Crummey powers lapse.

If an ILIT is created and/or administered in a manner different from the steps described above, the insured is increasing the risk that the IRS will attempt to attribute incidents of ownership to him or her.

To summarize, the insured should employ the following defensive strategies:

- The insured should not pay the policy premium before the ILIT is created.

- The terms of the ILIT should authorize but not direct the purchase of life insurance on the life of the grantor.

- The insured should retain no contractual rights, and there should be no trust provisions permitting him or her to acquire the policy held by the ILIT.

- The insured should not be the trustee and should not retain the power to become the trustee.

- The trustee should exercise clearly independent decision-making authority over the investment and disposition of trust assets.

FEDERAL GIFT TAXATION OF LIFE INSURANCE

LO 22.5   Explain the gift tax treatment of life insurance polices.

Gifts of life insurance are treated in the same way as gifts of any other asset as far as the annual exclusion or the split-gift provisions are concerned. The annual exclusion (or twice the annual exclusion amount if gift splitting) of gifted value per year per donee may be excluded from the gift-tax base when life insurance is gifted.

A donor often will continue to pay annual premiums even after an absolute transfer of the insurance has been made. Each premium paid subsequent to the policy transfer is considered a gift. As long as it is an outright transfer to a donee, the gift of the policy is a present-interest gift and the annual gift tax exclusion is applicable, not only to the gift of the policy itself but also to the gift of each premium payment as it is made. When gifts of life insurance policies are made in trust, however, the exclusion is forfeited unless the donee has an absolute and immediate power of withdrawal. With proper trust drafting, Crummey withdrawal powers are used to create a present interest for annual exclusion purposes.

Generation-Skipping Transfer Taxation of Life Insurance

Life insurance may also be subject to the federal generation-skipping-transfer tax. If life insurance proceeds are payable directly to, or may someday benefit, skip persons, the proceeds might be subject to the GSTT.

EXAMPLE

Grandmother makes a gift of a life insurance policy on her life to her grandson. The GSTT may apply to a gift of the policy to the grandchild.

The GSTT implications of life insurance trusts are more common and, in all probability, more difficult to avoid. The GSTT applies to trusts in two circumstances—taxable distributions and taxable terminations. A taxable distribution occurs if a distribution of trust income or principal is made to a skip (with respect to the grantor of the trust) beneficiary.

EXAMPLE

Grandfather creates an irrevocable life insurance trust for the benefit of his children and grandchildren. At Grandfather's death, the trustee is directed to hold the proceeds and to distribute as much income and principal to the various beneficiaries as the trustee in its discretion determines. If the trustee makes a distribution to any of the grandchildren, a GST taxable distribution has occurred.

A taxable termination occurs when either: (1) a trust terminates and all remainderpersons are skip persons, or (2) all interests in the trust held by nonskip persons terminate.

EXAMPLE

Suppose Grandfather, in the previous example, had instead provided that the insurance proceeds would be held in trust for his children with all income payable annually to his children in equal shares. At the death of Grandfather's last child, when the trust terminates and the remainder is distributed to his surviving grandchildren in equal shares, a taxable termination occurs.

PRACTICAL USES FOR LIFE INSURANCE IN ESTATE PLANNING

LO 22.6   Describe the practical uses for life insurance in estate planning.

There are many practical uses for life insurance in the estate planning context:

- estate enhancement (RLIT)
- estate liquidity (ILIT)
- grandparent-grandchild trusts
- equity of inheritance
- nonemployed spouse insurance

Revocable Life Insurance Trust

revocable life insurance trust (RLIT)

One useful estate planning device involves gifting a life insurance policy to a revocable trust. A **revocable life insurance trust (RLIT)** is advantageous because it can provide asset management and dispositive flexibility. Remember, however, that there are no tax benefits in using the revocable trust approach. For instance, the life insurance proceeds will be included in a decedent-grantor's gross estate for estate tax purposes because the grantor retained control over the policy within the trust until death. A revocable trust works extremely well in cases where estate-tax planning is not the life insurance plan's primary concern.

For example, a young couple with minor children might find a revocable trust to be helpful when the primary need for life insurance is estate enhancement. In this case, a revocable trust could be created to receive policy proceeds. At the death of the grantor-insured, the trust would become irrevocable and the trustee would then manage the proceeds for the surviving spouse, if necessary, and the minor children. If it is preferable for the surviving spouse to receive the proceeds outright, the revocable trust could be used as a secondary beneficiary to manage the proceeds for the minor children in the event of their parents' simultaneous deaths. In these circumstances, having the trust receive the proceeds avoids the need for a guardian of the minor's property to be appointed to manage the proceeds and the minor's other inherited property. The appointment of a guardian could cause delay and confusion. Moreover, the guardian might not have clear direction as to the disposition of the proceeds and other property for the minor's benefit.

Another common RLIT estate planning arrangement uses the RLIT in conjunction with the grantor's will that contains a pour-over provision. During his or her lifetime, the grantor creates a life insurance trust. The trust is named beneficiary of the policy(ies) on the grantor's life. At the grantor's death, the death proceeds are paid to the trust. In addition, the terms of the grantor's will require the residuary estate assets to be poured over into the life insurance trust (pour-over trust) when the grantor dies. Generally, the terms of the pour-over trust require it to be divided into two or three trusts: the marital trust (A trust), nonmarital trust (family, bypass, or B trust), and possibly, if the trust provides for three trusts, a QTIP trust (C or Q trust). In many instances, a funding formula in the pour-over trust for the marital and QTIP trusts results in the grantor's estate having no estate tax liability. The marital and QTIP trusts may receive assets from the pour-over trust in accordance with a funding formula that results in a zero estate tax for the grantor's estate. For some estate owners, the advantages of flexibility and control of an RLIT outweigh the disadvantage of inclusion of the life insurance in the gross estate.

Grandparent-Grandchild Trust

One commonly used technique is for a grandparent to purchase insurance on the life of a child for the benefit of his or her grandchildren. When the grandchildren are minors, use of a trust rather than an outright gift is preferable. In a typical arrangement, the grandparent creates a funded irrevocable insurance trust with a trustee owning the policy on the child's life. The trustee also pays premiums and designates the trust as beneficiary. From a general estate planning perspective, this type of arrangement should

- provide some reduction of the grandparent's potential estate taxes
- reduce the amount of insurance the child must carry
- keep insurance proceeds out of the child's estate
- enhance the estate the grandchild will receive at his parent's death

Nonemployed Spouse Insurance

There are many reasons why insuring a nonemployed spouse makes good estate planning sense. If the nonworking spouse is no longer living, someone must be paid for household and parenting services he or she previously rendered. Acquiring life insurance to offset those costs and losses could be an integral part of family estate planning. Another consideration is that if a nonworking spouse dies, a joint return for federal income tax purposes is no longer available to the survivor. The additional amount of income tax can be substantial over a period of years.

Gift taxes may also increase because the availability of the unlimited marital deduction and the ability to split a gift are lost.

For federal estate tax purposes, the death of the less-wealthy nonemployed spouse before the death of the working spouse can cause a considerable increase in the survivor's estate tax liability and a reduction in the net amount of property passing to children and other family members at the survivor's death as a result of the loss of the marital deduction. Although the marital deduction is available at the death of the first spouse, the deduction will not be significant if the deceased nonworking spouse has a relatively small estate.

> *Note:* Regulation of insurance products and services varies from state to state. In Florida, for example, regulations prohibit doing business with an unauthorized insurance entity. An unauthorized entity is an insurance company that has not gained approval to place insurance in the jurisdiction where it or a producer wants to sell insurance. These carriers are unlicensed and prohibited from doing business in that state. In most cases where these carriers have operated, they have characterized themselves as one of several types that are exempt from state regulation. It is the financial planner's responsibility to exercise due diligence to make sure the carriers for whom they are selling are approved by the department of insurance in that state.

CHAPTER REVIEW

Key Terms and Concepts

irrevocable life insurance
    trust (ILIT)
gift tax

revocable life insurance
    trust (RLIT)

Chapter 22: Review Questions

1. What are the main types of life insurance policies? [LO 22.2]

2. What is the primary distinction between term life and whole or universal life policies? [LO 22.2]

3. What is the importance of incidents of ownership with regard to life insurance policies and how is it determined? [LO 22.2]

4. What is the 3-year estate inclusion rule under federal estate tax law regarding the transfer of a life insurance policy? [LO 22.3]

5. Under what circumstances will life insurance proceeds be included in a decedent's estate? [LO 22.3]

6. Identify the estate planning advantages of an ILIT. [LO 22.4]

7. Describe the application of Crummey Power to ILITs. [LO 22.5]

8. What is the primary goal when using an ILIT? What is the primary drawback? [LO 22.4]

9. Explain how the annual gift tax exclusion can effectively be used in an ILIT. [LO 22.4]

10. What is the "present-interest dilemma" when a gift is made to an ILIT? [LO 22.5]

11. What are the five steps recommended to anyone who is establishing an ILIT? [LO 22.6]

12. Identify the potential benefits of an irrevocable life insurance trust (ILIT). [LO 22.5]

13. Explain how gifts of life insurance made to a trust can qualify for the gift tax annual exclusion. [LO 22.5]

14. What are the practical uses of life insurance in estate planning? [LO 22.6]

Chapter Twenty-Two Review Answers

1. The main types of life insurance policies are:

   - Term Insurance

   - Whole Life Insurance

   - Universal Life Insurance

   - Variable Life Insurance

2. Term life insurance provides coverage for a finite period of time, while whole or universal coverage are permanent policies that endure for the life of the insured, so long as premiums are kept in force. Notably, term life insurance generates no cash value while the latter three do.

3. Incidents of ownership help identify who actually owns a life insurance policy, which is crucial in determining whether proceeds will be included in a decedent's estate. Determining who possessed incidents of ownership requires consideration of who had the ability to receive the economic benefits of the policy.

4. Under federal estate tax law, gifts, including insurance policies, are typically included in the gross estate even if the gift was actually transferred before one's death. However,

federal law allows for a 3-year exclusion, by which any policy that is assigned or transferred to another person *more than 3 years* before the other person's death will not be included in the decedent's gross estate.

5. Under certain circumstances the proceeds may be included in the decedent's estate. These circumstances include:

    a. When proceeds are paid to the executor of the decedent's estate

    b. The decedent having an incident of ownership in the policy at the time of his/her death

    c. A transfer of ownership within three years of death (the three-year rule)

6. The ILIT provides the following advantages for estate planning purposes:

    *   disposition of the trust assets according to the grantor's terms

    *   efficient use of the grantor's gift tax annual exclusion

    *   efficient use of the grantor's GST exemption

    *   avoidance of estate taxation of the insurance proceeds

    *   avoidance of probate

    *   liquidity for the grantor's estate

7. The *Crummey* case has taught us that as long as a trust contains a power to demand distribution, a present-interest gift will be considered to have been made. This guarantees the availability of the annual exclusion. Therefore, since there will be a possible federal gift tax created: (1) by transferring existing life insurance policies into a trust, and/or (2) by gifting premiums to the trustee, the availability of the annual exclusion becomes very important because it is a method to reduce or even eliminate federal gift tax liability. Thus qualifying gifts to an ILIT for the annual gift tax exclusion is essential if the grantor hopes to maximize his or her potential gift and estate tax savings.

8. An ILIT should be used when the goal is exclusion of the life insurance proceeds from the estate of both spouses. The drawback to this arrangement is that the insured relinquishes any control over the policy.

9. Taxable gifts (gifts in excess of the annual exclusions and marital deduction) are returned to the donor's estate tax base as adjusted taxable gifts, even if the taxable gifts were fully sheltered by the applicable credit amount. Therefore, annual-exclusion gifts represent a rare opportunity to avoid the federal tax system entirely. If the grantor makes systematic annual-exclusion gifts to his children and/or grandchildren over a

number of years, a significant estate tax savings will result. If the donor is married and his or her spouse elects to split gifts each year, the transfer tax savings can be doubled by increasing the annual exclusion to $30,000 per donee (in 2019). The savings can be even greater if the annual exclusion gifts are made to an ILIT and invested in a life insurance policy covering the donor's life (or perhaps the lives of the donor and his or her spouse).

10. Unfortunately, annual exclusion from gift taxes is not available for all gifts. The rules of Sec. 2503 state that the annual exclusion is available only for gifts of a present interest. That is, an annual-exclusion gift must give the donee a present right of enjoyment. A problem arises in creating a present interest when a gift is made to a trust for the benefit of the donee-beneficiaries. If the trust does not provide for immediate benefits and delays income and principal distribution to a future date, the trust provides a future interest to the beneficiaries. An ILIT is a future-interest trust.

11. The five recommended steps for establishing an ILIT are:

    Step 1: The ILIT is executed before the final policy application is made and any premium is paid.

    Step 2: The grantor transfers funds to the ILIT (and makes further gifts, as necessary, when premium payments are due).

    Step 3: The trustee sends notice to the beneficiaries of their Crummey withdrawal rights. (This step is repeated each time additional gifts are transferred to the ILIT.)

    Step 4: The trustee applies for the policy on the grantor's life and is named as owner and beneficiary of the policy. (The insured participates in the transaction only for the purpose of establishing his or her insurability and signs only the "insured" signature block on the policy application.)

    Step 5: The trustee pays the policy's annual premium to the insurance company when the Crummey powers lapse.

12. The irrevocable life insurance trust can provide the following benefits:

    - Gift taxes can be avoided for premiums contributed to the trust.

    - Estate taxes can be avoided when the proceeds are received.

    - Generation-skipping transfer taxes can be avoided if the insured's exemption is allocated to the trust.

    - The insured's transferable wealth can be enhanced through leveraging.

- The expenses and publicity of probate are avoided for transfers to the trust.

- Estate liquidity can be enhanced by the trust.

- The grantor-insured can control the disposition of the proceeds before the fact through the trust provisions.

- Income taxes are avoided on the corpus buildup and receipt of proceeds.

13. For gifts of life insurance to an ILIT to qualify for the annual gift tax exclusion, the donee must have an absolute and immediate power of withdrawal. If the trust document provides for a Crummey demand/withdrawal power, the transfer will generally qualify for the annual exclusion.

14. There are many practical uses for life insurance in the estate planning context:

- estate enhancement (RLIT)

- estate liquidity (ILIT)

- grandparent-grandchild trusts

- equity of inheritance

- non employed spouse insurance

Chapter 23:

Postmortem, Health, and Special Groups Planning

Learning Objectives

An understanding of the material in this chapter should enable the student to do the following:

LO 23.1   **Describe the methods used for postmortem estate planning.**

LO 23.2   **Describe the types of powers of attorney and their purposes.**

LO 23.3   **Identify the documents used for health care planning.**

LO 23.4   **Explain how estate planning can be tailored to meet the special needs of elderly and incapacitated individuals.**

LO 23.5   **Describe some of the basic issues that pertain to estate planning for married couples and single individuals.**

LO 23.6   **Explain various estate planning arrangements for blended families and various living arrangements.**

POSTMORTEM ESTATE PLANNING METHODS

LO 23.1   Describe the methods used for postmortem estate planning.

While the term *estate planning* pertains to arrangements made during the estate owner's lifetime, planners must be aware that many of the methods and tax elections discussed previously are used for revising, adjusting, and fine-tuning an estate plan after the decedent's death. Some common postmortem practices are briefly discussed in the following summary.

Qualified Disclaimer

The disclaimer is a useful postmortem technique because it can be used to avoid estate tax and it serves to rectify predeath planning mistakes and legal drafting errors. When properly executed, the amount of property passing to one or more beneficiaries may be decreased in order to increase property passing to other beneficiaries.

Although disclaimers are a part of the common law of most states, many states have specific statutes relating to their use. The purpose of the qualified disclaimer under Sec. 2518 is to provide uniform federal requirements aside from state law requirements. State statutes may impose other additional rules for disclaimers to be effective under state law.

Disclaimers may be used to refuse a power or interest in property that an individual receives by gift, will, or operation of law. The disclaimer provides a 9-month period to evaluate and correct uncertainties such as the sequence and time of deaths and estate valuation estimates.

Because a disclaimed property interest passes to another person, the disclaimer can be used to redistribute property and readjust tax consequences. Although the disclaimant may not direct who the property passes to, they often know or may suggest who is "next in line" to receive it. In fact, disclaimers are usually used for the purpose of directing property to a specific recipient. For instance, a surviving spouse can disclaim unneeded marital-deduction property in order to use the full amount of the decedent-spouse's basic credit amount.

EXAMPLE

Jane and her two adult children are her Uncle Dan's sole surviving relatives. Jane knows that Uncle Dan is quite ill and that his will names her as beneficiary of his entire $3,200,000 estate and Jane's children as contingent beneficiaries. Jane has an estate of $3,725,000 in her own right. Jane plans to disclaim her inheritance after Uncle Dan dies and thereby make a nontaxable transfer to her children and avoid increasing the size of her own estate for estate tax purposes. In essence, Jane will be rewriting her uncle's will via the disclaimer.

It is also possible for a life-income beneficiary to disclaim property in order to accelerate the receipt of the property by the remainderperson.

EXAMPLE

Several years ago, Kate's Uncle George executed a will in which he created a testamentary trust for the benefit of Kate and her sons, Ron and Don. At Uncle George's death, Kate was to become the life-income beneficiary, and at Kate's death, the trust corpus was to pass to Kate's sons, Ron and Don. At the time of Uncle George's recent death, Kate made a qualified disclaimer of her life estate income interest. Kate's disclaimer accelerated the distribution of the remainder interests, causing the corpus to pass directly to Ron and Don.

Keep in mind that a disclaimer is not the same as a release. A release involves the relinquishment of a power or interest in property that has previously been accepted. A disclaimer, on the other hand, requires that the disclaimant must not expressly or by implication have accepted the disclaimed property interest or any benefits of the property interest. A disclaimant is not necessarily considered to have accepted property merely because title to the property vests in the disclaimant under state law at the time of the owner's death. However, if the disclaimant accepts rental income, interest income, or dividends from the property, the disclaimant is deemed to have accepted the property. Once the recipient of the property is deemed to have accepted the property, a transfer of the property to another constitutes a taxable gift.

One of the requirements of Sec. 2518 is that the disclaimer must be received by the transferor within 9 months after the date on which the transfer was made. For the disclaimant's protection it is advisable for the disclaimant to have some evidence of receipt and recognition of the disclaimer by the transferor or the executor of the transferor. Therefore, the disclaimer should include a form, signed and dated by the transferor, that the disclaimer was received.

EXAMPLE

Receipt of disclaimer by _____ (disclaimant's name) on _____ (date) _____ (signature of transferor/executor)

The uses, benefits, and advantages of the disclaimer are quite numerous. The primary advantages are derived from the flexibility and freedom it provides clients. It is a relatively straightforward, uncomplicated estate planning and corrective device as long as legal requirements are properly met.

Alternate Valuation Date

Another election available to the personal representative concerns the alternate valuation date. With this election, estate assets (with limited exceptions) can be valued 6 months after the decedent's date of death, providing the value of the assets on the later date is lower than the value on the date of death. By electing the alternate valuation date, the personal representative avoids paying higher estate taxes on estate assets that, overall, had a greater value at death than 6 months later. However, the income tax basis of the property is also set at the 6-month later date, meaning more income tax may be owed when the property is sold.

Current-Use/Special-Use Valuation for Real Estate of Closely Held Businesses and Farms

If certain conditions are met, IRC Sec. 2032A allows the personal representative to elect that a farm and certain closely held business property included in a decedent's gross estate be valued for estate tax purposes at its current- or special-use value (limited to an amount indexed for inflation) rather than at its highest and best-use value. Although this election decreases estate tax, the income tax basis of property is the lower special-use value, meaning more income tax may be owed when the property is sold.

Extension of Time for Payment of Estate Tax on Closely Held Business Interests

Under IRC Sec. 6166, the personal representative may elect to defer the payment of estate tax attributable to the inclusion of a closely held business in a decedent's estate. If the closely held business comprises more than 35 percent of the decedent's adjusted gross estate and the estate otherwise qualifies, estate taxes may be paid over a 14-year 9-month period. This tax payment deferral allows the surviving business members to retain and continue operating the business instead of having to sell it to pay estate taxes.

IRC Section 303—Stock Redemption

This IRC section allows an estate that contains stock to redeem a portion of or all of the stock for the purpose of paying funeral and administrative expenses and death taxes without the redemptions being treated as a dividend. This favorable tax treatment permits the estate to reduce its income tax liability.

Marital Deduction Qualification of QTIP Trust Property

The QTIP election is also made by the personal representative on the decedent's federal estate tax return. This election allows certain terminable property interests to qualify for the marital deduction.

The property is placed in a special (QTIP) trust and, to the extent it is not consumed or given away during the surviving spouse's lifetime, it will be taxable in the estate of the surviving spouse. Although the property is included in the surviving spouse's gross estate, the property passes according to the terms of the trust. The QTIP election permits the deferral of estate taxes on certain otherwise nondeductible terminable property interests until the death of the surviving spouse.

Election by Surviving Spouse to Split Gifts

A postmortem election to split gifts made by the decedent spouse during his or her lifetime benefits the decedent's estate in three ways: a reduction in gift tax liability, a decrease in estate tax liability, and—because transfer taxes are lessened—a greater portion of estate assets (that is, the amount of gift and estate taxes saved) passed to the beneficiaries.

Family Allowance

The family allowance is a small, limited sum of money set aside for the support of a surviving spouse and children during the time the estate is being administered. This property is not considered part of the distributable estate, is typically exempt from state death taxes, and may pass to the family whether or not it is needed.

Election Against Decedent's Will by Surviving Spouse

According to state laws called *elective share statutes*, surviving spouses are entitled to receive a statutorily specified minimum percentage of their decedent spouse's estate. Generally, a surviving spouse with living children is entitled to about one-third of the decedent spouse's estate and, if there are no children, to one-half of the estate. If a decedent spouse's will leaves a surviving spouse less than the state's statutory amount, the survivor can file an election with the probate court to go against the will in order to receive the higher amount. Making this election changes the decedent spouse's will because it results in a redistribution of his or her estate. The surviving spouse receives more than the will called for, and this in turn means other beneficiaries will receive less than under the will.

Deduction of Certain Administrative Expenses

The expenses of administering certain property included in the decedent's gross estate are generally deductible from either the federal estate tax return, Form 706, or the estate's federal income tax return, Form 1041. The greater tax savings determines which form to use. Only certain administrative expenses may be deducted on each form, however. Administrative costs deductible on either Form 706 or Form 1041 include expenses incurred in the collection, distribution, and preservation of probate assets and in the payment of estate debts. Court costs, executor's commissions, attorney fees, accounting fees, the costs incurred on the sale of estate property, and the excise taxes included in these sales (if a sale was necessary for estate settlement) are deductible on either form.

Deduction of Medical Expenses

A decedent's personal administrator or surviving spouse may elect to deduct the decedent's unreimbursed medical expenses on the decedent's final income tax return (Form 1040) or on the federal estate tax return form (Form 706), depending on the greater overall tax savings. For instance, if the decedent's estate is less than the basic exclusion amount (credit equivalent), the deduction would be lost, but if the expenses are taken on the income tax return, income taxes are saved. On the other hand, if the decedent's estate exceeds the exemption equivalent but there is no estate tax liability due to the basic credit amount and marital deduction, deducting the medical expenses on the decedent's final income tax return again saves taxes. If there is federal estate tax liability, higher taxes may result from deducting medical expenses on Form 706.

Executor's Fees as Bequest or Income

An executor may find it tax-advantageous to waive the executor's fee. If an executor receives a fee for administering a decedent's estate, the fee is deductible by the estate on the estate tax return (Form 706) or on the estate's income tax return (Form 1041); the fee, however, is taxable income to the executor. Executors who are also beneficiaries of the decedent's estate may wish to waive the fee. When the fee is waived, the estate is precluded from deducting that particular expense and the estate is thereby increased. More tax may be saved by the executor's receiving the fee income tax free as a bequest than by characterizing the executor's commission as a deductible expense of the estate.

POWERS OF ATTORNEY

LO 23.2   Describe the types of powers of attorney and their purposes.

Types of Powers of Attorney

durable power of attorney

special (limited) power of attorney

springing durable power of attorney

There are various types of powers of attorney:

- A **durable power of attorney** can be a valuable estate planning tool. It enables an individual (called a principal) to grant powers that remain in effect throughout the principal's incapacity.

- A **special (limited) power of attorney** enables the agent to act only with regard to one or more specific tasks or for a specified period of time.

- A **springing durable power of attorney** becomes operative only when a specified event occurs. The event is usually physical or mental incompetency or disappearance. A springing power of attorney is a solution for individuals reluctant to grant broad powers to another person while they are still capable of making decisions. It is important that the event triggering the power be carefully defined in the document. Most states recognize a springing power of attorney. Some states (ex. Florida) are mandating immediate powers of attorneys to avoid delays in usage, particularly for health care.

Of the three types mentioned, the durable power of attorney is the most useful for retirement and estate planning purposes. Therefore, the remainder of this section takes a closer look at some financial aspects of a durable power of attorney. (See Appendix C for a sample durable power of attorney.)

Advantages of a Durable Power of Attorney

There are many advantages to having a durable power of attorney. First, proper execution of this document can help to avoid the costs, delays, and emotional upsets of competency proceedings. Second, a court-appointed conservator or guardian may not be a person the principal would have chosen. Third, the activities transacted by an agent are private. In contrast, court supervision of a conservator's or guardian's actions on behalf of an incompetent involves records open to public scrutiny. A power of attorney can be advantageous in community-property states if one spouse becomes disabled and both spouses' signatures are necessary for community-property transactions.

Executing a power of attorney is relatively inexpensive and not time consuming due to the simplicity and availability of standard forms. Furthermore, a competent principal may revoke the instrument at any time. Assets do not have to be retitled or transferred. In most cases, it is not necessary to file or record a power of attorney with any governmental authority, although some states require recordation and other formalities for real estate transactions.

Estate Planning and Retirement Considerations. A durable power of attorney presents numerous retirement and estate planning possibilities. Retirement considerations include an agent's authority to exercise options under the principal's retirement plans (in this context the attorney-in-fact is referred to as an agent of the principal). Powers to be considered include powers to change beneficiary designations, elect payout options, satisfy spousal waiver requirements, and borrow from the plan.

Estate planning-type powers in a durable power of attorney can provide numerous transfer-tax benefits. For example, if there is authority to make gifts, an agent can use the federal annual gift tax exclusion (Sec. 2503(b)) to reduce the principal's gross estate by commencing or continuing a gifting program.

EXAMPLE

X, the father of five adult children, unexpectedly becomes incapacitated in December of last year. The doctors believe X's death is imminent. If X has executed a durable power of attorney specifically granting the authority to make gifts on X's behalf (and assuming no previous gifts from X to his children that year), X's agent could remove property valued at five times the annual-exclusion amount from X's estate by the end of that year and five more annual-exclusion amounts at the beginning of the next calendar year, providing X survives until then. With gift splitting and additional gifts to the children's spouses, grandchildren, and other relatives, it is possible for the agent to remove a substantial amount of property from X's gross estate completely free of transfer taxes.

Making gifts of appreciating property will help to avoid additional estate taxes generated by appreciation. (Note, however, that gifts of appreciating property carry over the donor-principal's adjusted basis for income tax purposes as opposed to receiving a step up in basis if held until the donor's death and included in the donor's gross estate.) With gifting authority, an agent can make tax-free gifts to the principal's spouse under the unlimited gift tax marital deduction to save gift and estate taxes. For example, an agent can transfer assets from a wealthy spouse to a less wealthy spouse to fully utilize the basic credit amounts in both estates. In larger marital estates, tax savings may also be achieved if estates are equalized to take advantage of lower estate tax rates in each estate. In addition, by gifting the proper type of assets, it may be possible for an estate to meet the mathematical tests required for a Sec. 303 stock redemption, a Sec. 6166 installment payout of taxes, and Sec. 2032A special-use valuation for a farm and certain real property used in a closely held business.

Advantages of Power of Attorney
- principal's alter ego
- privacy
- flexibility
- inexpensiveness
- simplicity
- acceptance over living will
- viability despite disability
- avoidance of incompetency proceedings
- estate planning tool

Litigation concerning powers of attorney and gifting issues, however, emphasizes the importance of an express authorization of the agent's power to make gifts on behalf of the principal, including any limitations on the group of potential recipients and amounts to be gifted. The IRS will not infer the power to make gifts from a broad grant of authority to an agent. When the agent is both a relative *and* a potential gift beneficiary, it is advisable to include a provision permitting gifts to relatives, including the agent. For the agent's protection from a possible claim by the IRS that the agent holds a general power of appointment, the agent's power to make such gifts can be limited. For instance, the agent's ability to make self-gifts can be limited to an ascertainable standard, noncumulative lapsing amounts not to exceed the gift tax annual-exclusion amount, or the greater of $5,000 or 5 percent of the principal's estate value. Another limitation could be the requirement of consent by an adverse party.

Another important estate planning consideration that a durable power of attorney may address is the agent's having authority to make disclaimers on behalf of a principal and having asset management powers that enable the agent to qualify a principal for Medicaid assistance.

HEALTH PLANNING

LO 23.3   Identify the documents used for health care planning.

Advance Medical Directives

advance medical directives

It is always prudent for estate owners, prior to advanced age, to have arrangements in place for health care decision making. Fundamental to the decision-making system is a statement declaring the owner's intent for the medical treatment he or she wants should incapacity arise. Durable powers of attorney for health care and living wills are referred to as **advance medical directives**. Although a relatively small percentage of the American public currently have some type of advance medical directive, these documents are receiving more attention due to new legislation, court decisions, practical experience, and a growing recognition that *health* planning is as important as *wealth* planning. Advances in medical technology that prolong life have increased fears of lengthy artificial life support and family financial disaster. Modern medicine can keep a person alive by artificial mechanisms even though the individual is unconscious and essentially nonfunctional. Life-sustaining procedures are used in cases of accident or terminal illness where death is imminent and recovery highly improbable. Advance medical directives have evolved in response to these situations. By executing an advance medical directive such as a living will and/or a durable power of attorney for health care (medical power of attorney), individuals may make arrangements and give authority to others to carry out their health care instructions. (Samples of these documents are included in the appendixes.)

Living Wills

living will

A few decades ago living wills were virtually nonexistent, and by 1984, only a few states had enacted living-will legislation. Practically all states now have statutes concerning the issues surrounding living wills. A **living will** addresses the inherent conflict of an individual's right to privacy and self-determination versus the medical oath to preserve life whenever possible. They apply to situations where the patient is terminally incapacitated or permanently unconscious and are limited to decisions concerning artificial life-support issues. Living wills have become the subject of public attention in recent years due to increased concerns about health and financial matters and the media coverage of certain right-to-die cases such as the *Cruzan v. Director (1990)* case in Missouri and the physician-guided suicide cases in Michigan.

State statutes, while similar, contain variations. One common requirement is a statement by one or more physicians that the declarant's death is, indeed, imminent. Individuals who execute living wills make a decision not to prolong the dying process, which may involve pain, suffering, and financial disaster for them and their families if recovery or life as they know it is no longer possible. An area in which state statutes vary concerns the definition of a terminal condition that will result in death.

There are many serious questions regarding the legal effect of living wills. It is important that state law be carefully examined. Actions taken by a state legislature could determine whether physicians and other health care personnel will follow living-will directives. The potential civil or criminal liability of physicians and licensed health personnel who act in accordance with living-will directives is an important legal issue involving the right to die. Most state statutes, however, grant immunity to medical providers acting in accordance with a patient's living will. Clearly, the law is still evolving in this area.

Advance medical directives also present moral considerations. Because the most fundamental mandate of a physician is to preserve life, a physician may consider that being party to a directive not to provide life support is contrary to medical training and principles. Also, persons executing or carrying out living wills may encounter personal obstacles of a religious or moral nature. In any event, concerns about the financial and emotional costs of artificially sustaining life are likely to result in an increasing number of individuals creating living wills in the future.

Medical Durable Powers of Attorney/Proxies

health care proxy

It is also advisable for estate owners to have a document appointing someone to act on their behalf with respect to personal medically related decisions—the idea being that the individual, while healthy and fully competent, expressed in writing (and ideally also verbally) his or her medical wishes and named someone to have the wishes carried out. This instrument is called a **health care proxy** or medical power of attorney. This document legally grants an agent, usually a close family member, the authority to act for the declarant and in the declarant's best interests in a medical context. The ideal situation is for the declarant to have expressed his or her wishes to numerous close family members at one or more times during the progression of family life.

At the present time, medical durable powers of attorney and health care proxies are statutorily authorized in all states. While the financial management advantages of a durable power of attorney have long been recognized, its use with respect to health and medical care is more recent. Because a durable power of attorney for health care covers a broad range of health care decisions, it may be an alternative or a supplement to a living will. A medical power of attorney, unlike a living will, may provide direction in nonterminal medical situations concerning such issues as: access to and disclosure of medical records and personal information; anatomical gifts; psychiatric care; releases of medical personnel; hiring and discharging household, medical, and companion help; and life-support provisions pertaining to mechanical respiration, cardiac resuscitation, organ transplants, blood transfusions, and withholding and withdrawing artificial nutrition and hydration. (Note, however, that the agent will be able to withhold or withdraw life support only when the principal's condition is terminal or death is imminent.)

Living Wills Versus Powers of Attorney

Living Wills	Powers of Attorney
• patient and physician only	• third-party agent necessary
• limited breadth and flexibility	• can cover broad spectrum of matters
• terminal condition necessary	• effective upon mere incompetency
Having Both Is Best	

If a patient has created an advance medical directive, such as a medical durable power of attorney, the individual acting on behalf of the patient is referred to as an agent, as mentioned above. If, however, the patient does not have an advance medical directive and has therefore not chosen an agent, the patient's family may choose a proxy to make medical treatment decisions for the patient. The proxy is someone who knows the patient well and knows what the patient's medical wishes are.

Today, there is federal legislation intended to encourage individuals to think about health care choices. As part of the Omnibus Budget Reconciliation Act of 1990, The Patient Self-Determination Act became effective in December 1991. The Act requires hospitals, nursing homes, health maintenance organizations, hospices, and home health care companies participating in Medicare or Medicaid to tell patients whether their state permits them to refuse life-prolonging treatment. Health service providers are required to note in the patient's medical file the patient's wishes to reject life support.

The Health Insurance Portability and Accountability Act (HIPAA) of 1996 and the regulations to this federal act became effective in April 2003. The regulations contain provisions on how health care information must be kept confidential and the circumstances under which individuals' health care information may be disclosed. Estate planners and estate attorneys drafting durable medical powers of attorney and advance medical directives must make certain the documents comply with the HIPAA privacy regulations to ensure the acceptance and effect of these documents. Previously existing powers of attorney and advance medical directives should also be reviewed for compliance and potential corresponding changes in state law with respect to HIPAA.

Although practically all states permit some form of legal advance directive for health care that can be used to direct at least some forms of psychiatric procedures, a relatively new legal instrument, referred to as a psychiatric advance directive (PAD), is also recognized by a majority of states. These directives are used specifically to document a competent person's instructions regarding future mental health treatment in preparation for the possibility of the declarant's later loss of mental capacity. More than one-half of the states have adopted specific PAD statutes.

CPR/DNR Directives

CPR directives

Cardiopulmonary resuscitation (CPR) is an emergency procedure that occurs when an individual's heart stops beating or when an individual ceases to breathe. In attempts to restart the heart or respiration, CPR typically involves compressing the patient's chest and using mouth-to-mouth resuscitation. In this emergency process, it is possible the patient's ribs may be broken and/or a tube may need to be inserted into the patient's neck to locate an air passageway. **CPR directives** are documents permitting an individual to refuse cardiopulmonary resuscitation.

DNR directive

A do-not-resuscitate (DNR) declaration is a type of CPR directive that exists in a hospital or nursing home setting. A DNR order is one in which either the patient or his or her agent limits resuscitative measures when and if the patient's heart and/or lungs no longer function. There are also statutes in some states that permit a CPR directive outside a hospital or nursing home setting. The purpose of this type of CPR directive is to limit paramedics or other rescue personnel in resuscitation efforts concerning the principal's heart or lungs in a home setting. Sometimes the subject of a nonhospital/nonnursing home CPR directive wears a necklace or bracelet stating, "No CPR." When an individual not in a hospital, nursing home, or hospice has a CPR directive, it is because the person is in a very advanced stage of illness. A CPR or **DNR directive** does not prevent other necessary medical procedures or limit pain control measures.

Five Wishes

Five Wishes

Another type of advance medical directive is called **Five Wishes**. This document is easy to understand and is often used to introduce conversations about the uncomfortable subject of terminal illness and dying. Five Wishes is a directive that has been recognized by the majority of states and a growing number of medical care providers and institutions. Physicians in states of acceptance will honor the Five Wishes form. It was created by known experts in the care of the terminally ill and the Commission on the Legal Problems of the Elderly of the American Bar Association. The intention of Five Wishes is to give seriously ill people a way to express their end-of-life wishes and to provide guidance for loved ones, care providers, friends, and clergy. Completion of the Five Wishes form helps to achieve emotional and psychological comfort to all concerned. The areas covered by the Five Wishes form are

- choice of health care agent
- medical treatment desired or not wanted
- care and comfort wishes
- personal treatment
- wishes for loved ones to know, including funeral and disposal of the body

Once this revocable, changeable form is signed and witnessed, it is a valid legal document in those states recognizing it. Executing Five Wishes revokes a previously executed advance medical directive or living will that the declarant may have had. Ideally, discussions on each of the five wishes have preceded its execution. Like any document of this nature, the form should be kept in a safe place in the person's home. Copies should be given to family members and other people who care about the declarant.

ESTATE PLANNING FOR THE ELDERLY AND INCAPACITATED

LO 23.4   Explain how estate planning can be tailored to meet the special needs of elderly and incapacitated individuals.

Another area of estate planning that deserves special attention is planning for elderly and incapacitated individuals. Although the proper emphasis of an estate plan might seem to be the distribution of property to the estate owner's heirs with the least tax liability, often the preservation of assets during lifetime is of far greater importance to the client than after-death issues. Preparing for the future financial and long-term care needs of the elderly, ill, and incapacitated presents some estate planning challenges. For instance, an estate plan that is oriented primarily toward passing property to the next generation becomes irrelevant if the estate is practically depleted by the cost of long-term care. On the other hand, retention of assets can prevent an estate owner from meeting Medicaid eligibility requirements. A comprehensive estate plan must address the implications of the client's potential need for long-term care.

One possible solution to achieving estate asset preservation goals and meeting long-term care needs is long-term care insurance (LTCI). However, most people do not purchase LTCI as the penetration rate in the U.S. is well below 10 percent as of 2019. For the owners of large estates, money expended to pay LTCI premiums escapes estate taxation. While it is established that long-term care costs may be deductible from the gross estate, there is no assurance that, without LTCI, lengthy long-term care will not exhaust or greatly diminish the assets in an estate. In addition to traditional LTCI, Medicare, Medicaid, hybrid products, Veterans administration, self-funding, and family members will provide a large amount of the long-term care funding. Over 70 percent of all people age 65 and over will need some long-term care services, and more than 70 percent of that will be provided informally and free by family members. Additionally, Medicaid is the largest funding source for long-term care expenses. However, generally only individuals with very little assets and income qualify for Medicaid coverage. There are some exemptions and protections for a spouse of a person who needs care. Medicare can cover a short period of long-term care services, but is not primarily designed to cover long-term care expenses.

The new hybrid long-term care policies can be a mix of life insurance and long-term care insurance–providing a dual benefit for estate planning purposes. These policies have become more popular in recent years, especially since the Pension Protection Act of 2006 helped ease concerns about 1035 exchanges of policies into the new policies.

Retaining Control With Trusts and Durable Powers of Attorney

Trust arrangements and durable powers of attorney are two devices that allow a client to have continued asset management despite incompetency. The trustee manages the trust property in accordance with the settlor's directions as established in the trust terms. For example, the settlor can grant the trustee the power to distribute income or principal at regular, preestablished intervals or at the trustee's discretion should the settlor later become incapacitated. Keep in mind, however, that trusts are used specifically for asset management; trustees cannot make personal health care decisions for an incompetent.

Durable powers of attorney can provide guidance for the personal care and financial decisions resulting from a client's incapacity.

Special Needs Trust (SNT)

special needs trusts

Special needs trusts are property-management devices used to protect the assets of individuals who anticipate long-term disability situations in the future. Often the subjects of special-needs trusts are children. Ethical considerations abound in discussions of special needs trusts because they entail arranging beneficiaries' financial interests to avail the beneficiaries of government-assistance programs such as Medicaid, Supplemental Security Income (SSI), In-Home Medical Care Services, and so forth. In other words, an individual's private assets are put in a special needs trust in order to keep those assets from being reached by the government for reimbursement. Insulation of the beneficiaries' assets is accomplished by having language in the document prohibiting trust principal from being used in substitution for governmental benefits. A few states view such trusts as against public policy and deny them legal recognition. If you want to leave money to a child or family member with special needs, you need to plan accordingly. Leaving them too much money or income could jeopardize their ability to receive federal aid. Always consult with an attorney when setting up a special needs trust or engaging in special needs planning. Special needs trusts are designed for beneficiaries with special needs. Special needs trusts are widely accepted and are an important part of the estate planning process for any parents with a special needs family member. In most states, special-needs trusts cannot be set up for someone over age 65, and in some cases cannot be funded for the individual after age 65. So if you want to set up a special needs trust for an adult child, make sure you do it before they reach age 65.

Elder Law Durable Power of Attorney

elder law durable power of attorney

In many instances, financial advisors and estate planners recommend that individuals have a financial plan in place in the event of later incompetency. A durable power of attorney may be a valuable addition to an estate owner's financial plans, especially in later years of life. There are some unique qualities that may pertain to a durable power of attorney for an elderly person—qualities and requirements to which an elder law attorney must be especially sensitive. Powers of attorney that are specifically for elderly clients are called elder law durable powers of attorney. Many of the reasons for such specificity involve the capacity of the elder client. Perhaps what drives an elderly client to execute an **elder law durable power of attorney** is that the principal is aware of the beginning or intermediate signs of one or more forms of impairment and therefore anticipates greater disability as time passes. Given the appropriate powers, the attorney-in-fact may expedite the principal's Medicaid eligibility, arrange for in-home or nursing home care, hire necessary health care personnel, employ companions, and so forth.

If the elderly client seeking the power of attorney displays signs of incompetency or the drafter has reservations about the client's mental capacity, the elder law attorney's choices are more limited. One solution may be to, with the client's consent, get a written opinion about the client's competency from the client's doctor(s), family, and/or other close acquaintances before proceeding to draft the document. If this fails, the attorney will have to work within the framework of prior instruments and arrangements. The choice of the most appropriate agent(s)—sometimes referred to as an attorney-in-fact—for elderly individuals is crucial. Protection from financial and personal abuse is paramount. In many cases, it is recommended that more than one agent be appointed with the requirement that one must approve the other's decisions or that the agents must be in agreement before decisions are made. Because the elderly client's children and/or spouse are often the agents under the power, having more than one caring family member has obvious built-in safeguards. On the other hand, having multiple agents (co-agents/co-attorneys-in-fact) may be cumbersome and result in more difficulty in reaching an agreement. If a spouse or other close family member is not particularly financially minded, a workable solution may be to appoint an independent financial agent along with one or more close family members as co-agents to achieve financial acumen balanced with personal knowledge. Careful drafting is, of course, necessary because a document with multiple agents should contain provisions for dispute resolution, hierarchy in decision making, and so forth. The issues that may be addressed in elder law durable powers of attorney are practically infinite, depending on the principal's particular circumstances. As an example, an important and common issue to resolve before a durable power of attorney becomes effective is whether the elderly principal wishes to remain in his or her home with caregivers during the remaining years of life. Clearly, elder law durable powers of attorney must be drafted with extreme care.

Sometimes, a client resists executing a durable power of attorney because of the perception that it is an admission of the inability to manage his or her own affairs. In such a situation, a springing power of attorney may be advisable. Because a springing power of attorney does not become operative until the time of the principal's incapacity, what constitutes incapacity for the particular principal should be carefully delineated in the document.

The combination of a trust and durable power of attorney allows the creator to indirectly maintain control of personal and financial matters when physical or mental limitations prevent the client from managing matters directly. An elderly client can retain personal dignity. A trust and durable power of attorney drafted with incapacity provisions may serve to avoid conservatorship or guardianship proceedings. Compared to a trust or durable power of attorney, these two court-supervised alternatives are expensive and time consuming, and they may undermine a person's self-esteem. Executing a trust or durable power of attorney, however, does not guarantee that the client will be completely protected from the appointment of a conservator or guardian. No matter how carefully the instruments are drafted, it is possible for court proceedings to result from a challenge to the estate owner's trust or durable power of attorney. For example, a disgruntled heir may claim that the client lacked capacity or was unfairly influenced by another at the time the document was executed and may seek to have it set aside.

Guardianship and Conservatorship

Judicial guardianship and conservatorship are more complicated, time-consuming, costly, and restrictive solutions to incompetency compared to the relatively simple agency relationship created by a durable power of attorney. A power of attorney reflects a voluntary, consensual agreement in which an individual (the principal) arranges for an agent (the attorney-in-fact) or named guardian to attend to the principal's personal care and property if the principal becomes incapacitated. Although one agent may be named to care for the principal, usually a relative or trusted friend becomes responsible for the care of the person while a bank or other entity oversees the property. In the absence of a durable power of attorney, a court proceeding may be held to establish incompetency to manage client's affairs. After hearing evidence of incompetency, a court may appoint a guardian or conservator to act on behalf of the disabled party, called a *ward*. The process is generally an unpleasant one that, in the end, results in substantial loss of a ward's liberties. In some cases, the term *guardian* pertains specifically to care of the person and the term *conservator* to management of the property. Sometimes, these terms are used interchangeably. The scope of the court-appointed guardian's powers to act for the ward may be broad or limited. Usually, however, the guardian has responsibility for the ward personally and the ward's property. It is the court supervision of the guardianship relationship that proves costly, time-consuming, and trying.

In addition to a durable power of attorney, other methods used to avoid judicial guardianship include joint ownership of property, advance medical directives, and trusts. When property is titled in more than one name, another party is already in place to manage the property, bank accounts, and so forth. As previously discussed, advance medical directives and living wills provide for health decision making prior to disability.

standby trust

Guardianship may also be circumvented with trusts. A primary benefit of a revocable living trust is that the trustee manages the trust property according to trust terms stated by the grantor. The trustee continues to administer the assets during the grantor's incapacity. Another type of trust used in planning for incompetency is a **standby trust**. A standby trust often works in tandem with a durable or springing power of attorney. The trust is unfunded until the grantor becomes incapacitated, and an attorney-in-fact funds the trust with assets of the grantor for the trustee to manage.

The planner should take reasonable precautions to determine that the client is competent at the time documents are executed. To ascertain an elderly client's mental competency, the planner should establish that the client has knowledge of his or her property, recognizes the purposes of meeting with the planner with regard to the property, and understands the arrangements to be undertaken. Documentation supporting the client's apparent capacity can be placed in the client's file. Trusts and medical durable powers of attorney provide the estate planner and the estate owner with a broad scope of permissible powers and the necessary flexibility to fashion incapacity-contingency plans.

Considerations Concerning Medical Assistance Programs

Another planning consideration is the possibility that the elderly client will inherit money or property from a family member's estate or receive death proceeds as the named beneficiary of a decedent's insurance policy. Since there is limited time to deal with the consequences of an unexpected increase in an elderly person's estate, such funds may cause greater estate tax liability than anticipated. In addition, if the recipient of the proceeds or inheritance is a Medicaid applicant, the property would be considered a Medicaid-available resource. Medicaid is a federal program that may help with payments for long-term care. Although Medicare is often thought of as being a federal system to which qualifying individuals are entitled because they had wages withheld and paid into the system, Medicaid is different. Taxpayers are not necessarily entitled to Medicaid. States obtain financial assistance from the federal government by administering their medical assistance programs in accordance with federal Medicaid rules. Certain levels of wealth or income determine whether or not a person qualifies to receive Medicaid assistance. The limits imposed on an applicant's assets and income are determined by the particular state.

Medicaid has sometimes been described as a welfare health care program. If an applicant or the spouse of an applicant is determined to have sufficient wealth to pay for health care, Medicaid will not pay for it. To be eligible for Medicaid benefits, an applicant must be in relative poverty as determined under the Medicaid rules. The following changes in the Medicaid laws after the enactment of the Omnibus Budget Reconciliation Act of 1993 (OBRA '93) are that applicants may be denied Medicaid benefits if they or their spouses: (1) have access to income in excess of a state's established maximum amounts, (2) have available assets in excess of permissible state-determined amounts, or (3) have made transfers of assets to other individuals within 60 months.

Older persons who make lifetime gifts to reduce their taxable estates based on estate planning advice may delay eligibility for Medicaid assistance if the gifts occur within a 60-month look-back period. If a client does not make gratuitous transfers within the appropriate time period before applying for Medicaid, transfers prior to that period will not cause disqualification. A properly drafted supplemental trust, also called a Craven trust, may be used to provide supplemental maintenance for a nongrantor beneficiary without triggering the beneficiary's loss of governmental assistance benefits. Note also that an applicant's disclaimer of an unexpected inheritance or insurance death proceeds to avoid being disqualified for Medicaid eligibility is likely to be unsuccessful because the particular state may consider the disclaimer to be a transfer for Medicaid eligibility purposes. *Clearly, that there are many ethical issues related to planning for eligibility for Medicaid.* Due to the complexities and recent changes in the Medicaid laws, the prudent estate planner should be well versed in Medicaid eligibility planning and other considerations specific to elderly or incapacitated clients.

ESTATE PLANNING FOR MARRIED COUPLES

LO 23.5   **Describe some of the basic issues that pertain to estate planning for married couples and single individuals.**

Estate planners may have to take special considerations into account when planning for married couples. In certain areas, U.S. law favors married status and treats a married couple as a single unit (for example, the unlimited marital gift and estate tax deduction and joint income tax returns), but a planner should be aware that the interests of a married couple may not be identical and may even be conflicting. Thus, one planner may not be able to fairly address the needs of both parties. In other words, just because a married couple seeks joint representation, the planner should not automatically conclude that the parties share identical objectives. Spousal estate planning and property disposition goals may be especially divergent and complicated when one or both have children from earlier marriages. Other areas of potential conflict may be: the existence of one or both spouses' community property, the subjection of marital or separate property to the claims of one spouse's creditors, reciprocal wills, the tax consequences of gift splitting, and the control or lack of control a surviving spouse will have over property after the first spouse's death.

Clearly, an estate planner for a couple must ascertain whether the interests of both spouses are the same or adverse. If both spouses are in agreement and appear to be comfortable using the same planner, joint representation of both parties should not be an ethical or practical problem. However, if there seems to be marital conflict, the planner should recommend that each spouse seek separate estate planning advice. When a married couple with differing estate planning goals still wants joint advice, all existing and potential conflicts should be disclosed, and the estate planner should obtain a written waiver or agreement from both parties concerning their joint representation for the planner's and the clients' protection. The agreement can establish some ground rules concerning the disclosure policy of each party's plan, documents, and joint and separate meetings. Addressing areas of potential conflict at the outset reduces the likelihood of problems for all parties. In keeping with current ethical concerns, some states require planners to send married couples a detailed joint representation letter outlining potential conflicts and to obtain the signatures of both parties before providing joint estate planning representation.

Separation and Divorce

Estate considerations also arise if spouses separate and divorce. In this situation, it is advisable, if possible, for each spouse to have an attorney or other professional advisor review the estate plans of both persons. This allows both individuals to plan more effectively for the benefit of any children from the union. Both former spouses should also execute new wills, even if their intentions upon death remain the same.

Frequently, an irrevocable life insurance trust is used in divorce situations to provide for a surviving spouse and children. Often, a trust is set up and the trustee purchases a policy on the life of the wealthier spouse, naming the surviving former spouse or children as beneficiaries. This arrangement can provide for the surviving beneficiaries' financial needs and, as long as the decedent former spouse did not hold any incidents of ownership in the policy or name the estate as beneficiary, the life insurance proceeds avoid inclusion in the insured-decedent's estate.

For gift tax purposes, divorcing spouses who enter into a written agreement addressing their marital and property rights may transfer marital or property rights to each other pursuant to the agreement free of federal gift taxation. Transfers of property between divorcing spouses that are incident to the divorce are not subject to federal gift taxation because the transfers and giving up of marital rights are treated as being made for full and adequate consideration in money or money's worth. The divorce, however, must occur within a 3-year period that revolves around the timing of the property-settlement agreement for the transfer to avoid gift tax.

Estate Planning for Singles

Eleven percent of adult women are widows. Widows, widowers, single parents, and confirmed singles over the age of 35 comprise almost 30 percent of the U.S. population, according to the Census Bureau. This group is reported to hold approximately the same percentage of the country's wealth. Estate planning for singles may present some unique, nonroutine planning situations that do not typically arise with married clients. There are often different psychological factors for single and married clients. For instance, some single clients, if they feel alone and vulnerable, may be less trusting. Therefore, more effort on the planner's part may be required to build rapport and establish trust. Single parents may be very dependent on child support payments to supplement income. Widows and widowers may be trying to live on monthly Social Security checks and small pension payments.

Older single people—but particularly widows and widowers—need to know or feel that they can act independently. Many fear becoming dependent on their children and other family members. They want to be able to take care of themselves for as long as possible. Older singles may gain a sense of independence, security, and confidence by knowing they have any or all of the following: certain investments, a living trust to manage their affairs if they become disabled, a durable power of attorney, a living will, an emergency or funeral fund, disability insurance, and long-term care insurance. A consolidated written list of accounts and their values can also provide a source of comfort to singles.

The estate planner needs to recognize when planning for singles that their estate planning objectives and needs are likely to be somewhat different from the goals of married couples and two-parent family households. He or she must plan differently for single clients who are financially responsible for minor children than for those clients with adult children who are attempting to manage the parent's finances or whose family members are asking for loans.

The individual who is left financially strapped as a result of becoming single has dissimilar concerns from the widow or widower who inherited substantial assets but is overwhelmed by the responsibility and complexity of the inheritance. Although planning for singles has some aspects in common (such as the loss of the marital deduction and gift splitting), the advisor must approach and analyze each situation individually and not according to a group stereotype.

Social Security Death Benefits

Social Security offers two different survivor benefits. First, it pays a $255 lump-sum amount to a surviving beneficiary, typically the spouse. This money was originally designed to help pay for things like the funeral home costs, but its not indexed and today does not help out a lot. The other survivor aspect of Social Security is the payment of benefits to surviving beneficiaries. A surviving spouse or ex-spouse can receive the benefits based on the deceased worker's benefits. A widow or widower can receive benefits if the survivor is at least age 60 (or age 50 he or she has a disability) within 7 years of his or her death. However, if you claim benefits at age 60, they will be reduced based on the survivor's full retirement age. In addition to the surviving spouse being eligible for benefits, certain minor children can also receive benefits. If there is an unmarried child under age 18 (or up to age 19 if still attending elementary or secondary school full-time) or if a child has a disability before age 22 and remains with the disability. While this usually applies to natural children, there are some instances where stepchildren, grandchildren, and adopted children can also receive benefits. Because Social Security has a survivor aspect to its benefits, it is important when claiming benefits to understand how the claiming decision will impact any survivor benefits.

ESTATE PLANNING INVOLVING BLENDED FAMILIES AND OTHER LIVING ARRANGEMENTS

LO 23.6   Explain various estate planning arrangements for blended families and various living arrangements.

Modern society has become more receptive to nontraditional living arrangements. Prevailing attitudes today encourage the acceptance of living styles that once were socially impermissible. Increasing rates of children being born to non-married couples, divorce, and remarriage have resulted in more flexible and tolerant views of family structures and living arrangements.

When advising married couples, estate planners have ample state statutory and case law for guidance. However, with the exception of a few states which recognize common-law marriages and court decisions addressing palimony claims, there is no legal point of reference for individuals who live together outside of marriage. Additionally, the recognition of common-law marriages has been in decline. In some states, like New Hampshire, the common-law marriage is only recognized after the death of one partner, creating some interesting planning opportunities and challenges. Simply living together is not sufficient to constitute a common-law marriage in those states that do recognize a common-law arrangement. A common-law couple must also publicly represent themselves as being married and meet other specific living requirements. Palimony lawsuits, on the other hand, are grounded on contractual claims for support after relationships have terminated. Discrimination law rather than marital law provides guidance for some other aspects of nontraditional living arrangements. Many of these cases arise from claims of different treatment due to sexual preference.

Just as the parties to a valid marriage can enter into agreements that delineate property ownership, rights, duties, expectations, obligations, and so forth in antenuptial or postnuptial contracts, unmarried persons who live together can also enter into cohabitation agreements. Such agreements can give structure to the living arrangements and may reduce the likelihood of palimony litigation if the relationship later dissolves.

Estate planners are sailing in relatively uncharted waters when planning for clients who are living together outside of marriage. As with married clients, a planner should at the very least suggest separate, independent planners for each of the partners to protect their rights and also to protect the planner from conflicts of interest and claims of malpractice. The planner has to factor into any estate plan for couples living together outside of marriage the fact that such relationships are more easily terminated by the parties than are marriages that are recognized under state law.

The presence of children adds to the complexity of estate planning for clients living in nontraditional arrangements. One of the partners may be the biological, custodial parent of children from a previous marriage or relationship. A nonbiological partner, however, may have formed a personal attachment to one or more of the children and may seek custody or visitation rights or may otherwise want to provide for them. Grandparents and other senior generation members may also be relevant in estate plans. Adoptions, stepchildren, half-siblings, surrogate births, artificial insemination, and in vitro fertilization all make the planning process even more complex. Typical methods that may be used to plan for children of a previous relationship include annual gift tax exclusion gifts, trusts for the children under the Uniform Transfers (or Gifts) to Minors Act, testamentary trusts, life insurance, and Social Security benefits.

Negative family reactions and hostility add yet another layer of problems to estate planning for unmarried couples, especially same-gender couples. To deter anticipated will contests or other actions, some couples have resorted to adoption by one of the adult partners of the other as his or her legal child.

Nonmarried couples may also have to contend with being denied visitation when a partner is in the hospital. However, this was eased in 2011, when new federal Hospital Visitation regulations were enacted, which allowed greater freedom for patients to designate visitors and more access to visitation by nonfamily members. Furthermore, a blood relative is more likely to be asked about a patient's medical wishes than a domestic partner is. The solution to both of these issues is a health care power of attorney (HCPOA) or a health care representative appointment (HCRA). If the patient-partner is unable to communicate his or her wishes, a living will used in conjunction with an HCPOA or HCRA that nominates the healthy partner as agent should protect the partner's wishes, including access to the patient-partner in the hospital.

In 2013, the Supreme Court in *United States v. Windsor*, 133 S. Ct. 2675, determined that the Defense of Marriage Act (DOMA) violated the U.S. Constitution and that the federal government would need to recognize any legally married same-sex couples. In 2015, a landmark Supreme Court Case held that it is a fundamental right for same-sex couples to marry. This right is protected by both the Due Process and Equal Protection Clauses of the U.S. Constitution. The case, *Obergefell v. Hodges*, requires that all states issue same-sex marriage licenses and recognize all other valid same-sex marriages that occur outside of the state. This opened up a lot of planning opportunities for same-sex couples. For instance, the DSUE (deceased spouse's unused exemption) allowance for portability of any unused lifetime exemption now applies to legally married, same-sex couples. Additionally, married same sex-couples can file taxes jointly as a married couple, use the state estate tax exemptions where applicable, receive Social Security spousal and survivor benefits, take property through state succession laws, have access to support statutes, election against the will rights, retirement plan joint and survivorship rights, and even some protections for Medicaid spend-down.

This does not mean that legally married same-sex couples can ease up on their planning because same sex couples now need to worry about things like community property laws, state succession laws, support obligations, family transfer limitations, and retirement plan requirements. However, planning has been significantly expanded and improved for same sex couples in light of the *Obergefell* decision. However, same-sex couples may still face discrimination, extra paperwork, and additional issues involved with setting up their estate plans. For example, be aware that many statutes and wills might say husband and wife and not spouse. Best practices now advise to use the term "spouse" rather than husband or wife when drafting documents.

Another issue can arise with hospital-visitation rights. However, in 2010 and 2011, President Obama and his administration, including the U.S. Department of Health and Human Services, issued regulations requiring any Medicare or Medicaid participating hospital to have clearly written guidelines for allowing designated visitors to have access to patients in hospitals, regardless of their legal relationship. Additionally, guidelines were created to allow for the creation of advanced directives, called health care proxies, which are documents that allow patients to designate who will be given visitation rights if they show up at the hospital. These forms can also serve as a health care power of attorney. As such, it is much easier now for same sex couples, married or not, to visit their loved ones in a hospital. However, planning is still required and same sex couples should be sure to set up the advanced directives. For any nonmarried person it's important, because hospitals tend to look to family members first to make health care decisions for someone who cannot make decisions for him or herself.

Addressing Estate Planning Concerns of Nonmarital Partners

The unavailability of the unlimited marital gift and estate tax deduction is the greatest tax planning hurdle to overcome in estate planning issues involving couples who are not considered to be legally married. Keep in mind that a nontraditional family can be any family or household in which there are at least two or more unrelated people, or, if there are related parties in the household, at least one person is related nonlineally, such as a brother or sister. Another variation of a nontraditional family is one with related family members where at least one lineal generational level is absent. For example, there are many households in which grandparents are raising their grandchildren without the parents of the child present. Other tax perspectives are necessary because tax matters cannot be postponed as readily without the marital-deduction option. There are, however, several common estate planning methods used for nonmarital partners.

Joint Tenancy with Right of Survivorship

Titling property as joint tenants with right of survivorship is one way of providing for a partner. At death, the property passes directly to the surviving party to the relationship.

Although holding property in joint tenancy with right of survivorship provides a certain sense of security for same-gender or other unmarried parties, there are some considerations with respect to this form of ownership that the individuals should be aware of, as follows:

- It may be possible for one of the unmarried parties to sever a joint tenancy.
- With bank accounts and certain other assets, either partner may be able to make withdrawals or obtain the property irrespective of his or her percentage of contribution to the account.
- The creation of a joint tenancy may cause gift tax liability.
- The joint-tenancy property may be reachable by the creditors of both partners.

Gifting

Outright transfers of property utilizing the annual exclusion, or the donor's basic credit amount if the transfer exceeds the annual-exclusion amount, avoid gift tax liability. (Of course, gift splitting is not an option in nonmarital situations.)

Testamentary Bequests

Provisions may also be made under a client's will for a partner with whom the client lives. (Clearly, federal and state marital deductions cannot be used by unmarried couples.) Will provisions, however, do not become irrevocable until death and could then be vulnerable to will contests by the decedent's lineal heirs. Challenges to a will are especially likely from the decedent's children from a marriage. Therefore, partners who desire to provide for each other under a will need to be aware that family members, even those who appeared to accept their deceased relative's significant-other person prior to death, may contest the will after the death of their family member. In this case, a revocable trust may prove more dependable for making sure property passes according to the partners' wishes. If the survivor to the relationship receives less than what was promised or expected under his or her partner's will, an election against the will is not available. If the decedent dies without a valid will, the survivor will not receive anything, since state intestacy statutes are based solely on blood relationships. Also, if either of the life partners wishes the other partner to be executor, the will should specifically nominate the partner because a court will often, in the absence of a specific nomination, be more inclined to appoint a sibling, parent, or child rather than the unrelated partner. The figure below shows the intestate distribution scheme.

Common Distribution Scheme of Interstate Succession

Surviving spouse takes 1/3; remaining 2/3 goes to children, or 1/3 to each. Child #2 prede-ceased decedent, so Child #2's share is divided equally, or 1/6 each, to each grandchild. If no children survived decedent, remaining 2/3 would pass to parents (1/3 each). If parents pre-deceased decedent, remaining 2/3 would go to their lineal descendants (brother and sister of decedent would receive 1/3 each). If no brothers or sisters of decedent survived, surviving spouse would get the rest. If there were no lineal decedents (including cousins), property would escheat to the state.

Revocable Trusts

Revocable trusts are excellent planning tools for unmarried partners to provide for each other by naming the partner as beneficiary. At the death of the grantor partner, the trust becomes irrevocable and the beneficiary partner receives the property or the income from the property according to the terms of the trust. The trust document may provide for alternates and may name a successor beneficiary in case the specific relationship is not sustained until the grantor's death.

Life Insurance and Retirement Plans

Life insurance and retirement plans may name the partner as beneficiary, thereby providing the partner with a sense of security during lifetime and with funds at the insured's and/or plan participant's death. If the same-gender partners are concerned about listing their partner as the beneficiary of benefits their employer provides, naming a trust with the partner as trust beneficiary may be a possible solution. Also be aware that retirement benefits may not be made available to a surviving unmarried partner the way they are to a surviving spouse. Life insurance on the life of the pension participant may be considered to supplant the loss of retirement benefits when the retiree partner dies.

Because a domestic partner generally does not have an insurable interest in the insured partner's life, the purchase of a life insurance policy on the partner's life may prove difficult. An ILIT, however, may be used to overcome the insurability-requirement obstacle and achieve the partners' goals. With an ILIT, the trust is the policyowner and the partner is the trust beneficiary. For grantor-partners concerned about the irrevocability element of an ILIT and a potential for the relationship to fail in the future, the trust may be drafted to contain provisions directing the policy proceeds to someone other than an estranged partner under specified circumstances.

GRITs

Another way an individual could transfer property to his or her partner is with a grantor-retained income trust (GRIT). Although Chapter 14 of the Internal Revenue Code (Sections 2701–2704) restricts tax benefits for GRITs between related parties, they can be a useful estate planning device for nontraditional couples. With a GRIT, the grantor-partner retains a value in the assets that is based on the terms of the trust. The values of the grantor's retained interest and the remainderman-partner's interests are determined under the Section 7520 rate at the time the GRIT is created.

For example, assume the grantor-partner, Martin, establishes a trust and funds it with $1 million. The funds are to be held in the trust for 10 years before the underlying property passes to his partner, Michael. Assume that the value of Martin's retained-income interest is approximately $695,000 and that Martin's taxable gift to Michael, as remainderman, is valued at $305,000 (the difference between $1 million and the $695,000 value of the retained interest). Martin has achieved his goal of passing the property to his partner but with less gift tax for Martin compared with the tax payable on an immediate gift of the entire $1 million.

In summary, change is prevalent as this multifaceted area of the law is undergoing continual adjustments to meet modern societal demands.

Ethical Dilemma

The ethical dilemmas presented in this text illustrate common scenarios that could present a financial or estate planner with an ethical predicament. The resolution of any dilemma, of course, depends on how one applies ethical codes, rules, and principles to the specific situation. The comments are meant to provide thought about these issues and not give a definitive resolution to them.

Charlie is an estate planner who just acquired a new client, Fred Rice. Fred recently became a widower. After meeting with Fred several times to discuss his estate objectives, Charlie began to question his client's mental competency. Not only does Fred seem to change his intentions each time they meet, he also appears to be ambivalent about the children he wishes to include or omit as estate beneficiaries. Exacerbating what Charlie believes is already a disturbing situation is an additional complication. Though he at times seems uncertain about how to leave his estate, Fred has occasionally stated that he wants to leave the largest part of it to his oldest daughter, Kate, who is known to be a notorious substance abuser. Fred appears to be completely unaware of his daughter's addiction.

- **What should Charlie do?**

A Possible Resolution

This is a difficult situation for Charlie. It could be that Fred is suffering from dementia, or it could be that he is suffering from the loss of his wife. Regardless, it is Charlie's responsibility to ensure that Fred has complete understanding of his choices and their ramifications before he can act on Fred's wishes. If Charlie refuses to carry out his wishes, Fred could go to a different estate planner. At the same time, it would be irresponsible for Charlie to carry out the wishes of someone truly suffering from dementia.

The troublesome nature of this situation is complicated because the amount of information that Charlie can reveal to anyone is limited by the constraints of confidentiality. In fact, it might be construed as a violation of confidentiality to even disclose that Fred is a client. If Charlie were to contact a family member in order to express his concerns surrounding Fred's mental competency, he should be careful not to reveal any privileged information (such as to whom Fred has considered or is considering leaving his estate).

Perhaps the most viable option is for Charlie to suggest that Fred have someone accompany him to their next appointment. He could indicate that some of the information is complicated. This would give Fred the opportunity to choose someone trustworthy to involve in his personal matters. Charlie faces another predicament regarding how to handle the situation with Kate. It would seem that he has an obligation to share this information with his client, even though he does not have definitive knowledge of her addiction. This is information that could influence Fred's decision making, and it was not revealed to Charlie in confidence. Charlie should be careful to present it as hearsay, though, not as fact.

Today, with the growing incidents of dementia, it is wise to proactively determine how the affairs of the elderly are to be handled.

CHAPTER REVIEW

Key Terms and Concepts

durable power of attorney	CPR directives
special (limited) power of attorney	DNR directive
springing durable power of attorney	Five Wishes
advance medical directives	special needs trusts
living will	elder law durable power of attorney
health care proxy	standby trust

Chapter 23: Review Questions

1. Cornelia and Conrad had been happily married for 46 years at the time of Cornelia's death 3 months ago. Their two adult children are Steve, a struggling musician, and Susan, a secretary who is helping to pay for her husband's graduate school education. There are no grandchildren. Although Cornelia and Conrad were not wealthy in their own right, over the last 15 years of her life Cornelia inherited property from relatives. At her death, Cornelia had an estate valued at $8.1 million, which includes her portion of the couple's residence and bank accounts titled jointly with right of survivorship. She left her entire estate to Conrad and, due to the unlimited marital deduction, there will be no estate tax. Until his wife's death, Conrad's only property consisted of the jointly held home and bank accounts, currently valued at $600,000. He is not knowledgeable about financial matters and has always lived simply. Conrad told the attorney handling Cornelia's estate that he does not want the burden of so much money. Explain why a disclaimer could be recommended as a postmortem estate planning device for Conrad. [LO 23.1]

2. Explain the methods frequently used for postmortem planning. [LO 23.1]

3. What are the postmortem benefits of a surviving spouse's election to split lifetime gifts of the decedent-spouse after the decedent-spouse's death? [LO 23.1]

4. Identify the different types of powers of attorney. [LO 23.2]

5. Explain what an advance medical directive is. [LO 23.3]

6. What are some of the special estate planning issues that may arise when planning for [LO 23.4]

    a. the elderly

    b. married couples

7. Identify steps that an individual may take to avoid the future possibility of judicial guardianship or conservatorship. [LO 23.4]

8. Explain what a standby trust is. [LO 23.4]

9. James and Jennie have lived together in a nonmarital relationship for several years and plan to continue this living arrangement for the rest of their lives. Both James and Jennie have children from earlier marriages. What are some frequently implemented estate planning methods that James and Jennie can use to provide financially—but separately—for their children? [LO 23.6]

10. Explain some of the problems that can arise with bequests to a surviving nonmarital partner under a decedent-partner's will. [LO 23.6]

11. Explain the tax treatment of the transfer of property between divorcing spouses that are incident to the divorce {LO 23.5}

Chapter 23: Review Answers

1. Although there will be no estate taxes due at Cornelia's death (because of the unlimited marital deduction), Cornelia's basic credit amount is being wasted unless the deceased spousal unused exemption amount (DSUEA) provision is used. In the absence of utilizing the DSUE provision and without the benefit of Cornelia's basic credit amount, there is likely to be a greater estate tax liability at Conrad's death (assuming he does not remarry) than is necessary. If Conrad makes a qualified disclaimer of some or all of the basic exclusion amount, the disclaimed amount of property will pass to their son and daughter and avoid estate tax liability at Cornelia's death. Thus—ignoring inflation and appreciation—as long as the value of Conrad's property is less than or approximates his own basic exclusion amount, little, if any, estate tax will have to be paid at his death.

2. Methods frequently used for postmortem planning:

    - Qualified disclaimers (Sec. 2518)
    - Special-use valuation for real estate of closely held businesses or farms (Sec. 2032A)
    - Installment payment of estate taxes under Sec. 6166
    - Stock redemption under Sec. 303
    - Alternate valuation date
    - Marital deduction qualification of QTIP trust property (Sec. 2056)
    - Gift-splitting election by surviving spouse
    - Family election
    - Election against decedent's will by surviving spouse
    - Certain administrative expenses deduction
    - Medical expenses deduction
    - Characterization of executor's fee

3. There are three benefits resulting from a postmortem election to split gifts made by a decedent spouse during his or her lifetime:

    - a reduction in gift tax liability
    - a decrease in estate tax liability
    - a greater value of assets pass to estate beneficiaries

4. There are various types of powers of attorney. A durable power of attorney allows the agent (also called an attorney-in-fact) to act for the principal despite the principal's incapacity and is an effective estate planning tool. A special or limited power of attorney is one in which the agent is granted the power to accomplish specific tasks or else is operative for only a certain period of time. A springing power of attorney is one that becomes effective only at the time of the principal's incapacity as expressly defined in the document.

5. Durable powers of attorney for health care and living wills are often referred to as advance medical directives.

6. a. Preparing for the future financial and long-term care needs of the elderly, ill, and incapacitated presents some estate planning challenges. For instance, an estate plan that is oriented primarily toward passing property to the next generation becomes irrelevant if the estate is practically depleted by the cost of long-term care. On the other hand, retention of assets can prevent an estate owner from meeting Medicaid eligibility requirements. A comprehensive estate plan must address the implications of the client's potential need for long-term care.

   b. A planner should be aware that the interests of a husband and wife may not be identical and may even be conflicting. Thus, one planner may not be able to fairly address the needs of both parties. In other words, simply because a married couple seeks joint representation, the planner should not automatically conclude that the parties share identical objectives. Spousal estate planning and property disposition goals may be especially divergent and complicated when one or both have children from earlier marriages. Other areas of potential conflict may be the existence of one or both spouses' community property, the subjection of marital or separate property to the claims of one spouse's creditors, reciprocal wills, the tax consequences of gift splitting, and the control or lack of control a surviving spouse will have over property after the first spouse's death.

7. In addition to a durable power of attorney, other methods used to avoid judicial guardianship include joint ownership of property, advance medical directives, and trusts. When property is titled in more than one name, another party is already in place to manage the property, bank accounts, and so forth. Advance medical directives and living wills provide for health care decision making prior to disability.

Guardianship may also be circumvented with trusts. A primary benefit of a revocable living trust is that the trustee manages the trust property according to trust terms stated by the grantor. The trustee continues to administer the assets during the grantor's incapacity.

8. Another type of trust used in planning for incompetency is a standby trust. A standby trust often works in tandem with a durable or springing power of attorney. The trust is unfunded until such time as the grantor becomes incapacitated and an attorney-in-fact funds the trust with assets of the grantor for the trustee to manage.

9. James and Jennie may make annual gift tax exclusion gifts to their children. They will not, however, be able to take advantage of gift splitting to increase the amounts of annual exclusion gifts because they are not married. If the children are minors, James and Jennie can also establish custodial accounts under the Uniform Transfers (Gifts) to Minors Act, or establish Secs. 2503(b) or (c) trusts naming the children as beneficiaries. Another solution to providing for the children would be to purchase life insurance on each of their lives, preferably through a trust arrangement such as an ILIT, naming the children as beneficiaries under the contract.

10. In some cases involving the wills of decedent nonmarried partners, the decedent's will may be more vulnerable to will contests by the decedent's surviving family members. Also, because the parties are not married, the marital deduction, right to elect against the will, and the right to receive property by intestacy are not available. In addition, the nomination of the decedent's life partner as executor of the decedent's estate is more likely to be challenged than in what are presently considered by some to be traditional living arrangements.

11. Transfers of property between divorcing spouses that are incident to the divorce are not subject to federal gift taxation because the transfers and giving up of marital rights are treated as being made for full and adequate consideration in money or money's worth. The divorce, however, must occur with a 3-year period that revolves around the timing of the property-settlement agreement for the transfer to avoid gift tax.

INDEX